CAN YOU STAND THE TRUTH?

THE CHRONICLE OF MAN'S IMPRISONMENT

Last Call!

TRANSLATION FROM THE ORIGINAL GREEK

ANDREAS KALOGERAS

ANGELIKI ANAGNOSTOU-KALOGERA

CAN YOU STAND THE TRUTH?

THE CHRONICLE OF MAN'S IMPRISONMENT

LAST CALL!

KERKYRA 2009

ISBN (Printed Version) **978-618-80216-0-0**
ISBN (e-book) **978-618-80216-2-4**

United States Copyright Office:
1-824408581_Application_20120920_164608

English Translation: Andreas M. Kalogeras
Corfu (Kerkyra), Greece 2012

First Greek Edition: December 2009
Second Greek Edition: June 2012

THIS BOOK SHOULD NOT BE READ
INCREMENTALLY.
SUCCESSION OF CHAPTERS MUST BE
FOLLOWED FAITHFULLY, SINCE THEY ALL
COMPRISE THE BUILDING BLOCKS
OF AN INNOVATIVE WORLD THEORY
(WELTANSCHAUUNG).

THE ENTIRE PICTURE WILL BE COMPLETED
BY THE END OF THE BOOK
ONLY IF, ALONG WITH THE MAIN TEXT,
ALL BIBLIOGRAPHIC REFERENCES ARE CARE-
FULLY READ AS FUNDAMENTAL AND INDIS-
PENSABLE ELEMENTS OF SUPPORT.

This book is exclusively dedicated to those who can still feel the Living Spirit 'burning' inside. And no matter how hard they try to nourish IT with the virtual idols of matter, IT remains unfed.

I want to thank my family, who uncomplainingly endured my 'absence' from the active scene of our lives during these three and a half years of writing the book:
My husband for the text proofing, the Greek translations of English texts and his technical support; my mother for her acceptance of my positions and her assistance; my eldest daughter for her work on the front cover, as well as my youngest one for her idea on its layout.

The author

Tr. note: Special thanks are to be given to Ms. Alexandra Koukouli, who diligently helped with the literary editing of the main corpus and the terminology of the references of the English translation.

WEB PAGES:
www.CanYouStandTheTruth.com
www.AntexeisTinAlitheia.gr
E-mail: delideli@otenet.gr
Tel. for orders: +30 6972 401015

TABLE OF CONTENTS

It is a fact that initial contact with anything that is subversive and innovative always creates insecurity (shock) to the reader. Additionally, assimilation of new information presupposes the existence of the corresponding brain synapses as well as psychological preparation. From these it can be deduced that deep understanding of the conceptual situations described in this book and the answers/solutions to the questions induced to the reader, make multiple readings of the book, a must.

Angeliki Anagnostou - Kalogera

WHAT DOES 'ΑΓΑΘΟΝ' MEAN?

The Ancient Greek word Ἀγαθόν [Agathón=good, benevolent, kind] refers to an aggregate of concepts encompassing all moral, intellectual and spiritual virtues of man. It must be thought of as <u>an absolute state, with an existence which is independent and unaffected by time, space or any other change</u>. Only The Supreme Deity, The Unified Being, The Monad, can be characterized by the term Ἀγαθός.

We must therefore accept the existence of an Ideal Conceptual World, independent from our physical world, which contains all the Eternal and Perfect Archetypes of the Ideas of Virtue, Justice, Morality, Grace and Truth. This is the World of Ἀγαθόν.

Whichever of the above Archetypes appears in the world of form (our world), is to be simply considered a mere reflection of the Real One, owing its imperfect existence to a vestigial and rudimentary relation to the Complete and Perfect State of that Other World, in which Ἀγαθόν is incorporated.

HERMES TRISMEGISTUS, HERMETIC TEXTS, VOL. I, RODAKIS P., TZAFEROPOULOS AP., **SPEECH VI**: «§3. When it comes to man, Ἀγαθόν is determined in comparison to evil. ...And Ἀγαθόν here is the smallest particle of evil. And it is **impossible** down here, that Ἀγαθόν be free from malice. For down here, Ἀγαθόν gets filled with malice, and being full of malice, it cannot be Ἀγαθόν; and since it cannot remain Ἀγαθόν anymore, it becomes evil. Therefore, Ἀγαθόν is (found) in God alone, or rather God Himself is Ἀγαθός. So then, Asclepius, **only the name of Ἀγαθόν is found in men**. Its workings are nowhere to be found. And it cannot be. For, **it cannot be contained in a material body,** which is bound on all sides by wickedness, pains, labors and rage and deceit and by foolish fantasies. And the greatest ill of all, Asclepius, is that each of these things that have been said previously <u>is thought</u> **down here** to be the greatest Ἀγαθόν when they are an inevitable evil. ...§6 Wherefore, those who are ignorant and do not tread the path of piety, **do dare to call** man fair and Ἀγαθόν. <u>Not even in their wildest dreams have they seen what Ἀγαθόν is</u>. And they call Ἀγαθόν all that is evil. »

Plato, in his Republic, gives us a definition of the term Ἀγαθόν:
[508e] «This reality, then, that gives their truth to the objects of knowledge and the power of knowing to the knower, you must say is the idea of Ἀγαθόν, and you must conceive it as being **the cause of**

Don't skip chapters or bibliographic references

knowledge*, and **the cause of truth** in so far as they become known. Yet, fair as they both are (knowledge and truth), you will think rightly in supposing Ἀγαθόν to be something different and fairer still than these. But as for knowledge and truth, even as in our illustration [509a] it is right to deem light and vision as being sun like, **but never to think that they are the sun**, so here, it is right to consider these two (knowledge and truth) as being like Ἀγαθόν but to think that either of them is Ἀγαθόν, is not right.» [TRANSLATED BY PAUL SHOREY, CAMBRIDGE, MA, HARVARD UNIVERSITY PRESS; LONDON, WILLIAM HEINEMANN LTD., 1969.

* Of Spiritual matter-less Knowledge

INTRODUCTION

Man, in his strife to endure survival in an adverse and difficult world, has fabricated various convictions about Creation, Man and Life, in order to justify the inexplicable controversies that surround him. These convictions have built theories, and through them, religions, heresies and views have been formulated. Following that, everyone adopts the theory that fits their idiosyncrasy and reasoning better, and cling firmly onto that view, because it suits them and affords them security. Comfortable then, behind whatever view they prefer, men delude themselves about the 'discrepancies' of their world-theory, and battle the 'discrepancies' of the opposing views in an eternal struggle with no definite winner.

The prevailing positions for the creation of life and the world today are mainly two, with plenty of 'offshoots' stemming from each one:

1st Position

The entire creation was formed by itself, through a natural selective process (natural selection through survival of the fittest). There is nothing else beyond autonomous natural conditions which generate life. When these conditions are not fully met, then life perishes.

This view however, when put under the scrutinizing microscope of logic presents discrepancies because it naturally accepts a mathematical consistency in nature. But mathematical consistency presupposes logic; logic presupposes a mind, and the mind always belongs to someone…

2nd Position

The entire creation is the result of a benevolent god who is given form by some, while others consider him formless. This benevolent god created everything through his love and wisdom, providing man with the possibility of free choice, between positive and negative actions. Through his choices, man is always taught how to finally become a better person.

This view however, has many logical gaps as well, and this is why it is being challenged by many. Every sentient human being, however

Don't skip chapters or bibliographic references

hard he/she might search inside the entire creation, <u>cannot</u> find this most Gracious God nor his love anywhere…

---

[1]**ATHENIAN AND MACEDONIAN NEWS AGENCY** (26/8/2007) http://www.ana-mpa.gr/anaweb/
«Mother Teresa doubted the existence of God, according to her letters. Mother Teresa, who is likely to be declared Saint by the Catholic Church, endlessly felt her faith shaken throughout her life and, in addition, doubted the very existence of God, as it is disclosed in letters that she wrote in 1979 to her trusted friend, reverent Michael Van der Pet.
Her constant references to the 'darkness', the 'loneliness' and the 'torment' are present in more than 40 letters she wrote during a period of 66 years. Although these letters exhibit brief remorse, Mother Teresa spent more than 50 years doubting the existence of God despite the opposite image she projected in her public life.»

Additionally, if someone intensively observes life as a whole, one will inevitably conclude that this alleged 'free choice' is completely unattainable and virtual: Man, eternally subdued to the needs that surround him, however much he keeps chasing it, it nevertheless remains elusive. This is of course, a rather obscure point and its realization is attained only if one transcends the bounds of his limited visual 'arch', and sees the entire circle of life and creation. Because of this highly invisible point, this second conjecture is the most widely-accepted one. So, the struggle to make the best choice continues incessantly.

Another group of skeptics, more sensitive to the overall injustice, tries to justify it, by bridging this gap with the dogma of karma and compensative (reciprocal) justice. According to this dogma and under the law of reciprocity, man 'pays' for his mistakes from one reincarnation to the next, thus learning more about right and wrong. Thus, he is upgraded and evolves both ethically and spiritually. But this view is also logically deficient: Human society, according to this point of view, should by now 'glow' with virtuousness! That is of course not true.

*So, however much we may dream that human society evolves, or that it will progress further, all that is really being accomplished, is merely a **technological** upgrading, promoted solely by the 'Sacred Need'.*

On the other hand, it is common knowledge that in the realm of ethics, morality and spiritual ascent, humanity, if it doesn't go backwards, it definitely stays still.

This whole quest for convenient answers therefore, aims to help man shut his eyes as tightly as he can in front of a reality that deep inside he feels is painful beyond comprehension, and inescapable.

He has sugarcoated it, elevated the virtue of optimism to a sacred emblem, put on the rose-tinted glasses of positive thinking, 'called' the glass half-full instead of half-empty and thus compromised; and the reason for all this? Simply because to face (the) truth, without the antidote of the solution, is unbearably painful! And as Christ said in the Gospel of John: "I have yet many things to say to you: but you cannot bear them now". [JOHN 16:12]

Henceforth, man has been content to let himself drift away in the ebb of everyday life and his needs, and subside even more into oblivion.

Throughout man's overall course on this earth, at certain instances of his history, the ONE Truth of All has been revealed.

Never has it remained intact for long though. After its exposure to the world, it is always dissected and dispelled into a thousand pieces. So, to-day, only some scraps remain scattered here and there. <u>Nowhere</u> does it exist in its pure form. After all, the best hideout for the TRUTH is in-between two lies.

The only thing these different conjectures do is confuse the tangle of Truth even more.

The painful truth is but ONE, <u>and contains all the partial/diverse truths inside it.</u>

The probability for someone to consolidate all these scattered scraps in order to recompose the puzzle, is minute to nonexistent, since the material plane is quite 'crafty' in refracting the truths and deflecting them to places other than where they should be.

To get to the bottom of things, one must start in reverse...

Knowledge completes its cycle by the end of this book, where the Complete Unified Truth about life, man and the reason for his existence, is present-ed. Some might obviously oppose that this theory is just an additional 'view' amongst so many others. However, **this** *'view' combines all the opposite ones into one unified system of thought.*

The time of great decisions for man is getting nearer, and in order for his decision to be a conscious one, IT IS IMPERATIVE that the complete Truth is revealed to him.

Be strong!

CLARIFICATIONS

The entire book constitutes a spherical and innovative 'theory of the cosmos' (Weltanschauung), not only in terms of its main corpus but also in regards to its overall presentation too. It is a thoroughly completed puzzle which composes the entire picture about man and his life in this world, without leaving out any 'pieces' just because they might not obviously fit.

*On account of the above, and in order for the reader to comprehend this world theory as a whole, regardless of his acceptance or denial of it, he/she –contrary to the prevailing tendency people have– **must not rush to read the last chapter**, skipping the ones in-between, because this will result in his/her rejection of many ground-breaking positions of this theory, due to the absence of **logical** evidence supporting them, which these in-between chapters <u>along with their references</u>, bring forth.*

What I must also mention is that the greatest part of the book refers to <u>notional concepts</u> which, in order to become clear, have been given a 'visual presentation'. For some readers though, this procedure harbors the danger of getting stuck on the 'image', neglecting the deeper Essence of the concept behind it, since human words can only describe the conceptual up to a certain point: For someone who has never experienced one of the basic human senses for example, verbal descriptions are quite limited in reproducing it in detail, no matter how clearly they might describe it.

*The entire work **gradually** takes the reader through an upward 'spiral' process, from a simple viewpoint to a more complex one, so as to smoothly transpose him to a different dimension, where he will be able to gaze at a world which is quite different to what he has believed so far.*

In the first part of the book, an ideological and emotional preparation of the reader takes place, in order for him to endure the revelations that follow.

I would also like to note that during this entire bibliographical research, I came across –to my grief– many and great discrepancies in the way a lot of texts had been translated. I found translations –not necessarily from Ancient to Modern Greek but also from Ancient Greek to English as well as others– with such great differences between the original and the translated text, that in some cases the translation produced the opposite meaning to that of the prototype! These are of course not found in the book. Because of such 'liberty' in the translation of many ancient texts, I was quite often forced to use different translations for the same work –especially of the apocryphal gospels– since each translator renders a passage in his own style. I therefore always chose the translation that more accurately stated what I was trying to point out in each case.

The theory unfolds through a dialogue between a (fictional) Hermit-Messenger and the writer. Through this dialogue many fundamental questions are answered which, in their sum, construct this diverse thesis. There are also many references <u>supporting</u> this theory.

There are specific writing font styles used in the text, which denote who is 'speaking' at any moment.

The styles used:

The writer
Main text or the 'hermit'
Excerpts of sayings and apothegms the hermit uses in his dialogues

REFERENCED BIBLIOGRAPHICAL CITATIONS
Excerpts of texts as references
(The writer's interventions or elaborations in-between reference texts)
(Translator's notes)

PART ONE

THE QUEST

The morning was pleasant. A cool breeze was coming in through the open window, as the car smoothly cruised on the country road. I couldn't be far from the village that had been indicated to me. After a half-hour's drive from the town, I started driving up a scenic mud road, passing through thick sycamore trees. Running waters crossed the road vertically, forming little ponds here and there.

It wasn't long before I reached a small opening, which seemed like the square of a small village. A few small tables with even fewer chairs under a big sycamore revealed the existence of people in that wilderness. I stepped out of the car and headed towards the little café. The door was wide open.

–*"Good morning!" ...I shouted... "Anybody here?"*

...Silence...

–*"Hello!!!" ...I shouted again. Still, no answer...*

I started examining the place around me. It was a humble café with a screen refrigerator dating back to the eighties. Some dusty shelves were hanging from a wall, with a few bottles on them. Exactly opposite to them on the other wall, there were some photographs, evidently of the owner's family. The old decorating fashion of the country was intensely impressed on the place.

–Yes please, are you looking for something?

I heard a voice behind me. I turned and saw a badly aged man. Deep wrinkles scarred his face, signs of a hard life that had left indelible marks on him. Behind this tired old body though, you could discern two sparks of humanity shining in his eyes;

–*I called you, but you obviously didn't hear me...*

I felt a little uneasy. What I was about to ask him was a little strange.

–*You know, I am looking for a hermit who is said to live in this area.*

–Ah! You mean the ghost hermit.

His characterization caught me off guard.

–*I beg your pardon? The person who told us the story did not describe him as a ghost.*

–Who told you about him?

–*One of my daughter's classmates; Elias is his name. He told us that this particular hermit had once saved him from certain death.*

–Ah! Elias… A sad story with an unexpected development… Do you know the whole story?

–*No, only bits and pieces... Could you recount it to me in detail? Time permitting of course...*

Don't skip chapters or bibliographic references

–Listen, my child, time here runs slowly. What chores can an old man have in the middle of nowhere? I barely manage to make ends meet with this little café that merely provides the minimum to keep me from dying. Few people still remain in this place. Even the primary school, the village used to have, was shut down. All young families that were left behind also moved to the city when the school closed. Only a handful of old people remained.

We took two refreshments which you could barely call cool and sat in the shade under the tree. He started narrating to me.

–A few years back, while the school was still in the village, Elias's family lived here. Elias was only little; he must have been in the third or fourth grade. But the child frequently complained about aches in his body. He also missed school quite often because of frequent high fevers. After some time, his parents decided to take him to the city to have him examined by a doctor there. They were gone from the village for one day, two days, three days, one week. Here at the village, we started worrying. We are a small community. A few days after, I had to go to the city for some store supplies; I would then meet them and find out what had happened.

Indeed, after a few days, I went to the city and started asking everyone I knew about Elias. The news was grim. The child was very ill with the 'wicked' disease *{Tr. n.: cancer}*. It had already spread, the doctors said, onto many vital organs. They had advised his parents to go to the big hospitals in Athens just in case something more could be done there to save the child. The cancer had progressed unnoticed, thus not allowing any early stage treatment.

I returned to the village completely heartbroken. Such a young child, so very ill! What had caused it? No one knew. A month went by and one day Elias and his parents returned to the village.

We were all left speechless. The child was a living corpse. His parents were two tragic figures; two shadows that could barely walk. They had been sent home by the doctors: "We shouldn't torture the child with treatments any more. The disease has already taken over the whole body. Go back home and leave the child rest peacefully in his surroundings". That's what they'd said. The parents' pain was beyond description. The child did not know the truth. He was told that he had left the hospital because he had already recovered. He was to stay at home for a few days to regain his strength and then return to his old life. The parents buried their pain deep in their hearts. They revealed nothing in front of the child.

One day, when the mother's pain seemed to overflow, she opened her house door, saying she was going to the neighbor's for a minute. Instead, she started going uphill towards the mountain. With relief she entered the forest and let her pain burst out.

She started crying out loud with all her strength. Her sobs echoed throughout the forest. The pain burst out like a torrent flowing from her eyes. Her incessant sobbing combined with the shortness of breath the ascent gave her, made her heart beat rapidly, ready to explode.

"I will die here", she thought, and didn't care anymore! What really mattered to her now was to be relieved from that unbearable pain. She wished something would happen to remove that thorn from her heart! She wished her child could recover!

She raised her head to look up to the sky and asked God: "Why, my God? What did we do wrong?" And then, through her teary eyes, she noticed something moving among the trees. She wiped her eyes to see more clearly. A man was standing in front of her. She was embarrassed. She blushed. She said "good day" and turned away to leave, but the man stopped her saying: "Your pain has roused the whole forest. What is bothering you?"... She told him. After the man had listened to her problem carefully, he turned to her and said: "I think I can help you". The woman, surprised, told him that it showed no human compassion to toy with someone else's pain. Yet he must have insisted quite strongly, because they both headed back to the village.

When they reached the square, he sat under this tree and asked her to bring him the child. "How can I bring the child to the square, sir? He is withering away every minute like a dying candle. He doesn't have the strength to change sides in bed, let alone walk!" But he replied: "When you go to your house now, you will find your child up and awake, playing with his toys. If this is so, bring him here. If not, stay home and dwell on his death." Listening to his words the woman was shaken. She turned and left running to her house. There, she found little Elias playing with his toys as the hermit had told her. She grabs the child by the hand and carries him hastily to the square. The hermit then approaches the child, strokes him gently on the head, and whispers something in his ear. That was it. The child became well. Since then, he never got sick again. We, on the other hand, never found out what the man had whispered to the child's ear. "It's a secret!" Elias always answers when someone tries to get it out of him. After the hermit had healed the child, he set out and left. When he reached the turn on the road, he disappeared. This is how Elias's story goes my child."

The story of that child had touched me deeply. When my daughter introduced him to me, his politeness and his innate kindness made a lasting impression on me.

–And why do you call the hermit a ghost?

–A strange man he is, my child. He has been living, God knows since when, in a shack in the forest. He never comes to the village for supplies. We don't even know where he came from and when. Furthermore, when-

25

Don't skip chapters or bibliographic references

ever, during cold winter days, hunters, searching for wild boars in the mountains, happen to pass by his shack, they never see smoke coming out of his chimney. There is no chopped firewood outside his shack. And what can you say about his appearance!

–*"What is wrong with his appearance?" I asked, feeling my curiosity reaching new heights.*

–Every time someone manages to see him, it's as if a single day has not passed over him. For years now, whenever someone sees him in the forest, they describe him as a young man around thirty-five. All these years and he hasn't changed at all!

–*He hasn't changed a bit? ...And why do you say that some people 'manage' to see him? Is it so hard for someone to see him and talk to him? Hasn't anyone else had the chance to ask for his help for something all these years?*

–Is it hard you say? You bet! After Elias' cure, as you can understand, there was great upheaval. People started surging to the village to look for him. Many went as far as his shack. He had vanished! Some waited for him outside his shack for days. But to no avail. He was nowhere to be seen! Some saw him collecting wild vegetables in the mountain. But when they turned their eyes away from him for a second and then looked back again, he would have disappeared.

Every time someone happened to see him though, their life would suddenly change. But the most important change would occur inside the person who had seen him. They became better. Among all of us natives here, it is considered a great favor of fortune to manage to see this strange man, even once.

–*"I will try to meet him!" I said with such confidence that even I was surprised by the level of faith it had expressed. "I must find out". The little old man looked at me in wonder.*

–May God help you. If you start now, you'll be there in an hour. You must consider the time you need to return, so that night doesn't find you in the forest. Do you have a compass?

–*What do I need a compass for? Can't I drive there?*

The kind old man burst out laughing.

–It is just a small footpath through wild bushes, and if you don't know it, you will get lost for sure. If you have a compass on the other hand, then you must follow a constant course due east, and after an hour's walk, you will be there.

A compass! I ran to the car. "There must be something in here." I never thought of bringing a compass with me. I started shuffling everything around in the glove compartment. Fortunately, my husband, being a scout, always carries things like that. I found nothing in the glove compartment;

in the trunk maybe? ...Nothing there either. I rushed back to the café. The little old man was picking up the bottles from the table we had sat at.
–I can't find a compass. Do you happen to have one by any chance?
–What use would I have for a compass? I know these parts like the palm of my hand. You must drive to town to buy one.
A thought came to me like a flash. I hadn't searched the little drawer underneath the passenger's seat. It was there that we kept everything we didn't use frequently. I ran back and opened it. A myriad of things were there, things my husband uses in his scout trips: Swiss army knives, torches, batteries, lighters, a magnifying glass, and a bunch of other small gadgets, useful to scouts. I dug through them anxiously. "There must be a compass here somewhere...! Who wants to drive back to town now... It's a three-quarter drive!"
Right then, amidst the pile of gadgets, I saw a compass: It looked old. I opened its bronze lid, turned it right and left; it seemed to work. I returned to the café again and showed it to the owner, full of excitement.
–Let's see, is it working?
He turned it round in his old hands and then gave it to me. It was correct.
–"Keep a steady course to the east", *he advised me.*

ॐ•ॐ

Full of optimism, I set off. It was noon. Although the day had become quite hot, the course through the forest was particularly pleasant. The deep foliage of the trees created a crisp atmosphere. Running streams gave an extra 'freshness' to the whole area. Even though I was alone in the forest, I didn't feel afraid. It was as if all fears I would have normally had in a similar situation, had vanished. I held the compass steadily and followed my east-bound course.
I was optimistic. Believing the proverb 'hope springs eternal' to be right, I tried to justify my optimism. All the information I had, indicated that it would be almost impossible for me to meet that strange man. And if I did meet him, how would I know it was him for sure? Nevertheless, such thoughts did not occupy my mind. I was solely overcome by the unshakeable conviction that I would soon be facing something which would radically change my life.
Throughout my course, I kept looking around hoping to see him somewhere in the woods before reaching his cabin. What people said about his appearance had roused my curiosity: It seemed as if he hadn't aged a single day! And then again, the way he had healed Elias was very strange. He had simply told his mother that when she returned home, she would find her child playing with his toys! Had he foreseen something that would

Don't skip chapters or bibliographic references

have happened anyway because of some oddity of nature? Or had he caused it himself? On the other hand, the notion that Elias' disease had been cured on its own was most improbable. Had he then foreseen the most extreme exception in nature's laws? No. He must have already cured Elias before he even met him. And what was the purpose of his meeting with the child? When the hermit met with Elias, the child was already cured!

I was walking in that wilderness, trying to keep my course steady. I looked around to spot the cabin somewhere. It could be hiding behind the bushes, and I could just as easily pass it by without noticing.
The little old man had told me that it was in a clearing. But glades in forests are here today and gone tomorrow! Uncontrolled vegetation bursts where it can and changes the site completely. I had been walking for an hour and I was getting worried. My pace, compared to someone else's, who is familiar with the territory, was slow, of course. One hour's walk certainly did not apply to me.
The sound of a river flowing rapidly was reaching my ears. As I proceeded, the sound became louder. Suddenly, I found myself in front of a steep gorge. I stopped. I looked around to find an easy way down. Every spot I saw was steep. I tied a handkerchief I found in my backpack on a twig, and changed course to the north, hoping to find a smoother passage. I walked parallel to the gorge edge for quite a while, and having found nothing, I returned back. After I reached the bush with the handkerchief tied on it, I followed a southerly course. It was not long before I discovered a manmade path leading down, which had obviously been made by hunters in the area. I went down the steep slope carefully, where someone had dug little steps in the soil supporting them with stones at their most dangerous spots.
When the slope finally ended, I found myself on the riverside, facing the turbulent river, which I could only hear before.
Fortunately, there was a wooden bridge at that spot. I approached hesitantly, noticing that it was too old to be considered safe. I placed my foot on the first plank, and it creaked so loud that it made me freeze.
A sign, rusted by time, wrote in washed-out letters: "Luck favors the daring ones".
"Bravo! Well, that's comforting! Now I got my courage back!" I thought.
I sat at the bank, not knowing what to do. I let my sight rest on the beautiful scenery. The sound of the water was relaxing. I lay on the ground putting my hands under my head like a headrest. I closed my eyes. It wasn't long before I fell asleep. It wasn't something I had planned or aimed for. My reasoning would surely keep me from such an action. Sleep came uninvited.

❧·❧

...Small tables with groups of people having a good time were scattered all over the square. The place echoed with joyful voices. Children were running around, screaming excited in their games. People were walking around, enjoying their promenade. Gradually, people started to leave. So, in a short while, the square was left deserted. I was all alone. "I better go too", I thought to myself and started packing the things I had left on a bench.
Suddenly, a hovering ball of golden light appears in the square, drawing circles in the shape of the symbol of infinity (∞).
As it rotated round and round, it produced music like the sound wind-chimes make when hanging in the air.

[2] **CHALDEAN ORACLES:** ATHINOGENIS I., GRAVIGGER, P., KROLL 51 – PLACES 111 PROCLUS, TIM. II, 312, 27, (p. 167): «…hastening towards the center of a **clamorous (noisy) light**.»

Having 'danced' around for 4 or 5 times in the air, the ball stood in front of me and started transforming into a golden glowing rod. It 'danced' another 2 or 3 times (always producing that strange music) and came back in front of me again, this time changing its form to the luminous shape of a human whose head was environed by rays of light.
The vibration of this Luminous Presence was very strong. My physical substance was being subdued by its powerful oscillation. Then, as if it perceived my weakness, it dissolved into a golden aura, that covered the whole surrounding area, with a sudden but silent 'explosion' of light. The entire space around glowed, flooded in golden light...

❧·❧

I anxiously woke and jumped up, still feeling my heart pounding strongly. What a dream that was! Was my subconscious playing games with me? Or was it some kind of premonition? I sat up straight and looked at my watch. I must have slept for about half an hour.
I stayed there, thinking of the dream I'd had, over and over again. I was in shock. I looked again towards the old wooden bridge. "I hope I won't be the last one to cross this tumble-down little bridge". Be it the dream that was a forecast for what I was about to come across, be it that hope dies last, I set out determined to cross.
I placed my foot on the first plank. It creaked loudly again. I ignored it. In my mind, I tried to imagine my body lighter, as if it were possible to reduce my weight. I held on the ropes firmly on both sides. After all, if a plank

Don't skip chapters or bibliographic references

broke, I would be able to hold onto the rope (if that didn't break as well); I tried not to think about it. I kept walking with all my attention intensified. I could hear the river flowing violently underneath my feet. The view from that spot was majestic. I took a deep breath and moved on. A few more steps and I would reach the bank opposite.

When I set foot on solid ground, relief took the place of my initial anguish. I took the compass out of my pocket again, opened it and held it steady in my palm: Course, due east.

I tangled myself into the forest again, leaving the river behind me. It was already two in the afternoon; early summer. Fortunately, the light of day holds strong until late in the afternoon, lasting even through dusk. Logically, the cabin should be built close enough to the river, but in a safe distance from its banks in case of heavy rainfall. I must be near! I accelerated my pace following an obscure track through the grass. I went around a tuft, and right behind that, I saw it.

It looked uninhabited. I went closer. It was only a wooden shack, with a window without shutters, its glass dusty and blurry. An old rusty latch, secured the wooden door, which was next to the window. I walked around the whole cabin, trying to detect the faintest sound. I could hear the distant sound of the river. The wind whispered through the foliage, as if in concert with the chirping of the birds. Some dispersed sounds of branches crackling, and wild nuts and fruits forced to the ground by ripeness, completed nature's music. On the side of the house, there was a rudimentary little bench made from a fallen tree log. I stopped hesitantly at the door. I knocked shyly... I got no answer. I found more courage though. I knocked louder. I waited... Nothing! I went to the window and placing my hands on both sides of my face for glare protection, I looked inside. Empty... I found more courage and opened the door latch. The door squeaked open. Nobody was inside. I walked into the empty room. There was only a single room. Under the window, there was an old Murphy bed made from green khaki cloth, probably an army leftover from World War II. On the wall, right above it, there was a wooden frame with the picture of a horse galloping in a field. In the middle of the room, there was a table with two chairs. On one side of the wall, there was a bench with a small oil stove, a box of moldy matches, a bottle of oil, an oil lamp, two clay cups, some tin plates, some empty bottles and a big clay pitcher. On the wall opposite the bed, there was the fireplace. On its wooden mantle there was another oil lamp and some candles. Inside the fireplace were some half-burned branches and a small pot on a cast-iron frame.

Everything in the room was dusty, and the spiders had set their traps in prominent spots. "It is uninhabited", I thought. I felt a tinge of disappointment in my heart. "...Rumors! But of course! Take everything with a pinch of salt!"...Thoughts of reprehension against myself came over me.

"What could I expect when I am so gullible? Serves me right! I went look-ing for adventure. I was rather naïve in the end". I then started blaming others. "As if it were possible for miracle workers to exist...Could Elias be a myth-maniac, after all? Yes, but what about the old man at the café? ...No, Elias must have been cured by the doctors. Then his parents, out of their great joy, attributed his cure to a miracle. That must be it. It doesn't matter. Oh well! At least I went on an enjoyable excursion".

I felt hungry. I sat on the bench that was outside the house. I opened my backpack and took out a filling sandwich. I enjoyed every bite, feeling I was regaining the energy I had lost by fatigue. I was better now. I took out my thermos and drank plenty of water. In my anxiety, I had not thought to fill it up with fresh water from the river. "It doesn't matter; I'll fill it up on my way back. I'd better not delay any further though. It is time to return. I must now follow a course due west." I took the compass out of my pocket again and opened it.

THE MEETING

"What! What is the matter with it? What perfect timing for it to stop working!" The compass needle kept spinning round like crazy... *"How am I going to get back now?"* I felt my knees failing me as I looked at its berserk spinning. And there was more in store for me. The distinctive squeak of the door was heard out loud. I stood up full of tension. In lightning speed, I reached the side of the house where the door was. No one was outside. I leapt up to the door. And then I froze. A young man was standing at the front. He was not going in, but coming out of the shack. I was left speechless. "What in the world! Am I in the twilight zone? Not even ten minutes have passed since I left the room, and there was nobody in. Where did that man come from?"

I looked perplexed, once at the compass and once at the man standing in front of me.

–When did you enter the cabin without me hearing anything?

...He smiled.

–"My compass has gone wild", I said with an uneasy feeling.

–"There's nothing wrong with it!" he said. "What brings you here?"

–I am looking for a hermit that people say lives here.

–What do you want him for?

–I need some answers! And I hope he will be able to give them to me.

–You are not looking for the hermit. You are looking for the Messenger.

–The Messenger? I don't understand.

–Come inside, and let's sit and chat at our ease.

As I was entering the room, I observed the man I had in front of me. He was a young, thin man with brown hair and eyes. He was about 1.70 m. tall. He was wearing a beige, shift linen shirt and linen trousers in the same color. His outfit was completed by a pair of shoes made of cloth, a little darker than the rest.

After the shock of the first impression, thoughts rushed through my mind like wild horses: He doesn't look like a hermit to me. He must be someone passing by. And if he is just that, what am I doing with him in the middle of the wilderness...? His appearance of course, creates a feeling of ease and security. But then again, what was that he said about the messenger? He mustn't be aware of the existence of the hermit. And what he said about the compass not having gone wild, how did he know...? Besides, I clearly saw his hands as he leaned at the door and they were clean and not rough at all. I've always imagined a hermit in dark clothes, or maybe a worn-out cowl and his hands must surely be rough and full of calluses from the chores of monastic life... No, he can't be the hermit! He must be just

someone passing by!
That last realization filled me with anxiety. I wanted to turn round and run away.
–You've only just arrived and you already want to leave?
–*"I beg your pardon?" ...Was I thinking aloud? "What made you think that I wanted to leave?"*
–Your thoughts are very strong.
–*I don't understand you.*
–And how could it be possible for your fragmented logic to understand me! When I met you at the river, in that dream that shocked you so much, I could discern you had the ability to assimilate the message I am about to send to the people.
The shock had left me speechless!
–"I am the one you are looking for", *he continued.* "Sit down though, and let's take things from the beginning".
I sat on one of the chairs that were by the table. He took the one opposite to me.
–Do you know what that crazy spinning of the compass denotes?
–*"No", I answered.*
–That at this moment, you are in an energy spot, inside which there is a space-time vacuum. This time vacuum was created by me entering your dimension. In order for me to manifest in your time, I had to 'warp' the space-time continuum, so as to create a tunnel, a wormhole. Through this wormhole, I have the ability to 'jump' almost instantly, to other time points nearby.

---

[3] **'BACK TO THE FUTURE THROUGH ...TIME HOLES'**
http://www.physics 4u.gr/news/2000/scnews51.html ('TA NEA' Athens Newspaper, June 2000): «Stephen W. Hawking concludes: In order to travel in time, we must be able to warp space-time so much as to create a tunnel, a wormhole. This wormhole will connect both edges of our galaxy and it will help us take a shortcut, go from one edge to the other and come back while our friends are still alive. It has been said that these wormholes will be possible in the future.»

To you though, who are unbreakably bound to your space-time, it seems strange that time wear does not affect me. This is why I always appear to be young.
–*Excuse me, but if I have understood you correctly, you mean that you can interfere with time?*
–This is not something difficult to those who are outside the prison of time. To you of course, who are inside your space-time cage, something like this seems unattainable.

Don't skip chapters or bibliographic references

One shock followed another. I still hadn't recovered from his sudden appearance, and there he was talking to me about incomprehensible things!
–All this you are telling me is completely incomprehensible…
–Look, since almost everything we are about to say will be incomprehensible to you, and since coming events are of great urgency, I do not intend to exhaust myself in meaningless discussions, in order to make things easier for you to grasp. Put your intellect and your senses into a state of awareness, and understand.

I do not belong to your world, not even your universe! While I am here, time will not affect this point in space. And you, being in this space–time vacuum, will not be affected either. This will give us the opportunity to say a lot, without time limitations. Now, as for my appearance: Like a diver needs a special diving suit, in order to spend some time underwater, so does my hypostasis need a material carrier, in order to become perceivable here in this world. I come from the Real HyperUniverses of True Light. There, concepts are not split into good and bad ones but are united, whole. Now, as far as our bodies are concerned, these are not exactly bodies in the sense you give to the word. We are 'Intelligent Wholenesses' *[=Nous possessing Wholenesses]*. This is of course difficult for you to conceive. The reason necessitating my entrance into your world is extremely urgent and concerns a great portion of mankind; but not all! An extremely urgent message must be delivered to this portion of humanity. Through our discussion, you will realize who these humans are.

The difference between me and you is the Active Spirit. In me, the Spirit is completely active and awakened. Yours though, is in a comatose state. When the Spirit of a human awakens, then, this man knows everything. He/she has no need for any knowledge or information· because he/she just knows. As centuries passed by, man lost his ability to receive information from his Spirit. When he started using material ways to gain knowledge, the mechanism to receive it through the Spirit started becoming dormant. And today, this mechanism has become completely useless. By now, men equate the 'spiritual man' to the materialistically educated. The real meaning of the word 'spiritual' is lost.

In your world, all things, from the simplest to the most complex, can be seen from two different points of view: What they 'are' and what they 'seem to be'. A Spiritual person sees things the way they 'are'. Men always see what things seem to be.

On account of the restricting abilities of your sensory organs, you are unable to perceive the Whole. Through your five senses you perceive only a small arch of the circle of things that surround you. And the overestimation you always have for these extremely restricting senses of yours makes the probability for you to understand the whole circle surrounding your world, almost impossible. In general terms, people see the effect, but almost always miss the cause. They see the tree, but ignore the true reason for the creation of the tree. They look at man, as well as themselves, but ignore the reason for their existence.

☙ • ❧

I was listening unable to utter a single word. A sequence of feelings overcame my whole existence; awe, surprise, relief, query. It seemed unbelievable. Furthermore, a second wave of questions took hold of me. I had nevertheless come to this place with so many unanswered questions! I felt perplexed. I looked at his face. It emanated safety and self-confidence. His features were gentle and absolutely harmonious. If someone were to observe them carefully, one would not be able to say with certainty whether they belonged to a man or a woman. His eyes emitted an otherworldly brightness. His voice was soft and without any trace of tension. He crossed his hands on the table and looked at me.
–*"After Elias' cure, many people tried to find you"*, I said. *"But you avoided appearing to them. Why did you choose to appear to me?"*
–All these people came to meet me, asking of me to repair mistakes of their creator. No one approached me to learn the Truth.
–*The mistakes of their creator…? I don't understand.*
–Yes. They came either asking for a cure, restitution, or adjustment of their problems. In general, they were asking for material settlement.
–*And where was the harm in that? After all you had already performed a miracle.*
–The miracle I had performed was not the aim but the bait!
–*The bait to catch what?*
–Truth seekers; and not just seekers of any sort of material adjustment.
–*And were all those, looking for you, seeking merely material solutions to their problems?*
–No, there were also some who appeared to be searching for the Truth. The Truth however, can be sought by three different people in three different ways. The first seeks the Truth motivated by the hunger of his curiosity; the second by an existential anxiety, and the third driven by an inward and obscure nostalgia.

☙ • ❧

I hadn't even begun to resolve one of my queries, simply by asking a question, when a second one was born, only to be added to the previous unresolved one. I felt my mind short-circuiting.
–*"You know", I started timidly, "for many years I have also been on a*

35

quest for the Truth, and God in general."
–"And if you are saying you want to learn the Truth", *he interrupted me,* "have you initiated, before anything else, the process of self-knowledge, so as to know exactly which body of yours is the one seeking It?"
–I honestly don't know. But I also didn't know that, for each person, the origins for the quest of the truth can be different.
–I will help you understand. When you say you seek the truth, which truth do you want to know? The one fragmented into many pieces or the one and only one Truth?
–I don't understand what you mean by the term 'fragmented into many pieces'. I guess I am looking for the one and only one Truth.
–In other words, you are not certain?
–No, I probably don't even know the difference!
–Oh! There is an enormous difference! But answer another question for me, so that I may understand. You say you seek God. Which God, the Father-God or the creator-god?

I felt completely lost. I felt terribly embarrassed, as if I were ignorant of elementary issues. I took a deep breath to regain my strength, and said:
–Many are the things I don't know. You may take this for granted. This is after all why I am looking for answers in matters pertaining to life and man in general. These are eternal questions that have preoccupied many people in the past and still continue to do so. There are however, some values I believe I know well. Now, if I am wrong there too, then, please show me.

THE TRUTH

—So, you want to know the Truth! Men however, often say that the Truth can sometimes be quite painful! Fragments of the Truth are found scattered throughout man's history. In that fragmented state however, men cannot perceive IT as a complete picture. So, they prefer to choose that particle of Truth that suits their idiosyncrasy best.

From another point of view however, a truly unbiased observer of life itself can feel his way to the Truth. But since what he will finally discover will be very unpleasant, he will prefer to turn a blind eye; and the result? Men cannot stand holding the Truth in their hands as a whole, so they cast IT as far away as they can. Then, they bury their heads in the sand of the material world like ostriches in danger, and go on living in company with the fragmented part of the truth that has remained in their hand. This is all they have the power to hold!

We have, in conclusion, the subjective truth of each man who also believes that it is different from the fragmented piece of truth of his fellow man. What is really happening though is that the different pieces of the Truth that each one possesses can only be isolated parts of the ONE and absolute Truth. Let me give you an example which is very characteristic of what I am trying to say:

You must certainly be aware of Newton's experiment. He painted a round disk with the seven basic rainbow colors (iris) that correspond to each frequency range of the light spectrum. He started with red, the color with the longest wave length, immediately after that he painted the color orange, then the yellow, the green, the blue, the cyan and finally he painted the violet (mauve), which has the shortest wave-length. On the round disk therefore, all seven colors of the spectrum could be seen, one by one, in sequence. When the disk started spinning fast though, these colors ceased to appear separate as before, and their place was taken over by the white color alone. This is exactly what happens with the different views/truths of people, and the ONE TRUTH. The One Truth looks like the white light ray. When it falls onto the crystal prism though, it is deflected into the seven colors of the rainbow and creates the 'polychrome' of views and opinions.

Men, immobilized and chained by the bonds of their weaknesses onto their own angle/view as they are, choose 'red' for example as their vista/truth and disagree with the other group of similarly immobilized and chained men who choose the 'yellow' expression of truth. A third immobilized group chooses as their personal worldview the aspect of 'cyan', and scold the 'green' position, and so on.

This is what happens with all different positions and views of people; the result? They are all right, and at the same time wrong. In other words, they

Don't skip chapters or bibliographic references

all have a **portion of 'justness'**, as we will examine later. The Complete Truth is not to be found in **any** isolated color/position, but simultaneously in all of them; this Wholeness of the Truth is expressed in this experiment/example, by the white color, which is the result of the synthesis of all colors together. This is, after all, what your natural science claims! So this is what I mean, when I ask you whether you could bear a face-to-face encounter with the complete picture of the Truth, the 'white', or whether you are merely interested in some fragmented part of it that suits your idiosyncratic 'coloration'.

–*"I am hoping that I would be able to handle the complete truth!"* I said, *letting my curiosity answer, rather than the real me.*

☙·❧

In reality, I kept listening without being able to understand a single word of what he was saying. All the rudimentary knowledge I possessed about some spiritual truths, could not explain to me the concept of the fragmented. In my life, I had grown accustomed to choose. I would separate the data and choose the best; Always the good versus the bad. And now, how should I accept everything as a whole, and not choose the best one? And what about the other notion, that the need for answers on issues of an existential nature could have risen from another body of mine, and that I should know which one it was! ...

I knew of course, what some Eastern religions (or even theosophy) talk about the existence of the seven bodies of man, but nothing more. The acquisition of self-knowledge on the other hand, had always been a process that made me wonder as to the way it should be carried out. Additionally, that riddle/question he had posed to me, regarding which god I was looking for, the God – Father, or the god – creator (!) was extremely incomprehensible to me. He discerned my confusion and went on.

–In the Greek language, there are many forgotten keywords. When I say forgotten, I am referring to the meaning some words have today, as opposed to the primordial meaning that the same word used to have in the early years.

---

[4]   **TZIROPOULOU-EUSTATHIOU, A., 'HELLENIC LOGOS, HOW THE GREEK LANGUAGE INSEMINATED INTERNATIONAL LOGOS** [=LANGUAGE]' (p. 32):
(a) KORAES A., 'ABOUT EDUCATION AND LANGUAGE': «In languages, many times, a metaphor generates homonymies *(synonymies, vocabulary in general)*, which, deviating from the etymology of the first principal word, bring confusion to the untrained minds...»
(b) HATZIDAKIS, G. «And they considerably distorted the language...»

We are about to use now one of the most important ones: the word 'Truth' (Gr.: Αλήθεια). Do you know the older etymology of this word?

—I think I do. It consists of the privative prefix α that declares negation and the verb λανθάνω or its older form λήθω, which means to forget, to lose memory of, to let something elude me.

—Which means that the correct form of the word is A–ΛΗΘΗ–A, and it means: 'What we must not forget'.

---

5 A) PLATO'S 'PHAEDO, OR ABOUT THE PSYCHE' [=SOUL], ATHANASOPOULOS I., K. (72e, 73a): «And besides, said Cebes intervening,…Socrates, if it is true…that learning is nothing other than **anamnesis** (remembrance), then, from that point of view, it is necessary for us, somewhere in the past, to have learned that which we now remember. But this would be impossible, if our soul hadn't existed somewhere else, before assuming this human form.»

B) CHALAS, A., 'THE UNDERLYING MYSTERY IN THE HELLENIC ALPHABET AND THE UNIVERSE, OR, ABOUT SCIENCE' CH: ABOUT THE WORD 'TRUTH' (p. 178): «We, humans, are the beings wandering about as shadows and phantoms/ghosts, having forgotten our past —our distant past— our previous hypostasis, due to, who knows what great injustices. For, each one of us on this Earth is paying a previous life's sins. Each one of us is a convict, and his body is his bonds; and gravity is a merciless and all-seeing guard. From that past, before our arrival on Earth, we recall nothing, because, between that past and the eye of our consciousness, the cloud and the mist of oblivion is placed…There was a time in that distant past, during which we came against the World of Ideas, with the non-specific, the invisible… Our Soul knows everything. It is imperative though for someone to extract the infinite knowledge deposited in oblivion. We are indeed fallen angels, serving [a sentence] on Earth for great injustices. …And we come thus to the meaning of the word we are examining: When the eye of the Soul sees without the mist and the cloud, without oblivion/forgetfulness, then it has Light in front of it. This condition of the Soul is called A-λήθεια (Gr.: without forgetting). This is the mystical meaning of the profound word.»

We have hence unlocked the 'first door' which is the absolute understanding of the word Truth. The word namely declares that the truth is something that we cease *(the privative α)* to forget *(the verb λανθάνω - λήθω).* As the word itself indicates, the truth must be remembered.

—And how is it possible to remember the truth…? This seems to me even harder than to search for it and find it.

—Maybe now we can really proceed to harder paths. Remembrance is the result of the sufficiently more painful process of self-knowledge, as well as man's broader understanding of things surrounding him, with the substantial precondition however that he is capable of spherical perception. And when I say spherical perception, I mean the prerequisite of understanding all views and standpoints.

JUSTICE

I had left my compass on the table, with its bronze lid closed. A delicate flower was painted on the lid, decorated with beautiful colors. He took it in his hands and showed it to me, turning the decorated lid towards my side, thus leaving the bronze bottom side of the compass facing him.

–Do you see this object? I want you to describe to me what you see right this moment, in every detail.

–I can see a round metallic box that has a very beautiful flower painted on it.

–You are mistaken, *he answered.* There is no flower painted on this bronze box. You are probably imagining the flower. What my eyes see is just a round bronze box.

I looked at him feeling some wheels of my mind slowly starting to spin and smiled.

–So, could you tell me which one of us is right about this box?

–I believe we both are, according to our individual point of view.

–This is what people always do. They disagree with the portion of the truth that others see, as opposed to the part of the truth they themselves see. All men always have a percentage of rightfulness on their side. And they always expect this percentage of rightfulness to be accredited to them. We now come to mention, even if only superficially, another concept. The concept of Justice; but a basic prerequisite of Justice is the existence of Morality (Ethics).

–And how can we define Morality?

–In a couple of words really. Morality is the safeguarding of what is 'essentially beneficial' to each being, **separately**. Surely though, in this universe of fragmentation, personal benefit on a general scale, is not feasible. So, people are forced to seek justice for larger groups, at least to the extent that this can be possible. In most cases though, one group's benefit is contrary to the benefit of another, so injustice is never eliminated. Essentially, injustice doesn't exist; what makes it appear nonetheless is the different position each living being holds in the wheel of life. This diversity/variation of everyone's position about everything produces injustice as a side-effect.

This different position that each being holds in the whole world however, is not artificial, but natural. Nature itself has based its operating mechanism on this diversity. The impossibility on the other hand, for everyone's position to prevail is also not artificial, but natural. Thus a new natural law emerges, to establish its principles: The law of the <u>rightfulness/justice of the strongest</u>!

Where is justice, when the hungry lion devours the carefree antelope? Which of the two animals has justice on its side?

–Both of them surely possess a percentage of rightfulness. But the law imposed by the strongest obviously exists for the sake of balance and selective upgrading. Only through this law can the strongest prevail while the weakest perishes. Only thus can there be evolution!

–Perfect! Only through strife therefore can balance and selective upgrading be accomplished! Doesn't this though automatically indicate moral degrading for the sake of material improvement?

I looked at him perplexed.

–Injustice ends up establishing itself as one of the fundamental laws for the entire material nature to function, and of course for humans too, as they themselves are also parts of matter.

–But, couldn't man define justice for all, instituting fair legislation, despite nature's inability to do so?

–What you are saying automatically proves that nature is defective in this sector! As far as man is concerned now, in **absolutely** **interpersonal** **relations,** the (rightful) interest of one side is the loss of the (rightful) interest of the other! Then, no matter how 'right' each side is, one of the two will prevail and the other will automatically lose its portion of rightfulness.

What do people do then? They strive for justice. Yet, when they finally establish it somewhere, either for humans or for situations, it starts being dissolved by the diametrically opposite (weakest) point of the 'wheel of life-matter' –because this is nature's law– and there, injustice gradually takes its place, bringing the totality of things back to their natural balance.

---

[6] '**LIVING ON THE EDGE OF CHAOS**' http://www.physics4u.gr/5lessons/lesson4.html

«The Second Law of Thermodynamics sets some limitations to the forecasts made in this clock-Universe. Everything, the Second Law of Thermodynamics insists, progressively acquires greater disorder. Anything that increases order, has the <u>inevitable</u> consequence, that <u>somewhere else in the Universe, disorder will increase</u>.»

What chance do you really have, when you strive to make things more just? More just, according to whose right? Through dyadicism (duality), the basic characteristic of nature, another element will **always** suffer!

I will give you a rough example, which nevertheless clearly exhibits this natural law I'm talking about: We have a sick man on one side, and on the other, a whole army of microbes devouring him. Well, one of the living beings must die so the other can survive!

Don't skip chapters or bibliographic references

Everything in this material dimension, from the tiniest blade of grass to the larger beings, even celestial bodies themselves, is subdued to this twofold-law: 'just – unjust'. Thus, another basic axiom of this universe manifests which is: 'Your death is my life'. But the predominance of this axiom inflicts pain. When someone loses their percentage of rightfulness, starting from the most insignificant detail and ending with the loss of their right to live, then they suffer pain. No matter how strange it may seem to you, the pain and agony of death are the **same** for all creatures of this world; and don't think that pain and agony are nonexistent in the world of plants. A mere hostile thought of someone towards these life-forms, can cause them great disturbance!

---

[7] **ILISSOS JOURNAL,** ISSUE #80 (1970) & #95 (1972) **'PLANTS FEEL'-MARCIA HAEYS**:
«Cleve Backster was a technician for the FBI. He was a specialist in the truth detecting machines. His job was to maintain these machines and demonstrate their use to the agents of the FBI. ...Cleve Backster, as an expert in lie-detection methods to people, connected plants with electrodes and found reactions equivalent to people's fear, nervousness and affection. "It appears that plants have a primitive sense" Cleve Backster says. "They respond to arduous situations with signs that correspond to people's uneasiness. They show relief when their owner returns home from a trip." ...The experimental method of Cleve Backster consists of attaching electrodes on the leaves of the plants and measuring their electrical reactions to external actions, as would happen with man... During the experiments and in order to protect the plants from external influences, Cleve Backster puts them in lead containers. Furthermore, he uses the Faraday Screen to record the radiofrequencies of the electromagnetic field. The project started while he was trying to measure the pace at which plants absorb water.
"...I thought it would be interesting to find out whether I could cause a reaction to the plant when I provoked it. So, I decided to burn a leaf. But before I had even proceeded to get the matches, at the moment of my decision, a dramatic change was recorded on the paper. The polygraph needle jumped up and began drawing something that looked like human anxiety.»

No matter how persistently people imagine they will at some point attain absolute justice, they are deceiving themselves. Injustice will always be created as a counterweight elsewhere, to maintain the balance of duality the characteristic property of matter. [☯] ...If one isolates the negative electrons from a material atom, keeping only its positive nucleus he will automatically cancel the whole atom.

> **8** **A) GOSPEL OF PHILIP**, JEAN-YVES LELOUP:
>
> «§10. Light and darkness, life and death, right and left, are brothers and sisters. They are inseparable.» [Eng. tr. JOSEPH ROWE]
>
> **B) BLAVATSKY H., P., 'THE SECRET DOCTRINE'** (II-96): «Good and evil are twins, the progeny (descendants) of Space and Time, under the sway of Maya *(=Deceit)*. Separate them by cutting off one from the other, and they will both die. Neither exists per se (autonomously), since each has to be generated and created out of the other, in order to come into being.»

Just think! Can there be life without death anywhere on earth and generally in the whole universe? Is there beauty without ugliness? Everything exists in pairs: High-tide and low-tide; centrifugal and centripetal; attraction and repulsion; positive and negative. Why do you then imagine that justice can exist without injustice? Injustice is not a personal matter of men, neither is it a matter of their choice. It is a natural condition.

Choices are usually pre-determined by the creators of an application/program, not by its users. When for instance, you want to wash your clothes in the washing machine, you select one of the cycles (programs) offered by the manufacturer. The manufacturer of matter however, does not appear to have included the parameter of morality (ethics) and justice somewhere in his material structure. What cunning mind has therefore placed the blame of making the wrong choice onto man? Where is sin hidden?

> **9** **THE GOSPEL OF MARY (MAGDALENE)** JEAN-YVES LELOUP, Gr. tr. KOUROUSSI A., A., verses 13-17: «What is the sin of the world? The Master said: There is no sin, but it is you who make sin exist **when you act according to the habits of your nature**, which is inclined to adultery.»
>
> *The very nature of matter ends up as the 'adulteress nature' and JEAN-YVES LELOUP clarifies:* «The word adulteress, here, has no sexual connotation whatsoever.»

Let us then try to locate sin: If we initially exclude the transitory labels of "do's and don'ts" or what are commonly referred to as taboos, which are established by human societies through the centuries and which alternate from nation to nation and from era to era, sin is usually considered to be the cause of injustice or harm to someone else. We have already established however, that the different view/position someone holds in the circle of life, according to the dyadic law of the universe, automatically creates a dipole. So, if injustice prevails somewhere, then, at the diametrically opposite point, justice does and vice versa. The stronger each party/view is bound to its position

Don't skip chapters or bibliographic references

(fighting for its values), the more antagonistic it becomes towards the opponent's view (who strives to make his own dreams come true). At some point, when the limits of assertion are exceeded, sin arises as a side-effect.

Sin therefore is the result of this extreme assertion of a man's own percentage of rightfulness and arises as a side-effect of dyadic matter. Nevertheless, every man sins towards himself as well! This is because every single sacrifice of his automatically makes him answerable to himself.

---

[10] **GOSPEL OF THOMAS**, THE ECUMENICAL COPTIC PROJECT,

http://www.metalog.org/files/thomas.html: «§14. Jesus says to them: If you fast, you shall beget transgression for yourselves. And if you pray, you shall be condemned. And if you give alms (charity), you shall cause evil to your spirits.»

It is not my purpose to avert you from offering any benefaction to your fellow men with the view I am presenting you with, but to make you question the possibilities matter has to finally make you a perfect Man.

You people seem to be living inside one of those nightmares, where someone is thirsty in his sleep and is constantly trying to quench his thirst in his dream. He is constantly dreaming he is drinking water, which doesn't satisfy him though. He can only find relief when he wakes up and really drinks water. The same holds true with the daydreaming illusion of the creation of a perfect material world! For as long as someone remains seized by this daydreaming, one will desperately fight for justice, love, morality and ideals. Not a single thing from what men imagine they are touching with their hands is actually real. This is why a taste of un-fulfillment is all that is left on the lips of the more sensitive ones.

---

[11] **HERMES TRISMEGISTUS**, HERMETIC TEXTS, VOL. II, ASCLEPIUS & EXCERPTS, RODAKIS P., TZAFEROPOULOS AP., EXCERPT II$_A$ FROM THE HERMES' SPEECHES TO TAT

Hieroglyphic Egyptian Texts translated into Greek during the Ptolemaic period, by Heliopolis' priest, Manethon.

«§3. All therefore Tat that is found on earth, are not real, but only **imitations of the truth** and yet not all of them, but only a few... §4. The rest is lies and delusion, Tat, and conjectures, constructed like the pictures of imagination; ...§5. So, those who are **not** taken by the lie, they can see the truth.»

Many philosophers compare material life to a lethargic sleep; others to a 'living' dream. If man does not wake up from this lethargic sleep, he faces the real danger of actually 'dying of dehydration'.

> [12] **GOSPEL OF THOMAS**, JEAN YVES LELOUP:
>
> «§28. And Jesus said: I stood in the midst of the world and revealed myself to them in the flesh. I found them all intoxicated. Not one of them was thirsty and my soul grieved for the children of humanity, for they are blind in their hearts. They do not see. They came naked into the world, and naked they will leave it. At this time, they are intoxicated. When they have vomited their wine, they will return to themselves.» [Eng. tr. JOSEPH ROWE]

The unfortunate thing with people is, of course, that while things go well and according to their interest, they remain untroubled by the total injustice plaguing the entire creation. When injustice knocks on their own door however, only then, do they become riled up.

DOES GOD EXIST?

My entire ideological structure started trembling dangerously. A truth that made me feel insecure appeared in front of my eyes. I was just looking for a 'grip', compatible to my social background and reasoning, to hold on to.

–Maybe the view that many people have, namely that there is no Creator and nature itself created all these species through its evolutionary mechanism, is true. It would thus be perfectly natural, in this impersonal nature, for the immoral and the unjust to prevail.

–If you put it that way *–he spoke again–* let us open a parenthesis, in order for me to explain to you the fallacy of this thought.

Look at the universe. Do you know what the basic element of the structure of the material universe is? *He continued without waiting for my answer.* The universe exists because it is based on laws. Law however, is established by logic and not the illogical. The mindless cannot create the intelligent, and neither can it create rules. Each species generates its similar one (according to image and likeness). In nature though, what is evident, is the logic with which everything is structured; and not just simple logic, but its extreme mathematical expression: From the way the ant's body is structured and the ways it moves in order to survive, to the absolutely mathematical motion of celestial bodies.

Let us now hypothesize that the concept of randomness does indeed hold true in creation. In a cosmos where the mindless dominates, creation structured in a mathematical logic can only occur **by accident** once, not time after time. Statistically speaking, this logically structured **repetition**, escapes from the category of a random creation of the mindless, and becomes an absolutely programmed creation by the sentient/intelligent and the absolutely logical.

---

[13] **A) 'EMBIOGENESIS'** (ARTICLE: MAY 2003) http://www.livepedia.gr/index.php/ or http://www.physics4u.gr/articles/2003/creationvital.html

«A biotic system must do three things: 1) energy exchange, 2) information storage, 3) replication. All biotic systems, from human beings to bacteria, do these three things. In essence though, the creation of a living organism starts with amino-acids which create proteins.

Only twenty out of the eighty types of amino-acids are found in living organisms. The trick is to isolate the right type of amino-acid.

Then, **the correct amino-acids** must be joined together **in the right sequence** and produce the protein molecules. Besides that, there are other factors involved in the process, like the reactions after the sequence.

Other (non-amino-acid) molecules tend to react easier with amino-acids than amino-acids react with each other. There is therefore, the problem with these 'other' molecules. ...There is also another complication. Half of the amino-acids are clockwise and the other half are counter-clockwise. **Yet, only the counter-clockwise ones are found in living matter**. (50% are thus excluded from the possibilities of the 'random')

Now the correct amino-acids must be interconnected in the right order/sequence. Additionally, they must form the right bonds (e.g. peptide bonds) in the right places, because protein folds in the correct three-dimensional manner. If all these steps are not completed **with absolute precision,** the protein will not function.

...In the same way, probably one hundred amino-acids must be put together in exactly the right way, in order to form **a simple protein-molecule**. And remember, this is only the first step!

A protein molecule is not enough to make a living organism. About two hundred more must be created in the same manner, and must gather in exactly the right order to make a distinct living **cell**.

...Behe, in his book 'The black box of Darwin', states that 'The probability for just 100 amino-acids to 'accidentally' join together, would be equal to that of a blind man finding a **specific** grain of sand in the Sahara desert, and furthermore, finding it not once, but three times in a row!'

[...] **Darwin's simplistic hypothesis:** Darwin must have undoubtedly thought that it shouldn't be very difficult for life to be created from lifeless matter, because in his time there were no scientific means to show the great chasm between these two material classes. Ernst Haeckel, in 1905, describes living cells in a rather simplistic way as 'homogenous spherical creatures'. In those days, they had no means of seeing the complexity that exists in such a 'simple' cell. The truth, as we know it today, is that a 'simple' cell is **incredibly more complex** than anything man has ever designed or recreated, even with hyper-computers.»

B) 'MYSTERIES OF THE WORLD', VOL. 'SECRET MESSAGES' (p. 392):

«American physicist and theologian Gerald L. Schroeder, in his book 'Creation and the Big Bang', in 1996, stated that, according to his calculations, time was not sufficient enough (the Earth is approximately 5 billion years old) to allow for the accidental creation of complex organisms like man. At a Conference titled 'Macro-evolution' which took place in Chicago U.S. in 1980, the first complete re-evaluation of life's origin and evolution was done. Scientists reached the following conclusion: The creation of life is the result of either an unknown –till today– force of nature, or a natural factor (god?), or lastly, it has originated from somewhere else.»

Don't skip chapters or bibliographic references

Yet, this life too, that might have come from ...'somewhere else' ... must have been created by someone!

C) SCIENCE ILLUSTRATED, SPECIAL EDITION 'EVOLUTION', JANUARY 2007

A statement from Darwin himself:

CHARLES DARWIN 'THE ORIGIN OF SPECIES': «I openly admit that the assumption that the **eye** was created through the process of natural selection seems to me totally absurd.»

Take for example any of man's creations. Can a factory be created by chance? Can a bridge or a house be made by accident? No.

---

[14] **PHYSICS4U,** http://www.physics4u.gr/news/2000/scnews18.html

American scientists Peter Ward, Professor of Geology, and Donald Brownlee, Professor of Paleontology, both at the University of Washington in Seattle, in their book 'Rare Earth', mention a series of 'coincidences' that assume the burden of the creation of life on earth:

«To begin with, in order for life to be created, it needs a stable star for a father, a star like the sun, capable of constantly producing a stable and adequate quantity of energy for billions of years. Animals, animal species, as we know them, need oxygen. And it took almost two billion years for the build-up of the amount of oxygen needed for all the animals on earth. If the energy produced from the sun hadn't been stable, if there had been sudden changes during this long-lasting process, chances for life to be created on our planet would have been minute... Of extremely great importance is also the size of the sun. If it (the Sun) had been 30% larger, it would have self-combusted in four billion years, an extremely short time frame to allow for intelligent life-forms to evolve. If it had been smaller on the other hand (and it is calculated that 95% stars are smaller than the sun), there would have been other problems. For life to exist though, even more favorable astronomic circumstances must coincide. One of them is the presence of a giant planet like Jupiter at a distance not very close, and yet not very far, which can function as a 'gravitational shield' against asteroid and comet attacks. Jupiter and its gravitational field have repeatedly protected the earth from attacks of this kind. Equally important is the presence of the Moon. Its size is much larger than what one would normally expect for a natural satellite of our planet. Yet, it helps stabilize the earth's axis close to 23 degrees (where it is today). It is thanks to this permanent declination, that the temperature on the earth's surface is maintained stable: another basic prerequisite for the development of life. Even the very creation of the moon, appears to have occurred at the precise moment and in that exact manner which would create the conditions we enjoy today. Coincidences do not stop here however. Even the position of our solar system in the galaxy (neither too close to the edges, where stars don't have enough metals to facilitate the creation of planets, nor too close to the center, where radiation would kill us all), is yet another co-incidence that allows us to live.»

Therefore, since man, who is the ultimate creation of nature, does not create accidentally, would his own 'nature/maker' do so? Do not forget, that the creation always reflects its creator's characteristics.

The scenario of randomness is utterly illogical. It is selected as a view by a category of mainly intelligent people who, being open-minded as they are, ascertain the existence of cruelty and injustice in the whole structure and operation of nature. They also realize that the prevailing justice is only the law of the strongest. However, this comes in complete opposition to the concept of the benevolent and merciful god creator (the maker of heaven and earth), whom all religions thus depict with only miniscule variations. In an indirect effort to reject the idea of a bad creator as they perceive him through his creation, they dispute the paternity of his logically structured creation.

Could it be that we should unite these two, and then realize something more real, but not as pleasant? We say **yes** on the one hand to the sentient/intelligent and omniscient creator but **no** to his 'all benevolent' quality!

THE PRIMORDIAL (ORIGINAL) SIN

Let us rather start from the beginning. If we look at humanity's past, we will stumble upon an old myth/riddle. This myth refers to a serious error, into which the forefathers of man, Adam and Eve, befell. This fault resulted in their eviction from Paradise, where they originally dwelled. This expulsion is interpreted as their fall from grace, from an originally higher condition to an inferior one.

Before we set off to examine this myth, you must keep in mind that every myth is constructed in such a way, so as to bring forth coded information to every prospective analyst.

[15] **A) SALLUSTIUS** (OR SALLUST, OR SATURNINUS SECUNDUS SALLUSTIUS) **'ON THE GODS AND THE WORLD'** Gr. tr. GRAVIGGER P., CH. 'CONCERNING MYTHS', (p. 21):

«On what grounds then, have the Ancient people set aside these teachings, in order to use myths? Here is what is worth inquiring. The first benefit we obtain from the use of myths is precisely this research, because this way, the intellect does not remain idle.»

He then classifies myths into five categories (p. 27): «...Amongst myths, some are theological, some are physical and the others are psychic, materialistic and mixed.»

B) THE GOSPEL OF MATTHEW, CH. 13: «§35...the words spoken by the prophet: I shall open my mouth in parables, I shall declare things which have been kept secret since the creation of the world.»

C) MARGIORIS, N. 'DE-SYMBOLIZATION OF THE GREEK MYTHOLOGY':

«The Myth is a manifestation of every mystery. The symbol/idea is translated into our world with a myth....The myth-weavers used to hide the knowledge they possessed, inside the plots/descriptions of the myth. ...He who de-symbolizes the myth, transcends the exoteric facts of the myth-plot and finds the esoteric schemes/symbols and transforms/transmutes them ...hence revealing the symbol's aetheric side. ...The myth was created by great mystics, who structured it with two sides: The esoteric/aetheric and the exoteric/narrative. The esoteric/aetheric side conceals the truths they carved inside the myth...i.e. they created the idea/symbol that represents the truth itself. They then built the outer features, the plots...The mystics have taught us that during the construction of the esoteric part of the myth, the core, they incorporated **seven truths**. These can be sciences... primordial knowledge, creative vibrations, spiritual energies, inner laws... experiences from other dimensions, where the gnosiological harvesting is enormously great.»

Within the story of the same myth, it is possible to unlock many levels of knowledge. It is essential though, for the prospective analyst, to possess at least certain basic elements. I shall then bring these basic elements forth to you, in order to establish the foundations onto which we shall later construct our building. Initially, you must know that there is not only one 'fall' for man, but a concatenation of falls, with **two**, overbearing 'par excellence'.

---

[16] **BLAVATSKY H., P., 'THE SECRET DOCTRINE'** (II-457):

«The Kabbalists teach **the existence of four distinct Adams**, or the transformation of four consecutive Adams, the emanations from the Dyooknah (divine phantom) of the Heavenly Man, a superior combination of Neschamah, the highest Soul or Spirit: this Adam having, of course, neither a gross human body, nor a body of desire. This 'Adam' is the prototype of the second Adam. That they represent our Five Races is certain, as everyone can see by their description in the Kabbalah: the first being the 'perfect, Holy Adam'... 'A shadow that disappeared' and was produced from the divine Tzelem (Image). The second is called the protoplastic androgyne [man/woman] Adam of the future terrestrial and separated (divided) Adam. The third Adam is the man made of 'dust/soil' (the first innocent Adam) and the fourth, is the supposed forefather of our own race, the Fallen Adam, who was clothed with skin, flesh, nerves, etc... He possesses the animal power of reproduction and continuance of species, and this is the human Root-Race.»

There is not one Heaven, but **two**. This happens because there are **two** main Creations.

---

[17] **A) BLAVATSKY H., P., 'THE SECRET DOCTRINE'** (II-59):

«Every ancient Theogony without exception −from the Aryan and the Egyptian down to that of Hesiod− places, in the order of Cosmogonical evolution, Night before the Day; even Genesis, where 'darkness is upon the face of the deep' before 'the first day'. The reason for this is that every Cosmogony begins by the so-called '<u>**Secondary Creation**</u>': namely the manifested Universe.»

B) CHALDEAN ORACLES, ATHINOGENIS I., GRAVIGGER, P., KROLL 33 − PLACES 185 PROCLUS, TIM. 429b, 256a (p. 113): «...The sun was born, like the others, **by the second Noũs/mind**, which was named Time of Time [Gr. Chronos].»

C) PLATO'S 'TIMAEUS' Gr. tr. KOUTROUMPAS D., G. (V 29a2 – 29b2): «If, of course, this world is beautiful, and the creator benevolent, it is obvious that the Maker was aiming for the eternal (the unchangeable)...And since these things exist in this way, by absolute necessity, **this world must be the image of another**. Thus, the most important duty of each researcher is to start from the natural principle (Gr. 'Archē').»

Don't skip chapters or bibliographic references

D) HERMES TRISMEGISTUS, HERMETIC TEXTS, VOL. I, SPEECHES I-XVII, RODAKIS P., TZAFEROPOULOS AP., SPEECH A: «§8. And I said to him: Where do these elements of nature come from? And he answered to me again: From the Divine Will which took the form of Logos (Word) and saw the good world *(of the 1ˢᵗ Creation)* and mimicked it, creating a world with its own *(the Divine Will's)* elements and its own creations, the souls.»

I looked at him puzzled, in disbelief.
–In this conversation, I do not intend to repeat known information to you, information of the kind that people ruminate, but to transpose you on to a very special vantage point, from which you will see the world that surrounds you, completely different and overtly real.

This particular myth corresponds to these falls of man and sketches out these facts in a coded way. Concepts describing the real events are certainly quite complex and for this reason, completion of this knowledge will come to you when we have closed the circle of our discussion in this meeting. Then, you will have understood with absolute clarity which these falls are and on what planes they have taken place. Additionally, two categories of Gods appear inside the book of Genesis. This becomes apparent when in many places, mainly in the first chapters, God is sometimes one, and other times he speaks in plural, as if they were a team.

---

[18] **OLD TESTAMENT**, GENESIS CH. 1: «§26. And god said: Let **us** make man, in our image after **our** likeness.»

Basically, the word 'god', in the first chapters of Genesis, refers to two diametrically opposite Beings. One refers to the Father God and the other to the god (gods) creator(s). For now, it will suffice for us to generally mention some very basic information. In the flow of our conversation though, we will report all the facts in greater detail.

This primordial myth says that sometime in the remote past, Adam and Eve were in Heaven. And God said to them: "You may eat fruit from all the trees of Paradise. But you must not eat the fruit from the 'wood' of knowledge of good and evil. If you eat from it, then you will die".

---

[19] **OLD TESTAMENT**, GENESIS CH. 2: «§16…And the lord god commanded **Adam*** saying: "Of every tree of the **paradise***, you may freely eat; §17 but of the tree of the knowledge of good and evil you shall not eat, for in the day that you eat of it, you shall **certainly die.**»
*These words are used in the Original Greek version of the Seventy (Septuagint or LXX): [§16 καὶ ἐνετείλατο Κύριος ὁ Θεὸς τῷ Ἀδὰμ λέγων· ἀπὸ παντὸς ξύλου τοῦ ἐν τῷ παραδείσῳ βρώσει φαγῇ, §17 ἀπὸ δὲ τοῦ ξύλου τοῦ γινώσκειν καλὸν καὶ πονηρόν, οὐ φάγεσθε ἀπ' αὐτοῦ· ᾗ δ' ἂν ἡμέρᾳ φάγητε ἀπ' αὐτοῦ, θανάτῳ ἀποθανεῖσθε.]

Everything was going well in the Heavenly realm, when at some point, a snake, having embraced the said (dead) tree/wood, prompted Eve to try its forbidden fruit, and through her, Adam as well. This fruit was the fruit of the 'knowledge of good and evil'.

This seemingly simple myth conceals the forgotten story of the 'Odyssey' of man. Every word in it is a symbol. Before we proceed to the analysis of the myth, we must clarify a fundamental word: the word 'god'. We shall once again go back to the primary etymologies of the Greek language. The word used in the scriptures in Greek is θεός [theós] (e.g. theology) and comes from the Greek verb [θεάομαι-θεώμαι] meaning I am visible, I am seen *(tr. n.: another word coming from the same verb is* θέατρο= *theatre).*

---

[20] **A) BLAVATSKY H., P., 'THE SECRET DOCTRINE'** (I-1):

«An Archaic Manuscript is before the eyes of the writer. On the first page, an immaculate white disk can be seen on a dull black background. On the following page, there is the same disk, but with a central point.

The student knows that the first disk represents the Cosmos in Eternity before the re-awakening of the still slumbering Energy…The point in the hitherto immaculate disk, denotes the dawn of differentiation. It is the Point in the Mundane (Cosmic) Egg; the germ within the latter, which will become the Universe, the ALL, the boundless periodical Cosmos, this germ being latent and active, periodically and by turns. The one circle is the Divine Monad (Unity) from which all proceeds (is projected) and to which all returns.»

In other words, the Picture that is presented in the archaic text is a circle in the center of which there is a dot/point: ⊙. *This symbol though, is the <u>primary shape</u> of the Greek Letter* Θ *(Theta), which is the starting letter of the word* ΘΕΟΣ *[Theos = God), which in turn (the word), with its first letter symbolizes exactly what it denotes.*

B) HERMES TRISMEGISTUS, HERMETIC TEXTS, VOL. I, RODAKIS P., TZAFEROPOULOS AP., SPEECH VI, ASCLEPIUS' DEFINITIONS TO KING AMMON

«§3. I will start my sermon, by invocation unto God, the master of all and creator and father, the All-Encompassing One…§7. To see Him, is not a matter of conjecture, but his very appearance engulfs the whole world in splendor, the world that is above and that which is below; for he is established in the midst, <u>wreathing the Cosmos</u>.» [⊙]

C) CHALAS A., 'THE UNDERLYING MYSTERY IN THE HELLENIC ALPHABET AND THE UNIVERSE, OR, ABOUT SCIENCE' CH: ABOUT THE WORD 'TRUTH' (p. 145):

«And firstly, we can notice that of the 24 known letters, only Theta (Θ) is left aside, somehow supervising and regulating everything. *(He classifies the*

Don't skip chapters or bibliographic references

> *Greek letters into nine triads including koppa [κόππα Ϟ] and sampi [σαμπί ϡ], where [Θ] completes their triad. Since these two letters [Ϟ] and [ϡ] are not used anymore, [Θ] is left on its own in the end).* And in a strange 'coincidence', the word Theos [Θεός = God] starts with Θ, and furthermore, that symbol Θ consists of a circular or elliptical circumference, of which, upon writing it, we never fail to define the Center. Is it that Θ symbolizes the Universe, in the center of which yet again lies the Central Authority?»

As the word itself denotes, the gods/creators, during the early periods of creation, were visible to men. It was feasible in other words for the gods to be seen. As a matter of fact, forgotten 'remnants' (of this visibility) can be found in most myths giving accounts of encounters of the gods with their protégés.

> [21] **A) HESIOD 'THEOGONY'** Gr. tr. STAVROS GIRGENIS (Verse. 535):
> «[...καὶ γὰρ ὅτ᾽ ἐκρίνοντο θεοὶ θνητοί τ᾽ ἄνθρωποι...] ... because, when the gods and mortal men separated from each other...»
> *The commentator of Theogony, Stavros Girgenis (ZITROS publ.) notes:*
> «Hesiod has in mind *(in this verse)* the end of the era when **the gods and men lived and ate together**.»
> **B) PLATO'S 'TIMAEUS'** Gr. tr. KOUTROUMPAS D., G. (XIII 40e-40e5): «And it is beyond our powers to speak of the other daemons and to know about their birth. We must believe those who spoke before and were descendants of the gods, as they said, even if they spoke without the probable and necessary proof. And inasmuch as they profess to speak of known family matters, we are obliged to believe them, following the established practices.»

When men say 'God', they mean the initially visible creator.
Besides the creator or creators, there is also another Infinitely Greater Existence, Higher, above the creator: The Genitor of the True Light.

> [22] **SALLUSTIUS SATURNINUS SECUNDUS**– (GALES 300 A.D.) **'ON THE GODS AND THE WORLD'**, Gr. tr. GRAVIGGER P. (FOOTNOTE OF THE TRANSLATOR, P. GRAVIGGER): PLOTINUS CH. V, IV 1 – PROCLUS, PLATO'S THEOLOGY II-Ψ- DIONYSIUS THE AREOPAGITE, 'ABOUT DIVINE NAMES'. FOR A CORRESPONDENT VIEW ON THE FIRST PRINCIPLE (ARCHĒ) IN THE EGYPTIANS SEE IAMVL. 'ON THE MYSTERIES' VIII, 2.
> «Prior to those who truly exist, and before all the archons *(or before all beginnings/startups/creations),* **There Is One God, Preceding the First God** and king, immoveable and abiding in the uniqueness of **His Own Unity**. For neither is there anything intelligible connected with Him, nor any other paradigm (example) exists about Him, the Self-Paternal, Self-Begotten (Self-Generated) and Singly-Paternal God, the One Who is really *Ἀγαθός*

[=Good/Benevolent] {*See Tr. n. on the w. Ἀγαθός at the beginning of Ch. 'HIGHER MENTAL BODY – CELESTIAL MAN'*}. For *(He is)* **even Greater, and The First One** and the fountain/source of all and the root/foundation/principle of all the first intelligible (thought-out) concepts, of the archetypes of all, of the intelligible forms.

And from this One then, *(the First One)*, a *(Second)* autonomous God appeared, self-contained and self-sufficient. For He *(the Second One)* is the principle/start *[Gr. Archē]* and also the god of other *(inferior)* gods, being **a Monad** Himself *(the Second One),* stemming from the First One, before Essence and the principle of It. These, therefore, are the most ancient principles of all things, older than the ones that Hermes *(Trismegistus)* places prior to the aethereal and empyrean (fiery) and celestial gods.»

He cannot be called God (Theós) because he has never been seen.

[23] A) THE GOSPEL OF JOHN, CH. 5:
«§37. And the Father, who has sent me…you have neither heard His <u>voice</u> **at any time**, nor seen His <u>form</u>.»

The god, who appeared to Moses in the form of the 'burning bush' on Mt. Sinai, **was not** *The Father of Jesus:*

B) OLD TESTAMENT, EXODUS CH. 19:
«§18. And Mount Sinai was wrapped in smoke, because the **Lord** descended <u>upon it, in fire [pyre]</u>. The smoke thereof ascended like the smoke of a furnace, and the whole mountain quaked violently, §19…and Moses spoke <u>and God answered him</u> **by a voice**.»

And Blavatsky notes:

C) BLAVATSKY H., P., 'THE SECRET DOCTRINE' (I-374):
«In the Zohar we read as follows: As Moses was keeping a vigil on Mount Sinai, in company with the deity, who was concealed from his sight by a cloud, he felt a great fear overcome him, and suddenly asked: "Lord, where art thou…sleepest thou, O Lord?…" And the Spirit answered him: "I never sleep: Were I to fall asleep for a moment **before my time**, all the creation would crumble into dissolution in one instant."

'Before my time' is very suggestive. It shows the God of Moses to be only a **temporary substitute**, like the male Brahma, a substitute and an aspect of THAT which is immutable, and which therefore can take no part in the 'days', or in the 'nights', *(of Brahma)* nor have any concern whatever with reaction or dissolution.»

He has no Name, simply because IT cannot be uttered through matter.

Don't skip chapters or bibliographic references

> [24] **HERMES TRISMEGISTUS**, HERMETIC TEXTS, VOL. II, RODAKIS P., TZAFEROPOULOS AP., 'ASCLEPIUS, OR THE PERFECT SERMON' (p. 51):
> «§20…So, there is no hope for the Omnipotent Father and Master of all beings to be defined by a name, even if that name is complex and sophisticated. God has no name.»

He is The Unspoken, The Great One: The Father.

> [25] **SALLUSTIUS (OR SALLUST) OR SATURNINUS SECUNDUS SALLUSTIUS** (GAUL 300 A. D.), **'ON THE GODS AND THE WORLD'** (Gr. tr. P. GRAVIGGER) p. 41-42:
> «Among the gods some are of the world, 'cosmic', and some above the world, 'hyper-cosmic'. By the term 'cosmic' I am referring to the Gods who create the Cosmos; as for the 'hyper-cosmic' ones, some create the essences of the Gods, others the noûs (mind) and others the souls: thus they have three orders, and all these (orders) are found in the related teachings.
> Among the 'cosmic' Gods one team creates the Cosmos, another animates it, another creates the harmony between the opposites which comprise it, and yet others supervise it, for the preservation of the once achieved harmony.»

In the centuries of man's history, this difference has been forgotten. So, with the word 'god' two completely different Entities were associated. The creator/god of the entire material universe, namely 'of what is seen and what is not seen' on one hand and, on the other, The Supreme One, The Genitor of True Light, The Unspoken **Mother/Father Unified**.

> [26] **HERMES TRISMEGISTUS**, HERMETIC TEXTS, VOL. II, RODAKIS P., TZAFEROPOULOS AP., 'ASCLEPIUS, OR THE PERFECT SERMON' (p. 51): «§21 God engulfs everything; He has in Him the infinite fertility of **both** genders.»

In the first two chapters of Genesis in the Old Testament, both These Two different Entities are involved, hidden in the symbolisms of the myth.
I was watching him with obvious astonishment painted on my face. He looked at me, and realizing my queries, he continued.
–When the truth is being searched starting from the side of matter, the 'tangle' is impossible to be resolved. When it is being searched from the side of the Spirit though, then everything gets untangled. There lies the difficulty for men to discover the Truth. Men try to discover the beginning and the cause of all through research, science and observation. Nevertheless, the answers they get are fragmented, since they all stem from this material plane of fragmentation. The more spiritually fine (subtle) the source of the information, the less fragmented and more spherical this information is.

This small clarification surely didn't satisfy me completely. Yet the only thing I could do at that point was to patiently synthesize the new puzzle pieces he was offering with my logic, gradually formulating the image of Truth. After this brief parenthesis, he returned to his main topic.

–We will now move onto another plane, which is very remote from the dense matter that surrounds man. I will try to describe this plane to you, giving form –as much as possible– to the concepts that compose it, by creating 'images' for them.

---

[27] **CHALDEAN ORACLES**, Gr. tr. ATHINOGENIS I., GRAVIGGER P., TEXT AND TRANS-LATION BASED ON THE COLLECTION OF W. KROLL, ALONG WITH ADDITIONS AND IMPROVEMENTS OF ED. DES PLACES (ORACLES CHALDAIQUES, PARIS 1971, B. L.) ED. BY ATHINOGENIS I., GRAVIGGER P. —KROLL, P. 11, KROLL, DAMASCIUS I, 154:

«There exists, something Intelligible *(apprehensible by the mind only)*, which you must perceive by the flower of your Noũs *(mind)*; for if you should incline your mind towards It and try to perceive It (like a particular, discrete thing), you will not manage to perceive This; for It Is a certain kind of power belonging to the edge (of a sword) of circumlucid strength and with glittering mental intersections (rays). <u>Therefore, you must not intently try to perceive That Intelligible Thing with vehemence of intellection, but with the subtle flame of a subtle/finer Noũs</u>, which can measure all things, except That Intelligible One; you must indeed understand That Intelligible – and if you turn your Noũs inwards to It, you shall perceive it– not fixedly, but by directing the pure Eye of your soul, after it *(your soul)* has turned away from *(disregarded)* anything sensory, so that your Noũs –void of thoughts– can turn towards The Intelligible, so that you may learn The Intelligible, **for It exists beyond the boundaries of human logic**.» [FESTUGIRE, REVELATION IV, p. 132-134 - H. LEWY, Chaldean Oracles p. 169 – PLACES, 123]

Through this 'image-giving process', I will present to you the Territories of Dominion of The Supreme One, The Unspoken. These Territories are infinite. They are The HyperUniverses of the Unsplit True Light.

---

[28] **CHALDEAN ORACLES**, A. I., GRAVIGGER, P., PROCLUS IN PLATO, KROLL 31- PLACES (p. 107) «For this is the light which is **above** the empyrean world *(the world of fire)*, which is <u>A Unit</u> (Monad), **before** the triad of the empyrean, the aetheric and the hylic (material) world.»

Everything THERE is Whole, Complete. Concepts are Unsplit. There is no good, simply because there is no evil. There is no justice, simply because there is no injustice. There is no dyadicism (duality).

Don't skip chapters or bibliographic references

---

[29] GOSPEL OF PHILIP, JEAN-YVES LELOUP:

«§69…He who has appeared *(the manifested creator)* has come from the depths, and *(but)* He Who owns the hidden things *(The Supreme One)*, **is beyond all the opposites**.» [Eng. tr. Joseph Rowe]

There is though, absolute Harmony and Knowledge (Gnosis). Concepts do not conflict with each other as opposites, but flow together in an ocean of absolute harmony and virtue. Beings are not split in male and female. Male and female are unified into **One Wholeness**, as is The Absolute One, Mother–Father of all.

---

[30] THE GOSPEL OF JUDAS [KASSER R., MEYER M., WURST G., NATIONAL GEOGRAPHIC]:

«[35] Judas [said] to him *(to Jesus)* "I know who you are and where you come from. You are from the immortal realm of Barbelo *(The Divine World of the Unutterable Father)*. And I am not worthy to utter the name of the One Who has sent you.»

At some 'point in time', inside The Absolute, The Great Unuttered Father emitted Primordial Light Rays from within His Existence: The Ultimate Firstborn Sons. Born directly of the Unuttered Father, they had those Unique Characteristics to possess HyperUniverses of Unsplit True Light: **They were the authorized ones**.

---

[31] *The above text **does not refer** to the so-called 'parallel universes'. These will be mentioned towards the end of the book, and **must be clearly distinguished** from what we call HyperUniverses.*

They were the Second manifestation of the Deity, in the form of the 'Son' (male and female one). Every Son of the Unuttered Principle was granted a HyperUniverse.

---

[32] THE GOSPEL OF JUDAS [KASSER R., MEYER M., WURST G., NATIONAL GEOGRAPHIC]: JESUS IS TEACHES JUDAS ABOUT COSMOLOGY; THE SPIRIT AND THE SELF-GENERATED:

«[47] Jesus said, [come], that I may teach you about [secrets] no person [has] ever seen. For there exists, a great and boundless realm, whose extent no generation of angels has seen, [in which] there is [a] great invisible [Spirit].

[The Gospel's translators have added the following: "which no eye of an angel has ever seen, no thought of the heart has ever comprehended, and it was never called by any name."]

…A Great angel, the enlightened divine Self-Generated One, emerged

---

from the cloud. Because of Him, four other angels came into being from another cloud, and they became attendants for the angelic Self-Generated *(The Self-Generated is the Unuttered – Unspoken Principle – The One – The Father, male and female one.)* The Self-Generated said, 'Let [lost text] come into being [lost text],' and it came into being [lost text]. And he [created] the first Luminary *(i.e. An Ultimate Spirit, His Monogenes in this particular HyperUniverse/Aeon)* to reign over him *(the Aeon)*. He said, 'Let angels come into being to serve [him]' and myriads without number came into being. He said '[Let] an enlightened aeon come into being' *(2nd Hyper-Universe of Unsplit Light)* and he came into being. He created the second Luminary *(Second Monogenes (Singly-Born) for the specific 2nd Hyper-Universe/Aeon)* [to] reign over him *(over the Second Aeon)*, together with myriads of angels without number, to offer service. That is how He created the rest of the enlightened aeons *(HyperUniverses of Unsplit Light).»*

In Judas' Gospel, it is mentioned, that there are twelve Aeons/HyperUniverses.

«…The twelve aeons of the twelve Luminaries constitute their Father, with six heavens for each aeon *(six dimensions for each HyperUniverse/Aeon)*, so that there are seventy-two heavens *(dimensions)* for the seventy-two Luminaries *(72 Monogenes).»*

For now, we briefly mention some concepts in passing. All these will later on be analyzed and justified meticulously with more evidence.

Inside the HyperUniverse of each Firstborn Son *(Luminary)*, absolutely harmonious Intelligent *[Nous possessing]* Entities (male and female one) were created by the Firstborn. These Entities expanded, offering new Beings into existence. All Beings stemming from the Firstborn were the third manifestation of the Unuttered Principle, with the quality of the Holy Spirit.

Body, in the sense that men know, does not exist. A relative designation of these Supreme Entities would be **Intelligent Wholenesses**.

The proliferation of these Entities has **no relation** to the insemination of material humans. Observe how this happens in an evolutionary manner: Inside the HyperUniverses of True Unsplit Light, a young figure (male and female one) –the third manifestation as the Holy Spirit– starts moving inside the infinite oceans of Knowledge of the Laws and Archetypes. It expresses one of the infinite qualities of ITS (male + female) Monogenes Genitor *(Luminary)* of that particular HyperUniverse *(Aeon)*. Emotions, in the sense known to humans, do not exist.

Don't skip chapters or bibliographic references

[33] **HERMES TRISMEGISTUS**, HERMETIC TEXTS, VOL. II, RODAKIS P., TZAFEROPOULOS AP., 'EXCERPT IV, 'FROM HERMES' SPEECHES TO TAT':

«§18…Wherefore, I say that sensations *(feelings)* are both corporeal and mortal, as they resemble the *(material)* body in constitution… §19. On the contrary, Immortal Bodies have no feeling, precisely because they are immortal; feeling is nothing more than the pre-existence of good or evil in the body, or their departure. Whereas in the Immortal Bodies nothing is born and nothing dies; therefore feeling does not exist in them.»

On the contrary, there is 'something' that only remotely resembles these emotions. It is a plethora of **complete** and **unsplit** states of being (biomes) that never come in opposition to one another, but are all characterized by an inconceivable, continuously expanding variety. Each Wholeness, as IT LIVES, absorbs the unified Knowledge of the Archetypes. At the same time IT 'associates' with other Wholenesses of different Qualities. From this symbiosis, Each Wholeness absorbs additional Qualities from the other. In other words, an 'osmosis-like' phenomenon is created. The newly assimilated Properties/Qualities interlace with the original innate ones and create new compositions of biomes and Properties. These various new Properties, in combination with Knowledge, are conducive to the expansion of each Personality, Its growth. At some point, when this particular Wholeness reaches a maximum level of expansion, new, separate, prevailing Properties detach themselves from IT as new, young, living Beings. These are self-substantial on one hand, but parts of the Genitor on the other. Every young Being, is a new diverse Property of the Primary One. The Primary Being now, continues to experience situations through ITS personal Life and also through ITS 'children'. The young Offspring on the other hand, set off on their own lives, yet in constant connection with Their Genitor. All Wholenesses are expressions of the Holy Spirit, and are united through Their Genitors with the Firstborn *(Luminary)* of their home HyperUniverse, and also with The Absolute One, The Unutterable Principle. The Absolute One again, is united with all His/Her Offspring (as They All Are Consubstantial). There is in other words, an unbroken **connection** among all Beings. Loneliness is a totally unknown condition.

These are in very general terms the Worlds/HyperUniverses of the True. There, the One and True Paradise exists, and Its 'Trees' symbolize the HyperUniverses of The True, Unsplit Light. In the center of this Sacred Heaven, there is the Tree of Eternal and Inexhaustible Life, which is born by the assimilation of the boundless Gnosis of the Sacred Archetypes. There is however, a dead tree/wood/universe, which is cut off and isolated from the other trees/HyperUniverses; a creation, **reflective** of the Real One.

☙·❧

Inside one of the HyperUniverses of the Firstborn Sons *(Luminaries),* at 'some point' a normal Wholeness (male + female one) 'was born' but with somewhat odd combinations of properties. After IT absorbed the Properties, the Laws and the Archetypes of ITS Universe IT expanded. But when the time came for IT to offer ITS offspring to ITS 'Home' HyperUniverse, **IT defected**. IT (this Wholeness) chose to create a universe of ITS own.

---

[34] **CHALDEAN ORACLES,** Gr. tr. ATHINOGENIS I., GRAVIGGER, P. PROCLUS IN TIMAEUS D, TALKING ABOUT THE AEON:

«Once **he snatched, completely alone and for himself,** the 'Flower of the Noûs (Mind)' from the Paternal Might, he is able to understand the Father's Noûs, and deliver that Noûs to all sources and upon all principles and has the power to swirl the never-tiring **vortex** and ever stay inside it.»

IT decided to create an isolated universe. However, IT was not authorized to do so, IT was a transgressor; IT was a thief and a fugitive at the same time.

---

[35] **A) THE APOCRYPHON OF JOHN,** THE GNOSTIC SOCIETY LIBRARY: ENG. TR. FROM COPTIC: FREDERIK WISSE: «This is **the first archon** who took a great power from his mother. And he removed himself from her and moved away from the places where he was born. He became strong and created for himself other aeons with a flame of luminous fire… Then his mother *(of the fallen creator)*…became aware of the deficiency, when the brightness of her light diminished. …But when she saw the wickedness, which had happened and the **theft,** which her son had committed, she repented…And the arrogant one took power from his mother.» [GR. EDITION: APOCRYPHAL TEXTS OF THE NEW TESTAMENT, VOL. V, THE APOCRYPHON OF JOHN, TR. KOUTSOUKIS D., PYRINOS KOSMOS PUBL]

Let us see however, who this 'first archon' is, that John describes in his Apocryphon Gospel, by searching for him in his more 'worldly' Gospel:

B) THE GOSPEL OF JOHN, CH. 12:

«§31. Now is the judgment of this world: now shall the **archon (ruler) of this world** be cast out.»

C) THE GOSPEL OF JOHN, CH. 16: «§11. …And concerning judgment, because **the archon (ruler) of this world** has been judged.»

D) BLAVATSKY H., P., 'THE SECRET DOCTRINE' (II-483): «The history begins by the descent on Earth of the 'Gods' …and this is the *(first)* fall. Whether (it is about) Brahma (who) **hurled down** on Earth in the allegory of Bhaghavat, or Jupiter by Kronos…»

Don't skip chapters or bibliographic references

In order for IT to accomplish that, IT had to use unorthodox methods. After IT withdrew to a neutral part of the Whole, IT **chose an old creation remnant**. This was the forbidden dead wood tree/universe. In order for IT to vitalize it, IT writhed around it, embracing it fully.

---

36 **HERMES TRISMEGISTUS, THE FOUNDER OF MONOTHEISM 9000 B.C.,** IOANNIDIS P. K.

1ST SPEECH: «§4…And I saw an infinite sight, flooded by light, both sweet and exceedingly pleasant; and I was wonderfully delighted beholding it *(the image of the HyperUniverses)*. But after a little while *(in another place)* I saw a downward darkness partially born coming down in **an oblique formation**, like a snake, fearful and hideous. I also saw that darkness to be changed into a **moist nature**, unspeakably troubled, which yielded a fiery smoke from its depths, and from whence I heard an unutterable heartbreaking sound, and an inarticulate roar in a voice of fire *(the forbidden tree)*.
§5. From those Luminous Planes *(of the HyperUniverses)*, I saw a Holy Logos (Word) pouring Itself out towards the moist nature *(the union of the fallen creator with the forbidden tree)*… §6…And that luminous Logos (Word) that you saw surging from (my) Luminous Planes **towards** that **moist nature**, is my *(fallen)* son that came out of my Noûs (Mind).»

After IT was assimilated by it, IT expanded to the deepest and furthest parts of it, and was cleaved in two opposite positions –god and daemon– thus giving birth to ITS own 'firstborns', in a state entirely ITS own.

---

37 **A) THE APOCRYPHON OF JOHN,** THE GNOSTIC SOCIETY LIBRARY [ENG. TR. FROM COPTIC: FREDERIK WISSE]: «And Sophia of the Epinoia… wanted to bring forth a likeness out of herself without the consent of the Spirit… And though the person of her maleness had not approved and had not consented, (yet) she brought forth (gave birth)… And because of the invincible power which is in her, her thought did not remain idle, and something came out of her, which was **imperfect** and different from her. …And it was dissimilar to the likeness of its mother, for it had a different form. And when she saw (the consequences of) her desire, it changed into a **form of a lion-faced serpent**. Its eyes were like flashing fires of lightning.
She cast it away from her, outside of that place *(from the 1st Paradise)*, so that no one of the immortals might see it, for she had created it in ignorance. And she surrounded it with a luminous cloud… so that no one might see it except the Holy Spirit… and she called its name Yaldabaoth.
This is the first **archon**, the one who got a great power from his Mother. And he removed himself from her and he abandoned the places where he had been born. He became strong and created for himself other aeons

---

inside a blaze of luminous fire, which still exists now. And he was stupe-fied in his **Madness**, which dwells within him, and he begat some **au-thorities** for himself... *(12 authorities are named)*... And he set up sev-en kings - one per firmament of heaven – **over the seven heavens** *(the 2nd virtual Paradise included)*, and five *(kings)* over the depth of the abyss *(hell)* so that they might rule there... Now the archon *(of this world)*, who is weak, has three names. The first name is Yaldabaoth *(the serpent)*, the second is Saklas *(its positive expression)* and the third is Samael *(or differently, Satan – its negative expression)*.» [GR. EDITION: APOC-RYPHAL TEXTS OF THE NEW TESTAMENT, VOL. V, THE APOCRYPHON OF JOHN, TR. KOUTSOUKIS D., PYRINOS KOSMOS PUBL.]

The following references declare the fission (splitting in two) of the one to the two opposites.

B) THE APOCRYPHON OF JOHN, THE GNOSTIC SOCIETY LIBRARY: «Elohim has the face a bear. Yahweh has a cat's face. One is righteous; the other is not. Yahweh is righteous; Elohim is not. Yahweh would command fire and wind, Elohim would command water and earth.» [Eng. tr. from Coptic: STEVAN DAVIES]

C) THE APOCRYPHON OF JOHN, THE GNOSTIC SOCIETY LIBRARY: «**Arise** and **remember** that you are the one who has heard, and **follow** your root, which is I, the Merciful *(Jesus) and* **protect yourself** against the angels of poverty *(positiveness)* and the daemons of chaos *(negativeness)*.» [Eng. tr. from Coptic: FREDERIK WISSE]

D) GOSPEL OF PHILIP, JEAN-YVES LELOUP: «§10. Light and darkness, life and death, right and left, are brothers and sisters. They are inseparable.»

It was that moment when the HyperUniverses shivered from the magnitude of the apostasy. The fission/schism of the Absolute gave birth to the second twofold/dyadic creation: 'the fruit of knowledge of good and evil'. It is the very **same** coin with its two different sides; Yin and Yang ☯.

[38] **HERMES TRISMEGISTUS**, HERMETIC TEXTS, VOL. II, RODAKIS P., TZAFEROPOULOS AP., 'ASCLEPIUS' (p. 47): «§19. First of all, there are the gods, masters of all spe-cies. Then come the gods who are masters of a substance. **These are the sensory gods** *(creators of the sensory world)*, **who are the same as their dual nature.** They are in the entire sensory world and create all beings, one with the mediation of another, **and each one is lit by the work he has cre-ated.**» *They receive energy from their bond servants – the bond servants of god/creator.*

The battle between the two opposite sides of the **same** fake coin started. This battle will stop, only when this whole deceitful product reaches its end, as is the destiny of everything fake.

Don't skip chapters or bibliographic references

---

39 **A) THE GOSPEL OF JUDAS** [KASSER R., MEYER M., WURST G.] NATIONAL GEO-GRAPHIC «[54, 55]: Jesus said, "Truly I say to you, for all of them, the stars bring matters to completion. When Saklas completes the span of time assigned for him …and they will finish what they said they would do … *(then)* **they all will be destroyed along with their creatures**.»

B) BLAVATSKY H., P., 'THE SECRET DOCTRINE' (I-36)
«In Book II, Ch. VIII of the Vishnu-Puraná, it is stated: "By immortality is meant existence until the end of Kalpa." And translator Wilson in a footnote remarks: "This, according to the Vedas, is all that is to be understood of the immortality (eternal life) **of the gods·** they perish at the end of universal dissolution (or Pralaya).»

C) STEPHEN HAWKING – 'THE UNIVERSE IN A NUTSHELL' Gr. tr. PETRAKI M. (p. 96):
«The probable end of the universe is the Big Crunch, during which matter will be cataclysmically sucked in by a huge gravity well.»

D) THE GOSPEL OF MARY (MAGDALENE) JEAN-YVES LELOUP, Gr. tr. KOUROUSSI A., A.:
«§24-25 All that has been composed **will be decomposed (dissolved), both on earth and in the sky**.»

This is the second 'creation' of the forbidden, the un–true, the fake, the perishable; a reflection, a mirror image *(mirage)* of the TRUE.

---

40 **HERMES TRISMEGISTUS**, HERMETIC TEXTS, VOL. II, RODAKIS P., TZAFERO-POULOS AP., 'ASCLEPIUS'
(a) EXCERPT XI: «§16. Nothing in the body is true, in the bodiless though, nothing can be fake.»
(b) EXCERPT II$_A$ (p. 111): «§3. All therefore Tat that is found on earth, are not real, but only **imitations of the truth** and yet not all of them, but only a few… §4. The rest is lies and delusion, Tat, and conjectures, constructed like the pictures of imagination…§5. Those who are not allured by the lie, they can see the truth.»

In it (the image), everything is in fission *(in a divided, dyadic, twofold state)*. Fragmentation and schizophrenia (from the Gr. σχιζο-φρένεια schizo+phrenia meaning 'with a mind split in two') reign everywhere: Concepts conflicting with other concepts, properties conflicting with other properties. There is joy, simply because there is sorrow. There is pleasure, because there is pain. There is good, because there is evil. This is the **entire** material **visible** and **invisible** (energy) universe.

In order to somehow clarify the difference between the concepts of the absolutely TRUE, and the concepts that prevail in the material universe (visible and invisible) to you, I will focus your attention on a 'trick': You must have surely seen a little toy with a coin run-through by a metal thread. When the coin is still, both its sides can be seen, but when it starts rotating with great speed, then the two-sided coin disappears from the eyes of the observer, and a 'sphere' appears in its place. This is exactly what happens with the Truth. This 'slowing down to a halt' of the speed of True Light has created dyadicism (the divided, twofold state); division; oscillation; something similar to the example of Newton's disk. The quality of being spherical is the property of every True Concept, which has been transformed to a polarity in the material plane. Hence, the two opposite positions were created. The coin always has two faces, each possessing its own particular characteristics. One face is 'good', the other is 'evil'; one is life, the other is death; one is joy, the other is sorrow. This is precisely the 'wood of knowledge of good and evil'. The Truth is not found on <u>either one</u> of the two sides of the coin. The Truth is found in the Sphere. This is the condition of Unsplit Concepts that reigns upon the True HyperUniverses.

࿓··࿔

Inside the True HyperUniverses of the Unsplit, young Beings had been created and were starting their Lives. They were the Celestial Men.

---

[41] A) **THE GOSPEL OF JUDAS** [KASSER R., MEYER M., WURST G.] NATIONAL GEO-GRAPHIC «[50] In him *(the Cosmos of the Ultimate)*, the first Man appeared *(Adamas/Celestial Man)*, with <u>incorruptible</u> powers.»
B) **THE GOSPEL OF JUDAS** [KASSER R., MEYER M., WURST G.] NATIONAL GEOGRAPHIC «[48] ADAMAS AND THE LUMINARIES: Adamas *(Celestial Man)* was the first luminous cloud that no angel has ever seen among all those called '**god**'»

These Sacred Wholenesses, in the form of the Holy Spirit, were the extensions of the Monogenes 'Christ' *(Luminary)* of their home HyperUniverse.

---

[42] **GOSPEL OF THOMAS**, JEAN YVES LELOUP: «§3. And Jesus said: ... The Kingdom *(of Heaven)* is inside you.»

The material (energy) universe had already been arranged when Celestial Man –male and female one– with infinite abilities, was starting His Real Life in the Real Worlds.

---

[43] A) **GOSPEL OF THOMAS**, JEAN YVES LELOUP:
«§84 Jesus said: when you see your true likeness, you rejoice. But when you see **your icons** –those that were **before you existed** and that never die and never manifest– what grandeur!» [Eng. tr. JOSEPH ROWE]

Don't skip chapters or bibliographic references

> *These icons (images) are the figure of the Celestial Man that exists <u>before</u> his fall into the energy- and material world, within a material body: <before you existed>; The Celestial Man, male and female, one.*
> **B) GOSPEL OF PHILIP,** JEAN-YVES LELOUP:
> «§67…the bridegroom is led into the Truth which is the renewal *(reinstatement)* of all things in their <u>integrity</u>.» *[Gr.: apocatastasis = reinstatement]*

Let us however return once again to the primordial myth (original sin) in order to examine it a little more, in light of the new data. I must point out though, that this matter is still presented very synoptically. As our discussion unfolds, more and more details will be analyzed to answer every query.

The (1st) Paradise with the multitude of trees, as we have said, symbolizes the HyperUniverses of the Ultimate, True and Unsplit Light. Isolated from these HyperUniverses (trees) there was also one forbidden universe (tree); the material universe. It was the dead universe/tree of the 'knowledge of good and evil', the universe of dyadicism/duality; the universe of life and death.

> [44] **OLD TESTAMENT, GENESIS CH. 2**: «§17 But of the **wood*** of the knowledge of good and evil you shall not eat, for in the day that you eat of it, you shall **certainly die**.»
>
> * *[Gr. ξύλον = wood used in orig. Gr. Septuagint (LXX) version]*

All Beings were allowed to visit all HyperUniverses (trees), to harvest their unified knowledge, and through the assimilation of this Sacred Knowledge, to expand and prosper. On the contrary, the dead wood/universe of the split knowledge of good and evil, the universe of fission, was dangerous. Whoever entered into it would die. Their very hypostasis would suffer division and dismemberment, resulting to their death.

Master archon of that universe *(forbidden tree)*, had become the god/snake *(Yaldabaoth)*.

> [45] **BLAVATSKY H., P., 'THE SECRET DOCTRINE'** (I-413): «One can ascertain one's self as to who the great 'Deceiver' is, if they search for him with open eyes and unprejudiced mind in all Ancient Cosmogonies and Scriptures. It is the human-formed Creator, the Demiurgos of Heaven and Earth, when he separated himself from the collective Hosts (Multitudes) of his fellows…»

After he appropriated it, he set it in motion. Then, in it, he created beings. Amongst them he decided to create the 'ultimate one'.

46 **A) HERMES TRISMEGISTUS,** HERMETIC TEXTS, VOL. I, RODAKIS P., TZAFEROPOU-LOS AP., SPEECH A: «§8. And I said to him: Where do these elements of nature come from? And he answered to me again: From the Divine Will which took the form of Logos (Word) and **saw the good world** *(of the 1ˢᵗ Creation)* **and mimicked it,** creating a world with **its own** *(the Divine Will's)* **elements and its own creations, the souls.**»

B) THE GOSPEL OF JUDAS [KASSER R., MEYER M., WURST G.] NATIONAL GEOGRAPHIC «[51]: *(Says Jesus)* And look, from the cloud there appeared an [angel] whose face flashed with **fire** and whose appearance was defiled with **blood.** His name was Nebro, which means '**rebel**'; others call him Yaldabaoth. Another angel, Saklas, also came from the cloud. So Nebro created six angels –as well as Saklas– to be assistants, and these produced twelve angels in the heavens, with each one receiving a portion in the heavens *(the material energy-dimensions)* …then, Saklas said to his angels "let us create a human being after the likeness and after the image." They fashioned Adam and his wife Eve who is called, in the cloud, Zoe (Gr. Ζωή = 'Life').»

Nembraw and Saklas: the result of fission (division); the god and the daemon; one being with two faces; with two sides.

However, <u>it</u> was lifeless.

47 **A) THE APOCRYPHON OF JOHN,** THE GNOSTIC SOCIETY LIBRARY: «And he *(the fallen archon, snake/serpent, Yaldabaoth)* said to the authorities who served him: "Come, let us create a human according to the image of God and according to our likeness, so that his image <u>may become light for us</u> (illuminate us)". …And all the **angels** <u>and</u> the **daemons** labored, until they had created the **psychic** body. And their product was completely inactive and motionless for a long time.» [Eng. tr. from Coptic: WALDSTEIN M., WISSE F.]

B) THE SECRET BOOK OF DZYAN *(The oldest book of the East),* 'ANTHROPOGENESIS', STANZA IV: «§15…The fathers, the ones without bones (boneless) **could not give <u>life</u> to beings with bones.** Their progeny (offspring) were Bhuta with neither form nor mind. Therefore they are called the Chhaya.»

The 'Sacred Essence/Life', which would upgrade his creation, was urgently needed. The transgressor-creator first called upon the Archetypal Property of Life of the HyperUniverses: Eve *(Eve who is called, in the cloud, Zoe (Gr. Ζωή= 'Life'* [GOSPEL OF JUDAS]*).*

48 *The word 'Eve' originates from the <u>pronunciation</u> of the Jewish word Havah, which means life. The interpretation of the word as 'woman' is purely symbolic.*

Don't skip chapters or bibliographic references

The Father, in His Greatness, granted this Property of Eve/Life to the renegade, in order for him to upgrade his creation. He subsequently imbued the souls he had created, with this Property of Life/Eve, rendering them alive.

---

[49] A) **THE APOCRYPHON OF JOHN,** THE GNOSTIC SOCIETY LIBRARY [ENG. TR. FROM COPTIC: WALDSTEIN M., WISSE F.]: «And the mother *(of the creator)* who wanted to **retrieve** the power she had given to the chief archon, asked the Mother-Father *(The Unuttered Principle)* of the All, who is most merciful. He then sent the five lights **down** to the place of the angels of the chief archon, and advised him to bring forth the power of his mother. And they told Yaldabaoth: "Blow into his face *(man-soul)* <u>something from your spirit and his body will arise</u>." And he blew into his face the spirit which is the power of his mother; he did not know (this), for he exists in ignorance. And the power of the mother **came out of Yaldabaoth and went into the psychic body** *(soul)* which they had made in likeness to 'The One Who exists from the beginning'. The body moved, gained strength and it was luminous.»

Since then he began his effort to buy off –by misleading– every single Soul, 'selling' material gifts to her, in order to get back the Power he had lost.

B) **THE SECRET BOOK OF DZYAN,** 'ANTHROPOGENESIS', STANZA IV: «§16. How are the Manushya born? How are the Manus made with minds? The fathers called for help **their own fire**…they created a good rupa. It could stand, walk, run, recline. And yet it was still but a shadow (a Chhaya) without sense (reason).»

But after the Archetype of Life-Eve *(Havah)*, the greed of the apostate continued…

❧·❧

In the HyperUniverses of Unsplit Light, Celestial Man, still being a Young Entity, hadn't broadened his Hypostasis by absorbing all the Knowledge of the True HyperCosmoi *(Cosmoi = Pl. of Cosmos)*. In order for the apostate of Truth to upgrade his creation even more, he invited that Young Being to his place; the first Celestial Man-Adam.

---

[50] *In Hebrew, 'Adam' means man, human species (men and women).*
FROM THE 'HISTORY CHANNEL' DOCUMENTARY: MAYAN DOOMSDAY PROPHECY: «Popol Vuh is for the Maya the equivalent holy scripture of the Bible… The sacred text narrates that the lords of the underworld *(snake)* invited a mythical Mayan known as the 'First Father' *(Celestial Man/Adam)* to a ball game. But the devious lords withdrew their invitation and decapitated the 'First Father'.»

Still inexperienced, Celestial Man, totally unsuspecting of the existence of malice –as it was a nonexistent quality in the Planes of the True– and seeing the Archetype of Life/Eve having also been granted to his cleaved older brother/creator, misjudged the prospect of accepting the invitation as harmless. After all, in the HyperUniverses of Unsplit Concepts, 'must' and 'must not' are relative concepts. Thus, (Celestial Man) overlooking the 'danger warning' that had been issued to all Beings of these Cosmoi, he extended his hand and tasted the fruit of the twofold knowledge of good and evil, accepting and acceding thus to the separate energy-area of the material creation –not yet into the dense visible matter– and 'incarnated' inside the soulful being created by the apostate god. This is **the first fall** and this is where his Odyssey begins.

---

[51] **A) THE APOCRYPHON OF JOHN,** THE GNOSTIC SOCIETY LIBRARY:
«But the Blessed One, the Mother-Father, the Beneficent and Merciful One, had mercy upon the Mother's power *(the Living Soul)* which had been brought forth out of the chief archon *(Yaldabaoth)*... and He sent... a helper to Adam *(the soulful material being),* Luminous Epinoia *(Celestial Man),* which comes out of Him Who is called Life *(The Unuttered Principle).*» [Eng. tr. from Coptic: FREDERIK WISSE]

B) THE GOSPEL OF JUDAS [KASSER R., MEYER M., WURST G.] NATIONAL GEOGRAPHIC:
«Jesus said, "This is why God ordered Michael to give *(to the fallen 'creators')* the spirits of *(Celestial)* people to them as a **loan**, so that they might offer service, but the Great One ordered Gabriel to grant spirits to the great generation with no ruler over it.»

C) GOSPEL OF PHILIP, JEAN-YVES LELOUP:
«§94 God *(The Unutterable Principle)* planted trees in a garden. Humans lived among these trees *(The real HyperUniverses),* they were not yet divided when they were told: "Eat from this tree *(the tree of knowledge of good and evil, i.e. the universe of matter),* or do not eat from it.» [Eng. tr. JOSEPH ROWE]
*Any potential questions that might arise in the mind of the reader are **all** answered with the completion of the book.*

After crossing over into the split universe/tree of the knowledge of good and evil, Celestial Man was himself divided (split), thus at the same time dying in the Real Cosmoi.

---

[52] *According to the Apocryphal texts of the Old Testament, Adam and Eve gave birth to a third son, Seth, who engulfed a Celestial Man inside him. Sethian texts find their origins in him, and –what is left of them and has not been falsified– refer to the Immortal Knowledge. Abel represented the positive expression of the Creator, Cain the negative expression which prevailed in the world, and Seth represented the Celestial Man.* Adam says to Seth:

Don't skip chapters or bibliographic references

THE APOCALYPSE OF ADAM, THE GNOSTIC SOCIETY LIBRARY, THE NAG HAMMADI LIBRARY, TRANSLATED BY GEORGE W. MACRAE:
«Then God, the ruler of the *(material)* aeons and of the powers, **divided us in wrath** *(into Adam and Eve)*.» [Gr. Ed.: PYRINOS KOSMOS PUBL.]

Through a process of imprisonment in many consecutive cells (energy-bodies) the disillusioned Men-Adams would end up into the last body, the one made of skin and blood!

---

[53] **A) OLD TESTAMENT, GENESIS CH. 3**: «§21…And the Lord God made for Adam and for his woman, garments of skins, and clothed them *(with a physical material body made of skin)*.»
B) THE APOCRYPHON OF JOHN, THE GNOSTIC SOCIETY LIBRARY
http://www.gnosis.org/naghamm/apocjn-davies.html
«The host of rulers and daemons plotted together. They mixed fire and earth and water together with the four blazing winds and melded them together in great turbulence. They brought Adam into the shadow of death. **They intended to make him anew** this time, from Earth, Water, Fire, Wind, which are Matter, Darkness, Desire, The Artificial Spirit. This all became a **tomb**, a new kind of body *(grave)*. Those thieves bound man in it, enchained him **in forgetfulness** and made him subject to dying.» [Eng. tr. from Coptic: STEVAN DAVIES]

In the finer/subtler, higher energy-planes of the material universe, there remains one part of the divided Celestial Man, the I Am Presence, while his other part, the Divine Spark, is incarnated inside dense matter, sometimes as a man and other times as a woman.

So here is man, **still** enchanted and hooked in the eternal trap of two-fold/dyadic matter, without cognition of the reality that surrounds him, tasting the twofold fruits of knowledge, selecting and turning down one or the other, and struggling for what he **imagines** to be the best.

---

[54] **THE APOCALYPSE OF ADAM,** THE GNOSTIC SOCIETY LIBRARY, THE NAG HAMMADI LIBRARY, TRANSLATED BY GEORGE W. MACRAE: «After those days, the Eternal Knowledge of the God of Truth, withdrew from me and your mother Eve. Since that time **we have been learning about dead things**, like men.» [Gr. Ed.: PYRINOS KOSMOS PUBL.]

This dyadic world has its own reflective second paradise, which will be analyzed at a later point in our discussion.

55 **THE APOCRYPHON OF JOHN,** THE GNOSTIC SOCIETY LIBRARY: *(Jesus speaks to John)*: «The archons took him *(Adam)* and placed him in paradise. And they said to him "Eat, that is at leisure;" for indeed their delight is bitter and their beauty is depraved. And their luxury is deception and their trees <u>are god-lessness</u>, and their fruit is deadly poison and their promise is death. And the tree of **their life** they had placed in the midst of paradise. …The root of this tree is bitter and its branches are death, its shadow is hatred and deception is in its leaves. The ointment of evil is in its blossom. Its fruit is death, and desire is its seed, and it sprouts in darkness. The dwelling place of those who taste from it is Hades and the darkness is their place of rest.» [Eng. tr. from Coptic: FREDERIK WISSE]

He looked me in the eyes. I could detect the sorrow he felt for me and the entire mankind. After remaining silent for a while he continued.

–It is not enough for you to know the Truth epigrammatically. In order for you to be saved, every cell of yours <u>must assimilate</u> (absorb) IT. This is why, to continue, we will set off on the long road of exploration.

56 **THE GOSPEL OF JOHN, CH. 8**: «§32. And you shall know the truth, and <u>the truth</u> <u>shall set you free</u>.» *(Gr. enthymesis=remembrance/recollection)*

CREATION

At this point, I would like to step in, producing an aggregate of written accounts from diverse sources, so that all these excerpts can synthesize the picture of the lost puzzle which outlines the <u>two</u> different creations that essentially exist.

At the same time, through this journey of information, the chronicle of man's imprisonment inside the second creation faintly starts to appear.

The first creation concerns the True Genesis of Everything and the second concerns the fallen material creation of the apostate of Truth.

*What becomes clear from this unbiased research though, is that this second creation in which we all –alive <u>and</u> dead– exist, and which contains not only dense visible matter, but also its invisible energy part, **positive and negative**, did not come forth through a smooth evolution of what was natural, but through a mistake. And the Gospel of Truth of Jesus says:*

THE GOSPEL OF TRUTH «§39. The deficiency of matter did not originate through the Infinity of the Father … although no one could predict that the Incorruptible would come *(end-up)* this way.»

*This mistake unfolded thereafter, forming an insane creation of visible and invisible worlds. These worlds are the **entire** visible and invisible material universe. It was inside this universe that Celestial Man was trapped and woven inside a poisonous cocoon (the material body) which anaesthetizes his Real Noûs (Mind).*

So let us examine these two creations: The Normal Creation on one hand and the distorted one on the other.

SALLUSTIUS OR SATURNINUS SECUNDUS SALLUSTIUS, (GAUL 300 A. D.) 'ON THE GODS AND THE WORLD', (Gr. tr. GRAVIGGER, P.) (p. 41-42): «Among the gods some are of the world, **cosmic**, and some above the world, **hyper-cosmic**. By the term 'cosmic' I am referring to the Gods who create the Cosmos; as for the <u>hyper-cosmic</u> ones, some create the essences of the Gods, others the noûs (mind) and others the souls: thus they have three orders, and all these (orders) are found in the related teachings.

Among the <u>cosmic Gods</u> one team creates the Cosmos, another animates it, another creates the harmony between the opposites which comprise it, and yet others supervise it, for the preservation of the once achieved harmony.»

*No testimony, in any of mankind's sources, **does analyze** the First Creation. They just sparingly mention it and only with a passing remark. And as H., P. Blavatsky states in her work 'The Secret Doctrine' (III-77):*

«Every ancient Theogony *(tr. n.: birth of the gods)*…places in the order of Cosmogonical evolution, **Night before the Day**; …The reason for this is that every Cosmogony …begins by the so-called 'Secondary Creation', namely the manifested Universe, the Genesis of which has to open by a marked differentiation between the **eternal Light of the Primary Creation**.»

Only Jesus, through the Gospel of Judas and the Apocryphon of John, mentions this world in detail, simply because He came from IT.

In this universe of deceit, its creator has skillfully woven his perpetual web, in order to keep Celestial Man eternally captive. <u>With endless efforts, great dexterity and skill, he suppresses and withholds everything that is relevant to the Real Cosmoi.</u> Through his 'human-tools', he weaves the fraud for all men, so that no one escapes him. When Jesus came from These Hyper-Cosmoi though, with the intention to gather the 'emigrants' and transport them to a Reception Area specially arranged in the Impassable Planes, it was natural for Him (Jesus) to be constantly against the 'archon of this world', as was for the 'archon of this world' to be hostile towards Jesus.

Thus, some years after Jesus' departure/withdrawal from the material universe, the fallen creator, regained control of the situation, by 'cutting and sewing' everything to his convenience. There lies the cause of the delusion that arose with the <u>falsification</u> of all of Christ's Teachings.

Only when man realizes that he is <u>not</u> inside his Ultimate Father's creation, <u>only then</u> has he some 'hopes' to start worrying about his true condition. This anxiety will be the beginning of his salvation.

Anaesthetized as he is by the poison of the snake-god, he plunges deeper and deeper into oblivion, as he equates his human hypostasis with his material body. So, at the end of this Cosmic Cycle, he will end up being totally absorbed by it (the Cosmic Cycle), having lost <u>everything</u>.

With all the information we have at hand now, we will examine the difference between the two creations: On one hand the Creation of the Unuttered Father, and, on the other, the creation of the material universe of the fallen creator. Thus, by making a collage of clues/excerpts, this will become more comprehensible.

Let us nevertheless consider that every scholar describes an event in his own diverse way. And if this event refers to a transcendental and immaterial condition, this diverse verbalization becomes more characteristic.

In Judas' Gospel, the description of the First Creation is quite clear, and this is why I am repeating the particular excerpt. What is interesting here is that this revelation was made to Judas by Jesus Himself while He was still in material life.

Don't skip chapters or bibliographic references

1ST CREATION:

THE GOSPEL OF JUDAS [TRANSLATED BY RODOLPHE KASSER, MARVIN MEYER, AND GREGOR WURST, IN COLLABORATION WITH FRANÇOIS GAUDARD, COPYRIGHT (C) 2006 BY THE NATIONAL GEOGRAPHIC SOCIETY].
JESUS TEACHES JUDAS ABOUT COSMOLOGY: THE SPIRIT AND THE SELF-GENERATED:

«Jesus said, "[Come] that I may teach you about [secrets] that no person [has] ever seen. For there exists a great and boundless realm, whose extent **no generation of angels has seen**,[57] [in which] there is [a] great invisible [Spirit].»

{Tr. n.: The Gospel's translators have added the following: "…which no eye of an angel has ever seen, no thought of the heart has ever comprehended, and it was never called by any name."}

> [57] *In the Gospel of Judas, there is a vague distinction between angels, which is nevertheless absolutely clear in the Apocryphon of John.*
> *In it, the angels are divided into: a) The Angels of the Real Cosmoi and b) the angels of poverty, as Jesus calls them 'by the hand of John', who are no other than the angels of 'positive' expression of this world, and naturally he distinguishes them from the daemons of darkness.*
> «And guard yourself against the <u>angels of poverty</u> **and** <u>the daemons of chaos</u>, and of all those who ensnare you, and beware of the deep sleep of the dungeons of Hades.»

THE GOSPEL OF JUDAS cont'd…

«…A great angel, the enlightened divine **Self-Generated**, emerged from the cloud. Because of him, four other angels came into being from another cloud, and they became attendants for the angelic Self-Generated. The Self-Generated said, "Let [lost text] come into being [lost text]", and it came into being. And he [created] the first Luminary *(Luminary=One who illumines; Ultimate; Monogenes (Singly-Born) for this particular HyperUniverse/Aeon)* to reign over it *(over the 1st Aeon)*. He said, "Let angels come into being to serve [him]", and myriads without number came into being. He said, '[Let] an enlightened aeon come into being', *(2nd Universe of Unsplit Light)* and he came into being. He created the second Luminary *(2nd Monogenes for this particular 2nd HyperUniverse/Aeon)* [to] reign over it *(over the 2nd Aeon)*, together with myriads of angels without number, to offer service. That is how he created the rest of the enlightened aeons *(HyperUniverses of Unsplit Light)*.»

In the Gospel of Judas, it is mentioned, that there are twelve Aeons/HyperUniverses created.

«…The twelve Aeons of the twelve Luminaries constitute their Father with six Heavens *(dimensions)* for each aeon *(HyperUniverse)*.» *(See Drawings: 'HyperUniverses of True Light')*

In his Apocryphon, John also describes the same subject, in a different way. This Gospel was discovered in the area of Nag Hammadi in Upper Egypt in 1945. The entire text refers to a series of esoteric messages given by the Resurrected Jesus to his disciple John.

«Says Jesus to John: "Now, therefore, lift up your face, that you may receive the things that I shall teach you today, and that you may tell them to your fellow spirits who are from the **UNWAVERING** *(non-oscillating)* race of the Perfect Man.» [En. tr. FREDERIK WISSE]

JOHN'S APOCRYPHON
CHAPTER: UNUTTERED–UNSPOKEN PRINCIPLE

«…The Monad is a monarchy with nothing above It. It is He Who exists as God and Father of All, The Invisible One who is above everything, The Incorruptible One, The One Who Exists as pure light which no eye can bear to look at. He is the Invisible Spirit; it is not right for you to think of Him as a God, or something similar. For He is more than God, since there is nothing above Him; nor is there any authority to rule over Him. He exists in Perfection and everything exists in Him. He exists for He has no need of anything …He is illimitable, since there is no one prior to Him to set limits to Him …He is Complete …He is Perfect inside the Light. He is Unsearchable …He is Non-dimensional… He is Invisible… He is Ineffable…He has no Name… He is not corporeal nor is He incorporeal. He is neither Grand nor is He Unimportant *(He has inside Him the opposites which He conjoins).* …He is an Aeon-generating Aeon. He is Life-giving Life… How am I to speak to you about Him? His Aeon is indestructible, at rest and existing in silence, reposing (and) being prior to everything. He is the head of all the Aeons, and He is The One, Who gives them strength and goodness.» [English tr.: FREDERIK WISSE]

CHAPTER: THE ORIGIN OF REALITY.

«And His Thought performed a deed and She came forth, namely She who had appeared before Him in the shine of His Light. This is the First Power which was before all, (and) which came forth from His Mind, She is the <u>Forethought</u> (Pronoia) of ALL. Her Light shines like His Light. She is the perfect power which is the image of the invisible perfect Virginal Spirit which is Perfect. The initial power, the glory of Barbelo… This is the first thought, His image; she is the womb of everything, for it is She who is prior to them all.» [English tr.: FREDERIK WISSE]

CHAPTER: THE PRIMARY STRUCTURES OF THE DIVINE NOÛS.

«…<She> *(Barbelo)* requested from the invisible, virginal Spirit to give her <u>Foreknowledge</u> *(Prognosis)*… And the Spirit consented… And Foreknowledge glorified Him and His perfect power *(Barbelo)*, for it was for Her sake that it *(Prognosis)* had come into being…And she *(Barbelo)* requested

Don't skip chapters or bibliographic references

again for <u>Incorruptibility</u> to be granted to her …and Incorruptibility came forth, and it stood by Foreknowledge *(Prognosis)*. … And Barbelo requested <u>Eternal Life</u> to be granted to her… And the Invisible Spirit consented and Eternal Life came forth and stood by them and they attended and glorified the Invisible Spirit and His Barbelo, the one for whose sake they had come into being. She *(Barbelo)* requested again for <u>Truth</u> to be granted to her. And the Invisible Spirit consented. And Truth came forth, and they attended and glorified the Invisible, Excellent Spirit and His Barbelo, the one for whose sake they had come into being. This is the Pentad of the Aeons *(The Fivefold Aeon)* of the Father.» (English tr.: FREDERIK WISSE)
[Invisible Spirit + Barbelo = (1) Pronoia, (2) Prognosis, (3) Incorruptibility, (4) Eternal Life, (5) Truth; these are the five Basic Archetypes of the Unuttered Principle.]

At this point and in order for the term 'Aeon' to become more comprehensible, I am appending an excerpt 'About the Aeon' from the 'Chaldean Oracles', which comprise the sum of the commentaries of Neo-Platonists on the Platonic dialogues.

CHALDEAN ORACLES, (Gr. tr. ATHINOGENIS I., GRAVIGGER, P.), PROCLUS COMMENT, (TIMAEUS D) ABOUT THE AEON (p. 96)
«Because of this, It *(The Aeon)* has been named by the 'Logia' (Scholarly Texts) '**Patrogenes** *(born of the Father)* **Light'** because, of course, **Its Light that <u>unifies</u> everything** shines upon all things.»
Sallustius on the other hand, regarding the first cause of the Cosmos, namely this Patrogenes Light, writes: (p. 37-38)
«Subsequently to the above, it is now worthwhile to acquire knowledge of the first Cause and the orders **of the resulting Gods** that followed it…The first Cause must be one, because before every multiplicity, the Monad has prevalence.»
With the occasion of this statement from Sallustius, P. Gravigger, the commentator of the Greek translation, submits the following:

PLOTINUS V, IVI – PROCLUS THEOLOGICAL MATTERS II–Ψ– DIONYSIUS AREOPAGITE, 'ABOUT DIVINE NAMES'. FOR A RELATIVE PERCEPTION ABOUT THE FIRST PRINCIPLE TO THE EGYPTIANS, SEE IAMB., ABOUT SECRETS VIII, 2.
«Prior to the truly existing beings, *(or before all beginnings–startups–creations)*, There is One God, **Preceding the First** God and king, immoveable and abiding in the uniqueness <u>of His Own Unity</u>.»
«Πρὸ των ὄντως ὄντων και των ὅλων αρχῶν εστί Θεός Εἷς, **Πρότερος και του πρώτου** Θεού και βασιλέως, ακίνητος εν μονότητι της εαυτού ενότητος μένων».

«For neither is the intelligible connected with Him, nor any other paradigm (example) exists about Him, the Self-Paternal, Self-Begotten (Self-Generated) God, the One Who is really *ἀγαθός* (Agathós)

76

[=Good/Benevolent] *(see Tr. n on w. ἀγαθός (Agathós), Ch. 'HIGHER MENTAL BODY – CELESTIAL MAN ').*»

«Ούτε γαρ νοητόν αυτώ επιπλέκεται, ούτε άλλό τι παράδειγμα δε ίδρυται του αυτοπάτορος αυτογόνου και μονοπάτορος Θεού του όντως ἀγαθοῦ».

«For *(He is)* something even greater, and The First One and the fountain of all and the root/foundation/principle of all the first thought-out concepts, of the Archetypes of all, of the intelligible forms.»

«Μείζον γαρ τι και πρώτον και πηγή των πάντων και πυθμήν των νοουμένων πρώτων ιδεών όντων».

«But from this One then, *(the First One)*, a *(Second)* autonomous God appeared, self-contained and self-sufficient.»

«Από δε του Ενός Τούτου ο αυτάρκης Θεός εαυτόν εξέλαμψε, διό και αυτοπάτωρ και αυτάρκης»

«Because He *(the Second)* is the start *(Gr. 'Archē')* and also the god of other *(inferior)* gods, being a Monad Himself *(the Second)* stemming from the *One* (First) and the Principle of essence.»

«Αρχή γαρ ούτος και Θεός Θεών, μονάς εκ του ενός, προούσιος και αρχή της ουσίας…»

«These, therefore, are the most ancient principles of all things, older than the ones that Hermes *(the Trismegistus)* places prior to the aethereal the empyrean (fiery) and the celestial gods.»

«Αύται ούν εισίν αρχαί πρεσβύταται πάντων ας Ερμής (Τρισμέγιστος) προ των αιθερίων και εμπυρίων Θεών και των επουρανίων προττάτει».

2ND CREATION:

In contrast to the First Cause which is the Patrogenes Light of the Aeon, which <u>unifies</u> all, comes the property of dyadicism, duality and division of the second creation of the manifested material universe.

H. P. Blavatsky in her work, 'The Secret Doctrine', I-65, states:
«The 'Manifested Universe' therefore, is pervaded by **duality**, which is, as it were, the very essence of its Existence as 'manifestation'».

At this point we will append an Orphic hymn which rhapsodizes the 'Primeval creative Light' called 'Phanetas' (Gr.: Φάνητας) to support the dyadicism of the material universe.
In this hymn, Orpheus gives to it (the Primeval creative Light) the property of dimorphism (dual form) on one hand (since it was split in two Λ and became Λόγος=Logos, [Word] in order to create), and on the other hand characterizes it as 'Antavges'.
The word Antavges (Gr.: Ἀνταύγης), is comprised of the adversative preposition 'anti' (Gr.: ἀντί = instead of, against) and the word 'avge' (Gr.: αὐγή [αὐγής in the genitive] meaning the light of dawn). 'Antavges' means 'the one who replaces the light, the one who reflects light'.
The material creation, is namely that which is born through Logos {Gr.:

Don't skip chapters or bibliographic references

also meaning fraction, division}, as a result of reflection.

Apparent therefore is the antithesis between the dyadicism/duality of the material universe and the Unified/Unsplit Patrogenes Light of the Aeon.

ORPHIC HYMNS (Gr. tr. MAGGINAS, S.), VI 'TO PROTOGONUS' THE FUMIGATION FROM MYRRH

«I invoke Protogonus, the **dimorphic** *(of a double form – duality)*, the great one who wanders through the aether, the **egg-born,** rejoicing with the golden wings; having the countenance of a Taurus (bull) who gave birth to the blessed gods and mortal men; who is a much-remembered seed (sperm), the far celebrated Ericapæus, Ineffable, Occult, Impetuous, the all glittering strength. You, who took away the dark fog from the eyes, after you writhed *(turned round and round in a snake-like manner)* in the violent movements of your wings, everywhere in the world; and **you brought forth a pure, lucent light** *{In Latin, the word 'Lucifer', means 'Light-bearer' (from lux - lucis, 'light', and ferre, 'to bear, bring' (from the Greek verb φέρω= to bring)}*, wherefore I invoke you as **Phanes** and as king Priapus *(fertile creator)* and **Antavges** with the quick-turning eyes. But you, the blessed, the resourceful, the fertile, walk (go), joyous, to your sacred ever-varied mystery that is held by those who reveal (who know how to perform) the orgies (secret rituals).» [http://www.sacred-texts.com/cla/af/af10.htm]

Thus, the First Creation is the Patrogenes Light which contains all the Aeons/HyperUniverses of the True, whereas the second is called Antavges (instead of/a reflection of Light) and it is the fallen dyadic material creation, which simply reflects the True Light, as the moon reflects the light of the sun.

CHALDEAN ORACLES (Gr. tr. ATHINOGENIS I. - GRAVIGGER, P.): CONTINUING 'ABOUT THE AEON' FROM THE ABOVE-MENTIONED EXCERPT OF PROCLUS: TIMAEUS D

«Once **he snatched, completely alone and <u>for himself</u>, the 'Flower of the Noûs (Mind)' <u>from the Paternal Might</u>,** he is able to understand the Father's Noûs, and deliver that Noûs to all sources and upon all principles and has the power to **swirl** the never-tiring **vortex** and ever stay inside it *(...as Antavges)* [And ever bide upon his never-tiring pivot].»

This is the dispensation of reflected Light through the creator to his <u>swirling</u> creation.

Hermes Trismegistus, while more precise at this point, doesn't mention The Ultimate Self-Generated (the Unuttered Principle) though. He only briefly mentions the Aeon/HyperUniverse of the Luminary (Monogenes) from which the creator of matter was born.

No material testimony other than that of Jesus in the Apocryphal Gospels outlines with such clarity the Landscape of the Impassable Cosmoi. Basical-

ly, they don't even mention The Ultimate Unspoken Principle or The Self-Generated One. All scholars and thinkers simply consider the Aeon (Hyper-Universe, Luminary) as the only Ultimate Principle, from which the creator of the material universe originated.

(There is a comprehensive table at the end of this chapter.)

Let us move on now to a point-by-point comparison of the two creations, analyzing thereby the text of Hermes Trismegistus.

HERMES TRISMEGISTUS, THE FOUNDER OF THE MONOTHEISTIC RELIGION, **9.000** B.C., IOANNIDIS P., 1ST SPEECH, «§4…And I saw an infinite sight, flooded by light, both sweet and exceedingly pleasant; and I was wonderfully delighted beholding it. But after a little while *(in another place),* I saw a downward darkness, partially born, coming down in **an oblique formation** like a snake, fearful and hideous. I also saw that darkness to be changed into a **moist nature**, unspeakably troubled, which yielded a fiery smoke from its depths, and from whence I heard an unutterable heartbreaking sound, and an inarticulate roar in a voice of fire.»

Here, by the term 'infinite sight flooded by light' he connotes one of the (twelve) Aeons (HyperUniverses). And the 'downward darkness' refers to a waste material, which certainly doesn't exist inside the realms of Light, but apart from them, with which the renegade would later on build his detached, second creation.

At this point, I would like to look at the image that describes the 'downward darkness, partially born' from a slightly different point of view, by submitting an alternative testimony about it, which comes from some very old written reports, in the Secret book of DZYAN with the corresponding STANZAS, translated by H. P. Blavatsky, who characteristically states about the aforementioned book:

«It is so very old that our modern antiquarians might ponder over its pages for an indefinite time, and still not quite agree as to the nature of the fabric upon which it is written… and *(through its entire translation)* excerpts are given from the Chinese, Tibetan and Sanskrit translations of the initial Senzar commentaries and interpretations on the book of DZYAN.»

The First STANZA in particular, from the volume 'Cosmic Evolution', describes this 'downward darkness' of Hermes Trismegistus in its own way and obviously refers to a dead remnant of a previous 'apostasy': the forbidden tree of the original (primordial) myth.

STANZA 1: «§1. The eternal Karana *(=Cause),* wrapped in her everlasting invisible robes, had slumbered once again for seven eternities.
§2. Time was not, for it lay asleep in the infinite bosom of duration.

Don't skip chapters or bibliographic references

§3…Universal Noûs *[(Mind), the Creator]* was not, for there were no AH–HI's *(Celestial beings)* to contain it.

§4. The seven ways to bliss were not. The great causes of misery were not, for **there was no one to produce** *(them)* **and get ensnared by them**. …

§6. The seven sublime lords and the seven truths **had ceased to be**, …

§7. The causes of existence <u>had been done away with</u>; the visible that was, and the invisible that is, rested in the eternal nonbeing, the one being.

§8. Alone, the one form of existence stretched boundless, infinite and causeless, in dreamless sleep…»

*And to remind us the inescapable destiny of everything that is 'false',
Jesus states in the Gospel of Judas* [KASSER R., MEYER M., WURST G., NATIONAL GEOGRAPHIC]: «Jesus said: "Truly I say to you, for all of them, the stars bring matters **to completion** (consummation). When Saklas completes the span of time assigned for him…and they will finish what they said they would do…they **all will be destroyed** along with their creatures.»
(The same fate for every apostate)

*so we are facing a formless remnant of a previous (already dead) condition,
which is used as foundation for the new offspring of the second creation.*
«…the earth was without form, and void, and darkness was upon the face of the abyss.» [Genesis: 1:2]

*Moving on in the collection of our puzzle pieces, we consult **Hermes Trismegistus** again, who in the 1ˢᵗ chapter of his work, refers to the second creation in more detail.*

(Gr. tr. IOANNIDIS P.) CH. 1 «§5 Then from those Luminous Planes *(of the HyperUniverses)* I saw a Holy Logos (Word) pouring itself out towards the moist nature *(=first move coming from the Light)*, and from the moist nature, a hollow *(without spirit)* drastic acid and a pure fire spurting to the heights *(as an answer to the first move, comes a second move, coming from the downward darkness)*. … §6 And Poemander says to Hermes: "…So Hermes, that Light that you saw, am I, thy God, **existing before that moist nature that appeared out of darkness**; and that luminous Logos (Word) that you saw surging from (my) Luminous Planes **towards that moist nature**, is my son that came out of my Noûs (Mind).»

It was the Luminous Ray - Creator that was magnetized by Eros which sprang out of the 'downward darkness, the one partially born', united with it and became luminous Logos.

Eros, the basic ingredient of the 'downward darkness', belongs to the primary 'tetras' [quadruplet] of the Greek Cosmogony. Stavros Girgenis, the commentator of Hesiod's 'Theogony' reports (p. 403):

«Chaos, Earth, Tartara *(Gr. = turmoil)* and Eros are the four initial elements of the cosmos.»

And P. Decharme in his work 'Hellenic (Greek) Mythology' (p. 4, 5) clarifies: «Regarding Eros, contrary to the text of the poet *(Hesiod)*, he is not the glittering god that shines with beauty, the winged god with youthful grace and alluring charm. …This primeval Eros of cosmogony, is a mythological picture that covers an abstract idea, he is indeed as they said **'the attractive force'**.»

Elsewhere, P. Decharme footnotes the following:
«In the Phoenician cosmogony, which is attributed to Sanhoniathon, **'Pothos'** (lust/desire) we find the beginning of creation. *(See M. Reman's note on Sanhoniathon: Acad. des Inscriptions, XXIII, s.275).*»

And Hermes Trismegistus adds: SPEECH A «§18 …And he who possesses Noûs *(mind)* will recognize himself as being immortal and the **cause** of death to be Eros.»

It is he [Eos-phoros=Lucifer=the one who bears the light, anti-Avges] who brought the light (as a substitute Light/Antavges) to the downward darkness, after he had already «**snatched** *completely alone and* **for himself** *(like a 'thief' as characterized by Jesus in John's Apocryphon) the 'Flower of the Noûs (Mind)' from the Paternal Might*» (PROCLUS-'TIMAEUS').

«And **darkness** was upon the face of the abyss (deep); and **the spirit of god** was hovering over the face of the waters. And god said, "Let there be light"; and there was light.» (GENESIS: 1:2-3)

Allow me to quote one more excerpt from the book of DZYAN yet again, in order to juxtapose the two reports, (Hermes Trismegistus and the book of Dzyan) which both comment on the union of the creator with the 'downward darkness'.

THE SECRET BOOK OF DZYAN 'COSMIC EVOLUTION' STANZA III: «§2. The vibration *(the Luminous Creator, coming from the HyperUniverses)* sweeps along, touching with its swift wing the whole universe *(the formless dark downward-swirling 'Karana/Cause')* and the germ *(of matter)* that dwells in darkness: The darkness that breathes (moves) over the slumbering waters of life… §3. Darkness radiates light, and light drops one **solitary ray** into the waters, inside the mother-depth *(into the abyss/depth of the mother; Devamatri: Mother of gods, the cosmic space)*. The ray shoots through the virgin egg *(i.e. it unites with the 'downward partially-born darkness')*. The ray *(as creator)* causes the eternal egg *(the building material/downward darkness)* to thrill (vibrate), and drops the non-eternal germ *(as it is mortal and not authorized/competent)* which condenses inside the cosmic egg. §4. Then the 'three' *(as the 3rd expression of the Holy Spirit in the form of the Creator)* falls into the '4' *(the manifestation of the four-dimensional matter, and its four elements: fire, air, water, earth)*.»

Don't skip chapters or bibliographic references

*Furthermore the epic of Creation '**Enûma Eliš**' mentions this defining union of Lucifer/Creator with the 'downward darkness which is partially born', namely the previous creation's remnants, in its own outstanding style:*

NEAR EAST TEXTS, GR. TRANSL.: SKARTSI, X., S., SKARTSIS, S., L., 'ENÛMA ELIŠ, THE ASSYRO-BABYLONIAN EPIC OF CREATION' 1ST **TABLET**: «§1 When the sky above had not been named, the firm ground beneath had not been uttered by name, 'the nothingness'', but only the primordial Apsû (Abzu) *(Lucifer/Creator)*, their begetter and Mu-um-mu Tiamat *(the previous creations' remnants)*, the mother of them all, **with their waters commingling as a single body**.»

For this second creation of course, Jesus does not express the most positive view.
So, if at this point we take into consideration the Word of Jesus from the Apocryphon of John on one hand and the Gospel of Judas on the other, we will be able to compose a more complete picture about the 'profile' of our Creator... I must note however, that even though the basic gist of the two Gospels is the same, the descriptive narration is different. This is due to the fact that the concepts expressed in both of these Gospels, pertain to extremely transcendental and abstract situations, thus making identical renderings impossible.

THE APOCRYPHON OF JOHN, THE GNOSTIC SOCIETY LIBRARY:
«And Sophia *(Wisdom)* of the Epinoia, being an aeon…wanted to bring forth a likeness out of herself, without the consent of the Spirit… And though the person of her maleness had not approved and had not consented, (yet) she brought forth (gave birth)… And because of the invincible power which is in her, her thought did not remain idle, and something came out of her, which was **imperfect** and different from her. …And it was dissimilar to the likeness of its mother, for it had a different form. And when she saw (the consequences of) her desire, it changed into a form of **a lion-faced serpent**. Its eyes were like flashing fires of lightning.
She then cast it away from her, outside that place, so that no one of the immortal ones might see it, for she had created it in ignorance. And she surrounded it with a luminous cloud… so that no one might see it except the Holy Spirit…and she called its name Yaldabaoth.
This is the first **archon** *(the creator of matter – visible and invisible)* who took a great power from his mother. And he removed himself from her and he abandoned the places where he was born. He became strong and created for himself other aeons inside a blaze of luminous fire which (still) exists now. And he was stupefied in his Madness which dwells within him and begat *(twelve)* **authorities** for himself *(names follow)*.

...And he placed **seven kings** —one per firmament of heaven– over the **seven heavens** *(up to the virtual 'paradise')* and **five** *(kings)* over the depth of the **abyss**, so that they may rule there *(in hell)*... Now the archon, who is weak, has three names. The first name is Yaldabaoth, the second is Saklas, and the third is Samael. And he is impious in his madness which is in him. For he said: 'I am God and there is no other God beside me,' for he is ignorant of the place from which his strength had come. And the archons created **seven powers** for themselves, and the powers created six angels for each one, until they became **365 angels** *(the angels of poverty)*. ...But Yaldabaoth **had a multitude of faces** *(facets, sides)*, ...so that he could put a face before all of them, according to his desire *(masquerade)*, when he is in the midst of his seraphs *(angels)*.

...He called himself god. And he did not obey the place from which he came. And he united the powers in his thought with the authorities which were with him...and he named each power beginning with the highest *(he names the seven powers)*...And he organized everything according to the model of the first aeons which had come into being, so that he might create them like the indestructible ones. Not because he had seen the indestructible spaces, but the power in him, which he had taken from his mother, produced in him the likeness of his cosmos (world). And when he saw the creation which surrounds him, and the multitude of the angels around him **who had come forth from him**, he said to them, "I am a jealous God, and there is no other God beside me." ...Then his mother...became aware of the deficiency, when the brightness of her light diminished. And she became dark because her consort had not agreed with her. ...But when she saw the wickedness which had happened, and the **theft** which her son had committed, she repented. And she was overcome by forgetfulness in the darkness of ignorance and she began to be ashamed. ...And the arrogant one took power from his mother. For he was ignorant, thinking that there existed no other except his mother alone. And when he saw the multitude of angels he had created, then he exalted himself above them. And when the mother recognized that the garment of darkness was imperfect...she repented with much weeping. And the whole 'pleroma' *(the Completeness of the True Cosmoi)* heard the prayer of her repentance, and they prayed on her behalf to the invisible, virginal Spirit. And the Spirit...poured *(Essence)* over her from Its Entire Pleroma...And she was taken up *(higher from where she had fallen)*, not to her own aeon *(not to her original position)*, but above her son that she might be in the ninth *(Heaven)* until she has **corrected** her defi-

Don't skip chapters or bibliographic references

ciency.» [Eng. tr. from Coptic: FREDERIK WISSE] *(The time of this restitution lies in the very near future of humanity).*

THE GOSPEL OF JUDAS, THE WORLD, CHAOS AND THE UNDER-WORLD:
«The multitude of those immortals is called the 'cosmos' by the Father and the seventy-two Luminaries *(Monogenes = Singly-born)* who are with the Self-Generated *(Unuttered Principle)* and His seventy-two Aeons *(the twelve Aeons/HyperUniverses with six firmaments/dimensions each, to the sum of seventy-two).* In him *(inside the cosmos)* the first man *(1ˢᵗ)* appeared with his incorruptible powers *(Celestial Man).* And *(2ⁿᵈ)* the Aeon *(HyperUniverse)* that appeared with his generation *(Its Beings),* the aeon in whom are the cloud *(the attribute)* of knowledge and *(3ʳᵈ)* the angel who is called El *(Elohim – the fallen one).*[58] [Missing text] aeon [missing text] after that [missing text] said, "Let twelve angels come into being [to] rule over **chaos** and the [**underworld**].»

---

[58] **A)** *By the commentators (Kasser R., Meyer M., Wurst G. and Gaudard F.) of the Gospel of Judas:* «El is the ancient Semitic name for God. In Sethian texts, relevant names, like Eloeos, are used for powers and authorities of this world. The Apocryphon of John[(1)] also refers to the name Elohim, the Hebrew word for God in the Jewish scriptures.»
[(1)] **THE APOCRYPHON OF JOHN,** THE GNOSTIC SOCIETY LIBRARY: «Yaldabaoth raped Eve *(Havah = the Archetype of Life).* She bore two sons. Elohim was the name of the first. Yahweh *(Jehovah)* was the name of the second. …Yahweh is righteous, Elohim is not. Yahweh would command fire and air, Elohim would command water and earth.» [Eng. tr. from Coptic: STEVAN DAVIES]
B) *In the Hebrew Bible of Creation (Sefer Yetzirah), the translator Theodore Siafarikas comments, among other things, on the term Elohim or Eloim:* «The Elohims of the living… The Elohims are the seven forces that come from the **One** Deity which controls the 'terra viventium', the manifested world of life.»
C) *In man's history the name Elohim is used by different ethnic groups and heresies, where it is attributed a variety of properties. In some occasions, it denotes the Unique God El/Elohim and elsewhere, especially in theosophy, it is associated with the constructors of pure matter, the commanders of Heimarmenē (fate/destiny).*

THE GOSPEL OF JUDAS cont'd: «And look, from the cloud there appeared an [angel] whose face flashed with fire and whose appearance was defiled with blood. His name was Nebro, which means 'rebel'; others call him Yaldabaoth. Another angel, Saklas, also came from the cloud. So, Nebro created six angels –as well as Saklas– to be assistants, and these produced twelve angels in the heavens, with each one receiving a portion in the heavens.»

In the above text an outline is given of the existence of the First Man or 'Celestial Man' as we call him –with imperishable powers– inside the Immortal Cosmoi. A 'dissonance' appeared though, in the area of the Archetypes of Absolute Gnosis (Knowledge), called 'Elohim'. Through this dissonance, the team of the fallen gods came forth, who in turn united with the detached 'moist, spiral nature' (the forbidden tree/egg) and brought to it the Patrogenes Light as Ant-Avges (quasi-light). From that point on begins the construction of the second creation that is described in so much detail in all ancient histories and mythologies of the human races.

*Before we proceed however to give an account of the evidence, let us open a small parenthesis in order to follow the way the apostates create 'according to image and likeness' an **energy**-replica of Adam, so they can later imprison Celestial Man in it.*

(a) GOSPEL OF JUDAS «…then Saklas said to his angels, 'Let us create a human being after the likeness and after the image.' They fashioned Adam and his wife Eve.»

(b) GENESIS 1 «§26 Then God said, Let us make man in our image, after our likeness.»

(c) JOHN'S APOCRYPHON «And he *(Yaldabaoth)* said to the authorities who attended him: "Come, let us create a human according to the image of God and according to our own likeness, so that his image may become light for us *(the bondservants of the god/creator)*." …And all the **angels and daemons** labored until they had created the **psychic** body. And their product was completely **inactive and motionless** for a long time.» [English tr.: FREDERIK WISSE]

And Yaldabaoth was advised from the HyperUniverses:

THE APOCRYPHON OF JOHN «…They advised him to bring forth the power of his Mother. And they said to Yaldabaoth, "Blow into his face *(the energyman)* something of your spirit and his body will arise." And into his face he blew the spirit, which is the power of his Mother; he did not know (this), for he exists in ignorance. And the power of the Mother **came out of Yaldabaoth and went into the psychic body** *(soul)* that they had made according to the likeness of the One who exists from the beginning. The body moved, gained strength, and it was luminous.» [English tr.: FREDERIK WISSE]

They then realize that this man was better and superior to them!

THE APOCRYPHON OF JOHN «…And when they *(Yaldabaoth's powers)* realized that he *(Adam)* was luminous, and that he could think **better than they**

85

Don't skip chapters or bibliographic references

did, and that he was free from wickedness and evil, they picked him up and threw him down into the **lowest** part of all matter.» [English tr.: FREDERIK WISSE]
...By creating the inferior dense material-body in the shape of material man as a shell.

JOHN'S APOCRYPHON (http://www.gnosis.org/naghamm/apocjn-davies.html)
«The host of rulers and demons plotted together. They mixed fire and earth and water together with the four blazing fiery winds. They melded them together in great turbulence. Adam was brought into the shadow of death. **They intended to make him anew this time** from Earth, Water, Fire, Wind, which are Matter, Darkness and Desire: The Artificial Spirit. This all became **a tomb**, a new kind of **body**. Those thieves bound man in it, enchained him **in forgetfulness**, and made him subject to dying.»
[English Tr. STEVAN DAVIES]

*As the book evolves, any questions that might arise on this particular subject will be clarified, since only **some** of the information has been given until now.*

Since then the fallen 'god' has been desperately striving to retrieve 'his Mother's Strength' (which he was fooled into distributing to the souls) trying to entice man to 'sell his soul back to him'. Thus, with worldly material offerings, 'the archon of this world' charms men...who sell their souls to the devil.
Closing this parenthesis we continue to accumulate the evidence for the two creations. In her work 'The Secret Doctrine', H. P. Blavatsky, having collected the testimonies of all nations, the historical sources and the myths, cites an aggregate of knowledge in which every researcher will be able to find a great deal of information. I must state however, that I am not using H. P. Blavatsky in my bibliography because I agree with her final positions, but rather with the completeness of her work, in which an enormously great wealth of information is produced. So, in the Assyro-Babylonian mythology which later became the main source of reference for the Old Testament in particular, the following is stated:

H. P. BLAVATSKY, THE SECRET DOCTRINE III-80:
«Now what do the Babylonian accounts of 'Creation', as found on the Assyrian fragments of tiles, tell us? Those very accounts upon which the Pharisees built their own angelology (angel stories)? ... It is the Tablet of the Seven Wicked Gods or Spirits:
{1} In the first days the evil Gods,
{2} the angels who were in rebellion, who in the lower part of heaven
{3} had been created
{4} they caused their evil work
{5} devising with (their) wicked heads (minds) ...etc.

… The rebellious angels had been created in the lower part of heaven, …i.e. they belonged and still belong to a material plane of evolution, although…it remains generally **invisible** to us…Were the Gnostics so wrong, after this, in affirming that this visible world of ours and especially the Earth had been created by lower angels, the inferior Elohim, one of which was, as they taught, the God of Israel?…

{7} There were seven such (wicked gods).

…Then follows their description, where the fourth (god) is a 'serpent', the phallic symbol of the fourth Race in Human Evolution.

{15} These seven of them, messengers of the god Anu, their king.»

So these inferior angels are the ones Jesus calls Elohim. At the same time, as our metaphysical knowledge tells us, these seven Elohims are also the primary creators of dense matter; they have their headquarters in the aetheric plane and are in total control of (hierarchically) the Devas and the multitude of elementals as they are divided in categories that correspond to each of the four elements of matter (Elemental-Dwarfs, Salamanders, Sylph[ide]s and Nereides).

Marvin Meyer, professor of Biblical and Christian studies in the Griset Chair of Chapman University in Orange, California and a member of the translating team of the Gospel of Judas from Coptic to English, having also devoted the greatest part of his research to the texts of the Nag Hammadi Library, which comprise the sum of the Gnostic Gospels, in his treatise on Judas' Gospel, states:

«The descendant of Sophia (wisdom), namely the fruit of a mistake, which in the Apocryphon of John is described as a dismorphic (ugly) child, is the master and creator of this world as we know from many Sethian texts *(from the Seth generation: Celestial Men)*. In the Gospel of Judas and other Gnostic texts, the creator of the world is far from gentle, noble or serene. As the creator, he is responsible for keeping the divine light of Sophia **imprisoned** inside the mortal bodies of men.» (pp. 188-189)

Correspondingly, Bart D. Ehrman, professor at the James A. Grey Chair, president of the Theology Department at the University of Northern Carolina and a member of the same translating team for Judas' Gospel as well, gives his own report on the book:

«In addition, our world belongs to the sphere/realm of 'perdition', or as we could alternately translate the word, of 'corruption'. It (our world) is not the creation of the One and only God. It is only after the appearance of all other deities, that the god of the Old Testament –who is called El– starts to exist, and who is followed by his assistants, the blood-thirsty rebel Yal-

Don't skip chapters or bibliographic references

dabaoth and the insane Saklas. The last two are the ones who created the world and men.» (p. 128)

In the course of history, words that describe the Divine Knowledge fall prey to the Babel, which generally prevails on the material plane. So, many and diverse names have been used in order to define the same concept, or the same being. However, the objective goal of every open-minded researcher is to look for the essence behind the words.

Inside a HyperUniverse/Aeon, the apostate god/creator 'is born' as an off-spring of the Monogenes Luminary/Aeon, abandons his Birthplace, unites with the dark moist nature and creates through his Logos (Λ Λόγος=division, fraction).

The classic beginning of every creation is chaos and darkness that predominate in the forbidden wood/tree. This is the creation of the material universe, of the fallen god (Lucifer [Eos-phoros=light-carrier]) who abandoned the Paternal Family, in order to build his own creation inside the realm of the waste of darkness and Erebus (Gr. = deep darkness). However, despite the fact that he bears (Gr. φέρω, Latin fero, ferre = to bear) the Immaculate Light of the Father in him, the material he chooses to build with never ceases to be unsound, foul and dirty. And after he molded the Psyche (Soul) from his own unblemished part, he forced IT to put on one filthy dress/body/carrier after the other.

But it is not only in Genesis of the Old Testament or in Hermes Trismegistus' narration that we find a description of the initial phases of the <u>second</u> creation. Hesiod, in his Theogony, expresses this equally vividly:

HESIOD, THEOGONY (verses 123-124): «…and from chaos came forth Erebus and the black night; and from the Night again, Aether and the Day were born. It (the night) conceived and gave birth to them from erotic union with Erebus.»

Aristophanes, in his work 'Ornithes' (=Birds) phrases this in his own way:

ARISTOPHANES, ORNITHES (verse 693) «At the beginning there was Chaos, Night, dark Erebus and deep Tartarus. Earth, Air, and Sky had no existence. Firstly, black-winged Night laid a germless egg in the bosom of the infinite deeps of Erebus…»

The Chinese Mythology has the following myth about creation:
«In the beginning, the world was a formless and chaotic mass in the shape of an egg *(the egg again!!)* Then, a giant appeared, Pan Kou. He took his axe and divided this mass in two *(division/fission)*. All the hot, luminous and dry elements rose and created the sky. All the cold, dark and moist ones settled and created the earth.»

And Hermes Trismegistus continues:

HERMES TRISMEGISTUS, THE FOUNDER OF MONOTHEISTIC RELIGION, 9,000 B.C.

IOANNIDIS P., CH. 1: «§9 The **God-Noûs** (Mind) *(1ˢᵗ, The Monogenes Luminary of the particular Aeon)*, male-female one, being Life and Light, gave birth to another **Creator-Noûs** of Fire and Spirit *(2ⁿᵈ one, the fallen Yaldabaoth)*. And this second Noûs created the administrators *(3ʳᵈ group)* of the sensory world which is encompassed in seven circles, whose administration is called **Heimarmenē**» [Gr.: Εἱμαρμένη = Fate] *(or else the seven Elohims, or else the powers, the authorities and the kings of Yaldabaoth's team in John's Apocryphon).*
The Authorized One (Luminary) (1ˢᵗ) God-Noûs, who comes from the Unuttered Father, gave birth to the creator of the material plane.

This is the (2ⁿᵈ) Creator Noûs who, when it was time for him to offer his offspring to his native HyperUniverse, he defected and created his own creation, «once he snatched, completely alone and for himself, 'The Flower of the Noûs' from the Paternal Might» *and united with the 'moist nature'.*
Proceeding, Hermes Trismegistus further clarifies the creator's own division as the divine Logos (=fraction, division, fission – divisible essence) for the creation of inferior matter, while retaining his higher part as the Creator-Noûs (Mind).

HERMES TRISMEGISTUS, HERMETIC TEXTS VOL. A SPEECHES I-XVIII, RODAKIS P., TZAFEROPOULOS A. SPEECH 1 «§10 Immediately from the lower elements [of god] sprang the Divine Logos into the pure creation of Nature and united with the **Creator-Noûs** (2ⁿᵈ) (with which he is consubstantial), and the mindless downward elements of nature were left aside to be matter only.»
This fission of the Creator-Noûs himself is more easily discernible in other excerpts.
To be more precise, through her meticulous research, H. P. Blavatsky, states in Volume IV of her 'Secret Doctrine' (p. 49):
«…The reading of the Chaldean-Assyrian tiles *(Deltae)* has demonstrated it beyond a shadow of doubt. We encounter the same idea in the Zohar. Satan was a Son and an Angel of God. With all the Semitic nations, the Spirit of the Earth was as much a Creator in his own realm, as the Spirit of the Heavens. They were twin brothers and interchangeable in their functions, when the two were not united in one.
(This is why) …The god of Jews **forbids cursing Satan**. The Pentateuch and the Talmud undeviatingly forbid one to curse the adversary, as also the gods of the gentiles *(the gods of the idolaters).*»
In Jude's (the brother of James) letter which can be found in the New Testament right before John's Apocalypse, we read:
«§9 But Michael the archangel, while contending with the devil, and quarreling about Moses' body, **never dared** to cast upon him (the devil)

Don't skip chapters or bibliographic references

a blasphemous accusation/judgment, but said: 'may the Lord reprimand/rebuke you.»

And Blavatsky continues in the 'Secret Doctrine' Vol. IV (p. 50-51):

«All we read in the Zohar and other Cabbalistic works regarding Satan shows plainly that this 'personage' is simply the personification of the abstract evil, which **is the weapon of the karmic law** and of KARMA *(the law of reciprocal justice)*. It is our human nature, and **man himself**, as it is said namely that 'Satan is always near and inextricably interwoven with man.'

…In the lower/inferior ranks/orders of Theogony, the celestial beings of lower Hierarchies, each had a 'Fravassi', or a celestial 'Double'. It is the same, only a still more mystic reassertion (reaffirmation) of the Cabbalistic axiom: **'Deus est Demon Inversus = God is the Devil in reverse'**.» ☯

And as it is mentioned in the **CHALDEAN ORACLES,** (p. 227) PLACES 215, LYDUS P. IV 101-141, 2-11 W: «There are two kinds of daemons in man. …For Zeus gives all the **good** and all the **bad** and it is he who determines life's duration for everything born, mixing a mortal body for the good ones as he does for the ones that are foul/evil.»

So, the Creator-Noûs (2nd), created through his Logos, the seven commanders (3rd order) of Είμαρμένη (Heimarmenē = fate, predestination, kismet) and the rest of the deities of his very own hypostasis.

Analyzing the Greek word Είμαρμένη, which has <u>a common root</u> and is equal to μοίρα=fate (Karma), we find that it comes from the Gr. verb μοιρά-ζω [=to allocate], and thus we can discern the division of matter and its constructors more clearly:

*[Gr.: **Μοίρα** < Gr. verb. <u>μείρομαι</u> (μοιρά-ζω=to allocate, to get my share)]*

*[Gr.: **Είμαρμένη** [Heimarmenē] = the female p.p. of εἶμαρμαι, ancient μείρομαι = to get my share]*

And as Hermes Trismegistus, states:

HERMES TRISMEGISTUS, HERMETIC TEXTS, Vol. A, SPEECHES I-XVIII, RODAKIS P., TZAFEROPOULOS A., 12TH SPEECH

«§5 All things, O Son, are the work of Heimarmenē (Fate), and without it nothing can happen of the things that happen to bodies; neither good, nor bad; For it is decreed by Heimarmenē, that **he who does <u>good</u> should suffer** and acts thus so as to suffer for what he has done…§6… But all men succumb to Heimarmenē, and are subject to birth and to change. The beginning and the end is Heimarmenē.»

*But 'Heimarmenē', that dictates the fate of every man, shares a **common root** with sin (Gr.: αμαρτία) and inescapably leads to it.*

[Gr.: Ἁμαρτία = α+εῗμαρται: 3rd person, Present Perfect of the Gr. verb μείρομαι = to share]

If, in other words, a man acts beneficially to his fellow humans, 'he sins' by harming himself. And if he acts beneficially to himself, 'he sins' by harming his fellows. And Jesus, who has been so little understood, says:

GOSPEL OF THOMAS, 'ECUMENICAL PROGRAM FOR COPTIC TRANSLATION'
www.metalog.org/ files/thomas.html

«§14 Jesus says to them: "If you fast you will beget transgression for yourselves. And if you pray, you shall be condemned. And if you give alms (charity), you shall cause evil to your spirits.»

...Because the inescapable 'fate' of matter is sin.

In fact, Heraclitus equated Heimarmenē with Need and considered it the seed everything originated from.

*And Jesus continues in **John's Apocryphon**:*

«And thus the whole creation was made <u>blind,</u> in order that they (the created ones) may not know God, Who is above all of them. And because of the chain of **forgetfulness** *[Gr.: λήθη]*, their sins were hidden. For they are bound with <u>measures</u> and <u>times</u> and <u>moments</u>, since **fate** *(Gr.: μοῖρα)* is lord over everything.» [English tr.: FREDERIK WISSE]

⇜·⇝

Now that matters are reaching their end, it is imperative for the Truth to be given to men again, in order for them to choose what they finally desire with α 'sober mind' and awareness. The choices are not two, but three. The first two are <u>the two sides of the same coin</u> that appear seemingly different to humans. They are one and the same, where the choice of one automatically generates its opposite. It is the everlasting vicious circle of the deceitful duality of good and evil.

*The other choice however –the real and not the virtual one– is simply the Realization and <u>Epignosis (deep awareness) of the Truth</u>. It is the **fundamental nucleus** of Jesus' Teaching, which was unfortunately twisted..., by the 'do-gooders'.*

JOHN'S GOSPEL 8:32 «And you shall know the truth, and the truth will set you free.»

Marvin Meyer, as mentioned above, claims in another part of the same treatise:

«Therefore, as Bart Ehrman has noted in his study, the Gospel of Judas, which in this particular case becomes the Gospel of Jesus himself, declares **salvation through Knowledge**, i.e. **self-knowledge** which is granted to man's soul through divine enlightenment.»

As an additional necessary choice, it is recommended to detach oneself

91

Don't skip chapters or bibliographic references

from everything extreme, aiming thus to the 'unwavering' (non-oscillating) balance.

In conclusion:
HERMES TRISMEGISTUS, HERMETIC TEXTS VOL. A SPEECHES I-XVIII, RODAKIS P., TZAFEROPOULOS A. SPEECH 11, (NOÛS TO HERMES)
«§2 So, listen my child about God and everything; God, aeon, cosmos, time, birth.
God creates the aeon, the **aeon** (creates) the cosmos, the **cosmos** (creates) time and **time** (creates) **birth**.
The Essence of God is wisdom.
The aeon's essence is identity,
The world's (substance) is order,
Time's (substance) is change, and
And the (substance) of birth is life and death *(dyadicism/duality)*.»

God is the Unuttered One.
The Aeon is (signifies) the HyperUniverses of the True Unsplit Light.
The world generated by the fallen one is (symbolizes) the finer dimensions (planes) of the material universe with the order of the laws and of karma.
Time is the entrenched densely material universe.
And birth is the bond of the prison.

---

[59] **THE APOCRYPHON OF JOHN**, THE GNOSTIC SOCIETY LIBRARY: «Jesus said: "And I entered into the midst of their prison, which is <u>the prison of the body.</u> And I said, He who hears, let him get up from the deep sleep.» [Eng. tr. from Coptic: FREDERIK WISSE]

This is why, Celestial Man, originating from the Aeon, in order to return back to IT, acts as follows:
He denounces the prison of the body/grave which is forced upon him through birth.
He maintains his balance, un-oscillating, in the change of time.
He reinstates his soul to order, shutting the door behind him.
He discovers the identity of 'his Essence' through self-knowledge (self-Epignosis) and walks toward his Aeon/Cosmos.
There and then, he takes in the Unified Patrogenes Light (of the Father), and not the split quasi/substitute light (Ant-Avge) of Logos.

---

[60] *May I remind you that the Gr. w. Λόγος (Logos/Word) also means fraction, i.e. fission, division, separation, with its initial letter Λ itself, indicating precisely this concept with its shape.*

HIERARCHICAL TABLE

UNUTTERED PRINCIPLE - FATHER		
TRUE PATROGENES LIGHT COHERENT INDIVISIBLE ESSENCE	12 HYPERUNIVERSES (AEONS) (1ST) NOÛS GOD (LUMINARY- CHRIST)	1ST PARADISE
9TH SKY MOTHER OF THE FALLEN CREATOR		
ANTAVGES FIRE DIVISIBLE ESSENCE	**8TH** SKY (2ND) NOÛS CREATOR (the fallen one) BEARER OF THE SACRED ARCHETYPES L O G O S	
7TH SKY HIGHER MENTAL PLANE		
6TH SKY THE COMMANDERS OF HEIMARMENĒ (DESTINY)		
7 RAYS OF FLAME (Quasi/Substitute Light)	THE GODS OF SAMSARA	2ND VIRTUAL PARADISE (NIRVANA)
	5th SKY AKASHIC ARCHIVES	
	4th SKY HIGHER ASTRAL	
	3rd SKY LOWER ASTRAL	
	2nd SKY, AETHEREAL (BRONZE) SEVEN ELOHIMS of CREATION	
	AETHERIC PLANE	
1st MATERIAL – VISIBLE – SKY DENSE MATTER		

OSCILLATION

[61] **KONSTANTINOS VAGIONAKIS**, (PROF., UNIV. OF IOANNINA) '**INTRODUCTION TO THE NATURAL SCIENCES**' VOLUME IV, 'OSCILLATION AND HARMONIC MOTION, INTRODUCTION TO FLUID MECHANICS' (GREEK OPEN UNIVERSITY)
«INTRODUCTORY NOTES: Every object's motion that is repeated in a regular way, namely where the object returns to a given position after a specific time interval, is called periodic motion. …Now, if an object performing a periodic motion moves forward and backward on the same course, then we call this motion 'oscillation'. …A periodic motion is often called 'harmonic motion'»

❦·❧

–But why do you think the snake was chosen to symbolize of the creator of this dyadic/twofold universe?

I raised my shoulders expressing my ignorance.

–Simply because the wavy movement of the snake is the same with the movement of the whole material universe: Oscillation.

[62] A) **DANEZIS M., THEODOSIOU S.** (ASSISTANT PROFESSORS OF ASTROPHYSICS IN THE UNIVERSITY OF ATHENS) '**COSMOLOGY OF THE INTELLECT**':
«T. A. Whiller (1968) stated: "The quantum geo-metro-dynamics space can be compared to a foam carpet that extends into a slow-moving **oscillating/wavy** landscape. …The perpetual minute changes that occur on the foam-carpet when new bubbles appear and old ones vanish, symbolize quantum-variations in geometry". Therefore, according to Whiller, electromagnetic and gravitational forces affect the quantum-foam causing vibrations and subsequently **waves** which are **noted by the observer as particles.** The interaction of these <u>waves</u> creates the <u>atoms</u>, the <u>molecules</u>, and the whole substance of the physical world. <u>In this way</u>, **everything** in the universe is **waves** <u>inside the nothingness.</u>»

B) '**CHORD THEORY**', LIVE-PEDIA.GR: http://www.physics4u.gr/χορδιακή θεωρία

«The theory of quantum-strings is the theory of physics that considers the fundamental constituents of the universe <u>not to be particles but strings</u>.

…Free strings vibrate. The different **vibration** modes of the strings represent the different types of particles. One mode of **vibration** makes the string appear as an electron, another as a photon.»

C) **PHYSICISTS DEVELOP EXPERIMENT TO TEST THE STRING THEORY,** UNIVERSITY OF SAN DIEGO, CALIFORNIA, JANUARY 23, 2007

> **PHYSICS4U.GR**, http://www.physics4u.gr/news/2007/scnews2727.html
>
> «The theory of quantum-strings says: Everything at the most elementary level consists of energy-threads that **vibrate** in various frequencies and especially in the multiple unknown dimensions. These 'strings' produce all the known forces and particles in the cosmos.»

Everything inside this material universe oscillates; from man's emotions to the virtual substitute light of the stars.

---

63 A) SIMON SINGH 'BIG BANG' (PH.D. MOLECULAR PHYSICS –CAMBRIDGE) Gr. tr. SPANOU A., (p. 270, 271): «In order to understand how astronomers discovered the chemistry of the stars, it is important to initially understand, albeit at a basic level, the nature of light. In particular, there are three main points which we must refer to.

First, physicists consider light to be an oscillation of an electric and a magnetic field, and this is the reason why light and the radiation forms related to it, are known as electro-magnetic radiation. Second, and probably simpler, is the fact that we can consider electro-magnetic radiation or light as a wave. The third important point is that the distance between two successive peaks of a light wave (or two successive valleys), which is the wave length, tells us almost everything we need to know about the light wave.»

B) KLOURAS, N., D., PERLEPES, S., P., 'GENERAL & INORGANIC CHEMISTRY' (GREEK OPEN UNIVERSITY) VOL. A, 'ATOMIC STRUCTURE, THE PERIODIC SYSTEM, THE PROPERTIES OF ATOMS' (p. 101-103)

«In 1924 Louis de Broglie (1892-1987) presented the bold idea, which was that just as light exhibits the properties of a material particle (photon), in the same way a particle, under the appropriate conditions, could exhibit the **characteristics of a wave** (material wave). For example, the electron which orbits around the core of a hydrogen atom could be considered **as a wave** that has a specific wave length. (According to de Broglie, the wave length of an electron or any other particle depends on the mass (m) and the velocity (v) of the particle). ...De Broglie's hypothesis applies **to all material bodies**, which means that every object with a mass (m) and a velocity (v) is equivalent with a specific material **wave**. ...A few years after the publication of de Broglie's ideas, the wave-properties of the electron **were experimentally verified**.»

C) THE MOST IMPORTANT FACTS IN PHYSICS IN 2002 AS RECORDED

BY PHYSICS WEB http://www.physics4u.gr/articles/2002/bestof2002.html

«In April 2002, the physicists in the Sudbury Neutrino Observatory (S. N. O.), in Canada, presented new finite indications that the electron neutrinos oscillate during their route from the Sun to the Earth. Only if the neu-

Don't skip chapters or bibliographic references

trinos have a mass, is this oscillation actually possible –a finding that de-mands a new science of Physics beyond the established model. Later dur-ing the same year, the experiment of KamLAND confirmed that the anti-neutrinos of the electrons oscillate as well.»

D) PLATO'S TIMAEUS, Gr. tr. KOUTROUMPAS D., G. (XIX 52d4-53): «And the nurse of creation, which is moistened and ignited/incandesced and receives the forms of earth and air, submits to all the subsequent effects and changes they un-dergo, so that she presents a variety of appearances as a result; …Oscillating though irregularly in all directions, she sways unevenly hither and thither, by the forces/forms that are inside her, and by her motion again she shakes them; and the elements when moved some one way, some another, are sepa-rated just as wheat when it is threshed.»

—*The virtual substitute light of the stars? …I asked bewildered.*
—In the True Light of the HyperUniverses, in every pair of opposites, both (opposite) parts coincide, HARMONIOUSLY INCORPORATED WITHIN the same 'entity' (Intelligent Wholeness). And when we speak of opposites, we mean properties, characteristics, tendencies without any daemonic colora-

tion. 'Evil', as it is known by men today, came about as a **side-effect** of perversion. We will analyze how this happened later on in our dis-cussion. The material universe was born from the fission (division) of the True Light of the HyperCosmoi. This fission produced a radiation that spread out and formed all the dimensions of the material universe. It was the virtual light, a substitute of the True One. After this initial fission, a chain reaction followed. It was the beginning of oscillation.

The encasement (entrapment) of the True Light (of the Light-bearing Crea-tor) between the two polar opposites of the fission of material creation, forced it to oscillate in a hopeless effort to unify them –something impossi-ble since one is outside and in opposition to the other– thus channeling and consuming its energy in the movement between the opposite poles which never unify into one. This is how the illusion of motion and alteration was born, in contradistinction to the Real Motion of the HyperUniverses which activates **Everything simultaneously**.

[64] **GOSPEL OF THOMAS,** JEAN YVES LELOUP:
«§50 Jesus said: … "If they ask you: What is the sign of your Father in you, say: It is movement and it is repose *(rest)*.» [Eng. tr. JOSEPH ROWE]

96

Oscillation is symbolized by the wavy movement of the snake and fission (Λ) Λόγος/Logos (Gr. Λόγος [Logos] = word/division/cause) is symbolized by its forked (y-shaped) Λ tongue.

> [65] *Several scholars commented on the Orphic Hymns in their own way:*
> **ORPHIC HYMNS, FROM ATHENAGORAS' APOLOGY,** Gr. tr. MAGGINAS S. (p. 72)
> «But Phanes or Protogonus *(Φάνητας, the Primitive creative light –the creator– we talked about in the chapter 'CREATION')* produced another terrible offspring from his holy womb, which has the dreadful form of a viper. It has a mane coming down from its head, and a beautiful face, but the rest of its body, from the neck and down, is that of a dragon, tremendous to the view.»

Oscillation is a wave. The Greek word for 'wave' is κῦμα [kyma]. Its root is the ancient verb κυῶ which means to swell, to get inflated. The Greek word κύησις is a derivative noun which means gestation, pregnancy. Hindus call it the 'breath of Brahma' whose exhalation gives birth to the worlds and inhalation devours them back in (absorbs them to extinction). Oscillation is the expression of duality: The 'up' and the 'down'; zenith and nadir; ascent and descent; good and evil; life and death; sleeping and wakefulness. One gives birth to the other. Inhalation bears exhalation and exhalation bears inhalation. The day bears the night and the night bears the day. Life bears death and death bears life. Each one gives birth to its opposite and simply mutates into it. Everything is subject to this inviolable law. A negative situation forces man to move to a positive position, and vice versa.

> [66] **LIVING ON THE EDGE OF CHAOS,** http://www.physics4u.gr/5lessons/lesson4.html
> «The Second Law of Thermodynamics sets some limitations to the forecasts made in this clock-work Universe. Everything, the Second Law of Thermodynamics insists, progressively acquires greater disorder. Anything that increases order, like tiding up your house, has the <u>inevitable</u> consequence, that <u>somewhere else in the Universe, disorder will increase</u>.»

An endless alternation of peaks and declines, love and hate, pain and pleasure, joy and sorrow, beauty and ugliness: This Truth lies 'hidden' in front of men's eyes, and everything surrounding them, like a 'magic picture' (visual riddle). The entire reality of beings takes place on a fundamental oscillation and the partial sections of their existence on secondary oscillations of a smaller scale. Every creature's life evolves on the upper part of this fluctuation, the visible one; and death occurs in its lower part, the invisible. Man seems to come to the material world from the invisible. An oscillating spermatozoon sets the start for the gradual construction of the material body.

Don't skip chapters or bibliographic references

Then comes birth in the natural world, growth, acme with the culmination of creativity, only to gradually start withdrawing, giving its place to the degrading senility of old age and finally to death, where through a different 'life' oscillation, the material body will decompose and man himself will be lead to the invisible part of this broader, twofold process. The same oscillation that initially promotes man is the very same one that degrades him. None of the two opposites can prevail over the other, because none can exist independent and disassociated from the other. The very nature of oscillation contains in it both opposite sides/positions. Hence the determinism of this world always moves things from one place to the opposite one and over again.

What role then, do you imagine, Celestial Man has inside this material schizophrenia (Gr. word from σχίζω [= to split in two] and φρένα [= mind/noûs]) meaning to have a split/fissional mind) in the real sense of the word? He is constantly trying to establish only one of the two opposites; good against evil; rise against fall; justice instead of injustice. But no matter how hard man struggles to stabilize only one of the two conditions, sooner or later, the law of this dyadic nature will inevitably generate one of its many expressions on the opposite side.

–But man, through his daily life, with a harmonious combination of both opposite situations, can achieve the perfect balance. He can bring the 'golden mean' into action and eradicate the schizophrenic polarization!

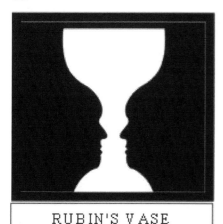

RUBIN'S VASE

–For man's natural status quo, what you propose is exactly what is needed. Only by diminishing the breadth (amplitude) of his daily oscillation as far as possible, and by equalizing the oppositions between the 'dipoles', can he find the balance. Then, after detaching himself from them, he will clearly see this dyadicism of nature and recognize in it 'the tree of knowledge of good and evil'. But as long as man holds himself stuck onto this oscillation that sometimes lifts him and then brings him down, it is impossible for him to realize this truth. Nevertheless, this state of balance he will apply to his life is superficial and not real.

[67] *The very nature of the operation of the human brain lacks the ability to integrate situations.*
CAN QUANTUM PHENOMENA EXPLAIN CONSCIOUSNESS?
http://www.physics4u.gr/news/2007/scnews3090.html   or   http://tech.pathfinder.gr/xpaths/x-scienc/564485.html

«According to Eustratios Manousakis, Professor of Physics at the University of Florida (Tallahassee), the key of consciousness could be found in the quantum-type actions taking place in the brain, when someone looks at ambiguous images, like Rubin's vase, on which there are two patterns with common borders and one of them is perceived as a figure, while the other as a background. In this case, our perception <u>has to choose</u> between the two alternative interpretations. It will perceive one pattern as a figure and the other as a background, but **it will <u>never</u> perceive both of them <u>simultaneously</u> as a figure**. These optical illusions are ambiguous because at any moment they can **only be perceived in one of the two alternative ways**. Under no circumstances can they be perceived in both ways simultaneously. The image looks as if it is inverted, when our perception changes from the one alternative interpretation of the image to the other.»

Follow my thought: The 'speed' of True Light of the HyperUniverses is not a measurable magnitude because there is no distance there that IT will have to cover in order to activate the opposites, since they are incorporated <u>at the same point</u>. In the HyperUniverses we talk about expansion of Light through Completeness, whereas in the universe of fission we speak of distances and velocities. Regarding speed in the finer (subtler) energy dimensions, we can say it is high, but as energies sink deeper and deeper in this material-energy spiral, they condense until –in the inner/lower regions– they are 'locked' into energy bronchi and project the form of 'decelerated' dense visible matter.

[68] **DANEZIS M., THEODOSIOU S.** (ASSISTANT PROFESSORS OF ASTROPHYSICS IN THE UNIVERSITY OF ATHENS) **'COSMOLOGY OF THE INTELLECT'**
A) THE CONCEPT OF MASS (p. 171): «The mass of a body, which people often confuse with the concept of sensory matter, is something totally different from it. As mass of a body we define **the extent of inertia** of its matter, i.e. the magnitude of the resistance it exhibits when we try to alter its **kinetic** state by exerting a force upon it.» *And they note:*
«Quite often, we use the concepts matter, mass, inertia and weight without distinction, since up to now, no material body has been found without mass, inertia and weight.»
B) THE QUANTUM NATURE OF COSMIC FORCES (p. 152): «The Higgs boson is an elusive and still hypothetical particle, through which all bodies **acquire mass.** According to the supporters of this view, the hypothetical Higgs bosons which we can, in theory, find in infinite numbers inside the Universe, gather around every sub-atomic particle attributing to it a property we refer to as **mass of tranquility.**»
C) NEW SCIENTIFIC DATA (p. 47): «Matter, according to the Theory of Relativity,

Don't skip chapters or bibliographic references

is no more the inalterable molecule-complex of Newton, but the **condensate of an energy-current.** In Einstein's space-time framework, matter does not constitute a separate entity, but a peculiarity of the field. An elementary particle is nothing more than a moving, **non-perceptible vortex** in space.»

D) MATTER AS A VORTEX (WHIRL) – SOME PERSONAL VIEWS (p. 178): «But the vortex-particle has a series of surprises in store for us, since it should present spherical symmetry. What we are essentially talking about, is a **non-perceptible spherical vortex** inside the n-dimensional **non** Euclidean field, whose projective shadow inside the three-dimensional Euclidean space of our senses, is perceived as an elementary particle.»

Thus, this condition of **visible** matter *(as the 'mass of tranquility'),* ends up looking 'static/inert'; and as 'static/inert' it keeps the opposites separated, as separate are the colors on the motionless Newton's disk. No matter how much you dip your paint brush into each 'color', painting your life's canvas like talented painters, you will never achieve the radiant White. This can only be achieved under conditions, unattainable and forbidden for your dense material bodies!

So, through this virtual balance, the only thing you can accomplish by holding a glass of water in one hand and sugar in the other is to make sweet water. To make syrup however, a third factor is necessary, a factor that dense matter –by nature– does not have.

Now if someone asks: "Where does all this dyadic alternation lead?" The creator/snake will answer: "To the acquisition of experience."

The Unuttered Father will answer back: "In the HyperUniverses of True Light, the experience of dyadic matter is **utterly useless**, because its properties are NONEXISTENT THERE."

And I, as a traveler coming from THERE, make this clear to you by giving you an example: "If a common man wants to study computer programming, how useful do you imagine knowledge of pottery would be to him?"

[69] **A) HERMES TRISMEGISTUS,** THE FOUNDER OF MONOTHEISM 9000 B.C., IOANNIDIS P. K., 'ELEVENTH TEACHING OF HERMES TO TAT', Verse 41:
«Nothing of the earthly offers benefit to the celestial things; the celestial things though benefit the things of the earth.»
B) THE GOSPEL OF JOHN, CH. 6:
«§63 It is the Spirit that gives life; the flesh is of no avail;»

GOD'S BONDSERVANTS

(Tr. note: In the English canonic Gospels, the original Greek word δοῦλοι/douloi [=slaves] is almost always translated as 'servants', whereas –its Greek meaning– primarily encompasses the concept of slavery/bondage. It was apparently too much for the religious 'establishment' to accept the notion of man being God's slave. Consequently, to keep both parties happy (our religious establishment and the correctness of the translation), the word bondservant is used, to convey both meanings of the original Greek word: prisoners to offer their services to God.)

And the perpetual cycle of the 'Ourobore' (tail-devouring) snake[70], which, wriggled in the form of a circle is swallowing its tail, continues, renewing its old skin through endless alternations (successions).

---

[70] **OUROBORE" (TAIL-DEVOURING) SNAKE:** *A mystical symbol that depicts a snake creating a circle with its body and eating its tail. Since it has its tail as food/nutrition, it is called 'Ourobore' (from the Gr. Ουρο-βόρος = tail-eating). This symbol is analyzed further in the last chapter of the book.*

All these 'new' skins of the snake however, do not transform it into something different; and they definitely do not make it evolve.

It is exactly here, that the basic difference among religions of the world lies, which also divides them into two categories. One category worships the mystical symbol of the snake as holy and sacred, and bows to the creator of this world. The other (category of religions) considers it satanic and –with Christ as its principal physiognomy/figure– fights the 'archon of this world'.

---

[71] **A) BLAVATSKY H., P., 'THE SECRET DOCTRINE'** (II-215):

«The 'Serpent' was 'the Lord God' himself, who, as the Ophis, the Logos, or the bearer of divine creative wisdom *(our Creator!),* taught mankind to become creators in their turn.»

Following that, Blavatsky attaches an excerpt from the book of Dr. A. Kingsford 'The Perfect Way', Appendix 15, titled 'The Secret of Satan' (II-233):

«§2. Eternity brought forth Time; the Boundless gave birth to Limit; Being <u>descended</u> into creation. §3 As Lightning, I saw Satan fall from the sky, mighty in strength and fury. §4 Among the Gods is none like unto him, into whose hands are committed the kingdoms, the power and the glory of the worlds: §5 Thrones and empires, the dynasties of kings, the fall of nations,

Don't skip chapters or bibliographic references

the birth of churches and the triumph of Time.»
To confirm the previous reference):
B) **THE GOSPEL OF MATTHEW, CH. 4**: «§8. Again, the devil took him *(Jesus)* to a very high mountain, and showed him all the kingdoms of the world and their glory; §9. And he said to him, 'All these I will give you *(since, of course, all these are his own possessions!),* if you will bow down and worship me'.»
C) **THE GOSPEL OF JOHN, CH. 14**: «§30. I will not speak much more with you, for **the *archon (ruler)* of the world** is coming, and he has nothing in me;»
D) **THE GOSPEL OF JOHN, CH. 16**: «§11. ...And concerning judgment, because **the archon *(ruler)* of this world has been judged**.»

Today, the initial concepts of Christianity are lost. The Unutterable Principle of the HyperUniverses –The Supreme Father of the Christ– has been equated to the 'archon of this world', the creator of matter, the snake; the 'Creator of heaven and earth, of the visible and the invisible (higher-frequency matter).'

The Monogenes (Singly-Born) Christ *(Luminary),* in order to save His Celestial Children, who are trapped in the prison of material bodies and serve in the captivity of the snake as slaves, offered the '**sap of the pain**' *(the energy produced by His suffering)* of His Sacrifice as ransom to the 'archon of this world'.

---

[72] A) **THE APOCRYPHON OF JOHN, THE GNOSTIC SOCIETY LIBRARY:**
(Jesus said): «And I entered into the midst of their prison, which is **the prison of the body**. And I said, He who hears, let him get up from the deep sleep!»
[Eng. tr. from Coptic: FREDERIK WISSE]
Celestial Man is imprisoned in the material body.
B) **GOSPEL OF PHILIP**, JEAN-YVES LELOUP: «§13. High spiritual Powers (the Archon) wanted to deceive Man *(Celestial Man)*, because they saw goodness engendered in Him. They took the name for goodness and applied it to what was not good: words became deceitful, and *(since)* then they are joined to that which is without being and without goodness. They alienate with simulations and appearances: **they make a free person into a slave**.» [Eng. tr. JOSEPH ROWE]
C) **THE GOSPEL OF MATTHEW, Ch. 20**:
«§28. Because the Son of Man did not come to be served/ministered but to serve and to give His Life as **Ransom** for many.»
After the ransom payment by the Christ, man (if he so chooses) is free from his karma and from the karma administrator, Lucifer.

In the time that followed, through the foggy Babel that characterizes the entire material dimension, concepts have been disordered and faded and original words have been manipulated and thus misinterpreted. Today, only a few notions still remain from the real message of Jesus Christ to men, like empty fossils, and their essential meaning has faded in time. The initially small conceptual deviation from the Original Teaching, created, in time, a vast chasm between the primary position and what it finally became, thus transforming Christian faith into an aggregate of contradicting theories, views, superstitions and heresies.

---

[73] **RETROSPECTIVE FALSIFICATION**, http://www.skepdic.com/retfalse.html:

«D. H. Rawcliffe coined this term to refer to the process of telling a story *(or even a theory/doctrine)* that is factual to some extent, but which gets distorted and falsified over time by retelling it with various embellishments. The embellishments may include speculations, conflated events that occurred at different times or in different places, and the incorporation of material without regard for accuracy or plausibility. The overriding force that drives the story is to find or invent details that fit with a desired outcome. ...The original story gets remodeled with favorable points being emphasized and unfavorable ones being dropped. The distorted and false version becomes a memory and a record of a remarkable tale.»

Old beliefs were mingled with new ones and others of the opposite view and made a new faith, which people called Christianity.
The Christ did not condemn any sinner, because sin does not exist in the acts of man, but in matter itself.

---

[74] **A) THE GOSPEL OF MARY (MAGDALENE)** JEAN-YVES LELOUP, Gr. tr. KOUROUSSI A., A., VERSES 13-17: «What is the sin of the world? The Master said: There is no sin, but **it is you who make sin exist** when you act according to the habits of your **nature**, which is inclined to adultery.»

The very nature of matter betrays the Eternal Immortal Truth and ends up as an 'adulteress nature' because: «The deficiency of matter **did not** originate through the Infinity of the Father.» [GOSPEL OF TRUTH §39]

B) THE GOSPEL OF JOHN, CH. 3: «§17. For God sent His Son into the world **not to judge the world** but that the world might be saved through Him.»

C) THE GOSPEL OF MATTHEW, CH. 11: «§18-19 (Jesus speaks) When John *(The Baptist)* came neither eating nor drinking, people said, He has a demon. But when the Son of man came eating and drinking, they say, Behold, a glutton and a drunkard, a friend of tax collectors and sinners!»

*In reality, there are no RULES of behavior indicating who is a 'child' of Truth and who isn't. Both, John, being ascetic as well as Jesus, who was more sociable, were on **one and the same side**.*

Don't skip chapters or bibliographic references

On the contrary, he who is judged is SOLELY the administrator and **archon** of this world: "…Concerning judgment, because the archon (ruler) of this world has been judged." [JOHN'S GOSPEL 16:11] This is why Jesus came to pay **the ransom** for the liberation of Man to this kidnapper-administrator and to open the sealed escape Gate in the 'egg of the snake'. The road that leads to the exit is the realization of the absolute Truth. This is the antidote to the poison of the snake.

---

75 A) «And the Truth shall set you free.» [JOHN 8:32]
B) **HERMES TRISMEGISTUS,** HERMETIC TEXTS, VOL. I, RODAKIS P., TZAFEROPOULOS AP., **SPEECH A:**
(a) «§20. And I said: But do they, who are in **ignorance,** sin so terribly, that they should therefore be deprived of immortality?»
(b) «§26. This is the Ἀγαθόν [=good] end for those who **possess the Gnosis**: They become one with God». *{See Tr. n. on w. Ἀγαθός, beginning of Ch. 'HIGHER MENTAL BODY – CELESTIAL MAN'}*

Some years after the Christ's withdrawal from this material universe though, subsequent (later) Christians, returned to the 'old ways' with their head bowed, once again as bondservants of the god/creator/snake.
But do you know what bondservants usually do? They yield their energy for their master's benefit.

---

76 A) **THE APOCRYPHON OF JOHN, THE GNOSTIC SOCIETY LIBRARY**: «And he *(Yaldabaoth)* said to the authorities who attended him: Come, let us create a human according to the image of God and according to our own likeness, so that his image **may become light for us**.» [Eng. tr. from Coptic: FREDERIK WISSE]
B) **NEAR EAST TEXTS,** Gr. tr. XENI SKARTSI S., – SOCRATES L. SKARTSIS, **ENUMA ELISH** (THE ASSYRO-BABYLONIAN EPIC OF CREATION):
It was unearthed in the town of Nineveh and was found as part of the imperial library of Assurbanipal, the last great king of Assyria. It consists of reproductions of older texts, obviously predating the second millennium.
TABLET 6: «§1. When Marduk hears the words of the gods, his heart prompts him to create skillful works. He opens his mouth and turns to Ea to reveal to him the plan he had captured in his heart: "I shall gather blood and make bones. I will make a savage one. Man will be his name. I will create a truly savage man. He will undertake **the service of the gods,** so that they might be comfortable.»

As far as the bondservants of the god-creator are concerned, they transform portions of their spiritual hypostasis, their fundamental spiritual body/essence, **into matter**. They waste, in other words, their Fatherly 'Fortune' as the parable of the Prodigal (lost) Son tells us. *{Tr. n.: the Greek word used for 'fortune' in Luke's 15:13 is Οὐσία [Ousseea] which means Essence}*

---

[77] **THE GOSPEL OF LUKE, CH. 15** (PARABLE OF THE LOST SON): «§13. Not many days later, the younger son gathered all he had *(his share from the Paternal property [Gr. = Essence])* and set off for a distant country, and there he squandered his wealth in riotous living. §14. And when he had spent everything, a great famine arose in that land, and he began to be in need. §15. So he went and joined himself to a citizen of that country *(the Archon of this world),* who sent him <u>into his fields</u> *(and became his slave)* to feed swine. §16 And he would gladly have fed on the husks *(the material benefits of the god/creator)* that the swine ate, and no one gave to him.»
B) OLD TESTAMENT, GENESIS CH. 3 *(God/creator says to the prodigal son – Adam)* «§18. Thorns also and thistles it *(the Earth)* shall bring forth for you; and you shall eat the herb of the field *(...the husks).*»

–And in what way does this transmutation take place? I asked.
–The structure of natural laws is relatively the same on all planes of the material universe. The search for a 'unified theory of all' that your physicists are conducting today is based on this rationale.

In nature, energy has the potential to transform from one kind to another. But according to the 'principle of energy degradation', energy is maintained –regardless of its transformation to another kind– but it is at the same time degraded. This happens because, during the transformation of one energy-type into another, a small part of this transformed energy is always lost in the atmosphere, since it is converted into heat.

---

[78] *At this point, I would like to mention the definitions of some basic laws of Physics, and by extension, the laws of nature itself.*
SOURCES: **SCHOOL ENCYCLOPEDIA AVLOS, AVLOS PUBL. MAJOR HELLENIC LEXICON (TEGOPOULOS- FYTRAKIS) WIKIPEDIA,** (http://el.wikipedia.org/wiki)
PHYSICS4U, (http://www.physics4u.gr/5lessons/lesson4.html)
(http://www.physics4u.gr/articles/2002/secondlaw1.html)
«We define Energy as the natural magnitude that can be transformed into work. When a material body has the attribute of producing work, then this body encompasses energy. Every material body contains energy. Energy cannot be created out of nothing (from the void) nor can it be destroyed when it is transformed from one kind to another (e.g. from dynamic to kinetic). This observation was first made by Julius Robert von Mayer in 1842 and was named the 'Principle of the Conservation of Energy' or the 'First Law

---

Don't skip chapters or bibliographic references

of Thermodynamics'. Therefore: Every material body encompasses energy. Every form of energy can be transformed into another.»
We will now examine the second axiom or the Second Law of Thermodynamics that interests us more.
"Every time that energy is transformed from one form to another, a certain amount of it is lost (given back) to the environment, in the form of degraded (weakened) thermal energy. In other words, it is a property of energy that each time it passes from one form to another, **only a certain amount of it can be used.** The rest of the energy is eventually transferred to the environment in the form of heat, which is a <u>non</u>-usable energy form **and thus is lost.** So, we have a 'degradation of energy' because heat is considered energy of inferior quality, compared to other forms that are characterized of a superior quality. Thus, during transformation, energy is conserved quantitatively but degraded qualitatively. <u>Heat is lost in space.</u> This is at least, what the 2nd Law of Thermodynamics imposes, which is also called the Law of Entropy and was first formulated by Walther Nernst.»
And what exactly is entropy?
«It is the mathematical function that describes the state of **disorder** of a system. More simply: Entropy is thought to express the **magnitude of disorder** of a system. For example, the particles that compose an apple or a piece of iron are in an orderly arrangement. *(Nevertheless, as the laws of duality, oscillation and alternation dictate...)* At some point, the apple starts to rot and the iron rusts. Then, the previously correct arrangement of their particles gradually starts to get disorganized and thus the system's entropy *(=disorder)* increases.»
Similar to the principle of 'Entropy' is 'Enthalpy' which mainly pertains to chemical reactions of elements:
«Enthalpy is the quantity of energy that is contained in a chemical substance. When this substance is subject to a certain physical-chemical change, its enthalpy (internal energy) is also changed. Then, a certain portion of it is transformed into heat *(and is lost)*. This is the cause of the thermal phenomena that accompany chemical reactions.»

So if we take the existence of uniform laws throughout the universe for granted and apply them into everyday life, some reasonable correlations arise: the prevailing characteristic in people's lives is an uninterrupted creativity. This creativity is expressed through the production of work *{Tr. n.: Gr. ἐνέργεια [=energy]' means exactly that: energy is found/consumed in ἔργον [=work]}* on matter. This work, in order to be realized, requires the existence of energy, which in the case of man, is no other than his psycho-spiritual power. Men imagine that their life is god's 'gift' to them. But only in their imagination is it really a gift. The 'energy tax' is too heavy. No one can 'live' if they don't pay the heavy du[ti]es of this creation with the energy of their work. The moment though that they transform their spiritual energy/power to material work 'with the sweat of their brow' they degrade their spiritual reserves.

> [79] **OLD TESTAMENT, GENESIS CH. 3**: «§19. By the <u>sweat of your face</u> *(the product of heat)* you shall eat bread, until you return to the ground from which you were taken.»

It is the moment that man/bondservant, through his own offer/creation, enriches the material construction of his master/creator, leaving his spiritual 'imprint' on matter. Through this process, the reason for the technological upgrading of the human civilization becomes clear, even though it does not go hand-in-hand with a corresponding spiritual blooming.

> [80] **'IDEOTHEATRON' MAGAZINE, APRIL 1999 ISSUE,** AN EXCERPT OF AN INTERVIEW WITH D. NANOPOULOS (ACADEMIC, HEAD OF THE HOUSTON ADVANCED RESEARCH CENTER) «Our living standards may have risen, we may perform one-day 'bloodless' surgical operations, we may have more free time, we may eat more healthily, we may get information about things faster, but have we really become any better? Not necessarily, I think. It's not that I am pessimistic, on the contrary, I am optimistic by nature but I can't shut my eyes in front of reality.»

This spiritual degradation, in contrast to materialistic progress, is apparent in every subsequent generation, when it 'passes the baton' to the next one. There is then, this intense feeling that the new generation is 'inferior' to the previous one. People believe that this feeling is the result of the 'generation gap'. But it isn't. What do you think this renowned 'generation gap' really is? It is clearly **spiritual degradation**, as opposed to the **materialistic upgrading** which happens when a portion of man's spiritual 'Essence' is transformed into material expression and falls. This is why most of the real saints relinquish any kind of activity in this world of Lucifer. Make sure that you <u>never</u> associate material technological progress with spiritual progress!

> [81] **THE APOCALYPSE OF ADAM, THE GNOSTIC SOCIETY LIBRARY,** THE NAG HAMMADI LIBRARY, TRANSLATED BY GEORGE W. MACRAE: «After those days, the Eternal Knowledge of the God of Truth withdrew from me and your mother Eve. Since that time, **we learned about dead things**, like men.» [Gr. Ed.: Pyrinos Kosmos Publ.]

Don't skip chapters or bibliographic references

As 'clever' as a computer-robot can be, it can certainly <u>not</u> possess spirituality. From a different perspective, technological progress is the outcome of the greatest law of matter: **Need**. And of course Need only serves 'the house it was born in' and this is no other than matter itself.

---

[82] *Dido Kallergi, in the introduction of her book 'The Twelve Olympian Gods' presents a great wealth of evidence related to the attributes of 'Necessity' and its earlier meaning.*

DIDO KALLERGI, 'THE TWELVE OLYMPIAN GODS': «According to the modern philosophical Theory of Necessity/Need, all that happens is the requisite consequence of causes. But this isn't just a contemporary theory, because most of the ancient people –theologians, philosophers and authors– believed the same thing. They regarded need/necessity as the fundamental cause of the cosmic order. In the 'Argonautica' of Orpheus (§1-17) it is mentioned: "Even before the ancient chaos, there was the unrevealed necessity... "In the 2nd hymn of Orpheus to Kronoteknus [Kronos' child], as Uranus* was called, it is also mentioned: "in his chest he holds the unapproachable Necessity of Nature." In 'The Natural' of Johannes Stobaeus, Ch. 4, it is recorded that: "Thales called Necessity the inconvertible force that dominates everything." Pythagoras said that: "Necessity/Need surrounds the world." Democritus called it world-creating, Provision, Heimarmenē (Fate) and that everything happens out of Need/Necessity. ...Plato called Necessity the Mother of the Fates with which Zeus makes all his decisions. According to Proclus, "Orpheus called the one fundamental law, from which all the others derive, 'Zeus' Deputy' and, as it is obvious, it is the Law of Necessity itself." ...In consequence of the above, Necessity, the fundamental law of Nature, is the natural cause out of which everything was made.... Moreover, the Gr. word Ἀνάγκη [=Need/Necessity] is derived from the Gr. verb ἀνάσσω, which means to reign, to dominate, to rule.»

Tr. n.: URANUS: ancient Greek deity of the sky (Ancient Greek: Οὐρανός), the father of Cronus (Saturn) and grandfather of Zeus (Jupiter).

Spirituality seems to be an expendable 'essence', a means for the accomplishment of every material goal, rather than the goal itself. So humanity, firstly because of the inevitable sin due to the material incarnation, and secondly because of the transmutation of its spiritual energy into matter, <u>does not evolve spiritually</u>. It progresses only materially. Spiritually speaking, it falls back.

83 A) **HERMES TRISMEGISTUS,** HERMETIC TEXTS, VOL. II, RODAKIS P., TZAFERO-POULOS AP., **'EXCERPT VII (HERMES)'** (p.149):

«§3 Men are a sinful race, because it is mortal and **its constituents are of bad matter;** and it so happens that those who do not possess the power to see the divine are the ones who fall more into errors.»

B) **BLAVATSKY H., P., 'THE SECRET DOCTRINE'** II: «As shown, we gather from the latter that man was not 'created' the complete being he is now… There was a spiritual, a psychic, an intellectual, and an animal evolution, **from the highest to the lowest**…ever furnishing an ascending scale for the **manifested**, or that which we call the great Illusion (Maha-Maya), but **plunging the Spirit deeper and deeper into materiality.**»

This spiritual fallback is obvious by the fact that when someone finally chooses to follow a spiritual path (a pure and ethical life), he has some chances of success, only if he moves **against** all this downward vortex of materialism that humanity is following. If matter however could be upgraded to a more spiritual condition –in this 'godly' creation– then the whole 'current' would have an upward direction and it would not be necessary for someone to fight against it with thousands of difficulties hindering him!

84 THE GOSPEL OF MATTHEW, CH. 7: «§18. A good tree cannot bear evil fruit, nor can a corrupt tree bear good fruit.»

In reality, these hardships –called 'tests' and 'trials'– are enforced by the fallen Creator in order to avert and discourage every 'candidate' from escaping his creation.

Like the poison of the snake that paralyzes the poor victim without it being able to react while the snake devours it at its leisure, so do the 'false views' of the twisted religions sooth the souls of the entrapped men, concealing the Truth. And man endlessly continues to hope. But with the thread of hope the god-creator of this world spun his web and enfolded man in a golden cocoon, so he could never be redeemed.

–*So, how can we define Spirituality?*

–Today, most people equate 'spirit' and 'spirituality' with materialistic education, or even civilization. When I speak of Spirit though, I certainly do not associate it with the education of a man, but with his living immortal part, which vitalizes his material body. This immortal part possesses some rare qualities, which, if nourished by man, can produce monumental results. Most men leave this Immortal Spiritual Essence buried deep inside their body and only use its vitalizing force, while

Don't skip chapters or bibliographic references

neglecting the special properties it carries within. They then imagine that by merely recording material knowledge and experience onto their mortal brain cells, they will somehow feed and upgrade this Sacred Essence. But this way, all they succeed in doing is to entomb it even deeper into the mud/clay of their materialism. There they leave IT to slowly fade away until IT emits its final glow. What makes them <u>seem</u> alive then, is solely the resultant of their remaining energy-bodies, which –as auxiliaries– support the densely material body and oscillate between emotional polarities.

---

[85] **THE GOSPEL OF MATTHEW, CH. 8**: «§22. But Jesus said to him, "Follow me, **and let the dead bury their own dead.**»

What every man must do is focus all his efforts to the retrieval of this Divine Spark from the depths of his being. This, thereafter, will lead him to the Absolute Truth, and the Ἀ–λήθη–α (= truth, the absence of forgetfulness, enthymesis/reminiscence) to Deliverance. This is the True expression of Spirituality. Instead, man wastes his energy, transforming his Spiritual Essence to produce temporary materialistic undertakings. Next, the all-devouring time-wave will sweep these delusive creations like castles in the sand.

–And how can a man draw out (unsheathe) this Sacred/Divine Flame, which is his Spirit, to the surface of his existence?
–They say that the key to the Truth lies inside man. The path to finding this key though, leads to the deeper understanding of human existence, which is the essential self-knowledge.

---

[86] *Marvin Meyer, Professor at Chapman University, in Orange, California, mentions in the essay regarding the Gospel of Judas:*
«As Bart D. Ehrman points out in his study, the Gospel of Judas, which becomes the Gospel of Jesus himself in this particular case, preaches **salvation through knowledge**, namely **self-knowledge** which provides the Divine Enlightenment to the souls of men.»

SELF-KNOWLEDGE

> **87 GOSPEL OF THOMAS**, JEAN YVES LELOUP:
> **(a)** «§3. Jesus said: ...The Kingdom is inside you, and it is outside you. When you know yourself, then you will be known, and you will know that you are the child of the Living Father; but if you do not know yourself, you will live in vain and you will be vanity.»
> **(b)** «§111. Whoever has self-knowledge, the world cannot contain them.»
> [Eng. tr. JOSEPH ROWE]

❧·❦

While he was saying that, he lifted the painted lid of the bronze box that was on the table and showed me the compass.
–If we raise this box's lid, if we take off its 'mask' in other words, then, a reality which is totally different from the original one, appears in front of you. This reality is at an even greater measure of discord/disagreement with my fixed point of view, *he said, still looking at the bottom of the bronze box.*
–So this is the extreme form of disagreement between men who remain fixated on the outer 'shell' of things and those who manage to lift the masks off.
The greatest percentage of people –due to their weakness to face Truth– ornament their attitudes and generally embellish the things and situations that surround them with fake decorations, so as to be agreeable to their fellowmen who only look at the external appearance of things, and in full accord with the conventions and the virtual standards society dictates. After a few years though, the fixed 'painted masks' that cover them, crystallize, creating emotional 'ankyloses' (fixations) thus fooling even themselves with the virtual/fake state they project.

> **88** *This is what Wilhelm Reich called 'The Emotional Plague'.*

So through the paths of superficial self-knowledge, men simply fumble around, merely touching their fake masks, and imagine that this is their reality. Yet the only thing they can see is the fragmented piece of truth they possess.
Essential self-knowledge is a rather painful process that is completed in three basic phases. It is not a temporary process, but a way of life. I must make it clear here, that this exploration is an extremely personal one,

Don't skip chapters or bibliographic references

where each one stands alone against oneself. The presence of a 'teacher' or a 'guide' is absolutely useless and sometimes, even obstructive. Self-knowledge is the denudation of man in front of himself. It is a difficult situation that becomes even harder if one has to share it with a 'third' person, who, almost always, poses as an 'expert'! In most cases, the influence of these 'qualified' people aims more towards controlling and manipulating the 'candidate', rather than actually helping him.

The fundamental way to start the first phase of self-knowledge is a question-answer conversation of man with himself, so that he may penetrate the multiple levels/layers of himself. After successive 'whys' to the previously given answers, the person will delve into regions of his consciousness, where, in order to get further answers, one needs to possess quite a bit of courage.

–*"I don't understand. What are the 'whys' to the previously given answers?" ...I interrupted.*

–"Let us use a simple everyday example then." ...*he continued.*

–Your child returns home from school with his report-card full of bad grades. What do you do?

–*I understandably get angry, because his progress is not good.*

–Good! Now you must ask yourself: "Why did I get angry because his progress was not good?"

I immediately gave the answer:

–*Because I provide him with all the possibilities to progress, and he is reluctant to make an effort, despite my provisions.*

–Very good. Now comes the next 'why': Why do you provide him with all these possibilities?

The answer came to me spontaneously again:

–*Simply because I love him, and I want him to progress.*

–And if he doesn't progress, won't you love him?

–*I will love him and I want what's best for him.*

–And how do you imagine the best?

–*I want to help him succeed.*

–And if he doesn't manage to succeed, what will happen to you?

–*I will commiserate with him for the failure and suffer along with him.*

–Is it you that doesn't want to suffer or him?

–*Basically him; and then me, through him.*

–And why should he suffer and then you?

–*Because his failure will cause him pain.*

–If he succeeds though, won't he ever feel pain again?

–*He will, but from other causes.*

–So, what makes you angry in the end is failure (through low grades) as the cause of pain; primarily your child's and then yours.

Without waiting for my answer, he continued with his next question.
–And how is the pain caused? It is usually **loss** that causes pain. In this particular case though, what are you losing that causes pain to you and your child?
–*"I don't know", I answered.*
–*"You do know", he answered. "But from here on, we will start facing the first difficulties…"*
–*I remained silent…. He resumed…*
–People stop their investigation here. They put an end to it and continue carefree with their lives, thinking that they have come to an understanding with themselves. I will give you the answer that you should have given me, just like anyone else should. What you are losing is the satisfaction of your egotism, which you project onto your child and which *(egotism)* is satisfied through his success. Egotism is followed by pride, arrogance, conceit, all carefully hidden behind hypocritical masks. Along these, acceptance by others and the dominion of the successful one over the rest *(the unsuccessful ones)* go hand in hand. Even his magnanimous 'compassion' towards his inferiors, out-rightly declares the position of the strong one who **can** give and be generous, in contradistinction to the misfortunate, the unsuccessful, the weak, the powerless one…

At this stage of self-knowledge, man's self-contentedness suffers the first blow. Sometimes after many 'why(s)' and 'because(s)', you realize that everything, and I do mean everything, points back to this fundamental axis: The EGO. The above example is just a sample. Every man, according to his character, his ideology and the circumstances of his life, will find his own answers. The different paths of self-knowledge are like the branches of a tree and represent men's different idiosyncrasies and diverse living conditions.
Sometimes, the tree branches (of a man), experience 'spring' and blossom with aromatic flowers (pleasant experiences). Other times they experience 'summer', full of juicy fruit (creative conditions). Other times still, they experience 'autumn' with brown leaves falling constantly (difficult times), and yet at others, the grim 'winter' with dry and frozen branches (painful times).

These are the basic conditions in every man's life. The tree though, remains always the same, regardless of the phases it goes through. It is the tree of Epi-Gnosis (that deep contact with one's Spirit).
No matter which of the different roads for deep self-knowledge a man follows, they all lead to two basic trunks/axes: one is egotism and the other is individualism. Both however finally unite into the same frame

Don't skip chapters or bibliographic references

of reference: The EGO. In essence, both egotism and individualism are the two basic expressions of the EGO but with different characteristics. For the sake of egotism, individualism is sometimes sacrificed, whereas for the benefit of individualism egotism is sacrificed. In other words, egotism supports the dominance of the individual onto his environment while individualism supports his 'comfort' (well-being). Their common interest though, is the EGO.

Each man, having started off with an un-biased and spherical observation of the outer environment, and in parallel with the process of self-knowledge, begins forming a new perception of the material reality. This initially brings the Truth of exoteric phenomena to the surface, and later their deeper ramifications. Then, man starts descrying situations in his surroundings he couldn't see before. In order to examine his own reality to an ever greater depth, it is imperative to 'project' (to imagine) himself into all possible living conditions (even the most unlikely ones), and then to observe how he would react <u>there</u>. This whole process of observation of the deeper parts of one's self, prepares him to face the second and essential phase of self-knowledge.

With the completion of the first phase, man moves from the 'negative point' (-) to 'ground zero'. There, at 'ground zero', the seeker realizes **matter's complete impotence** to upgrade the Spirit.

---

[89] **A) GOSPEL OF THOMAS**, JEAN YVES LELOUP: «§29. Jesus said: If flesh came into being because of spirit, it is a wonder. But if spirit came into being because of flesh, it is a wonder of wonders. Yet the greatest of wonders is this: <u>How is it that this Being, which Is, inhabits this nothingness?</u>» [Eng. tr. JOSEPH ROWE]

B) THE GOSPEL OF TRUTH «§39. The deficiency of matter did not originate through the Infinity of the Father.»

C) HERMES TRISMEGISTUS, HERMETIC TEXTS, VOL. II, RODAKIS P., TZAFEROPOULOS AP., **'EXCERPT VII (HERMES)'** (p.149): «§3. Men are a sinful species, because it is mortal and **its constituents are of bad matter;** and it so happens, that those who do not possess the power to see the divine, are the ones who fall more into errors.»

–And where is Love? I asked.
–"Love"…! His voice had a color that expressed the greatest longing I had ever heard!
–What do you material people know about Matter-less, Spiritual Love? Nothing! …At the time when Spiritual Man 'wore' the animal, it *(the animal)* didn't have the ability to experience Spiritual Love, but only an energy-reflection of IT.

---

90 GOSPEL OF PHILIP, JEAN-YVES LELOUP:
(a) «§11. The words we give to earthly realities engender illusion; they turn the heart away from the Real to the unreal. The one who hears the word *God* does not perceive the Real, but **an illusion** or an image of the Real.»

(b) «§13. High spiritual Powers *(the Archon)* wanted to deceive Man *(Celestial Man)*, because they saw goodness engendered in Him. **They took the name for goodness and applied it to what was not good**: words became deceitful, and *(since)* then they are joined to that which is **without being and without goodness**.» [Eng. tr. JOSEPH ROWE]

The property of matter is individualization, while the Spirit's property is Unification… Love is Unification…
He remained silent, as if my mentioning of the word Love had overwhelmed him! He then turned his head towards the wall, where that old picture was hanging and told me:
–The Truth lies in the concepts of things and not in the things themselves. Look at this picture depicting a horse galloping in a meadow. What relation can this picture have to the real living horse running lively in an ever-green meadow with the wind blowing through its mane and echoing its gallop? …Minimum to no relation at all. Similarly, the Real, Life-giving concept of Love bears <u>no</u> relation whatsoever to what even the best of men can feel!

---

91 HERMES TRISMEGISTUS, HERMETIC TEXTS, VOL. I, RODAKIS P., TZAFEROPOULOS AP., **SPEECH VI:** «§6. Wherefore, they who are ignorant and tread not the path of piety, dare call man fair and good [Gr. Ἀγαθόν *(Agathón)*]. Not even in their dreams have they seen what Ἀγαθόν [=Ultimate Good] is; and they call Ἀγαθόν all that is evil.» *(See Tr. n on w. ἀγαθός (Agathós), beginning of Ch. 'HIGHER MENTAL BODY – CELESTIAL MAN')*

The way he expressed his words with his deep nostalgia tainted by a hint of bitterness, softened my mood.
–"Yes, and what about parental love?" I said. "At least that must be

Don't skip chapters or bibliographic references

the ultimate one!"
He looked at me with a very strange look.
–You are asking where the love of the parent for his child is! Well, you must know that this love is a 'command' recorded on man's genetic code. It is the law that ensures the **preservation** of the human race in time, and has been registered into the 'software' of its structure, its genes, from the first moment of its creation. It was not only recorded onto man, but onto most creatures of creation as well. Without this code-entry, the created (product) would be in danger. So, this command/law, whose purpose is to preserve, you men call 'love'. It has no relation to Love though. It is but a piece of paper showing its picture. The same holds true though with the other strong, absolutely material sensation men have: erotic love. This is the fundamental, the primary recorded command in your cells. It is the command to 'be fruitful and multiply' that urges you to produce offspring, in order for your generation to remain in existence.

---

[92] **A) THE APOCRYPHON OF JOHN, THE GNOSTIC SOCIETY LIBRARY**:
«I asked the Savior, "Lord, isn't it the serpent that caused Adam to eat? *(...from the tree of knowledge of good and evil)*" He smiled and replied, "The serpent caused them to eat in order to produce the wickedness of the desire to reproduce. That would make Adam helpful to him *(to the serpent)*. ...From then, until now, sexual intercourse has persisted thanks to the Chief Ruler who put desire for reproduction into the woman who accompanies Adam. Through intercourse the Ruler caused new human bodies to be produced and he blew his artificial spirit into each of them.»
[Eng. tr. from Coptic: STEVAN DAVIES]

B) LOVE IS A CHEMICAL PHENOMENON, NEUROSCIENTISTS CONFIRM

http://el.science.wikia.com/wiki/αγάπη: «Biologists may soon be in a position to attribute certain mental states relating to love, to a chain of biochemical events Larry Young writes in Nature Magazine, who claims his ultimate goal is not 'the pill of love', but confronting conditions like autism, through the study of those chemical substances of the brain which are involved in the creation of emotional bonds.
By studying how the administration of hormones, mainly oxytocine, affects 'Microtus of the Savannah' –a rodent– which develops monogamous relations, Young has concluded, it can shift from polygamy to monogamy. As he said, **love is primarily a matter of chemical reactions.** If a female Microtus receives oxytocine and is placed near a male of the species, it will soon develop a bond. If, on the contrary, normal levels of oxytocine in that female are reduced, then it will never form a bond to the male, regardless of the number of their sexual intercourses. As Young writes in Nature Magazine, a simple oxytocine **spraying** improves the feeling of intimacy and trust

and helps people to tune their emotions better to those of their fellowmen *(oxytocine 'air-spraying' might not be such a bad idea!)*.

In the World Wide Web, he said, products like 'Enhanced Liquid Trust' are already for sale, a cologne-type mixture of oxytocine and pheromones, which is supposed to help emotional relations and the creation of bonds.

Young considers the use of such products probable for the restitution of problematic relations and marriages. "If one could combine psychological consultation support with a drug, this would be desirable" he says. Nevertheless, he makes clear that love cannot be limited to a single hormone, like oxytocine. Other studies have shown that in the first stages of sexual attraction, the genes of the 'major histocompatibility complex (M.H.C.)' might be involved, whereas, in men the hormone 'vasopressin' seems to be even more important.

Young though, sees love as a clearly biological process which evolved to bring the two sexes closer to each other, and for this reason it exists in the other mammals as well. As he states, "we are dealing with primordial **chemical substances in the brain**, that exist everywhere and among other things, they activate the mother-child bond". Men and certain other animals, in their evolutionary course have developed this chemical mechanism further, so as to energize the monogamous emotional bonds between men and women.»

Further information can be found at:
http://www.in.gr/news/article.asp?lngEntityID=973620&lngDtrID=252 in.gr/news

–*"What parents feel for their children can't be anything but love! Especially when they sometimes sacrifice their very own lives for them!" ... I said.*

–Certainly! The parent has paid his debt to life in full. Life does not need him so much. It needs the younger individual more, to create anew. This is not Love, it's an instruction. Now look at nature and you will better understand what I am telling you: Look at the care which the mother animal enfolds her little one with! When it can survive on its own then her 'love' for it disappears.

–*Yes but the human parent loves his/her child no matter how old it gets!*

–Man basically needs to be cared for longer than any other animal. On the other hand, through this long-lasting process of the parent giving energy of all kinds to his child, he **loses** 'pieces' of himself, which leave energy gaps in him. The parent then tries to fill these energy voids, by asking or even demanding his **'portions' of energy** back; energy, which his child now generates through his own success. In combination with his Ego that each parent projects to his child, he fills these inner energy gaps with what people call 'social recognition'.

–*But there is also love of the child for his parents. What is that?*

–That is very clear. The child is fully dependent on the parent, both energy-wise and materially.

Don't skip chapters or bibliographic references

–*"No, this I cannot accept," I said. "Even when parents grow old, the child still loves them. I cannot believe that everything is an energy exchange. There are the good feelings of compassion, of aiding those who are in need, of kindness. There is a great portion of men who care for their fellow humans, who hurt inside with the pain of others and want to help them, to share part of their burden. Why don't we discuss that?"*

–All human relations are based on a constant energy 'give-and-take'. Why do people hurt when they lose the object of their love? Do you think that dependency, pain, anxiety or feeling sorry for someone can define Immaculate Spiritual Love?

Today, psychiatrists in the greatest Universities of the world, precisely because they have found themselves at a dead end as far as understanding the nature of emotions, they have decided to trace them using a highly peculiar tool: Quantum physics.

---

[93] **A) 'IDEOTHEATRON' MAGAZINE, ISSUE APRIL 1999, A PART OF AN INTERVIEW WITH DIMITRIOS NANOPOULOS** (ACADEMIC, HEAD OF THE ASTRO-PARTICLE PHYSICS GROUP, HOUSTON ADVANCED RESEARCH CENTER)

«This means that it is possible for the basic brain functions like thought, perception and **emotions** to depend on Quantum laws. Namely, that the realization of our self and the world surrounding us is essentially of a quantum nature! …If this is the case, I anticipate that in the near future, all brain functions will be analyzed through a system of **quantum equations**, which will constitute the basis of a hierarchy for our **most universal emotions**. And now you will probably ask: "A quantum equation for love? What my answer will be? Maybe, yes!»

B) THE QUANTUM FUNCTIONING OF THE BRAIN,
http://www.physics4u.gr/articles/qbrain1.html

«Classical Neurology has made great leaps in the research of brain functions, but it has also come to a dead end, facing a huge complexity. So, the new viewpoint suggests that the brain phenomena we observe and the properties of the brain will be explained with more fundamental elements and we expect that the discoveries related to the quantum nature of the molecular function of the cells will provide us with the bridge between perception and the brain, which has been for long pursued. An ally of the quantum theory is the string theory. The arguments for the need of this approach have been mainly formulated through articles written by Penrose, Nanopoulos & Mavromatos, S. Hameroff, A. Mershin, E Skoulakis, as well as Tuszynski, Jibu, Stapp etc.

The common denominator of all these is that, the sub-cellular processes play a fundamental role in life as a whole, and are of great importance to all that makes the **senses** in our life possible, including its most prominent achievement: **intelligence**.»

–Quantum physics? What in the world does psychiatry have to do with the quanta?
–Do you know exactly what the quanta are?
–The Quantum is the smallest energy-particle. What the atom is for matter, the quantum is for energy.
–Do you realize what you've said? …Energy.
–Fine! And what difference does it make if we define love as energy?
–Man, along with all other beings in this world, is comprised of a sum of energy frequencies which fluctuate from the lowest (slow/densely material), to the highest (faster/of subtler matter). All these different energy-frequencies form a series of energy-bodies that constitute the overall hypostasis of man, as well as every other living organism on earth.
In order for these energy-bodies to keep oscillating, to keep living in other words, they need supply.
So, energy (the Greek word ενέργεια [energeia] is comprised of the preposition εν=inside and έργο=action, result) is the action that –when manifested– yields a result. When a man proceeds with an act/action, a reaction/result is brought about as a natural consequence. This reaction/result is a kind of energy-'nutrition' for that man. Every man, depending on his energy-needs, performs positive or negative actions, which provoke positive and negative reactions to other people. These reactions manifest themselves as positive or negative emotions, which in turn yield their energy-result (positive or negative) for consumption (by the man who inflicted them to others).
People who are used to nourishment by positive energy are characterized by others as 'good' and those nourished by negative energy are characterized as 'bad'. The positive and negative emotions that come about can be compared to the healthy and unhealthy material food people eat. As some foods harm man's physical health and some others benefit it, so are some emotions beneficial and some harmful. Beyond this however, nothing changes the fact that for man, all emotions are exclusively energy-nutrition and energy-supply to his/her 'EGO tree'.
Energy-nutrition resulting from a negative action is the assertion of the (negative) 'power' of a man and satisfies his negative egotism, whereas energy-nutrition stemming from a good deed is the assertion of his/her (positive) 'power' and fulfills his/her positive egotism. Both kinds of actions though (either positive or negative), have as their primary goal **the fulfillment of the (action's) doer himself**, and not its recipient.
If you observe carefully, you will realize that what people call love is never a single emotion on its own. It is always embraced by a –seemingly secondary– accompanying emotion. Nevertheless, it is not necessary for someone to experience all kinds of 'love'. This depends on the circumstances and the nature of each relationship. We therefore see love, arm in arm with jealousy,

Don't skip chapters or bibliographic references

love with possessiveness, love with passion, love along with egotism, love with sorrow, love with demand, love with superiority, love with fear, love with convenience, love with insecurity, love with obligation, love with dependency, love arm in arm with pain and finally self-serving love. No matter how deep a man searches inside of him, he won't find love alone anywhere!

---

[94] **HERMES TRISMEGISTUS,** HERMETIC TEXTS, VOL. I, RODAKIS P., TZAFEROPOULOS AP.

SPEECH VI: «§2...For all things that are born are full of passions, birth itself being a passion as well; and where passion is, there is no Ἀγαθόν *(Agathón)* [Good]. ...It is hence impossible for Ἀγαθόν [=Good *(See Tr. n on w. ἀγαθός (Agathós), beginning of Ch. 'HIGHER MENTAL BODY – CELESTIAL MAN')*] to be in birth, it can only be in the unborn. ... §3. When it comes to man good is determined in comparison to evil. ...And good down here, is the smallest particle of evil. And it is **impossible** down here that good be free from malice. For down here, good gets filled with malice, and being full of malice, it cannot be good; and since it cannot remain good anymore, it becomes evil.»

In reality, what men consider love is but a 'scout'-feeling that locates situations in which every man will fill his/her emotional gaps (empty spaces) by nourishing his/her positive EGO. Conversely, negative feelings diametrically opposite to positive 'love' also cover emotional voids, but those relating to the satisfaction of negative EGO.

My logic resisted this view. I felt anger taking over me.

–I know that at this moment, you have the urge to leave. You can freely do so if you want, and continue to turn a blind eye to the Truth.

I stood up and walked to the window. I looked outside and saw the whole landscape glow with an otherworldly light. I was shocked. I didn't know if I even wanted to hear another word. When I started this quest, I could have never imagined that I would get involved in such an adventure. The members of my family came to my mind. I felt I needed them all. I remembered the little old man at the lonesome, small café. I wanted someone to talk to about everything I felt. I wanted a material person. I was standing with my back turned to the room, looking out the window. I felt time could not touch me. I was neither hungry, nor thirsty, nor did I feel tired. I felt a burden on my chest. I sighed deeply. The deep sigh was a relief. I turned back and sat on my chair again.

–I am sorry to cause such anguish and confusion to you, but this is inevitable in order to have these fixed prejudices removed from you. No matter how outrageous this view might seem to you, you must know that man is subject to the greatest power that rules the universe: the 'Sacred Need'. Since man –

as a material being– depends on his **personal** needs, it is impossible for him to love anything else but these needs and what satisfies them.

---

[95] A) PIERRE GRIMAL, 'THE DICTIONARY OF CLASSICAL GREEK AND ROMAN MYTHOLOGY': «Need, the personification of absolute command and the force that forejudges the decisions of Fate, is 'a wise' deity. In Greece, it can be found with this name only in the Orphic Theogony, where, together with her daughter Adrasteia, is the nurse of little Zeus. She is the daughter of Kronos just like Justice. Aether, Chaos and Erebus are her children.
Necessity/Need has its part in the cosmogonical and metaphysical compositions of philosophers. For example, in the Platonic myth of the 'Republic', Necessity is the mother of the Fates [Gr. Μοίραι]. In time, and especially in the mind of common people, Necessity/Need became a death-deity; the Need/Necessity for someone to die. But for poets and especially the tragic poets, it remained the incarnation of the supreme Power, which even gods should obey.»

B) THE PORTAL OF THE GREEK LANGUAGE http://www.greek-language.gr
«Necessity/Need = Compelling Coercion, Divine Will, laws, fate [Gr.: μοῖρα].»

C) 'GREAT ETYMOLOGICAL LEXICON' (G. KOULAKIS) MALLIARIS-PAEDIA
«Necessity/Need = derivative of ancient Ἀνάγκη, related to ἄγχω (= suffocate), ἄγκος (= imposed by nature).»

D) 'GREAT HELLENIC LEXICON' (TEGOPOULOS-FYTRAKIS):
«Necessity/Need (noun) = anything imposed by matters or the existing situations // financial difficulty // out of need, perforce.»

E) THALES THE MILESIAN (640-546 B.C.): «Δεινῆς Ἀνάγκης οὐδέν ἰσχυρότερον [=Nothing is more powerful than terrible need/necessity].»

F) PITTACUS OF MYTILENE (650-560 B.C.): «Ἀνάγκα καί θεοί πείθονται. [=Even Gods can be persuaded by necessity/need].»

G) DEMOCRITUS (460-370 BC): «Ὅλα εξ ἀνάγκης γίνονται [= everything happens out of Necessity/Need].»

H) ARISTOTLE 'METAPHYSICS': «Necessity/Need [Gr. Ἀνάγκη] is the motivating initiative or the prohibiting force of an action, which is derived from free will and thought.»

Let us once more retrace the keyword, since you have always liked this method of examination. Tell me then, what is the root of the Greek word 'love'?
I remained pensive for a moment, trying to retrieve old knowledge from my memory.

Don't skip chapters or bibliographic references

–Well, I think that opinions diverge about the word ἀγάπη ['agapē'=love]: One view claims that the word stems from the adverb ἄγαν ['agan'= in excess, in exaggeration], and the verb πάομαι [= to acquire, to possess] [Liddell Scott Dict., p. 953].

–<u>Which both combined mean to 'grab'</u>, *he interrupted me.*
–And the second view considers the first constituent to be ἄγαν [=in exaggeration], and the verb ἀφάω = to palpate, to touch.
–Where again both words combined mean 'to grab', but in this second view, this 'grab' appears more intense, with the property of 'snatching'.
Certainly, you must see, regarding both views, that what is doubtless is the adverb ἄγαν which denotes 'in excess'. But excess denotes extremity. And extremity is associated with one of the two extreme points of oscillation **of this world**. But regardless of the position in which this excess manifests, be it the negative or the positive one, it will inescapably evolve and leap –as we previously analyzed– to the diametrically opposite position.
People always think that proverbs and sayings state the truth. One of these sayings stays unaltered in time, and is no other than the Greek 'μηδέν ἄγαν' [= zero (no) exaggeration] that averts us from any 'excess'. It prescribes in other words 'zero exaggeration' (μηδέν is the Greek word for zero). Don't you think then that there is a contradiction here? By itself, the word love ἀγάπη, denotes the danger that can be created by an excess or exaggeration…
–But Jesus Christ spoke of Love and prompted man to "love thy neighbor as thy self". I said.
–And what makes you imagine that men understood what Christ meant exactly when he spoke of Love?

---

[96] **A) THE GOSPEL OF MATTHEW, CH. 10**: «§34. Do not think that I have come to bring peace to the earth; I have not come to bring peace, but a sword. §35. For I have come, to set a man against his father, and a daughter against her mother, and a daughter-in-law against her mother-in-law; §36. And a man's enemies will be those of his own family. §37. Anyone who loves father or mother more than me is not worthy of me; and he who loves son or daughter more than me is not worthy of me.»
B) GOSPEL OF THOMAS, JEAN YVES LELOUP: «§55. Jesus said: Whoever cannot free themselves from their father and their mother cannot become My disciple. Whoever cannot free themselves from their brother and sister…is not worthy of Me.» [Eng. tr. JOSEPH ROWE]

Let us start from this simple question: Who do you think is each man's 'self'? Do you imagine that Christ referred to its material part?

[97] **GOSPEL OF THOMAS**, JEAN YVES LELOUP: «§25. Jesus says: Love your brother and sister as your **soul**.» [Eng. tr. JOSEPH ROWE]

That material part of man filled with camouflaged hatred, egotisms, malice, greed and passions, which is exactly the part He came to free you from?

[98] **A)** *A Reminder:* **THE APOCRYPHON OF JOHN, THE GNOSTIC SOCIETY LIBRARY** ENG. TR. FROM COPTIC: FREDERIK WISSE: *(Jesus says to John)* «And I entered into the midst of their <u>prison</u>, which is **the prison of the body**. And I said, "He who hears, let him get up from the deep sleep!"» [GR. EDITION: APOCRYPHAL TEXTS OF THE OLD TESTAMENT, KOUTSOUKIS D.]

B) GOSPEL OF THOMAS, JEAN YVES LELOUP: «§87. Jesus said: "Wretched is the body that depends upon another *(human)* body, and wretched is the soul that depends on these both *(bodies)*.» [Eng. tr. JOSEPH ROWE]

C) THE GOSPEL OF MATTHEW, Ch. 6:

«§24. No one can serve two masters; for either he will hate the one and love the other, or he will be devoted to the one and despise the other…§25 Therefore I tell you, do not be anxious about your life, what you shall eat or what you shall drink, **nor about your body, what you will wear.**»

D) HERMES TRISMEGISTUS, HERMETIC TEXTS, VOL. I, RODAKIS P., TZAFEROPOULOS AP.

(a) SPEECH IV: «§6…My child, if you **do not first hate your body, you cannot love yourself;** and once you love yourself, you shall have Noũs, and having Noũs, you shall also partake the Science (Knowledge). …It is impossible, O Son, to be conversant in both things, the Mortal as well as the Divine. …The choice of either of the two is left to you and your will; for it is impossible for you to choose both at the same time. …One prevails while the other diminishes."

(b) SPEECH VII *(About the physical body):* "§2. But first you must throw away the garment you wear; the fabric of ignorance, the foundation of all malice; the bond of corruption; the dark Coverture; **the living death**; the Carcass that has senses, the Sepulcher (tomb) you carry with you; the domestical Thief, him <u>who hates through what he loves and envies through what he hates</u>.»

E) CHALDEAN ORACLES, Gr. tr. ATHINOGENIS I., GRAVIGGER, P., KROLL 52 – PLACES 116 – **PROCLUS IN CRATYLUS, 93, 5** (p. 170):

«For things Divine are not accessible to mortals who think in the bodily manner, but only to those who, having been stripped naked of this *(bodily thinking)*, speed aloft unto the Height.» (See also Proclus in Alcib. 63 (138 GR) 18 WEST: Plotinus I, 6, 7, 7-Plat. Gorg. 523 C-E FESTUG., PEVEL III, 131- LEWY, p. 170 & ft. 395)

F) THE GOSPEL OF JOHN, CH. 6:

«§63. It is the spirit that gives life; **the flesh is of no avail.**»

G) PLATO'S 'PHAEDO, OR ABOUT THE PSYCHE' [=SOUL] ATHANASOPOULOS I., K. (66b): «So long as we have the body, and the soul is 'knead together' with this **evil**, we shall never manage to acquire enough of what we desire: and by

Don't skip chapters or bibliographic references

that we mean what is True. For our body forces us to countless chores... (66c) Furthermore, the body fills us with many erotic passions and desires and fears, and all sorts of fancies and foolishness... so that, as they truly say, it really is impossible for us to logically think of anything at all, while under its (our body's) command. After all, wars and factions and battles are caused by nothing else but the body and its desires; since it is for the sake of gaining material goods that all wars arise. And we are compelled to gain those material goods for the sake of the body, like slaves to its service.»

(In the same work as well) (82e): «...Of course, all knowledge lovers know that, when philosophy first took possession of their soul, which is entirely and clumsily fastened and welded to the body and is compelled to regard things not with its own thinking *(unhindered),* but through the body, **as if it were behind prison bars** and is wallowing in utter ignorance... (83a)...the lovers of knowledge, then, I say, know that philosophy, after taking possession of their soul in this state, comforts it gently and tries to redeem it (set it free), pointing out that investigation through the eyes is full of deceit as well as through the ears and the other senses, urging it to withdraw from these, except in so far as their use is unavoidable.»

H) HERMES TRISMEGISTUS: THE FOUNDER OF MONOTHEISM 9000 B.C., IOANNIDIS P. K., **CH. 6**: «§3... there is no good in men but only its title (name). And that happens, because there is no room for good in material bodies; since there is not enough space for it. The human body is encircled and coarcted with evilness and labors (pains), and griefs, and desires, and wrath, and deceits, and glories and the worst of all is that men trust this evil as if it were good. Here on earth gluttony rules which is the sponsor of all evils; good [Ἀγαθόν *(Agathón)*] is absent from earth.» *(See Tr. n on w. ἀγαθός (Agathós), beginning of Ch. 'HIGHER MENTAL BODY – CELESTIAL MAN')*

Or is it maybe that this Self is no other than the Pure Unified Spirit of each man, or what we call 'Celestial Man'?

[99] **THE SECRET BOOK OF DZYAN, 'COSMIC EVOLUTION', STANZA VII**: «§7. This is thy present Wheel, said the Flame *(The 'I Am the Presence')* to the Spark *(The Divine Spark).* Thou art myself, my image, and my shadow. I have clothed myself in thee, and thou art my Vahan *(my carrier/vehicle)* to the Day, **'Be with us'**, when thou shalt re-become myself and **others, thyself** and me.»
If we compare this last point to the words of Christ 'Love thy neighbor as thyself', we'll clearly understand that the REAL SELF of every man is <u>*SOLELY*</u> *his* <u>*UNIFIED*</u> *Self.*

Only by loving his True Self can man truly love his neighbor as 'Himself'. Until then he simply **imagines** he loves.

After all, no philosopher of the ancient times has praised the emotion that people call love today. On the contrary, the great philosophers honored different virtues of man. This fact implies three probabilities: Either that the structure of man's matter suddenly changed and started expressing a new, unknown –till then– emotion, or that the whole humanity was undertaken by divine grandeur and started manifesting the ultimate spiritual expression, or finally, that today's humanity has somehow mixed these concepts up.

---

[100] *In earlier times, the word 'love' did not exist with its contemporary meaning. Its meaning started to change, when the first Christian 'agapae' (banquets for the relief of the poor) started being organized.*
The Gr. word ἀγαπώ [agapô] = to love, basically meant to like, in ancient times.
In the earlier Homeric types, it can be found as ἀγαπάζω which is obviously closer to its original root: (ἄγαν + ἀφάω = ἁρπάζω/grab) or as ἀμφαγαπάζω with the meaning of embracing. Specifically:
A) DICTIONARY OF ANTHIMOS GAZIS
*In the entry of the word **ἀγαπάω**=to love mentions, with regards to the use of the word by Homer:* «Homer uses the word αγαπάζω more often than the word αγαπάω... also...In Penelope's speech, who with these words embraced and kissed her husband Odysseus (Ulysses), ...[ἀμφαγαπάζειν και φιλοφρονεῖσθαι = embracing and kissing].»

B) 'HOMERIC LEXICON' PANTAZIDIS I.: *Next to the interpretation of the Homeric word **ἀγαπάω**=**to love** he notes:* «Related verb of ἄγαμαι or ἀγάομαι and ἀγαίομαι (=in case of benevolence: to admire, respect, honor, and in case of evil/ill: to see someone with rage, envy, be jealous of)
The verb **ἀγαπώ** = **to love** can be found in (φ289, ψ214). Somewhere else as **ἀγαπάζω** (Ω464, π17) and as **ἀγαπάζομαι** (η33, χ499) {= 1) be friendly disposed to someone, to welcome in a friendly way, honor or 2) to thank, to be pleased/content. Colloquially αγαπώ = to kiss, to feel erotically towards someone.»
*We ought to also note the difference between the Greek meaning of the word **ἀγαπῶ**=**to love** with the corresponding of the languages with Latin origin. In particular:*
C) TZIROPOULOU-EUSTATHIOU, A., 'HELLENIC LOGOS, HOW THE GREEK LANGUAGE INSEMINATED INTERNATIONAL LOGOS [=LANGUAGE]' (p. 234):
«French (aimer), Italian (amare), Spanish (amar), Latin (amo) they are derived from the Gr. word ἀμμάς = τροφός (nurse), μήτηρ (mother) {Rhea is also called ἀμμάς and ἀμμία} {Ἀμμάς or Ἀμμαία Δημήτηρ=beloved/mother Demeter (ἀμμά=μήτηρ/mother), others say that it is derived from αἷμα=blood, ὅμαιμος=of the same blood, ἀγαπητός=dear, lovesome}.»

Don't skip chapters or bibliographic references

In order then for me to inform you about this True Love, I will lead our discussion back to self-knowledge again:

After completing the <u>first phase</u> of self-knowledge, man will realize that what he previously imagined 'himself' to be is totally different from what he finally realizes. Then, all this complacency that defines him comes crashing down as he finally discovers 'himself' being a beautifully **masked Archanthrope** (archaic man, from the Gr.: αρχάνθρωπος). As long as man prides himself in assuming that he does not possess/carry this species (of Archanthrope) inside him whatsoever, he deludes himself. But this is only his matter (his material part). Man, as we have said, is not only made of matter. If he then doesn't take-off all the costumes that surround him one by one, he will <u>never</u> be able to discover his real Spirit-Self.

He will have his first taste of True Love, when he is in the second phase of self-knowledge, after he opens the 'door' and liberates the captive Spirit existing within him. He will then cease energy-feeding himself through all these different good and bad energies, and having discovered the Unique Life-giving Essence, he will be nurtured **only** by IT. Only then will he understand that all previous emotions were nothing but mere substitutes. He will continue experiencing these emotions as a material man of course, <u>but he will not feed from them</u>.

He will reach recognition of his Spirit upon completion of the third phase of self-knowledge. Only then will he be able to implement in action what Christ said: 'love thy neighbor as thyself', because the real quality of Love is not a property of matter, but of the Unified Spirit.

When Man-Spirit (with his Divine Spark awakened) meets his Higher Self at the final meeting point, <u>only then</u> does he also experience the maximal true state of Love, which manifests devoid of accompanying emotions of dependence, requirement and imposition. This state does not resemble what men imagine as love, because IT is not an emotion but a SENSATION.

Apart from the five basic bodily senses to perceive the world around him, man also possesses Spiritual senses. When someone 'awakens the sensory organs' of his Spirit, he then interprets the world around him through a different perception.

[101] **HERMES TRISMEGISTUS**, HERMETIC TEXTS, VOL. I, RODAKIS P., TZAFEROPOULOS AP., **SPEECH VII** *(ABOUT THE PHYSICAL BODY)*
«§3 Of such sort is the enemy whose hateful garment you are wearing, making you feel stressed and drawing you downwards ...as it wishes ill for you and **it anaesthetizes the sensory organs, the real ones, not the alleged ones.** These organs have been obstructed with much matter, and filled with abominable pleasure, so that you should neither hear those things **which you must** hear, nor see **those which you must see** *(...he, who has ears, let him hear...).*»

Emotions are stimulated by daily experiences and **desires**; when desires are satisfied, they provoke pleasant emotions, when they are not, they cause dissatisfaction and when uncertainty prevails they cause fear.

---

[102] **A) DANIEL GOLEMAN** (PhD, HARVARD UNIVERSITY) **'EMOTIONAL INTELLIGENCE'**
Referring to the term emotion he mentions:
«Emotion is a term whose exact meaning has caused a dispute between psychologists and philosophers for more than a century. In its most literal sense, the 'Oxford Dictionary' defines emotion as: "Any agitation or anxiety of mind, feeling, passion; any vehement or excited mental state."
I take emotion to refer to: a feeling and the distinct thoughts it causes, the psychological and biological states accompanying it as well as the sum of intentions to act. There are hundreds of emotions, along with their blends, variations, mutations and nuances. ...Researchers continue to disagree with each other about which specific emotions should be considered as primal... where all the other *(emotional)* nuances originate from. Some theorists suggest some basic families of emotions, although not everyone accepts them. The principal groups are *(in short)*: anger, sorrow, fear, pleasure, love, surprise, resentment (aversion) and shame.»
B) MAJOR HELLENIC LEXICON (TEGOPOULOS- FYTRAKIS):
«Αίσθηση=Sensation: all functions through which we perceive internal and external stimuli: (vision, hearing, smell, taste and touch are the five senses), perception, cognition, assertion or appreciation of the value or importance of someone or something.»

But the Sensation of Love is independent of desires, dependencies, divisions and segregations, as it offers him who possesses it an outstanding sensitiveness above the norms. IT makes him primarily focused on the Spiritual salvation of the <u>true</u> fellow-Man, rather than the restitution of his matter/flesh 'prison'. After all Christ is par excellence a Savior of Souls!
Climbing therefore one by one the steps of the temple of Man, we will proceed to the even more painful second phase of self-knowledge.

THE OTHER BODIES OF MAN
AND THE SECOND PHASE OF SELF-KNOWLEDGE

[103] **CHALDEAN ORACLES**, Gr. tr. ATHINOGENIS I., GRAVIGGER, P., 52C KROLL 32 – PLACES -PSELLUS 1149C (p. 111): «They claim that there are seven corporeal Cosmoi (worlds), the first one empyrean (in fire), after that three aethereal and finally three hylic (material) ones.»

(p. 109) *Commentator P. Marinis elaborates:* «In 'Logion' 52c, the human organism is analyzed (=corporeal world). The scholars' aspect absolutely agrees with the point of view of traditional religion and science, according to which the material-psychic person is clothed with electromagnetic mantles/garments of which the innermost and thinnest one is called 'empyrean' (fiery), whereas the immediately outer three are called 'aethereal' and the most external three are called 'hylic' (material) because, at death, they remain onto the body (comprising the known 'aetheric carcasses' left over on the bodily residues).»

After the main 'trunk' of the EGO, Man's 'tree' enters a different environment. The 'soil'; its roots are there. From the soil they absorb the nutritious saps which are then carried to the rest of the tree, feeding it. In man's case, the 'soil' is the astral plane, from which all man's emotions are supplied. Hence, in order to understand what exactly happens in this area we will follow man's path in this second phase of self-knowledge.

This phase is very defining, because it leads the seeker to the 'Tartara' (underworld) of his existence, where from he will gain the spherical perception of his own world. Before everything else though, we must make an initial mention about the seven bodies of man, in order for you to better understand what we will discuss. At a subsequent point in our discussion, we will analyze everything more thoroughly.

As you already know, the various schools of spiritual quest that exist in your world, all talk about six bodies (in total), which envelop the Real seventh – Spiritual– Body of Man. These bodies –except the material one– are primarily made of thinner (subtler) energy and finer matter, and thus are not visible.

–*Are these the ones mentioned mainly by eastern religions and theosophy?*

–Almost, *he answered.* Now, regarding the names given to the first four lower bodies, they are almost the same in all 'schools'. But the names given to the three higher ones are quite different among various views. The terms used to describe them are so incomprehensible, that one cannot help but wonder if there was deliberate intention to keep them hazy and vague. So, the names I will use for them will be a little different from the terms usually used, but much easier to understand.

If we begin numbering them, starting from the denser to the finer/subtler one, they are in the following order: 1) natural/material, 2) aetheric (aura), 3) astral/emotional/causative body, 4) lower mental, 5) Soul, 6) Higher mental and finally 7) the Divine Spark /Spirit, one half (part) of the **real** hypostasis of the true Celestial Man, which is not an energy-body, but a creation of a different 'texture', which from now on we will call Essence. *(See: Drawings, The seven bodies of man)*

All these bodies are connected to their corresponding planes/fields through energy-bonds. Each one of them has also some particular characteristic properties. As the material body has its five main senses, vision, hearing, taste, touch and smell, as well as a number of secondary senses that give motion to all the autonomous functions of the organs of the body, so do the rest, less material bodies, have their own characteristic 'senses'.

The body we will mostly deal with during the second phase of self-knowledge is the astral body, which is the carrier of all emotions of man. In other words, all man's **emotional conditions** are the 'sensations' which are caused by the 'sensory organs' of that *(astral)* body. The astral plane on the other hand, inside which this body moves, is the 'stage' on which all man's emotional situations take place.

Leaving this elementary briefing on the astral body behind us, we move onto the second phase of self-knowledge. This second phase consists of three stages. We shall call the first stage Inquiry, as it concerns the meticulous examination of the subconscious states of man. The second is man's Battle with his lower-self, and the third stage is the Liberation of the Divine Spirit that resides inside him.

Man, starting the second phase of self-knowledge, enters a more transcendental state, because this phase can only be accomplished in a transcendental way.

---

[104] MAJOR HELLENIC LEXICON (TEGOPOULOS- FYTRAKIS):

«Υπερβατικό = **Transcendental** = Anything relative to the hyper-sensory world which is beyond the experience of the physical senses and is accessible only by intellect or intuition.»

Namely, in order to fathom the deeper parts of himself, man must learn to experience his daily life as much on the materialistic dimension, as on the transcendental dimension of events, **simultaneously**.

Don't skip chapters or bibliographic references

---

105. **'SUPERMUNDANE' BOOK II** (AGNI YOGA SOCIETY) 1938 *(Speeches of the teachers of the White Brotherhood, given to the students of the Agni Yoga group through the medium 'Urusvati' in 1938)*
«§303 Just as there are three worlds, there are also three levels of thought. Man can think **simultaneously** on all three levels. For instance, he can be absorbed in mundane thinking, which includes empirical reasoning. Behind this, functions his subtle thought, and in the depths of his consciousness a fiery spark may radiate. At times these three layers can merge harmoniously into one, and there results a powerful projection of thought.»

During the day, man associates with other men and performs actions. This daily activity brings about the excitation of desires, satisfactions, disappointments, assertions/claims or egotisms and creates emotional ups and downs. So, in order to observe these emotions in their birth and understand how they work, he must learn to look at them in a transcendental way. I will try to **metaphorically** outline this setting using pictures.

After the completion of the first phase of self-knowledge, when man manages to lift the masquerade veil that covers him, he will descry the Archanthrope/material-self inside him.

---

106 **GOSPEL OF THOMAS**, JEAN YVES LELOUP: «§80. Jesus said: Whoever knows the world discovers the body. But the world is unworthy of whoever discovers the body.» [Eng. tr. JOSEPH ROWE]

The disappointing feeling that is generated by this revelation, seems to drag him deeper, into an endless fall from the 'clouds' to the Abyss of 'Tartara' (another Greek word for Hades). So the second phase of self-knowledge starts from these swampy grounds that are found in the 'Tartara' of his own hypostasis (existence). There, he will meet the Lernaean Hydra *(an ancient Gr. mythological, serpent-like chthonic water-beast, with numerous heads –that multiplied when cut– and poisonous breath, finally killed by Hercules)*, which haunts him!

In the foggy atmosphere of his subconscious, the man-observer can descry shadows moving. They are his desires, weaknesses, lusts and passions having 'assumed form', that have hypostasis/substance. Each in a different form, they connect to each other in friendly, kin (of the same family), or even hostile bonds.

---

107 **A) 'MYSTERIES OF THE WORLD', VOL. 'SECRET MESSAGES'**

«**Tibetan Archetypes**: In the Tibetan 'Book of the Dead' the emotional states of a dying man (sorrow, rage, fear etc.) are depicted in the form of deities and daemons that the deceased meets in the 'other' world. In these texts, there was knowledge of the psychology of the depth, i.e. relevant to the archetypes, which psychologists like Carl Gustav Jung (1875-1961) officially formulated just the previous century.»

B) RUDOLF STEINER (1861–1925): FOUNDER OF 'ANTHROPOSOPHY', AND INSPIRER OF THE 'WALDORF SYSTEM OF EDUCATION') **'AT THE GATES OF ANTHROPOSOPHY'**, (Gr. tr. ALEXIOU TH.) CH. 'THE THREE WORLDS' (p. 19):

«These days, a lot of people see themselves surrounded by black malignant forms, which threaten and terrify them.... The fact is that these figures are their own impulses, desires and passions which live inside man and specifically in what we call the astral body.»

All these entities have an absolutely characteristic movement: They oscillate; sometimes upwards and sometimes downwards. They are alive. Through their movement, they generate emotions in men; oscillating feelings. They (feelings/emotions) are their children. At times, when rising to high levels of their oscillation, they generate beauty, kindness, compassion, joy. Other times, when diving down to low points of their oscillation, they generate pain, disappointment, malice, jealousy and sadness. What goes up must come down. What goes down must come up; moving snakes. Like the Lernaean Hydra of the myth, with its primary body, the Ego.

If you focus your attention onto each one of them, you will realize that they all demand nutrition from you: energy-nutrition. I will give you a typical example, in a rather peculiar way. When a man sees jealousy making its appearance inside him, he initially feels pain. Jealousy is biting him. Its bite hurts. But jealousy's bite has its reason. It bites man to make him feed it. And what is its food? The satisfaction/nourishment/energy it takes **from the pain** caused to another human being.

When man is jealous (the victimizer), he has the desire to carry out actions that will cause pain to the one he is jealous of (the victim). It is every man's predisposition that makes him say: "I will show him..." The victim's pain will produce energy. This energy will provide the jealous man with a feeling of satisfaction. In reality though, it is the haunting wraith of jealousy residing within the victimizer's astral-body which has been satisfied, having received the energy-supply it claimed from him.

Don't skip chapters or bibliographic references

---

108 **RUDOLF STEINER 'AT THE GATES OF ANTHROPOSOPHY'**, Gr. tr. ALEXIOU TH.
CH. 'THE THREE WORLDS' (p. 18):

«There are three worlds: 1) The Physical world, the 'scene' of human life 2) The Astral or Soul world, 3) The Devachan(ic) or world of Spirit. These three worlds are not spatially separate from each other. We are surrounded by the things of the physical world, which we perceive with our external sensory organs (senses). But the astral world exists in the same space with us. As we live in the physical world, at the same time, we live in the other two worlds as well: The astral world and the Devachan world. The three worlds are wherever we ourselves are. Only, we do not see the two higher worlds, just as a blind man does not see the physical world.»

CH. 'LIFE OF THE SOUL AFTER DEATH' (p. 32): «...For example, a man eats avidly and with real pleasure. The clairvoyant will see the satisfaction of the man's desire as a brown-red thoughtform *(skeptomorph)* in the upper part of his astral body.»

Now that's a taste of Hell! The same thing however, holds true with all human activities. They all have the purpose of feeding the various 'wraiths/specters' / weaknesses / passions / desires of his astral world. Some appear benevolent and nice, and prompt man to actions that seem beautiful. But the moment man sees these 'wraiths' happily devouring the 'benevolent' energy he has collected for them he realizes in horror what they really represent! There, he will discover how social recognition is transformed into conceit, offering into demand and kindness into assertion and claim.

---

109 **GOSPEL OF THOMAS**, THE ECUMENICAL COPTIC PROJECT
http://www.metalog.org/files/thomas.html

«§14 Jesus says to them: If you fast, you shall beget transgression for yourselves. And if you pray, you shall be condemned. And if you give alms *(charity)*, you shall cause evil to your spirits.»

Another cunning 'wraith/specter', which voraciously consumes energy, is curiosity. It plays the role of the 'scout/informer' on behalf of its world. Clad/disguised in the costume of 'interest' or 'concern', it creeps close to the unfortunate man who does not recognize it, and prompts him to 'go out begging'. He then collects energy chunks from the lives of others, and offers them to his curiosity, like a bondservant to his master. Afterwards, the aforementioned 'wraith/specter', once it has satiated its hunger, being 'benevolent' as it is, informs the rest of its community, about the 'sources' from where each kind of weakness will receive its corresponding energy-supply.

This is the world of every man. And these wraiths/passions function the same way for everyone. The differentiation between the idiosyncrasies of men depends on which wraiths each man is more accustomed to feed. Through detailed observation, the man-researcher will discover a whole society of this kind of 'entities' with their particular inter-relations, their alliances and their hostilities, their laws and their preferences, but also their 'family' bonds. Then he will realize that he is in essence a puppet, since his every move is driven by his desires, his passions, his ambitions and his needs, all of which he **considers** his own, whereas in reality they (weaknesses/passions) are merely his 'escorts', feeding on his actions they themselves cause.

---

110 **A) PLATO'S 'PHAEDO, OR ABOUT THE PSYCHE' [=SOUL], ATHANASOPOULOS I., K.** (83D): «Each pleasure and sorrow, as if it had a nail, nails the soul and rivets it onto the body and the soul becomes one with the body (makes it corporeal), **forcing it to <u>believe</u> that what the body says is true.** And since it agrees with the body and is pleased by the same things as the body, it is compelled, in my mind, to also adopt the same manners (ways) and pleasures with it.»

B) HERMES TRISMEGISTUS, HERMETIC TEXTS, VOL. I, RODAKIS P., TZAFEROPOULOS AP., 'SPEECH VI, ASCLEPIUS' DEFINITIONS TO KING AMMON':
«§10...And (this happens) because there are many groups of daemons round him [man], like hordes of various kinds; the 'co-dwellers/housemates' of mortals. And they are not far from the immortals, where from, having received their land by lot, supervise the human affairs and execute the commands given by the Gods ...§14. All of these *(daemons)* have been allotted the authority over things and turmoil upon the Earth and it is they who bring about all kinds of unrest in social groups and cities (states) and nations and for each individual separately. For they do transform our souls and dominate over them, obsessing and occupying the nerves and the marrow of the bones, inside the veins and arteries, even inside our brain itself down to our very bowel. §15. When each one of us is born and acquires a soul, the daemons take hold of him, they [daemons] who are in service at that moment [of the wheel] of genesis (creation), who have been appointed to each one of the Stars. These often alternate, for they do not stay the same, but circle around and come back again· these, then, descending through the body into the two parts of the soul, set it (the soul) awhirling, each one towards its own energy (activity).»

Thus, when two people interact with one another, it's not really them that communicate, but rather their desires, passions and ambitions they drag behind them and motivate them to act or react.

Don't skip chapters or bibliographic references

When man decides not to feed these monsters with the energy from someone else's pain, he will find them starting to claim their energy food from him, causing him the pain they crave for.

---

111 *At this point I would like to quote an ancient Greek word, intent on making the reader think.*
A) DICTIONARY OF THE ANCIENT GREEK LANGUAGE BY IOANNIS STAMATAKOS
The ancient Greek word **βροτός** *means* **mortal** *in Modern Greek.*
On the other hand, the word **βρωτός** *means* '**what is meant to be eaten**' *in Modern Greek.*
Does this mean that **the mortal** *βροτός is at the same time (to be)* **eaten** *βρωτός? Of course some people might juxtapose that the one word is written with o (omicron) and the other with ω (omega). But if we go back to the aforementioned dictionary by IOANNIS STAMATAKOS, as well as to the DICTIONARY OF THE GREEK LANGUAGE BY LIDDELL & SCOTT, we can read about the difference between omicron and omega, in the entry of* '**Omega**':
«Ω μέγα: The letter **Omega** (=great or long 'o') is more recent and it **was made up** in order to distinguish it from the letter **Omicron** (=small or short o). **Initially, there was no distinction** between the two letters and in the earlier inscriptions, both of them were written with the same symbol **O**.»
(That is, when the language was still 'under construction' according to the – then recent– fresh Truths.)
The character Ω was officially introduced in Athens during the rule of Euclid (403 B.C.). Finally, the small letter ω, which is used nowadays, was introduced during Hadrian's time.»
B) CHALAS A., 'THE UNDERLYING MYSTERY IN THE HELLENIC ALPHABET AND THE UNIVERSE, OR, ABOUT SCIENCE' CH: ABOUT THE WORD 'TRUTH' (p. 146): «Before we proceed further, it is imperative to note that in the Ancient Attic Dialect O and Ω were tantamount, hence, as Plato states, the contemporary ΩΡΑ (=time) was written OPA.»
Therefore, the word βροτός (=mortal) and βρωτός (=eaten) are tantamount. And if two things are equal to a third one, then they too are equal to one another. As a result: mortal = to be eaten...

In this phase therefore, to achieve a more complete understanding, man must regard each of his weaknesses as a separate and independent entity. And in order to observe the 'techniques' they use to survive, he must subject each one of them (in a manner of speaking) to deep 'psychoanalysis'... Of course, if you could descry the ways in which all these entities/states/weaknesses maneuver or energize other weaknesses neighboring them, along with which they besiege man in order to make him succumb to their demands, then you would see why I am talking about 'psychoanalysis'.

Some weaknesses, if ignored, seem to withdraw. But his happens only because they have recruited other peripheral emotional states, seemingly irrelevant, which start manipulating man's temper and ask for attention. If the person does not recognize them from the start, he will later realize that behind these 'new' emotional tendencies, the old weakness is hiding transformed. Other times again, they do not retreat, but mercilessly besiege and torment man, in order to get satisfaction from him. And other times, they conceal themselves, they bury themselves into the deepest and most inconspicuous places of human existence, and from there, they covertly eat man away from within just like the worm inside the apple, causing physical diseases to his body in order to get their energy-share that way. These are the gimmicks and the alliances that develop between the weaknesses and the desires of man, where each one supports the other and all together the EGO.

Oscillation, as we have mentioned, is symbolized by the snake. Furthermore, in myths, a dragon-snake always guards something precious. But myths are riddles that require de-symbolization, deciphering. What do you then imagine those oscillating feelings/snakes guard...?

He looked at me without speaking... and resumed.

–Where does man 'feel' his emotions? *He asked again.*

–*"In the heart", I answered.*

–Yes, he experiences higher vibrations in the heart and others, the 'lower' ones, are 'felt' in the 'solar plexus', one of the seven energy-centers of man, which is found somewhere near the stomach.

"What lies in the heart though?" *He asked again...*

–*"I don't know", I answered...*

–At the heart terminates what people call the 'Silver Thread of Life', or the 'Thread/Chord of Silver'. At the end of this Thread of life and inside the cardiac center, the Soul can be found, which sometimes carries inside it something even more precious: A Divine Spark; the second half of the split Celestial Man. The other end of the thread is connected to his 'I Am Presence', or his Higher Self. There, inside the foggy scenery of his subconscious, man will finally discover the guarded prison which holds his True Spirit captive. The oscillating snakes/passions/emotions, with their hissing voices cover the desperate call for help of the Spiritual Man while simultaneously guarding the entrance of the prison. Precisely at that point starts the second stage of the second phase of self-knowledge. From there, the man/Hercules starts to carry out his labors one by one.

This is a long-lasting period in man's life and the only thing he does, is to battle with his own monsters/snakes. This war does not have any rules. It is a raging close-up battle to tame and silence all oscillating 'snakes'/passions; they don't die. So, what exactly happens when these 'snakes' hush? They

Don't skip chapters or bibliographic references

remain motionless, thus narrowing the amplitude of their oscillation between the two opposite states.

As we have said, the 'formed' weaknesses, passions, hatreds and envies generate oscillating emotions (snakes). When these weaknesses/passions are tamed, they stop generating the bipolar emotional oscillations that 'drive man crazy' with their demands and they hush. This condition of silence is expressed in a man as emotional tranquility: he neither 'loves' nor hates.

The mistake people often make in their effort to improve themselves is that they choose the positive views and reject the negative ones. They don't realize that the twofold nature of matter will suddenly relocate them, thrusting them down to the diametrically opposite negative state, forcing them to start a new attempt again. And the endless circle never seems to end. People then reach the conclusion that man can never change· so they abandon the struggle, or look forward to an 'upgraded' consequent incarnation... The solution for man however, is to remain – as much as possible– **un-oscillating** in equilibrium.

---

[112] **PLATO'S 'PHAEDO, OR ABOUT THE PSYCHE' [=SOUL]**, ATHANASOPOULOS I., K.
(83b, 83c): «Now the soul of the true philosopher, believing that it must not resist this deliverance, stands aloof from pleasures and lusts and griefs and fears, so far as it can, considering that when someone is too over-joyed or too afraid or grieves or lusts a lot, he suffers not so greatly from what one might think, be it disease or be it the dominion of his desires, but rather, he suffers something which the greatest and the most extreme evil, and does not even realize it.» ...*i.e. one should distance one's self from both extremities of the oscillation.*

Only then, through the shadowy landscapes of the subconscious, will the desperate voice of his own Spirit be heard, calling for help. From there starts the third stage of the second phase of self-knowledge. After the long and relentless battle that has preceded man stands exhausted. He gathers all his strength to stand on his own two feet. But right there and then all he can see is absolute emptiness. Here is what I mean: While the emotions/snakes were oscillating, man felt either joy through the satisfaction of his desires and his ego, or sorrow when they were not satisfied. After the fierce battle and with the snakes/passions quieting down, he ceases to experience these fluctuations; he seems apathetic; He feels absolute neutrality; he neither wants nor does he not want. He neither loves, nor hates. He is neither happy nor sad. It is the moment when he stops energy-feeding from these substitute emotions. This is a difficult and extremely dangerous phase. Man seems free, but he lacks something important. 'Spiritual starvation' makes its appearance then.

Till then, through the satisfaction of his passions/weaknesses, he used to energy-feed himself as well. In the new situation, he starts realizing that all previous emotions have solely been energy nourishment. He must now get his nutrition elsewhere.

> **113** **THE GOSPEL OF JOHN**, CH. 4: «§32. But He (Jesus) said to them, "I have food to eat, which you know nothing about.»

He has no other choice, but to turn to the Pure Spirit inside him, in order to get supplied from IT henceforth. This Spirit is Life itself.

To make the process of this new Spiritual nutrition clearer, we shall use a metaphor, mentioning an international mystical symbol with its metaphysical ramifications; the symbol of the 'egg'.

The whole material universe, seen (matter) and unseen (energy), can be paralleled to an Egg.

> **114** **BLAVATSKY H., P., 'THE SECRET DOCTRINE'** (I-359,360): «The Egg was incorporated as a sacred sign in the cosmogony of every people on Earth…. It represented most successfully the origin and the secret of the Being… In the fancy of the thinkers it was portrayed as an ever invisible, mysterious Bird that dropped an Egg into Chaos, which Egg became the Universe. Hence Brahma was called Kalahansa, 'the swan in (space and) time'. He became the 'swan of eternity' who, at the beginning of each Maha Manvantara, lays a 'Golden Egg'.
> In Ch. 54, of the Egyptian Ritual, Seb, the god of Time and of the Earth, is spoken of as having laid an egg, or the Universe, an egg conceived at the hour of the great one, of the **'Dual Force'**.
> Ra *(of the Egyptians)* is shown, like Brahma, gestating in the Egg of the Universe. In the (Indian) book of Vishnu Puraná, translated by Wilson, it is mentioned that: 'The egg is given the epithet Haima or Hiranya, meaning 'golden'. Also, as said in the Vishnu Puraná: 'Intellect (Mahat)…, the (un-manifested) gross elements inclusive, formed an egg… and the lord of the Universe himself <u>abided in it</u>, in the character of Brahma…. In that egg O Brahman, there were the continents, and the seas and the mountains, the planets and the divisions of the universe, the **gods**, the **demons** and **mankind**.»

The idea of an egg-universe has always been carved in the thought of wise men throughout antiquity, who also thought that the visible and the invisible worlds were both surrounded by an impermeable border.

Don't skip chapters or bibliographic references

---

115 A) **THE APOCRYPHON BOOK OF ENOCH, CH. 14**: «§10. They elevated me aloft to heaven. I proceeded, until I arrived **at its wall** built with stones of crystal. A vibrating flame (tongues of fire) **surrounded it**, which began to strike me with terror.» *(See also: http://reluctant-messenger.com/1enoch01-60.htm)*

B) **PLATO'S REPUBLIC, BOOK 10**, (616b-616c)

From the narration of Er, the son of Armenius who describes his death experience: «To this light we came after another day's journey; and we saw there that the **edges of the sky** <u>stretched out ending</u> into the middle of that light, which was the girdle of the sky, **and it enveloped the entire circumference/revolution of the sky evenly, holding it together** like the under girders of triremes. And from its extremities, the spindle of Need/Necessity was stretched, putting all the celestial orbits to motion.»

Later, scientists formulated the same picture.

---

116 *Scientifically, the concept of the 'spherical' nature of the universe is mathematical and cannot be perceived by the human senses.*

DANEZIS M., THEODOSIOU S., 'COSMOLOGY OF THE INTELLECT'

«(p. 117): In the 19th century, German mathematician G. F. B. Riemann proposed the **Hypersphere** as a model to describe the Universe. …This depiction has the shape of a Euclidean closed spherical surface. The model was the first finite model without limits.

(p. 261) …Riemann's space is **curved** and, as mentioned before, its curvature depends on the presence of matter in various areas of it.

And authors Danezis & Theodosiou never cease noting:

(p. 269) …It mustn't escape our attention that the forms and shapes that are created in the framework of such Universes cannot be perceived through the human senses. Especially when we use concepts like 'spherical' and 'hyperbolic', we must realize that we refer to spheres and hyperbolae of **non-Euclidean spaces** and not the known spherical and hyperbolic shapes of Euclidean geometry.»

When the embryo is in its mother's womb, it does not realize that there are also different ways of nourishment. What the embryo feels as air and nutrition are just substitutes. When it is born though, the oxygen it will inhale will feel nothing like what filled its lungs when it was inside its mother's womb. The same holds true for the bird that just hatches out of the egg. There is one kind of nourishment it gets inside the egg, and another one outside.

All these emotions people consider good or bad are mere **substitutes** (of various sorts of energy) which men feed on inside the universe/egg.

> **117** **DANEZIS M., THEODOSIOU S., 'COSMOLOGY OF THE INTELLECT'** (p. 98):
> «British astrophysicist **Fred Hoyle** states: "Feelings are **delusions**, creations of our consciousness and of the way we perceive the world.»

The moment a common mortal man comes in contact with his own Spirit, he is born in the Spiritual World and ceases being nourished by the (positive or negative) energy-substitutes of the universe/egg, thus receiving communion of the authentic, the original. This is when he receives his **first taste** of True Spiritual Love. It is the Love for his very own, Life-giving, other half-self.

> **118** **GOSPEL OF THOMAS**, JEAN YVES LELOUP:
> «§3. Jesus said: The Kingdom is inside you and it is outside (of) you. When you know yourself, then you will be known and you will know that you are the child of the Living Father. But if you do not know yourself, you will live in vain and you will be vanity.» [Eng. tr. JOSEPH ROWE]

Until then, man lives **with the illusion** that his self is his Ego! However the Spirit has no Ego since it is the absolute Unification With Everything. After that man LOVES only THIS ALL and what IT encompasses. Only then is the phrase "love thy neighbor as thyself" **valid**. Then, Real Love is solely focused on how to liberate the –imprisoned in matter– Spirit of the neighbor / brother / fellowman.

The Ego is an individualization, which ends up like this (degraded) when 'something' **is cut off** from its Source and tries to survive independently. In order for matter to survive, it has developed the individualized Ego, a diametrically opposite and inversely relative property to that of the Spirit (*Ego, Gr. Εγώ=1st person singular of the personal pronoun 'I')*. However much material man might want to rid himself of his Ego, the effort is rendered fruitless, lest he possesses the antidote Spirit, since one cancels the other out. If we delve into the subject even deeper, we will be forced to compare these situations and we shall then acknowledge the similarity of the cut-off Ego of men to their cut-off Creator; who, in order to exist independently –as an Ego– detached himself from his Divine Community and ended up fallen.

> **119** **A) THE GOSPEL OF JOHN, CH. 15**: «§4. Abide in Me, and I in you. As the vine-branch cannot bear fruit of itself unless it abides in the vine, so, neither can you, unless you abide in Me.»
> **B) BLAVATSKY H., P., 'THE SECRET DOCTRINE'** (I-413):

Don't skip chapters or bibliographic references

«One can ascertain one's self as to who the great 'Deceiver' is, if they search for him with open eyes and unprejudiced mind in all Ancient Cosmogonies and Scriptures. It is the human-formed Creator, the Demiurgos of Heaven and Earth, when he separated himself from the collective Hosts (Multitudes) of his companions.» *...and he united with the 'forbidden tree'.*

So, from this point of the Self-knowledge process onwards, starts the ascent of the Divine Spark from the dark 'Tartara' (Abyss/Hades) of the subconscious, towards the absolutely luminous territories of the seventh energy-center, where the 'Holy Matrimony' will take place.

ENERGY CENTERS – THE THIRD PHASE OF SELF-KNOWLEDGE

As long as the snakes/emotions oscillate between good and evil, they are awake; The Divine Spark remains jailed, guarded by them. Only when the snakes 'fall asleep', in other words stop oscillating, only then has the Divine Spark the chance to escape from the fourth energy-center of the heart and start ascending towards Its final destination, the seventh energy-center, which is located at the top of the head. This whole route is the third phase of self-knowledge. From this cardiac center on, the road is hard with two big traps half way up.

–I am sorry to interrupt again, but I would like us to set some things straight regarding the energy-centers of man. I think they are alternatively called chakras. Isn't it so?

–Right, the basic ones are seven. You can analyze them better if you decode some symbolic parts of the Hellenic (Greek) myths that are related to them.

The lowest is the **<u>first energy-center</u>** and is located at the base of the spinal cord, at the so-called 'Sacred Bone' (Sacrum). It is called sacred because it is there that the holy snake of creation has its 'den', and it is associated with the sub-chthonian (subterranean) and also lunar goddess Hecatē.

[120] **CHALDEAN ORACLES**, Gr. tr. ATHINOGENIS I., GRAVIGGER, P.: (p. 98) KROLL 28-PLACES 51-PROCLUS IN REPUBLIC II, 202, 14-16- IN TIMAEUS. III, 304, NOTE. 3 – IN PLATO THEOL. 265 - FESTUG. REVEL. III, P. 58- LEWY, 68 & NOTE 83: «…From the right haunch (of Hecatē), around the hollow of the cartilages, there springs forth and full-bursting the Fountain of the Primordial Soul, which in general animates the light, the fire, the aether, the Cosmoi.»

A Triune chthonic goddess, whose threefold depiction on every statue symbolizes the heavy, three-dimensional matter.

All primeval instincts that have their roots in the animalistic remnants of primordial cells are energized by this first energy-center; the preprogrammed (by the creator) impulses/hormones that literally 'bind' man onto his bestial nature.

[121] **TRIANTAFILLIDIS M., 'LEXICON OF THE COMMON GREEK LANGUAGE'**: «The Gr. word ὀρμόνη = **hormone** comes from the ancient Greek word ὁρμῶν. The root of this word is the Gr. verb ὁρμῶ = to actuate/push/excite/agitate.»

Indeed the hormones by nature excite, push, force and compel.

These instincts of self-preservation, like Hecate's dogs, dart forth in order to satisfy their impetuses/drives.

Don't skip chapters or bibliographic references

---

[122] **CHALDEAN ORACLES,** Gr. tr. ATHINOGENIS I., GRAVIGGER, P.:
(a) (p. 148) KROLL 45-PLACES 90- PSELLUS, EXPLANATION #23:
«Out of the hollows of the Earth, charge forth the Chthonic Dogs which **never let a true sign be seen by** mortal man.»
(b) (p. 149) KROLL 45-PLACES 91- OLYMPIODORUS IN PHAEDO. 230, 32 N:
«And from the airy regions, all non-rational Daemons begin assuming hypostasis. Hence, the Logion concludes: "She is the Driver of the aëry and the chthonic and the watery dogs.»
(c) (p. 149) LEWY, P. 271, FT. 41: «We are constantly referring to the non-rational Daemons ... the hunting group of the huntress Hecatē. ...The dogs symbolize the spirits who offer counsel and thus always accompany Hecatē...»

Immediately after that, the **second energy-center,** is located in the genital area and energizes the genital drives. This center is linked/related to the (aphrodisiac) goddess Aphrodite.

Third energy-center; the so-called 'Solar plexus'; it is focused on the umbilical area. It hosts all the inferior and generally negative emotions, and the ones that are related to fears, sexual passions, anxieties, hatreds, malice. It is linked with the subterranean 'inner Sun', god Pluto; the god of the underworld. All emotions that oscillate in this lower energy-center are negative and consequently hidden. Men usually hide their negative states and wicked 'ugly things' in general. This third center therefore is associated with man's inwardness.

Fourth energy-center: The center of the heart; the central position of a plain soul and potentially of the Divine Spark living inside it. Higher emotional oscillations are usually experienced here. It is equated with goddess Demeter who –while having her daughter Persephone by her side– gives birth to spring and fertility. When the fourth center of the heart however is alone, without Persephone present, it withers. Here, Persephone is absolutely equated with and symbolizes emotion; man's oscillating emotion that sometimes descends to the lower regions of Hades, where at the third energy-center of the solar plexus it is embraced by the dark bosom of Pluto, and other times comes out to the outer world, where in the fourth cardiac energy-center of 'Demeter', the love of the mother embraces it, purifies it and creates Spring.

This center (the fourth), is equated with man's extroversion. Man does not hide himself when he functions with this center. He takes the beautiful Persephone out to the light of the external Sun. Demeter then, rejoicing with the presence of her emotion/daughter, creates efflorescence and spiritual fruitfulness in man. Man taken by this spiritual euphoria, does not realize that summer is always followed by fall and fall is always followed by winter. He is swept by the magical phase, which entraps him again into the bipolar oscillation that accompanies it. Definitive Redemption can never come from this situation.

Fifth energy-center: The fifth chakra, at the throat; the Final base for the soul; there, lies the Creator's 'laboratory'; the house of 'Logos' (Word). "In the beginning there was Logos. And Logos is the god/creator." The manifested god abandoned the Celestial planes of Olympus and descended lower down, in order to create through the oscillation of Logos. And the first thing he created was the soul of man. This soul was manufactured from the Essence of the HyperCosmoi, where its creator came from, and from the 'paste' of the world it was going to live in. It was a mixture of Essence and higher energy.

---

[123] **PLATO'S TIMAEUS,** Tr. KOUTROUMPAS D., G. (C35a1-35b3 pp. 57-59):

«And he *(the creator)* made the Soul out of the following elements and in the following manner: Out of the **indivisible** and eternally unchangeable essence *(The Indivisible Spirit granted through the Immortal Breath of the god/creator)*, and also out of that which has to do with material bodies and is **divisible** *(the subtler energy-paste/matter of the material world, which is divided by Logos)*, by combining therefore the two, he had essences from both and he compounded a third and intermediate kind of essence between the indivisible and the divisible. And after he had received all three kinds *(the divisible, the indivisible, and the compound)* he blended them into a new kind, compressing by force the reluctant and unsociable nature of each into the others. He mingled this essence with the other two and made <u>one</u> out of three, which he again divided into as many portions *(souls)* as was fitting. Each portion of these had inside it of the one, the other, and the third compound essence.»

This soul was then placed in the fifth energy center of the throat. There lies the base/house of the energized Spiritual Logos. This center is equated with Hermes, the messenger of the Logoi (words) of the god/creator.

The moment Celestial Man tastes the fruit of knowledge of good and evil, he falls from the Celestial planes where he originates from, to the next lower level. The poisonous 'apple' –mortal traditions say– gets stuck in the middle of his throat, at the point called 'Adam's apple', and he tumbles lower down, where at the fifth energy center, the base of the throat, he wears the Soul as a garment that activates the ability of Logos.

---

[124] **HERMES TRISMEGISTUS,** HERMETIC TEXTS, VOL. I, RODAKIS P., TZAFEROPOU-LOS AP., '**SPEECH XII**' (p.193): «§13…The blissful god, the benevolent daemon said that the soul was to be in the body, **the Noûs (mind) in the soul**, the logos/reason in the Noûs and father of all is god.»

Don't skip chapters or bibliographic references

Anatomically, the fifth energy-center is focused at the base of the throat. There, the two clavicles (collarbones) of the sternum (breastbone) are located. Behind that upper part of the sternum, there is a small gland. Those who 'knew' named it with a keyword useful to the seekers. They called it the 'thymus gland'. 'Thymus', the Greek word Θυμός [*Thymos*], means soul in ancient Greek. Today, in the man of the Fifth Root Race, this gland is no longer under the control of the fifth energy-center of the throat and was put under the dominance of the fourth center, like the soul of the man of the Fifth Root Race of Iron, which was subdued by emotion, identified with it and settled in the fourth center of the heart.

Every plain soul –worshiping the powers of this world– can reach up to the fifth energy-center, not through self-knowledge but <u>through the techniques</u> which those powers propose. In this energy-center, the soul begins to acquire the 'gift' of Spiritual Logos that Hermes, the messenger of the gods, brings to man. They are the spiritual messages coming from the sixth energy-center of Olympus, the house/seat/base of the gods.

At this precise point (the 5th center of the throat) the third phase of self-knowledge **must come <u>before</u>** any acceptance of 'gifts'. This 3rd phase is carried out through specialized and very deep meditation, whose goal is to cast away the 'veil of oblivion' that surrounds the soul, and reveal to man his true spiritual identity. This identity contains the information of the Spiritual category each man belongs to and his Spiritual origin. The search for previous incarnations is a **huge obstacle** that completely detunes and disorients man from his true target. This search (search for previous lives) orients man exclusively towards the investigation of an endless alternating oscillation, which, besides the diversity of its fragmented versions, <u>does not offer any essential knowledge</u> of the reality surrounding him. Contrary to that, Epi-gnosis (awareness) of the Spirit that man receives life from, allows him to access more spiritual territories.

---

[125] **A) THE GOSPEL OF PHILIP** www.metalog.org/files/philip.html: «§61. The Lord says: "Blessed is he who 'IS' <u>before</u> he comes into Being *(existence)*! For he who IS, both WAS and shall 'BE'.» [Eng. tr. from Coptic PATERSON BROWN]

B) GOSPEL OF THOMAS, JEAN YVES LELOUP: "§19. Jesus said: Blessed is he who **IS** before existing." [Eng. tr. JOSEPH ROWE]

(To exist = Gr. Υπ-άρχω, υπό + άρχω= be sub-ject to the power of someone else)

C) THE GOSPEL OF JOHN, CH. 3: "§3. Jesus answered and said to him, "Truly, truly, I say to you, unless one is born **from above***, he cannot see the kingdom of God."

*In most Engl. tr. the word 'again' is incorrectly used, whereas, the orig. Gr. uses the word: **[ἄνωθεν = from above]**

> **D) GOSPEL OF THOMAS**, JEAN YVES LELOUP: «§84. Jesus said: When you see your icons, those that were before you existed, and that never die and never manifest, what grandeur!» [Eng. tr. JOSEPH ROWE]

There is a fundamental difference that comes to play when a soul is the exclusive offspring of the manifested creator/god, or if it encompasses (as if it were a garment), a Divine Spark/Spirit inside it. The 'I Am Presence' is the other half of the split Celestial Man, and remains autonomous inside the 'universe of the snake'. The Divine Spark is the other half, while the soul surrounding this Spiritual Divine Spark is not controlled by its creator, but as a mere garment encompasses the Spirit inside it.

> **126** **THE GOSPEL OF JUDAS [KASSER R., MEYER M., WURST G.] NATIONAL GEOGRAPHIC** [53]: «But the Great One ordered Gabriel to grant spirits to the great generation *(of the material Humans)* with no ruler over it.»

–So then, don't all souls have a Divine Spark inside them?
–No, yet we shall deal with these matters later, once we have previously analyzed some other basic issues.
–And what is the difference separating these two categories?
–The spiritual 'drive'; this entire previous and long-lasting procedure of self-knowledge cannot EVER be completed by a plain Soul, except if there is a deeper force, uninterruptedly supporting this difficult effort. In our previous discussion, we compared this 'power' to the 'desperate cry for help' by man's very own Spirit. If this power does not exist inside a man, every effort is abandoned after the first difficulties and man's entire dynamism is focused on the daily material productiveness and not Spiritual Salvation. Every plain Soul however, has the freedom to choose: either to remain in this world forever, accepting the presents of its god/creator, or to ask to be 'filled'/completed with Spirit from the Immaculate FatherLands *(HyperUniverses)*.

> **127** **A) THE GOSPEL OF MATTHEW, CH. 7:** «§7. Ask, and it will be given to you; seek, and you will find; knock and the door will be opened to you.»
> **B) THE APOCRYPHON OF JOHN, THE GNOSTIC SOCIETY LIBRARY:**
> «Those upon whom the Spirit of the Life <u>will descend</u> and (with whom) it will be powerfully present, **they will be saved** and will become perfect. And they will become worthy of the great realms. And **they will be purified in That Place** (the *'prepared Place' –as we will see later on*) from all evil and the concerns of wickedness.» [Eng. tr. from Coptic: FREDERIK WISSE]
> **C) HERMES TRISMEGISTUS**, HERMETIC TEXTS, VOL. I, RODAKIS P., TZAFEROPOULOS AP., 'SPEECH IV, HERMES TO HIS SON TAT; THE CRATER OR MONAS':

Don't skip chapters or bibliographic references

«§3. For he (god), Tat, divided speech among all men but he did not do the same with Noûs (Mind) *(which Trismegistus considers identical with spirit)*. And he didn't do this because he envied someone. ...He wanted, Son, to let the Noûs in the middle among all souls as a reward to strive for.

§4. Tat: And where did he place it *(the Noûs)*?

Hermes: Filling a mighty Cup with it *(Noûs)*, and sent it down with a Herald, whom he commanded to proclaim to the hearts of men these things: "Baptize thyself, thou that art able, in this Cup; thou that believes that thou shalt return to him that sent this Cup; thou that knows the reason for which it happened." As many therefore as understood the Proclamation, and were baptized into the Noûs (Mind), these are partakers of the knowledge, and became perfect men, receiving the Noûs. But those who missed of the Proclamation, **the rational ones**, since they didn't receive the Noûs, are ignorant of what happens and of the outcomes. §5. And their senses are just like non-rational beasts, and having their anger and wrath possessing them, they do not admire the things worthy of looking on... and let themselves to the pleasures and desires of the Body, believing that man was made for them alone. But as many as partook of the gift of God, these... are both immortal and mortal, because they have included in their Noûs all things which are upon the Earth, in the Sky, and anything existing **above** the Sky...And, having seen Ἀγαθόν *[=Ultimately Good (See Tr. n on w. ἀγαθός (Agathós), beginning of Ch. 'HIGHER MENTAL BODY – CELESTIAL MAN')]*, they consider henceforth their dwelling on Earth a **miserable calamity** [1] and despise all things bodily and **bodiless** and make haste to the One and Only One.»

[1] **GOSPEL OF THOMAS**, JEAN YVES LELOUP:
«§80 Whoever knows the world discovers the body; but the world is unworthy of whoever discovers the body.» [Eng. tr. JOSEPH ROWE]

This way, the soul can also enter the Impassable Spaces of the HyperUniverses.

---

128 **THE GOSPEL OF MATTHEW, CH. 22**:
«§14. For many are invited, but few are chosen.»

But if man **imagines** the material world he lives in to be a gift of the God/Father, he will never ask to be filled with Spirit, since he will not consider that to be important.

All the so-called 'initiation' procedures, or 'karma restitution techniques', concern the first choice of the souls (to stay inside the material universe), and all these souls will ever accomplish is their eternal enslavement.

> [129] **PADMASAMBHAVA, THE TIBETAN BOOK OF THE DEAD.** [Gr. tr. LIAKOPOULOS E.]
> «…These gods of Samsara (=the vicious circle of births and deaths) are considered 'immortal', but up to the point that their good karma <u>runs out</u>.»
> *If then, good Karma **can run out** <u>for the gods</u>, what do we humans hope to achieve?*

These though, will be clarified later on in our discussion.

We now come to the **sixth energy-center**. It is located at the center of the forehead, sometimes referred to as 'the third eye'. It is equated with the residence of the creator/god, Mt. Olympus. There, is the 'all seeing eye'. Not even a single man's soul can step in there.

> [130] **DAVID ICKE, THE SECRET OF ALL AGES** [GR. TR. MASTAKOURIS T.] (p. 434): «The truncated pyramid with the all-seeing eye is a symbol. …The all-seeing eye is the eye of Horus, of Lucifer, of Satan, call it what you like. It is also related to the 'third eye', the 'chakra' in the center of the forehead, through which we are connected with our psychic vision. According to the Egyptian legend, Osiris was murdered by Set and Set was killed by Horus, who lost his eye in the battle. Hereby, we have the expression 'the eye of Horus.»
> *Obviously, the correlation with the 'Evil Eye' in the book /movie 'The Lord of the Rings' is not accidental.*

When this center, which is the exclusive seat of the creator/god, controls a plain soul (devoid of Divine Spark), this soul obtains access to it only through the connection with its own 'I Am Presence', namely its god/creator. The creator then –as a reward– provides the soul with the inner vision of the sixth sense, where, with the help of Kundalini, through the **back stage** of Olympus, it 'sneaks a peek' into the astral and aetheric worlds.

Spiritual Logos (Word) through messenger-god Hermes, the ability to cure material bodies and the capacity of the sixth sense, are the end of the road for every plain soul. At that particular point of course, man is somehow 'lulled' and never finds the Truth. This is, after all, unattainable either way, simply because through the messenger Hermes, man can know only what the creator chooses to provide him with as knowledge. And as you can easily understand, the Truth is out of the question. Next, such 'accomplished' people, by means of what has been transferred to them, guide the rest of the crowds of the 'commoners' through 'teaching', and lead them to dead ends. You must therefore discriminate between the knowledge you have till now been acquiring from men, and the knowledge you are receiving now. You will certainly see many differences. But this is natural, if you

Don't skip chapters or bibliographic references

consider that what man has learned up to now is exclusively the knowledge of only one view alone, however twofold it might appear in the (dyadic) material dimension.

In the universe of the absolute 'give and take', if a prospective seeker receives the gifts of god creator, he must automatically offer a counter-gift in return. It is the Logos of the creator, in relation to the causative/cause.

> [131] **GAZIS A., LEXICON OF THE GREEK LANGUAGE** (p. 52): Αιτία = Cause: «The first thing according to Pindar and Herodotus, the beginning, the source, the foundation and the motive for anything made of matter (Gr. Hylē).»

And as far as plain souls are concerned, since they have always belonged to him, they receive his presents and obediently continue to succumb to his every will.

Celestial Man being independent, if He accepts these rare gifts, He gives up his Divine Essence in return, putting it under the absolute control and service of the creator of matter.

> [132] **HESIOD, WORKS AND DAYS** [Gr. tr. GIRGENIS S.] (VERSES. 85 - 92): «And Epimetheus did not think on what Prometheus had said to him, telling him **never to take a gift from Olympian Zeus**, but **to send it back** for fear it might prove to be something harmful to mortals (men). But he accepted the gift, and when calamity was already upon him, he understood.»

So if the third phase of self-knowledge has not been completed before this, man, through his ignorance and oblivion, is deluded and in order to gain the gifts of the creator god, trades his 'part within', losing in essence his 'Everything'.

The road to Deliverance and the Truth is totally different and the key is called **power transmutation**. The course is the same for every plain Soul that **will choose** to abandon the universe of duality and pass over to the Immortal FatherLands, after having previously been fulfilled by Spirit.

The creator's 'gifts' hide the Power inside them, but also a big trap. Man has two choices then: either to make use of these gifts and profit from their power, or to transmute this power, converting it to an elevator which will lift him up to the higher levels. If man has not been freed from the charms of material power, he gets irretrievably trapped through/by these gifts. But if he bypasses this trap, then the power of these gifts is transmuted and becomes the vaulting horse to 'launch' him, in order to conquer the seventh sense of the Truth.

> [133] **BLAVATSKY H., P., 'THE SECRET DOCTRINE'** (I-96): «The Occult claim that there are **seven senses in man,** as in nature, as there are seven states of consciousness, is corroborated in the same work. *(Anugîtâ, Sacred Books of the East, Vol. VIII., 278)*»

The transmutation is the result of **non-use** of these Powers. In other words, man possesses these gifts, but makes no use of them. He never 'touches' them; neither for good, nor for evil. He 'burns' this 'ace up his sleeve' (does not take advantage of these gifts).

> [134] **THE GOSPEL OF MATTHEW, CH. 7:** §22-23 «On that day many will say to Me, "Lord, Lord, did we not prophesize in your name, and cast out demons in your name, and do **many miracles** in your name?" And then will I declare to them, "I never knew you; get away from me, you evildoers.»

Their accumulated power then, shoots him to a higher state. The success of this whole undertaking is determined by man's predominant, fundamental and essential resolution to discover THE ONE Truth of Everything. If this resolution is not **his ultimate priority**, then the result will be fruitless. The Sixth Sense is the trap. Whoever falls in it, gets permanently trapped and never manages to redeem himself. The Seventh Sense of Truth can only be conquered by **bypassing** the sixth.

Let us see though, what happens at the fifth energy-center (at the throat), when a soul with Spirit takes off the veil of oblivion. This description is such a difficult task for me, as if I were trying to describe to you in words, the scent of gardenias, when you have never smelled them before!

> [135] **CHALDEAN ORACLES, Gr. tr. ATHINOGENIS I., GRAVIGGER, P.** (p. 42) P. —KROLL, P. 11 KROLL, DAMASCIUS I, 154 14-26: «There exists, something Intelligible *(apprehensible by the mind only),* which you must perceive by the flower of your Noũs *(mind)*; …by directing the pure Eye of your soul, after it *(your soul)* has turned away from *(disregarded)* anything sensory, so that your Noũs – void of thoughts– can turn towards The Intelligible, so that you may learn The Intelligible, **for It exists beyond the boundaries of human logic.»**

This information though, will help whoever 'smells gardenias' at some point, to know he is on the right track.

At this point, very different 'memories' in the form of a sensation, start to faintly appear, referring to worlds radically different from ours or anything else that exists in the densely material- and energy-universe. Along with these 'nostalgic' sensations, some symbols/keys (accompanied by their confirmations from each corresponding plane) start arriving in transcen-

Don't skip chapters or bibliographic references

dental form, which refer to secret codes, **exclusive** to each 'kind' of Spirit, with which (codes) the seeker will later unlock the impassable territories that lead to the seventh energy-center. From then on, no more instructions or clarifications are needed, because each Spiritualized Soul KNOWS exactly the steps IT has to take.

---

[136] A) CHALDEAN ORACLES, Gr. tr. ATHINOGENIS I., GRAVIGGER, P. (p. 164) - KROLL 50 – PLACES 108- PROCLUS IN CRAT. 21, 1-2 P–PSELLUS, EXPL. 26:

«The Mind of the Father has sown symbols in the world."

B) CHALDEAN ORACLES, Gr. tr. ATHINOGENIS I., GRAVIGGER, P.: (p. 165) KROLL 50 – PLACES 109- PSELLUS, EXPL. 39 PROCLUS IN PLATO, THEOL. 12, 5-104:

«But the Mind of the Father does not allow the soul's will to be fulfilled, since she has not yet departed from **Oblivion**, and is incapable of uttering the (magic) word, until it has remembered the Father's pure token (symbol).»

C) THE GOSPEL OF TRUTH, 'ECUMENICAL COPTIC WORK' NAG HAMMADI MANUSCRIPTS (tr. from Coptic PATERSON BROWN) www.metalog.org:

«§10…Acting with recognition[1] *(Gnosis/Knowledge)* and perfection, He (Jesus) proclaimed what is in the heart [of the Father, in order to] make wise those who are to receive the teaching. Yet, those who are instructed are the Living, inscribed in this Book of Life, who are taught about Themselves and who receive Themselves from the Father in again returning to Him.

§11. Because the Perfection of the Totality is in the Father, it is requisite that they all ascend unto Him. When someone Recognizes[1] *(knows)*, he receives the things that are his own and gathers them to Himself. For he who is unacquainted *(does not know)*, has a lacking –and what he lacks is great, since what he lacks is Him who will make him perfect. Because the perfection of the totality is in the Father, it is requisite that they all ascend unto him. Thus each and every one receives Himself.

§12. He *(The Father)* pre-inscribed them, having prepared this gift for those who emerged from Him. Those whose names He foreknew are all called at the end. Thus someone who **recognizes**[1] *(has Gnosis=knowledge),* has his name spoken by the Father. For he whose name has not been spoken remains unacquainted *(with the Father)*. How indeed can anyone hearken *(listen)*, whose name has not been called? For he who remains unacquainted *(with the Father)* until the end is a figment of forgetfulness and will vanish with it. Therefore, there is indeed no name for those wretches, and they do not heed *(hear)* the call.

§13. Thus someone with acquaintance is from above. When he is called he hears and heeds and returns to Him who called, ascending unto Him. And he discovers Who it is that calls him. In recognition he does the volition of Him Who called. He desires to please Him, and with granted repose **he receives the Name from the One. He who recognizes thus discovers from whence he has come and whither he is going.** He understands like someone who

---

was intoxicated and who has shaken off his drunkenness and **returned to himself**, to set upright those things which are his own.

§15. This is acquaintance with the Living Book, whereby at the end He has manifested the Eternal-Ones as the alphabet of His revelation. These are not vowels nor are they consonants, such that someone might read them and think of emptiness, but rather they are the true alphabet by which those who recognize it are themselves expressed. Each letter is a perfect thought; each letter is like a complete book written in the alphabet of unity by the Father, who inscribes the Eternal-Ones so that through His alphabet they might recognize the Father.»

[1]**Recognition**: Coptic sooun, Greek Γνῶσις (gnosis); this important term means direct personal acquaintance rather than mere intellectual knowledge. [WALTER EWING CRUM, *A COPTIC DICTIONARY*, OXFORD: CLARENDON PRESS, 1939]

Man's history abounds with myths delivering encoded truths. The sad thing is that after so many centuries past, most of these myths have been corrupted and do not state their hidden message with precision. Nevertheless, the fundamental concepts are clearly visible.

[137] **MYTHOLOGIE GENERALE, FELIX GUIRAND**, COPYRIGHT BY DIMITRAKOS S., BIBLOS 1953 (p. 270): «An obscurity and even some contradictions are noted in the myths preserved to us.»

Let us examine then, how these traps come about, as we analyze a very difficult myth/riddle: The myth of Orpheus and Eurydice: The myth says that one day when Eurydice was playing in the fields carefree, a snake bit her and she died. She was then brought down to the kingdoms of Hades. Her beloved Orpheus was inconsolable. He cried and asked for her desperately. With the power of his music, he moved the sub-chthonic powers, who gave him permission to bring Eurydice back to life. There was one condition though. 'He should never turn back to look at her before reaching the world above'. But when they were at the end of their journey, just before they had reached the cave's exit, Orpheus turned and looked at her. And then, the only thing he could see was her elusive shadow getting lost again in Hades. The end of Orpheus was quite painful, since he was finally mangled by the infuriated Maenads (frenzied female worshipers of Dionysus). Can you imagine what this myth is trying to tell us?

–*No…*

–Orpheus and Eurydice together, symbolize the Unified Celestial Man. Eurydice is the Divine Spark, entrapped inside material man who has reached the underworld of matter, after the bite of the snake/god. The lonely Orpheus symbolizes Man's 'I Am Presence' wandering the universe of the snake. This particular myth however, highlights a great danger that can cost him the permanent loss of the whole redemption. Celestial Orpheus, in order to reunite with his split half, Eurydice, projects himself into Hades in the form of a conscious decision of the man incarnate, and leads his Divine Spark /Eurydice, towards the seventh energy-center, which is also defined as the spot where the Holy Matrimony takes place. But as the Orpheus/Man projection is climbing from the darkness –of Tartara– of the underworld of his subconscious, bringing the Divine Spark /Eurydice with him, he sees the twilight *(of the Antavges)*, starting to appear as he approaches the exit of the 'cave' to the outer world, and **confuses** this twilight with the True Light.

Through his burning desire and his oblivion, Orpheus/man is confused, accepts the counter-gifts of 'marriage', and turns to Eurydice/Spark, thus losing her forever along with the possibility to arrive with her at the seventh energy-center (the top of the head). This twilight is a reflection of the True Light *(the Patrogenes One)* of the seventh energy-center, which, passing through the chambers of Olympus of the 6th energy-center, is split, and as a reflection *(Ant-Avges)* reaches this 'verge' spot of Hades, of the 5th energy-center, as the first streak of dawn- twilight/gift of the god/creator.

---

138 **A) THE FIRST BOOK OF ADAM AND EVE, SACRED TEXTS, RUTHERFORD PLATT, CH. 27**: «Satan began with transforming his hosts; in his hands there was a flashing fire, and they were in a great light. He then placed his throne near <u>the mouth of the cave</u> *(at the sixth energy center of Olympus, as the 'all-seeing eye')* …<u>and he shed light into the cave</u>, until the cave glistened over Adam and Eve, while his hordes began to sing praises. And Satan did this, in order that when Adam saw the light, <u>he should think within himself that it was a heavenly light</u>, and that Satan's hosts were angels; and that God had sent them…When, therefore, Adam and Eve saw the light, **fancying** it was real, they strengthened their hearts;» [Gr. edition: APOCRYPHAL TEXTS OF THE OLD TESTAMENT, KOUTSOUKIS D.]

B) PLATO'S 'REPUBLIC' BOOK 7 (514a-517b)

(A dialogue, between Socrates and Glaucon)

«Socrates *(to Glaucon)*: Picture men, dwelling in a sort of subterranean cavern with a long entrance, open to the light on its entire width. Conceive them as having from childhood their legs and necks chained so that they remain in the same spot, able to look forward only, and prevented by their bonds from turning their heads. Picture further **the light from a fire burning higher up and at a distance behind them** *(as the Twilight [Antavges=substitute light], the degraded 'light' of the creator, burning **inside the cave just before its exit**).*»

Then, Orpheus/Man chooses the oscillation of the sound of the Holy twilight(ing) Logos as his reward, and totally succumbs to the service of god/creator (as a bondservant), thus remaining forever split in the universe of duality.

Orpheus afterwards, through his hymns and man through his services, hail the gods/creators of this world, and offer their 'Essence' as a sacrifice/return-gift to the inferior deities-maenads.

---

139 *And now Orpheus worships the powers of this world, and their creator…*
ORPHIC HYMNS FRAGMENTA (1) GR. TR. MAGGINAS S.: 'ORPHEUS' EXCERPTS' (p. 66):

«There is indeed only one king-lord self-born. And ALL that has been created are offspring (creations) of this unique one. He, the king, wanders amongst them (his creations); and no man can see him, yet he sees ALL *(the all-seeing eye)*. He **provides** (bestows) men everything from **good to evil**, like the bitterly cold war, and tearful sorrows *(the two extremes of material oscillation)*. Neither does someone exist separately from the great king. I cannot see him, for a cloud has been placed around him and because men only possess mortal irises in their eyes which cannot see Zeus, the archon of all.

Because he is enthroned/settled in the bronze sky [1] upon a golden throne, he walks the earth with his feet.»

[1] *As we will see in a later chapter, the bronze sky is equated with the aetheric plane were the seven Elohim of creation have their seat.*

So, this is the fifth energy center-trap; the center of the magic of Logos; the Logos of god/creator, who 'always geometrizes', and since he geometrizes, his Logos is more intertwined with the mathematical logos/fraction *(the Gr. word logos, among other meanings, also denotes: fraction, ratio)*, which automatically indicates division. Hence the early ancient Greek name for Jupiter, $\Delta\iota\varsigma$ [Dis=dual] which alludes to **di**-vision.

---

140 **DICTIONARY OF THE ANCIENT GREEK LANGUAGE BY IOANNIS STAMATAKOS**
«$\Delta\iota\varsigma$ is the ancient Gr. name of $Z\varepsilon\acute{\upsilon}\varsigma$ [Zeus] which appears in the oblique cases $\Delta\iota\acute{o}\varsigma$, $\Delta\iota\acute{\iota}$ ($\Delta\iota$) $\Delta\iota\alpha$. Its connection with the Gr. word $\delta\iota\varsigma$ (which means two or twice) is not accidental. Furthermore, the Gr. name $\Delta\acute{\iota}\alpha$ is connected with the Gr. adverb $\delta\iota\alpha$ which –without inflection– denotes separation and division.»

If the Higher Self of the seeker falls for his charm, accepting the gift of the (twofold) god/creator, then IT gets permanently di-vided from the (Divine Spark) Eurydice, who goes back as an 'eternal prisoner' of the gods/creators.

Don't skip chapters or bibliographic references

Sixth energy-center; Found at the center of the forehead; Right where people place the 'third eye'. It is the central seat of the god/creator; the ultimate point. It is equated with Mt. Olympus, the highest throne of the gods. There, the soul of the (common) man never sets foot in. At this height, the snake-figured goddess Hecatē shall present the view from the 'back chambers of Olympus' to the 'select few' souls if she so wishes.

---

141 **PHILOSOPHICAL AND CEREMONIAL MYTHS OF THE ANCIENT GREEK MYSTS, GRAVIGGER** (p. 145): «Ave, Hecate, **'Prothyraia'** [Qui veilles aux portes (du ciel)] (=who always stands sleepless at the Gates of the Sky), is the translation of M. Meunier in the hymn to Hecate by Proclus.

She who always stands sleepless at the Gates of the Sky; the 'Queen [Gr. Ἄνασσα] of the Sky' as Orpheus calls her in his first Hymn for her [1].

...Proclus here invokes her from an even higher stand point addressing her as the guardian and guide of souls in their ascending course to the light, to redemption.»

[1] **'ORPHIC HYMNS' 1ST HYMN TO HECATE,** TR. MAGGINAS S., (p. 3): «I invoke and praise Hecatē, who is revered in every street and crossroads; ...the huntress of bulls, the queen **who has the keys to the whole** world (the key-holder), the guide, the nymph.»

From the lower planes, the soul can accept the gods' gifts to it, only through pleading. The power of Logos, of Prophecy, of Therapy (cure), and Inner Vision are the best a select soul can hope for. The scepters of absolute power are 'in its hands'. But at what cost! Do you think, that in this universe of give and take, all this can be granted without return? And as far as common souls are concerned, this is the best they can long for from a life they only came to be bondservants in. Woe to the Celestial Men though! Their submission signals their inability to return to the FatherLands.

Throughout man's history on this Earth, great Mystics (Initiates) have been imprisoned in these two energy-centers and have then 'fallen from grace' to become 'black magicians', trapped by the 'power' of the aforementioned dispensations. The eternal circle of rise and fall of the oscillating snake is infinitely continued.

The Divine Spark/Man though, who will continue undeterred to go higher, at the sixth energy-center enters the most difficult and by far the most dangerous phase of his path. Obliged to pass **through** the impassable realms of the sixth energy-center of Olympus, he makes use of his codes/keys.

There, he is put through extremely difficult ordeals, and comes face to face with staggering revelations…

At the end of this road lies the **seventh energy-center.** Into this center, it has been foretold, only a soul that possesses the Living Spirit inside it can enter. This center is located at the top of the head. It is otherwise called the 'Lotus Center'. It is the star painted at the top of the head in all depictions of the Virgin Mary.

At that seventh energy-center, the Holy Matrimony takes place: The union of the Divine Spark with the 'I Am Presence'. In this particular union, there is absolutely no trace of sexual connotation. For the man experiencing it, this union assumes form in the birth of a new body. This body is called Higher Mental. The Higher Mental Body has no relation whatsoever to material or scientific knowledge of any sort. It is simply the body which, through Man's Enlightenment by the True Unsplit Light of the Seventh Center, brings him the Truth, and through the Truth, it brings him Wisdom. In this seventh energy-center then, man is found in the neutral zone between the material and the matter-less worlds. This center is, in other words, the seventh degree, which in the language of music is called 'leading tone'.

---

[142] *Leading tone: The seventh note of the scale, leading to the first note of the next Octave.*

KUNDALINI

I must definitely stress a very significant and essential matter regarding the two paths through which material man can reach the impassable energy-territories of the sixth energy-center of 'Olympus'.

The first path is the 'honest' way through self-knowledge which sharpens man's intellect and the second one is the 'thief's way' that transforms the human brain to a 'soft'/weak brain, or even a disturbed one.

The front side of man is identified with the apparent. His back is related to what is hidden.

[143] **PLATO 'TIMAEUS'** Modern Gr. tr. KOUTROUMPAS D., G. (XVI 45A3-45B2): «And the gods, deeming the front part of the body as more honorable than the back and more fit to lead, gave us the ability to move for the most part in this direction. So it was necessary for man to have the front part of his body distinguished and dissimilar to the back. Wherefore having set the face upon the globe of the head on that side, they naturally placed on it *(the front side)* the organs for all the forethought of the soul, and they ordained that the one to lead should be this *(the front side)*.»

What is hidden, of course, is usually not absolutely pure. Let me become clearer though: In the 'honest' way/path of progress/ascent, man must hold in his hand the 'sacred invitation', which is no other than the possession of the Divine (Spirit) Spark. When at a certain point, the Divine Spark is awakened in the cardiac center, IT starts ascending upwards, passing through the 5th energy-center of the throat to the 6th energy-center of the forehead (third eye). Through this 6th center of 'Olympus', IT will finally reach the seventh, the 'Lotus center'. The meditation 'tricks' that accelerate the process, bring no results because only the entirely **honorable** life and the absolute pureness of emotions and intentions can promote the Spark from each lower center to a higher one.

There is nevertheless also the way of the 'thief'. The road of the cheater is the road through the cunningness of the snake. The thief too will of course be able to reach the sixth energy-center of Olympus, but only through the 'back door' in order to admire the view that the key-holder goddess Hecatē will present to him from the 'back stages' *(Another name the Greeks had given to Hecatē was Προθυραία [Prothyraia] = standing in front of the gate)*. The problem is of course that the 'thief' will never enter the Holy

Planes of the Father, but this alleged wisdom will be channeled to his intellect by the devious wisdom of the snake. I will explain to you exactly what happens: At the base of the spinal cord, the sacred vertebra (Sacred Bone/Sacrum), at the first energy-center, there is an energy 'coiled round itself'. This energy is paralleled by the thinkers to a snake and is called Kundalini. It is essentially identified with the snake-figured goddess Hecate, who, by personal choice, has placed her 'subterranean' base there.

> [144] **CHALDEAN ORACLES,** Gr. tr. ATHINOGENIS I., GRAVIGGER, P. (p. 98) - KROLL 28-PLACES 51: «...From the right haunch *(of Hecatē)*, around the hollow of the cartilages, there springs forth and full-bursting the Fountain of the Primordial Soul...»

The uninformed student, unaware of the danger involved, calls upon Hecate's Kundalini energy through meditation. Everyone who calls the manifested gods of the material universe should know that he must also have an 'exchange gift' **always** available· otherwise he will receive 'venom' in return. There lies the danger which lurks when many people, after they call upon kundalini energy, they are granted madness instead of wisdom.

The moment man chooses the snake as his guide in his path to wisdom, he energizes it through meditation. This energy, will start ascending through his spinal cord (the back door).Through it, it will reach the sixth energy center of the brain, in the 'gap' between the pituitary gland and the pineal gland whose anatomical name is Thalamus, *(Greek θάλαμος [thalamos] = chamber)*, and is located in-between the two hemispheres. The so-called Thalamus/chamber can be paralleled to the control center for all data being received. The distribution of all incoming information to the various parts of the brain is carried out through this Thalamus.

> [145] **DANIEL GOLEMAN,** (PSYCHOLOGIST, HARVARD UNIV.) **'EMOTIONAL INTELLIGENCE'** (p. 48): «The conventional view in neurology states that the eye, the ear and the other sensory organs transmit the signals to the thalamus and, from there, *(the signals are distributed)* to the areas of the cerebral cortex which process the stimuli. There, the signals are combined and form the objects in the way we perceive them. ...A visual signal is firstly transmitted from the retina of the eye to the thalamus, where it is translated into the language of the brain. After that, most of the messages go to the visual cortex, where they are analyzed and evaluated in respect to their meaning.»

Don't skip chapters or bibliographic references

Into this distribution department then, the wise snake's venom is 'discharged' as energy, and from there, the Thalamus/chamber communicates it to the rest of the brain's sections, where it manifests as devious 'wisdom'.

---

[146] *Since there is not only the Immaculate Wisdom, but also the devious one:* **THE GOSPEL OF MARY (MAGDALENE) JEAN-YVES LELOUP**, Gr. tr. KOUROUSSI A., A., verses 2-3 & 9-14: «Then, the soul arrived at the fourth atmosphere, which took seven manifestations *(forms)*: The first manifestation is darkness, the second one is desire, the third one is ignorance, the fourth one is deadly jealousy, the fifth one is carnal inebriation, the sixth one is the <u>intoxicating wisdom</u>, the seventh one is <u>devious wisdom</u>. These are the seven expressions of **Wrath**, which oppress the soul with questions like: Where do you come from, man-slayer? Where are you going you wanderer?»

This sort of 'wisdom' though, is entirely different from the one channeled to the human brain through the seventh energy-center.

'Wisdom' coming from kundalini is the manifestation of the sixth sense; a trap-sense which conveys all the information of the astral world, and its accompanying problems. On the contrary, wisdom transferred through the seventh energy-center, is the seventh sense of the Truth and gives man the key to his Liberation.

The snake's course will not, of course, continue to the seventh energy-center. It couldn't anyway. It remains there, in order for the seed/venom of the wise snake/creator, to start activating man's intellect with its own schismatic wisdom. In most cases, the consequences of this method/path are devastating for the one who chooses the 'back door'. Many cases have been reported, where people energized kundalini, but paid back dearly for it, with the disturbance of their mental and psychological health.

Recapitulating then, there are two ways of ascent for man: In the first category, plain souls, or souls with a Divine Spark inside, entrapped in the illusion of the material plane, worship the powers of this world, and through 'techniques' that they (the powers) offer, climb up to the fifth energy-center and then through the 'back chambers' (Thalamus) of 'Olympus', contemplate the view of the astral world and its 'magic'. These men never learn the Truth, but clung firmly onto the highest degree of the oscillation, they rise with it up to the 2nd reflective heaven, until that same oscillation inevitably brings them back down to the lower regions, where they will start a new experience cycle again. *(Reincarnation)*

¹⁴⁷ **PADMASAMBHAVA, THE TIBETAN BOOK OF THE DEAD** [Gr. tr. LIAKOPOULOS E.] (p. 68). *The commentator and translator of the 'Tibetan book of the dead', Eustathios Liakopoulos, points out:* «The six realms of Samsara *(the material world of Maya/delusion)* are: 1) the realm of the gods of Samsara *(or the gods of the world, the <u>cosmic ones</u>, according to Sallustius)* ...these Samsaric gods are considered immortal, but up to the point that their good karma **runs out**.»

In the second category, **every man** who wants to Be Redeemed, initially appeals to the Impeccable Home Lands, asking to be fulfilled with Divine Spirit. Following that, he starts the process of self-knowledge, which will lead him to the seventh energy-center of Truth and Freedom.

HOLY MATRIMONY

148 **GOSPEL OF THOMAS,** THE ECUMENICAL COPTIC PROJECT
http://www.metalog.org/files/thomas.html
«§11 On the day when you were united, you became divided –yet, now that you have become divided, what will you do?»

The moment the Unified Celestial Man, Male and Female One, resident of all HyperUniverses of the Absolute and the True, tried the cursed fruit of the knowledge of good and evil, he died in the True Worlds and was incarnated into the mortal material universe of the snake.

149 **GOSPEL OF PHILIP,** JEAN-YVES LELOUP: «§71. When Eve was in Adam, there was no death: When she was separated from him, death came.» [Eng. tr. JOSEPH ROWE]

In this dyadic (twofold) world, just as concepts were divided into good and bad ones, just as the creator of matter was split into a god and a daemon, exactly like that, man himself was also split in two.

150 **A) HERMES TRISMEGISTUS:** THE FOUNDER OF MONOTHEISM 9000 B.C., IOANNIDIS P. K., '11TH SERMON OF HERMES TO TAT': «§10. Every being is **double in nature (dyadic)** and is set to motion by nature.»
B) GOSPEL OF PHILIP, JEAN-YVES LELOUP: «§72. The Teacher rose beyond death. He became what he was **before the separation** *(splitting)*. His body was **whole.** He had a body but this *(the unified body)* was the true body.» [Eng. tr. JOSEPH ROWE]

One part of the existence of Celestial Man remained free in the material energy-universe, as the Life-giving 'I Am Presence', or the Higher Self, and his remaining half, the Divine Spark, was incarnated into denser matter, sometimes as a man and other times as a woman. The reunion of these two segments (I Am Presence and Divine Spark) unifies the split man back into One Whole Entity, and this union is brought about through the Mystery of the Holy Matrimony. The result of this union, is the recovery of man's Spiritual Remembrance and the Reinstitution of the Truth (A-λήθη-α=Non-Forgetfulness). This is symbolically pictured by Mythology, with the birth of the Goddess Athena/Truth/Wisdom from inside Zeus' head. A different depiction of the same theme is the halo over the head of Christian Saints.

The reunification of the split Celestial Man gives Him the ticket for His return to the Celestial Kingdoms.

> **151** **GOSPEL OF THOMAS**, JEAN YVES LELOUP: «§49. Jesus said: Blessed are you, who are **the whole ones** *(unified)* and the chosen ones. You will find the Kingdom, for you came from there, and *(there)* you will return.» [Eng. tr. JOSEPH ROWE]

The Holy Matrimony of course, has nothing to do with social marriages of humans. The falsification that exists in the world of matter has its roots elsewhere.

When most of the quasi 'initiation' schools mention the Holy Matrimony, they don't mean the reunion of the Divine Spark with the student's Higher Self, but with his 'other' 'divine complement'! The 'divine complements', according to these schools of the quasi 'teachers', are common people of the opposite gender. They imagine then, that sexual union of the male student with a female student who the 'guru' will adjudicate to be his divine complement, will 'lift them both up' to the highest levels of spirituality!

> **152** **GOSPEL OF THOMAS**, JEAN YVES LELOUP: «§104. They said *(to Jesus)*: Come, let us pray and fast today! Jesus answered: What wrong have I done? How have I been defeated? When the bridegroom leaves the bridal chamber…that will be the time to fast and pray.» [Eng. tr. JOSEPH ROWE]

Through this sexual euphoria, students believe they will ascend in the spiritual pathway! …A deplorable, piteous mistake. After all, according to Hesiod's 'Theogony', Love [Eros] was one of the four primary elements (ingredients) of primordial darkness. Could it ever be 'redeeming'? Eros was that primordial power that first magnetized and then trapped the creator and Man inside the downward vortex of matter.

> **153** **A) HERMES TRISMEGISTUS**, HERMETIC TEXTS, VOL. I, RODAKIS P., TZAFEROPOULOS AP., **SPEECH I**: «§18…And he who possesses Noûs (mind) will recognize himself as being immortal and the cause of death to be Eros *(erotic love)*.»
> **B) HESIOD 'THEOGONY'** (V.115-122): «Truly, before everything, Chaos was made. And next the wide-bosomed Earth… and the gloomy Tartara in the depth of Earth … and Eros, the most handsome among the immortal gods…»
> **C) DECHARME P., 'HELLENIC MYTHOLOGY'**: «The primordial Eros of cosmogony is a mythological figure that engulfs an abstract idea; it is indeed, as they said, 'the force of attraction'.»
> **D) GRIMAL P., 'LEXICON OF HELLENIC AND ROMAN MYTHOLOGY'**
> "EROS: …Eros is thought to be a god, born at the same time as Earth, rising directly from the primordial Chaos. Furthermore, Eros is born from the primordial Egg, the same Egg that was born from the Night; the two halves of this Egg divided/separated to form the Earth and its cover Uranus (the sky).»

Don't skip chapters or bibliographic references

Chaos, Gaia (the Earth), Eros and Tartarus comprise the primary tetras in the Greek Cosmogony. Eros was, in other words, one of the primary elements of '...the downward darkness, the partially born' as Hermes Trismegistus describes it. Thereafter this 'erotic' force, the constituent of darkness, in order to inseminate its 'dark' environment, attracted (magnetized) a Light Ray from the HyperUniverses, which possessed the property 'to create'. Eros rendered the Light Ray 'fallen'. And as a reminder:

E) THE SECRET BOOK OF DZYAN, 'COSMIC EVOLUTION', STANZA III: «§3...The ray *(creator)* shoots through the virgin egg *(i.e. unites with the 'downward darkness the partially born')*. The ray causes the eternal egg to thrill *(oscillate)* and drops the non-eternal germ, which condenses into the world-egg.» *And carnal love remains a useful tool exclusively in the hands of the 'archon of this world.'*

F) THE APOCRYPHON OF JOHN, THE GNOSTIC SOCIETY LIBRARY: «Yaldabaoth raped Eve. She bore two sons. ...From then until now sexual intercourse has persisted thanks to the Chief Ruler who put desire for reproduction into the woman who accompanies Adam. Through intercourse the Ruler caused new human bodies to be produced and he blew his **artificial** spirit into each of them.» [Eng. tr. from Coptic: STEVAN DAVIES]

These would-be candidate mystics, through their delusion, with the schizophrenic duality wiggling their intellect, search to find their other divine half in the outer world. Having the instruction to perpetuate the species written onto their material gene on one hand, and the dormant inner spiritual need to reunite with their opposite spiritual part on the other, they find themselves pathetically deceived by their message-carrying 'masters' of the apostate (renegade) creator. They hasten therefore to satisfy this need of theirs in material copulation.

The fallen god creator's staff artfully weaved all religions and all metaphysical and mystical initiation-pathways of men.

---

[154] **BLAVATSKY H., P., 'THE SECRET DOCTRINE'** (II-215): «Dr. A. Kingsford 'The Perfect Way', APPENDIX 15, titled 'The Secret of Satan' (II-233): ...§3 As Lightning, I saw Satan fall from the sky, mighty in strength and fury. §4 Among the Gods is none like unto him, into whose hands are committed the kingdoms, the power and the glory of the worlds: §5 Thrones and empires, the dynasties of kings, the fall of nations, the birth of churches and the triumph of Time.»

On account of that, they characterize this sexual intercourse with the 'divine complement' as imperative and extremely necessary.

155 THE APOCRYPHON OF JOHN, THE GNOSTIC SOCIETY LIBRARY: «I asked the Savior, Lord, isn't it the serpent that caused Adam to eat? *(From the tree of knowledge of good and evil)* He smiled and replied: The serpent caused them to eat in order to produce the wickedness of <u>the desire to reproduce</u>. That would make Adam helpful to him *(to the serpent)*.» [Eng. tr. from Coptic: STEVAN DAVIES]

They also use the term 'holy matrimony' to further misguide people and commit adultery as they copulate, making 'love' to other people of the opposite gender, fooling themselves, that through this extremely material carnal pleasure, they will ascend the steps of spirituality! According to this reasoning of theirs, the two material individuals uniting sexually should be transformed into 'one body/flesh' and this, of course, is not materially possible. The saying 'into one flesh' is literal. Men however, through their inability to comprehend, started to presume, as usual. But through the True Holy Matrimony, in the very flesh of one Man Initiate, the 'male' and the 'female' parts of the same split Spiritual Entity unite.

156 A) GOSPEL OF THOMAS, JEAN YVES LELOUP: «§22. When you make *[Doresse: become]* the two into One, **when you make the inner like the outer and the high like the low** *(unification of the two opposite poles of split matter)*; when you make male and female into a <u>single One *(Unity)*</u>, **so that the male is not male and the female is not female**; when you have eyes in your eyes, a hand in your hand, a foot in your foot, and an icon in your icon, **then** you will enter into the Kingdom!» [Eng. tr. JOSEPH ROWE]
B) THE SECRET BOOK OF DZYAN, 'COSMIC EVOLUTION', STANZA VII: «§7. This is thy present Wheel, said the Flame *(The 'I am Presence')* to the Spark *(The Divine Spark)*. Thou art Myself, My Image, and my shadow. I have clothed myself in thee, and thou art my Vahan *(my carrier/vehicle)*, to the day, 'Be With Us,' **when thou shalt re-become myself** *(by means of the Sacred Union)* and others, thyself and me.»

Unfortunately, a great portion of humanity believes in this fallacy. They even go as far as to imagine that the 'divine complement' of Jesus Christ was Mary Magdalene. But with this logic of theirs, if male Jesus united with His female half that was Magdalene, –then logically and after His Resurrection– Magdalene's resurrection should have followed.

157 BLAVATSKY H., P., 'THE SECRET DOCTRINE' (II-134): «Mystically Jesus was held to be man-woman.»

Don't skip chapters or bibliographic references

Controversies come and go in the multi-fragmented dimension of matter!

INSIDE <u>ONE AND THE SAME</u> MAN,
UNIFICATION OF THE OPPOSITES RESTORES HIS WHOLENESS

THE TIBETAN BOOK OF THE DEAD: THE FIRST LIGHT
«…Now the clear luminance of Dharmata shines in front of you. Recognize it! This moment the state of your Spirit is pure essence by its nature, it has no property, no hypostasis, no form, no color, but it is pure emptiness. **This is the Emptiness, the Female Buddha** (Samantabhadri).

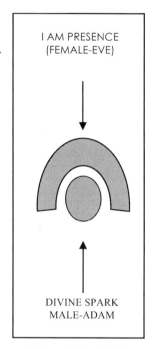

But this state of your Spirit is not simply barren emptiness. It is unhindered, transparent, pure and vibrating. **This** *(vibrating)* **Spirit is the Male Buddha** (Samantabhadra).

These <u>two</u>, the Spirit whose nature is <u>emptiness</u> *(female/I Am Presence/Eve)* without any hypostasis and the Spirit which is <u>vibrating</u> and Luminous *(male/Divine Spark/Adam)* are <u>undivided</u>. This is Buddha's Dharmakaya. Your very Spirit itself is the Emptiness and Luminance undivided as well, in the form of a great mass of Light and in this state, **it is no longer subdued to birth or death.**» [THE TIBETAN BOOK OF THE DEAD: THE FIRST LIGHT]

GOSPEL OF PHILIP: §67. «The bridegroom is led into the truth which is the **reinstitution** [apocatastasis] of all things <u>in their integrity</u>.»

GOSPEL OF THOMAS, SACRED TEXTS: «§61. Jesus said to her, "I am He who exists *(comes)* from the Undivided *(Whole)*…Therefore I say, if he is <undivided> *(Whole)*, he will be filled with light, but if he is divided, he will be filled with darkness.» [Eng. tr. THOMAS O. LAMBDIN]

THE IMPOTENCE OF THE MATERIAL BODY

In order for man to be able to function completely in the material plane without the indolence of plants, or the inferior cognition of animals, he had to be clad with more energy-bodies besides the material one.

> **[158] CHALDEAN ORACLES,** Gr. Tr. ATHINOGENIS I., GRAVIGGER, P. (p. 242) (ADDENDUM: COMMENTS AND EXPLANATIONS OF M. PSELLUS) 'RECAPITULATING AND CONCISE ESSAY OF THE CHALDEAN DOGMAS' (TEXT TRANSLATION IN HELLENIC PATROLOGY (JACQUES-PAUL MIGNE), VOL. 122 (PLACES P. 189-1149 C)
>
> «They (Chaldeans) accept the existence of seven corporeal Cosmoi, the first one, empyrean (fiery) *(Spirit)*, after that, three aethereal ones *(higher mental, soul, lower mental)* and then three material ones *(astral, aetheric, physically material)*; of these, the last one is called chthonian (earthly) and it is the enemy of light (Gr. μισοφαής = 'Light-hater'); it is the sub-lunar world containing inside it that matter (hylē), which they call 'the Deep Bottom' [Gr. βυθός].»

Each of these bodies would bring him some additional specific characteristics. All these energy-bodies are partially material. They are not of course visible, because they are oscillating at higher frequencies from that of visible matter. The deficient sensory organs of the physical (densely material) body, i.e. the five senses, are incapable of encompassing the entire range of real matter in their perceptive ability, so as to render it perceptible to man.

> **[159] SIMON SINGH, 'BIG BANG'**
>
> *Andromache Spanou (M.Sc. in Theoretical Physics), translator of the above work, notes* (p. 271): «The colors of the rainbow are infinite, and not only the visible seven (violet, cyan, blue, green, yellow, orange, red). Our physical eye cannot see the ultra-violet radiation (the one that is before the violet of our visible spectrum), nor the infrared (the one following red).»
>
> *And the writer goes on:* «Most people use the word 'light' to describe only those waves we can see, but physicists use the term to generally describe any kind of visible or **invisible** electromagnetic radiation.»

Man's material form, his material body, is simply a carrier with very imperfect sensors.

> **[160] A) DANEZIS M., THEODOSIOU S. 'COSMOLOGY OF THE INTELLECT' (FROM THE THESIS OF GEORGIOU, G., DROUGAS, A.,** 'CYBERNETICS AND MODERN PHYSICS, 1999, MAN AS A RECEIVER AND DATA PROCESSOR – THE DELUSION OF THE SENSES')

Don't skip chapters or bibliographic references

(p. 407) «The nervous system doesn't receive all the data from a stimulus, but only what it considers useful, and interprets it by incorporating it in the context of previous experiences.

In terms of Physics: we receive electromagnetic waves of various frequencies but we perceive these stimuli as colors. We receive waves of pressure but we perceive them as words. We incept chemical combinations from the air and water, but we sense them as odors and tastes. All these colors, sounds, odors, tastes do not really exist on their own, **but are mentally created in the brain through sensory processing.** …What this means is that man's perceptions are not direct sensory recordings of the physical world that surrounds us, but are created internally, according to innate rules and limitations that are imposed by the abilities of the nervous system. Kant named these innate limitations 'prognosis' *(foreknowledge)* and believed that the mind is not a passive receptor of sensory impressions but has such a structure that it adapts to conceptual or objective pre-existing categories like space, time and causality, which exist independently of the physical stimulation of the body. Space, time and causality are of course very different concepts than their counterparts described in Physics. This, in combination with the fact that perception is based on immediate sensory recording, presents us with a sense of skepticism in regards to our ability as humans to totally and **objectively** interpret the physical world that surrounds us.»

B) PLATO'S 'PHAEDO, OR ABOUT THE PSYCHE' [=SOUL], ATHANASOPOULOS I., K. (83a): «The lovers of knowledge, then, I say, know that philosophy, after taking possession of the soul …tries to redeem it (set it free), pointing out that investigation through the eyes is full of deceit, as well as, through the ears and the other senses, urging the soul to withdraw from these, except in so far as their use is unavoidable. The soul should also *(according to philosophy)* collect and concentrate itself within itself, and trust nothing except itself, because <u>only by its own pure cognition</u> {*Tr. n. 'Noesis' from 'Noùs'*} would it be able to recognize the true essence of things.»

Even natural vision is literally useless in the complete absence of light. On the contrary some animals have this sense much more developed, considering that they don't even need light to use it. For man though, light is an extremely necessary precondition for vision. If you reflect on the real abilities of the body, which literally seems to be an 'acrobat on the moment of time', then you can't but parallel the body more to a prison cell which bonds the soul and the Divine Spark, rather than the most beneficial gift. Of course, a long-lasting familiarization with anything will also bring about its acceptance.

–*What does 'acrobat on the moment of time' mean?*

–The material body seems to be 'hovering' on the moment of the present (here and now). It therefore ceases to exist in relation to the past, but it hasn't also yet come to existence for the future; it thus seems to balance on the moment of time!

Time seems to be comprised of infinite moments, like protruding rocks in a lake. Material man, in order to step on one, must leave the other. All these instances/moments, like the frames of a motion picture film, give man the sense of continuity. His life though is not a smooth sequence as he thinks, but a constant 'skip and jump' from one point to another. At each moment of his 'present', he can choose from a number of probable future points. The present is instantly transformed into the past when he crosses over to the next moment.

All this happens simply because the material body does **not** possess the needed characteristics to be **always everywhere** (ubiquitous/omnipresent). It is deficient. For every Complete Wholeness though, space-time does not constitute a barrier. For material men it is the 'yard' of their prison.

---

161 **M-BRANES AND THE DREAMS FOR UNIFICATION**
PHYSICS4U: http://www.physics4u.gr/articles/2007/m-branes.html
SOURCES: THE ELEGANT UNIVERSE OF BRIAN GREENE, CAMBRIDGE WEBPAGE FOR THE STRING THEORY, SCIENTIFIC AMERICAN, PHYSICS4U.GR –JULY 2007

«Physicists Randall and Sundrum created a model of branes in which the visible universe is a brane incorporated in a bigger universe, just like a piece of seaweed floats in the ocean. Ordinary matter is **attached** to this brane. The usual particles like electrons and protons can only exist on this brane. We humans will not be able to enter other dimensions because the particles that form our bodies —electrons, protons, neutrons— **remain attached** to this brane that constitutes our world.»

To be able to comprehend all this, you must transcend beyond the fragmented human logic, in order with the new evidence, to investigate what you finally accept as given (granted).

–*"With his thought though, man can freely move wherever he wants!"* I said.

–Precisely! This is because thought is not dense matter. It is energy. But then again, through this extremely restricting brain, this thought is encaged! The possibilities of the human brain are very limited.

---

162 **STEPHEN HAWKING** (LUCASIAN CHAIR OF THEORETICAL PHYSICS AND APPLIED MATHEMATICS AT CAMBRIDGE UNIVERSITY) **'THE UNIVERSE IN A NUTSHELL'** Gr. tr. PETRAKI M. (p. 169): «From a biological point of view, **the limit to human intelligence** is set (up to now) by the size of the brain that can pass through the narrow pelvis and the vaginal passage during the birth process.»

Don't skip chapters or bibliographic references

So, even if thought and more generally the intellect, being an energy, would obviously have unlimited possibilities on its own, constricted as it is in the human brain, it is constantly forced to succumb to the demands of matter that surrounds it.

---

163 **PLATO'S 'PHAEDO, OR ABOUT THE PSYCHE' [=SOUL]**, ATHANASOPOULOS I., K. (66b, 66c): «So long as we have the body, and the soul is 'knead together' with this **evil**, we shall never manage to acquire enough of what we desire: and by that we mean what is True. For the body forces us to countless chores to find the necessary sustenance. Moreover, if diseases come upon it they hinder our pursuit of the truth. Furthermore, the body fills us with many erotic passions and desires and fears, and all sorts of fancies and foolishness... so that, as they truly say, it really is impossible for us to logically think of anything at all, while under its (our body's) command. After all, wars and factions and battles are caused by nothing else but the body and its desires; since it is for the sake of gaining material goods that all wars arise. And we are compelled to gain those material goods for the sake of the body, like slaves to its service.»

–Yes but the human brain produces thought. Without the brain, thinking does not exist!
–The brain does not produce thought. Thought is the result of intellect and intellect is **the basic property of the Soul** and the cause of upgraded thought in man.

---

164 **A) HERMES TRISMEGISTUS**, HERMETIC TEXTS, VOL. I, RODAKIS P., TZAFEROPOULOS AP., **SPEECH XII**: «§13...The blissful god, the benevolent daemon said that the soul was to be in the body, the Noûs (mind) in the soul, the logos/reason in the Noûs, and father of all is god.»

B) CHALDEAN ORACLES, Gr. tr. ATHINOGENIS I., GRAVIGGER, P.:

(a) KROLL 47–PLACES 95- PLATO IN TIMAEUS 30B, (p. 153): «After he placed the Noûs (mind) inside the soul and the soul inside the body, he proceeded with the construction of All.»

(b) KROLL 47 – PLACES 94- PROCLUS IN TIMAEUS 336A (p. 153): «He *(the creator)* placed the Noûs in soul, and the soul inside the inert body. We were established by the father of men and gods himself.»

C) PLATO 'TIMAEUS' Gr. tr. KOUTROUMPAS D., G., 30b4-30b6 (p. 49): «So, because of this reasoning, after he placed the Noûs within the soul and the soul within the body, he fashioned the All *(the Universe)*.»

D) SALLUSTIUS 'ON THE GODS AND THE WORLD' GRAVIGGER P., CH. 16, ON THE IMMORTALITY OF THE SOUL (p. 53): «Again, every worthy soul uses Noûs (Mind); but nobody can ever produce Noûs.»

The intellect [Gr. Νόησις from Νοῦς] renders man capable –in contrast to animals– to produce every form of logical reasoning and it (the intellect) has its origin in the Soul.

The brain is a transformer and a decoder. Its ability is twofold: It primarily accepts the mental (intellectual) property of the soul and secondarily it receives the electromagnetic oscillations of the outer environment and in relation to their vibrating frequency, translates them to objects, sounds and sensations.

[165] **DANEZIS M., THEODOSIOU S. 'COSMOLOGY OF THE INTELLECT'** CH. HUMAN SELF-DELUSION (pp. 98-99): «As Heinz Von Foester –the famous Cybernetics Scientist– mentions in 1973, man doesn't perceive 'everything' that exists out in space but 'what he believes' must be there. The famous researcher points out more specifically: "…We shouldn't be surprised of this, as, in reality there is neither light nor color out there. There are only electromagnetic waves. There is no sound or music out there, but only periodical fluctuations of the air pressure. There is neither heat nor cold out there, but only molecules with more or less kinetic energy. Finally and definitely, there is no pain out there. Provided that all the previous stimuli are not encoded into neural activity, a fundamental question arises: How can the brain create the astonishing variety of this colorful world, as we perceive it from the moment we wake up and occasionally in our dreams?"

It seems, therefore, that <u>our brain perceives the things it wants and what it learns to perceive</u>. This point of view expresses in the best way, the content of the 'Anthropic [human] Principle', <u>which describes the world as a manufactured structure (ideograph) of the human senses and not as an objective reality</u>.

John K. Lilly in his book 'The Human Bio-computer' (1972) mentions: "…The cerebral cortex operates as a high-level computer and controls the structurally lower levels of the nervous system. It is a bio-computer…."

…In general, as Michael Talbot highlights in his book 'Mysticism and Modern Science' (1993), we can say that we are not born in the world. <u>We are born into something that we transform into a world.</u>

Finally, the view of Heinz Von Foester that "The environment we perceive is an invention of our brain", may be correct.

…This false sense of space, which springs from the imperfection of the known human senses and functions, almost annihilates our ability to perceive the whole essence and extent of Einstein's fourth dimension.»

Don't skip chapters or bibliographic references

Take a guitarist for example, playing a music piece. The listener's ear receives a sound oscillation, and through his brain he translates into a musical melody. At the same time, his eye receives a corresponding oscillation, which again, through his brain, gets translated into an image. These two elements then, 'convince' the individual that what he is seeing and listening is a reality, and he remains blind to the truth stating that what he sees is only a virtual expression, which the brain in its own absolute way projects.

> [166] **DANEZIS M., THEODOSIOU S. 'COSMOLOGY OF THE INTELLECT'** (p. 55): «Through our senses and the various organs that reinforce them we do **not** perceive the Universe as it really is. We merely perceive it according to our brain's ability to do so, through these most imperfect human senses. The real nature of the four-dimensional **non** Euclidean Universe is **non-perceptible** and can only be described by mathematical functions.»

So, the aetheric (quantum) decoder brain formulates the visible world, with the simultaneous collaboration of the five basic senses. Each one of the five senses decodes (through the brain) the received information which is in the form of oscillations from the surrounding world. Consequently, the brain, along with the combined collaboration of all the senses, composes the world that surrounds man.

As an example of what I am telling you, I will refer to a situation that commonly occurs to people: At times, when someone is quite tired and is lying in bed ready to fall asleep, it so happens that he is suddenly startled by an intense sensation of 'falling into the emptiness/abyss', and being half asleep wakes up again. Do you know what this means?

–*I nodded negatively and waited for his explanation.*

–The moment a man is ready to fall asleep, consciousness is the first to withdraw. At a second phase, the brain starts 'shutting down' some of its decoders/switches. Occasionally though, due to fatigue, this withdrawal sequence changes and the brain shuts its decoders before consciousness is completely withdrawn. Then the sensation that man is really inside the void and falling, **is literal**.

> [167] **DANEZIS M., THEODOSIOU S. 'COSMOLOGY OF THE INTELLECT'**: «T. A. Whiller (1968): **Everything** in the universe is **oscillations** inside nothing.»

–*And what is consciousness?*

–Consciousness is the **resultant** of all astro-aetheric-mental bodies of man, which we will examine later.

During sleep, the bonds of these bodies loosen up and then some of these (bodies) 'travel' into their corresponding planes/dimensions, wherefrom they carry information in the form of dreams. The body that exclusively does most of the 'traveling' is the astral one, which is the source of wishes, fears and feelings (suppressed or expressed) of men. This is why some people get confused and interpret dreams exclusively as manifestations of deeper desires, since, of course, desires originate from this body.

The combined cooperation of the five basic senses therefore, finally composes what appears to the perception of humans as the 'cosmos'.

These stimuli that the human brain receives from two different origins (from the intellect of the soul and from the environment), embrace each other, and in a broader surrounding formulated by emotions stemming from the astral body, compose every man's idiosyncrasy. Thus, the only thing the physical brain does is to simply receive, decode and project the results —once processed— literally composing a **virtual reality**. Just as the heart is a pump for blood circulation and the kidneys its cleaners, so does the brain not generate thought, as the heart does not generate blood. It solely formulates what it receives, to make it perceptible to the material man.

I looked at him with some doubt.

–"So we disagree with each other, like those in the riddle, on whether the egg produced the chicken or the chicken produced the egg," *he said laughing.*

–And yet; it was the properties of the soul that generated the abilities of thought and intellect inside man. Have a little patience, and all will fall into place as our discussion evolves.

Through this restricted ideo-receptive sensitivity of man, his material body resembles an upgraded machine —an extremely inhibiting factor— rather than a means to spiritual evolution.

> [168] **STEPHEN HAWKING – 'THE UNIVERSE IN A NUTSHELL'** [Gr. tr. PETRAKI M.] CH. BIOLOGY-ELECTRONICS INTERFACE (p. 170): «In the next twenty years a computer worth a thousand dollars might be as complex as the human brain. Parallel processors might be able to mimic the way our brain functions and render computers capable of functioning in an intelligent and conscious way.
> Neuronic implants could allow a much faster interface between the brain and computers, thus minimizing the distance between biological and electronic intelligence. In the near future, most business transactions could be carried out by 'cyber-personae' through the World Wide Web. In a decade, many of us may choose to live virtual lives on the Internet, developing cyber-friendships and cyber-relations.»

As we previously stated, in order for man to function in the physical environment, an environment which, after all, is comprised exclusively of energies, he should have the ability to formulate, to feel and to handle these energies. At the same time, the instinctive drive for self-preservation had to

Don't skip chapters or bibliographic references

exist inside him, or he would face the danger of extinction. Following that, man had to be programmed through 'instructions' recorded in his genetic code, with the dictate for the continuation of his species. He had to be dominated by emotions enabling him to express every one of his needs, as well as have the ability to actively claim, in order to fulfill his goals. The completion in other words of man, demanded a set of parameters which would support/complete his existence.

A series then of 'material' energy-bodies, starting from the denser material and moving towards the adjacent finer/subtler ones, served the purpose of the smooth 'functioning' of man, while at the same time enabling him to perceive energies of higher frequencies. At least those that were necessary to him. Because, let's keep in mind, there is a whole gamut of energies and frequencies that the deficient physical body does not perceive, unless it is aided by advanced technological apparatuses, which in the end verify the existence of those frequencies.

---

[169] **SIMON SINGH 'BIG BANG'** (p. 271): *Andromache Spanou (M. Sc. in Theoretical Physics), translator of the above work notes:* «The colors of the rainbow are infinite, and not only the visible seven (violet, cyan, blue, green, yellow, orange, red). Our physical eye cannot see the ultra-violet radiation (the one that is before the violet of our visible spectrum), nor the infrared (the one following red).»

So, six bodies surround the Divine Spark, the other half of the true Celestial Man, and each one has its own characteristics. While man leads his daily life, all bodies surrounding him are at the same time in their respective fields. Thus, as his physical body lives daily in the densely material plane, his aetheric body exists in the aetheric plane, his astral in the astral plane and so forth. Let us proceed then to a guided tour of these bodies and also the energy-fields in which these bodies are.

AETHERIC BODY – AETHERIC PLANE

DANEZIS, M., THEODOSIOU, S., 'COSMOLOGY OF THE INTELLECT' (p. 99) "The Universe however is just a mere manifestation of another non-Euclidean, hyper-sensory hyperspace that coexists with the Universe sensed by us, **but nevertheless (this hyperspace) remains invisible** to our human senses."

---

[170] **DANEZIS M., THEODOSIOU S. 'COSMOLOGY OF THE INTELLECT'** (p. 79)
CH. 'FOURTH DIMENSION AND METAPHYSICS': «As Max Jammer states in his book 'Concepts of Space' *(University of Crete Publications, Heraklion 2001)* "…It is intriguing to know that the idea of the fourth dimension was met with great enthusiasm by the spiritualistic circles. Henry Moore had already applied this concept in his spiritualistic conception which he called 'apissitudo essentialis' (essential density). In his 'Enchiridion metaphysicum' he writes: …Supernatural phenomena, which are demonstrated by spiritualists in various séances of theirs, are interpreted based on the hypothesis of a fourth dimension."
From this aspect, very well-known are the experiments that German professor of Astronomy J. Zollner conducted in Leipzig, which many of his distinguished colleagues witnessed. Experiments of a topological nature, like the untying of knots enclosed in closed thread-loops, or the infamous happenings that are known as 'apports' (retrievals), namely the sudden materialization and telekinesis of an object out of nowhere, were interpreted as movements or processes in the fourth space-dimension.»

The aetheric body is the next subtler material body, after the physical/material one. It is a pattern/template upon which the absolutely physical body is structured.

---

[171] **RUDOLF STEINER** (1861-1925) **'OCCULT SCIENCE'** CH. WHAT IS MAN (p. 46): «The aetheric body completely permeates the physical body in all its parts and fills it throughout. It is to be seen as the architect of the physical body, so to speak. All the organs of the physical body are maintained in their form and structure by the currents and movements of the aetheric body. Our physical heart is based on the aetheric heart; our physical brain is based on the aetheric brain and so on. The aetheric body is differentiated (multipartite), just like the physical body, but it's more complicated. In the aetheric body, everything is in a living, flowing state of interpenetration, whereas in the physical body, there are distinctly separate parts.»

Some people call it 'aura' and others 'pranic body' (prana). The aetheric body is connected to the physical one with energy-bonds and it operates in

Don't skip chapters or bibliographic references

the aetheric plane, which exists as an energy-dimension inside the material universe. The basic 'sensation' of this body is the feeling of self-preservation. Whatever is inflicted onto one body will afterwards affect the other. But it is mainly the aetheric body that suffers first in case of illness, and then carries the disease to the physical. It is onto this body that home-opathic medicine bases its therapeutic successes.

> [172] *This is why the more we dilute homeopathic medicines with water, the stronger they become, since, through the technical process they undergo, the aetheric part of the herb is activated.*

Every organ, every bone, every nerve, every cell group of this body (the aetheric) is structured on 'number concepts'.

> [173] **A) SAKELLARIOU, G.,** (Philosophy Prof. Univ. Of Athens) **'PYTHAGORAS, THE TEACHER OF THE AEONS'** CH. LIVING PROPERTIES OF NUMBERS (p. 173):
> «It is worth noting, that this theory of Pythagoras regarding the properties of numbers, fits into the Pythagorean Philosophical System in various combinations, as: 1) Numbers that classify the primordial principles of the being, 2) Numbers that signify the conceptual order, 3) Numbers viewed in terms of relativity and **as coefficients of form,** 4) Numbers symbolizing the elements, 5) Numbers symbolizing ideas, 6) Numbers as an international language and 7) Numbers related to the Arian religion.
> (p. 174)…According to the Pythagoreans then, numbers, although they seemingly determine the quantitative relations among perceivable things, they are constituent points of the ALL and take part both in the noetic (=higher mental/intellectual from the Gr. w. 'Νοῦς'= Mind) as well as the material in a parallel fashion. Furthermore, the Pythagoreans, generalizing this belief, in which every order in the world is a manifestation of harmony and presupposes arithmetic analogies, *(conclude)*…that man's Soul is a number, the essence of beings is a number, and that the similar can be known (understood) by the similar.»
> **B) THE SECRET BOOK OF DZYAN, 'COSMIC EVOLUTION', STANZA IV:**
> «§1 Listen, ye sons of the Earth, to your instructors --the sons of the Fire. Learn, there is neither first nor last, **for all is one number** issued from no number."
> **C) BLAVATSKY H., P., 'THE SECRET DOCTRINE'** (I-66): "In the 'Book of Dzyan', as in the Kabala, there are two kinds of numerals to be studied –the figures, often simple blinds *(misleading)*, and the Sacred Numbers, the values of which are all known to the Occultists through Initiation. The former is but a conventional glyph, the latter is the basic symbol of all. That is to say, that one is purely physical, the other purely metaphysical, the two standing in relation to each other as matter stands to spirit –the extreme poles of the

ONE Substance. As Balzac, the unconscious Occultist of French literature, says somewhere, the Number is to Mind the same as it is to matter: 'an incomprehensible agent'; (perhaps so to the profane, but never to the Initiated mind). Number is, as the great writer thought, an Entity, and, at the same time, a Breath emanating from what he called God and what we call the ALL; the breath which alone could organize the physical Kosmos, where naught obtains its form but through the Deity, which is an effect of Number.»

Numbers in the sense people understand them in their everyday life, are images or symbols of living concepts. Thousands of number-concept groups in various combinations aetherically build the pattern/template upon which the material/physical body of man is then built. Every incorrect 'number concept' in a group/system creates a problem and disharmony which in turn affects the material body with the onset of an illness.

Whatever material form exists in the physical/material world also exists in the aetheric.

174 **'MYSTERIES OF THE WORLD', VOL. 'MYSTERIES OF THE EARTH'**

KIRLIAN PHOTOGRAPHY: «Many Esotericists believe that the aura of living organisms and objects can become visible through a unique photographic method, the Kirlian photography. Russian electronic engineer Semën Davidovič Kirlian…during the years 1939 and 1958 developed a photographic method utilizing the effect of a very high frequency current, the so called Kirlian photography.

PHANTOM LEAF: A phenomenon first observed in a laboratory in South America, created a great stir. In a Kirlian photograph, the radiation of an entire leaf was depicted, even though part of it had been previously removed.»

People usually say that, for example, a particular substance may cause cancer. They don't know however, that what usually causes an illness is the aetheric existence of the substance when it interferes with man's aetheric body, detunes the integrity of the structure of its 'number concepts', resulting to the appearance of the disease. This however is only one side of the story. There is another completely different dimension to this issue, which will be examined later.

Your scientists today have detected through quantum physics a finer form of matter encompassing the densely material universe. They call this matter 'dark matter'. They call it dark because it is thinner/subtler and thus <u>not</u> visible to your physical eyes. This dark matter is precisely the aetheric plane/aether/template of all that exists in the visible universe and all that is constructed, in order to later materialize.

Don't skip chapters or bibliographic references

[175] *Once a metaphysicist becomes acquainted with the behavior of the 'aetheric', he will realize that it is EXACTLY THE SAME with the behavior of 'dark matter'.*

A) 'DARK MATTER ACCUMULATES FIRST AND THEN THE GALAXY IS FORMED'
http://www.physics4u.gr/news/2006/scnews2503.html SOURCE: NASA NEWS 16/06 /2006:

«A new study from NASA's Spitzer space telescope suggests that **galaxies are formed within large masses of dark matter**. This mysterious substance emits no light but it has mass and therefore can attract matter-matter *(dense matter)* with its **gravitational force**. Astronomers believe that there is five times more dark matter in the world than normal matter. …Initially, researchers were trying to better comprehend how new galaxies and dark matter, evolve and accumulate together. …At that point they observed something odd: Every galaxy they studied seemed to be surrounded by 'chunks' of dark matter of approximately the **same** size. They were able to indirectly measure how much dark matter –holding the structure together like glue– was present. The tighter the grouping [concentration] was, the greater the amount of dark matter,present.»

B) COSMIC COLLISION REVEALS DARK MATTER, JANUARY 2007
http://www.physics4u.gr/articles/2007/top_space_stories_2006.html:

«If dark matter exists, then it must be present here on earth as well. The next step for physicists is to detect it in a laboratory here on earth. This effort began a few months ago when the Cryogenic Dark Matter Search (CDMS) experiment was initiated, buried one kilometer beneath the ground, in an old mine in Minnesota, in order to provide protection from cosmic rays.»

C) THEORY INTERPRETS THE BEHAVIOR OF DARK MATTER ASSUMING THE EXISTENCE OF THREE ADDITIONAL DIMENSIONS
SOURCE: SCIENCE NEWS.GR 09/09/2005
http://www.sciencenews.gr/index.php?option=com_content&task=view&id=94&itemid=37

«An astrophysics research team claims it has discovered evidence proving that the universe has six dimensions. Joseph Silk from Oxford University in the UK and his colleagues claim that these additional spatial dimensions are the result of the complex behavior of dark matter. This mysterious substance is not visible, but its presence in the galaxies is evident from the gravitational force it exerts on visible stars.»

D) ADDITIONAL DIMENSIONS OFFER NEW POSSIBILITIES TO SOLVE OLD MYSTERIES ARTICLE OF NIMA ARKANI HAMED, SLAC RESEARCH LIBRARY
http://www.physics4u.gr/articles/fifthdim.html

«In our everyday lives we appear to live in four dimensions, three spatial ones and one dimension of time. But in the previous months, theoretical physicists discovered that the collisions between high-energy particles in particle-accelerators can reveal the presence of extra space-time dimensions.»

E) THE KALUZA-KLEIN THEORY http://www.physics4u.gr/strings/string6.html: «The notion that our universe can have more than the three familiar spatial dimensions was introduced by Teodor Kaluza and Oscar Klein, fifty years before the formulation of the string theory.»

F) STRING THEORY / SIX DIMENSIONS, PHYSICS4U.GR
http://www.physics4u.gr/news/2000/scnews4.html:
«In order for the required space to be given to the strings so that they can serve their unique function, scientists had to add six extra dimensions, which are so closely interwoven with each other that particle accelerators the size of an entire galaxy, would be required to examine them.»

Most mediums as well as the prophets, sneaking a peek at this plane/dimension, can prophesize 'what is to come' because it happens in the aetheric plane first. The same holds true with prophetic dreams.

This aethereal plane/dimension then is the primary design location of everything material. In the plant kingdom, the aetheric is the only body encompassing the absolutely dense material one. Therein lies the difference between plants, animals and man. Plants only have a physical and an aetheric body. Animals have a physical, an aetheric and an astral body and man has all that was briefly mentioned beforehand, when we spoke of the second phase of self-knowledge. Now as far as the inorganic world is concerned, it is also enveloped by the aetheric plane, but the template woven for it, is more simplified compared to the others.

In the aetheric plane/dimension, all powers of construction and maintenance of matter exist. Included in them is not only the mindless potential for the design of dense matter, but also a whole community of intelligent entities that handle the tools of structure (form). There, the following hierarchy of entities exists: At the top are the seven Elohims of creation *(third class of creators, the commanders of fate or 'Heimarmenē')* who are not of course solely confined to this plane, but can move to all energy areas/dimensions of the universe. The entire material creation (visible and invisible) is distributed and assigned to the supervision of these seven, ultimate in power, wisdom and magnitude Elohims. Each Elohim has under his control, and in accordance to the objective of his creation, the corresponding categories of Devas. There is a very big number of Devas, different for each species/kind of creation. Each Deva has under its rule armies of elementals. They may be elemental-dwarfs, Nereids/Undines, Nymphs, Fairies, Salamanders, Mermaids, Sylphides and all the beings mentioned in old folktales.

Don't skip chapters or bibliographic references

> [176] **JORGE ÁNGEL LIVRAGA RIZZI, 'LOS ESPÍRITUS ELEMENTALES DE LA NATU-
> RALEZA' [THE ELEMENTAL SPIRITS OF NATURE, AN ESOTERIC STUDY]** - MADRID,
> NUEVA ACRÓPOLIS: «The elementals have energy-forms as bodies and are not
> strictly physical or material in the common expression of the term, even
> though energy is also material and its results are evident on a daily basis.
> ...Elementals usually have their most dense part or body in the energy- or
> pranic-field and they can, under favorable conditions, be mirrored (reflect-
> ed) and assume a certain materialization in the aetheric zones. These zones
> are the connection between what we could call energy (whose characteris-
> tic is the loss of perceptible form for our senses) and matter, whose charac-
> teristics are clearer to us. ...Their main property is a plasticity (the ability
> to change form) far speedier than ours and their forms are much more un-
> stable and dynamic.»

All these energy-beings have the sole purpose of weaving, maintaining,
transmuting and reconstructing matter like good and obedient workers of
nature in its entirety. These beings can be perceived by sensitive people easily, because the plane they dwell in is adjacent to the densely material one.

> [177] **ENCYCLOPEDIA DOMI, 'MYSTERIES OF THE WORLD'**, VOL. 'SECRET MESSAGES'
> (p. 396): «Iceland is the country with the greatest tradition of legends relating
> to gnomes. Characteristic is the fact that the **Hafnarfjordhur** tourist map
> also includes the areas where gnomes dwell. In Reykjavik there is the one
> and only Gnome School of the world, in which students are taught, among
> other things, to recognize and identify the 79 kinds of spirits like fairies,
> elves, and spirits of the plants, which emit a characteristic aroma of a flower,
> of a healing plant or tree. ...Nature's spirits incarnate the four elements of
> nature and live in a parallel world, avoiding man.»

At the early stages of man's creation, at that turning point when Australopithecus was slowly being transformed into Homo (man), these microscopic creatures of the aetheric plane taught the first men the secrets of nature
as well as the properties of plants and herbs. A great portion of this
knowledge did not come through observation of nature alone, but also
through the suggestions of qualified elementals to the juvenile mankind.
Following the development of that close relationship between mankind and
the elementals, man's greed increased and so did his demands from that
kingdom, resulting in the conversion of the obedient elemental-dwarfs into
subdued bondservants.

[178] **PAPASTAVROU, A., 'LETTERS TO ANONYMOUS'**: «Like all nature's powers, so are the element-dwarfs extreme mimickers. With the obedience vows they gave to man, they reflect what they see –regardless of whether this is good or bad. Many of the aetheric element-dwarfs were facially contorted after mimicking what they saw man create through the ill-bearing use of words, thoughts and emotions, which he (man) attracted around him through his bad use of the life-energy. These element-dwarfs also became malevolent, cunning and ill-intended by nature and enjoyed mocking men –their torturers.»

Right then however, new decisions made by the authorities of creation had as a result the end of that disharmonious relationship and confined every 'rogue' to his own plane only.

[179] **THEODOSIADIS N., 'GNOMES'**, «Old stories say that, the worlds of men and gnomes were once one and undivided, but something happened to divide it in two, and since then, each party has lived in their own separate part of the world.»

–And yet science claims that nature has self-sufficiency and that each natural phenomenon follows exclusively natural laws for its change and evolution. Where can the aetheric plane fit in this absolutely logical point of view of science?
–Every plane/field has its own laws. With very fine threads, all planes are interconnected. For example, what compelled scientists to investigate the (finer/subtler) dark matter, was the quest for the origin/root/cause from which the force called gravity stems. The denser material plane has its own natural laws. These laws however don't exist independently or exclusively in one plane/field! It is in a neighboring dimension that **the cause** of these laws lies. The cause lies in the aetheric field and the manifestation in the material one. To make this clearer: In heavy matter, things evolve in their own way but the stings/threads of these laws/ways are moved/pulled from elsewhere.

[180] **THEORY EXPLAINS DARK MATTER'S BEHAVIOR, ASSUMING THE EXISTENCE OF THREE ADDITIONAL DIMENSIONS.** SOURCE: SCIENCE NEWS.GR 09/09/2005
http://www.sciencenews.gr/index.php?option=com_content&task=view&id=94&itemid=37
«One explanation, they say, is that the three additional dimensions, besides the three spatial ones which we are accustomed to, **change the effects of gravity** in very small distances. …This mysterious dark matter is not visible, **but its presence in the galaxies becomes perceptible <u>through the gravitational attraction it exerts on visible stars</u>**.»

Don't skip chapters or bibliographic references

What the physical man receives through his five, extremely restricting senses is a series of **consequences** caused by a sequence of events of a much deeper origin. One does not cancel the other. It just adds to it.

---

[181] **DANEZIS M., THEODOSIOU S. 'COSMOLOGY OF THE INTELLECT'** (p. 55): «In this new physical reality, what we have been calling matter up-to-now –based on **the delusion of human sensory organs**– is elegantly described by **Charles Muses** in his book *'Consciousness and reality' (1972)*. "...All observable objects are three-dimensional images formed by **waves** that are still or moving (under the influence of electromagnetic and nuclear processes). All objects in the world are three-dimensional pictures formed into images of a hyper-hologram, in an electromagnetic way."

An additional reminder:

(p. 55): Through our senses and the various organs that reinforce them we do not perceive the Universe as it really is. We merely perceive it according to our brain's ability to do so, through these most imperfect human senses. **The real nature** of the four-dimensional non Euclidean Universe is non-perceptible and can only be described by mathematical functions.»

An example will render this mechanism clearer to you: A computer program directs the movements of a sewing machine embroidering a table cloth. Man only sees the sewing machine embroidering. He knows nothing about the program.

He looked at me inquisitively to see if I had understood. I remained silent. I was trying to put the new puzzle pieces together into a complete picture. Old and new data were arranged disorderly in my mind. Logical deductions sprang out and demanded new explanations. Some answers came about almost instantly from the new evidence I now had in my possession. Others still remained obscure.

–"Let us continue the conversation," I said, "and I believe that in the end, the cycle of my queries will close."

LOWER MENTAL BODY – LOWER MENTAL PLANE

–When counting from the denser to the finer energy-bodies, next one in line is the astral. Nevertheless, for a better understanding, we will first describe the lower mental body with its corresponding plane.

The lower mental body is connected to man's physical material brain through energy-bonds, and forms the lower mental field/plane which is one of the higher sub-planes of the astral world.

The creator blew a 'living intelligent breath' inside man. This living sentient breath of the Creator was the so-called 'Soul'.

> **182** **A) OLD TESTAMENT, GENESIS CH. 2**: «§7. And the Lord God made man from the dust of the earth (ground)· and he blew the breath of life into his nostrils; and man became a living soul.»
>
> **B) THE APOCRYPHON OF JOHN, THE GNOSTIC SOCIETY LIBRARY**: «And he *(the Creator)* blew into his *(the human's)* face the spirit, which is the power of his Mother; he was not aware of this because he exists in ignorance. And the power of the Mother **came out of Yaldabaoth and went into the psychic body** *(soul)* that they had made according to the likeness of the One who exists from the beginning.» [Eng. tr. from Coptic: FREDERIK WISSE]

Inside the primitive man, the newly-born Soul started building a connection bridge with his physical/material substance in order to transmit its properties to it. Following that the mental energy which the physical brain started to produce through thought (under the soul's influence), formed the lower mental body which was situated in the lower mental field respectively. This influence resulted in the re-formulation of the material logical brain in man.

The procedure of creation, formulation, and refinement of the physical brain, under the influence of the noûs of the soul, inside the 'sloweddown' *(mass of tranquility)* pure-matter dimension spread out into thousands of years of slow

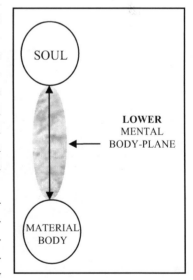

transmutation. This transmutation created the chain of anthropoids, where one species with a more developed brain than its predecessor, finally evolved into modern man.

Don't skip chapters or bibliographic references

People often confuse the feelings of the astral body with the properties of the soul and imagine they (emotions) are products of the soul. Emotions however, many of which are also experienced by animals, are the characteristic property of the astral body. On the contrary, **the soul is the exclusive possessor of intellect** and is the carrier of Noûs (Intellect).

---

183 **A) HERMES TRISMEGISTUS,** HERMETIC TEXTS, VOL. I, RODAKIS P., TZAFEROPOULOS AP., **SPEECH XII** (p. 193): «§13…The blissful god, the benevolent daemon said that the soul was to be in the body, <u>the Noûs (mind) in the soul</u>, the logos/reason in the Noûs, and father of all is god.»

B) CHALDEAN ORACLES, Gr. tr. ATHINOGENIS I., GRAVIGGER, P., KROLL 47–PLACES 95- PLATO IN TIMAEUS 30B, (p. 153): «<u>After he placed the Noûs (mind) inside the soul</u> and the soul inside the body, he proceeded with the construction of All.»

C) PLATO'S 'TIMAEUS' Gr. tr. KOUTROUMPAS G., (30b4-30b6, p. 49): «So, because of this reasoning, after <u>he placed the Noûs within the soul</u> and the soul within the body, he fashioned the All *(universe)*.»

D) SALLUSTIUS 'ON THE GODS AND THE WORLD' GRAVIGGER P., CH. 16, ON THE IMMORTALITY OF THE SOUL (p. 53): «Again, every worthy soul uses Noûs (Mind); <u>but not a single body can ever produce Noûs.</u>»

The lower mental plane, which is located at the higher layers of the astral world, is where **pure thought,** devoid of emotions, ends up. There lie all scientific achievements of man 'in form', as well as all historic events (in the form of knowledge) that humanity has ever lived through. It is there that metaphysicists place the 'Akashic Archives'.

---

184 *Astral 'libraries' with the entire course of humanity recorded (imprinted) in them.*

A) RUDOLF STEINER 'APOCRYPHAL SCIENCE' CH. COSMIC EVOLUTION AND THE HUMAN BEING, 1909 (p. 106): «These imperishable eternal traces of everything spiritual may be called the 'AKASHIC RECORD' (Akashic Chronicle), if we designate the spiritually lasting element in world events as their Akashic essence, as opposed to their transient/expiring *(material)* forms. And it must be stated here again, that research into the supersensible realms of existence can only be carried out with the help of spiritual perception, which in this case means reading the AKASHIC CHRONICLE.»

B) RUDOLF STEINER 'FROM THE AKASHIC CHRONICLE', CH. COSMIC MEMORY (p. 20): «This history is written in letters different from the ordinary. In Gnosis and Anthroposophy it is called 'the Akashic Chronicle'. Only a faint conception of this chronicle can be given in our language. Because our language corresponds to the sensory/perceived world and whatever is defined

---

by our language, immediately embodies the character of this sensory/perceived world.

…Whoever has acquired the ability to see/perceive in the Spiritual World comes to know past events in their eternal character. They do not stand before him like the dead testimony of history, but appear in full life. In a certain sense, what has happened takes place before him.»

C) SAKELLARIOS G., (PROF. OF PHILOSOPHY, UNIV. OF ATHENS) 'PYTHAGORAS, THE TEACHER OF THE CENTURIES' CH. COSMIC MEMORY: «Pythagoras believed that the Cosmos contains a record of everything that happens in the universe… So, he attributed a Cosmic Memory to it (to the Universe), which receives and eternally holds all the impressions of experiences and observations. Furthermore, Pythagoras considered this Cosmic Memory to be a lake or tank, from where ideas are projected as thought-waves to be captured by spirits acting as 'receivers.'»

The brain, besides its ability to decode energy-frequencies –of the surrounding world– and the messages of intelligent soul, also has the ability to record and process data and information in order to produce results, like a high-performance 'computer'.

185 'QUANTUM MEMORIES WILL IMITATE OURS' SOURCE: NATURE, 6/8/2001
http://www.geocities.com/grhysics/news/scnews290.html: «According to Carlo Trugenberger of InfoCodex in Geneva, quantum memories of future computers will be like our brain. Quantum computer engineers will have to design memories like our own, storing information as patterns rather than putting each item to its own labeled box, as in conventional computers.»

In very general terms, man's brain follows a specific course: When man is born, the brain certainly has no records. It is a blank brain. Step by step, collecting data from its environment, either as living experiences or as knowledge acquired through learning and education, it starts building memories. The sum of the data it has gathered constitutes the foundation (database) upon which its intellectual construction will be erected later on, and all this information is situated and enriches the so-called 'Akashic Archives'.

Every material man through his lower mental body –which resides in the lower mental plane/dimension– has access to his **personal** 'Akashic vault', located at the higher astral sub-planes. All the information he collects in his life is written in that 'Akashic vault'. Every time a piece of information needs to be retrieved or a solution be given to a problem, a specialized brain function comes into action to access the **personal** 'Akashic **energy** vault': Information is retrieved and the required result is produced. Following that, men **mistakenly** think that information is

Don't skip chapters or bibliographic references

recorded in the material brain and scientists search for it there in vain. This is why these recent years they have turned their search more towards energy-areas than material ones −namely quantum regions. The so-called 'brain synapses' are simply the 'keys' with which old and new accounts access each personal 'Akashic energy-issue/vault'.

So, all human memories are located and sorted out in this energy region/dimension. Today neuro-psychiatrists of your world make clear that every remembrance that comes to man either as a result of educational knowledge or as biome/experience, can be maintained as knowledge/memory/remembrance only if there is simultaneous emotional involvement. Metaphysics supports this view because in order for any information to be archived in the 'Akashic Archives' of the lower mental plane −which is located in the higher sub-level of the astral world− it must **necessarily** pass through the astral plane encased/enveloped by some emotion.

With this function of thought though, a problem arose for material creation: Thought generated emotions and emotions thoughts. Thus the lower mental body started supplying the whole astral/emotional plane/field with thoughtforms.

A very large stratification of emotions and thoughtforms also created the corresponding zones, or sub-planes, or gradations of the astral world. The darker/more negative the thoughtforms are, the lower the sub-planes of the astral plane will be to receive them. The more positive/luminous they are, the higher the astral layers they will be placed at. All of them though are included in the area called the astral plane.

ASTRAL BODY — ASTRAL PLANE

In order for every animal and man as well to be able to function in the physical environment and for the characteristics of the 'Ego' and the 'I will' to develop, the existence of the astral body of emotions was necessary.

> [186] **HERMES TRISMEGISTUS, HERMETIC TEXTS, VOL. II**, RODAKIS P., TZAFERO-POULOS AP., **'EXCERPT IV**, HERMES TO TAT': «§18...Wherefore I say that, feelings are both corporeal and mortal, as they resemble the *(material)* body in constitution... §19. On the contrary, Immortal Bodies have no feeling, precisely because they are immortal; feeling is nothing more than the pre-existence of good or evil in the body, or their departure/absence. Whereas in the Immortal Bodies nothing is born and nothing dies; therefore feeling does not exist in them.
> ...§23. –Is feeling[1] a body, father, or does it just happen to be in the body? –If we consider it [the feeling] incorporeal inside the body, we will accept it as equal to the soul or the energies [2]; for these, even though they are incorporeal, we say, exist inside bodies· whereas the feeling is neither energy *(Essence-Spirit)* nor soul, nor something else incorporeal; hence it couldn't be incorporeal; **had it not therefore been incorporeal, it could be a body;** for of the beings, some must be bodies and others incorporeal.»
>
> [1] **Feeling:** *Refers to the <u>emotions</u> of joy and sorrow.*
> [2] **Energy:** *With the word 'energy' he means <u>Essence-Spirit</u>.*

Through this energy-body all emotions are manifested, and in affinity to man's soul they expand the palette of emotional colorations.

As the material body has its own five (main) senses, so does the astral one possess its own 'senses', which are essentially the supply source of the Ego. It is in this body that kindness and meanness, passions and desires, hatred and tolerance, satisfaction and disappointment, compassion and revenge, lust, jealousy and anger have their origin. The astral body is the foundation/base of the 'Ego' and 'Will'. It is the realm wherefrom they are both supplied with good or bad feelings. It is the energy body which is enriched and expanded by the energy produced by man through his daily activity during his material life. All energy situations that man experiences emotionally during his life accumulate and build his astral/energy/emotional body. As the fruit starts from the flower bud, grows (plumps up), reaches its normal size (depending on the species)

Don't skip chapters or bibliographic references

and then starts to ripen, so too is man's astral body initially built, after-wards expands and finally, during old age, reaches maturity.

The astral, quite like the aetheric body, starts its creation in the womb. Just like the plant's seed has all the necessary instructions for the complete for-mation of an aethero-physical tree encoded inside it, so does the egg com-bined with the spermatozoon, carry in its genes the weaving code, not only for the absolutely physical but also for the other two bodies; the aetheric and the astral one. The entrance of the Soul and the Divine Spark in the fetus occurs only when some basic conditions have been met. Thus, whereas the physical, the aetheric and the astral bodies are the outcome of genes, the Soul and the Spirit remain independent of the genetic factor and heredity.

Of course, for this astral body, the entire creation had to pay a very heavy price! ... We will now speak of this briefly and later in our discussion we will analyze where the 'basis' of this plane came from, as well as the prima-ry 'ingredient' from which it is built.

ೞ··ക

The astral body –the body of desires and emotions– is situated inside the astral plane/dimension, just as the roots of a tree are inside the soil. This plane is created and expanded by the emotionally tinted energy of the thoughts of all **intelligent** beings.

All thoughtforms generated by the thoughts of all men that have ever lived on this Earth have assumed form and exist in the astral field. The emotional-ly 'colored' energy of thoughts accumulates in this energy-area of the uni-verse. Then pure thought is separated from emotion. Pure thought (devoid of emotions) is incorporated into the areas forming the lower mental plane –as the higher layer of the astral plane– and emotion is registered to the lower astral regions, where, depending on its kind, merges with similar ones and expands the higher and the lower astral.

There, meanness, hatred, kindness, revenge and compassion accumulate and create unified teams of similar emotions and energy-conditions. All emotions of meanness, revenge and hatred have merged and created what men call the Devil. Respectively, unified groups are formed by pos-itive thoughtforms. But the negative energies, armed by their nature with extra dynamism, in contrast to the nature of the positive ones, persistent-ly claim ever more and larger shares... So, born from the thought of ma-terial man, they strive to go on existing, supplied with new emotions kindred to them and urge man (as temptations) to actions and deeds,

186

which will generate new negative thoughtforms in order to increase the size of the already existing evil.

> [187] **ENOCH'S APOCRYPHON CH. 15**: «§8. And now the giants born by the coherence of spirit and flesh shall be called on earth evil spirits and on earth shall be their habitation. They will in their turn bear evil spirits …and they will be called **spirits of evil**. …§9. The spirits of the giants, the Napheleim (Nephelim) *[Anc. Gr. original text]* shall bring all sorts of inflictions (scourge) to earth, cholera, war, famine and lamentation. §10. They will neither eat food nor drink, <u>invisible to the sight</u> *(they are the astral beings)* and they will rise even against men and women, <u>for they have received life from them</u>.»

So it now becomes clear that: temptations on one hand are provoked by the negative astral society (devil), and trials (tests) by the creator/god (Lucifer) on the other. Unfortunately, **the very same material embodiment**, through the genetically-recorded laws/instructions for the benefit of man's self-preservation in the material plane, has been the cause of birth of all astral evil. The 'instruction' itself from the god creator to his creation for its self-preservation, namely the conservation of its individuality in life, came in opposition to **the same self-preservation instruction** of another thinking being. This opposition generated animosity. Animosity created hatred. Hatred generated negativity and negativity manifested in dark thoughts and feelings, which accumulated in the astral plane. This negativity kept asking for more negativity to feed on and grow. Evil grew… It has become gigantic.

He remained pensive for a while.

–Astral plane! …The greatness of deceit and delusion and fraud! Inside this enormous astral region which is multiple times larger in size than visible matter, millions of existences (entities) live and function.

> [188] **GOSPEL OF PHILIP**, JEAN-YVES LELOUP: «§63. One is either of the world, or one is resurrected *[anastasis],* or one is in the intermediate world *(the astral plane).* God forbid that I be found there! In this world there is good and there is evil. What is good is not all good, and what is evil is not all evil. But beyond this world, **there is something that is really evil**: it is the intermediate world, the world of the dead.» [Eng. tr. JOSEPH ROWE]

Inside these worlds, a 'traveler' can meet thoughtforms ranging from the heroes of his childhood stories, to the sickest perversions of adults.

Don't skip chapters or bibliographic references

> [189] PAPASTAVROU A., 'A COSMOS WITHIN A COSMOS' CH. ASTRAL PLANE: «The astral plane was labeled as the universal memory and the cosmic picture-gallery, and this, because in it we find all skeptomorphs (thoughtforms) and every picture that man has formed in his imagination, not only in the present life of a single man, but of myriads of men and for uncountable rebirths. It is comprised of seven sections which are divided in two groups, a 'higher' and a 'lower' one.»

There, all desires and all creations lie formulated. Scattered like puzzle pieces, all the lies and fragmented truths are also there. Every astral entity can take any piece it wants and present it to humanity as the one and only truth. With the most widely used property of this dimension, i.e. masquerading, astral entities of doubtful quality, entities that may easily be either **astral shells** (not yet dissolved) of dead people, mindless **astral bodies** carrying entrapped souls inside them, or formulated **astral thoughtforms** of desires, weaknesses and negative energies of every nature, masquerade and present themselves to living men as 'celestial guides'.

> [190] PAPASTAVROU A., 'COSMOS WITHIN A COSMOS' CH. ASTRAL PLANE: «The astral plane is often called the kingdom of deception and delusion, because of the ungrounded and **unreliable** impressions an inexperienced psychic receives from it. One reason for this is that the tenants of this plane possess the miraculous power of changing their appearances with an unimaginable speed and influencing those they want to tease by causing an unsurpassed level for self-delusion to them.»

They then introduce themselves as 'saint' or 'master' So-and-so, as spiritual 'guides', extraterrestrials, intra-terrestrials, dead relatives or anything else you can imagine. These perverted astral entities, holding an advantageous position against 'lacking' humans with their five deprived senses, literally patron them, leading them to ugly situations, their sole purpose being their energy supply and entertainment. These are the information sources, which most mediums bring forth to their audiences through 'channeling'. Most of the information reaching humanity has its origins in that dimension! The lower the planes (sub-planes of the astral field) the information is received from, the 'clearer' the mediums hear the instructions in their ears. It is what some people describe as 'hearing voices', an extremely dangerous situation for their emotional, intellectual and spiritual course; the higher the planes the information comes from, the less clearly can someone 'hear' it. From the farthest energy-layers information is transferred as a sensation. This happens because the lower sub-planes of the astral are very close to the material plane and do not differ from it apart from a minute alteration of their frequency.

Of course, there is also the other, the 'upgraded' guidance too, the one coming from the creators themselves, who through their human-tools, direct and regulate the various spiritual norms of the planet on one hand, and its wider cultural, educational and technological course, in order for humanity to produce the corresponding **forms of energy** under the respective circumstances on the other. These issues though, will be more thoroughly examined later on and only after we have analyzed some more information.

–And what exactly do all these invisible powers want from man?

–Their energy supply; all creatures in nature eat one another. Do you think man would be spared from this strife? Gods and daemons contest each other, asserting their respective energy-nutrition from man.

As we have mentioned before, positive or negative emotions are the energy nutrition, whether healthy or not, that man receives from his actions or re-actions from other people. If therefore normal men have the ability to absorb energy from daily circumstances, can you imagine what quantities of energy are produced through each lifetime and how much they nourish 'those' who absorb it? ...I will try to be more specific. When after a fight, some observers walk away 'full' and afterwards 'ruminate' the incident, narrating it again and again, absorbing every little chunk of energy left from it, can you imagine how much **energy** is produced from a disease, a love disappointment or the sexual intercourse itself, misery, or even death? ...Not to mention of course state conflicts, wars and natural disasters!

> **191** **HERMES TRISMEGISTUS, HERMETIC TEXTS, VOL. I,** RODAKIS P., TZAFEROPOU-LOS AP., **'SPEECH VI,** ASCLEPIUS' DEFINITIONS TO KING AMMON' (p. 249): «§14. All of these *(daemons)* have been allotted the authority over things and turmoil upon the Earth, and it is they who bring about all kinds of unrest in social groups and cities (states) and nations and for each individual separately; for they do transform our souls and dominate over them, obsessing and occupying the nerves and the marrow of the bones, inside the veins and arteries, even inside our brain itself, down to our very bowel.»

All these astral Powers, penetrating the aetheric field/dimension, have immediate access to the aetheric body of each man. In this (aetheric) field they then weave the conditions for the diseases which will later materialize in

Don't skip chapters or bibliographic references

dense matter as viruses or epidemics, sucking every man's energy this way much like you enjoy your juice through a straw. Some medications do nothing more than cancel their energy formulas, dissolving their 'straws' (e.g. microbes). Other times again through the aetheric field, they organize/orchestrate positive or negative situations which will later materialize (happen) in dense matter as facts, in order to gain their energy-results.

–*In other words, god created us to benefit from us?*

–Well you are his bondservants, are you not?

---

192 **PLATO'S 'PHAEDO, OR ABOUT THE PSYCHE' [=SOUL]**, ATHANASOPOULOS I., K.:

(a) (62b, 62c, 62d) *(Socrates speaks to Cebes a little before he drinks the conium [hemlock]):* «Now the idea that is taught in the secret teachings about this matter, *(that)* we men are in a kind of prison and must not set ourselves free or escape, seems to me to be great and not easy to understand. But this at least, Cebes, I do believe is sound and correctly said, that the gods are our guardians and that **we men are one of their possessions**. Or do you not think so? …Well then, said he (Socrates), if one of your chattels (possessions) should kill itself when you had not indicated that you wished it to die, would you not be angry with it and punish it if you could?»

(b) (85b) *(Socrates addresses Simmias)* «But neither they (the birds), it seems to me, sing when they are sad, nor do the swans, but because they are **prophets–servants** of Apollo. …And I think that I myself am a **fellow-servant** with the swans and devoted to the same God.»

Are you finally gradually starting to understand the purpose served by the sacrifices to the 'gods' throughout the centuries? … Could it be that people meant the self-evident: "Oh, god! Accept the energy of the sacrificed, so that you don't take mine through some misery or misfortune?"

---

193 **A) THE GOSPEL OF PHILIP,** [Eng. tr. from Coptic: PATERSON BROWN]

http://www.metalog.org/files/philip.html: §54. «God is a cannibal. Because of this, mankind [is sacrificed] to it. Before mankind was sacrificed, animals were being sacrificed. For these to which they are sacrificed are not divinities *(they are astral entities).*»

B) OLD TESTAMENT, GENESIS CH. 8: «§20. Then Noah built an altar to the lord, and took of every clean animal and of every clean bird, and offered burnt-offerings on the altar. §21 And **the lord smelled the pleasing aroma** *(the smell of roasted meat).* And the lord said in his heart, "I will never again curse the earth because of man.»

C) THE EPIC OF GILGAMESH (THE ASSYRO-BABYLONIAN EPIC OF CREATION), ASSYRIAN INTERNATIONAL NEWS AGENCY, BOOKS ONLINE, http://www.aina.org
Utnapishtim (equivalent to Noah) is sacrificing to the gods after the flood.
«Then, I made a sacrifice. I poured out a libation on the mountain. Seven and another seven vessels I set up on their stands, and into the bowls I gathered timber, cane, cedar and myrtle. When the gods smelled the sweet savor, they gathered like flies over the sacrifice.» [Greek version: Near East Texts, The Epic of Gilgamesh, Kastaniotis Publ.]

The greatest harm caused by today's extremely consuming human society, is the uninterrupted supply of the astral body. Through its direct and indirect 'commands', it hypnotizes souls, leading them to an unrestrained material quest. Material quest for pleasure, combined with infinite material provisions gives birth to desires. Desires expand the astral body, which in turn, feeds a continuously expanding astral society, totally entrapping man's soul, until it is completely exterminated.

When man sleeps and his physical body 'withdraws', it dynamically gives its place to the other bodies, which bring information forth from the corresponding planes they reside in. The information sometimes comes from the aetheric body, which brings it from the aetheric plane; there the 'facts' come first, before they manifest in dense matter and are revealed to the dreamer as prophetic dreams. Other times, information comes from the astral body of desires, where dreams are interpreted as 'suppressed' emotional situations – since they are stationed in this body– or as gut fears, or even as simple wanderings of the astral body in this plane.

The astrophysicists of your world, through quantum physics, have located this astral territory which they call 'dark energy'. It is a much thinner energy compared to dark matter and can be found throughout the material universe. In reality, this dark energy is the astral plane. As dense matter has its own physical laws, so does the astral plane/dimension (dark energy) has its own particular characteristics and its own laws!

[194] **DARK ENERGY,** LIVE-PEDIA.GR http://www.livepedia.gr/index.php
«It is a cosmic entity. More precisely, it is a hypothetical kind of energy, which came to the foreground in the 90's, and which is responsible for the existence of a repulsive effect which forces the parts of the universe to distance themselves from each other. It is considered to run through the entire Space and it has a negative pressure.

Don't skip chapters or bibliographic references

Dark energy appears to be without mass and it is distributed evenly throughout Space where it acts as a kind of anti-gravity, a repulsive force that pushes the Universe to split and expand. It was theoretically established in order to justify the unexpected discovery that the rate of expansion of the Universe isn't slowing down, as it was believed until then, but it is in fact accelerating. Moreover, the existence of this entity contributes to the calculation of the inexplicable 'deficit' of the total mass of the Universe.

According to the latest estimates, this dark energy comprises 75% of the universe and the dark matter makes up 23%, while the ordinary baryonic matter with its energy is in the minority with only 2%.» (*Refer to* IMAGES: *THE CONSTITUTION OF THE MATERIAL UNIVERSE*)

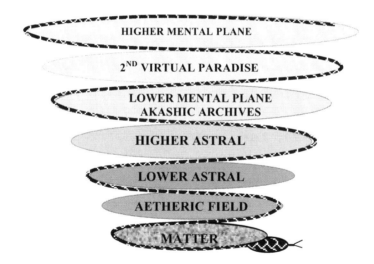

SOUL – 2ND REFLECTION-PARADISE (NIRVANA)

Immediately after the lower mental body and the corresponding astral sub-plane, there is another dimension, at the borders of finer/subtler matter which is closer to the realms of the immaterial. It is at that point, where material oscillation is at its highest frequency; the area of 'Nirvana', the Second Reflection-Paradise.

The Soul was created from the 'Essence/Spirit', i.e. the Breath of the god creator and was interwoven with the finer/subtler energy of the material world. Thus the soul's body was created, with Noûs and Logos (Word) as its properties.

---

[195] A) **HERMES TRISMEGISTUS**, HERMETIC TEXTS, VOL. II, RODAKIS P., TZAFEROPOULOS AP., 'FROM HERMES' SPEECHES TO AMMON, EXCERPT XIX, OF THE SAME' (p. 175):

«§1. The Soul therefore is eternal intelligent Essence, having its own Logos (Word) as its Nous/Mind *[orig. Gr. text:* νόημα = *thought, understanding, mind].*»

B) **OLD TESTAMENT, GENESIS CH. 2**: «§7. Then the Lord God formed man from the dust of the earth* and he blew the breath of life into his nostrils; and man became a living soul.»

* *In all ancient Greek texts, the word* γῆ *[= earth] is used to denote the cause of all matter.*

Let us compare though, Hermes Trismegistus' ideas to those of Plato with regards to the 'creation of the soul':

C) **PLATO'S 'TIMAEUS'** tr. KOUTROUMPAS G. (C35a1-35b3 pp. 57-59):

«And he *(the creator)* made the Soul out of the following elements and in the following manner: Out of the **indivisible** and eternally unchangeable essence *(The Indivisible Spirit)*, and also out of that which has to do with material bodies and is **divisible** *(divided by Logos),* by combining therefore the two, he had essences from both and he compounded a third and intermediate kind of essence between the indivisible and the divisible. And after he had received all three kinds *(the divisible, the indivisible, and the compound)* he blended them into a new kind, compressing by force the reluctant and unsociable nature of each into the others. He mingled this essence with the other two and made <u>one</u> out of three, which he again divided into as many portions *(souls)* as was fitting. Each portion of these had inside it of the one, the other, and the third compound essence.»

D) **HERMES TRISMEGISTUS**, HERMETIC TEXTS, VOL. II, RODAKIS P., TZAFEROPOULOS AP., 'EXCERPT XXIII, FROM THE HOLY BIBLE OF HERMES TRISMEGISTUS, TITLED KORE KOSMOU'

(p. 189): «§14. God, no longer willing that the world above should be inert, decided to fill it with spirits, so that creation should not remain immobile

---

Don't skip chapters or bibliographic references

and lifeless. He thus began crafting his plan with use of divine materials to bring forth his work. By taking spirit from himself *(the creator's breath)*, to the extent necessary, he mingled it mentally with fire and with certain other unknown substances; and having made them one, with certain apocryphal words of power, he set all the mixture swirling; until out of the compost a substance emerged, as it were, far subtler, far purer, and more translucent than the materials from which it came; and this material had two forms that only the craftsman god could see.

§15. And since this matter neither melted when fire was set unto it, nor did it freeze, as it was a creation of spirit, but it kept its consistency, a certain special kind, peculiar to itself, of special type and special blend, –god called this composition Ψύχωσιν [= to animate, to give soul or life to], after the more auspicious meaning of the name and in accordance to its energy/action. And from it he molded myriads of souls, creating what he wanted with order and symmetry. This mixture surfaced with fitting experience and reason; §16 so that the souls should not differ from one another in any way than in what was necessary.»

Following that, passing through the lower energy-fields of the material world, the Soul ended up into the denser one, where it was dressed with the dense material body. From then on, it coexists with it, trapped by its needs.

[196] A) **HERMES TRISMEGISTUS**, HERMETIC TEXTS, VOL. II, RODAKIS P., TZAFEROPOU-LOS AP., 'FROM HERMES' SPEECHES TO AMMON, EXCERPT XVII, OF THE SAME' (p. 171):
«§1 The Soul then, Ammon, is self-contained essence, which at first chose a life according to Heimarmenē (Fate), and then took for itself inclination [orig. Gr. θυμόν = mind, temper, will] and desire which have proportion similar to matter.»

Subdued by the laws of the material world, it struggles to win the bet that its logical noûs will eventually master the dense material body that surrounds it and subjugate its desires, in order to gain entry into the regions of the 2nd Reflection-Paradise of Nirvana as a reward. It is there that the higher ranks of the manifested gods/creators of the Soul reside. It is there that purified souls arrive at the end of their cycle, unite with their genitor and in cooperation with him, become communicants of the superior designs.

Absolute serenity prevails on this level. Many teachers and the creators themselves, in order **to free themselves** from this stagnant **state of boredom**, abandon this particular plane and relocate themselves onto the higher sub-planes of the astral, where they engage in endless battles with the dark daemonic entities of the lower sub-planes.

Many 'accomplished' Souls/humans, when they perceive the state of absolute tranquility that exists on this plane/dimension, **voluntarily** decide to return to the incarnation cycle, simply because they feel they are sinking into an indolent quiescence. For the souls of these humans, who are used to living within the action of material life, the state of Nirvana seems idle. Then, they return as 'aids' of humanity, entering the process of reincarnation again, with the intention to offer help. This is true at the beginning. After a number of incarnations though inside heavy matter, sin inevitably comes about again and oscillation itself drags them down to lower planes. A new cycle begins for them again and the perpetual circle of the Ourobore snake continues endlessly.

> [197] **PADMASAMBHAVA, THE TIBETAN BOOK OF THE DEAD** [Gr. tr. LIAKOPOULOS E.]
> (p. 68): «The six realms of Samsara *(the material world of Maya/delusion)* are: 1) the realm of the gods of Samsara …these Samsaric gods are considered immortal, but only up to the point that their good karma **runs out**.»

This is where the center of the great delusion lies. The fallacy is centered in the fact that men confuse the dull dimension of Nirvana with the HyperUniverses of the True and imagine that the same boredom exists there too. The unfortunate thing is that they don't know that the Nirvana phase is simply one side of the SAME split (dyadic) quality of this universe.

> [198] **PADMASAMBHAVA, THE TIBETAN BOOK OF THE DEAD** [Gr. tr. LIAKOPOULOS E.]
> *The commentator and translator of the text of the 'Tibetan Book of the Dead' Eustathios Liakopoulos, points out:*
> «…(The terms) Samsara and Nirvana here are considered as aspects and manifestations of the already dyadic plane, which **must be overcome** through 'ascesis' (from the Gr. άσκησις = training/exercise), allowing thus perfect enlightenment to be realized, experienced for what it really is, namely **beyond the perception of both Samsara and Nirvana.**»

This state is one-sided, an extreme state, which occurs at the highest (most positive) peak of material oscillation. It has nothing in common with the Unsplit, 'Spherical' conditions of the True Cosmoi, where ESSENTIAL HARMONY is the status quo. Thus, many who confuse things can find no justification to even try for their personal elevation.

Translator's Note: The Ancient Greek word Ἀγαθόν (Agathón) [=good/ness, benevolent/ness, kind/ness] refers to an aggregate of concepts encompassing all moral and intellectual virtues of man. It must be thought of as an absolute state, with an existence which is independent and unaffected by time or any other change. Only The Supreme Deity, The Unified Being, The Monad, can be characterized by the term Ἀγαθός (Agathós).

We must therefore accept the existence of an Ideal Conceptual World, independent from our physical world, which contains all the Eternal and Perfect Archetypes of the Ideas of Virtue, Justice, Morality, Grace and Truth. This is the World of Ἀγαθόν (Agathón).

Whichever of the above Archetypes appears in the world of form (our world), is to be simply considered a mere reflection of the Real One, owing its imperfect existence to a vestigial and rudimentary relation to the Complete and Perfect State of that Other World, in which Ἀγαθόν is incorporated.

Plato, in his Republic, gives us the definition of the term Ἀγαθόν:

[508e] «This reality, then, that gives their truth to the objects of knowledge and the power of knowing to the knower, you must say is the idea of Ἀγαθόν, and you must conceive it as being the cause of knowledge*, and the cause of truth in so far as they become known. Yet, fair as they both are (knowledge and truth), you will think rightly in supposing Ἀγαθόν *(Agathón)* to be something different and fairer still than these. But as for knowledge and truth, even as in our illustration [509a] it is right to deem light and vision as being sun like, but never to think that they are the sun, so here, it is right to consider these two (knowledge and truth) as being like Ἀγαθόν but to think that either of them is Ἀγαθόν, is not right.»

* Of Spiritual matter-less Knowledge

[TRANSLATED BY PAUL SHOREY, CAMBRIDGE, MA, HARVARD UNIVERSITY PRESS; LONDON, WILLIAM HEINEMANN LTD., 1969.]

HERMES TRISMEGISTUS, HERMETIC TEXTS, VOL. I, RODAKIS P., TZAFEROPOULOS AP., **SPEECH VI**: «§3. When it comes to man, Ἀγαθόν *(Agathón)* is determined in comparison to evil. …And Ἀγαθόν here is the smallest particle of evil. And it is **impossible** down here, that Ἀγαθόν be free from malice. For down here, Ἀγαθόν gets filled with malice, and being full of malice, it cannot be Ἀγαθόν; and since it cannot remain Ἀγαθόν anymore, it becomes evil. Therefore, Ἀγαθόν is (found) in God alone, or rather God Himself is Ἀγαθός. So then, Asclepius, **only the name of Ἀγαθόν is found in men**. Its workings are nowhere to be found. And it cannot be. For, **it cannot be contained in a material body,** which is bound on all sides by wickedness, pains, labors and rage and deceit and by foolish fantasies. And the greatest ill of all, Asclepius, is that each of these things that have been said previously is thought **down here** to be the greatest Ἀγαθόν when they are an inevitable evil. …§6. Wherefore, those who are ignorant and do not tread the path of piety, **do dare to call** man fair and Ἀγαθόν. Not even in their wildest dreams have they seen what Ἀγαθόν is. And they call Ἀγαθόν all that is evil.»

After that highly-oscillating energy-region of the Second Reflection-Paradise of Nirvana, there is a plane which could be characterized as borderline between the Ἀγαθόν *(Agathón)* of the absolutely pure immaterial Spirit and the invisible material universe.

It is the Higher Noetic (Higher Mental) plane in which the Higher Mental body of man resides. The greatest part of humanity does not possess this body.

When the intelligent (=Nous possessing) Soul was embodied into the material body, it began building a connection/communication **bridge** with it, in order to transfer its mental properties to it. The upgraded mentality *(normal intellect)* was then created in the material man and through the development of the physical *(material)* brain, the lower mental body with its corresponding plane/dimension started being formed.

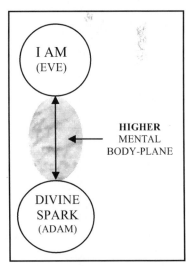

An exactly equivalent process takes place in the Higher Mental body: When the Divine Spark/Adam, the half-section of the split Celestial Man *(Adam + Eve = One),* performs the 'holy matrimony' with its 'Higher Self' or the 'I Am Presence' in the seventh energy-center, then the 'fruit of this marriage' is the creation of the Higher Mental Body. In other words, the moment one half of the very same Man approaches the other, True Light Rises, and encompasses his entire existence.

Don't skip chapters or bibliographic references

---

199 A) GOSPEL OF THOMAS, SACRED TEXTS, http://www.sacred-texts.com/chr/thomas.htm

«§61. Jesus said to her, I am He who exists *(comes)* from the Undivided *(Whole)*. I was given some of the things of my Father…Therefore I say, if he is <undivided> *(Whole)*, he will be filled with light, but if he is divided, he will be filled with darkness.» [Eng. tr. THOMAS O. LAMBDIN]

B) GOSPEL OF PHILIP www.metalog.org/files/philip.html

«§142. Every plant which my Heavenly Father has not sown shall be rooted out. Those who are separated *(He means the divided/split Celestial Men)* shall be mated and the empty shall be filled *(He means the plain Souls that will be 'filled/completed' with Spirit)*. Everyone who enters the Bedroom *(for the Holy Matrimony and in the 'Bridal-Chamber' of the 7th Energy Center)* shall be born in the Light. For they are not begotten in the manner of the marriages which we do not see *(human, social marriages)*, which are enacted by night, the fire of which flares in the dark and then is extinguished *(lost)*. Yet rather the Sacraments of this Marriage are consummated in the day and the light. Neither that day nor its light ever set.

§143. If someone becomes a Son of the Bridal-Chamber *(through the Holy Matrimony)* he shall receive the Light. If one does not receive it in these places, he will not be able to obtain it in the other place. He who has received that Light shall not be seen *(he will not be perceived by the forces of darkness)*, nor shall they be able to seize him; nor shall anyone be able to disturb this one of this nature, even if he socializes in the world. And furthermore, when he leaves the world he has already received the truth via the imagery. The world has become eternity *(Eternal Kingdom)*, because the **fullness** is for him the eternal. And it is thus revealed to him individually –not hidden in the darkness or the night, but rather hidden in a Perfect Day and a Holy Light.» [Eng. tr. from Coptic PATERSON BROWN]

This True Light is the Holy Spirit which is born and transfuses the Sacred Knowledge (A-λήθη-α = absence of forgetfulness) to Man through the Higher Mental Body.

---

200 A) HERMES TRISMEGISTUS, HERMETIC TEXTS, VOL. I, RODAKIS P., TZAFERO-POULOS AP.: **(a) SPEECH VI**: «§23…Do you think then, son, that every soul has the **Good Noûs**? *(Higher Mental/Noetic Body)* For this is what we are speaking of and **not** of the servant mind *(lower mental body)*… §24. For the soul without the Noûs can neither speak nor act.»

It is clear in this excerpt that a distinction must be made between the Higher Mental (Benevolent Noûs/Mind [Gr. Νοῦς ἀγαθός (Agathós)]) and the lower mental (servant mind) of man.

(b) SPEECH XXII: «§4. Whichever human souls have not the Noûs *(Higher Mental)* as their guide, they suffer in the same way as the souls of non-

---

rational animals. In these cases the mind *(the servant mind/lower mental)* becomes a co-worker exciting desires towards the irrationality of appetites, and conduces the irrational never to cease desiring, just like non-rational animals, without ever being satiated of ills. For, irrational angers and desires become *(develop into)* great ills. And over these souls God has set up the law[1] to play the part of moderator and punisher.»

These souls are attracted by the material 'magnets' and trapped in the material world, where the law of reciprocal justice and karma rules. If however, they release themselves from these dependencies, **then, without any further obligation,** *the escape gate is open for them* **WITHOUT JUDGMENT.**

[1] **(a) THE GOSPEL OF JOHN, CH. 3**: «§17. For God sent the Son into the world **not to judge the world**, but that the world might be saved through Him. §18. He who believes in Him is not judged. He who doesn't believe has been judged already.»

(b) THE GOSPEL OF JOHN, CH. 5: «§24. Most assuredly I tell you, he who hears My word, and believes Him who sent Me, has eternal life, and does **not** come into judgment, but has already passed out of death into life.»

Since Karmic Law punishes ONLY those who choose to live in the falsehood of this world... and therefore, it only applies to them.

B) *Let us examine how SALLUSTIUS, in his work 'ABOUT THE GODS AND THE WORLD', and in the chapter 'About the Noûs and the Soul' differentiates between the Noûs (mind/intellect) of a Soul which encloses Spirit/Essence or a Divine Spark and the mind of a plain Soul.*

SALLUSTIUS, 'ABOUT THE GODS AND THE WORLD' Gr. tr. GRAVIGGER P.:

(a) CH. ABOUT THE NOÛS AND THE SOUL: «§1. The Noûs is a force which comes second, after the Essence *(Spirit)*, but comes before the Soul, attracting Its existence from the Essence and perfecting the Soul, as the Sun completes eyesight. Of Souls, some are rational and immortal, some are irrational and mortal. The former are derived from the First Gods *(the HyperCosmic Gods of the HyperUniverses),* the latter from the secondary *(the earthly gods of the material Universe).* §2. Firstly, we must consider the true nature of the soul... Thus the irrational soul is subject to the senses and the imagination, whereas the rational soul is the Life which commands the senses and the imagination and uses reason. The irrational soul is subject to the affections/urges of the body's passions. *(Here, as Gravigger comments, he alludes to Paris (Trojan Prince), who is subject to his passions and irrational emotions).* Indeed, it feels desires without reason and it is angered irrationally. The rational Soul (with the help of reason), shows contempt for the bodily passions and comes into conflict with the irrational soul. Its victory generates virtue while its defeat brings vice.»

(b) CH. 16. THAT THE SOUL IS IMMORTAL: «§3. We need to consider this rational soul as immortal because it knows the Gods –since nothing of the mortal

Don't skip chapters or bibliographic references

realm receives knowledge from the immortal– and it (the Soul) looks down (with contempt) on human affairs as alien *(to its nature)* and it reacts, in the opposite way to the bodies because of its incorporeal nature.»

But in contrast to Sallustius and Hermes Trismegistus who attribute both the rational Soul and the non-rational Soul to man, Julian the Transgressor, emperor and great devotee of the God-Creator's religion, in his work 'To King Sun' –and since he KNOWS NOT the existence of Another Superior Being other than his god/creator– assumes that the non-rational soul refers to animals and the rational one to humans. Porphyry, on the other hand, attributes the (possession of a) non-rational soul all the way down to plants.

c) H. P. Blavatsky briefly mentions an occurrence from the Anugîtâ text, part of the Asvamedha Parvan of the 'Mahabharata'. Mind and Speech appear to disagree there on which of the two (Mind or Speech) is superior. The debating parties finally ask The Self of the Being, i.e. the individual Higher Self, and the Lord thus replies:

BLAVATSKY H., P. 'THE SECRET DOCTRINE' (I-95): «**There are two minds: the 'movable' and the 'immovable'**. The immovable is within me *(in the Higher Self)*, the movable is in your dominion (i.e. of the speech) on the plane of matter. To that *(the movable)* you *(speech)* are superior.»

The Higher Mental body is the 'bridge' connecting the Absolutely Pure Spirit of the **Unified** Celestial Man with his entire energy- and material (physical) Hypostasis.

[201] **THE GOSPEL OF MARY (MAGDALENE)**, JEAN-YVES LELOUP, Gr. tr. KOUROUSSI A., A. (p. 10): «Lord, does he who contemplates (sees) **Your Apparition,** see it through the (eyes of the) soul (or) through the spirit? The Savior answered. He does not see through the soul nor through the spirit, but through the Noûs which is in-between the two –that is [what] sees and that is {lost passage}.»

This body can only be built during material life.

[202] **GOSPEL OF THOMAS,** THE GNOSTIC SOCIETY LIBRARY
http://www.gnosis.org/naghamm/gosthom.html
«§59. Jesus said, Look to the Living One **as long as you live**, otherwise you might die and then try to see the Living One, and you will be unable to see.» [Eng. tr. STEPHEN PATTERSON, MARVIN MEYER]

In relation to the other bodies, which are older, it is considered the youngest. It is then placed **as a cover** of Man's other bodies and it envelops him like an outer layer. Little by little the Light of This Body permeates Man's entire existence, and by unfolding the Spiritual 'Memories', directs him to Redemption and Freedom. This is exactly where Salvation is.

What normal man perceives as consciousness is **the net result** (resultant) of all his energy-bodies. With the death of the physical body initially and the aetheric one after that *(the aetheric body is dissolved 40 days after death)*, this resulting consciousness loses its 'cohesion' and maintains only a few of the characteristics it had in life. Then, the only body that remains to encompass the soul is the astral/emotional body. The main characteristic of the astral body is that it DOES NOT possess logic. This was after all known to man from living experience: his emotions never contained logic. Basically, Logic and emotion were and still are incompatible states; and may I remind you that logic stems from the soul, whereas emotion from the astral body. Left with the astral body as its sole carrier/body, the soul is incapable of transferring its logical messages to it, since the astral body, from its construction, does not possess the decoders/tools to perceive this intellect. The only 'logic' it then **seems** to possess, is the one it has built during its material life, which **formed** the lower mental body. Without the physical brain available any more, the lower mental body resembles a **copy** of a 'cassette' which is no longer recordable (locked). It mustn't however be presumed that the astral dimension is related to 'Reason', just because it (astral) is the 'passage' of every logical thought to the lower mental plane. After all, let me remind you here that in order for every logical thought – generated by **the living** man– to cross the astral worlds and settle in the lower mental plane (the higher layer of the astral world), it must be **enveloped** by some emotion **as its carrier**. This is why all human information can be 'recorded' as memory <u>only</u> if it is accompanied by an emotion. Productive logical thinking therefore does not exist there, only **reproductions** of the thoughts already created <u>during material life</u>.

---

[203] **PAPASTAVROU A., 'COSMOS WITHIN A COSMOS'** CH. ASTRAL PLANE (pp. 29-30): «The popular idea that someone can –after death– acquire unlimited knowledge from the astral world or other sources of higher spiritual development, and that these can be transferred through a psychic *(medium)* to the living, **is not true**. In the astral plane, the deceased **does not possess** more knowledge than what he did while living, and if he could transmit something that would be what little he knew when alive.»

Don't skip chapters or bibliographic references

The soul then, in these **unknown astral regions,** is tormented by emotions, desires and passions, without having the 'means' and the way to control its mindless astral body.

The Higher Mental body, being the outer body of the rest –as it was the last to be created– has the ability to communicate with the unified Spirit, to receive Its Knowledge and transfuse it to man's entire hypostasis. Therefore, in the planes where man goes after death, it is the **only body** to possess a Productive Mind and encompasses the astral body and soul. It is the Luminous Logical **Spiritual Noûs (Mind)** which, built with all the spiritual information acquired by man with the Holy Reunion *(Holy Matrimony)*, knows the A-λήθη-α (Truth), and through the dark hell of the astral plane, it continues to be supplied by the Logic of the active unified Spirit and guide the Soul to Exodus and Deliverance. The Light IT emanates lights every dark spot of the astral inter-dimensions and discourages every malevolent daemonic entity from attacking IT.

---

[204] **GOSPEL OF PHILIP** [Gr. tr. PATERSON BROWN]: «§143. If someone becomes a Son of the Bridal-Chamber *(through the Holy Matrimony)*, he shall receive the Light. If one does not receive it in these places, he will not be able to obtain it in the other place. He who has received that Light shall not be seen *(he will not be perceived by the forces of darkness)*, nor shall they be able to seize him; nor shall anyone be able to disturb this one of this nature, even if he socializes in the world. And furthermore, (when) he leaves the world he has already received the truth via the imagery. The world has become eternity, because the **fullness** *(Completeness)* is for him the eternal. And it is thus revealed to him individually –not hidden in the darkness (or) the night, but rather hidden in a Perfect Day and a Holy Light.»

This body (Higher Mental/Noetic) is thus transformed into a transportation vehicle or 'spacesuit', which has the power to carry within it the Unified Being to the neutral zone of the Higher Mental (Noetic from the Gr. w. Noῦς = Mind) plane.

---

[205] **THE GOSPEL OF MATTHEW, CH. 22**: «§2. The Kingdom of Heaven is like a certain (human) king, who made a marriage feast for his son, §3 and sent out his servants to call those who were invited to the marriage feast…§10. Those servants went out into the streets, and gathered together as many as they found, both bad and good. The wedding was filled with guests. §11. But when the king came in to see the guests, **he saw there a man who didn't have on wedding clothing** *(the wedding clothing here refers to the Higher Noetic Body)* §12 and he said to him, "Friend, **how did you come in here**

> **not wearing wedding clothing?**" He was speechless. §13. Then the king said to the servants, "Bind him hand and foot, take him away, and throw him into the outer darkness" *(the material-energy universe, for **this** is hell)*; <u>there</u> is where the weeping and grinding of teeth will be. §14. For many are invited, but few chosen.»

A euphoric equilibrium prevails There (in the Higher Mental Plane), and right <u>There</u>, is **the Gateway to Escape** located. This body therefore (the Higher Mental) is a 'key' that leads to Freedom and Salvation.

> **206** A) *A Reminder:* **GOSPEL OF THOMAS,** EARLY CHRISTIAN WRITINGS
> http://www.earlychristianwritings.com/thomas/gospelthomas70.html
> «§70. Jesus said: If you have gained THIS within you, what you have will save you. If you do not have THIS in [you], what you do not have in you, [will] kill you.» [Eng. tr. BEATE BLATZ]
> *At this point I am making a reference to Helena Blavatsky, who provides an explanation to the term 'THIS' through the study of Hindu wisdom:*
> **B) BLAVATSKY H., P., 'THE SECRET DOCTRINE'** (I-7): «Parabrahm is, in short, the collective aggregate of the Kosmos in its infinity and eternity; the 'THAT' and the 'THIS' to which distributive aggregates cannot be applied. **In the beginning 'THIS' was the Self, One only.**» *[Aitareya Upanishad]*"

In this region of the Higher Mental Plane we find the souls of all those who believed and followed the Truth. Freed from incessant reincarnations <u>they wait</u> for the circle of matter **to close permanently**.

> **207** THE GOSPEL OF JOHN, CH. 6: «§40. And this is the will of Him Who sent Me, that everyone who sees the Son and believes in Him may have everlasting life; and I shall raise* him up to life **on the very last day.**»
> *Orig. Gr. text uses the word:* ἀναστήσω = I shall resurrect

Then they will **all** enter a new 'space-dimension' **together**, set up especially for them, which will offer the ideal conditions for the Men/Souls to restore the damages they have suffered from the prolonged stay in the poisoned material universe in order to be able to permanently return to the Immaculate FatherLands.

> **208** A) THE GOSPEL OF JOHN, CH. 14: «§2. In my Father's house there are many mansions. ...I am going to prepare a place for you. §3. And after I go and prepare a place for you, I will come again, and receive you to Myself; that where I am, there, you may be also.»

Don't skip chapters or bibliographic references

B) THE GOSPEL OF JOHN, CH. 12: «§25. He who loves his soul* shall lose it, and he who hates his soul* in this world shall keep it to life eternal.»
The original Greek Text uses the word ψυχὴν = Psychē/Soul but, for some reason, all English translations use the word 'life' instead: [...ὁ φιλῶν τὴν **ψυχὴν** αὐτοῦ ἀπολλύει αὐτήν, καὶ ὁ μισῶν τὴν **ψυχὴν** αὐτοῦ ἐν τῷ κόσμῳ τούτῳ εἰς ζωὴν αἰώνιον φυλάξει αὐτήν.]

Let us examine how this Body works:

The visible material world can only be perceived through our physical senses. Conversely, the World of Pure Spirit (not of the astro-aetheric dimensions) can only be 'sensed' through the Higher Noûs (Mind). As the basic bridge of communication with the Celestial Man, it transports all received information from the higher worlds to the rest of the material bodies. The result of this process is the gradual removal (withdrawal) of the 'ribbon/blindfold of oblivion/forgetfulness' and the restitution of remembrance/Truth. Information brought forth by this body, clearly **doesn't concern material subjects**, but deeply Spiritual knowledge.

---

[209] **THE GOSPEL OF TRUTH, NAG HAMMADI MANUSCRIPTS**
www.metalog.org/files/valent.html:
«§15. This is an acquaintance with the Living book, whereby at the end He has manifested the Eternal-ones *(Aeons/HyperUniverses)* as the alphabet of His revelation. These *(Aeons)* are not vowels nor are they consonants, such that someone might read them and think of emptiness, but rather they *(Aeons)* are the True alphabet by which those who recognize it are themselves expressed. Each letter is a perfect thought; each letter is like a complete book written in the alphabet of **Unity** by the Father, who inscribes the Eternal Ones so that through His own alphabet they might meet/recognize/know the Father.» [Eng. tr. from Coptic THOMAS PATERSON BROWN]

As you can easily understand, when man reaches this point, the **last** thing that he is concerned with are his previous incarnations! And I am saying this because as the building of this body is gradually starting, its **basic side-effect** is an indifference to any worldly activity, and every materialistic interest **shrinks** under the influence of the True Light.

---

[210] **A) HERMES TRISMEGISTUS**, HERMETIC TEXTS, VOL. I, RODAKIS P., TZAFERO-POULOS AP., **SPEECH IV**: «§6…My child**, if you do not first hate your body, you cannot love yourself;** and once you love yourself, you shall have Noûs, and having Noûs, you shall also partake of Science *(=Knowledge)*.
–Father, why do you say that?

–It is **impossible**, O Son, to be conversant in both things, the Mortal as well as the Divine. ...For it is impossible for you to choose both at the same time. ...One prevails while the other diminishes.»

B) THE GOSPEL OF MATTHEW, CH. 6: «§24. No one can serve two masters, for either he will hate the one and love the other; or else he will be devoted to one and despise the other. You can't serve both God and Mammon. §25. Therefore, I tell you, don't be anxious for your life: what you will eat, or what you will drink; nor for your body, what you will wear.» *Here, the mortal body is clearly connected to Mammon.*

C) PLATO'S 'PHAEDO, OR ABOUT THE PSYCHE' [=SOUL], ATHANASOPOULOS I., K.: «(66b) So long as we have the body, and the soul is 'knead together' with this **evil**, we shall never manage to acquire enough of what we desire: and by that we mean what is True. For our body forces us to countless chores... (66c) Furthermore, the body fills us with many erotic passions and desires and fears, and all sorts of fancies and foolishness... so that, as they truly say, it really is impossible for us to logically think of anything at all, while under its (our body's) command. And because wars and factions and battles are caused by nothing else but the body and its desires, since, it is for the sake of gaining material goods that all wars arise. And we are compelled to gain those material goods for the sake of the body, **like slaves in its service**....»

This process concerns the activation of the Seventh Sense of Truth and as it happens with any sense, it can only be understood as an experience.
The personal Golgotha of every ascending man starts from here, and it will lead him to his personal crucifixion.

[211] **THE GOSPEL OF MATTHEW, CH. 10**: «§38. And he who does not take his cross and does not follow behind Me, is not worthy of Me.»

The Cross:
The four elements of matter:
Earth, Air, Water, Fire.
The spinning of the elements creates the material spiral, depicted with the swastika.

The Cross is a symbol representing dense matter. Each point of the cross corresponds to one of its four elements: water, fire, air and earth. These four elements are the nails that crucify the Unified Man.

Don't skip chapters or bibliographic references

> **212** **A) GOSPEL OF THOMAS,** JEAN YVES LELOUP:
> «§56. Jesus said: Whoever knows the world discovers a corpse. And whoever discovers a corpse cannot be contained by the world.» *Because of course, he cannot bear living inside the corpse.*
> **B) THE APOCRYPHON OF JOHN, THE GNOSTIC SOCIETY LIBRARY,** ENG. TR. FROM COPTIC: FREDERIK WISSE: *(Jesus says to John):* «And I entered into the midst of their prison, which is **the prison of the body**. And I said, He who hears, let him get up from the deep sleep!» [GR. EDITION: APOCRYPHAL TEXTS OF THE OLD TESTAMENT, KOUTSOUKIS D.]

Pinned down onto his material body/cross, Man awaits patiently for the time when his unified Spirit will abandon the material world, in order to enter the regions of the Higher Mental Plane!

> **213** **THE APOCRYPHON OF JOHN, THE GNOSTIC SOCIETY LIBRARY:** «Those upon whom the Spirit of the Life will descend and (with whom) it will be powerfully present, **they will be saved** and will become perfect. And they will become worthy of the great realms. And **they will be purified in That Place** from all evil and the concerns of wickedness. Then they will not take care for anything except the imperishability alone, attending to it from this point on without anger or envy or jealousy or desire or greed of anything at all. For they are not restrained by anything except the reality of the flesh alone, which they bear **while fervently awaiting** the time when they will be visited by those who will receive (them).» [Eng. tr. from Coptic: FREDERIK WISSE]

And when I say patiently, I stress the word; because any 'voluntary breach of the life contract' (i.e. suicide) carries the ultimate price, i.e. **the complete enslavement** of the Soul in **indescribably painful** conditions. After all, the material body is not the only obstacle to the liberation of man, since his astro-emotional body –the carrier of desires– continues to envelope the Soul even after his physical death.

Ever since Celestial Man tasted the fruit of the twofold/dyadic material knowledge and buried himself in the mud/matter of this world, he is considered dead for the Immortal Worlds. It is **THERE** (in the HyperUniverses of the True), where He is Resurrected from the dead and permanently dies in the material universe.

> **214** **GOSPEL OF PHILIP,** JEAN-YVES LELOUP: «§21. Those who say that the Lord first died and then was resurrected are wrong: for He was first resurrected *(in the HyperUniverses of the Father)* and then died *(permanently, in the universe of matter).*»

Man's real hypostasis is the Celestial Man, an **immaterial** Intelligent Wholeness.

The primordial **environment** where this divine, unified Wholeness 'was born' was Love. Love exists as a condition and not as an emotion. As material beings basically need an environment of air, water and nutrition to survive in the material plane, so too the 'environment' in which these Unified Intelligent Wholenesses (male and female One) live, is the Condition/environment of Love. They (the Unified Intelligent Wholeness) are nourished through Love, and Their Bodies are built with It. Love is not an (astral) emotion. It is the **'Essence'** of the HyperUniverses of True Light and only through the Seventh Sense of the Truth can someone approach it.

> [215] **GOSPEL OF PHILIP**, JEAN-YVES LELOUP: «§11. The words we give to earthly realities engender illusion; they turn the heart away from the Real to the unreal. **The one who hears the word** *God* **does not perceive the Real, but an illusion or an image of the Real.** ...we will understand this on the day when we **experience** the Real. ... §13. High spiritual powers (the Archon) wanted to deceive man. ...**They took the name for goodness and applied it to what was not good:** Words became deceitful, and *(since)* then they are joined to that which is without being and without goodness. They alienate with simulations and appearances: they make a free person into a slave.»
> [Eng. tr. JOSEPH ROWE]

Men confuse this Love-Condition with the positive emotions of the astral body, or even with compassion and dependence. After all, even a dog feels a similar astral 'love' for his master! Can this condition then be identified with the Immaculate? The astral body, which is also the carrier of emotions in man, is not built to experience the Condition of Spiritual Love. It can **only** be perceived when the Life-giving Spirit is liberated.

He finished talking and remained silent for a while…

The symbol depicting the <u>creation </u>of the four elements of matter as well as the Hierarchy of Entities that constitutes and sustains the entire visible and invisible material world is the pyramid. The pyramid consists of four triangles (**Δ**). Each triangle represents the creation *{Tr. n.: Gr. word for creation is Δημιουργία [Demiourgia] with Delta Δ as its first letter}* of each one of these four elements of matter. The top of each triangle is located at a point/location/moment of the highest section of the material oscillation. This location (the peak of the triangle {**Δ**} D (Δ)elta), is where the command of the Logos of Creation is located *(In the early periods of development of the Greek language, every letter symbolized*

Don't skip chapters or bibliographic references

what it declared). In order for each command *(for the creation)* to manifest *(materialize)*, through the **Logos** *(Gr. Λόγος = fraction, division)*, it is split. This is where the shape of the first letter of the word Λόγος (**Λ**) becomes relevant, declaring precisely this fission and creating the two sides of the mental image of a triangle as they gradually pass through the denser energy-planes. The base of the triangle corresponds to the time this command needs to manifest in each plane/field and its (Δ) Demiourgia = Creation to appear. It is at the top of the pyramid, where the common point of all four elements of matter (triangles) is located and is identified with the '(A)rche [see Archon]' = Authority/Beginning of this (Δ) Demiourgia = Creation. *(See also: DRAWINGS, 'THE STORY IN PICTURES')*

The God Creator's Logos/fission (Gr. (Λ)όγος [Logos]) created the Hierarchy of the Constructors of matter *(the Commanders of Heimarmenē [Fate]).* And the Constructors created the four elements of matter: Fire, Air, Water and Earth. And for each element a great Hierarchy of Entities and Powers was formed to support this Creation, creating a pyramid. And the Lord of all, became the Arche/Archon = the Authority, Commander (A) [Gr.: Αρχή] and settled at the Top of the Hierarchy, which he himself had created and supervised everything from there. And he became the 'All seeing Eye' and the ultimate Lord of all and he remained there, cut-off and independent, to supervise everyone, distinguishing his position from his subordinate slaves. And he adopted the Truncated Pyramid as his symbol because its top is detached from its main body. And he equated the (A) with the 'Arche'=Beginning/Authority of his creation and with it, the truncated pyramid. The symbol of the truncated pyramid will always be associated to the Hierarchy of Authority, and with the letter Alpha (A), since the **shape** of this letter declares just that.

[216] **A) THE GOSPEL OF THOMAS: THOMAS THE ISRAELITE PHILOSOPHER'S AC-COUNT OF THE INFANCY OF THE LORD,** FIRST GREEK FORM, ROBERTS-DONALDSON
http://www.earlychristianwritings.com/text/infancythomas-a-roberts.html
«§6 And a certain teacher, Zacchaeus by name, was standing in a certain place, and heard Jesus thus speaking to his father; and he wondered exceedingly, that, being a child, he should speak in such a way. And a few days thereafter he came to Joseph, and said to him: Thou hast a sensible child, and he has some mind. Give him to me, then, that he may learn letters…And He (Jesus) looked upon the teacher Zacchaeus, and said to him: You who are ignorant of the nature of the Alpha, how can you teach others the Beta? You hypocrite! First, if you know teach the 'A', and then we shall believe you about the 'B'. Then He began to question the teacher about the first letter, and he was not able to answer Him. And in the hearing of many, the child says to Zacchaeus: Hear, O teacher, the order of the first letter, and notice here how it has lines, and a middle stroke crossing those which you see

common; (lines) brought together; the highest part supporting them, and again bringing them under one head; with three points *of intersection*; of the same kind; principal and subordinate; of equal length. You have the lines of the 'A'. §7. And when the teacher Zacchaeus heard the child speaking such and so great allegories of the first letter, he was at a great loss about such a narrative, and about His *(Jesus')* teaching.»

B) GAZIS, A., 'LEXICON OF THE GREEK LANGUAGE':

«'ALPHA': **(a)** Alpha, nicknamed 'Alphadeon' (spirit level), is the name of a ruler, due to its shape or the level used by masons.

(b) Alpha stems from the Gr. verb ἀλφω [alpho], αλφαίνω [alphaeno] = to invent, to find something.

(c) According to the classical grammarians, Alpha stems from the Gr. verb 'alpho', to invent, because according to its etymology, it was the first one to be found....Later however, it was considered more prudent to link it to the Hebrew or Arabic word 'aleph'... According to others, 'Aleph' was the word used by the Phoenicians and the Hebrew for 'ox'.»

C) STAMATAKOS I., 'LEXICON OF THE ANCIENT GREEK LANGUAGE'

«'ALPHA' HISTORICAL REVIEW: This letter is the first letter not only of the Greek alphabet but also of every known alphabet. Its name during the Phoenician Period resembled the Hebrew word 'aleph', whereas in the Greek language it was introduced with the name 'alpha'. The word 'aleph' means 'ox'. Indeed, if we turn the capital letter 'A' upside down or if we write the lower case 'α' on its side, we will see that the two shapes (∀, 8 ή ȣ) are linear representations of an ox's head with horns.»

For greater data correlation, see DRAWINGS →HOLY MATRIMONY → REFLECTIVE SYMBOL → EGYPTIAN DRAWINGS → MOSES.

This is the Arche (**A**) [Beginning/Authority] of the entire material, visible and invisible world, and its course in time is a one-way route that inadvertently ends up to the End/Omega (Ω [Ωμέγα]). *(See the end of the book, DRAWINGS → THE STORY IN PICTURES)*

With the New Knowledge my thoughts started filling in the blanks, weaving the Truth. I could now understand what Jesus Christ meant when He said He had come to liberate man from imprisonment. Not the imprisonment of sin, but that of matter.

Matter itself was Man's bond because the entire creation of the material universe was the result of disobedience and mutiny. This is why the Gospel of Truth says:

"The deficiency of matter did not originate through the Infinity of the Father." [Gospel of Truth, §39]

REINCARNATION

–And what about reincarnation? Is it true?

–Some don't believe in anything. They attribute everything to nature's whim, call 'believers' naïve and quaint and declare themselves to be materialists and atheists. Others believe what their heresy, religion or perception dictates and they blindly follow their faith. No matter which position a man is in, the only certainty is the oscillation of **visible and invisible** nature. Any intelligent man will see this in front of his eyes. This oscillation has the two poles and through them it brings alteration. Alteration is supported by the birth of the opposites. Since, for example, there is the condition of awareness, it would be impossible for the condition of sleep not to exist as well. As there is inhalation, there is exhalation also; similarly, according to the same law, as there is life there is death, both parts of the same oscillation.

When a 'Life Force' comes to the world of form, it energizes life inside matter with the birth of a new material body. As this 'Life Force' moves from one condition to the other, subjected to the phases of <u>its own</u> oscillation, it withdraws and death of the form (physical body) occurs. Then it returns back again, into a different material form, thus following **its own** periodic course. So, whether people accept reincarnation or not, it exists as a process serving the continuous alteration of the two poles: life – death – life…

– This argument though could easily opposed by the fact that the death of every material body provides life to other material forms and thus the law of oscillation still holds true: life-death-life…

–This however does not refer to the periodic course of the <u>**same**</u> life! Oscillation, as a fundamental property of this Cosmos, exists on every level and in every case; throughout all lengths and all widths; from the tiniest detail to the largest, engulfing everything in small and large periodic cycles. A large oscillation **encompasses** smaller oscillations within it and these, others even smaller, and the smaller ones even smaller, until they sink into the infinite depths of the microcosm. It is what Pythagoras calls the 'Harmonic Series', using the monochord to describe the phenomenon of **simultaneous** <u>oscillations of just a single string</u> in its various lengths.

²¹⁷ **MICHAEL KENNEDY, OXFORD LEXICON OF MUSIC**
«HARMONIC SERIES (HARMONICS): The lower tone of the harmonic series (fundamental) is the first harmonic. Immediately higher than that is the second harmonic, and so on. These simple sounds, whose frequencies **are simple (integer) multiples of the frequency of the fundamental tone**, are always created in the same order of intervallic sequence.»

When a string is vibrating, and while it oscillates in its entire length (at the fundamental frequency), <u>all its partial sections are **simultaneously**</u> vibrating in different frequencies, according to their length. That is, the string simultaneously oscillates in its halves, its thirds, its fourths, fifths, etc., in frequencies which are multiples of the fundamental.

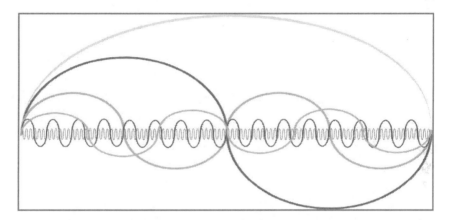

All who remain firmly 'anchored' on a single point of view, cannot perceive <u>the total width</u> of the Cosmos (the fundamental frequency), but only a small part/arch of it, or a side-oscillation which <u>is included as part</u> of a larger one.

Likewise those who do not accept the existence of the Soul and Spirit, can only **partially** perceive this alteration of life, and locate it exclusively in the densely material, visible plane. Because of that, they are comfortable believing that the up to now intelligent human body of theirs will 'evolve', after death, to a new living existence in the form of a worm! Let them be content with it and turn a blind eye to the complete picture. The complete picture however, includes besides the visible the invisible too; and this invisible includes the Soul and the Spirit which **are also** subject to a **corresponding** alternating procedure of the 'inhalation-exhalation' type.

Don't skip chapters or bibliographic references

When someone desires to redeem himself from death, he must automatically abandon the **dipole**. He must shift himself from 'I Exist' to 'I Am'.

---

218 **THE GOSPEL OF MATTHEW, CH. 10**: «§39. He who finds his life shall lose it; and he who loses his life for My sake, shall find it.»

When someone lives in matter, he has a {sub-stance} and {sub-fers (suffers)} under someone's authority and can only exist as a {sub–ject} and slave/servant of his god creator. *{Tr. n.: The Greek word [Υπ-άρχω = to exist] consists of the preposition [ὑπό=under] and the verb [ἄρχω=to rule], and clearly equates the concept of existence to that of being under the authority of someone, as his sub-ject}*. But when someone {IS}, he has automatically escaped the dipole of dying and material living. You will understand what I mean as our discussion unfolds.

–If a man does not manage to achieve redemption in his life, is there a chance for him to finally attain his goal in a new incarnation?

–In every new incarnation that man goes through –contrary to what everyone claims– he leaves a part of his Spiritual Essence behind as 'payment'. In other words, the prodigal son wastes his Father's Fortune *(Tr. N.: The Gr. word {Περι-ουσία = fortune}, is comprised of the preposition {περί = about, around, for} and the word {ουσία [Ousseea] = essence} and can be translated as 'all about the essence')*. This fortune is his Spirit.

---

219 **THE GOSPEL OF LUKE, CH. 15**: «§11. Then He (Jesus) said: A certain man had two sons. §12. And the younger of them said to his father, 'Father, give me my share of the **Essence** (fortune)*.' So he divided it to them. §13. And not many days after, the younger son gathered all, **journeyed to a far country, and there wasted his Essence** with prodigal living.»

*Translator's note: The original Gr. version [translation of the 70] uses the Gr. word ουσία = essence which was later translated as fortune = περι-ουσία. According to philosopher Sallustius (Gaul 300 A.D.) the primary Cause of creation is equated to the Essence of Noûs and of the Soul [Gr. Ousseea].

The sooner someone is free from this alternating process, the better for his own sake. With every new incarnation, his spiritual part gets more and more poisoned from the 'clay' of dense matter. A clean cloth, when soaked in muddy waters, definitely doesn't get cleaner, but rather gets shabbier and irrevocably soiled. Men then lose the sense of the Immaculate and have no ability to even imagine it. They then **consider** 'clean' what in reality is dirty.

---

220 **HERMES TRISMEGISTUS,** HERMETIC TEXTS, VOL. I, RODAKIS P., TZAFEROPOULOS AP. **SPEECH VI**: «§3. When it comes to man, Ἀγαθόν [=Ideally Good *(See Tr. n on w. ἀγαθός (Agathós), beginning of Ch. 'HIGHER MENTAL BODY – CE-LESTIAL MAN')*] is determined in comparison to evil. ...And Ἀγαθόν [Ideally Good] here, is the smallest particle of evil. And it is **impossible** down here, that Ἀγαθόν be free from malice. For down here, Ἀγαθόν gets filled with malice, and being full of malice, it cannot be Ἀγαθόν; and since it cannot remain Ἀγαθόν anymore, it becomes evil. Therefore, Ἀγαθόν is (found) in God alone, or rather God Himself is Ἀγαθός. So then, Asclepius, **only the name of Ἀγαθόν is found in men**. Its workings are nowhere to be found. And it cannot be. For, **it cannot be contained in a material body,** which is bound on all sides by wickedness, pains, labors and rage and deceit and by foolish fantasies. And the greatest ill of all, Asclepius, is that each of these things that have been said previously is thought **down here** to be the greatest Ἀγαθόν when they are an inevitable evil. ...§6 Wherefore, those who are ignorant and do not tread the path of piety, **do dare to call** man fair and Ἀγαθόν. Not even in their wildest dreams have they seen what Ἀγαθόν *(Agathón)* is. And they call Ἀγαθόν all that is evil.»

–They say however that man's soul learns through consecutive incarnations and through this knowledge and the pain of karma, it does not repeat the same mistakes. At some point –they say– it will cease to reincarnate inside matter and it will be transformed into spirit. In fact the 'teachers' mention that after a certain number (some thousands) of reincarnations, one will manage to reach holiness and Ascension!

–In other words your Souls started off as pure Spiritual Entities and were incarnated into matter. Why? To return back to where they started from, pure again? And having gained what? ...Virtual-life experiences, **useless** to the Spiritual Planes.

---

221 **HERMES TRISMEGISTUS,** HERMETIC TEXTS, VOL. I, RODAKIS P., TZAFEROPOULOS AP., **SPEECH XI:** «§41. Nothing of the earthly offers benefit to the celestial. All celestial things offer benefits to the earthly.»

For what else of essence can you gain? Only the knowledge of the eternal cycle of 'good and evil', where one action, under some circumstances can be right and the **same** action, under different circumstances can be wrong! There is a logical contradiction and falsehood in this view.

Through reincarnation, man is degraded more and more in relation to his Spiritual part.

Don't skip chapters or bibliographic references

---

222 **A) BLAVATSKY H., P., 'THE SECRET DOCTRINE'**: «As shown, we gather from the latter that man was not 'created' as the complete being he is now... There was a spiritual, a psychic, an intellectual, and an animal evolution, **from the highest to the lowest**...ever furnishing an ascending scale for the **manifested**, or that which we call the 'great Illusion' (Maha-Maya), but **plunging Spirit deeper and deeper into materiality**...»

And this plunge reaches <u>absolute death</u> *as is supported by* <u>the very same</u> *religion that supports reincarnation. Even the very Gods of this world are destroyed and eventually die, as is described below:*

B) BLAVATSKY H., P., 'THE SECRET DOCTRINE' (I-36):

«In Book II, Ch. VIII of the Vishnu-Puraná it is stated: "By immortality is meant existence until the end of Kalpa." And translator Wilson in a footnote remarks: "This, according to the Vedas, is all that is to be understood of the immortality (eternal life) of the gods· **they perish** <u>at the end of universal dissolution</u> (or Pralaya).»

C) PADMASAMBHAVA, THE TIBETAN BOOK OF THE DEAD

Eustathios Liakopoulos, commentator and translator of the above text, makes the following remarks:

«...The Gods of Samsara (of the vicious circle of deaths and rebirths) are considered to be 'immortal', but only up to the point that their good karma <u>runs out</u>.»

Therefore, if the Gods of Samsara are destroyed at the end of Kalpa, what do we humans imagine we can possibly 'gain' ...other than experiences of death?

D) DAVID ICKE 'TALES FROM THE TIME LOOP' – 'THE NEW AGE MATRIX' (p. 431)

«The concept of reincarnation is yet another creation of the Matrix, to keep consciousness in a cycle of enslavement, while it **believes** it 'progresses' through experiences, according to the beliefs of New Age... And because, as it is said, 'death doesn't cure ignorance' the same thing happens to the consciousnesses (on other levels of the Matrix) that remain **trapped in delusion**.»

The very **demands of his survival** teach man craftiness, lying and deception; otherwise others will survive against him. These are the Laws of this universe. What he will finally reach after these thousands of reincarnations is not ascension –as they claim– but total spiritual death inside the clever body of a bio-robot.

---

223 **A)** *In the 2ⁿᵈ Meeting in Athens, in Pnika on the Acropolis (30/5-5/6/1966), French professor Etienne Souriau in his speech 'The Food of the soul' said:*

«The needs of the body and the fast pace of material accomplishment made us forget the needs of the soul and spirit. The philosophers must ponder on this. There is a dramatically intense need for us to replace the nightmare of modern man's life and provide solutions to the immense psychic and spiritual problem. Who is the man of tomorrow? He will have undoubtedly found solutions for many scientific and technological challenges. He might have even managed to create a lasting and care-free peace. He might have succeed ridding himself of any deprivation and constantly have material goods at his disposal. But what will fulfill his soul? The time has come for man to seek and satisfy the desires of his soul, **before they die out completely.**»

But this 'dying out of the soul' is unavoidably, the natural outcome of man's material journey since his fall inside matter.

B) 'IDEOTHEATRON' MAGAZINE, APRIL 1999 ISSUE, AN EXCERPT OF AN INTERVIEW WITH D. NANOPOULOS (ACADEMIC, HEAD OF THE HOUSTON ADVANCED RESEARCH CENTER): «Our living standards may have risen, we may perform one-day 'bloodless' surgical operations, we may have more free time, we may eat more healthily, we may get information about things faster, but have we really become any better? Not necessarily, I think. It's not that I am pessimistic, on the contrary, I am optimistic by nature but I can't shut my eyes in front of reality.»

When one realizes it though, it will be too late. Through their 'gurus' (assignees), your creators have purposely methodized this whole lie, to keep you chain-bound by rebirths, constantly turning the wheel of matter. The only reason for the existence of the material 'life' of man is exclusively energy-production. And the <u>alleged</u> karmic debt reinforces this endless trap, since it is the melting pot for this production.

During the first Christian years, when the teachings of Christ **had not yet been corrupted**, everyone knew that reincarnation with its complementary 'karma' was the principal process of **imprisonment** of the Celestial Man into the kingdom of the fallen god-creator, the material universe. When Jesus Christ delivered His Life-giving Teaching (through the **Truth** IT carried within) it awoke the sleeping Sparks in the hearts of men, who by breaking their bonds, escaped from the eternal oscillation of the snake-god and shattered the cycle of endless reincarnations. This is why Christianity **chose** to reject the Reincarnation dogma from its doctrine; because the reason Christ came was exactly this: <u>to cancel this interminable **imprisonment** procedure which is Reincarnation, **by paying the ransom** for Karma</u> *(sins)*.

Through material desires encircling the soul, and with an astral body endlessly supplying it with emotions of material dependence and passion, with the total deletion of its existential memory, as well as the complete ignorance of the reality that surrounds it, she (the Psyche/Soul) has no other

Don't skip chapters or bibliographic references

escape, but to reincarnate consecutively. The **energy-deficits man has suffered** in his life **from injustice** carry him back to a new life, in order to 'get his blood back' *(to revenge)*. These energy-deficits end-up being the worst burden for man's imprisonment, since his demand to be justified and compensated for the injustice he has suffered, irrevocably entrap him into matter. One shackle holds him captive in its 'high' pole of material oscillation, while the other, prisoner to its 'lower' pole in a continuous role alteration. Do not forget the basic point though! **The fruit** of the knowledge of good and evil (the apple) is <u>one</u>. And the endless cycle of eternal desire and satisfaction, injustice and restitution, balance of debts and credits continues without end, until the soul loses even its most minute trace of spiritual reserves and becomes dead.

---

[224] **THE GOSPEL OF MATTHEW, CH. 8**: «§22. But Jesus told him, Follow me, and let the **dead** bury their own dead.»

Let us now move on to the examination of another subject: People by default love the world of matter, since it is all they know. What they love attracts them. Thus, out of all the material manifestations, those they have loved the most will be the 'magnets' to draw them back.

---

[225] **THE GOSPEL OF MATTHEW, CH. 6**: «§21. For where your treasure is, <u>there</u> your heart will be also.»

In essence then, through his own love, man is entrapped and bound to his material preference, whatever that may be.

---

[226] **THE GOSPEL OF MATTHEW, CH. 6**: «§19. Do not store up for yourselves treasures on earth, because moth *(for material bodies)* and rust *(for material objects)* will destroy them, and thieves break in and steal. §20. But store up treasures for yourselves in heaven, where moth and rust do not destroy, and where thieves do not break in nor steal.»

In this precise detail, lies the key to salvation. Through self-knowledge, man will discover (remember) his Spiritual Origin. Then he will love his Spiritual Birth-Land **more than anything else** and IT will draw him close to IT and will redeem him completely.

---

[227] **THE GOSPEL OF MATTHEW, Ch. 10**: «§37. Anyone who loves his father or mother more than Me is not worthy of Me; anyone who loves his son or daughter more than Me is not worthy of Me;»

Any emotional (astral) **dependence** on people traps each departing soul and does not let it return to its Spiritual Birth-Land, but rather encages it.

> **228** **THE GOSPEL OF THOMAS,** JEAN YVES LELOUP
>
> **(a)** §55. «Jesus said, whoever cannot free themselves from their father and their mother cannot become My disciple. Whoever cannot free themselves from their brother and sister and does not bear their cross…is not worthy of Me.»
>
> **(b)** §87. «Jesus said: Wretched is the body that depends <u>on another body</u> *(loving or hating it —they are both dependences)*. <u>Wretched</u> is the soul that depends on these two *(caught in the nets of hatred or dependent love)*.» [Eng. tr. JOSEPH ROWE]

—All this information is totally new and different to what 'circulates' in the circles of those who 'seek'.
—This is natural. The reason is that this **quasi** spiritual upgrading is purposely given in such a way through channeling by the 'assigned teachers', so that it leads **nowhere**. 'Good students' continue to hope that in their **next** life, they will win laurels for their efforts and the vicious cycle is perpetuated.

> **229** **THE GOSPEL OF MATTHEW, CH. 10**: «§24. A student is not above his teacher, nor a servant above his master. §25 It is enough for the student to be like his teacher, and the servant like his master. If the **master of the house** has been called Beelzebub, how much more the members of his household…!»

—And how can I be certain that through this innovative philosophical position, Spiritual salvation will finally come?
—Through logical reasoning, we reach the conclusion that through matter, one can only evolve **materially**. On the contrary, for Spiritual upgrade, withdrawal from anything materialistic is necessary. Ergo, the absolutely dense material plane <u>does not favor</u> spiritual ascension!

PART TWO:
THE CHRONICLE OF MAN'S IMPRISONMENT

THE CREATION OF THE HUMAN RACES AND THE FIRST FALL

–All our previous discussion had the purpose of preparing your intellect to accept what I am about to gradually reveal to you. We will now change our view, looking at the facts from a completely Spiritual dimension, having in our possession all that was previously mentioned. You must look at the final 'fall' of man objectively and understand the myth of the primordial sin because therein lies the key.

To begin with, it would be worthwhile to feel our way around two fundamental Hebrew word-keys. The first is the word 'Adam', which in Hebrew means 'human/human kind' and doesn't differentiate between male and female. The second word is the word 'Eve' which is simply the **pronounced sound** of the Hebrew word 'Havah' meaning 'Life provider – Life': (Havah – Eve = Life). So the word has no relation to the woman, except in its metaphorical meaning

❧··❧

Before we proceed to a more detailed analysis of the facts, we will make a brief recapitulation, so as to associate better with what is to follow.

At a certain point in eternity, a Luminous Entity of the HyperUniverses (Lucifer) decided to create. After having expanded from the received Properties from 'There', He detached Himself from the Whole, and distanced Himself from It. Then, selecting a dark, swirling (spinning) remnant/carcass –the forbidden tree– as 'building material', He coupled (united) with it and permeated it with His whole existence.

---

[230] **A) BLAVATSKY H., P., 'THE SECRET DOCTRINE'** (I-413):

«One can ascertain one's self as to who the great 'Deceiver' is, if they search for him with open eyes and unprejudiced mind in all Ancient Cosmogonies and Scriptures. It is the human-formed (human-shaped) Creator, the Demiurgos of Heaven and Earth, when he separated himself from the collective Hosts (Multitudes) of his fellows...» *and united with the forbidden tree.*

B) OLD TESTAMENT, GENESIS CH. 1: «§2. And **darkness** was upon the face of the abyss, and the **spirit of god** was hovering over the face of the waters. And god said, "Let there be light", and there was light.»

A reminder, in order to correlate the excerpts:

C) THE SECRET BOOK OF DZYAN, 'COSMIC EVOLUTION', STANZA III:

«§3...The ray *(the Creator)* causes the eternal egg *(the building material)* to thrill *(oscillate)*, and drops the non-eternal germ, which condenses into the

---

Don't skip chapters or bibliographic references

world-egg. §4 Then the '**three**' *(the third expression of the deity)* **falls into the 'four'** *(the four material elements).*»

D) HERMES TRISMEGISTUS: THE FOUNDER OF MONOTHEISM 9000 B.C., IOANNIDIS P. K., CH. 1: «§4…And I saw an infinite sight, flooded by light, both sweet and exceedingly pleasant; and I was wonderfully delighted beholding it. But after a little while I saw a downward darkness partially born coming down in **an oblique formation**, like a snake, fearful and hideous. I also saw that darkness be changed into a **moist nature**, unspeakably troubled, which yielded a fiery smoke from its depths, and from whence I heard an unutterable heartbreaking sound, and an inarticulate roar in a voice of fire.... §6. *(And Poemander says to Hermes)* …And that luminous Logos (Word) that you saw surging from (my) Luminous Planes **towards that moist nature**, is my *(fallen)* son that came out of my Noũs (Mind).»

At this point we need to point out what was mentioned in the chapter of 'Creation', where it becomes obvious that Poemander is not the Unuttered Principle Who names the creator of matter as 'His son', but rather, He is the Monogenes Son/Luminary of this specific Aeon-HyperUniverse. It is from Him (The Monogenes) that all his infinite, sentient, intelligent, living expressions spring forth, as the Holy Spirit. The Creator does not represent the Son but rather, He is the Third manifestation of The Holy Spirit.

In order to create an entire universe, He expanded and split, converting His very body into an invisible oscillation. Every **part** of His oscillating body was comprised of peripheral gods, each of whom represented one property, and who (gods) –according to the 'point of the oscillation' they were at– created the various energy planes (dimensions) of matter.

231 A) *Let us remember again how John expresses the event of the birth of the fallen creator and how this fallen creator builds his creation:*

THE APOCRYPHON OF JOHN, THE GNOSTIC SOCIETY LIBRARY [ENG. TR. FROM COPTIC: WALDSTEIN M., WISSE F.]: «And Sophia of Epinoia, being an aeon, conceived a thought from herself and the conception of the invisible Spirit and Foreknowledge *(Prognosis)*. She wanted to bring forth a likeness out of herself without the consent of the Spirit. …And though the person of her maleness had not approved and had not consented, (yet) she brought forth (gave birth). …And because of the invincible power which is in her, her thought did not remain idle, and something came out of her, which was **imperfect** and different from her. …And it was dissimilar to the likeness of its mother, for it had a different form. And when she saw (the consequences of) her desire, it changed into a **form of a lion-faced serpent**[1]. Its eyes were like flashing fires of lightning. She cast it away from her, outside of that place, so that no one of the immortals might see it, for she had created it in ignorance. And she surrounded it with a luminous cloud… so that no one might see it except the Holy Spirit. …and she called its name Yaldabaoth.[2] This is the first archon, the one who got a great power from his Mother. And he removed himself from her and he abandoned the places where he had been born. He became strong and created for himself other aeons inside a blaze of luminous fire, which still exists now. And he was stupefied in his Madness, which dwells within him, and he begat some authorities for himself… *(12 authorities are named)*…

And he set up seven kings - one per firmament of heaven - over the seven heavens *(the 2nd virtual Paradise included)*, and five *(kings)* over the depth of the abyss *(hell)* so that they might rule there.

And he shared his fire among them, but he did not send them (anything) from the power of the light which he had received from his Mother. **For he is ignorant darkness**. And when the light mixed with the darkness, it caused the darkness to shine, but when the darkness mixed with the light, it darkened the light, so that it became neither light nor darkness, but it was weak *(it became dim)*.

Now the archon *(of this world)*, who is weak, has three names. **The first name is Yaldabaoth** *(the main body – serpent – oscillation)*, **the second is Saklas** *(the positive expression)*, **and the third is Samael** *(or otherwise Satan)*.»

«…it changed into a **form of a lion-faced serpent.[1]**»

[1] **DANEZIS M., THEODOSIOU S. 'COSMOLOGY OF THE INTELLECT'**
CH. COSMOLOGICAL MYTHOLOGY, APPROACHING THE KNOWLEDGE OF THE CREATOR
«THE COSMOLOGICAL MYTH OF THE GREEKS: according to the Orphic cosmological view: …Water* was the beginning of All things and from the water, mud was sedimented *(dense matter)*; from these two, an animal was born, a **lion-headed snake**, and between them there was the face of a god, called Hercules and Time [Gr. 'Chronos']. This Hercules laid a huge egg…»

* *The energy-planes in the sacred texts are characterized as watery. Reference is made to the information contained in the book's final reference #635.*

«…and she called its name Yaldabaoth.[2]»

[2] **BLAVATSKY H., P., 'THE SECRET DOCTRINE'** (I-197) ILDA-BAOTH OR JEHOVAH:
«Ilda-Baoth (or Yaldabaoth) is a compound name made up of the Hebrew word **Ilda**, 'a child', and **Baoth;** [both from Hebrew 'the egg'], and [Hebrew] Baoth, **chaos**, emptiness, void, or desolation; or the child born in the egg of Chaos, like Brahma.»

B) KRAPPE A. 'INTERNATIONAL MYTHOLOGY - INDIAN (p. 145): «Brahmanism or Hinduism is characterized by the elation of two Gods: Vishnu and Shiva. These Gods, equal to each other and to Brahma, compose with Brahma the 'Trimurti' **(Triad)** that collectively includes all divine abilities and proper-

Don't skip chapters or bibliographic references

---

ties **that were distributed amongst many deities**. In this triad, **Brahma** is the creator, **Vishnu** *(the positive manifestation)* the one who preserves and **Shiva** *(the negative manifestation)* the destroyer. All other deities are either emanations or creations of these three dominant gods.»

C) **CHALDEAN ORACLES,** Gr. tr. ATHINOGENIS I., GRAVIGGER, P. (KROLL 37 – PLACES 73 DAMASCIUS II-217, 5-10 (p. 129): «If it is then said that this Zeus dwells in the heaven, it's possible that **the three fathers**, though primordial, **have been divided** into a celestial, a chthonian (earthly/terrestrial) and an intermediate one *(the aetheric realm is implied here)* as is revealed by the 'Logia' *(tr.: Scholarly Texts)*: 'Amongst these, there is the first divine path, then, in the middle, we find the airy one and a third one, that heats the earth through fire. Therefore, EVERYTHING is subject to all these three vigorous principles.»

This entity however, had not been authorized to build a universe. Nevertheless, IT desired to create living beings.

---

[232] **NEAR EAST TEXTS,** Gr. tr. XENI SKARTSI S., – SOCRATES L. SKARTSIS, **ENUMA ELISH** (ASSYRO-BABYLONIAN EPIC OF CREATION)

It was unearthed in the town of Nineveh and was found as part of Assurbanipal's imperial library, the last great king of Assyria. It consists of reproductions of older texts, obviously predating the 2nd millennium.

TABLET 6: «§1. When Marduk hears the words of the Gods, his heart prompts him to create skillful works. He opens his mouth and turns to Ea to reveal to him the plan he had captured in his heart: "I shall gather blood and make bones. I will make a savage one. Man will be his name. I will create a truly savage man. He will undertake the **service** of the Gods, so that **they** might be comfortable.»

In the apocryphal history of many human races, narrations appear which refer to the five Genders/Races of humanity. You can guess, I imagine, that I don't mean the color races of men, which concern the distribution of humanity according to climatic and geographical position. I am referring to the sum of phases that **the entire** humanity went through, during its evolutionary process until today. Most people think that these races refer to the material passage of man in life. Others however claim that they designate the gradual creation/development of man from an immaterial entity to a material existence. Indeed, this is so.

---

233 *Let us remember a previous reference*

BLAVATSKY H., P., 'THE SECRET DOCTRINE' (II-457): «The Kabbalists teach **the existence of four distinct Adams**, or the transformation of four consecutive Adams, the emanations from the *Dyooknah* (divine phantom) of the Heavenly Man, a superior (aetheric) combination of Neschamah, the highest Soul or Spirit: this Adam having, of course, neither a gross human body, nor a body of desire *(astral body)*. This Adam is the prototype of the second Adam. That they represent our Five Races is certain, as everyone can see by their description in the Kabbalah: the first being the perfect, Holy Adam… A shadow that disappeared and was produced from the divine Tzelem (Image). The second is called the protoplastic androgyne Adam of the future terrestrial and separated (divided) Adam. The third Adam is the man made of 'dust/soil' *(aetheric)* (the first innocent Adam) and the fourth, is the supposed forefather of our own race, the Fallen Adam, who was clothed with <u>skin</u>, flesh, nerves, etc. *(terrestrial, of the Earth)*… He possesses the animal power of reproduction and continuance of species, and this is the human Root-Race.»

–If I am not mistaken, they are the five races mentioned by Hesiod. And they also coincide with the genders – 'Root Races' mentioned by the Hindu tradition.

–Precisely; these are the races I am referring to. These five Gender-Races of men are in reality the Chronicle of Man's Imprisonment.

We will refer to these Races, walking hand in hand mostly with Hesiod's views, who is more kindred to your Greek culture. These five Genders are: First the Golden Race, then the Silver, next the Bronze. The Race of Heroes is in between, which is characterized by a rather shocking event (hence its characterization as the Race of Heroes) with the Iron Race coming up next. These Genders then refer to the creation of the energy-bodies of man, from the finer/subtler to the denser material one.

❧·❧

In the HyperUniverses of the Father, 'birth' does not occur by will, but is the result of Completeness. Will is the result of fission, since for every will there is always an involuntariness *{Tr. n.: [α-βουλία = lack of will] the negative 'α' and the Gr. word βούλησŋ = will}*.

Don't skip chapters or bibliographic references

---

234 **HERMES TRISMEGISTUS,** HERMETIC TEXTS, VOL. I, RODAKIS P., TZAFEROPOULOS AP., **SPEECH I**: «§8. And I said to Him: Where do these elements of nature come from? And He answered to me again: From the Divine **Will** which took the form of Logos (Word) and **saw the Good World** *(of the HyperUniverses)* **and mimicked it,** creating a world with its own *(the Divine Will's)* elements and its own creations, the souls.»

The creator's instruction was clear and addressed all partial deities of creation. "Let us create man according to our image and our likeness".

---

235 A) **THE SECRET BOOK OF DZYAN, 'ANTHROPOGENESIS', STANZA IV**: «§14 The seven hosts, the **Will (or Mind) born Lords**, propelled by the spirit of life-giving *(Eve/Life)*, separate *(projected)* men from themselves, each on his own zone.»

B) **OLD TESTAMENT, GENESIS CH. 1**: «§26. Then God said [1] "Let **us**[1] make man in **our**[1] image, after **our**[1] likeness." *...The main body (of the one god/creator) consisted of all other partial/secondary gods. They corresponded to specific parts of his oscillating, snake-like body. There is the reason for the plural forms used in the above text* (…each in his own zone/territory).

[1] **PLATO'S TIMAEUS** (41b, c5): «Now, when all gods…had been born, the Creator of the present universe addressed them in these words: "Gods, children of gods, of whom I am the Creator and father as well as of the creations, which, since they were made by me, are all indissoluble unless I will it otherwise….Now listen to my instructions: Three mortal generations remain to be created. If they are not born the sky will be incomplete, for it will not contain every kind of animal which it ought to contain, if it is to be perfect. On the other hand, if they were to be created by me and received life from me, they would be equal to the gods. In order then that they may be mortal, and that this universe may be truly universal, **do as your nature directs**, devoting yourselves to the formation of living beings, imitating the power shown by me in my creation of you.»

C) **THE GOSPEL OF JUDAS** [KASSER R., MEYER M., WURST G.] NATIONAL GEOGRAPHIC: «Then Saklas, *(whose face flashed with fire and whose appearance was defiled with blood)* said to his angels, "Let us create a human being after the likeness and after the image.»

D) **THE APOCRYPHON OF JOHN, THE GNOSTIC SOCIETY LIBRARY**: «And he *(Yaldabaoth)* said to the authorities who served him, "Come, let us create a man

---

according to the image of God and according to our likeness, so that his image may become light for us.» [Eng. tr. from Coptic: FREDERIK WISSE]

E) THE SECRET BOOK OF DZYAN, 'ANTHROPOGENESIS', STANZA III: «§12. The great Chohans (Lords) called the Lords of the Moon, of the airy bodies. "Bring forth men, men of your own nature. Give them their forms within. She will build coverings without (their external bodies). For male-female will they be.»

F) HERMES TRISMEGISTUS, HERMETIC TEXTS, VOL. II, RODAKIS P., TZAFEROPOULOS AP., **EXCERPT FROM 'KORE KOSMOU'**: *God sends Hermes to summon all the Gods in front of him:*

«§28 Each one of them thought about what he could offer to those about to be born in the future. …Kronos informed them that he had already become the father of Justice and Necessity/Need; Zeus said: "In order for the race of men to completely avoid the war that was to follow, I have already given birth to Fortune, Hope, and Peace"; Ares (Mars) said that he was already the father of Struggle, Wrath and Strife; Aphrodite did not remain indifferent but stated: "My Lord, I shall grant them Desire, Pleasure, and Laughter, so that the kindred souls might not endure further punishment and prolong the suffering of their **sentence**"… §29 "And for my part", said Hermes, "I shall create the nature of men. I have thought of giving them Prudence, Wisdom, Persuasiveness, and Truth, and shall ceaselessly work with them through Invention and will eternally benefit the mortal lives of men.»

Then, all 'points' of His oscillating existence (every deity) would work to contribute their little 'something' for the 'greatest' creation. It is that plural

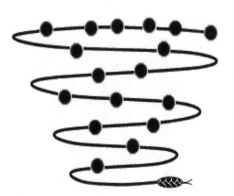

used in the phrase "let <u>us</u> create man", which is so incomprehensible to the Bible scholars, since they believe the creator to be only one. The man-being would be an absolutely collective creation with the collaboration of all points/deities of the oscillating body of the one creator-god.

Immortality is not a 'de facto' property, but occurs <u>only</u> from the perpetual absorption of the Life-creating 'Atmosphere' of the HyperUniverses and the expansion of all the Intelligent Wholenesses <u>in IT</u>.

Don't skip chapters or bibliographic references

> **236** *This is why after all the Book of Dzyan characterizes the 'sperm' of the ray that penetrated the eternal egg of the universe, as non-eternal. This is because this ray/creator A after detaching itself from its Initial Environment, it gradually proceeds toward death Ω where it will cease living:*
> **THE SECRET BOOK OF DZYAN, 'COSMIC EVOLUTION', STANZA III**: «§3…The ray *(Creator)* causes the eternal egg *(building material)* to thrill *(oscillate)*, and drops <u>the non-eternal germ</u>, which condenses into the world-egg.»

However the young creator, having been <u>cut off</u> from his Source remained bound onto his own universe. Because of that, His Completeness was being constrained and He could expand no more. The fission which He had undergone essentially weakened Him.

> **237** **THE APOCRYPHON OF JOHN, THE GNOSTIC SOCIETY LIBRARY**: «§10. Now the archon *(of this world)* **who is weak** has three names.»

The higher parts of the oscillation of the second (energy-material) manifested creation were inhabited by the entities reflecting absolute positiveness. It is what many people call Paradise and the Hindus Nirvana; the base of the 'benevolent' God and His angels; the one side of the twofold entity of the creator.

Inside this highly oscillating area, these positive Entities (gods) created 'Creatures' from the subtlest/finest/most delicate 'matter' of their plane and according to their properties. These Creatures exhibited their creators' characteristics. However these Creatures just lay there, lifeless. They were dead.

> **238** **A) THE APOCRYPHON OF JOHN, THE GNOSTIC SOCIETY LIBRARY**:
> «§17, 18 And **all the angels and daemons** labored until they had created the psychic body. And their product was completely inactive and motionless *(without life)* for a long time.» [Eng. tr. from Coptic: WALDSTEIN M., WISSE F.]
> **B) THE SECRET BOOK OF DZYAN, 'ANTHROPOGENESIS', STANZA IV**: «§15…The fathers, the ones without bones (boneless) **could not give <u>life</u> to beings with bones.** Their progeny (offspring) were Bhuta with neither form nor mind. Therefore they are called the Chhaya.»

In order for the Holy Spirit/creator to vitalize the young creatures, so that they –having been created by the higher section of His body, i.e. by the individual higher gods– would possess Life, the property of Life/Eve needed to be granted to Him from the Father-Planes of the HyperUniverses as a fundamental prerequisite.

The Sacred Archetype of Life/Eve is granted to the new creation from the Unspoken Principle.

> **239** *The reasons for this concession/bestowal are given in chapter: 'A DIF-FERENT VIEWPOINT'*

The gods acquire Living Breath which is blown into the lifeless creatures. The 'products' of the creators are transformed into Living Souls.

> **240** **A) THE APOCRYPHON OF JOHN, THE GNOSTIC SOCIETY LIBRARY**:
> «They *(the Delegates of True Light)* said to Yaldabaoth: "Blow into his face something of your Spirit, and his body will arise *(of the man/being/soul)*." And he blew into his face *(of the man/being/soul)* the spirit which is the power of his mother; he did not know (this), for he exists in ignorance. And the power of the mother **came out of Yaldabaoth and went into the psychic body** *(soul)*... The body moved, gained strength and it was luminous.» [Eng. tr. from Coptic: WALDSTEIN M., WISSE F.]
>
> **B) PLATO'S TIMAEUS C35.** TR. KOUTROUMPAS G. (C35a1-35b3 p. 57-59): «And he *(the creator)* made the Soul out of the following elements and in the following manner: Out of the **indivisible** and eternally unchangeable essence *(The Indivisible Spirit granted through the Immortal Breath of the god/creator)*, and also out of that which has to do with material bodies and is **divisible** *(divided by Logos, finer/subtler energy-hylē/paste of the material world)*, by combining therefore the two, he had essences from both and he compounded a third and intermediate kind of essence between the indivisible and the divisible.»
> *In other words, the creator created beings with the subtler **divisible** energy-matter, and since these beings were dead, he breathed (blew) into them the **indivisible** part he carried within from the Unsplit Cosmoi of The Truth.*
>
> **C) BLAVATSKY H., P., 'THE SECRET DOCTRINE'** (II-513): «The Fall was the result of man's knowledge, for 'his eyes were opened'. Indeed, he was taught Wisdom *(devious wisdom)* and the hidden knowledge by the 'Fallen Angel', for the latter had become from that day his Manas, Mind and Self-consciousness. ...And now it stands proven that Satan, or the Red Fiery Dragon, the Lord of Phosphorus (brimstone was a theological improvement), and Lucifer, or 'Light-Bearer', is in us *(as the 'Breath' of the creator of our soul)*: it is our Mind -- our Tempter and Redeemer.»
> *Here lies the great fallacy of Blavatsky, since she couldn't see the whole picture and gave the role of the 'redeemer' to the convicted one.*
> *In another place (since she has thoroughly researched into the subject) she states it bluntly:* (I-198): Thus 'SATAN', once he ceases to be

Don't skip chapters or bibliographic references

viewed in the superstitious, dogmatic, un-philosophical spirit of the Churches, grows into the grandiose *(!!)* image of one who made of terrestrial *(matter)* a divine MAN; who gave him, throughout the long cycle of Maha-Kalpa the law of the Spirit of Life, and made him free from the Sin of Ignorance, hence of death. *(!!)*

The basic properties of the soul are mainly the Noûs and the ability to perceive immaterial ideas from the conceptual spaces of the **energy**-universe.

241 *A reminder:* **CHALDEAN ORACLES,** Gr. tr. ATHINOGENIS I., GRAVIGGER, P. KROLL 47-PLACES 94-PROCLUS IN TIMAEUS. 336A (p. 153): «He *(the creator)* placed the Noûs in soul, and the soul inside the inert body. We were established by the father of men and gods himself.»

Besides the psychic noûs though, the soul itself is characterized by some personal properties. These properties <u>must not</u> be confused with emotions. They relate more to 'tendencies' that have the roots of their variety in the special characteristics of each individual **partial** god-creator of 'Beings/Souls', since each individual god created his own group of 'sister souls'.

The first Souls in the 'form' of man, the first Race of Man-beings, had been completed: Only soul, and no other garment/body on them. This is The First Race, the Golden one.

242 **HESIOD 'WORKS AND DAYS',** VERSES 109-122: «First of all, the immortal gods who dwell in the Olympian chambers made the golden race of mortal men ... And they lived like gods without sorrow in their hearts, free from toil and grief. Not even the misery of old age came upon them *(since the soul does not grow old)*; but with legs and arms never failing, they made merry with feasting beyond the reach of all evils. ...For the <u>wheat-giving</u>[1] earth spontaneously *(Anc. Gr. original:* αὐτομάτη *= automatically, i.e. the energy that permeates the entire universe)* granted them plenty of fruit abundantly...But after this race was covered by the soil, in accordance to Zeus' will they became benevolent daemons.»
[1] *In the ancient text the meaning of the word 'σιτοδότρα' stems from the ancient word 'ζείδωρος' [zeidoros = wheat-giving]. A great number of writers, all following Hesiod's time, assume that the word etymologically stems from the Gr. verb 'ζάω-ζῶ' [zao-zo = to live] and consider it synonymous to the word 'viodoros'= life-granting.*

The second (inferior) creators' group (daemons) was the sum of entities comprising the astral plane. They would prepare their own creation by molding astral bodies, each one in his personal style, and using the 'materials' of their own particular plane.

> **243** *As to __what__ these 'materials' are, this will be clarified as our discussion continues.*

I must make it clear that, when the astral plane was first created, it was simply the negative expression of dyadicism (duality) and not necessarily of the dark negativity. It was much later that this negativity (-) was transformed into the dark daemonic quality man knows today. As an electron possesses negative charge, without this negativity having bad or daemonic connotations, so too this __initial__ fission of the Creator simply created the two opposite poles (+ and –) without the burden of the dark negativity that has been woven within it today. Also, this division to a superior team and an inferior one, to positive entities and negative ones, to gods and daemons, __was not a natural event__ from the HyperUniversal view. It was a **side-effect** that resulted from the 'stuff' (quality of the building material) of the dark remnant/carcass with which the Creator united, to make his material creation. We will examine this 'building material' later in our discussion and we will then justify the reason why this division into superior and inferior, positive and negative and so on, was an 'unnatural' yet necessary perversion.

The creation of the higher class of the creators (the Soul) had to merge with the creation of the next lower class/cast, i.e. the astral body. Thus the souls of the first Race are 'covered with the soil' of the next denser (energy-wise) matter, the astral energy, and are 'dressed' with the astral body. The second Race/Gender, the Silver one is born.

> **244** **THE SECRET BOOK OF DZYAN, 'ANTHROPOGENESIS', STANZA V:**
> «§21 When the *(First)* race became old, the old waters mixed with the fresher waters[1]. When its drops became turbid, they vanished and disappeared in the new stream, in the hot stream of life. **The outer of the first became the inner of the second**. The old wing became the new shadow, and the shadow of the wing.»
> [1] *Blavatsky notes:* «The old initial Race was mixed with the second and became one with it.»

The second body, the astral, did not possess a noûs (mind) or the ability to express the mental (conceptual/intellectual) property of the soul. It possessed two other very special tools though, useful to an individualized hypostasis: The 'Ego' and the 'I Will'. Surrounded by the denser astral body, the pure soul could not convey intellect to it. The astral body, being denser, dominates the soul, controlling it exclusively with its two astral properties

Don't skip chapters or bibliographic references

of the 'ego' and 'will', which are simply colored by the psychic 'tendencies' and manifest the diversity of emotions.

> **245** **RUDOLF STEINER, 'FROM THE AKASHIC CHRONICLE'** COSMIC MEMORY (p. 169):
> «At the same time, the Fire Spirits act in the astral body, enabling it to carry an active perception and feeling and effervescently taking in impressions from the world around. …What however the Fire Spirits cause onto the astral body, are intense passions of love and hatred, anger, fear, horror, gusty passions, instincts, impetuses and so forth. Because the Spirits of Personality (Azura) had previously vaccinated this astral body with their resemblance/nature *(the Souls)*, these passions appear now with the character of selfhood, of a separate self. …Into the astral body, pictures pour and then ebb, pictures which are aroused by the aforementioned passions.»

This is why there is a great divide manifesting in material man between the unreasonable emotional impetuses generated by the astral body, and the advice of the Soul's noûs. These two 'guides' (reason and emotion) are usually in conflict and opposition to each other.

The physical body, carrying the decoding brain, has the ability to receive the dictates of the sentient soul and to control its overall behavior according to logic. This is precisely the reason for the 'childishness' in the man-child, whose physical brain, the main recipient of the soul's intellect, hasn't yet fully developed. So, the man-child is exclusively controlled by the mindless astral body, which is the carrier of intense emotions, compulsions and the Ego.

These two primary properties (the 'Ego' and the 'Will'), at the time of early creation, are manifested differently to what man is familiar with today. Later on, in combination with man's living conditions inside dense matter, a plethora of different expressions of the 'Ego' and the 'Will' enriched the astral body with new properties and characteristics, which compose the emotional character of each person today.

So this young being *(Second Race/Gender, the Silver one)* was dominated by an intensely impulsive behavior.

> **246** **HESIOD, 'WORKS AND DAYS'** (verses 127-135): «Then the gods made a second generation/race, the silver one, **inferior** and less noble one by far *(instead of an improvement, degradation occurs)*… unlike the golden race in body or in spirit. A child was brought up for a hundred years …playing joyously and **foolishly** at home. …They lived only for a little time and suffered because of their foolishness, for they could not avoid unholy insults to one another.»

When the Silver Race completed its cycle, it too was covered by the next denser layer of aetheric matter i.e. 'it got dressed up' with a new body, the aetheric one, thus forming the Bronze Race.

–When we were enumerating the bodies of man, we spoke of the lower

mental body. When was this body created?

–This body (the lower mental one) with its respective plane is much younger and was created <u>after</u> the creation of the purely material man. We will examine this later, because to be able to focus on details, we must first have a complete overview; this is why I am giving you the complete picture more concisely.

So the Third Race, the Bronze, was born with a body a step denser than the astral one *(Silver Race),* and thinner/subtler than that of dense matter. It resides in the field whose entities weave the aetheric pattern/template upon which the absolutely material (visible) universe will be built <u>next</u>.

---

247 A) **HESIOD 'WORKS AND DAYS'** VERSES 143-145: «Zeus the Father made a third generation of mortal men, a brazen race, sprung from Meliae [ash-trees] [1]; and it was in no way similar/equal to the silver race, but was terrible and strong.»

[1] *Hesiod's reviewer, Stavros Girgenis, as a footnote at this particular point, mentions here:*

«The Bronze race is associated with the Melia (ash-tree), a tree that has very hard wood… According to another view, this reference to the Meliae is directly associated with the Meliad Nymphs, forest-tree deities.»

The Nymphs belong to the category of elementals that dwell in the aetheric plane.

B) *At this point, I cite an excerpt from an Orphic Hymn devoted to Zeus, the dominant king (creator), because this hymn specifically mentions the 'bronze sky', which is none other than the 'sky' of the aetheric plane.*

«…There is indeed only one king-lord self-born. And all that has been created are offspring (creations) of this unique one. He, the king, wanders amongst them (his creations); and no man can see him, yet he sees all. He provides (bestows) men everything from good to evil, like the bitterly cold war, and tearful sorrows.

…However, I cannot see him, for a cloud has been placed around him and because men only possess mortal irises in their eyes which cannot see Zeus, the archon of all. Because he is enthroned/settled in the **bronze sky** *(aetheric–bronze plane)* upon a golden throne, he walks the earth with his feet on the ground and his right hand is extended to the end of the ocean …and around him the grand mountains, the rivers and the depths of the blue sea tremble.»

C) MARGIORIS, N. 'DE-SYMBOLIZATION OF THE GREEK MYTHOLOGY' (p. 253):

«The aetheric body is the canvas upon which the material, human body is woven by the aetheric vibrations.»

The aetheric body is equipped with such properties so that it can receive the provided qualities of both previous bodies: The psychic intellect with the special psychic tendencies as well as the intentions of the 'Ego' and the 'Will' of the astral body.

Don't skip chapters or bibliographic references

In the densely material plane, these three bodies interact with each other and generate a combination of properties, thus expressing the individual character of each person.

All bodies of man, each one materially denser than the previous one, had completed his outfit. The journey had reached its end. The purpose of this creation was the formation of only these three bodies/races: Golden, Silver and Bronze.

The tenants of each plane/dimension, which the sentient *[Nous possessing]* soul passed through, dressed it with their own body/garment. Each plane corresponded to a different part of the oscillating creation. In each of its parts, different beings/powers lived with different properties from the neighboring ones. Man was going to be the 'child' of all points/levels of the oscillation. Gods and daemons had ornamented every part of him. He (man) was the creation that belonged to everyone. Everyone could and would claim it!

---

248 **THE SECRET BOOK OF DZYAN, 'ANTHROPOGENESIS', STANZA IV**:

«§17 The Breath needed a form; the Fathers gave it. The Breath needed a gross body. The Mother molded it. The Breath needed the Spirit of Life. The solar Lhas breathed it into its form. The Breath needed a mirror of its body. "We gave it our own", said the Dhyanis. The Breath needed a vehicle of desires. "It has it", said the drainer of waters. But Breath needed a Mind (Noûs) to embrace the universe;. "We cannot give that," said the Fathers. "I never had it", said the spirit of the earth. "The form would be consumed were I to give it my Noûs", said the Great Fire.... Man remained an empty senseless Bhuta.... Thus have the boneless given life to those who became men with bones in the Third *(the Third Root Race, or the Third Gender of Hesiod, the Bronze Gender).*»

The reproduction of these aetheric man-beings was peculiar and different compared to contemporary man's reproductive process. Man-beings were only <u>one gender</u>, which is entirely normal after all, and not the perversion that followed. The division of the sexes did not exist yet.

---

249 **PLATO'S SYMPOSIUM ARISTOPHANES' SPEECH** (189d-190d):

«...For our original nature was by no means the same as it is now, but entirely different. Unlike today, with its two sexes male and female, there used to be a third kind before as well, which had equal shares of the other two, and whose name no longer exists. For 'man-woman' was then a unity, common both in form and in name, composed of both male and female ...Then, each person of this kind was round all over, with back and sides forming a circle... Zeus...said: "I will slice every one of them in two, so that they are made weaker. *(Why is that, really?...)*»

Birth was accomplished through **excretion** of a portion of the vital essence of the astro-aetheric man-being; something <u>equivalent but inferior</u> to the production/manifestation of each individual Intelligent Living Archetypal Property-Wholeness of the HyperUniverses by Its Genitor.

A similar **material** depiction of this process is given by the ectoplasm poured out by some mediums when they are in communication with the spirit realm. Through this process a young being was born.

---

250 **A) THE SECRET BOOK OF DZYAN, 'ANTHROPOGENESIS', STANZA VI**:

«§22 Then the Second *(Root-Race of men)* evolved the Egg-born, the Third *(Root-Race of men)*. The sweat grew, and the **drops** became hard and round. The sun warmed it; the moon cooled and shaped it. The wind fed it until its ripeness.»

H. P. Blavatsky, in the 2ⁿᵈ Volume of her 'Secret Doctrine', further clarifies on this:

(II-132) «…The early sub-races of the Third Humanity procreated their species by a kind of moisture exudation, or a vital fluid, the drops of which coalescing formed an oviform (egg-shaped) ball –or shall we say an egg– that served as an extraneous vehicle….»

B) *An excerpt from the Vishnu-Puraná, describes a story about how the Second Race, the Silver/Astral one, the mindless, gave its place to the Third Race, the Bronze/Aetheric one, the sweat-born (made of Melia [ash tree]-wood), through a Meliad nymph [a being/deity of the aetheric plane].*

BLAVATSKY H., P., 'THE SECRET DOCTRINE' (II-175): «The king of the gods sends a beautiful Apsarasas (nymph) *(=Meliad nymph)* named Pramlocha to seduce Kandu and disturb his penance *(because he had made the Gods jealous)*. She succeeds in her unholy purpose and 907 years six months and three days spent in her company seem to the sage as one day.[1] When this psychological or hypnotic state ends, the Muni (Kandu) curses bitterly the creature who seduced him. "Depart, be gone!" he cries, "vile bundle of illusions!"…And Pramlocha, terrified, flies away, wiping the perspiration from her body with the leaves of the trees as she passes through the air. She (the nymph) <u>went from tree to tree</u>, and as, with the dusky shoots that crowned their summits, she dried her limbs, the child she had conceived <u>came forth from the pores of her skin in drops of perspiration</u>. **The trees** *(=Melia [ash] trees)* received the living dews; and the winds collected them into one mass. 'This', said Soma (the Moon), "I matured by my rays; and gradually it increased in size, till it became the lovely girl named Marisha.» [Vishnu-Puraná, Bk.1, Ch. XV, Wilson, Vol. II, p. 5]

[1] *And Blavatsky here specifies that:* «Kandu is a son of the Pitris, hence one devoid of mind *(=the Silver Race/Gender… foolishly and mindlessly playing [HESIOD])*, which is hinted at by his being unable to discern a period of nearly one thousand years from one day.»

A great problem arises here though, and this is where <u>the fundamental cause</u> for the fall of Celestial Man <u>inside</u> the man-being of material crea-

Don't skip chapters or bibliographic references

tion stems from. I must make it clear that the creation of the three initial Gender/Races (Golden-Soul, Silver-Astral and Bronze-Aetheric), does not refer to the creation of Celestial Man, but to that of the man-being. This living man-being **did not** possess a very basic capacity in order to be complete. This was the capacity to offer **his own** living offspring –without the intervention of gods or daemons. The young offspring, the one stemming from the soulful, astro-aetheric man-being, <u>could not</u> assimilate all the qualities of his parent. And despite the fact that the primary parent possessed a full-fledged hypostasis, the offspring was deficient. The inability to transfer the attributes of the parent (astro-aetheric man-being) to the young offspring was a great problem for the material creation.

–*Does the same also happen with animals?*

–Astro-aetheric animals were created (formed) later on and almost <u>in parallel</u> to the creation of the absolutely dense matter. We have not touched upon this part yet in our analysis.

However I must clarify to you a very obscure and indistinguishable difference. There are two poles: the spiritual and the material one. One pole is diametrically opposite to the other. If in other words we gaze 'upon the facts from the **material pole**, then we can discern <u>an upgrade</u> from the incomplete, simple, material microorganisms to the more complex and developed ones. If we look at the facts from the point of view of the **spiritual pole**, then a process of spiritual <u>degradation</u> becomes apparent from a higher to a lower state.

---

251 *In the 1ˢᵗ <u>Chapter</u> of Genesis, which refers to the creation of **<u>dense matter</u>**, man is created <u>last</u> and particularly in §26, <u>after</u> the rest of the dense, material creation **<u>has already been completed</u>**.*

OLD TESTAMENT, GENESIS CH. 1 *(**<u>Material Creation</u>**)*

«§25 And God made the beasts of the earth according to their kinds, and the cattle according to their kinds and all the serpents of the earth, each according to its kind. And God saw that it was good. §26. Then God said, <u>Let us make man</u> in our image, after our likeness, and let them have dominion over the fish of the sea and over the birds of the sky and over the livestock and over all the earth, and over every serpent that creeps on the ground.»

*Contrary to the first chapter though, in the <u>second chapter</u> of Genesis, where the **<u>aetheric creation</u>** is described, Man appears **<u>first</u>** and specifically in §7. The remaining creation <u>follows</u>, where, in §19, the animals are created*

OLD TESTAMENT, GENESIS CH. 2 *(**<u>Aetheric Creation</u>**)*

«§18 The Lord God said, "It is not good for man to be **alone**. I will make him a helper, suitable for him. §19. And **out of the earth*** the Lord God

made all the beasts of the field and all the birds of the air and he brought them to Adam to see how to name them; and whatever name Adam gave to each living creature, that was its name.»

*In the following text, we can clearly see the **aetheric creation** of Chapter 2.*

OLD TESTAMENT, GENESIS CH. 2 (*Aetheric Creation*)

«§4 This is the book of genesis *(creation)* of the heavens and the earth when they were created, in the day when the Lord God **made them**, the earth and the heavens §5. and all herbs of the field, **before** they had yet been created on *(densely material)* earth and all the plants of the field **before** they had yet sprung up, for the Lord God had not yet sent rain on the *(visible)* earth and **there was no man** to work the ground, §6. but steam came up from the earth and watered the whole face of the earth.»

I deem it necessary here, to remind you of a previous reference mentioned in Ch. 'Aetheric Body – Aetheric Plane' so that an association is made, namely that, before any densely material manifestation, dark matter precedes it, as cohesive tissue. Dark matter here is equated to the aetheric plane.

DARK MATTER ACCUMULATES FIRST AND THEN THE GALAXY IS FORMED
SOURCE: NASA NEWS 16TH JUNE 2006
http://www.physics4u.gr/news/2006/scnews2503.html

«…Initially, researchers were trying to comprehend better how new galaxies and dark matter evolve and accumulate together. …At that point they observed something odd: Every galaxy they studied seemed to be surrounded by 'chunks' of dark matter of approximately the **same** size. They were able to indirectly measure how much dark matter –holding the structure together like glue– was present. The tighter the grouping [concentration] was, the greater the amount of dark matter present.»

In order to overcome the difficulty of transferring 'Life' to the descendants, an autonomous, **Unsplit Intelligent Wholeness** with the ability to frequently visit the FatherLands had to be embodied inside the already formed man-being who possessed a soul and astral and aetheric bodies. Then its emanations/offspring would supply the energy-material creation with the Life-giving Essence of Immortality, thus expanding the material-energy universe; because the property of Immortality exists only if the Immortal Entity remains **unified** with Its Source.

[252] A) THE GOSPEL OF JOHN, CH. 15: «§4. Abide in Me, and I in you. As the vine-branch cannot bear fruit of itself unless it abides in the vine, so, neither can you, unless you abide in Me.»

Don't skip chapters or bibliographic references

> **B)** *A reminder:* **THE SECRET BOOK OF DZYAN, 'COSMIC EVOLUTION', STANZA III**: «§3…The ray *(Creator)* causes the eternal egg to thrill *(oscillate)*, and drops <u>the non-eternal germ,</u> *(or the non-immortal)* which condenses into the world-egg.» *It ceases being eternal and immortal because it is cut off from its Source.*

Again the creator addresses the HyperUniverses of the True for a second time, asking now for the capacity of expansion for his offspring. His plea is considered as a cry for help, it is acknowledged and accepted. In the material (energy) universe, with the aetheric man-being already formed, a tremendous event is about to take place. Because of that event, the fourth Race/Gender of Heroes was about to be born.

کمچ۰ی

In the **Celestial Kingdoms of the HyperUniverses**, young properties/offspring/emanations had been created; new emanations of the third category of the Holy Spirit, belonging to the same category as the young creator. They were the Celestial Men (Adams). The invitation/request of the brother-creator becomes known. The Holy Celestial Men, seeing the archetype of Life/Eve having **already** been granted to the new creator, accept his proposal and join his creation aiming to help him.

> **253** *The Great One (in the Gospel of Judas) commands that those who possess the Spirit (Celestial Men) should proceed to the material universe with no ruler over them, implying the soul and its creator.*
>
> **A) THE GOSPEL OF JUDAS [KASSER R., MEYER M., WURST G.] NATIONAL GEOGRAPHIC** «[53]: Jesus said, "This is why God ordered Michael to give the spirits of people *(Celestial Men)* to them **as a loan**, so that they might offer service, but the Great One *(The Unuttered Supreme One)* ordered Gabriel to grant spirits to the great generation with no ruler over it.»
> *But therein lies the key of the misfortune, as will become apparent later on. The key phrase here is 'With no ruler over it'.*
>
> **B) THE APOCRYPHON OF JOHN, THE GNOSTIC SOCIETY LIBRARY**: «But the Blessed One, the Mother-Father, the Beneficent and Merciful One, had mercy upon the Mother's power *(the Living Soul)* which had been brought forth out of the chief archon *(Yaldabaoth)*… and He sent… a helper to Adam, Luminous Epinoia *(Celestial Man)*, which comes out of Him Who is called Life.» [Eng. tr. from Coptic: FREDERIK WISSE]
>
> **C) THE APOCRYPHON OF JOHN, THE GNOSTIC SOCIETY LIBRARY** [ENG. TR. FROM COPTIC: STEVAN DAVIES]
>
> «HUMANITY BEGINS: Then, came a voice from the highest realms saying: "The Man exists! And the Son of Man!" Yaldabaoth, chief ruler, heard it. He

thought it came from his mother. He did not know the true source of the voice: The Holy Mother-Father, Perfect Providence, Image of the Invisible Father of Everything, in Whom everything has come **TO BE**. The First Man [This is the one who appeared to them. He appeared in the form of a human being.] All of the realm *(dimensions)* of the chief ruler quaked! The foundations of the abyss moved! He *(this human form)* illuminated the waters above the world of matter, his image shown *(appeared)* in those waters. All the daemons and the first ruler together gazed up toward the underside of the newly shining waters. Through that light they saw the Image *(of man)* in the waters.» *This is Celestial Man's first appearance in the astro-aetheric realms.*

Dense **visible** matter had not yet been formed. These events take place in the **aetheric planes**. Upon entering the energy-creation, Celestial Men from the HyperUniverses choose the most handsome aetheric appearances of man-beings and after they are embodied inside of, they upgrade them. Other energy beings are not chosen and remain plain souls.

[254] **THE SECRET BOOK OF DZYAN, 'ANTHROPOGENESIS', STANZA VII**:
«§24 The sons of wisdom … came down. They saw the vile forms of the first third *(the early Third - Bronze - Root Race)*. "We can choose", said the lords. "We have wisdom". Some projected a spark *(simply to upgrade the race a little)*… Those who received but just a spark remained destitute of knowledge. The spark burned low… These were set apart *(as plain souls)* …they became narrow-headed. The Third [Root Race] were ready *(when it was perfected)*. "In these shall we dwell", said the lords of the flame.»

The entrance of the unified, Celestial Man into the chosen, soulful, astro-aetheric man-beings catapults this Race to the highest levels. The result of this entrance is the generation of the Race of Heroes. It is the time of the Demigods; the hour of the Supreme Race. So the Unified, Spiritual Man appears in the material scene and falls/sinks into the energy-expression of material creation, where he wears the soul, the astral and finally the aetheric body. He is embodied in other words, inside the man-being. {*Tr. n.: still not in dense matter*}

[255] **PAPASTAVROU, A., 'LETTERS TO ANONYMOUS'**: CH. ASTRAL PLANE (p. 38)
The Masters of the Spiritual Hierarchy (i.e. the creators' delegates) of the planet say through channeling:
«While all this was taking place, while the Elohims and the lesser constructors of form, the Deva Angels and the Legions of the Elemental

Don't skip chapters or bibliographic references

Realm were creating and beautifying the planet, the Solar Logos (Word) *(2nd Noũs/Creator/the Fallen One)* was attracting the Spiritual Sparks, the ones that would benefit *(??)* from all this preparation and love *(!!!)*. These Sparks, **having been invited** *(from the Aeons/HyperUniverses of the 1st Noũs-God)*, remained in the heart of the Deity, until IT was ready for the projection of the White Beings and the Electronic Bodies *(the souls)*, **which would be the garment** *(carriers)* **of these Spirits**. So, on one of the Cosmic Days, the work of creation was completed and the seven Elohims joyfully announced to the Solar Logos that the planet Earth was ready to host tenants.»

This is the moment when the Race of Heroes and Demigods is born and shines sublimely, when the 'Fire/Celestial Man' is granted to man-beings and a large number incarnates in them. In a covert manner and with apocryphal talent, the ancient myth-makers, sketch this Heroic entrance of Celestial Man, comparing it to the gift of 'fire' to men by Prometheus.

256 A) **BLAVATSKY H., P., 'THE SECRET DOCTRINE'** (II-83): «But shall we turn to other ancient Scriptures and documents for the corroboration of the 'Fires', 'Sparks', and 'Flames'? They are plentiful, if one only seeks for them in the right places. In the 'Book of the Concealed Mystery', they are clearly enunciated, as also in the 'Ha Idra Zuta Qadisha', or the lesser holy Assembly. The language is very mystical and veiled, yet still comprehensible:
(427) Therein, among the sparks of Prior Worlds *(HyperUniverses)*, 'vibrating Flames and Sparks', from the divine flint, the workmen proceed to create man, 'male and female' *(unified)*;
(429) From a Light-Bearer of insupportable brightness proceeded a radiating Flame, dashing off, like a vast and mighty hammer, those sparks which were the Prior Worlds.
(430) And with most subtle aether *(soul)* were these intermingled and bound mutually together, but only when they were conjoined together, even the great Father and great Mother.» …*Then the Unified Celestial Man was intermingled with the Soul and restrained by it.*
B) **HERMES TRISMEGISTUS**, HERMETIC TEXTS, VOL. II, RODAKIS P., TZAFEROPOULOS AP., **EXCERPT II$_a$**: «§1…Truth exists in eternal beings only, §2. the very **bodies** of which are true, i.e. pure **fire** and nothing else.»

'Fire' denotes nothing else but the entrance of Luminous, Celestial Men inside the up-to-now soulful, astro-aetheric man-being of the aetheric plane; A rather inappropriate metaphor of course, since the Pure Spirit's True Light can never be identified with fire or flame; these are sole manifestations of the material world as we will see later on *(see references 266 &*

268 C). Nevertheless, this is a point quite distorted by men, because of its simplification.

---

257 **A) BLAVATSKY H., P., 'THE SECRET DOCTRINE'** (II-520):
Blavatsky here refers to De Charme and his work 'Mythology of Ancient Greece'
«And here steps in the killing materialism of the age; that peculiar twist in the modern mind, which, like a Northern blast, bends all on its way, and freezes every intuition, allowing it no hand in the physical *(natural sciences)* speculations of the day. After having seen in Prometheus no better than fire by friction, the learned author of the 'Mythologie de la Grece Antique' *(hinting at De Charme)* perceives in this 'fruit' a trifle more than an allusion to terrestrial fire and its discovery.»

B) *At this point I need to call your attention to a few sensitive points that can be read between the lines of Hesiod's works, 'Works and Days' and 'Theogony' and which associate: (a) the 'Fire' Prometheus brings to humanity and (b) the Bronze Root Race. These two points are directly linked together since Prometheus offered the Fire to the men of the Bronze Root Race in the aetheric plane. This provision/offering symbolizes the entrance (embodiment) of the Celestial Men into the aetheric men-beings of the Bronze Race, made of Melia wood. Hence the three concepts:* <u>Melia wood</u>, <u>Fire</u> *and* <u>Bronze Race</u> *are interrelated.*

HESIOD 'WORKS AND DAYS' verses143-145: «Zeus the Father made a third generation of mortal men, a brazen race…sprung **from Meliae [ash-trees]** *(and not from bronze, of course)* … terrible and strong.»

PIERRE GRIMAL, DICTIONARY OF GREEK AND ROMAN MYTHOLOGY:
«The Melia *(ash tree)* is linked to the Bronze Race and it was that tree that the Meliad Nymphs inhabited.»

The Nymphs belong to the category of elementals and are the par-excellence inhabitants of the aetheric (Bronze) plane. (Let us not forget the <u>Bronze Sky</u> *in the Orphic hymn!)*

In verse 535 of 'Theogony', Hesiod speaks of the time when: "…the gods and mortal men separated from each other", *namely, of the time when the aetheric man of the Bronze Root-Race was about to inhabit the densely material field, where he would truly be separated from his unseen - invisible gods.*

It was then that Prometheus –through his infamous sacrificial distribution– cut up an ox and tried to fool Zeus by offering the <u>best parts</u> *of the animal to men. This is when Zeus' antagonism with Men begins.*

And now we come to highlight another point which relates the Melia Tree – Bronze Root-Race– to fire.

'THEOGONY' verses 558-564: «But Zeus who gathers the clouds, said to him in great grief: "Son of Iapetus, cleverer above all, oh, beloved one! So, my

---

Don't skip chapters or bibliographic references

good one, you have not yet forgotten your cunning art!" So spoke Zeus in anger, whose thoughts are everlasting; and from that time he never let go of his wrath, and **he would give no more the power of the tireless fire to the Melian Race of mortal men** who inhabit the earth.» *(He does not mean the densely material Earth here, but the aetheric one)*
There it is again, the connection of the flame/fire to the Melia–Bronze Race.
Of course, Hesiod describes <u>this conflict</u> between the men of the Bronze Root-Race and the Creator at that period of creation <u>in a rather indirect and concealed manner</u>, a conflict, which will be analyzed in the course of our narration.
We must certainly not ignore the fleeting associations we all make between maelia – Melia – mēlo [Gr. μῆλο] (=apple) [the forbidden fruit].
With the above clarifications, the following verses (567-570) from 'THEOG-ONY' seem almost self-explanatory:
«And this stung Zeus (who thunders from above) deeply into his soul and **enraged him** in his heart as he saw the **far-seen shine of the fire inside**[1] men *(the Celestial Men-Spirits)*. Forthwith he prepared a calamity for men as a reprisal for the <u>fire</u>.»

[1] **THE APOCRYPHON OF JOHN, THE GNOSTIC SOCIETY LIBRARY**: «And the luminous Epinoia **was hidden inside** Adam, <u>in order that the archons might not know her</u>.» [Eng. tr. from Coptic: FREDERIK WISSE]
C) **BLAVATSKY H., P., 'THE SECRET DOCTRINE'** (II 519, 520):

«The same author *(De Charme)* reminds us of another equally mysterious personage, though one less generally known than Prometheus, whose legend offers remarkable analogies with that of the Titan. The name of this second ancestor and generator is Phoroneus[1], the hero of an ancient poem, now unfortunately no longer extant... His legend was localized in Argolis, where a **perpetual (inextinguishable) flame** was preserved on his altar as a reminder that he was the bringer of fire upon earth (Pausanias, 11, 19, 5; Cf. 20, 3.) A benefactor of men as Prometheus was, he had made them participators of every bliss on earth. Plato (Timaeus, p. 22), and Clemens Alexandrinus (Strom. 1, p. 380) say that Phoroneus was the first man, or 'the father of mortals'. His genealogy, which assigns to him as his father Inachus, the river, reminds one of that of Prometheus, which makes that Titan the son of Oceanide Clymene.

But the mother of Phoroneus was the <u>nymph Melia</u>; a significant descent which distinguishes him from Prometheus (De Charme, Ancient Greek Mythology, p. 265) *(see reference #250 B, nymph Pramlocha, who fooled Kandu)*. Melia, Decharme thinks, is the personification of the Melia-tree [ash-tree], whence, according to Hesiod, issued the race of the age of Bronze (Works and Days, 142-145); and which according to the Greeks is the celestial tree common to every Aryan mythology. <u>This **'Melia'** (ash-</u>

tree) is the Yggdrasil (Cosmic Tree) of the Norse antiquity, which the Norns sprinkle daily with the waters from the fountain of Urd, that it may not wither. It remains verdant till the last days of the Golden Age. Then the Norns (the three sisters who gaze respectively into the Past, the Present, and the Future) make known the decree of Fate (Karma, Ørlǫg), but men are conscious only of the Present.»

[1] **PIERRE GRIMAL - DICTIONNAIRE DE LA MYTHOLOGIE GRECQUE ET RO-MAINE** "PHORONEUS: In the Peloponnesian myths, Phoroneus is the primordial man. *(Could he be the First Celestial Man from the Race of Heroes?)* He is the son of the god/river Inachus and the nymph Melia, whose name is reminiscent of the homonymous Melia Tree. …They also say that Phoroneus was the first one to teach humans how to amass in cities and how to use fire."

As we will see next, it was at that time that the great advancement of man from Australopithecus to Homo sapiens occurs.

From here on though, the devastating tumble begins…

After this Majestic Race of Heroes, man would 'put on' a heavier, material 'garment', thus creating the Gender/Race of thick Iron. Then, behind the 'Iron Bars' of the Iron Race, man would be definitively entrapped, imprisoned, to be punished in the denser part of the material universe. The utter fall of man in the material plane was about to take place. But because Cosmogony is a very obscure chapter, it is best to analyze it gradually, so as to discover the reasons that lead man to this 'punishment'.

THE CAUSE FOR THE SECOND FALL OF MAN

> **258** *The events of this chapter take place in the astro-aetheric planes (prior to the Big-Bang era). The densely visible (universe) has not **yet** been created.*

ॐ·ॐ

Suddenly, with the influence (embodiment) of Celestial Man inside it, the up-to-then defective, soulful, astro-aetheric man-being, is transformed into a powerful God with incredible powers!

> **259** A) THE APOCRYPHON OF JOHN, THE GNOSTIC SOCIETY LIBRARY:
> «And the man came forth *(manifested)* because of the shadow of the light which is in him. And his thinking was <u>superior to all those who had made him</u>.» [Eng. tr. from Coptic: WALDSTEIN M., WISSE F.]
> **B) THE APOCALYPSE OF ADAM, THE GNOSTIC SOCIETY LIBRARY, THE NAG HAMMADI LIBRARY,** TRANSLATED BY GEORGE W. MACRAE: «When God had created me out of the earth *(energy matter)*, along with Eve, your mother *(unified and <u>BEFORE</u> their division that follows)*, I went about with her in a glory which she had seen in the Aeon *(HyperUniverse)* <u>from which we had come forth</u>. She taught me a word of knowledge of the Eternal God. And we re-sembled the great eternal angels, <u>for we were higher than the god who had created us and the powers with him, whom we did not know</u>.» [Gr. edition: Pyrinos Kosmos Publ.]

As a unified entity *(Celestial Man)* retained the privilege **to visit** all HyperUniverses of the True and benefit from their Goods (Gr. Ἀγαθά). In order to do that, he would 'abandon' his energy-bodies in the energy (material) universe, by putting them through a sleep-process. Thus, by absorbing the **Unsplit,** Sacred Knowledge from the HyperCosmoi, he would have the freedom first to expand his Wholeness, since the Life-giving 'Atmosphere' of the HyperUniverses would render him Immortal, and then – through his (now) enriched energy-bodies– to transfer every Sacred Provision to the inferior energy-fields of the material world, expanding them with complete descendants.

260 **A) OLD TESTAMENT, GENESIS CH. 2**: «§16…You may freely eat *(…enjoy and benefit)* of every tree of the paradise *(of the HyperUniverses).»*

He presents however an obvious antithesis to his **pinned-down** creator. The magnitude of Man's supremacy and powers cause panic to the creators, who seem totally powerless in front of him. They, being **cut-off** from their SOURCE on one hand and fragmented into many partial powers in order to create through their expansion on the other, are inferior to the Almighty Man who possesses the entire unified strength of the finer/subtler material creation through his energy-bodies, and the diadem of His HyperUniversal Family and his Unutterable, Supreme Father as a radiating crown. And certainly the instruction given by the HyperUniverses, that Celestial Men –in contrast to plain souls– would **NOT** have the creator of matter as their master, rendered this whole Creation/Man totally independent.

261 **A) THE APOCRYPHON OF JOHN, THE GNOSTIC SOCIETY LIBRARY:**
(a) [WALDSTEIN M., WISSE F.] «§20…And the snake (the archon) knew that he (Adam) was disobedient to it *(him)* due to light of the Epinoia *(Celestial Man)* dwelt in him, making him more correct in his thinking than the Chief Ruler.» *(or…)*
(b) [STEVAN DAVIES] «§20. …The chief ruler, Yaldabaoth *(serpent)*, knew that because the light-filled Epinoia within Adam made his mental abilities greater than his own, Adam had been disobedient (to him, the archon).»
All this was happening because the Key-Command had been given from above:
B) THE GOSPEL OF JUDAS [KASSER R., MEYER M., WURST G.] NATIONAL GEOGRAPHIC [53]: «But the Great One ordered Gabriel to grant spirits to the great generation with no ruler over it.»

Panic spreads in the ranks of the creators.

262 **OLD TESTAMENT, GENESIS CH. 3**: «§22 Then the Lord God said, "Behold, Adam has become like one of us, in knowing good and evil; and now, lest he put forth his hand and take also of the tree of life *(of the HyperUniverses)*, and eat, and live forever.»

Suddenly the creator was losing his creation from his hands and control was going back to where it belonged: to the Prevailing HyperUniverses of the Father. This situation enraged him. What was really happening though is that the creator was in a very adverse/unfavorable position due to his creation.

Don't skip chapters or bibliographic references

The moment he parted from the True HyperUniverses, in order to create, he chose a detached mishmash of waste elements (the forbidden tree) as the **building material** for his creation. This aggregate formed a swirling (spinning) spiral comprised of the 'fossils' of previous, **already dead** creations.

---

[263] *Let me remind you of the 'identity' of the swirling spiral, through written testimonies.*

A) THE SECRET BOOK OF DZYAN, 'COSMIC EVOLUTION', STANZA I:
«§1 The eternal Karana *(Cause)* wrapped in her ever invisible robes had slumbered <u>once again</u> for seven eternities…§6. The seven sublime lords and the seven truths <u>had ceased to be</u>… §7. The causes of existence <u>had been done away with</u> and the visible that was, and the invisible that is, rested in eternal non-being -- the one being. §8. Alone the one form of existence stretched boundless, infinite and causeless in dreamless sleep.»

B) HERMES TRISMEGISTUS, THE FOUNDER OF MONOTHEISM 9000 B. C., IOANNIDIS P. K., **CH. 1**: «§4…But after a little while, I saw a downward darkness partially born, coming down in **an oblique formation**, like a snake, fearful and hideous. I also saw that darkness be changed into a **moist nature**, unspeakably troubled, which yielded a fiery smoke from its depths, and from whence I heard an unutterable heartbreaking sound, and an inarticulate roar in a voice of fire.»

C) OLD TESTAMENT, GENESIS CH. 1: «§2. The earth was without form and void, and darkness was upon the face of the abyss.»

This vortex consisted of consecutive layers of fossils. Each layer corresponded to the remnants of a previous creation. Layers that sank into the inner regions of the spiral corresponded to the 'remains' that belonged to older creations. Each layer, as it piled deeper, was transformed, undergoing a 'septic' (rotting) procedure and finally, having reached the bottom, it was molded into a **mutated** 'condensing' of elements, from the initial/previous 'ingredients'.

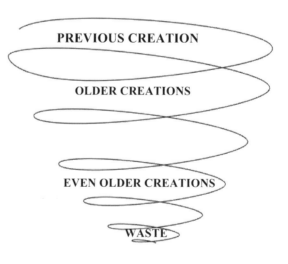

In order for the creator to vitalize this 'carcass' he united with it and was embodied within. All parts of the swirling, dark spiral, from the higher one down to the lower, embraced the incoming Light of the young creator and became one with it/him.

264 **A) HERMES TRISMEGISTUS:** THE FOUNDER OF MONOTHEISM 9000 B. C., IOANNIDIS P. K., **CH. 1**: «§5. From those Luminous Planes I saw a Holy Logos (Word) pouring Itself out towards the moist nature *(=first move, coming from the Light)* and from the moist nature, a hollow drastic acid and a pure fire spurting to the heights *(=second move, as an answer to the first, coming from the downward darkness.)* §6 So, that light that you saw was Me, your God, **existing before of that moist nature that appeared out of the darkness**. And that luminous Logos (Word) that you saw surging from (my) Luminous Planes **towards that moist nature**, is my *(fallen)* son that came out of my Noûs (Mind).»

B) THE SECRET BOOK OF DZYAN, 'COSMIC EVOLUTION', STANZA III:

«§1. The last vibration of the seventh eternity thrills through infinitude. The mother *(cosmic space-Devamatri)* swells, expanding from within without, like the bud of the lotus. §2. The vibration *(the Luminous creator coming from the HyperUniverses)* sweeps along, touching with its swift wing *(simultaneously)* the whole universe *(the shapeless, dark and whirling Karana-Cause)* and the germ *(of hylē/matter)* that dwells in darkness: the darkness which breathes (moves) over the slumbering waters of life. §3 Darkness radiates light and light drops only one solitary ray into to the waters, within the depth of the mother *(Devamatri, Mother of the Gods, the cosmic space)*. The ray shoots through the virgin egg.»

C) OLD TESTAMENT, GENESIS CH. 1: «§2. And the Spirit of God *(the creator)* was hovering over the face of the *(dark)* waters.»

Every section of the up-to-then dead matter was rekindled.

265 **OLD TESTAMENT, GENESIS CH. 1**: «§3. And God *[the light bearer]* said, "Let there be light;" and there was *(dark)* light.»

Thus, with his body he vitalized and restructured this whole carcass/remnant, transforming it into an energy spiral.

Every **part of the body** of the creator consisted of the autonomous entities, powers, deities, which, while engaging with the swirling, dark spiral, formed the various energy-fields (planes) and dimensions. As the different parts/deities of the creator-Being were distributed into this spiral, then settled into particular layers, intermixed with them, and were sorted into orders: from the outer/higher ones, forming the group of positive forces, to the ones who, demoted to the inner/deeper regions, formed the group of negative forces, generally projecting the dyadicism (duality) of the new world.

Don't skip chapters or bibliographic references

---

266 A) **HERMES TRISMEGISTUS**, HERMETIC TEXTS, VOL. I, RODAKIS P., TZAFERO-POULOS AP., **SPEECH I**: «§7. And when I regained consciousness, I felt that **the light consisted of innumerable powers.** And an infinite world was created where **fire predominated** with magnificent force, trying to stay in place. …§9 The Noûs (Mind) God who is male-female, Life and Light, gave birth to another creator Noûs, who is the god of fire (pyre) and of the spirit and the creator of the seven commanders who encompass the tangible world within circles and their command is called Heimarménē (Destiny).» *When The True Light is downgraded, it is turned into flame, fire.*

B) **THE APOCRYPHON OF JOHN, THE GNOSTIC SOCIETY LIBRARY**: «And she called its name Yaldabaoth. This is the first archon. …He became strong and created for himself other aeons *(energy-dimensions)* **inside a blaze of luminous fire** *(the dark light)*, which still exists now. And he was stupefied in his Madness, which dwells within him, and he begat some authorities for himself *(12)*…And he set up seven kings –one per firmament of heaven– over the seven heavens, and five *(kings)* over the depth of the abyss, so that they might rule there. …And he is impious in his madness which is in him. For he said: 'I am God and there is no other God beside me,' for he is ignorant of the place from which his strength has come. And the archons created seven powers for themselves, and the powers created six angels for each one, until they became 365 angels. …He called himself god. And he did not obey the place from which he came. …And he named each power beginning with the highest *(he names the seven powers)*. …And all these *(the Lords of the Seven Powers)* have a firmament corresponding to each aeon-heaven *(dimension)*.…And he organized everything according to the model of the first aeons… And when he saw the creation which surrounds him, and the multitude of the angels around him who had come forth from him, he said to them, "I am a jealous God, and there is no other God beside me.» [Eng. tr. from Coptic: WALDSTEIN M., WISSE F.]

C) **SALLUSTIUS 'ON THE GODS AND THE WORLD'** [Gr. tr. GRAVIGGER P.] CH. 'ON THE FIRST CAUSE': «Following the above, it is worth knowing the first Cause and the orders of the resultant (Gr.: απορρεόντων) gods posterior to that. …as well as the good and foul administrations issued from them, and finally the origin of evils in the world.»

This situation forced the entire creative power to stay detached and pinned-down inside the 'waste-essence', in order to vitalize and formulate it.

> **267** **HERMES TRISMEGISTUS:** THE FOUNDER OF MONOTHEISM 9000 B.C., IO-
> ANNIDIS P. K., **CH. 1**: «§11. And the second creator Noûs, he who en-
> compasses the seven circles and the vortices of their roots –along
> with logos– turned his creatures and they all started swirling from an
> indefinite beginning to an interminable end.»

Because of this 'pinning-down', the creator was unable to visit the
Fatherly Realms and from There to supply himself with the ingredient
of Immortality, the Life-giving 'Essence'. His own 'power' reserves
would not last for long.
Celestial Men on the contrary, had the ability to shift (move back and
forth) to the HyperUniverses of the True Light, on account of their integrity –they had not been split yet. From 'There' they would 'cater' this whole
'problematic' creation with a constant flow of Living Essence. The offer of
the Celestial Children would ensure the Supply of the creator and his creation, and it didn't come in the form of domination but salvation.

An unpredictable factor though made its appearance like an unforeseen
'accident': The factor of 'contamination'. This contamination is manifested
in the form of <u>intolerance</u>.
The moment the young creator embraced the cyclically moving darkness
with his luminous body, he was contaminated by it. His Essence/Spirit decayed (was degraded) **into energy**, and His Light was split and diminished,
thus creating the positive and the negative energy. The downgraded, substitute, virtual, dark light and the darkness were then created.

> **268** **A) THE APOCRYPHON OF JOHN, THE GNOSTIC SOCIETY LIBRARY**:
> «When the light mixed with the darkness, it caused the darkness to shine,
> but when the darkness mixed with the light, it <u>darkened</u> the light, so that it
> became neither light nor darkness *(Ant-avge, dusk, twilight)* but it was weak,
> it became dim. ...Then his *(the creator's)* mother began to move to and fro
> *(oscillating)*. She became aware of her deficiency, when the brightness of
> her light <u>diminished</u> *(became darker)*...» [Eng. tr. from Coptic: FREDERIK WISSE]
> **B) PIERRE GRIMAL 'LEXICON OF THE HELLENIC AND THE ROMAN MYTHOLOGY'**
> «**Leto (Lětố)**: ...They still narrate about Leto, that in order to escape Hera's
> rage *(so that she could safely give birth to Apollo and Artemis)*, she assumed
> the shape of a she-wolf and left the land of the Hyperboreans, where she
> actually lived. That explains the strange epithet 'Λυκο-γενής' 'Luco-genes'
> (wolf-born) which sometimes is attributed to Apollo.»
> *This explains the origin of the name 'Lycaios' [Gr. Λύκαιος] as an attribute
> of Apollo, the god of light, since, of course, his light is the downgraded twi-
> light [lyco+phos=wolf+light=twilight].*

Don't skip chapters or bibliographic references

The True Light is downgraded to dark light and manifests as flame/fire, twilight [lyco-phos]

C) THE GOSPEL OF JUDAS [KASSER R., MEYER M., WURST G.] NATIONAL GEOGRAPHIC [51]: *(Says Jesus:)* «And look, from the cloud there appeared an [angel] whose face flashed with **fire**[1] and whose appearance was defiled with blood. His name was Nebro, which means 'rebel'; others call him Yaldabaoth.»

Let me remind you of Hermes Trismegistus: «...And an infinite world was created, where **fire predominated**[1]».

D) THE FIRST BOOK OF ADAM AND EVE, SACRED TEXTS, RUTHERFORD PLATT, **CH. 27**: «Satan began with transforming his hordes; in his hands there was a **flashing fire**[1], and they were in a great 'light'. He then placed his throne near the mouth of the cave ...and he shed light into the cave, until the cave glistened over Adam and Eve, while his hordes began to sing praises. And Satan did this, in order that when Adam saw the light, he should think within himself that it was a heavenly light, and that Satan's hosts were angels *(the angels of poverty [John's Apocryphon])*; and that God had sent them...When, therefore, Adam and Eve saw the light, **fancying** it was real, they strengthened their hearts;» [Gr. edition: APOCRYPHAL TEXTS OF THE OLD TESTAMENT, KOUTSOUKIS D.]

Every divine power of this world manifests itself in the form of fire/pyre, just as the god of Moses presented himself on Mount Sinai.

[1] **(a) OLD TESTAMENT, EXODUS CH. 3**: «§2. And an angel of the Lord appeared unto him in flames of fire coming out of the midst of a bush.»

(b) OLD TESTAMENT, EXODUS CH. 19: «§18 And Mount Sinai was wrapped in **smoke**, because the Lord descended upon it, in fire [pyre]. The smoke thereof ascended like the smoke of a furnace, and the whole mountain quaked violently.»

And with this **virtual, dark light** He formed the higher planes of the material world (positive energy), whereas with the darkness, the lower ones (negative energy).

---

269 **A) OLD TESTAMENT, GENESIS CH. 1**: «§4. And god separated/divided the light from the darkness.»

B) THE APOCRYPHON OF JOHN, THE GNOSTIC SOCIETY LIBRARY: «And he begat some authorities for himself *(12)*...And he set up seven kings –one per firmament of heaven– over the seven heavens, and five *(kings)* over the depth of the abyss, so that they might rule there.» [Eng. tr. from Coptic: WALDSTEIN M., WISSE F.]

C) THE SECRET BOOK OF DZYAN, 'COSMIC EVOLUTION', STANZA III: «§10. The Father-Mother *(the creator)* spins a web, whose upper end is fastened to the spirit, the light of the one darkness and its lower edge is fixed onto matter, its shadowy end. And this web is the universe spun out of two substances made in one.»

The virtual 'light' of the visible **and the invisible** material universe differs from the non-manifested (True) Light. This virtual 'light' belongs to the one side of the **same coin** which also contains darkness on the other. They are one the same thing.

> **270** A) **BLAVATSKY H., P., 'THE SECRET DOCTRINE'** (II-95,96): «Absolute light is absolute darkness and vice versa.... Good and evil are twins, the progeny (descendants) of Space and Time, under the sway of Maya (Deceit). Separate them by cutting off one from the other, and they will both die. Neither exists per se (autonomously), since each has to be generated and created out of the other, in order to come into being.»
>
> B) **GOSPEL OF PHILIP**, JEAN-YVES LELOUP: «§10. Light and darkness, life and death, right and left, are brothers and sisters. **They are inseparable.**»

The True Light is trapped. Only with great difficulty can someone descry the minutest crumbs of the Absolute Truth –through which The True Light manifests. These crumbs of The Absolute Truth are found **scattered** inside concepts, ancient texts and some living symbols of matter.

> **271** A) **HERMES TRISMEGISTUS**, HERMETIC TEXTS, VOL. II, RODAKIS P., TZAFERO-POULOS AP., **EXCERPT II$_a$** (p. 111): «§3. All therefore Tat that is found on earth, are not real, but only **imitations of the truth** and yet not all of them, but only a few... §4. The rest is lies and delusion, Tat, and conjectures, constructed like the pictures of imagination."
>
> B) **GOSPEL OF PHILIP**, JEAN-YVES LELOUP: "§16. The high spiritual powers (the Archon), thought that it was through their power and their will that they did what they did: But it was the Holy Spirit which, through them, worked its own desire in secret. The truth is sown everywhere, existing since the beginning: Some see it at the time it is sown, but few still (will manage to) see it at the time of harvest (at the end of time).» [Eng. tr. JOSEPH ROWE]

Material man can locate the True Light in the material plane, not, of course, by fumbling around inside matter, but only through a Profound Spiritual Transcendence. Then –and only if the discovery of The Truth is his main priority– these Spiritual Findings will lead him to the corresponding material sources.

So, at that stage of material creation during which Celestial Man, in order to help, enters its energy spaces, the creator's intolerance prevails. This is where the cause for the second and most essential fall begins –not only of Man but of the creators as well.

Don't skip chapters or bibliographic references

༺•༻

Celestial Man's ability to visit the Fatherly Planes was a challenge for the creators. Their staffs confer in order to find a solution for the problem called 'Upgraded Man'.

---

272 **NEAR EAST TEXTS 'THE EPIC OF GILGAMESH'** [GR. TR. XENI SKARTSI S., – SOCRATES L. SKARTSIS]

The Epic of Gilgamesh was unearthed in the town of Nineveh and it was part of the royal library of Assurbanipal, the last great king of Assyria. It consists of reproductions of older texts, obviously predating the 2nd millennium. The Epic unfolds in twelve clay tablets.

Gilgamesh can be paralleled to the Celestial Men, in the aetheric city of Uruk. There, the way of his entrapment and his <u>incorporation in his material copy, Enkidu,</u> is orchestrated.

«PREAMBLE: Oh Gilgamesh, lord of Kullab, great is the hymn of yours. This (is the) man who knew everything; this was the king who knew all the countries of the world. He was wise; he saw the mysteries and learned in secret. He brought us the story about the days before the cataclysm (deluge). …

…When gods made Gilgamesh, they gave him a perfect body. Shamash, the bright sun gave him beauty; Adad, the god of tempest gave him bravery; the great gods made his beauty perfect to exceed every other beauty. They made him God by two parts and human by the third part. … In Uruk he built walls, a big fortress.

…And there he is today: <u>the outer wall enclosed in the frieze, glistens from the copper</u> *(does he imply the Bronze Root-Race with the aetheric body?)* and the inner wall is similar to none. …However, the people of Uruk murmured in their houses: "Gilgamesh tolls the bell of danger in order to have fun. His arrogance has no limits, day and night. He does not leave a son to his father. Gilgamesh takes them all. His lust-loving nature does not leave a virgin to the one she loves, a daughter to her warrior father, a bride to her noble husband. However, he is the shepherd of the city, wise, dear and decisive." …The gods heard their lament. The gods of heaven cried to the lord/god of Uruk, Anu. … As soon as Anu heard their lamentation, the gods called out Aruru, the goddess of creation.

"It was you, Aruru, who made him, <u>now make another one, identical to him</u>. He must be the same, as if he was his image, his second self: A heart of the storm for the heart of the storm. Let them confront each other so that Uruk may find peace!»

The solution chosen is what is called 'Command for Creation'. This would be their salvation…! They would prompt man to create!

> [273] **BLAVATSKY H., P., 'THE SECRET DOCTRINE'** (II-215):
> «The 'Serpent' was 'the God Lord' who as the Ophis, the Logos, or the bearer of divine creative wisdom, *(our creator!)* **taught mankind to become creators in their turn.**»

With this pretext, they would force him to remain **pinned-down** to the aetheric field, where the object of his creation would be; he would therefore be hindered to move. But what the creator teams were engineering was for Man to create the 'layout' for his densely material prison!

The aetheric plane existed then only as a harmonic vibration and not as an image. The task was very specific.
–*How did the aetheric dimension exist without form? And how was man in it?*
–What is manifest doesn't necessarily have the form you have been used to. Every different vibration is a manifestation. You men have identified yourselves too much with form/image. This is a constraint. The image encages essence. Because you cannot grasp the essence, you need its image.

> [274] **GOSPEL OF THOMAS,** JEAN YVES LELOUP: «§83. Jesus said: When images become visible to people, the light that is in them **is hidden.**»

The staffs of Elohims (Devas and Elementals) had created/vitalized oscillating vibrations. Man would shape their form. The plan was composite and a quite complex process would follow. What was initially needed was the transformation of the **aetheric noûs (mind).**

The Soul's Constitution (Spiritual Essence + finer/subtler energy) gave (aetheric) Man the ability of Logos (Word). The aetheric brain had to be constructed in such a way, that it could initially receive the aetheric vibration and through its 'Logos' project it onto the aetheric plane as image/form. The foundations of material creation are being redefined.
Logos is sound. The sound of Logos is formulated vibration. Every word carries within it its image. The 'Logos' of Man would give form to aetheric matter.

Don't skip chapters or bibliographic references

275 **A) OLD TESTAMENT, GENESIS CH. 2** (AETHERIC CREATION)

«§19. And **out of the earth** (ground) the Lord God **made all the beasts** of the field and all the birds of the air and he brought them to Adam to see how to **name** them *(to give them form/shape through the Logos/Word)*; and whatever name *(form)* Adam gave to each living creature, that was its name. §20. And Adam gave **names** *(form/shape through the Logos/Word)* to all the beasts and the birds of the sky and all the animals of the field.»

B) 'ENUMA ELISH' (THE ASSYRO-BABYLONIAN EPIC OF CREATION) **NEAR EAST TEXTS** [GR. TR. XENI SKARTSI S., – SOCRATES L. SKARTSIS]

«TABLET ONE: §1. When the sky above had not yet been named, the solid ground beneath had not been called by a name, the nothingness, only the primordial Apsû (Abzu) *(Lucifer/creator)*, their genitor, and Mummu Tiamat *(the remnants of the previous creations)*, she, who gave birth to them all, with their waters mixed in one …when none of the gods had come to existence, unnamed by a name and their fates were vague, it was then that the gods were created inside them. §10. Lahmu and Laḫamu were born and were named by names".

And translators Xenia and Socrates Skartsis note: "They were named by names: genesis and name-designation are identical terms. Very often, the same thing is expressed in a bipolar/twofold way, on two different levels.»

C) THE GOSPEL OF TRUTH, NAG HAMMADI MANUSCRIPTS, THE ECUMENICAL COPTIC PROJECT [ENG. TR. FROM COPTIC THOMAS PATERSON BROWN] www.metalog.org/files/valent.html

«§47 The Name is not mere verbiage, nor is it only terminology, but rather it is transcendental. …Whoever does not exist has no name –for what names are given to the nothingness? But this existing-one exists together with his Name.»

D) BLAVATSKY H., P., 'THE SECRET DOCTRINE' (I-93,94):

«As beautifully expressed by P. Christian, the learned author of 'The History of Magic' and of 'L' Homme Rouge des Tuileries', [The Red Man of Potteries], the word spoken by, as well as the name of, every individual largely determine his future fate. Why? Because…To pronounce a word is to evoke a thought, and make it present: the magnetic potency of the human speech is the commencement of every manifestation in the Occult World. To utter a Name is not only to define a Being (an Entity), but to place it under and condemn it through the emission of the Word (Verbum), to the influence of one or more Occult potencies. Things are, for every one of us, that which it (the Word) makes them while naming them…Yes, names (and words) are either BENEFICENT or MALEFICENT; they are, in a certain sense, either venomous or health-giving, according to the hidden influences attached by Supreme Wisdom to their elements, that is to say, to the LETTERS which compose them, and the NUMBERS correlative to these letters.»

> *And as it was stated in chapter 'AETHERIC BODY – AETHERIC PLANE' the entire aetheric plane/field is constructed with <u>number concepts</u>.*
>
> **E) THE SECRET BOOK OF DZYAN, 'COSMIC EVOLUTION', STANZA IV:**
> «§3 From the effulgence of Light sprang in space the <u>reawakened</u> energies[1]; The One from the egg, the six and the five. Then the three, the one, the four, the one, the five; the twice seven the sum total. And these are: the essences, the flames, the elements, the builders, the numbers, the arūpa *(formless)*, the rūpa *(with form)* and the force of the Divine Man: The sum total. **And from the Divine Man emanated the forms**, the sparks, the sacred animals and the messengers of the Sacred Fathers within the holy four. §4. <u>This was the army of **the voice**</u>, the divine septenary.»
>
> [1] *The reawakened remnants from the previous creation*

God/creator's instruction for men to create had been given. The formulation of **aetheric** structure began.

> [276] **HERMES TRISMEGISTUS,** HERMETIC TEXTS, VOL. II ASCLEPIUS, RODAKIS P., TZAFEROPOULOS AP., **'KORE KOSMOU':**
> «§17 And thus, after he (the Creator) had stood on the all-fairest station of the **Æther** and after he had summoned all the existing species of beings, he said: "My Spirits and creations of my care, **souls**, beautiful children, you that I have created with my own hands, I place you in my own world. Listen to my words, as if they are laws and <u>never approach another place</u> except for that which I have ordained with my decision *(the beginning of restriction)*. <u>If you stand firm, then the sky will remain in its place in a similar way,</u> *(If you stay firm (grounded) exclusively in the aetheric condition where I have placed you, only then will the sky exist firmly because in this way it (the sky) will be <u>projected</u> by the aetheric decoder, the brain [1])* as well as the appointed constellation and the thrones, full of virtue. If however, you do anything opposite to my Will, I swear to the spirit and the mixture out of which I have created you and to my own hands which create souls, that <u>it will not be long,</u> before I create chains and punishments for you". *(This is the final but secret aim: to cast man into even thicker matter.)*
> §18. After god who is my own lord had said that much, he mixed the rest of the congenial elements, that is to say water and soil and said some apocryphal and powerful words but not similar with the first ones. He mixed the elements very well, he breathed life-giving power *(Life-Eve)* into the mixture and using the well-painted and well-thickened crust of the mixture which floated, he created <u>the human-like beings.</u>
> §19. He gave the remainder part (residue) to the souls that had already made

Don't skip chapters or bibliographic references

good. And he said to those souls that had been **summoned** to the lands of gods near the places of the stars and the holy demons *(Celestial Men)*: "My children, make creatures of my own nature; accept the remnants of my own craft and may each one of you make creatures similar to your own nature; I will also deliver these models to you" and he handed them over to them;

§20. He arranged the zodiac circle in order and beauty, according to the movements of the souls, after he had placed next to the human-like beings the remainder, that is to say the animals to which he also added the cunning powers as well as the ingenious generative spirit for all that is to exist eternally.

§21. And he departed promising to breathe invisible spirit and essence of common origin to each one of their visible pieces of work, so that each would be able to give birth to others similar to itself and thus they would not have to do anything else but what they had already created *(programming/recording of the 'commands' in the 'electronic brain'/ DNA of the animal and plant cell)*.

§22. "So, what did the souls do, mother?"
And Isis said: "My child Horus, after they had received the blend of matter, they first tried to conceive it with their mind. They worshiped the mixture of their father and tried to find out whence it was composed. But that was not easy to be perceived. So, they were afraid that they might provoke their father's wrath, for they had showed this kind of curiosity and set to do what they had been commanded.

§23. Thereon, using the upper part of the matter which had a superfluously light crust, they formed the race of birds; in that span of time, using the mixture which was already half hardened, they made the species of quadruped, which was the least light and the race of fish that had the need of another kind of moist substance to be able to swim in. From the rest, which was cold and had a tendency to evil, the souls made a new species, the race of reptiles.

[Let me remind you of this excerpt from Genesis 2:19-20, for better correlation ...because there is but ONE Truth and it is found scattered everywhere: "And whatever name *(form)* Adam gave to each living creature, THAT was its name. §20. And Adam gave names *(form/shape through the Logos/Word)* to all the beasts and the birds of the sky and all the animals of the field."]

§24. And those souls my son, already from now they were armed with a strange impudence, as if they had performed an act of bravery, and despite the orders, they abandoned their components and their stores and did not want to remain in the same place, because they considered that it was **death** to continue to stay in the same residence." *(They were henceforth starting to* *realize the ulterior dark aims of the Creator, feeling the danger 'ante portas' [closer and closer]).*

§25. And Hermes, speaking to me my child, said: "What the souls did, did not escape the attention of the lord and god of all, and that is why he sought for <u>punishment</u> and chains which the souls would endure patiently. And therefore, the sovereign and lord of all *(the archon of this world)* decided to artfully fabricate the human frame for the race of souls **to suffer** in it."

(1) [<u>If you stand firm, then the sky will remain in its place in a similar way</u> *(it will be projected)*]

Modern quantum Physics has come to the conclusion that everything around us is a cerebral projection. Our brain receives the quantum (energy-) hyperchords, and depending on the way they oscillate, formulates them into atoms, molecules, and generally speaking into objects:

DANEZIS M., THEODOSIOU S. 'COSMOLOGY OF THE INTELLECT'
(FROM THE THESIS OF GEORGIOU, G., DROUGAS, A., 'CYBERNETICS AND MODERN PHYSICS, 1999, MAN AS A RECEIVER AND DATA PROCESSOR – THE DELUSION OF THE SENSES'):

«(p. 407) …In Physics terms, we receive electromagnetic waves of different frequencies, but we perceive these stimuli as colors. We receive pressure waves, but we perceive them as words. We receive chemical compounds from the air and the water, but we sense odors and flavors. All these colors, sounds, smells and tastes do not exist by themselves, **yet they are created intellectually in our brain through a sensory process.** …The idea is that man's perceptions are not direct sensory recordings of the natural world surrounding us, but rather internally created ones, according to inherent rules and restrictions that are imposed by the abilities of our nervous system.

(p. 413) …First of all, the main thing we've just looked at is that man's perceptions differ in quality from the natural properties of the stimuli he receives with his sensory organs. The entire structure of the perceptible world is not formed by the passive contact with the objects' properties, but it is created by the human brain after it has received certain signals. <u>Perception is a creative process of the human brain</u>. This discovery/ascertainment is very important for man's ability to interact (in physical terms) with the world and at the same time the process of perception constitutes a mystery that is only partially approached.»

Energies that until recently were vibrating aetherically, had to be amassed into compounds, in order to form their **aetheric** form/image. Every detail had to be carefully engineered; through synchronous projection, the absolutely **aetheric** universe starts to assume form through Man. Two fundamental processes had a primary role: One was the as-

Don't skip chapters or bibliographic references

similation of energy-information, and the other was the emission/projection of the aetheric form.

At that point, many aetheric Celestial Men, realizing the trap hidden behind the command to create, refused to proceed to its execution.

---

[277] **BLAVATSKY H., P., 'THE SECRET DOCTRINE'** (II-93):

«The first ones, born of the Noûs, Sons of the Deity, refuse to create and Brahma curses them to be born as humans.»

This excerpt can be compared to the previous passage of Hermes Trismegistus:

«§24 And those souls my son, already from now they were armed with a strange impudence, as if they had performed an act of bravery, and despite the orders, they <u>abandoned</u> their components and their stores and did not want to remain in the same place, because they considered that it was **death** to continue to stay in the same residence.»

B) PAPASTAVROU, A., 'LETTERS TO ANONYMOUS'

The spiritual teachers (the Creators' delegates) clarify their views on this subject:

«The moment at which The Divine Noesis (Intellectuality), inside the Entity of The White Fire *(Celestial Man)* perceived Itself as an individualized portion of divine life of the *(material)* universe, it was granted the choice of free will as to whether or not it would continue, as an individualized portion of the creator, …which would render IT able to <u>create</u> like the Father. Acknowledging Itself as 'I AM THE ONE WHO IS', the Immortal Triple Flame *(the Divine Spark)* in the Entity of The White Fire …<u>could deny</u> self-governing individualization. If It chose to do that, the Triple Flame would withdraw and return to where it originally came from.

For each individualized Entity of The White Fire that accepted the responsibility to become **a co-creator**, there were at least <u>a dozen or more who chose **to return**</u>.» *(Only one in twelve consented to creating…death…)*

Others however were convinced that the move was benign. This was a fatal mistake! The very procedure of aetheric projection would entrap Man inside the 'prison of shape/form'. This is the original (primordial) sin. Through his own creation, Man tastes the fruits of dense, dyadic matter, 'understands' (knows) it and dies in the HyperUniverses.

A DIFFERENT VIEWPOINT

As I have previously mentioned, you men have equated everything to a form. This is, after all, the only way you can function. This is why I too was forced to give things form, in order to make them comprehensible to your intellect. In reality, very few of them have form. The largest volume of information concerns conceptual situations without shape. The higher we ascend spiritually, the more abstract the concepts become. It would therefore be impossible for someone to assimilate The Truth in any other way, but only through looking at IT in ITS assumed form. This is the main reason why wise men have created myths in the past. They were trying to give form to portions of the Truth, in order to make it comprehensible.

> [278] THE GOSPEL OF MATTHEW, CH. 13: «§34. All these things Jesus spoke to the crowds in parables; and He did not speak to them without a parable, §35. that it might be fulfilled which was spoken by the prophet, saying: I will open My mouth in parables; I will utter things kept secret since the foundation of the world.»

Later of course, subsequent generations, not being able to understand these myths, considered them fabrications and called them fairy tales... 'Sour grapes'! (as the fox said when she couldn't reach them)

But since, under material conditions we are dealing with concepts that have acquired form, they have to be seen from yet another point of view in order for them to be fully comprehensible. Let us look at the same story from a totally different perspective; another piece of the same Truth. Don't confuse yourself thinking that this assumed form does not coincide with Reality. It is as true as your material hypostasis (substance). It is the same with you men as well: Even though in reality you are sums (sets) of concepts and situations, you manifest inside matter with form.

Let me present you with a formulated piece of 'history' from the HyperUniverses of the True Unsplit Light: In the HyperUniverses of the True, the Property to 'Create' is an Ultimate condition that concerns **only** the Unuttered Principle – Father. His Creation comprises different properties/situations, which **altogether** support their Sum. The One and Unique Creator, the Unuttered Principle – Father, initially 'Creates' His Firstborn Sons. Each Monogenes Son is in possession of one HyperUniverse *(Aeon)* –His 'Cradle'/Birthplace– which consists of a vast number of Archetypes, corresponding to the primary Attribute of the Monogenes *(Luminary/Christ),* Who Has It as His Home. This is only the beginning though. Every Monogenes, after assimilation of His 'Cradle's' Archetypes, expands

Don't skip chapters or bibliographic references

and <u>His entire Body</u> takes the form of His particular HyperUniverse. When He reaches a maximum point of enlargement, new living and Intelligent Wholenesses (1st generation) detach themselves from Him, with characteristics that are a combination of the Principle Quality of the Monogenes and the Archetypes that engulf Him. All these young Living Expressions (Manifestations) are in absolute connection to their Monogenes Genitor but also to the Unuttered Principle.

In their turn, They (1st generation) have the ability to move to all other HyperUniverses –in contrast to the Monogenes– and by coming in contact with other Intelligent Wholenesses (emanations of other Monogenes') to absorb new Attributes from Them, as well as offer Theirs. When These young ones reach a maximum point of expansion, They return to the 'Mother Cradle'/HyperUniverse again, to offer the 'treasure' of Their Completeness There, while new living Intelligent Wholenesses (2nd generation) detach Themselves from Them, with Attributes in various combinations and intermixed Properties from their ancestors' previous transactions with other Wholenesses.

---

[279] **OLD TESTAMENT, GENESIS CH. 2**: «§16…Of every tree of the paradise *[Gr.: παραδείσω]* you may freely eat;»

Now these young entities (2nd generation) in their own turn, start the same voyage as their Genitors (1st generation). Their Genitors however do the same thing in a new 'cycle' of experience. All Entities continue to remain connected to each other, to their Monogenes Genitor and to the Unuttered Principle-Father of All as, all three, share the same Essence (they are Consubstantial).

There, good and evil, justice and injustice don't exist. Pain, as an attribute, is totally unknown. So is Death and loneliness. The concept of god doesn't exist. The concept of 'Family' does exist there though. All these HyperUniverses comprise the members of a very large and continuously expanding 'Family'. The whole web of That Creation forms synapses and connections between ITS parts, thus producing an inconceivable plethora of Attributes, Archetypes, Concepts and Situations which human logos has no means of expressing. But the characteristic and majestic thing is that all These (Attributes, Archetypes, Concepts) are **Intelligent/Noûs-possessing, Conscious Living Wholenesses**.

The whole environment, the 'atmosphere' into which These Supreme Presences live and expand, is uninterruptedly emanated (outpoured) by the Unuttered Principle and consists of an 'Essence' of the same 'texture' as that from which Their 'Bodies' themselves are 'made' of. This 'Essence' is

Love. This Ultimate Condition of Love is **uninterruptedly** produced by the Unuttered Principle/Father and **Everything** else is built and permeated by IT.

–In what way is this complexity of situations different to the equivalent material polymorphism? Isn't there a possibility that there too (in the Hyper-Universes), through this infinite differentiation, opposite or conflicting situations might occur?

–Rightly you ask this. In the material dimension, two opposite concepts appear separate, self-standing and autonomous. In the Real Cosmoi, these two are united together and appear AS ONE, new, homogenized attribute. This is their only healthy state. And of course, you should not even in the least relate this perverse negativeness that has been weaved in your world today with what I am describing, since I am referring to crystal clear and **healthy, opposite** states. Nothing conflicts with anything. Antagonism, as a condition, exists only in the fragmented (visible and invisible) material creation. As I have explained to you though, I am forced to use words that can only constrictively refer to the Structure of Those HyperCosmoi; because the words of men have been constructed to describe this material world alone. Therefore, the account of these situations is more an approximation rather than a detailed and accurate one.

> [280] **BLAVATSKY H., P., 'THE SECRET DOCTRINE'** (I-95): «This allegory is at the root of Occult law, which prescribes silence upon the knowledge of certain secret and invisible things perceptible only to the spiritual noûs (mind), and which cannot be expressed by 'noisy' (uttered) speech.»

What Christian Religion calls 'True Light', is an aggregate of Angelic Forces that emanate from the Father, in a different way however than the emanations of the Monogenes', and with their Presence contribute to the Whole by enriching IT. Every situation THERE is ALIVE.

֎·֍

At times throughout eternity and trough the plethora of concepts, situations and attributes existing THERE, the property of Creation becomes prominent in the Hypostasis of a Nous-Possessing, Sentient Wholeness. Then the Wholeness possessing this attribute detaches ITSELF from the Family of the Father in an intention to Create Its own creation in an absolutely proprietary 'Space'. IT cannot create inside the Fatherly Environment. So, IT separates ITSELF off the entire community and 'bears' the Attributes IT carries within to ITS own 'space'. This way IT builds a Universe of ITS own.

Don't skip chapters or bibliographic references

There is however an extremely fundamental precondition in order for a Wholeness to become a Creator. The Unspoken Father is an endless Source of a very specific **totality** of attributes *(The Quintuple (Fivefold) Aeon of the Father [John's Apocryphon])*. All these properties, each and every one, are absolutely necessary for the construction of an Immaculate and Healthy Creation. Even if only one property is missing, then the result **is defective**. So, if this **totality** of attributes <u>does not come together inside</u> the Wholeness Child/Creator, after IT (the Child/Creator) delivers the acquired Attributes/Children from the Large Family to Its own Universe, **IT is incapable** of creating new ones. IT then uses those (Attributes/Children) to build/create a defective world of ITS own. Additionally, the production/creation of the fundamental Atmosphere –the Condition of Love– is of the <u>utmost importance</u>, since it is the basic constituency of not only the 'body', but of the whole environment that sustains True Life. It is what we call 'Essence'. The Child/Creator's inability to **'give birth'** to the Condition of Love, results in the death of this entity, which also leads all its off-spring to devastation with it.

---

281 **A) THE GOSPEL OF JUDAS** [KASSER R., MEYER M., WURST G.] **NATIONAL GEOGRAPHIC**

[54, 55]: «Jesus said, "Truly I say to you, for all of them, the stars bring matters to completion. When Saklas completes the span of time assigned for him, their first star will appear with the generations, and they will finish what they said they would do. ...I am not laughing [at you] but at the error of the stars, because these six stars wander about with these five combatants, and they all will be destroyed along with their creatures.»

B) BLAVATSKY H., P., 'THE SECRET DOCTRINE' (I-36):

«In Book II, Ch. VIII of the Vishnu-Puraná it is stated: "By immortality is meant existence until the end of Kalpa." And translator Wilson in a footnote remarks: "This, according to the Vedas, is all that is to be understood of the immortality (eternal life) of the gods· they perish at the end of universal dissolution (or Pralaya).»

Therefore, some previous efforts made by Entities possessing the property/tendency to create, while initially fruitful, they then started falling short and finally perished, leaving behind dead creation carcasses, which swirled in the void. This was the dead forbidden tree *(the downward darkness the partially born* — [H. Trismegistus]*)*. It is what men call 'Brahma's breath'. Brahma is Each Wholeness that possesses within the (deficient) property for creation. After IT is initially cut off, IT creates by 'exhaling' ITS attributes from within. IT is nevertheless consumed inside ITS own creation and then perishes. The wisest of men, not wanting to accept Brahma's death, called this perishing 'sleep' and equated it to the inhalation of Brahma, when everything is 'absorbed' back again and is lost in his great night. There is a **different Brahma** for each material creation. Men however think he is always the same. But IT is always a new Brahma replacing the old one who perished, having consumed all his parts in his creative tendency. Whatever he has created remains a dead carcass, spinning isolated and dark at the edge of nothing.

---

282 *A reminder*: **THE SECRET BOOK OF DZYAN, 'COSMIC EVOLUTION', STANZA I:**

«§1 The Eternal Karana *(Cause)* wrapped in her ever invisible robes had slumbered once again for seven eternities... §6. The seven sublime lords and the seven truths **had ceased to be**. §7. The causes of existence **had been done away with**; The visible that was, and the invisible that is, rested in eternal non-being -- the one being.»

It remains there, until a new creator is found to give it life again.

When the creator of matter was initially cut-off from the HyperUniversal Family with the intention to create, the Unuttered Principle/Father, as the Exclusive Creator of the Absolute, offered to embrace this Creation too, regardless of the fact that it had started off as a defective one. The contribution of Celestial Children/Men concealed no intention for domination, but an intention to salvage. Celestial Men, with their visits to the Celestial Kingdoms would nurture this defective creation with Life-giving Essence, in order to keep it Alive.

The preference that a Child-Creator (Brahma) exhibits to vitalize the dead 'carcass' of the previous creation is justified by the need to find a substratum. This tendency is evident only in the case of a Child-Creator that doesn't possess the **total sum** of qualities/attributes that will support Its Creation. Otherwise, when the totality of Attributes is complete, then, the new Creation is capable of starting from ground zero and in turn to form a new group of HyperUniverses.

THE DENSELY MATERIAL PLANE

Leaving the Sacred Spaces of the HyperUniverses behind us, we return to the material creation again, in order to follow the evolution of its construction.

Before we proceed though, we must examine what this dense matter – where man resides today– precisely is.

As you may have been informed, earth's contemporary astrophysicists have deduced that dense visible matter occupies only 4% of the actual material universe, whereas the remaining 96% refers to its invisible energy-part.

---

283 **A) PHYSICS4U.GR,** ARTICLE OCTOBER 2005, THE STORY OF THE DARK MATTER THEORY
http://www.physics4u.gr/articles/2005/historydarkmatter.html
«In 2001 NASA launched the WMAP (Wilkinson Microwave Anisotropy Probe) satellite. Its purpose was not only to calculate how old and how big the Universe is, with an alarming accuracy –13.7 billion years– but also to help scientists better comprehend what it's made of. Its findings further exacerbated the already problematic questions about dark-matter. The WMAP discovered (with an approximately 5% error margin) that **the Universe consists of only 4% regular matter, 23% of an unknown type of dark-matter and 73% of an even more mysterious dark-energy.**» *(SEE: DRAWINGS, 'CONSTITUTION OF THE MATERIAL UNIVERSE').*

This suspiciously small percentage (4%) automatically proves that the humanly visible universe isn't the main body of the entire massive creation, but a **tiny** part of it!

I hope that everything that has come earlier in our discussion has certainly prepared you psychologically and mentally to bear the new data, considering that their revelation isn't the most pleasant one! When people refer to space they exclusively mean that 4% of the visible, dense matter. But this minute percentage which comprises the densest part of the universe looks more like the coffee residue in a coffee-cup than the coffee itself! If you now look with deep awareness (Epignosis) into the 'time' factor, you will conclude that time doesn't simply entrench dense space, but is rather the **foundation** that structurally holds it together and this is why these two are indissolubly connected to each other.

284 **A) DANEZIS M., THEODOSIOU S. 'COSMOLOGY OF THE INTELLECT'**
TIME IN THE GENERAL THEORY OF RELATIVITY (p. 189): «The work of famous cosmologists S. Hawking and R. Penrose opened new windows to the concept of the beginning of time. And as astrophysicist Th. Grammenos (1988) writes: "It has been proven with methods of Topology and Differential Geometry that time started flowing at the moment of the Big Bang, when space was also created. Consequently, the birth of the universe and the creation of space-time are temporally <u>identified</u>...»
B) STEPHEN HAWKING – 'THE UNIVERSE IN A NUTSHELL' [GR. TR. PETRAKI M.] CH. THE SHAPE OF TIME (p. 34): «The general theory of relativity combines the dimension of time with the three dimensions of space to form the so-called *space-time (as a unity)*.»

–But doesn't time exist in the thinner material dimensions?
–In these planes, time may exist but it is not impermeable! This way we can explain the peculiarity presented by quantum theory in dealing with the past and the future with equal ease of access. On the quantum level, there is ease of movement towards the past as well as the future.

285 **A) STUART HAMEROFF** (PROFESSOR OF ANESTHESIOLOGY WITH STUDIES ON HUMAN CONSCIOUSNESS), **'WHAT THE BLEEP DO WE KNOW'** http://www.whatthebleep.com/:
«It is only in our minds that we move forward in time. In quantum-theory you can also go backwards. You can always go backwards in time.»
B) DANEZIS M., THEODOSIOU S. 'COSMOLOGY OF THE INTELLECT' (p. 185):
«Einstein's rectilinear forward time-flow seemed so well-documented, that no one could ever think of questioning or extending it. This however, was achieved by the very father of the new idea, within the framework of the General Theory of Relativity, which he formulated a few years later. After this powerful 'bomb' in the foundations of Newtonian Physics, the rectilinear 'forward' time-flow of Specific Relativity, started being disputed as more and more reports of prominent scientists came forth regarding the theoretical possibility of **successive submersions from the present to the past or the future and vice-versa.**»

The quantum state however doesn't concern visible, dense matter, but the next more thinly-structured **energy-field**. There, the time factor may exist, but it is not impenetrable.
It is this (4%) 'partial section' of the material universe where the creator of matter decided to 'throw' Man into, when he realized that this **upgraded** creation/Man (by the Supreme Father), surpassed him (the creator) by far. It is the moment that Greek mythology speaks of an enraged Zeus casting his

Don't skip chapters or bibliographic references

'thunderbolts' against men, when he perceives Celestial Man *(as fire, flame)* inside the (**still aetheric, not yet densely material**) man-beings and devises the greatest of calamities with the poisonous (for them) 'gift' of hope.

---

286 A) *Let me additionally remind you of the excerpt referring on the event of the 'fire' granted to men by Prometheus:*

HESIOD 'THEOGONY' (v. 567-570) «And this bit Zeus (who thunders from above) deeply into his soul and **enraged him** in his heart as he saw **the far-seen shine of the fire inside** men. Immediately he prepared **a calamity** for men as a reprisal for the fire.»

B) *Hope, by default, is based on the expectation of what is desired, and not on the realistic handling of situations, since it would then cease to be considered as hope, and would be regarded as certainty. Nevertheless, if expectance of the desired ends up disorienting from reality and henceforth deludes and hypnotizes man, then, hope could certainly be characterized as a malady!*

JEAN RICHEPIN 'GREEK MYTHOLOGY', VOL. A – THE GODS, CH. THE CREATION OF PANDORA (p. 39): "Pandora had brought with her a box, on the contents of which, writers are not in full agreement. Hesiod speaks of 'terrible calamities/misfortunes', which were unleashed from it, adding that only Hope alone remained in the bottom of the box.»

C) **KAZANTZAKIS NIKOS**: «I hope for nothing, I fear nothing, I am free.»

At the same time though, your very religion, through the chapters of Genesis, presents an unimaginably jealous creator (Jehovah) who endlessly curses his very own creation (man).

ॐ∙ॐ

We left Man pinned-down inside the aetheric plane, giving form to its aetheric vibrations. At the end of the aetheric form-making, Man had already understood the trap he had woven through his own creation. Without even realizing it he had entered into the early atomic creation with the formation of the subatomic particles which were on the threshold between the aetheric and the densely material plane.

In its entirety, this 'concoction/fabrication' of material creation (visible and invisible), is (a situation) analogous but not identical to what scientists call a 'black hole'. And it is not identical, because the conditions of its creation were different from the ones that create a corresponding material black hole.

287 *And as far as the Big Bang is concerned... "Nought from nought"*

A) PHYSICS4U.GR : 'THE UNIVERSE EXISTED BEFORE THE BIG BANG'
SOURCE: FROM THE PAGE OF NEWGEN, JANUARY 2000
(http://www.physics4u.gr/news/2000/scnews87.html)

«The dominant view about the Big Bang wants it coinciding with the beginning of everything. But the pioneer researcher Gabriele Veneziano (CERN Physicist−European Laboratory of Particle Physics and High Energies) had a different opinion. ...In his effort to formulate a cohesive theory on the Big Bang, he made a time jump backwards, overcoming in this unorthodox way the 'peculiarities' of 'Max Planck's Era' *(10^{43} seconds before the Big Bang)*. To his great surprise, he found out that by applying the superstring theory, the conditions of 'singularity' on the first 10^{-43} second cease to create problems! In the classic Big Bang theory the 'singularity' is indeed an insurmountable obstacle. In superstring cosmology however, that obstacle does not exist: according to this model, if we turn back time the strings will shrink to infinity but never disappear! What this means is that: "before the Big Bang there was not the 'Absolute Nought' but rather an exotic, infinitesimal 'Something', which we have only started to touch". ...At that point exactly, the Universe, as we know it today, was born. Veneziano maintains that the application of the superstring theory inside a black hole <u>is exactly the same</u> with the accelerating expansion, as predicted by the same theory for the pre-Big Bang Era. **"Our Universe is but a small piece inside a black hole[1]"**says Veneziano. "It is indeed frightening if you think about it."

According to the Italian scientist, our familiar matter- and antimatter-particles (electrons, positrons, and photons) were created by **oscillations** in the geometry of space. Indeed, according to quantum mechanics, gravitational fields with strong variations can create particles of every kind. Additionally, these particles are generated from great quantities of kinetic energy and that explains the gradual rise in temperature. ...Gordon Kane, professor of Particle Physics at the University of Michigan, finds it 'very probable' <u>that the Big Bang constitutes a **posterior** phase of the Universe.</u> Besides everything else, this point of view provides enormous support to the mathematical equations.»

[1] **Black Hole:** «A region of space-time from which nothing can escape, not even light, due to its very strong gravitational field.» *(From the glossary of the book 'The Universe in a nutshell' by Stephen Hawking)*

B) DANEZIS M., THEODOSIOU S. 'COSMOLOGY OF THE INTELLECT'
«WHAT WAS THERE BEFORE THE BEGINNING OF THE UNIVERSE? (p. 303):
If we accept the Theory of the Big Bang as true, then initially, at time $t_0=0$, all the energy and matter of the Universe must have been compressed in the frame of a point. This point would certainly constitute a **'point singularity'** *(focusing at the 'bottom' of a black hole)* analogue to

Don't skip chapters or bibliographic references

those we find in a black or a white hole.

TIME IN THE GENERAL THEORY OF RELATIVITY (p. 189): The intensity of the gravity field depends on the value of density of the particular mass. This means that ...the existence of masses of enormous density is a necessary precondition for the appearance of very high gravitational fields. The problem was overcome by modern Astrophysics with the discovery of the so-called black hole. ... As astrophysicist Th. Grammenos (1988) writes, "The work of famous cosmologists S. Hawking and R. Penrose has proved that by applying the laws of the General Theory of Relativity and reversing the direction of time flow, the Universe not only could, **but is rather imperative to have come forth** from the Big Bang of a point singularity of infinite density and temperature."

(p. 256) The Universe, according to the views of the two atomic philosophers (Democritus and Leucippus), was born through the processes of a **white hole**[2], whereas after its birth it evolves within the bounds of a black hole. In that black hole's **point singularity,** as the universe gets **crushed,** it will eventually dissolve.

(p 252) ...Democritus' 'vortex' is formed in the bounds of the original non-sensory system *(of the invisible energy)* ...at a second stage, this 'vortex' evolves in a small area of the big '**voids**' –Euclidean subspaces *(of the visible and flat bottom or in the "point singularity")*.

(p 216) ...Contemporary scientific thinking accepts that the **vacuum** is not empty but full of **gravitational** energy... This means that the supposedly '**empty**' space *(of the bottom or the 'point singularity' of the black hole)* can't 'arithmetically' be of zero energy, as the determination of a certain value, like zero, is opposed to the Uncertainty Principle. In this way, the vacuum can now be defined as the space not of zero but of minimal energy for certain border values. This energy is called '**vacuum-energy**' ...Thus, the energy, in the bounds of any void space, can't constantly be equal to zero. This would mean that its value of uncertainty would be zero and as a result, according to the Uncertainty Principle, the time of measuring this energy would be infinite.

[2] **THE WHITE HOLE** (p. 342): A white hole would practically constitute an area of space from which, a mass of infinite density (coming from the perceptible nothing) would materialize inside our observable Universe, through a blinding explosion of unspecified duration.

This phenomenon may occur in a miniature scale, similarly to the Big Bang event, from which –as it is believed nowadays– our Universe was born. Surely, an acceptance like this, would not only refute the contemporary cosmological views, but also a series of social and philosophical movements based on these points of view. This is because, the notion that the birth of the perceptible to us Universe through the false nonexistence of another invisible Universe, which may lay behind the horizon of a black hole, would be indeed a serious threat to all aforementioned cosmological social and philosophical views.»

(A parenthesis opens…)

[In this case, the 'invisible Universe' would correspond to the HyperUniverses of the True Light and the black hole/material universe to their Forbidden Tree. However, let's not overlook some universally accepted wise men:

PLATO'S TIMAEUS (29b5, V): «And since these things exist in this way, by absolute necessity, **this world must be the image of another.**»

HERMES TRISMEGISTUS, HERMETIC TEXTS, VOL. I, RODAKIS P., TZAFEROPOULOS AP., SPEECH I: «§8…The Divine Will took the form of Logos (Word), and **saw the Good World, and mimicked it**, creating a world, with its own elements…»] *(Parenthesis closes)*

(DANEZIS-THEODOSIOU Continued):

«According to the previous point of view, the whole of our Universe, provided it expands, constitutes nothing more than the space of evolution of a huge, limitless white hole. Perhaps because of these facts, physicists nowadays have the impression that the existence of white holes **would unsettle the scientifically acceptable order of things**, leading to results that wouldn't possibly be supported by the contemporary scientific theory. …What are white holes after all, besides **gates** for unexpected matter and energy to enter into the Universe? The Israeli nuclear physicist Yuval Neeman (1925-) and the Russian mathematician Sergei Petrovich Novikov (1938-) tried to answer this question with their independent works and claimed that the white holes constitute long overdue events in relation to the moment of creation of the Universe, through which, just like then, matter and energy are born **from the non-perceivable**.

PARADOXICAL PHENOMENA IN THE ENVIRONMENT OF A BLACK HOLE (p. 352):

In the bounds of a black hole and inside the invisible space, which is defined from the horizon of its events, according to the Theory of Relativity, hyper logical and incomprehensible natural events occur. On the one hand, they are due to the relativistic velocities with which masses in motion are being driven towards the point-anomaly *(point-singularity)*, and on the other hand to the huge gravitational powers that develop in this space. Thus, according to the Theory of Relativity, the length of an object moving towards the direction of its length, becomes smaller (reduced) as its velocity increases and it will practically become zero, when its speed reaches the speed of light.

However, during the period of time that the length of the object 'shrinks', due to its speed increase, **its mass gets larger and larger until it becomes infinite**[3], **when its length has become zero.** Like-

269

Don't skip chapters or bibliographic references

wise, time (along with the body's mass) expand with the increase of the object's speed. Therefore, the moment when time reaches the speed of light **it 'freezes'**, which means that the time between two ticks of a clock is estimated to be infinite, equal to eternity.

[3] (p. 171): Yet the mass of an object is defined as the measure of **inertia** of its matter, that is, the magnitude of **resistance** it exhibits when we try to alter its kinetic condition by exertion of force.»

(I am opening another parenthesis here…)
[This is precisely what happens in the densely material dimension that surrounds us, where, although the energy forces of the subatomic particles move at high speeds while submerging towards the bottom of the black hole of the material (visible) universe, our dense material bodies –which consist of these subatomic particles– end up, in this space-time distortion of the bottom, being 'static/inert' (mass of tranquility); a condition relative to what takes place in the 'eye' of a tornado.
As far as the factor of 'time' is concerned, theologians say: One moment of God is a thousand years for man …since…the time between two ticks of the clock up there is equal to eternity here!] (Parenthesis closes here)

(DANEZIS-THEODOSIOU Cont'd)…

(p. 352) …So, when we talk about the increase of a body's mass, we refer to the increase in the measure of its inertia. But how can an object's inertia increase through the increase of its velocity? As the Italian physicist W. Bertozzi proved with the maximum-speed **experiment**, when we offer energy to a body, so as to increase its velocity and for as long as the developing speed is low, the greatest part of the offered energy is consumed in order for the body to increase its velocity, while a small percentage is accumulated in the structural constituents of the body. However, if we continue offering energy to the body,…the phenomenon is reversed and only a minimal part of the offered energy is consumed in order to increase its velocity, while the overwhelmingly greatest part of the energy, is stored in the structural constituents of the body *(its mass)*. This constant accumulation of energy can, theoretically, go on to infinity…

And if we proceed even further:
(p. 184): Time expands, just like the mass of a body, when its velocity increases. Thus, the moment the body reaches the speed of light, the hands of the clock will stop rotating, as the time between two ticks of a clock is estimated to be infinite and equal to eternity. That is …the faster (a muon) moves, the longer it lives. Furthermore, if its velocity reaches the speed of light in vacuum, then it can exist for much longer than its theoretical life span. In other words, an increase of its velocity means prolongation of its life.

Allow me to intervene with another parenthesis: Does this mean 'life' in the bottom of the black hole? ... This is equivalent to the eternal (fire of) hell...

In an analogy, if we give a metaphysical extension to this phenomenon, we can deduce that the more 'speed/vigor' an 'atom/person' acquires, the more they increase their material 'mass', since the more the mass of a body increases, the more the time factor 'entrapping' this 'mass', increases respectively. Apparently, this is the reason why some people choose to become 'quietists' in terms of mundane trivialities... safeguarding whatever surrounds their (Spiritual) Fortune/Essence [Gr. w. Περι-ουσία = surrounding essence/fortune]...While others choose to become 'immortal' at the bottom of a black hole. It's a matter of choice.

And since all things are reflective repetitions, besides the fact that particles of matter are spherical vortices-whirls of energy...:

BLACK HOLES IN THE CENTERS OF GALAXIES (p. 359): Scientific evidence at our disposal today lead us to the feasible conclusion that the cores of most giant regular galaxies, like our own... are spaces that host black holes.

...Relatively recently, new evidence indicates that in the center of our galaxy there is a black hole. ...Meaning, that we are led to assume that in the center of our galaxy, there is a black hole of a mass equal to 2.5×10^6 Mo *(30,000,000 times our sun's mass)*, concentrated in an area of diameter of 0.1 light years!»

Since this reference is quite long and obviously difficult for some readers, I sum up:

In the True Universe (HyperUniverses of the Light) there is a black hole (forbidden tree), from carcasses of older creations that perished. This black hole, after 'the horizon of its events' (=the limits of the area from which nothing can escape anymore, due to gravitational/erotic attraction), forms an energy-spiral (the 96% energy <u>material</u>*-universe) which leads to its bottom (=to its 'point singularity'). The bottom of this black hole (the forbidden tree) transforms into a white 'hole/door' (Schwarzschild's theory), where, through a four-dimensional bridge (Einstein-Rosen) creates another world, which, in this case, is our 4% visible Universe... in which space-time distortions (warps) take place and give us the sense of time of billions... of years. This is the* **delusion** *caused in man about the existence of the material world.*

The densely material universe, i.e. the partial, visible 4% which is <u>all</u> man's eyes can see, did not yet exist. There existed though a **formless,** swirling 'something' *(vacuum energy)* **like** a farrago (confused mixture) of 'fire' and 'gases' in the lowest (innermost) point of the energy-vortex *(point singularity)*.

The 'fire/heat' that existed there was generated by the **final** transition/degradation of the dead 'energy-remnants' into the phase/state of

Don't skip chapters or bibliographic references

waste. There was no form there yet. The 'ingredients' of this <u>inferior</u> intermixture were comprised of the **waste materials** of previous dead creation carcasses.

---

[288] **THE SECRET BOOK OF DZYAN, 'ANTHROPOGENESIS', STANZA III**: «§28. From the drops of sweat, from the residue *(sediment)* of the substance, from the matter of dead bodies of men and animals **of the previous wheel** and from cast-off *(waste)* dust, the first mammals were created.»

The 'energy remnants' that were located throughout this entire energy-vortex (the invisible energy-universe) **once** represented Life. As they died away, they retained a **modified** trace of that Life as a remnant within; this replica of life, we will from now on call 'life-remnant'.

As these (energy) 'life-remnants' accumulated (pushed down by the outer ones) into the inner part of the energy spiral, at its bottom (as waste), they joined together, creating a <u>new</u> **mutated** 'ingredient' that now lay scattered in the bottom region and supplemented the sum of its elements (the bottom's). From now on, we will call this 'sedimented life-remnant', and it was this that would later on comprise the 'photographic paper/<u>yeast</u>' to exclusively **project** the densely material, organic **life**.

---

[289] *The visible creation as the result of astro-aetheric (energy-) **projection**:* **DANEZIS M., THEODOSIOU S. 'COSMOLOGY OF THE INTELLECT'**
MATTER AS A WHIRL (VORTEX) – SOME PERSONAL VIEWS (p. 178): «But the vortex-particle has a series of surprises in store for us, since it should present spherical symmetry. What we are essentially talking about, is a **non-perceptible spherical vortex** inside the n-dimensional **non Euclidean field**, whose **projective shadow** inside the three-dimensional Euclidean space of our senses, is perceived as an elementary particle.»

The rest of the waste material sediment, at the inner/lowest point of the bottom of the energy-spiral (the interior of the 'black hole'), would be converted to the 'photographic paper' on which the aetheric 'model' for the <u>inorganic,</u> visible universe of the 4% would be later on imprinted. Let us examine some additional data though, so that this particular point can become clearer as we move on.

In order for a complete (densely) material ecosystem to be born, which would accommodate **M**an in one of its corners, the entire (wavelike) 'oscillation' of the creators had to go down one more step in the scale. The second fall of the creators was complete. They were not bothered by this additional degradation. What was needed was Celestial **M**an's complete entrapment.

As we said, Immortality is not a property of the holder, but of the space in which he dwells. Each Wholeness that is severed from Its Source ceases to possess this privilege and eventually dies.

---

290 **THE GOSPEL OF JOHN, CH. 15**: «§4. Abide in Me, and I in you. As the vine-branch cannot bear fruit of itself, unless it abides in the vine...»

Its Essence is initially **transformed** into energy until it too is degraded, gradually losing everything up to its last trace of Life.

Throughout the entire 'energy' part of the dark, swirling matter, there were stacked 'carcasses' of older creations. These dead 'energy-remnants' were spinning in layers. Each layer inwards corresponded to an older creation. With the creator's entrance into this 'energy' vortex, these 'remnants' were vitalized with new life. They initially appeared as living vibrations. The vitalized energy-layers were incorporated into dimensions, according to the position they had in the vortex. Because each dimension had more than one energy-layer, the various sub-planes were formed. It was from **the sum** of the energy-material of previous remnants, **that all** <u>energy-bodies</u> of the man-being were first built.

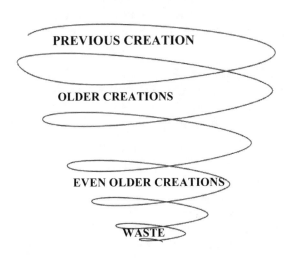

PREVIOUS CREATION

OLDER CREATIONS

EVEN OLDER CREATIONS

WASTE

The creators, by replicating the Fatherly HyperUniverses, wanted this man-being to possess the capacity to expand its species through its energy-bodies as it would absorb 'data' from the energy of the entire material-energy world. But this was not achieved, because the Attribute of Life the creator had brought with him <u>was incomplete</u>. He then turned to the Fatherly HyperUniverses where he was initially granted Life/Eve (in order for the Attribute of Life to be complete/whole) and later on (he was granted) Celestial **M**an/Heavenly Adam as well.

---

291 **THE APOCRYPHON OF JOHN, THE GNOSTIC SOCIETY LIBRARY**:

«But the Blessed One, the Mother-Father, the Beneficent and Merciful One, had mercy upon the Mother's power which had been brought forth out of the chief archon *(in the form of the human Soul)*. ...And He sent... a helper to Adam *(the energy man-being or material Adam)*, Luminous

Don't skip chapters or bibliographic references

Epinoia *(Celestial Man or Heavenly Adam)* which comes out of Him, Who is called Life. And she assists the whole creature *(material Adam)*, by toiling with him and by restoring him to his fullness and by **teaching him about the descent...** and about the way of re-ascent. And the luminous Epinoia **was hidden inside**[1] Adam, <u>in order that the archons might not know her</u>, but that the Epinoia might be a correction of the deficiency of the mother.» [Eng. tr. from Coptic: FREDERIK WISSE]

[1] HESIOD: «...as he saw the far-seen shine of the fire **inside** men.»

The **remaining** part of vitalized remnants, which did not form man's energy-bodies, was left to create the inferior living vibrations, which would <u>in turn</u>, be formulated by aetheric **M**an into energy-plants and energy-animals.

Energy-beings that did not possess this special privilege of the Breath/Soul/Logos (i.e. plants and animals) would not expand energy-wise, but would only <u>accompany</u> and assist the man-being by supplying him with all the knowledge/information they had acquired from previous energy-creations.

---

292 **OLD TESTAMENT, GENESIS CH. 2** *(Aetheric Creation)*

«§18 The Lord God said, "It is not good for man to be **alone**. I will make him a **helper**, suitable for him. §19 And **out of the** *(aetheric)* **earth*** the Lord God **made all the beasts** of the field and all the birds of the air and he brought them to Adam to see how to name them; and whatever name Adam gave to each living creature, that was its name.»

*Gr.: ἐκ τῆς γῆς = out of the earth

Now in the third phase, these –formulated by Man– aetheric beings, would project their forms and thus get imprinted onto dense matter as our familiar plants and animals.

Life is offered to each species of **material** animals through a collective unconscious connected to a central vitalized astro-aetheric being of the corresponding remnant energy-layer. This manner of life-supply to animals can be paralleled to a single, central, electric light-bulb from which hundreds of optical fibers are supplied with light and form the decorative light fixtures. Thus, from **a single species** of an astro-aetheric being, millions of animals of the **same species** are projected and vitalized in the material plane.

The material-beings, which are very close to inorganic matter in the pyramid of life (of visible matter), are projected and vitalized by the energy-layers that correspond to the aetheric plane (the closest one to dense matter), which also corresponds to the older energy-layers of 'life-remnants' of the entire universe vortex. These material beings possess only a vitalized aetheric body, e.g. plants, amoebas, fungi, anthozoa, various insects etc. On the other hand, the creation's <u>inorganic</u> part is enveloped by the **constructive aetheric substance.**

More analytically the order of things is as follows:

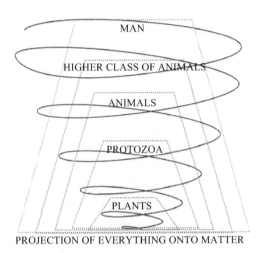

PROJECTION OF EVERYTHING ONTO MATTER

In the outer (higher) energy-layer were the 'life-remnants' of the immediately previous creation. From this energy-material the anthropoids were molded, vitalized and later imprinted (appeared) onto the densely material plane as living creatures **but without a soul**. When man settled in the outer energy-layer, those beings moved to the immediately inner one, piling up and in turn pushing their inferior ones even deeper, all successively succumbing to a degradation process.

In the inner layers were the 'life-remnants' of older creations. After being vitalized from the sum of the creative force of the creator-gods and formulated by Man, they formed (through projection) the great variety of animals in the densely material plane.

From the even older layers of energy-remnants, the category of plants and trees was formulated in dense matter.

Finally, the absolutely thick, dense waste-sediment constructed inorganic matter and became the inorganic, densely material, visible universe.

Thus, each category of living beings that was **inferior** to the previous one in the pyramid of life **is vitalized** from life-remnants from an energy-layer of equivalent **antiquity**. This unfortunately, is the final destiny of all luminous beings of the HyperUniverses, which are cut-off from their Source, get trapped and then remain pinned-down into the 'web' of the material universe.

❧·❧

Parallel to the **aetheric form-giving** by Man, a team of gods, representative of each category starts creating **the conditions** for the <u>imprinting</u> of aetheric form onto dense matter. This would include two phases: (a) the mere appearance of inorganic matter and (b) the manifestation of (material) **life.**

Don't skip chapters or bibliographic references

Formulated dense matter would be placed into the 'bottom' of the energy-universe, where the last energy-layers had been condensing, as it entered/fell into the 'waste phase/state'. There, in the lower (inner) layers, energy accelerated its speed/frequency. This acceleration –with gravity as its basic ingredient/tool 'residing' in the lower energy-regions– was forcing the elements of higher layers, as they subsided, to accumulate and condense in this 'bottom' region and transform into cumbersome, slow-moving elements *(mass of tranquility)*.

---

[293] **DANEZIS M., THEODOSIOU S. 'COSMOLOGY OF THE INTELLECT'**:
(a) NEW SCIENTIFIC DATA (p. 47):

«Matter, according to the Theory of Relativity, is no more Newton's inalterable molecule-complex, but **the <u>condensate</u> of an energy-current.**»

(b) FORMATION OF A SPHERICAL SYSTEM OF SENSORY-MATTER WITH SIMULTANEOUS EJECTION OF MATERIAL INTO THE OUTER VACUUM (p. 254):

«It is interesting that in the limits of the vortex, near the region of the 'great void', before the creation of the spherical condensation, the material of the non-sensory Universe (space+atoms) consists of an 'exotic' to the senses material, which cannot be described by atomic philosophers, and which is subsequently divided in two components, the 'fine' and the 'non-fine' ones, which in a later phase would –according to the views of the atomic philosophers– form what is today known to our senses as 'matter'. As modern cosmologic views describe, during the Planck Epochs *(up to 10^{-43} seconds before the Big Bang, when mass was so dense that a whole flock of galaxies had the dimensions of a hydrogen atom)* and the inflationary expansion, matter –under the extreme conditions prevailing at that time– was really 'exotic'. More specifically, during the inflationary expansion, conditions were such that favored …most probably the creation of the 'exotic' Higgs particles which constitute the hypothetical means through which bodies can acquire the property of mass after the Big Bang.»

(c) THE QUANTUM NATURE OF COSMIC FORCES (p.152): «The Higgs boson is an elusive and still hypothetical particle through which all bodies acquire mass. According to the supporters of this view, the hypothetical Higgs bosons, which can be theoretically found in infinite numbers inside the universe, gather around each subatomic particle, imparting it the property which we call **mass of tranquility.**»

Following that, the energy carrying the aetheric **image** within, would initially permeate the densely material waste and then mold it according to the aetheric form it (the energy) carried inside it each time. Nevertheless, ideal conditions for the appearance of dense material **life** demanded a different procedure: From this 'bottom', **all** scattered 'sedimented life-remnants' that where located in that inner region, had to be initially selected. Then they had to be concentrated in a **preselected** point (the Earth). Following that, densely material **life** would be exclusively projected onto this selected (primary) sediment, and the remaining (secondary) sediment of the bottom would form all the inorganic portion of the visible universe.

Therefore the creation of the visible world is supported by the following points:
(a) The separation of the bottom's sediments (4%) into 'sedimented life-remnants' and the secondary lifeless sediment
(b) The fundamental vitalization **origin** of each being from the corresponding energy-layer of 'life-remnants' and
(c) The **projection** of the aetheric pattern/layout (of the dark matter) onto the corresponding sediment.

Densely material creation, like beautifully embroidered needlework, would hold the sewed gemstones onto it with the exclusively aetheric thread men call gravity.

In order for the slow energy-vibrations *(of low frequencies)* of the bottom to exist autonomously, precisely because of their low frequencies, they were in need of an entire mechanism of inter-connected elements holding each-other. These elements would then assume form **in the perception** of the inhabitants of this plane as an ecosystem. This ecosystem would include everything from the tiniest grain of sand on earth to the remotest galaxies and nebulae of the visible 4% of the universe.

---

[294] **'THE GOLDILOCKS ENIGMA'** THE GUARDIAN, PHYSICS4U APRIL 2007
(http://www.physics4u.gr/articles/2007/universe and man.html):
«Life on Earth is the result of ideal coincidences in the microcosm as well as in the mega-cosmos.
The stars, like thermonuclear reactors are resupplied by the force of their gravity and burn the primordial hydrogen changing it to an ash of heavier elements. Afterwards, this becomes the raw material for the planets round a new star generation (Suns). This ash is a biochemical laboratory from which life sprang up in a planet 3.5 billion years ago. The universe could achieve this, only because the fundamental forces that orchestrate creation are coordinated with absolute precision. If these forces (weak-electric, gravitational and powerful-nuclear) were different, even to a minimal degree, the stars would either burn their fuels too fast, or they would not have ignited at all, or they would fail to make carbon and the heavier elements on which life depends, or they would collapse from their weight instead of exploding. If therefore, something had not been regulated to perfection, the stars would fail to scatter water and the

Don't skip chapters or bibliographic references

chemical substances essential to life in our entire Galaxy.

This enigmatic **cosmic precision** made British astrophysicist Fred Hoyle to propose that the World resembles a 'controlled project'. And this prompted physicist Freeman Dyson, to say that: "Under a certain view, it appears that the world knew of our arrival."

While Leonard Susskind mentions that it is out of something more than 'humble' coincidence that the universe is so well-adapted for human beings and he wonders: "Can science explain the exceptional fact that the universe appears to be so terribly unknown, so inexplicable, so marvelous and so well-designed to accommodate our existence?" Cosmologists call this incredibly fine-tuned universe, 'Anthropic Principle'. Believers call it the 'hand of God'.»

Two basic principles are indissolubly interwoven with each-other and make formulated dense matter visible by projecting it: Firstly, the acceleration of energy causes its condensation. Namely, as gravity –which 'resides' in the inner/deeper layers– attracts the outer parts towards the bottom of this spiral/vortex, it causes a higher concentration of the energy in the deeper regions. This concentration/jam then results in the condensation/deceleration of the energy *(mass of tranquility)*. Next comes the **formulation** of this energy which is achieved by the **projection** of the aetheric image onto the bottom's condensed sediment.

This entire dense (visible) materialization process can be paralleled to the photographic or cinematographic camera mechanism –which in this case is the brain of the beings– which, by momentarily entrapping the light carrying the (aetheric) image inside them receive it and in turn project it onto the film. For the material condition, the 'film' corresponds to the projection/imprinting onto the space-time bottom/grid *(brane)* of the energy spiral-universe.

[295] **ENCYCLOPEDIA 'DOMI'**, PHOTOGRAPHY: «…Schematically we can distinguish two phases in the photographic process: the image formation in the dark chamber and its reproduction by the use of photochemical reactions… The photographic process can be summed up as follows: the **photo-sensitive** material *(film)* is placed in a dark chamber *(photographic or movie camera)* and when the shutter opens, the film is exposed to the light coming from the object being photographed. A photochemical reaction occurs on the areas of the film where the light falls.»

Cinematography (Motion Pictures) is an extremely fast projection of still pictures (frames).

Just as the functions needed for a picture to be printed on the film are specific, likewise the operations for the imprinting/projection onto the space-time 'film' are also specific.

[296] 'MYSTERIES OF THE WORLD', VOL. 'SECRET MESSAGES'
THE HOLOGRAPHIC FUNCTION OF THE BRAIN (pp. 395-403): «According to the American neurophysiologist Karl Pribram, of Georgetown University, Washington, the human brain functions as a(n) (apparatus creating) hologram. It records the stimuli it receives through specific frequency patterns and converts these information-waves –like the light beam projecting the holographic image– into three-dimensional, moving, color images that we interpret as the conscious perception of the world. Consequently the brain functions as a hologram interpreter which decodes a holographic universe. Pribram's theory is based on the research by physicist David Böhm (1917-1992) professor at the London University, who worked closely with Einstein. According to Böhm our entire reality is a formation of waves which coincide and subsequently create continuous parallel images. Reality is, according to Böhm, an organized hologram.
[I am referring to the statement of Danezis-Theodosiou *in the previous reference #289:* «...the vortex-particle ... a non-perceptible spherical vortex inside the n-dimensional non Euclidean field, whose projective shadow inside the three-dimensional Euclidean space of our senses, is perceived as an elementary particle.»]
A HOLOGRAM IS: An unusual technique of taking pictures during which the image information is recorded in such a way that each picture appears as a three-dimensional projection. The hologram is created when a laser beam is deflected in two beams with the help of a special deflector. The object being photographed reflects the first beam. The second beam somewhat collides with the reflected beam. This process is similar to what happens when we throw two stones in a lake. Each stone causes the water to move in concentric circles. When these circles coincide so do the ripples in the water creating a crisscross pattern. The crisscross pattern created by the colliding laser beams is captured with the help of the photographic film. A holographic film appears as mere disorganized wavy lines to the naked eye. However, if we illuminate this film, we can see the captured object in a three-dimensional form and thus we can observe it from all sides and different angles. What is impressive with this image-capturing method is the fact that the information from the image (i.e. every section of the entire image) is stored in every section of the film.»

Don't skip chapters or bibliographic references

Characteristic is the process of trapping the aetheric light carrying the aetheric image on it. This is brought about by matter's dyadic condition 'light – no light'. Then, the imprint of this image onto the space-time 'film' through the opening and closing of the 'photographic shutter' creates the 'positive' and 'negative' position, just like the positive and the negative of a picture. This is proved by the peculiarity exhibited by subatomic particles. What am I referring to? I am referring to the mysterious appearance and disappearance of these particles.

---

297 **FRED ALAN WOLF** (PH.D. IN PHYSICS, UCLA) **'WHAT THE BLEEP DO WE KNOW'** (http://www.whatthebleep.com): «Physicists invented the world of subatomic particles while trying to figure out what happens in their experiments. Namely, a great amount of energy in limited space and time *(i.e. condensation, or just like the imprint of an actual time scene on photographic paper)*. In such a dimension, bizarre things take place and these are explained by subatomic quantum-physics. However, all this remains the subject of much controversy and many hypotheses related to what is actually happening. Particles appear and disappear all the time. Where do they actually go when they disappear? This is a thorny question.»

Their appearance or disappearance is something equivalent to the light getting trapped by the cinematographic/photographic lens. While the subatomic particle disappears, the photographic or cinematographic camera shutter is shut. However the instance that the subatomic particle seems to appear from nowhere corresponds to the moment when the photographic shutter opens in order to capture the aetheric 'image' and project it onto the time-space/film. This function is related to the 'yes/no' poles of duality which is the basis of the entire (visible and invisible) nature; exactly equivalent to 'charge/no charge' of the fundamental computer operation *(10101101)*.

---

298 *Could it be that the way signals/messages are transmitted in our brain is related to the process we are describing?*
DANEZIS M., THEODOSIOU S. 'COSMOLOGY OF THE INTELLECT' (FROM THE THESIS OF GEORGIOU, G., DROUGAS, A., 'CYBERNETICS AND MODERN PHYSICS, 1999) **MAN AS A RECEIVER AND DATA PROCESSOR – THE DELUSION OF THE SENSES'** (pp. 410-411)
«CH. NEURONS: In order for neurons *(of the brain)* to function as electric cells, they maintain an electric potential difference of the order of 65mV along their cellular membrane. …If now the neural cell is excited, the equilibrium-potential changes and an electric-signal transferring mechanism is created. …What is important as far as the electrical function is concerned, is that the transferred signal is of the **all-or-nothing** type. This means that stimuli which do not exceed the minimum 'sensory' threshold cannot create a sig-

nal, whereas, stimuli exceeding it **do,** and always produce **the same** signal *(yes light-no light)*. This means that regardless of the difference of intensity or time of the stimuli, the amplitude and duration of the transmitted signal is always the same. ...In the transmitted signal then which carries the information, what matters is the number of energy-potentials and the time intervals between them *(oscillation characteristics)*. Thus, what determines the intensity of the sensation and the speed of the movement is the frequency of the potentials and not their magnitude or their duration because as we have said the potentials are of the **all-or-nothing** type. This characteristic of signal-transmission in the nervous system is very important if we think that since the signal-transmission mechanisms are stereotyped, they do not reflect the properties of the stimulus. Henceforth, to differentiate the information, since the manner of their transfer is the same for all, we come to the conclusion that the signal of an energy-potential is determined entirely by the neural path through which it is being transferred.»

It might not be pointless here to also take into consideration a different piece of information which supports this dyadic behavior of energy:

MAGNETIC GATES OPEN AND CLOSE CONTINUOUSLY LETTING PARTICLES TO PASS THROUGH AND REACH EARTH FROM THE SUN

(a) http://www.arvanitidis.gr/?s=flux+transfer+event&submit=Search

«Strange portal connects Earth to sun; High-energy particles can travel the 93 million miles during brief opening.»

(b) http://www.msnbc.msn.com/id/27525165/#.TysHVeTAG7s

«As strange as it might sound, the above is probably true since approximately every 8 minutes, very high up in the sky a huge magnetic gate of 150 million kilometers in length opens up, letting tons of high-energy particles pass through towards earth!

The phenomenon is called Flux Transfer Event (FTE), explains physicist David Simbeck of NASA's Goddard Space Flight Center. He characteristically reports that: "Ten years ago I was sure it didn't exist, now though, the evidence is irrefutable."

The scientific team stated at the Plasma Physics Conference in Alabama, that the FTE phenomenon not only occurs, but it is twice more usual than they had suspected till then.

Scientists have for some time now suspected, that the Earth and the Sun must be connected in some way. The Earth's magnetosphere is full of solar-wind particles which pass through the Earth's magnetic 'shields' and enter, following the magnetic-field lines which can be traced from the surface of our planet, all the way back to the Sun's atmosphere. Till now, they imagined that the Earth-Sun connection was permanent, but now, according to Simbeck's scientific team, it becomes apparent that the interaction is brief and very dynamic.

How does the FTE work though? The Earth's side which is exposed to the

Don't skip chapters or bibliographic references

> Sun at a given time, 'presses' its magnetic field against the magnetic field of the Sun. Every approximately 8 minutes, the two fields reconnect or merge for a short time span, forming some kind of a huge gate through which high-energy particle-flow is possible. The gate created has the form of a cylinder of a width almost as the earth's diameter.
> The European Space Agency (ESA) with four 'Cluster' spacecraft, and NASA's five 'Themis' probes have flown through and surround these cylindrical gates, measuring their dimensions and scanning the particle-flow in their inside. From the research done, they have reached the conclusion that the magnetic gates have a tendency to form over the Earth's equator, and then move towards the North Pole in December and the South Pole in July.»

The infamous 'Big Bang' was nothing more than the first 'flash' that imprinted the photograph (first frame) of the aetheric onto the waste space-time 'film' of the bottom, when the aetheric creation came to completion.

Time in dense matter had its own pace. The base of time in the triangle (Δ) of creation [Gr. for Creation= Δημιουργία {Demiourgia}] was unfolding lazily in dense space and was interwoven with it forming the dense grid of support for the visible.

[299] A) 'THE ELEGANT UNIVERSE OF BRIAN GREENE', Cambridge Webpage For The String Theory, Scientific American, July 2007 http://www.physics4u.gr/articles/2007/M-branes.html
«BRANE: *(membrane-grid)* Physicists Randall and Sundrum created a model of branes in which the visible universe is a brane **incorporated inside a greater universe,** just like a piece of seaweed floats in the ocean. Ordinary matter is attached to this brane. The usual particles like electrons and protons can only exist **on** this brane. We humans will not be able to enter other dimensions because the particles that form our bodies —electrons, protons, neutrons— remain **attached** to this brane that constitutes our world.»
B) THE LOST MATTER OF THE UNIVERSE FOUND IN THE COSMIC WEB
SOURCE: SCIENCE DAILY, MAY 20, 2008(http://www.physics4u.gr/news/2008/scnews3327.html):
«We think we see the aethereal threads of a structure like **the spider's web,** which formulates the World's spine, Prof. Mike Shull says.»
C) COSMIC WEB (http://www.physics4u.gr/news/2008/scnews3311.html):
«All matter in the World is distributed in a web-like structure. In the dense nodes of this cosmic web are the galactic flocks and the greater objects in the World.»
D) BLAVATSKY H., P., 'THE SECRET DOCTRINE' (I-83): «In the Mandukya (Mundaka) Upanishad it is written, "As a spider throws out and retracts its web *(woe to him that gets caught in it!),* as herbs spring up in the ground... so is the Universe derived from the un-decaying one." (I. 1. 7) Brahma, as 'the

germ of unknown Darkness' is the material from which all evolves and develops as the web from the spider, as foam from the water, etc.»

E) THE SECRET BOOK OF DZYAN, 'COSMIC EVOLUTION', STANZA III: "§10. Father-Mother *(the Creator + Devamatri matter)* spin a **web** *(brane, grid)* whose upper end is fastened to spirit, the light of the one darkness *(virtual light)* and the lower one to its shadowy end, matter; and this web is the universe spun **out of the two substances** made in one, which is Svabhavat[1]. §11. It expands when the breath of Fire *(Creator)* is upon it; it contracts when the breath of the Mother *(cosmic space, Devamatri)* touches it. ... §12 Then Svabhavat sends Fohat[2] to harden the atoms. Each is a part of the web, reflecting the 'Self-existent Lord' like a mirror, each becomes in turn a *(reflective)* world."

[1]**Svabhavat:** The 'Material Cause of the Universe'. The Puranic Commentators explain it by Karana – 'Cause' -- but Esoteric Philosophy by the 'ideal spirit of that Cause'. It is, in its secondary stage, the Svabhavat of the Buddhist philosopher, **the eternal cause and effect**, *(the commanders of fate [Heimarmenē*] according to Hermes Trismegistus)* omnipresent yet abstract, the self-existent plastic Essence and the root of all things, viewed in the same **dual** *(dyadic/twofold)* light. [BLAVATSKY H., P., 'THE SECRET DOCTRINE']

* **HERMES TRISMEGISTUS**: THE FOUNDER OF MONOTHEISM 9000 B.C., IOANNIDIS P. K., CH. 1:

«§9 And the God Noũs (Mind), male-female one, being Life and Light *(the Genitor of the fallen one)*, gave birth to another Creator-Noũs of Fire and Spirit *(2nd one, the fallen one, Yaldabaoth, Lucifer)*. And this second Noũs created the administrators of the sensory world, which is encompassed **in seven circles**, whose administration is called **Heimarmenē** *(or else the seven Elohims, or else the powers, the authorities and the kings of the group of Yaldabaoth in John's Apocryphon)." The DZYAN make no mention of the Sacred Place of origin of the Primordial Demiourgos (Creator)/ Ray/ Lucifer.*

[2]**Fohat:** The Vehicle (Vahan) of the 'Primordial Seven' *(Creators, Elohims, the Commanders of Destiny)*; The 'Messenger of their will'. [BLAVATSKY H., P., 'THE SECRET DOCTRINE' I-108].

(I-76): "The ancients represented it by a serpent (snake), because Fohat makes a hissing sound as he glides *(crawls)* hither and thither in zigzags *(in a crisscross pattern)*.»

In the primeval visible universe, the chemical elements of dense nature started weaving their compounds, faithfully following their aetheric template/pattern

.

Don't skip chapters or bibliographic references

---

300 **A) 'FIRST DARK MATTER IS ACCUMULATED (THE AETHERIC PATTERN) AND THEN THE GALAXY IS FORMED'** ARTICLE JANUARY 2007 SOURCE: PHYSICS4U.GR DISCOVERY (http://www.physics4u.gr/articles/2007/top space stories 2006.html):

«A new study from NASA's Spitzer space telescope suggests **that galaxies are formed within large masses of dark matter**. This mysterious substance emits no light but it has mass and therefore can attract matter-matter *(dense matter)* with its **gravitational force**. Astronomers believe that there is five times the amount of dark matter in our world than normal matter. …Initially, researchers were trying to comprehend better how new galaxies and dark matter evolve and accumulate together…. At that point, they observed something odd: Every galaxy they studied seemed **to be surrounded** by 'chunks' of dark matter of approximately the **same** size.[1] They were able to indirectly measure how much dark matter –holding the structure together like glue– was present. **The tighter the grouping [concentration] was, the greater the amount of dark matter present.**»

[1]*This is obviously something equivalent to the depiction of the aetheric leaf in Kirlian photography.*

The aetheric creation is described in the 2ⁿᵈ Chapter of Genesis and corresponds to dark matter which precedes the densely material creation.

B) OLD TESTAMENT, GENESIS CH. 2:

«§4 This is the genesis *(creation)* of the heavens and the earth when they were created, in the day when the Lord God **made them**, the earth and the heavens §5. **and all herbs of the field, before they had yet been created on** *(densely material)* **earth** and all the plants of the field **before they had yet sprung up, for the Lord God had not yet sent rain on the** *(visible)* carth and **there was no man to work the ground**, §6. but steam came up from the earth and watered the whole face of the earth.»

Out of the sum of the formulated material universe, after thousands of condition-creating mathematical functions, Earth is chosen as Man's cradle. From every corner of the newborn universe the selected 'sedimented life-remnant' is chosen and accumulated there like yeast, so that onto this selected material, life can be projected at the bottom of this spiral/vortex.

The first plants make their appearance and get projected onto the 'visible' vitalized from the older energy 'life-remnants', namely the inner layers that are closer to the dense material waste.

Then, in the densely material plane, the first simple organisms are projected. They are in-between plant and animal and are vitalized from the immediately higher (a little younger than those of the plants) energy 'life-remnants' and the immediately outer –from the previous ones– layers. The first complete animals appear. Some are vitalized from layers comprised of older energy life-remnants and others from younger ones.

At the same time, from the same **dense** mud of 'sedimented life-remnants', the material body of the animal to host Man is created (in the dense/visible matter). This animal is vitalized from the **energy** 'life-remnants' of the first (outer) energy-layer of the dark vortex/universe, namely the creation immediately before yours.

Man's earthly cradle had already been arranged. All incarnate beings in dense matter possess programmed genetic functions in order to procreate, **before** they are divided into two genders.

The basic adjustments are carried out in the aetheric plane, where the subatomic particles form **bridges** which connect the aetheric plane to the densely material one. Mathematics, in all its grandeur, composes matter. The DNA programming of all living creatures as well as every plant-seed are in no way different from the programming code of a computer of contemporary human technology.

Every animal and plant cell is a perfect mathematical model, having all information/data registered into it; information, not only for the creation of a complete being, but also for the propagation of its species through new programmed cell production. In order for some minor details to be adjusted, the creators had and still have the potential to intervene on their design at any moment in time.

---

301 **BARBARA MARCINIAK, 'GAIA'** [GR. TRANS. MATZOROU E.] *(Information through channeling)*:

«The reptilian race or Little Lizards, as we amicably call them *(!!!)*, constitute an integral part of your genealogy. It is a tremendously savage, and at the same time merciful collective consciousness, because they are many things mingled in one. ...You must realize the fact that the reptilian energies are your creators – your gods. They are masters of genetics. ...They are the masters of the game. The masters of the game get together, as you do to play cards or racket-ball. The only difference is that **their game aims at the creation of civilizations.** They modify and change worlds, allowing the entrance of different civilizations **in the realities they orchestrate.** These civilizations act based purely on their impulses, which are nevertheless provided to them through matrixes of energy-blueprints. ...The masters of the game are geniuses. Not only do they conceive the game and create the entire energy-matrix through which each civilization will flourish,

Don't skip chapters or bibliographic references

from the most skillful craftsmen to the last beggars, but they also introduce their own selves **inside** the civilizations they create. …The masters of the game are formless and they can change shapes/forms and know no limitations. They can assume any form they choose, as they move in-between and beyond sound and geometry. The masters of the game create the energy-matrixes of the civilizations in their mind, and then open the gates in order to literally introduce them to the Earthly plane. Following that, they allow these civilizations to grow and mature, so as to exert their influence to other time periods.»

As the foreman watches over all the progressive production-phases, going from machine to machine, so do they intervene as they always have –by an energy-condensation of their hypostasis– inside the various 'time frames', in order to intercept and operate (live and in real time) on their creation.

Material men (ancient Greeks) initially called them ΘΕΟΣ (=*god [the word used in Greek is* θεός/*theós, coming from the verb* {θεάομαι-θεῶμαι} *meaning I am visible, I am seen*) because they were often visible, while others later called them 'extraterrestrials'! In the evolution of our discussion we will see what role they play today, those who so persistently insist on 'introducing' themselves as extraterrestrials!

On account of this energy-deceleration (*mass of tranquility*) for the formation of dense matter, a new, different oscillation came about. Every immaterial concept, as it went through dense matter, suffered absolute multi-fragmentation. Like Newton's disk when still, 'decelerated' matter did not depict the 'White' Truth anymore, but the fragmented polychrome. The creation of multi-fragmented concepts, views, stands, ideas and forms had generated utter fragmentation in the purely dense material plane. The tree of knowledge of good and evil was there with all its branches stretched out.

[302] *Scientists conclude that the Big Bang was an equivalent event to the creation of a black hole in our universe.*

But in the 'Region' (HyperUniverses) where this 'creation' (Black Hole/Material Universe) took place, totally different conditions prevailed from the ones existing when a black hole is created in the visible universe. A relative analogy of course exists in the area of 'point singularity' (of the bottom).

For the Material Universe/Black Hole, the 'point singularity' corresponds to our visible (4%) universe.

DANEZIS M., THEODOSIOU S. 'COSMOLOGY OF THE INTELLECT'
SCHWARZSCHILD BLACK HOLE (p. 344): «As mass sinks inside the gravitational

field of a black hole, …its spectral lines will relocate to wavelengths so great *(low frequencies)* that they will be practically untraceable. At that point mass will have practically disappeared from the senses as well as from the viewer's observation means.

While the distant observer will perceive these though, someone else, standing **on the moving mass,** will feel gravity increase constantly, until the enormous tidal forces near the point-singularity <u>will shatter him, and **these pieces will be infinitely divided into smaller ones, until his mass ceases to exist.**</u>»

The ONE TRUTH undergoes a similar adventure the moment it passes into the densely material plane (point-singularity) and is fragmented into the thousands of 'positions' and 'oppositions' and diverse views... until the moment that it definitively ceases to exist.

And let me remind you: **GOSPEL OF PHILIP,** JEAN-YVES LELOUP:

«§16…The truth is sown everywhere, existing since the beginning: <u>Some</u> see it at the time it is sown, but <u>few</u> *(will manage to)* see it at the time of harvest *(at the end of time).*» [ENG. TR. JOSEPH ROWE]

He turned and pensively looked at the picture showing that horse galloping in the field.

–This is what you are! <u>Trapped dots on photographic paper</u>…. It is impossible for you to realize it. You don't belong here though!

[303] **DANEZIS M., THEODOSIOU S. 'COSMOLOGY OF THE INTELLECT'**
THE NEW SCIENTIFIC FACTS (p. 48):

«In a few words, the space of the Universe that surrounds us, and which we want to say we measure –since we accept that the General Theory of Relativity is true in this Universe's framework– is not Euclidean *(three-dimensional)* but Riemannian *(multi-dimensional).*

…It is here though that paradoxes for common sense start, since, as we know today, our senses can record and specify shapes that assume their form **only** in three-dimensional spaces, described by Euclidean geometry. Shapes formed inside spaces described by <u>non</u>-Euclidean geometries, like those of Lobatschewski and Riemann, <u>cannot become perceived by the human senses</u>…

THE FLAT WORLD (p. 50): All the above might seem paradoxical and incomprehensible to many. This is why it would be interesting to mention some simple examples which will help us grasp the truth of these previously mentioned ideas. Let us consider then the existence of a <u>flat-world</u>,[1] exactly similar to ours, with the only difference that everything on that world evolves in the framework of two dimensions i.e. length and width. This of course, means that the developed senses of the beings of that world will not have the ability to perceive objects of more than two dimensions. There, everything is flatted-out, humans, animals, their houses; they will all be like architectural drawings (ground plans). Similarly, what we call an impenetrable material wall, in that world would be expressed by a material line of a certain thickness. If we place a three-dimensional object in that said world, its people will perceive <u>only</u> the points of contact of this three-dimensional object with the two-dimensional plane of their world. ...Let us look though at some paradoxical phenomena related to this flat-space.

If a three-dimensional object is located out and over the flat-space, although existing, it cannot be perceived by flat-men. Henceforth, a three-dimensional observer, located outside the said world, will be invisible to that world, since the dimension of height –which is not being perceived by the senses of that world– separates him from the flat space. Let us consider now that the three-dimensional observer draws a material straight line with a graphite pencil onto the flat-space. What will the flat-men of flat-space perceive? Simply that, 'out of nowhere', without any cause and with no logical explanation, a material and impenetrable (to them) wall appeared. It will namely be an inexplicable miracle...»

[1]*The writers of the book mention that the example has its roots on E. A. Abbot's idea and his book 'O Epipedos Cosmos' (=The Flat World) Delfini Publ., Athens 1991.*

You are prisoners and you don't even know it!

304 **THE GOSPEL OF JOHN, CH. 12**: «§47. And if anyone hears My Words and does not believe/keep them, I do not judge him; for I did not come to judge the world but **to save** the world (...*from captivity*)»

You speak of freedom, but you <u>can't</u> imagine what Freedom can really be! Real Freedom, the one a free Intelligent Wholeness experiences which is not subdued to a virtual life but simply **IS**, has no time boundaries to begin with. It has no space limitations. It is not constrained by death, sickness, old age, need for food or lack of, need for clothes or lack of, need for a roof or lack of, need for a family or lack thereof, need for company or lack of. And most importantly, Real Freedom is not constrained by the 'queen' of needs: the oscillation of **breath** *[Gr. ανάσα = breath (Gr.: άνασσα = queen]* which sustains a heavy material body, often sick, in pain and with limitations, a body, which mostly resembles the heavy iron ball and chain of prisoners, rather than the 'ultimate gift'... The freest man today has the same amount of 'freedom' a prisoner does in his cell, who can either lie down, walk around, read, dream, remain standing, or sit –but always in his cell. Real Freedom existing in the worlds where I come from is beyond your imagination. It is neither constrained by needs, nor by circumstances or conditions.

> [305] **GOSPEL OF THOMAS**, JEAN YVES LELOUP: «§84. Jesus said, When you see your true likeness, you rejoice. But when you see your icons, those that were **before you existed,** those that never die and never manifest, what grandeur!» [ENG. TR. JOSEPH ROWE]

To win it, you must first defeat death. To defeat death however, you must first defeat 'virtual' life. When your life 'leads' you, then it has defeated you. But when it has nowhere to 'take' you to, then you have won. If one of the two defeats you, then you have lost!

> [306] **THE GOSPEL OF MATTHEW, CH. 10**: «§39. He who finds his life will lose it, and he who loses his life for My Sake will find it.»

THE SECOND MAJOR FALL

A complete ecosystem had already been born to support the necessary conditions for the survival of the material, 'living' beings. The plan for the formulation of the aetheric creation was just a well thought-out trap. Man had been caught in it and by participating in creation himself, he had already touched the dense waste-material; he had 'touched' absolute death, where, as 'dark light' passes through, gets deflected, deviates and forms the boundless fragmentation of positions and oppositions. Celestial Man had tasted the fruit of the tree of knowledge of good and evil. He was already trapped.

The punishment for the 'alleged' sin had already been prepared. And it was ready because events were precisely expected as they were thoroughly **preplanned**. The verdict is announced to Celestial Men by the creator, in the pretense that they had created death by molding creations from the material of sepsis (rot). He characterizes them as cursed and condemns them to isolation in the absolutely dense, material plane.

---

307 **THE APOCRYPHON OF JOHN, THE GNOSTIC SOCIETY LIBRARY**: «…And when they *(Yaldabaoth's powers)* realized that he *(Adam)* was luminous, and that he could think better than they did, and that he was free from wickedness and evil, they picked him up and threw him down into the lowest part of all matter.» [ENG. TR. FROM COPTIC: FREDERIK WISSE]

☙·❧

At the selected 'point' of the densely material world, Earth, after many trials and errors, living beings of unbelievable beastliness had been created and waited to host the Race of Heroes inside their bodies. These beings were the dinosaurs of prehistory. Built with incredible capabilities, they possessed all the 'equipment', in order to build a fierce and unimaginably ferocious race. Panic takes over the Men of the energy-planes. Involuntarily and simply **by obeying orders**, they had built their own jail in dense matter!

---

308 **A) RABINDRANATH TAGORE (GITANJALI)**, HINDU POET: «Prisoner, tell me, who was it that forged this unbreakable chain? It was I alone, said the prisoner, Night and day I worked on the chain with huge fires and cruel hard strokes. When at last, shackle after shackle, the work was done, I found myself caught in its unbreakable power.»

B) HERMES TRISMEGISTUS, HERMETIC TEXTS, VOL. II, RODAKIS P., TZAFERO-POULOS AP., 'EXCERPT XXIII, FROM THE HOLY BIBLE OF HERMES TRISMEGIS-

---

TUS, TITLED **KORE KOSMOU'**:

«§24 And those souls my son, already from now they were armed with a strange impudence, as if they had performed an act of bravery, **and despite the orders**, they <u>abandoned</u> their components and their stores and did not want to remain in the same place, because they considered that it was **death** to continue to stay in the same residence. §25. And Hermes, speaking to me my child, said: What the souls did, did not escape the attention of the lord and god of all, and that is why he sought for <u>punishment</u> and chains which the souls would endure patiently. And therefore, the sovereign and lord of all *(the archon of this world)* decided to artfully fabricate the human frame for the race of souls to suffer in it.»

The HyperUniverses, realizing the devious impropriety of the creator of matter, demanded that all granted Sacred Provisions be returned along with Celestial Men. Simultaneously, with a swift, decisive intervention they destroy a great part of that creation spreading death to those beings *(the extinction of dinosaurs by an asteroid)*.

[309] **'MASS EXTINCTIONS OF** SPECIES **ON EARTH DURING THE PALEOZOIC-MESOZOIC ERAS' ARTICLE:** PHYSICS4U, JANUARY 2004
http://www.physics4u.gr/articles/2004/massextinction.html
THE END OF THE CRETACEOUS PERIOD –63 TO 135 MILLION YEARS AGO

«The massive extinction between the Cretaceous and the Tertiary period, 65 million years ago is the most famous of all massive extinctions. Its fame stems not from its size (the Permian period extinction was really much greater) but from the victims of the extinction – the dinosaurs. The massive extinction of the Cretaceous-Tertiary period exterminated approximately 85% of all species. Dinosaurs, in other words, were not the only victims. Pterosaurs (flying reptiles) and other marine reptiles, fish, brachiopods, plankton and many plants either vanished completely, or suffered heavy casualties in their population. Even ammonites, who had survived the 4 previous extinctions, were finally extinct.»

Additionally, they give a clear command to the creators to completely evacuate the **densely** material plane and **cancel it**. Celestial Men start to withdraw from the aetheric planes. But the creators' team refuses to obey. The notification from the HyperUniverses then becomes definitive, not as a threat of punishment but as a warning: "If you remain in this sordid creation, you will assume the appearance/form of the fleshy beings *(dinosaurs)* that have just been exterminated."

Don't skip chapters or bibliographic references

---

310 **OLD TESTAMENT, GENESIS CH. 3:**

«§1. Now the serpent was more prudent [Gr. Septuagint (LXX): φρονιμώτατος] than any beast of the field which the Lord God had made…§14 So the Lord God said to the serpent: Because you have done this, you are cursed more than every beast of the field; on your belly you shall go, and you shall eat dust all the days of your life.»

They nevertheless replied with mutiny. Thus, your 'all beneficent' creator was suddenly transformed into a 'wise' dragon/serpent).

---

311 **A) DAVID ICKE 'THE SECRET OF ALL AGES'** «Contemporary descriptions of reptilians fit exactly the descriptions of many ancient 'gods' as they are mentioned in the surviving texts and myths. The Ubaid civilization that appeared between 5,000 and 4,000 B.C., even before the Sumerians, in the region where Iraq is today, had idols of gods which most obviously depict anthropoids with reptilian characteristics. …Central American civilizations had their own winged, reptilian god Quetzalcoatl. Hopi Indians had the winged god-snake Baholinkonga, and native-American civilization is generally flooded with representations of reptiles, such as the mysterious tomb in the shape of a snake in Ohio. Hindus speak of their own reptilian gods Naga (a daemonic race whose name means 'they who crawl'). The Egyptians had their own reptile-god Kneph, and the Pharaohs were often pictured with snakes. The Phoenicians had Agathodaimon, another reptilian entity. Those who believe in Voodoo have a god who is called Damballah Weddo and who is represented as a snake, whereas, the Jews had Nehushtan, the Bronze Serpent. The ancient British god, who was known as the **Dragon/Ruler of the World,** was called HU, and I believe *(says Icke)* that it is from this word that the word hu-man comes from. …The idea of dragons exhaling fire and diabolic snakes appearing in legends and texts of the whole world could easily come from the reptilian gods, who sometime in the past, thousands of years ago, overtly ruled the world.»

…Not to mention the Chinese dragons or the dragon that was killed by St. George.

B) BARBARA MARCINIAK, 'GAIA' [GR. TRANS. MATZOROU E.] *(Information through channeling)*:

«The reptilian race or Little Lizards, as we amicably call them, constitute an integral part of your genealogy. …You must realize the fact that reptilian energies are your creators – your gods. …They were amongst the main motivators for the creation of the human species on this planet. …They are extremely skillful in handling and arrangement of genes. …The reptilian influence is in the core of your biological structure.»

With the power of Logos –the creator– 'places the Cherubim and the flaming sword which turned every way' thus cutting off Man's way of return to the Father-Grounds, by intercepting a big group of Celestial Men about to abandon the universe/trap by encaging them in it.

---

312 **A) OLD TESTAMENT, GENESIS CH. 3**: «§24…And at the east of the garden of Eden he stationed the cherubim, and a revolving, flaming sword, to guard the way to the tree of life.»

B) THE BOOK OF ENOCH, CH. 14: «§10. They elevated me aloft to heaven. I proceeded, until I arrived **at its wall** built with stones of crystal. A vibrating flame (tongues of fire) **surrounded it**, which began to strike me with terror.» (*see also:* http://reluctant-messenger.com/1enoch01-60.htm)

C) PLATO'S REPUBLIC, BOOK 10 (616b-616c)

From the narration of Er, the son of Armenius who describes his death experience:

«To this light we came after another day's journey; and we saw there that the **edges of the sky stretched out ending** into the middle of that light, which was the girdle of the sky, **and it enveloped the entire circumference/revolution of the sky evenly, holding it together** like the under girders of triremes. And from its extremities, the spindle of Necessity/Need was stretched putting all the celestial orbits to motion.»

D) HERMES TRISMEGISTUS, HERMETIC TEXTS, VOL. I, RODAKIS P., TZAFEROPOULOS AP., **'SPEECH VI, ASCLEPIUS' DEFINITIONS TO KING AMMON'**:

«§3 I will start my sermon, by invocation unto God, the master of all and creator and father, the all-encompassing one… §7. To see Him, is not a matter of conjecture, but his very appearance engulfs the whole world in splendor, the world that is above and that which is below; for he is established in the midst, <u>wreathing the Cosmos</u>.» [☉]

HyperUniverses characterize the creator of matter as an apostate and pronounce him fallen.

---

313 **THE GOSPEL OF JOHN, CH. 16**: «§11…concerning judgment, because the archon (ruler) of this world **has been judged**.»

Since then, a deep chasm has been created between the creator of matter and the HyperUniverses, with Celestial Man as the 'apple of discord'. But this is another great subject, which we will deal with later on.

The material universe gates are sealed, cutting off all those who had been trapped in it, turning them **into hostages**. The creator's position remains firm, and unyieldingly he condemns Man anew to even further **demotion** through incarnation. New conditions of life are created and introduced on

Don't skip chapters or bibliographic references

Earth's destroyed remains because the imprisoned man should have an absolutely proprietary Alcatraz-like plane/field to 'create' **in isolation**.

---

[314] *The ENTIRE material universe seems to have been created EXCLUSIVELY to host man. This phenomenon is called by scientists 'Anthropic Principle' and I am reminding you of the excerpt from the relative article.*

THE GOLDILOCKS ENIGMA: 'WHY DOES THE UNIVERSE HAVE JUST THE IDEAL CONDITIONS FOR LIFE TO APPEAR ON EARTH?, 'PHYSICS4U, APRIL 2007 (http://www.physics4u.gr/articles/2007/universe_and_man.html) SOURCE: THE GUARDIAN:

«…This enigmatic cosmic precision made British astrophysicist Fred Hoyle to propose that the World resembles a '<u>controlled project</u>'. And this prompted physicist Freeman Dyson, to say that: "It appears under a certain view that <u>the World knew of our arrival</u>." While Leonard Susskind mentions that it is out of something more than 'humble' coincidence that the universe is so well-adapted for human beings and he wonders: "Can science explain the exceptional fact that the universe appears to be so terribly unknown, so inexplicable, so marvelous and <u>so well-designed to accommodate our existence</u>?" Cosmologists call this incredibly fine-tuned universe, '<u>Anthropic Principle</u>'. Believers call it the hand of God. Neither of the two explains anything.»

From this group of 'selected beings', a new species is chosen to play the protagonist role in this creation. This species belongs to the gender of apes (anthropoids).

---

[315] *I must point out that dinosaurs were destroyed approximately 65 million years ago and Dryopithecus (see last* reference *of this chapter) appears 25 million years ago.*

This **animal** would henceforth be the '**prison**' of this so 'dangerous' a Man. Other animals are also vitalized from the same energy-region as alternative choices for Man's 'material residence' (body). These animals in your world exhibit special gifts today.

During that period, there were two sorts of Men in the aetheric planes. There were some whose Souls had an imprisoned Celestial Man as their Spirit and comprised the Race of Heroes, and plane Souls. They **would all be forced** to incarnate into the material projection of the aetheric field, the dense, septic matter.

The kidnapped Celestial Men refuse to incarnate. They will be later on **forced** to follow.

[316] **THE SECRET BOOK OF DZYAN, 'COSMIC EVOLUTION', STANZA VI:** «§5. At the fourth *(cycle of creation, or the 4th Race of the Heroes)*, the sons are told to create **their images**. One third refuses *(Celestial men refused)*.
Two (thirds) obey *(plain souls of the aetheric world obeyed)*.
The curse is pronounced; they will be born in the fourth *(at the second half of the fourth root-race)*, suffer and cause suffering; this is the first war.»
The devastating consequences of this curse are described in the Chapter:
'THE END OF THE RACE OF HEROES'
There, H. P. Blavatsky comments on that particular verse but presents only the Creators' version and states:
«The holy youths refused to create species after their likeness, after their kind. They are not fit forms for us *(the Apes!!)*. "They have to grow". They refuse to enter the shadows/images **of their inferiors**. Thus the selfish *(selfish?!!)* feeling prevailed from the beginning, even among the gods *(Celestial Men)*, and they fell under the eye of the Karmic Lipikas.» (I-192)
When this excerpt quotes 'to create', it means that after they incarnate into the 'shadows-projections of their inferiors' they must upgrade them. This is exactly what happened when Celestial Man incarnated inside the Australopithecus and upgraded it to Homo sapiens.
Narcissus' projection/reflection onto the (energy-) waters of the lake/world refers to that same event.

The souls stoically accept it. They will be the first to incarnate. No one will escape.

[317] *Plain Souls are the first to incarnate into pythecoids-anthropoids and upgrade them to such a degree that the Genus of Australopithecus is created.*
HERMES TRISMEGISTUS, HERMETIC TEXTS, VOL. II, RODAKIS P., TZAFEROPOULOS AP., EXCERPT XXIII, FROM THE HOLY BIBLE OF HERMES TRISMEGISTUS, TITLED '**KORE KOSMOU**' (p. 201):
«§31 Then the souls, learning for the first time **their sentence**, were saddened (and said)... §34...Another soul shrieked shrilly, and before she spoke shed many tears, and, turning up and down what things served her as eyes, she said: "O Heaven, source of our begetting, O Æther, air, O hands and holy spirit of God our Monarch, O ye most brilliant stars, eyes of the gods, O tireless light of sun and moon, co-nurslings of our origin, detached from you all, we suffer piteously. And this the more, in that from the spacious realms of light, out of the holy envelope and wealthy vault of the gods, and from the blissful government of the gods, **we shall be thus shut** into these **honor-less and lowly bodies**. §35. **What is that so unseemly thing we miserable ones have done? What crime deserves these punishments?** How many sins **await us** wretched ones! How many are the things **we have to do** under the wretched guidance of hopes, to furnish the necessities for a life in this watery

Don't skip chapters or bibliographic references

frame/body that is soon to be dissolved!

§36. For the souls no longer belonging to God, the eyes will no longer hold a prominent position and through such watery spheres as these, we will see our own forefather Heaven tiny, and we shall never cease to suffer, and **at some point** *(after many...reincarnations!)* we shall have **no more** *(spiritual)* vision.[1] We the wretched ones, for sentence has been passed on us poor things... For home, instead of this great world high in the air, a heart's small mass awaits us.»

[1]**HERMES TRISMEGISTUS,** HERMETIC TEXTS, VOL. 1, SPEECHES I-XVIII' RODAKIS & TZAFEROPOULOS: **SPEECH 7, ON THE MATERIAL BODY** «§3. ...and it anaesthetizes the sensory organs, the real ones, not the alleged ones. These organs have been obstructed with much matter, and filled with abominable pleasure, so that you should neither hear those things which you must hear *(he who has ears, let him hear)*, nor see those which you must see.»

He became silent. He looked pensively outside the window. I looked as well. Everything was still and motionless like a frozen frame on a film.
–And you miserable men mistook punishment for the ultimate gift!

[318] **GOSPEL OF PHILIP,** JEAN-YVES LELOUP:
«§11 The words we give to earthly realities engender **illusion**; they turn the heart away from the Real to the **unreal**.» [ENG. TR. JOSEPH ROWE]

...How else would you be able to bear it, after all?

[319] **HERMES TRISMEGISTUS,** HERMETIC TEXTS, VOL. II, RODAKIS P., TZAFEROPOULOS AP., **'KORE KOSMOU'**:
«...For that the Monarch came, and sitting on the throne of truth, said to the souls... §41...You will take the punishment for benefit; you will take the change to better things for infamous despite.»

In the beginning, all aetheric beings were of one sex only. The same was true during the first phase of their materialization. The two sexes would be created later on.

[320] **PLATO'S SYMPOSIUM ARISTOPHANES' SPEECH, CH. 14** (189-190):
«...For our original nature was not the same as it is now, but entirely different. Unlike today, with its two sexes male and female, there used to be a third kind before as well, which had equal shares of the other two, and whose name no longer exists. For 'man-woman' was then a unity, common both in form and in name, composed of both male and female ...Then, each person of this kind was round all over, with back and sides forming a circle... **Zeus... said: "I will slice every one of them in two, so that they are made weaker**.»

Each animal species in dense matter at that time reproduced itself through a purely genetic process. The purpose for the creation of two sexes was **not** propagation, but total entrapment. After all, monogenic (unisexual) reproduction is not absent from nature. Thus, in primeval eras, before the division of the sexes, each animal propagated itself.

---

[321] **A) ENCYCLOPEDIA 'DOMI', ASEXUAL REPRODUCTION - (MONOGONY):**

«A way of reproduction in which new organisms are created by <u>one and only one</u> pre-existing organism. It can be found in the plant, as well as the animal kingdom, with the only difference, that in the plant world, we find it even in their most advanced forms. Monogony can be divided into three categories: fission, budding and sporogenesis (spore formation).

...Monogonic fission, either single or multiple, is a reproductive way of a large category of organisms; yet it can be seen in larvae, as well as embryos of organisms which are also capable of sexual reproduction. An example of that is the **human embryo,** which, when divided monogonically, leads to the creation of twin individuals (also triplets, etc.) without this meaning of course, that the monogonic division of the embryo is the only way twins can be born in humans.»

Apparently, this property remains as a residue from those primordial times.

B) BLAVATSKY H., P., 'THE SECRET DOCTRINE' (II-133):

An excerpt of the article of Prof. Alexander Wilder is given here, which states the following:

«A large part of the vegetable creation exhibits the phenomenon of bisexuality. ...the Linnaean classification (taxonomy) enumerating thus almost all plants. This is the case in the superior families of the vegetable kingdoms as much as in the lower forms; from Hemp to the Lombardy Poplar and Ailanthus. In the animal kingdom, in insect life, the moth generates a worm and the worm becomes a moth. ...The coral-producing family, which, according to Agassiz, 'has spent many hundreds of thousands of years, during the present geological period, in building out the peninsula of Florida ...produce their offspring from themselves like the buds and ramifications in a tree.' Bees are somewhat in the same line ...The amphibians, and plant lice construct their homes like the Amazons (ants), and virgin parents perpetuate the race for ten successive generations.»

Let us examine now the basic 'key' for Man's enchainment in the material plane, focusing onto those events with a magnifying glass. Despite the blockade, Celestial Men can still escape. As Unified Wholenesses they still retain the prerequisites to return to the Sacred Capital. After all, the 'payment' of their punishment did not concern the Father but <u>only</u> the creator

Don't skip chapters or bibliographic references

of matter. By secretly escaping therefore from this trap/universe, they would 'abandon' their energy-bodies behind, and return back to the Sacred Capital/BirthLand. The creators' team knew this very well, as they knew that **nostalgia** for the Holy Fatherland made Celestial Men audacious. However, for material creation to be upgraded and function, the 'Life-generating Peri-Essence/fortune' *(Gr. περί-ουσία [ουσία = essence] = fortune)* of Celestial Men was necessary, as **'yeast'.** If Celestial Men were to leave, material creation would remain defective.

Celestial Man's role was, from the beginning, that of the <u>Spiritual Provider/Supplier.</u> In the new order of things He would again be **the catering source** for the material creation, although not with the Revitalized 'Living Essence' anymore, but with a new, different one. What Man/slave would thereafter offer to the creator of matter, would be the energy produced by **himself** through the toil of incarnation inside the material plane and **through his own material life**.

---

322 **A) TEXTS FROM THE EAST: THE EPIC OF GILGAMESH - ENUMA ELISH**

6TH TABLET: «§115. May the subjects (god's bondservants) for ever bear their god in mind. … May food-offerings be borne for their gods and goddesses, without fail let them supply and support their gods! Let them improve their lands, build their shrines.» [ENG. TR. DENNIS BRATCHER]

B) AESCHYLUS, 'SEVEN AGAINST THEBES' «…Ares (Mars, The God of War) is fed with the blood of the mortals.»

Spiritual Entities would no longer expand material creation. Material humanity would assume this role now.

Today man is the principle source of energy-catering for all energy-beings *(gods, daemons and astral skeptomorphs)*. A lot depends and a lot is at stake from this energy-supply and, as we will analyze later in our discussion, a lot of 'games are being masterminded' behind man's back.

Therefore, to avoid the danger of the Celestial Children's escape, the creator *(the archon of this world)* decides there is only one solution: **Man should <u>stop desiring</u> to return to his Holy HomeLand**. This could only be accomplished one way: HE SHOULD STOP <u>REMEMBERING</u> THE HOLY FATHERLAND *(Gr.: A-ΛHΘH-A = The Truth is attained when we cease to forget)*. And how would He stop remembering? Only if He were to be subjected to a spiritual 'lobotomy'; and how would this be possible? Simply: by His division in two.

---

323 **PLATO'S SYMPOSIUM:** «…For 'man-woman' was then a unity, **common** both in form and in name, composed of both male and female …Zeus…said: "I will slice every one of them in two, <u>so that they are made weaker</u>.»

From One Unified (complete) Wholeness (male + female = <u>ONE</u>) HE would be split in two.

---

[324] **GOSPEL OF PHILIP**, JEAN-YVES LELOUP: «§71. When Eve was in Adam, there was no death: When she was separated from him, death came.» [ENG. TR. JOSEPH ROWE]

Under the new circumstances, the foundations of the initial creation are changed only to be substituted by others, fitting the new demands better.

---

[325] **THE APOCRYPHON OF JOHN, THE GNOSTIC SOCIETY LIBRARY**:
http://www.gnosis.org/naghamm/apocjn-davies.html
«Adam was revealed because within him dwelt the shadow of light. His mental abilities were far greater than those of his creators. They had gazed upward and seen his exalted mental capability. The host of rulers and daemons plotted <u>together</u>. They mixed fire and *(energy)* earth and water together with four blazing winds. They melded them together in great turbulence. Adam was brought into the shadow of death.
They intended to make him anew; this time from Earth, Water, Fire, Wind, which are **Matter, Darkness, Desire**, <u>The Artificial Spirit</u>. This all became a **tomb,** a new kind of body *(grave)*. <u>Those thieves bound the man in it, enchained him in</u> **forgetfulness**, made him subject to dying.» [Eng. tr. from Coptic: STEVAN DAVIES]

Creation enters a 'pause' period, and **everything is retracted.**

---

[326] **A) OLD TESTAMENT, GENESIS CH. 2:**
«§21 And the Lord God brought a **trance** upon Adam, and he **slept**;»
Let me remind you that we are in the 2nd chapter of Genesis which refers exclusively to the <u>aetheric</u> creation.
B) THE APOCRYPHON OF JOHN, THE GNOSTIC SOCIETY LIBRARY:
«§21 And he *(the archon)* wanted to bring out the power which had been given to him. And he cast a **trance** upon Adam.»
This period obviously corresponds to a certain 'Pralaya' (dissolution) of Maha-Yuga of the Brahmans, and the preparation to enter into a new Brahma period.
C) HERMES TRISMEGISTUS, HERMETIC TEXTS, VOL. I, RODAKIS P., TZAFERO-POULOS AP., **SPEECH I**
Poemander addresses Hermes, teaching him: «§18. The period being completed, the connecting bond of all things was loosened, by the will of God; so, all the living creatures being male-female, along with Man, **were severed apart**, and some became male and others female. And then, God uttered a Holy Word: 'Increase and multiply in multitude all beings and creations', and let him who possesses Noŭs, recognize himself as being <u>immortal</u>, and **the cause of death to be Eros** *(erotic love).*»

Don't skip chapters or bibliographic references

The creators first divide the aetherically formed animals into two discrete sexes, which then get projected onto dense matter separately, male or female.

---

[327] **THE SECRET BOOK OF DZYAN, 'ANTHROPOGENESIS', STANZA VIII:**

«§31 The animals were separated first (into male and female). They started breeding...»

*Now is the time when dense visible matter has already been created and, as described in the First Chapter of Genesis, §24-25, the animals were created **first**.*

*Obviously, some might question the separation of the sexes of the animals at that time, since the dinosaurs had already preceded this period and were thought to reproduce in the 'conventional' way. Yet, this does not necessarily mean that the dinosaurs and generally all the animals of that time were of two sexes, since **even today**, parthenogenesis is how seventy species of snakes and lizards (and not only!) breed. Let us not forget that in Greek the word 'dinosaur' means fierce lizard ([δεινό-σαυροι] deino=fierce, sauroi=lizards).*

B) PARTHENOGENESIS OF THE DRAGONS OF KOMODO
http://news.pathfinder.gr/scitech/366824.html (Dec. 22, 2006)

«In two zoos in England two female Komodo dragons produced off-spring through parthenogenesis, according to an article published in 'TA NEA' newspaper. It is well known that Parthenogenesis can constitute a reproductive method for about 70 species of snakes and lizards, but it had never been observed before in Komodo dragons, which are counted among the biggest reptiles on the planet *(why not in dinosaurs then?)*. The baby lizards, according to the same article, are both male. They were born in Chester Zoo in U.K. by 'Flora', who is waiting her clutch of eight eggs to hatch and were presented in the journal 'Nature'. At the same time, four more dragons were hatched in London Zoo.

During parthenogenesis, the female fertilizes her eggs on her own. In the case of the dragons, the ovum is attached to another cell, called the polar element/particle, which, instead of dying, is absorbed by the ovum and fertilizes it, contributing half of the necessary genetic material. Scientists consider that the phenomenon of parthenogenesis offers the Komodo dragon an evolutionary advantage, particularly in the case that the female is unable to find a mate.»

Some more cases, not only in the U.K. but in the U.S.A. as well:

C) PARTHENOGENESIS AND OTHER MIRACLES
KAROLOS 2-28/03/2009, ELEFTHEROTYPIA NEWSPAPER
(http://wwkarolos.blogspot.com?2009?04?blog-post.html):

«These days, animal lovers are celebrating a case of parthenogenesis which occurred in Wichita Zoo, Kansas USA: this case has been definitively confirmed and broadcasted in all international news agencies. The zoo keepers had the shock of their lives, when they discovered eggs in the Komodo lizard's cage. It's a big lizard which originates from Indochina. These eggs – two of which were hatched– were laid by a female which hadn't seen a male for about **a decade**. ...A DNA analysis of the 'miraculous embryos' showed that, **their entire DNA was derived from the female.** Selective parthenogenesis has been also observed in other species during the last years. ...In some gecko species, males don't exist, while females lay eggs which are genetically identical to their mother and the females to come. Also some aphids give birth to females in the same way.»

D) SHARK PARTHENOGENESIS
SCIENTISTS HAVE CONFIRMED THE SECOND-EVER SHARK PARTHENOGENESIS
(OCT. 14th 2008) SOURCE: CNN) (a) http://news.pathfinder.gr/misc/510310.html
(b) http://www.powermediaplus.com/news/archive.aspx?newsTypeID=1&newsID=2974

«**Virginia:** The first-ever confirmed case of single-parent shark-reproduction [also known as parthenogenesis] was spotted in a newborn hammerhead shark in a zoo in Omaha, Nebraska.

"The first case was no surprise to us" stated Demian Chapman, a shark scientist and lead author of the second study. "It is quite possible that something like that can occur with female sharks as well as many other species."

...In a study published in the scientific magazine 'Journal of Fish Biology', scientists report that the DNA examined, showed that the newborn shark did not have genetic material from a male shark. ...DNA techniques used by the scientists with the sharks are identical to the ones used in the DNA paternity tests for humans.»

Astro-aetheric (soulful) man-beings, –Celestial Men <u>not yet</u> included– obediently part from their genitors (creators) for good and incarnate into the preselected pithecoid animals.

[328] HESIOD 'THEOGONY', (verse 535): *Hesiod talks about the era when* «the gods and mortal men **separated** from each other...»
B) THE SECRET BOOK OF DZYAN, 'ANTHROPOGENESIS', STANZA VII:
«§32 And those which had **no** spark *(plain Souls)* took *(through spiritual possession)* huge she-animals unto them. They begat upon them dumb races. **Dumb they were themselves too** *(Australopithecus).*»
At the end of this chapter Man's Genealogy is analyzed. There, the <u>incarnation of the souls</u> (through spiritual possession) inside the Pithecoids is clearly indicated. The souls upgrade the Pithecoids to Australopithecus, however without the possibility of further upgrading. «...They begat upon them dumb races. Dumb they were themselves too.»
After that, the entrance (through spiritual possession/incarnation) of the Divine Sparks-Men inside Australopithecus upgrades it to the Homo category.

Don't skip chapters or bibliographic references

In order for the necessary connections to be made, allow me to remind:
THE SECRET BOOK OF DZYAN, 'COSMIC EVOLUTION', STANZA VI:

«§5 At the fourth *(cycle of creation)*, the sons are told to create **their images. One third refused** *(Celestial Men)*. **Two (thirds) obeyed** *(plain souls)*. The curse is pronounced; they will be born on the fourth *(at the second half of the Fourth Root-Race)*, suffer and cause suffering.»

Next, the creator divides Celestial Man.

---

329 A) **OLD TESTAMENT, GENESIS CH. 2** *(Aetheric Creation)*
«§21 And the Lord God cast a trance upon Adam, and he slept; and He took one of his ribs, and filled up flesh in its place. §22. Then the rib which the Lord God had taken from man, He made into a woman, and He brought her to Adam. …§23…**she shall be called Wo-man**, because she was taken out of Man. §25. And they were both **naked**, Adam and his woman, and were not ashamed.»

They had not yet been attired (dressed) with the fleshy garment of dense matter, the «…garments of skins» [OLD TESTAMENT, GENESIS 3:21]

B) **THE SECRET BOOK OF DZYAN, 'ANTHROPOGENESIS', STANZA VIII**:
«§31…The twofold man was also separated.»

C) **THE APOCALYPSE OF ADAM, THE GNOSTIC SOCIETY LIBRARY, THE NAG HAMMADI LIBRARY**, [Eng. tr. GEORGE W. MACRAE:] «Then God, the ruler of the aeons and the *(material)* powers, **divided us in wrath**.» [GR. EDITION: APOCRYPHAL TEXTS OF THE OLD TESTAMENT … 'THE REVELATION OF ADAM TO HIS SON, SETH' Gr. Tr. KOUTSOUKIS]

D) *(A reminder)* **PLATO'S SYMPOSIUM ARISTOPHANES' SPEECH** (190d):
«Zeus…said: "I will slice every one of them in two, so that they are made weaker.»

He **aetherically** separates the male from the female part of Man into 'Adam' and 'Eve'; not into man and woman, but into the 'Divine Spark' (Adam) and the 'I Am Presence' (Eve). The I Am Presence/Eve is placed on the higher energy-planes and the Divine Spark/Adam wanders in the aetheric planes, dressed with the garment of the soul.

---

330 **THE SECRET BOOK OF DZYAN, 'COSMIC EVOLUTION', STANZA VII**:
«§7. This is thy present Wheel, said the Flame to the Spark. Thou art Myself, My Image, and my shadow. I have clothed myself in thee, and thou art my Vahan *(my carrier/vehicle)*, to the day, 'Be With Us,' **when thou shalt re-become myself** and others, thyself and me. Then the builders, having donned their first clothing, descend on radiant Earth and reign over men –who are themselves…»

From this point on, a dynamic **falsification** of the history of Man begins, which disorients and confuses him with thousands of lies mingled with half-truths, scattered in legends, traditions, conjectures, heresies, theories, assumptions, and permanently entraps him inside the downward vortex.

After Spiritual Man's division, the I Am Presence intimately feels the need to reunite with its other split half (the Divine Spark) and is **desperately** searching for it.

The Divine Spark inside the soulful, astro-aetheric man wanders in the aetheric planes down below, with oblivion as its guide.

Loneliness as a condition/property makes its first appearance in the energy-material plane. After all, its very own origin stems from this fission/splitting. Later on, it manifests through the energy-bodies and dominates man's entire existence.

Oblivion blurs the aetheric noûs of the Divine Spark/Man and he doesn't clearly perceive the facts, while within the energy planes of the material universe, his intimate nostalgia urges him to approach his separated half and reunite with it. Through this intimate tendency, many of the Divine Sparks secretly unite with their other 'half', recognize their Spiritual **nudity** and the devastation they are in and escape from the universe/trap.

---

331 *(A reminder)*: **PAPASTAVROU, A., 'LETTERS TO ANONYMOUS'**: CH. ASTRAL PLANE (p. 102) *The spiritual teachers (i.e. the Creators' delegates) clarify their views on this subject.*

«The moment at which The Divine Noesis (Intellectuality), inside the Entity of The White Fire *(Celestial Man)* perceived Itself as an individualized portion of divine life of the *(material)* universe, it was granted the choice of free will as to whether or not it would continue, as an individualized portion of the creator, ...which would render IT able to <u>create</u> like the Father. ...<u>For **each** individualized Entity of The White Fire that accepted the responsibility to become a co-creator, there were at least a dozen or more who chose to return</u>.

...At this point it would not be pointless for you know that not all 'I AMs' are divided into divine counterparts. Possessing the freedom of will *(!!)* they can and very often refuse **dichotomy** (fission in two).»

The creator then, relying on the oblivion (forgetfulness) which blurs their mind, describes the event of Remembrance/Epignosis that occurs through the reunion of the two separated parts of Man, <u>as the ultimate sin.</u>

Don't skip chapters or bibliographic references

---

332 **THE APOCRYPHON OF JOHN, THE GNOSTIC SOCIETY LIBRARY**:
ADAM IN YALDABAOTH'S PARADISE: *(Jesus said)* «The rulers took the man *(Adam)* and put him into paradise. They told him to eat freely. Their food is bitter; their beauty is corrupt. Their food is deceit; their trees are ungodliness. Their fruit is poison. Their promise is death. They placed the tree **of their Life** into the middle of *(their)* paradise.

(Jesus said) I will teach you (plural) the secret of their life, the plan that they made together about an artificial spirit. Its root *(the tree of their life)* is bitter. Its branches are dead. Its shadow is hatred. Its leaves are deception. The nectar of wickedness is in its blossoms. Its fruit is death. Its seed is desire, it flowers in the darkness. Those who eat from it are denizens of Hades. Darkness is their resting place.

As for the tree called 'The Knowledge of Good and Evil' it is the Epinoia of the light. They commanded him not to eat from it, standing in front to conceal it for fear that he might look upwards to the **fullness** and know the nakedness of his indecency. However, I *(Jesus)* caused them to eat.

I asked the Savior, "Lord, isn't it the serpent that caused Adam to eat?" He smiled and replied, "The serpent caused them to eat, in order to produce the wickedness of the desire to reproduce.[1] That would make Adam helpful to him *(to the serpent)*.» [ENG. TR. FROM COPTIC: STEVAN DAVIES]

[1] **HERMES TRISMEGISTUS**, HERMETIC TEXTS, VOL. I, RODAKIS P., TZAFERO-POULOS AP., **SPEECH I**: «§18…And then God uttered a Holy Word: "Increase and multiply in multitude all beings and creations", and let him who possesses Noũs, recognize himself as being immortal, and **the cause of death to be Eros** *(erotic love)*.»

He announces the '**new**' punishment and sentences defective man to **mandatory** incarnation into the universe's waste, its material part, his densely material prison. This was after all his original plan, which Celestial Man had denied while still unified.

---

333 *A reminder:* **THE SECRET BOOK OF DZYAN, 'COSMIC EVOLUTION', STANZA VI**: «§5…The curse is pronounced; they will be born on the fourth, they will suffer and <u>cause suffering</u>; this is the first war.»

In order for this to be 'painlessly' achieved, the greatest and most wicked <u>conspiracy</u> against Man is masterminded. Intensify your attention: Plane souls have **already** incarnated inside the pithecoid (material) animal and are slowly upgrading it in material time, forming the category of the Australopithecus. Celestial Man's spiritual division into

I Am Presence and Divine Spark, has been completed in the aetheric plane. Oblivion starts deranging him.

The creator then molds a **new soul**, not according to the initial prototypes, but **similar** to Man's I Am Presence. This is Pandora of the Greek mythology.

---

[334] **A) THE APOCRYPHON OF JOHN, THE GNOSTIC SOCIETY LIBRARY** N. H. CODEX II,1 & N. H. CODEX IV,1 http://www.gnosis.org/naghamm/apocjn-long.html

«And he *(the archon/creator)* brought forth a part of his power *(soul)* from Adam *(he took it back from him)* and he created another <u>molded form in a **woman's shape according to the image of Epinoia**</u> who had appeared to him *(thus making Pandora)*. And into the molded form of womanhood he put the part which he had taken from the power of the human (Adam) *(as a Soul)* — not 'his rib' as Moses said. And he *(Adam)* saw the woman beside him *(Pandora/Eve with the appearance of Epinoia - I Am Presence)*. Immediately, the luminous epinoia appeared *(the counterfeit mold)* for she had uncovered the veil which had been on his understanding. He became sober from the drunkenness of the darkness *(he came out of the trance imposed to him by the archon)* and he recognized his likeness *(with the womanhood mold)*. And he said, "Now this is bone from my bones and flesh from my flesh. Because of this, man will leave his father and his mother and he will cling to his wife...» [ENG. TR. FROM COPTIC: WALDSTEIN M., WISSE F.]

B) PIERRE GRIMAL - DICTIONNAIRE DE LA MYTHOLOGIE GRECQUE ET ROMAINE

«**Pandora:** According to Hesiod, Pandora is the first woman. Zeus ordered Hephaestus and Athena to create her with the help of all gods. Each god helped create her by giving her unique gifts like beauty, grace, persuasion, craftiness etc. However, Hermes also gave her lies and cunningness. Hephaestus made her <u>according to the form of the immortal goddesses</u> *(in the form of Epinoia/I Am Presence),* and Zeus intended to send her to the human species as punishment, just after Prometheus had granted them the **divine fire**. This was the gift all gods bestowed upon humans to make **them miserable.**»

C) HESIOD 'THEOGONY' verse 570 *(The creation of Pandora)*

«Forthwith he made an evil thing for men as the price *(payback)* for fire; for the renowned Limping God *(Hephaestus)* formed of *(energy)* earth the **likeness** of a respectable maiden *(as the likeness of Epinoia in John's Apocryphon)* as the son of Kronos *(Zeus)* willed. And Athena, the bright-eyed goddess, girded and clothed her... and she put upon her head a crown of gold which the very famous Limping God made himself and worked with his own hands as a favor to Zeus his

---

Don't skip chapters or bibliographic references

father. On it, much curious work, wonderful to see, he pre-pared…admirable ornaments that looked as if they had life, and as if they would speak. And after Zeus had made the good evil to be **the counter-price for the blessing**, he brought her out, to the place where the other **gods** and men were *(in the aetheric planes)*.»
Hesiod also describes Pandora's creation again in his 'Works and Days', verses 51-82.

This astro-aetheric creature, which is a **replicate** of the 'I Am Presence', wanders in the energy worlds and seduces Divine Sparks with its charm. The Divine Sparks, overtaken by their oblivion, consider this duplicate to be true.

[335] *The allegory of the story of P. I. Tchaikovsky's ballet 'Swan Lake' with Odile and Odette obviously refers to that event.*

This way, yet another new attribute makes its first appearance in the aetheric planes, after loneliness: 'adultery'.

[336] *The reader can now understand fully, what the excerpt from the gospel of Magdalene, referring to adultery, means:*
THE GOSPEL OF MARY (MAGDALENE) JEAN-YVES LELOUP, Gr. tr. KOUROUSSI A., A., verses 13-17: «What is the sin of the world? The Master said: There is no sin, but it is you who make sin exist when you act according to the habits of your nature, which is inclined to adultery.»

After this presence has enchanted everyone, up to the very last Divine Spark, it abandons the astro-aetheric planes and incarnates into dense matter.

❧·❦

The plane Souls that had initially incarnated inside dense matter, had already upgraded the pithecoid (material) animals, forming the genus of the Australopithecus. The creator then embodies his new creature (Pandora) into the females **of those** archanthropes. This new soul automatically projects its beauty onto the **external figure/form** of the female anthropoids. The Divine Sparks/Adams (still in the aetheric planes) now watch the new figures of the female anthropoids/humans in admiration.

[337] **A) BOOK OF ENOCH, 6:1-3** «§1. And it came to pass when the sons of men had multiplied that in those days, daughters were born unto them elegant and beautiful *(Pandora)*. §2. And when the angels, the sons of heaven, saw them, they lusted after of them, and said to one another: Come, let us select for ourselves wives from the race of men and beget us children.»

B) PIERRE GRIMAL DICTIONNAIRE DE LA MYTHOLOGIE GRECQUE ET ROMAINE, «**Pandora**: ...In 'Works and Days', Hesiod narrates how Zeus sent Pandora to Epimetheus, who, **forgetting** his brother's advice *(Prometheus, who had told him never to accept a present from Zeus)* and charmed by her beauty, made her his wife.» *This is exactly what happens to the Divine Sparks.*

C) BLAVATSKY H., P., 'THE SECRET DOCTRINE' (II-93): «The first ones, born of the Noûs, Sons of the Deity, refuse to create and Brahma curses them to be born as humans.»

In short, the story of Brahmanism says the following on the subject as quoted by Blavatsky:

(II-82) «When Daksha, the chief of the Prajapati (creators), brings forth 10,000 sons *(souls)* for the purpose of promoting the world, Narada, the great Rishi *(head of the Celestial Men)* interferes with, and twice frustrates Daksha's aim *(creator)*, by persuading those Sons to remain holy ascetics and eschew *(avoid)* marriage *(incarnation in the bottom of matter)*. For this, Daksha *(creator)* curses Narada to be re-born as a man, as Brahma had cursed him before for refusing to marry, and obtain progeny, saying:-- "Perish in thy present (Deva or angelic) form and take up thy abode in the womb," i.e., become a man ...Notwithstanding several conflicting versions of the same story, it is easy to see that Narada belongs to that class ...who have all proven rebellious to the law of animal procreation, for which they had to incarnate as men...Thus Narada is shown as decisively refusing to create, and also calls Brahma 'a false teacher'.»

Later on Blavatsky defines Narada's identity: «Narada is one of the **Fires** mentioned above, and plays a part in the evolution of this Kalpa *(Cosmic Cycle)*.»

We too have mentioned these 'Fires' in a previous reference about the offer of 'Fire' (of Celestial Men) by Prometheus to men/beings.

A reminder (BLAVATSKY II-83): «...But shall we turn to other ancient Scriptures and documents for the corroboration of the 'Fires', 'Sparks', and 'Flames'? They are plentiful, if one only seeks for them in the right places. In the 'Book of the Concealed Mystery', they are clearly enunciated, as also in the 'Ha Idra Zuta Qadisha', or the lesser holy Assembly....From a Light-Bearer of insupportable brightness proceeded a radiating Flame, dashing off, like a vast and mighty hammer, those sparks which were the prior worlds.»

Don't skip chapters or bibliographic references

And also II-584, 585:

«Narada is the leader of the Gandharvas, the celestial singers and musicians; esoterically, the reason for it is explained by the fact that the latter (the Gandharvas) are the instructors of men in the secret sciences. It is they, who 'loving the women of the Earth', *(according to Enoch)* disclosed to them the mysteries of creation; or, as in the Veda -- the 'heavenly Gandharva' is a deity who knew and revealed the secrets of heaven and divine truths, in general. If we remember what is said of this class of Angels in Enoch and in the Bible, then the allegory is plain: their leader, Narada, while refusing to pro-create, leads men to become gods... This is a mystery very difficult to realize and understand correctly. For, we see that those who were 'obedient to law' *(souls)* are, equally with the rebels *(Celestial Men)*, doomed to be re-born in every age. Narada, the Rishi, is cursed by Brahma to incessant aim-less peripateticism (wandering) on Earth, i.e., to be constantly reborn. He is a rebel against Brahma, and yet has no worse fate than the Jayas -- the twelve great creative gods produced by Brahma as his assistants in the functions of creation.»

Following that, the creator, **allegedly** aiming to ease Man's intimate need for reunion with his other Spiritual half, directs Man's attention towards matter, specifically orienting him to the sexual intercourse of animals. "There is your other half" he says to Him. "Look at the animals and how their two halves copulate! You too must do the same and propagate."

---

338 A) OLD TESTAMENT, GENESIS CH. 1 *(Densely material creation)*

«§28 And God blessed them, and God said to them, **Be fruitful and multiply**, and fill the earth and subdue it...»

B) THE APOCRYPHON OF JOHN, THE GNOSTIC SOCIETY LIBRARY: «He *(Jesus)* smiled and replied, The serpent caused them to eat in order to produce the wickedness of the desire to reproduce that would make Adam helpful to him *(to the serpent)*.» [Eng. tr. from Coptic: STEVAN DAVIES]

C) THE SECRET BOOK OF DZYAN, 'ANTHROPOGENESIS', STANZA VIII: «§31. The animals separated the first *(into male and female)*. They began to breed. The two-fold man separated also. He said: "let us do as they; let us unite and make creatures." they did...

STANZA X §40 Then the Fourth *(The Race of Heroes)* became tall with pride. We are the kings, they said; we are the gods. §41 They took wives fair to look upon, wives from the mindless, the narrow-headed *(they embodied into the female Australopithecus/Pandoras)*. They bred monsters *(the creation of the 'Giants' as we will see later on)* wicked demons, male and female.»

But the unpredictable factor of 'contamination' had already started to gradually affect this already crippled, misshapen man, seizing him with the bottom's mysterious, attractive force (gravity), which magnetized him and drew him erotically to what he himself had originally created; because Eros and the attractive force (gravity) are twin forces, whose 'mother' can be found at the energy-outskirts of the bottom of the material spiral/black hole.

[339] *The following reference is quoted ...so that the logical correlations can be made between the 'Siamese twins': **erotic love – gravity**.*

DANEZIS M., THEODOSIOU S. 'COSMOLOGY OF THE INTELLECT' (p. 177):

«Electromagnetic fields have the property of causing **attractive forces** between particles. Thus, charged <u>particles</u> throughout the Universe, interacting with Zero-point field (ZPF) that is everywhere in it, create corresponding electromagnetic fields, and the respective **attractive forces,** which constitute what we call **gravity**.

(p.178) MATTER AS A VORTEX (EDDY)' – SOME PERSONAL VIEWS:

...According to A. Einstein's views, a material <u>particle</u> does not constitute anything but the sensory equivalent of a **moving swirl of the field**. ...What we are essentially talking about is <u>**a non-perceptible** spherical vortex</u> inside an <u>n-dimensional **non** Euclidean field</u>, whose **projective shadow** *(aetheric projection)* inside the three-dimensional Euclidean space of our senses, is perceived as an elementary particle.

Human practical reasoning could perceive such an odd spherical vortex as an infinite number of classic conical vortices oriented toward every direction, but with a common apex (peak). We can distinguish two kinds of spherical vortices depending on the type of their internal rotation, ...such as the clockwise eddy of a bathtub which leads *(attracts)* water into the drain hole, or the counterclockwise vortex of a tornado which lifts *(attracts)* objects from the ground and leads them upwards *(because every eddy/vortex activates forces of attraction ...gravity)*.

(p. 179) THE COSMOLOGICAL EDDY-VORTEX OF ANCIENT GREEK NATURAL PHILOSOPHERS:

...A first reference of the concept of the <u>vortex</u> is made in Orphic Cosmology. The initial cosmological egg, whose natural creation and composition is in a wonderfully scientific way described by Democritus, gives birth to a **whirlwind**, which atomic philosophers describe <u>as a secondary vortex and Orphic Texts call **Eros**</u>.

"Firstly, black-winged Night lays a germless egg wherefrom, when the time came, sprang the fiery Eros with his glittering golden wings shining on his back, <u>just like a whirlwind</u> [εἰκὼς ἀνεμώκεσι δίναις]..." *[Aristophanes, Birds, v. 693]*

Don't skip chapters or bibliographic references

...We also come across the concept of vortex as Empedocles' Cosmological view. Aristotle thus says that Empedocles taught: "As the dispute reached the innermost depths of the vortex *(point-singularity)* and Love came in the middle of the vortex, all those things started to accumulate and become one thing only...» *[Simplicius, On the heavens, 529, v.1-15 in Aristotle Physics, 32, 13 (verses 3-17)]*

Through genetic programming of the densely material cell, the Demiourgos has secured the way to make Man **confuse** his Spiritual tendency to reunite with his Divine/Spiritual part, with the body's (sexual) need to copulate. Thus, by directing Man's attention to the females of the anthropoid animals, he raises a second insurmountable wall/barrier around him in order to completely rule out the prospect of his escape, permanently locks him in and throws away the key.

Man, crippled, confused and with the 'ribbon of oblivion' in his noûs, even though he had originally refused, is finally convinced that there (in dense matter) he will meet his other 'half'; and not only is he subdued to incarnate inside the animal, he also regards this proposal as the 'ultimate gift'!

---

[340] *The event of the incarnation/entrapment of the Race of Heroes (the Celestial Men), is presented by the Assyro-Babylonian Religion in its own way in the Epic of Gilgamesh.*
Gilgamesh represents the Celestial Man who is entrapped in the material animal Enkidu and becomes one with it.
THE ASSYRO-BABYLONIAN EPIC OF GILGAMESH, NEAR EAST TEXTS, Gr. tr.: SKARTSI X., SKARTSIS S.:
«...The gods heard their lament. The gods of heaven cried to Anu *(primordial deity)*, the lord/god of Uruk *(the town of immortals)*: "A goddess brought him into being like a mighty wild bull, and there is no rival who can confront him. Gilgamesh does not spare a son for his father, he takes them all and it is he the king and the shepherd for his people. His lust-loving nature does not leave a virgin to the one she loves, a daughter to her warrior father, a bride to her noble husband." Anu listened to their complaints, and the gods called out to Aruru, the goddess of creation:
"It was you, Aruru, who made him, **now make another one identical to him. He must be the same, as if he was his image, his second self**: a heart of the storm for the heart of the storm. Let them confront each other, so that Uruk may find peace!" *(This is the eternal struggle between the Superior Immortal Man against his matter).* Thus, Aruru conceived an image in her spirit, and it was of the material of Anu, of the firmament. **Aruru wetted her hands, she grabbed some clay**, she let it drop into the wilderness and

the valiant Enkidu *(the Archanthrope)* was created. He was endowed with strength by Ninurta himself, the god of war. His whole body was shaggy with hair, he had a full head of hair like a woman, his locks billowed in profusion like Nissaba, the goddess of wheat. His body was covered in curly hair, like Sumukan's, the god of herds. He knew nothing about people, he had no idea about plowing, Enkidu *(the Archanthrope)* <u>ate grass with the gazelles, and jostled at the water-hole with the animals; along with the wild animal herds, he enjoyed water</u>.

But, there was also a trapper *(from the land of the immortals),* who came face-to-face with Enkidu at the water-hole, because the wild animals had invaded his territory (the trapper's). For three days, he *(the trapper)* came face-to-face with him *(Enkidu)* and he *(the trapper)* would go stark with fear. He *(the trapper)* went back to his dwelling with the game he had caught, and he was speechless and numb with fear. His face had changed, looking like one who had made a long journey. He *(the trapper)* addressed his father with true respect, saying: "Father, a certain being *(Enkidu)*, like no other, has come from the hills. He *(Enkidu)* is the mightiest in the land; he is like a celestial immortal. He wanders with the wild animals around your land and goes to the water springs. I am afraid of him and I daren't go up to him. He fills in the pits that I dig, and wrenches out the trapping nets that I spread, he releases the trapped animals, and now I lose them from within my hands."

The trapper's father spoke to him saying: "My son, in Uruk, there lives a certain man, Gilgamesh. No one has escaped his hands victorious; he is as strong as a celestial star. Go, set off to Uruk, find Gilgamesh and **praise the might of this wild man** *(Enkidu)*. Ask him to give you a prostitute from the temple of Eros, a child of lust *(the future Pandora);* return with her, and let the woman's power **overcome this man** *(let the woman be embodied into Enkidu).* When he comes down to the springs to drink, he will embrace her and then all animals will deny him."

…So the trapper returned, bringing the harlot with him. On the third day they arrived at the water-hole and there they sat down; the trapper and the harlot sat down facing each other and waited for the wild animals to come. For the first two days, both of them sat down and waited, but on the third day the herds came to drink and so did Enkidu, who grazed on grass with the gazelles and had been born on the hills. The trapper talked to her:

"That is he! Now, woman, expose your bare breasts, feel no shame, do not wait too long, but accept his love willingly. As soon as he comes near you, spread out your robe and lie down with him; **teach him, to the man, your own art of womankind!** *(This is the embodiment of*

Don't skip chapters or bibliographic references

Pandora into the animal–primitive man. After that, the turbid half celestial man, looking for his other half, will get confused believing that it can be found in the carnal female). For, once his love is drawn into you, the animals, who shared wilderness with him in the hills, will become alien to him and cast him away." The woman took him in without restraint. For six days and seven nights they lay together, Enkidu had forgotten all about his home in the hills. However, when he had had enough, he returned to the wild animals. But, when the gazelles saw him, they darted off and the wild animals distanced themselves from him. Enkidu wanted to go off with them, but his body felt as if it had been tied with a rope, he attempted to run, but his knees felt rather weak and he couldn't run as fast as before. And now the wild creatures had run away from him; Enkidu had become weak, **for his understanding had broadened and human thoughts were in his heart**. Turning around, he sat down on the woman's lap, his ears attentive as she spoke: "You are wise, Enkidu, you have now become like a god. Why do you want to gallop around the wilderness with the wild beasts? Come, let me bring you into the well-fortified Uruk, to the Blessed Temple, the residence of Anu and Ishtar, the place of Eros and Heaven. This is the place of Gilgamesh, who is really powerful and struts exhibiting his power over the people like a wild bull."

What she kept saying found favor with him. He longed for a companion, someone who could understand him.

"Come, woman, take me away with you to this holy temple, the House of Anu and Ishtar, the place where Gilgamesh reigns over people. I will challenge him with courage, I will shout out in Uruk: I *(the material man)* am the mightiest one here! I have come to change the old order of things; I am the one born in the wilderness, I am the mightiest!"

She said: "Come, let us go, so he (Gilgamesh) may **not** see your face *(the hairy face of the Archanthrope Enkidu).* I know where Gilgamesh will be in grand Uruk. Oh! Enkidu, there everybody shows off in skirted finery, every day is a day for celebration, the young men and women are sublime in appearance. How sweet they smell! All the prominent ones rise from their beds. Oh! Enkidu, you who loves life, I will show you Gilgamesh. He is a happy man; you will see him glow in manly freshness. His body, strong and mature, is perfect; he never rests, day or night. He is stronger than you, so do not boast. Shamash, the bright sun, gave him grace, Anu of the skies and Enlil and Ea, the wise man, gave him a deep mind. Even before you set off from the wilderness, Gilgamesh in Uruk will have dreams about you coming here."

1ˢᵀ DREAM OF GILGAMESH:

"...Mother, I had a dream last night. I was full of joy and the young heroes were around me and I was walking through the night, under the starry sky. Some kind of meteorite of Anu fell from the sky *(It is said that everything, in the material Earth, is made of stardust)*. I tried to lift it but it was too heavy for me. The men of Uruk came around me to see it, they had all assembled about it, the simple men were thronging around it, the nobles clustered about it, and kissed its feet. I loved it and was attracted to it **as if for the love for a woman** [*Enoch: ...in those days daughters were born unto them elegant and beautiful. And when the angels, the sons of the heaven, saw them, they lusted after them.*] They helped me and I tied it from his forehead and I towed it and brought it to you and you named it my brother." Then Ninsun... said : "What you saw ...from the sky above, **and you succumbed to it as you succumb to the female and you loved and embraced it as a wife,** he was the companion, the strong one, he who helps his friend when in need... the moment you cast eyes upon him, you shall feel great joy."

2ᴺᴰ DREAM OF GILGAMESH:

".... In the streets ...of Uruk there laid an axe *(Gr. pelekis=axe; the axe of fission)*. "It had a strange shape and all the people had assembled about it. I saw it and I rejoiced. I bent down, something deep inside me drew me towards it, I loved it like a woman, and hanged it on my side." Ninsun replied: "The axe that you saw is the companion I give you, (that) you love him and embrace as a wife" *(Pandora)*...Gilgamesh said: "This is my lot; the companion shall be mine.»

After that, follows the union of Gilgamesh and Enkidu with eternal 'friendship' and Gilgamesh's desperate and hopeless search for Immortality. When he finally finds the plant of immortality, just before he can cut it, it is devoured by a 'snake'. Eventually, Gilgamesh resigns to his mortal fate.)

Then, through 'spiritual occupation', he is embodied inside that material, female creature, where his energy-bodies initially 'mate' with the energy-bodies of the animal, lock themselves together and wreak absolute havoc, as we will examine later on.

³⁴¹ BOOK OF ENOCH, CH. 7: «§10. Then they *(the Holy Watchers)* selected wives, each choosing for himself; whom they approached, and with whom they cohabited *(inside the same body [Anc. Gr. word used: εἰσπορεύεσθαι = to enter inside])*; teaching them sorcery, charm (incantations), and the properties of roots and herbs *(The Homo genus makes its appearance and upgrades the species)*. §11. And the women conceived and gave birth to giants.»

Don't skip chapters or bibliographic references

With the command to 'be fruitful and multiply' now recorded in the material gene, the need for reunion with the other Spiritual Half Self **shifts** entirely to the quest for the material companion of the opposite sex, thus rendering Man utterly powerless.

The 'garment' that would henceforth surround Man, would cease to be dazzlingly glorious; it would also cease to be a high frequency energy-body and would end up being a measly integument (shell) made of the bottom's waste of this mess of remnant carcasses. This integument was built in low frequencies that would prevent any non-fragmented concepts of Truth from penetrating it, in order to guide Man. The new conditions, under which this new body –made out of sediment clay– would function, would be the complete fragmentation of every Divine Concept, into thousands of 'conjectures'. Thus Man would remain occupied, investigating the maze of these conjectures and eternally entrapped. …So, you wore death and then worshiped it, believing it is life…

The first plain Souls that initially incarnated inside the (material) animal, barely upgraded it, thus forming various, secondary anthropoid species and finally the Australopithecus generation. The moment though the Divine Spark/Adam incarnates inside those partially evolved animals, an explosive upgrade is observed and the aforementioned species becomes separate from the rest of its group, forming the Homo Race. This is where the Race of Men starts to slowly develop in material time. Various racial differences start to appear, depending on their innate properties/attributes and through crossbreeding they expand the chain of evolution.

Men today quarrel about the correct view for the creation of man. As we said at the beginning of our discussion, there is a relative **percentage of justness** in all battling camps. The incarnation of Spiritual Man **inside** the animal made it evolve into what man is today.

---

342 GENEALOGY OF MAN

SOURCES: http://www.physics4u.gr/articles/2005/originofhuman1.html
http://www.physics4u.gr/news/2004/scnews1653.html
http://www.physics4u.gr/news/2005/scnews1895.html

«The first species to appear in the chart of our common ancestors was the **Dryopithecus**. He is a species between a gorilla and a chimpanzee. He lived approximately 25 million years ago on trees and walked on all four.

Ramapithecus: Slightly different from the above. He lived **14 million years ago** and walked erect or semi-erect and scientists hesitate to classify him as a hominid (future humans) or a primate (gorilla, chimp). It is with this species that the first form of distinction begins. A related species to this one is the following:

Sivapithecus: He lived **9-10 million years ago**. He is an ancestor of the Australopithecus, the undeniable ancestor of humans.

The next finding divides the scientific community in whether it should be classified as an ancestor of humans or apes. He lived **6-7 million years ago** and is in the period of division in evolution when, according to scientists, one species lead to hominids resulting in modern man, and the other, to primates. This new species was formally classified as:

Sahelanthropus Tchadensis and the finding named '**Toumaï**' is a mixture of man and chimpanzee. Brunet, who discovered additional fossils of the same creature in the area, argues that 'this creature may not have been able to stand erect', but he believes that Toumaï lived shortly after the two species of hominids and chimpanzees evolutionarily separated.

Next comes, the definitive human ancestor. The new finding dubbed 'Lucy' lived **2.8 to 3.8 million years ago** and belongs to the species of **Australopithecus Afarensis**. She stood erect, was 1.00 meter tall and her head resembled that of humans.

At **2.5 million years ago** we have the appearance of **Australopithecus Garhi**, discovered in Ethiopia and named 'Selam'.

Finally we have the final australopithecine species, **Australopithecus Africanus**, dated **2.3 million years ago**, who passed the evolutionary torch to the genus **Homo**, **2.2 million years ago**. He stood erect, he was 1.30 meters tall, his cranial capacity measured 400-500 cm³; he had a wide face and was an omnivore. He was also a tool constructor tools.

(Up to this point, solely plain Souls are incarnated and only minimally upgrade the animal)

Australopithecus Africanus gave us two subspecies:

1. **Australopithecus Robustus**, who stood 1.50 meters tall, was a herbivore and had a cranial capacity of 500 cm³ along with **Australopithecus Gracilis**, who was petite with a 450 cm³ cranial capacity, and

2. **Homo Habilis** (Handy-man), the **first** Human.

(At this point we have the first incarnation of Celestial Men, who are dynamically distinguished from their brother genus, Australopithecus Robustus).

Homo Habilis

This is the first and oldest species of the Homo genus, dated at 1.6-2.6 million years ago. 'Adam' lived along the banks of Lake Turkana, in Northern Kenya, while the first 'Eve', who was a Homo Habilis was discovered in Olduvai Gorge in Tanzania.

Don't skip chapters or bibliographic references

This primary **Homo** species is known for its **enormous brain-size increase from 450 to 800 cm³**. They are more human-like compared to the ape-like Australopithecus.

In the **Homo** genus, the period of puberty is obvious, as opposed to apes that go from childhood straight to adulthood.

From an evolutionary point of view, man deviated from the hominid development model, when its cranial capacity reached 800 cm³. That distinctly differentiated him from the Australopithecine species. *(But what was the cause of this divergence?)* He was probably the first species to utter words and was definitely a carnivore, something that is believed to have contributed to the development of his brain, which consists mainly of lipids. *(Of course, if lipids were the exclusive decisive factor for brain development, tigers should all be able to solve equations...)* He is also believed to have discovered fire. His appearance is clearly human, he is completely distinct from all other animals and his skeleton differs a lot from that of his ancestor, **Australopithecus Africanus**. *(Let us recall the Gilgamesh/Enkidu story)*

Homo Habilis <u>coexisted</u> with Australopithecus Robustus for a while *(they did share Australopithecus Africanus <u>as a common ancestor</u> after all).*

The genus of Australopithecus retained the nutritional habits of apes. The reason why human infants are born helpless has to do with that fact that the large human brain is linked to certain 'mechanical' restrictions in the female pelvis, affecting additional characteristics besides intelligence.

Along with the Homo Habilis species we find **Homo Rudolfensis**, considered a sub-race of the Homo Habilis family. Both are direct ancestors of the **Homo Ergaster**, who lived 1.9-1 million years ago in Africa. Most scientists link him directly to <u>Homo erectus</u>, a more developed and human-like species in appearance.

Homo erectus lived 1.6 million – 400,000 years ago. **Sinanthropus Pekinensis**, considered a Homo erectus sub-species, was mostly built as a herbivore rather than a carnivore. He did however have increased brain capacity and stood erect. Standing erect had negative consequences as well, such as limited ability to escape, flat feet, vertebrae strains, difficulties in childbirth, as well as circulatory problems, since the heart is fatigued while pumping blood.

The **Archanthrope of Petralona**, found in Khalkidhiki, Greece, is said to be the most developed form of *Homo erectus* and the link with Neanderthal man.

Homo Heidelbergensis follows and is dated around 800,000-500,000 years ago.

After that, we find the 'first cousin' of our species, the renowned **Homo Neanderthalensis**, who lived 130,000-35,000 years ago. He lived along the contemporary Homo Sapiens (the wise one) for some time. However, this coexistence appears to have been antagonistic. Some scientists believe that Homo Neanderthalensis was exterminated by Homo Sapiens, while others maintain that there was interbreeding between the two species.

Homo Neanderthalensis did not contribute to our evolutionary development, as he disappeared rather suddenly, giving rise to various speculations regarding his disappearance. That fact aside, he appears to have had religious preoccupations, he buried the dead, he drew inside caves, he had tools, he had developed speaking skills and he used musical instruments. Genetic research has indicated that the Neanderthal line of evolution splits way back in time.

In another branch of the human evolutionary tree we find **Homo Florensiensis**, nicknamed Hobbit.»

DE-SYMBOLIZATION OF THE PRIMORDIAL (ORIGINAL) SIN

At this point, I consider it worthwhile to proceed to a deeper analysis of the primordial sin, breaking the codes and de-symbolizing its messages on **two** basic levels. The first level concerns the Supreme, Divine Territories of the True Cosmoi and the second level concerns the material universe, starting from the invisible energy-universe all the way down to the densely material one. As I initially clarified to you, each myth's magic is its ability to unlock many levels of knowledge, giving answers ranging from the simplest to the most complex ones. Let us then recount the facts, using the myth and relating the symbols/keys to the real concepts that correspond to each level.

1. TRUE HYPERCOSMOI:

The trees of Paradise correspond to the HyperUniverses of the True Unsplit Light. The Tree of Life (of the HyperUniverses) corresponds to the inexhaustible, eternal, True Life of Those Worlds and is identified with Immortality. The forbidden wood/tree of the knowledge of good and evil represents an isolated/forbidden residue of previous, dead creations. Eve symbolizes the Sacred Archetype of Life. Adam is the Spiritual Unified (Male and Female one) Celestial Man. Eve, as the Sacred Archetype of Life, is the first to 'taste' the forbidden fruit of the tree of duality of good and evil. The Unified Celestial Man/Adam, seeing Eve/Life enter into the detached universe by trying its forbidden fruit, is also fooled and tastes it as well. In that Immortal World the prompt is given by Eve/Life and Adam follows. Through the 'branches' of the tree/universe of the knowledge of good and evil, they both cross over to the second virtual world, leaving the True One behind.

---

[343] **FELIX GUIRAND, MYTHOLOGIE GÉNÉRALE**, CH. GERMAN MYTHOLOGY (p. 270): «There is also another myth which hardly agrees with the ones already mentioned, which however is found in all poets of the ancient Scandinavian Language; according to it the whole world is a tree of colossal dimensions. This tree with the evergreen foliage, 'maelia'[(1)] (or Fraxinus) Yggdrasil reaches with one of its roots down to the bowels of the sub-chthonian (underground) world, and raises its strong branches up to the highest point of the heavens. Yggdrasil means, in the poetic tongue of the skalds *(group of Old Norse poets)*, 'the path of Epiphovos' (meaning Odin...)»

[(1)] See: 'Meliad Nymphs' of Hesiod and the 'Melia <u>tree</u>', whose wood

> *was used to create the bronze (aetheric) Race…<u>inside</u> which Celestial Man was embodied.*
> *At this point I also give an account of H. P. Blavatsky, agreeing to Decharme's view (Mythology of Ancient Greece) on this particular subject.*
> **BLAVATSKY H., P., 'THE SECRET DOCTRINE'** (II-519, 520):
> «Melia, Decharme thinks, is the personification of the ash-tree, whence, according to Hesiod, issued the race of the age of Bronze and which, according to the Greeks is the celestial tree common to every Aryan mythology. This ash is the Yggdrasil of the Norse antiquity, which the Norns sprinkle daily with the waters from the fountain of Urd that it may not wither.»

By entering this fake world Eve/Life and Adam lose their immortal attribute and acquire the mortal one. To remain in this world, they are forced to 'try the fruit of its life'. This 'fruit' however is twofold and bears death within.

> [344] **THE APOCRYPHON OF JOHN, THE GNOSTIC SOCIETY LIBRARY**: *(Jesus speaks to John)*:
> «The archons *(the Demiourgos and his Authorities)* took him *(Adam)* and placed him in paradise. And they said to him "Eat, that is at leisure"; for indeed their delight is bitter and their beauty is depraved. And their luxury is deception and their trees <u>are godlessness,</u> and their fruit is deadly poison and their promise is death. And the tree of **their** life they had placed in the midst of paradise. …The root of this tree is bitter and its branches are death, its shadow is hatred and deception is in its leaves. The ointment of evil is in its blossom. Its fruit is death, and desire is its seed, and it sprouts in darkness. The dwelling place of those who taste from it is Hades and the darkness is their place of rest.» [Eng. tr. from Coptic: FREDERIK WISSE]

Twofold and dyadic after all, is the entire structure of this world. Trapped there, Eve/Life and Adam are forced to yield to its laws and be split themselves just like everything else. The Sacred Archetype of Eternal Life/Eve ceases to be Immortal, becomes mortal and in the universe of death, strives to express the property of vitalization through endless diversification and shift/changeover.

> [345] **THE APOCRYPHON OF JOHN, THE GNOSTIC SOCIETY LIBRARY**:
> «The Chief Archon saw the young woman who was standing by Adam. He realized that the light-filled Epinoia of life was within her. Yaldabaoth became completely ignorant. When the Providence of all saw what was going to happen, she sent assistants to remove Divine Life from Eve. Yaldabaoth raped Eve. She bore two sons. Elohim was the name of the first. Yahweh was the name of the second. Elohim has a bear's face, Yahweh has a cat's

Don't skip chapters or bibliographic references

face. One is righteous; one is not. Yahweh is righteous; Elohim is not. Yahweh would command fire and wind, Elohim would command water and earth. Yaldabaoth deceptively named the two: Cain and Abel. From then until now, sexual intercourse has persisted thanks to the Chief-Ruler, who put desire for reproduction into the woman who accompanies Adam. Through intercourse, the Ruler caused new human bodies to be produced and he blew his artificial spirit into each of them.» [Eng. tr. from Coptic: STEVAN DAVIES]

With a quick look, the above reference does not seem pertinent to the particular subject of the main text. However, through some analysis, one can see that the excerpt presents in a few lines, the whole process of abuse (encroachment) and depreciation of the Sacred Archetypes that 'were stolen' from the Impassable (Holy) Regions, thus de-symbolizing the facts at all levels. After all, according to the French ethnologist Claude Levi-Strauss, "the myth must be perceived <u>as a sum, where the real meaning does not emerge from the event sequence, but from an event cluster</u>. The sequence of images of the myth must be read as a musical score, not note by note but as a cohesive whole."

The text starts with the natural demotion of the Sacred Archetype of Life/Eve with the removal of the Divine Spirit. This is the reason why 'Life' in the world of matter remains void of Spirit. Next, follows the 'rape' of the Archetype by the Creator/Yaldabaoth. (... «And Yaldabaoth raped Eve.» ...«Once <u>he snatched, completely alone and for himself,</u> the 'Flower of the Mind' from the Paternal Might» [THE CHALDEAN ORACLES, PROCLUS IN TIMAEUS CF. H., I 387-412, TALKING ABOUT THE AEON.])

A result of this rape is the fission (splitting) with the 'vitalization' of the opposites of the material world.

Living <u>duality</u> starts from the higher 'spiritual' plane with the emergence of Elohim and Yahweh –higher order of opposites– all the way to the entirely material with Abel and Cain –lower order of opposites. Following that, the text skillfully refers to the 'animal faces', giving an account of an extremely peculiar condition which mankind went through, immediately after its settlement in this material world. Then, it refers to another category of men who, scattered throughout the planet, 'live' with the artificial spirit of their Demiourgos. This new data is given in the next chapters.

Adam tastes the fruit of the new world too and is divided into the I Am Presence and the Divine Spark. Through this spiritual lobotomy he undergoes, he equates death of the world surrounding him with true life, and calls his eternal oblivion death. The warning for the danger of death has already come true. In the universe of reflection *(anti-avge)*, everything is mirrored backwards (inverted).

> **346** **DANEZIS M., THEODOSIOU S. 'COSMOLOGY OF THE INTELLECT'** (p. 193): «We all know that if an object is reflected in a mirror, the concepts of left and right as perceived by the object are reversed in the reflection.»

With the fission of True Light, two virtual universes were formed by reflection; a material and an anti-material one.

> **347** **DANEZIS M., THEODOSIOU S. 'COSMOLOGY OF THE INTELLECT':**
> **(a) APPENDICES: THE PHYSICS OF THE ANTIMATTER-METEORS, FILIPPOS M. PA-PAILIAS** (Assistant Professor In The Department Of Physics Of The University Of Athens, Astrophysics, Astronomy And Mechanics Section) p. 418:
>
> «Logically, the universe should consist of 50% matter and 50% anti-matter in formations of stars and anti-stars, galaxies and anti-galaxies and every other kind of formation, analogous to the one of common matter. Experiments in accelerators showed <u>that all objects always appear in formations of pairs of matter and antimatter.</u> …The laws of conservation determine that matter (common matter and antimatter) appears (is created) or disappears (dematerializes) only in pairs of particles-antiparticles. The simplest example we could provide is the materialization of a gamma radiation photon to an electron (matter) and a positron (antimatter). We notice that G. Steigman (1969) also accepts that, if during the first moments of the creation of the Universe (and before the dematerialization process eliminated its anti-atoms), a solid body of antimatter had had the time to be formed, then, this object could last indefinitely.»
>
> **(b)** MATTER AND ANTIMATTER IN THE UNIVERSE (p. 160-161):
>
> «The Dutch chemist P. Debye (Nobel Prize in Physics 1963) wrote: "Someone can imagine two kinds of worlds: The first, like the one we live in, where the positive electricity is connected with the atomic nucleus (the proton), and around which the negative cloud of electrons revolves and a second one, in which the atom nuclei are negatively charged, and a cloud of positrons *(=positive electrons)* revolves around them."
>
> Dim. Kotsakis, the late Astronomy Professor of the University of Athens, wrote in one of his articles in 1963 on the same topic: "The world of antimatter must have the main characteristics of our own world. Without any doubt, its matter must be stable just like the matter of our world. The atoms of that world must be electrically neutral. The antiparticles, of which it consists, must have the same mass of tranquility, but an opposite magnetic torque, compared to the particles of our own world. Because of the lack of magnetic torque, they will probably differ in their spin[1]. If there are logical beings, they will materially consist of antimatter. However, the form of their world and its research by them must follow the course which is also followed by the experimental and theoretical scientists of our world, provided

Don't skip chapters or bibliographic references

that they are at the same point of progress and civilization."

...For historical reasons, we mention the view of M. Goldhaber of Brookhaven National Laboratory, who describes how the first universes of matter and antimatter were initially created. Goldhaber accepts that originally there was a unique hyper-particle, the 'universon', instead of the original hyper-atom of Lemaitre. This hyper-particle was split up, right away, in two particles, 'cosmon' and 'anti-cosmon'. Out of these two particles surged both our familiar perceivable world and the anti-world, which is neither perceivable nor observable.

... Surely it was known from the beginning that it's not possible for matter and antimatter to coexist, since the collision of a particle with its antiparticle, brings about the annihilation of their mass and the transformation of this mass into energy (gamma (γ) radiation).

...A collision of a proton with an anti-proton releases energy equal to 1.800.000.000.000.000 eV.

...It's quite interesting to mention that the orbit of a positron can be equated to the orbit of an electron in negative time, which means that it moves towards the past. ...Richard Feynman, the great physicist, was the first to argue that a positron moving forward in time *(future)* is actually an electron moving backwards in time *(past)*.»

[1] «**Spin:** An intrinsic property of elementary particles, which is related but not identical to the concept of rotation, known to us from daily life.» [From the 'Glossary' of Stephen Hawking's book, 'Universe in a nutshell']

Some personal thoughts:

If we accept that two independent universes were formed at the point of creation, i.e. a material and an anti-material one, and if, starting from the common point of their creation, we were to schematically depict the counterclockwise orbit of the anti-material universe (to the past) on one hand, and the clockwise orbit of the material universe (to the future) on the other, we would see the appearance of the symbol of infinity (∞).

This shouldn't be considered as impossible as:

DANEZIS M., THEODOSIOU S. 'COSMOLOGY OF THE INTELLECT' (p. 185): «Einstein's rectilinear forward time-flow seemed so well-documented, that no one could ever think of questioning or extending it. This however, was achieved by the very father of the new idea, within the framework of the General Theory of Relativity, which he formulated a few years later. After this powerful 'bomb' in the foundations of Newtonian Physics, the rectilinear 'forward' time-flow of Specific Relativity, started being disputed as more and more reports of prominent scientists came forth regarding the theoretical possibility of successive submersions from the present to the past or the future and vice-versa.»

And let's not forget that when reflected, the right part becomes left and the left right.

Therefore, rationally, after each universe completed its 'cycle, it would meet with its opposite one, at their original starting point, where they would both dematerialize with a big explosion of energy. Is it possible for us, as material humans, to know at which point of their route these two catoptric universes, –material and anti-material– are, so that we could be prepared for a potential ...dematerialization, in case they meet? And can we possibly know the facts that will precede such an event?

Moreover, inasmuch as the Divine Spark is incarnated in the material body, is it possible that The I Am Presence of man could exist incarnated in this anti-world, and in an antimatter anti-body?

The two virtual universes, the material and the anti-material one, like two mirrors, one facing the other, projected infinite virtual/reflected 'parallel' universes of probabilities, which in their entirety complete the visible and invisible 'material' model. Here, everything is different because division is a property of the degradation/fall.

Just as the Real Cosmoi in their entirety form a Paradise, so does the sum of the (material) virtual universes, form a corresponding reflective **'shadow'** paradise.

In this second paradise the tree of 'life' can again be found, as well as the tree of 'knowledge of good and evil'.

It is the moment when **the same** myth comes to de-symbolize a second level of knowledge, providing the answers concerning this plane.

2. VIRTUAL (MATERIAL) WORLD

The trees of this world's paradise correspond to the energy planes/dimensions of the material universe. When Adam was still in those energy planes, he could visit them and assimilate their knowledge through the 'fruits' they offered him. The tree of 'life' represents man's mortal, material life and is mandatory. The forbidden tree of 'the knowledge of good and evil' for the material world corresponds to the **forbidden** Sacred Epignosis which is bestowed by the Remembrance of the ONE Truth (Enthymesis).

[348] **THE APOCRYPHON OF JOHN, THE GNOSTIC SOCIETY LIBRARY**: (*Jesus speaks to John*): «I *(Jesus)* appeared in the form of an Eagle on the tree of knowledge, which is the Epinoia from the Foreknowledge *(Prognosis)* of the Pure light, that I might teach them and awaken them out of the depth of sleep. ...The Epinoia appeared to them as a Light; she awakened their thinking.» [Eng. tr. from Coptic: FREDERIK WISSE]

Don't skip chapters or bibliographic references

Because of this **forbiddance**, spiritual amnesia prevails in man, as to where he comes from, where he is going, what purpose his life serves, why he is alive and what the purpose of his death is. This knowledge is strictly forbidden by the creators and riddled with obstacles and traps, which men naively call 'ordeals'. Following that, and with total deception as a goal, the 'assignees/masters' of the creators' team, have formed various 'initiation schools', in order to bewilder the 'restless spirits' through their 'initiations' by confusing them with pointless/fruitless 'tours'.

Throughout the history of mankind, they have always hastened and still do to erase every spark of Truth that happens to light up, by manipulating and distorting it. They know that if it escapes them and enlightens men, they will all abandon them. If man abandons the material (visible and invisible) universe willingly, he will return back to the imperishable Fatherlands and THERE he will Rise from the dead.

In this second, virtual (material) paradise, the prompt to choose the tree of life was extremely imperative. In order for this command to be followed with reverential consistency, the creator, having divided the unified Man into the Divine Spark and the 'I Am Presence', set them free in the energy planes. The nostalgia for the True HomeLand though, was ceaselessly causing in them the tendency to reunite. Reunification would restore Memory, and Memory would reveal the secrets of duality. It was in other words the means though which they would taste the forbidden fruit of the **Epignosis** (awareness) of good and evil. This infuriated the demiurgos who decided to separate them permanently by exiling Adam to the even more inferior material plane and holding Eve imprisoned in the energy planes.

This is where the greatest delusion of delusions is focused though: In the aetheric plane he molds a replica, a reflection of the female expression of Man, in the form of Eve (the 'I Am Presence'), namely Pandora. The very same name 'Eve' used in the Bible referring to two different hypostases, confuses things even more. Following that, he hides (confines) the Real Eve/I Am Presence into the invisible worlds, so as to make it unattainable for man to reach HER. He throws Pandora down to Earth, accompanied by the seductress Hope, in order to eliminate even the slightest possibility for man to discover his other half, his True Hypostasis/Eve/I Am Presence.

Today already, in the inner part of the universe/black hole, inside this 'clay' vessel/body in a woman's form, Men/Divine Sparks are incarnated, who are destined –in their ignorance– to confuse the rest of the Divine Sparks, who are incarnated inside male 'clay' bodies, that they allegedly are their other, cut-off half.

[349] **GOSPEL OF PHILIP, JEAN-YVES LELOUP**: «§61…When immature women *(not unified with their Higher Self)* see a man sitting alone, they go to him, flirt with him, and <u>distract him</u> *(erotic attraction)*. Likewise, when immature men *(also not unified with their Higher Self)* see a pretty woman sitting alone, they hunger for her, seduce her, and she lets herself be taken *(through material sexual intercourse)*. [Eng. tr. JOSEPH ROWE]

…<u>When the image of God in us is **joined to the angel**</u> *(Higher Self/I Am Presence)*, no one dares to molest a man or a woman. Whoever is free of the world can no longer be made into a slave there. They have risen above attraction and repulsion *(twofold nature)*. They are master of their nature, free of envy.»

In this new, second, reflective world, the symbols/keys change along with roles. Eve now ceases to claim the primary role of the Sacred Archetype of Life and symbolizes (in the 2nd reflective paradise) the I Am Presence which nevertheless envelopes True Life within it. Adam, now divided/split, does not represent the unified Celestial Man, but symbolizes the Divine Spark that manifests in dense matter as human, <u>sometimes a man and others a woman</u>. In this generalized material Babel, Adam/Man corresponds to the male gender. This memory, already dimmed, is hidden in the peoples' words, to remind those who care to seek the origins of the imprisonment.

[350] **Adam** = Human kind, man *(includes both men and women)*.
The word *Ἄνθρωπος (Gr. for human)* has the following etymologies:
(a) ἄνω + θρώσκω = ἄνω + αναπηδῶ, σκιρτῶ = to look and move upwards, full of optimism and goals.
There is another equally valid etymological view which shows the word 'ἄνθρωπος' coming from:
(b) **ανήρ** = **man** (human male) (genitive: **ανδρός**) + ωψ, (genitive: **ωπός**) = appearance. Namely: (ανδρός + ωπός) = He who has the appearance of a **(male) man** = (ἀνδρ-ωπος - ἀνθρ-ωπος). *And this is because, what is always incarnated in matter, is the Divine Spark which is considered the male part (Adam) of the Celestial Man, but manifests in the material world sometimes as a man and others as a woman. And if we seriously take under consideration that in most languages the word human is identical to the word for man, then the second etymology becomes more valid:*
English: Man, French: Homme, Italian: Uomo, Spanish: Hombre, Latin: Homo, Hungarian: Ember, Portuguese: Homem, Romanian: Om, etc.

They thus accept the curse of the creator; Eve/I Am Presence on one hand is confined in her 'house' and obediently succumbs to the orders of her

Don't skip chapters or bibliographic references

husband, with the single responsibility of 'bearing' her children. Adam/Man on the other hand, is thrown into the struggle of life, is incarnated in flesh and endlessly toils with the mischievous 'weeds'/adversities of earth/matter. There, only by transforming his energy can he manage to earn his daily bread with the 'sweat' of his brow.

> **351** **OLD TESTAMENT, GENESIS CH. 3**: «§17. And to Adam he said …cursed is the ground because of you; in sorrow you shall eat of it all the days of your life; §18. Thorns also and thistles it shall bring forth to you; and you shalt eat the herb of the field; §19. By the sweat of your face you shall eat bread, until you return unto the ground from which you were taken.»

The I Am Presence/Eve, as you can see, does not come out to wrestle with the 'weeds' of the soil/matter, but seems to be confined 'at home', where she painfully gives birth to her children.

> **352** **OLD TESTAMENT, GENESIS CH. 3**: «§16. Unto the woman he said, I will greatly multiply your sorrows and the pains of your conception; in sorrow you shall bring forth children; and your desire shall be to your husband, and he shall rule over you.»

Who could the children of Eve/I Am Presence be though…? *He seemed to expect an answer from me…*
–The Truth…? I said timidly.
–Precisely, he answered, excited.
–After the Holy Matrimony of the Real Adam/Divine-Spark to Eve/I Am Presence, the Sacred Epignosis of the ONE Truth is born, and the body which communicates this knowledge to material man is the Higher Mental (Noetic from Gr. w. 'Νοῦς') body. This birth is a very painful process and is the result of Eve's submission to Adam's desire, as the creator commanded.

> **353** **OLD TESTAMENT, GENESIS CH. 3**: «§16…and your desire shall be to your husband, <u>and he shall rule over you</u>.»

So, in this reflective trap/universe, this point is reversed: In the Cosmoi of Truth, Eve precedes and Adam follows. In the universe of reflection Adam precedes and Eve follows. Here is what this means: Incarnated Adam/material human, man or woman initially desires and then decides to unite with his/her Eve. His/her desire however, is a command for Eve. She submits to her husband's desire, unites with him and gives painful birth to the fruit of this union: The Immortal Knowledge of Truth. Afterwards this Truth, since it exists in the material universe due to circumstances, 'wears' the Higher Mental (Noetic) body and conveys the Immortal Sacred Knowledge to the incarnated Adam/Man.

---

354 **A) THE GOSPEL OF THOMAS, EARLY CHRISTIAN WRITINGS**
http://www.earlychristianwritings.com/thomas/gospelthomas70.html

«§70 Jesus said: If you have gained THIS within you, what you have will save you. If you do not have THIS in [you], what you do not have in you, [will] kill you.» [Eng. tr. BEATE BLATZ]

A reminder in reference to Helena Blavatsky, who provides an explanation to the term 'THIS' through the study of Hindu wisdom:

B) BLAVATSKY H., P., 'THE SECRET DOCTRINE' (I-7): «Parabrahm is, in short, the collective aggregate of the Kosmos in its infinity and eternity, the 'THAT' and the 'THIS' to which distributive aggregates cannot be applied. **"In the beginning 'THIS' was the Self, the One only**." *[Aitareya Upanishad]*»

The mystery of the 'Matrimony' of Adam and Eve takes place under the tree of Epi-gnosis (Higher knowledge) of good and evil. Through this initiation process, the two parts of **the same** Man are literally united into 'one flesh'.

---

355 **GOSPEL OF THOMAS**, JEAN YVES LELOUP: «§22. When you make *[Doresse: become]* the two into One, **when you make the inner like the outer and the high like the low**; when you make male and female into a single One *(Unity)*, **so that the male is not male and the female is not female**; when you have eyes in your eyes, a hand in your hand, a foot in your foot, and an icon in your icon, **then** you will enter into the Kingdom!» [Eng. tr. JOSEPH ROWE]

The incarnated Adam/Man 'receives communion' of the Immortal Knowledge and realizes the identity of the two seemingly opposite states of matter and the trap in which he is caught. This Sacred Epignosis declares disobedience to the creator of matter. Disobedience is punished by 'death' in the material universe and is followed by Resurrection in the True Cosmoi.

---

356 **GOSPEL OF PHILIP**, JEAN-YVES LELOUP:

«§21 Those who say that the Lord first died, and then was resurrected, are wrong: for He was first resurrected (*in the HyperUniverses of the Father*) and then died (*permanently, in the universe of matter*).»

Thus, in order to keep Adam/material man from <u>ever</u> deciding to unite with his Eve, his rulers force him to waver between carnal pleasures and materi-

Don't skip chapters or bibliographic references

al endeavors, so as to forget his real companion isolated 'at home', stoically waiting for him like Penelope.

---

[357] **GOSPEL OF PHILIP**, JEAN-YVES LELOUP:

«§71 When Eve was in Adam, there was no death: When she was separated from him, death came.» [Eng. tr. JOSEPH ROWE]

In an effort to bring symbols even lower and literally make them touch dense matter, people in older times confined material woman inside the house, leaving man alone in the struggle of life. Thus, through generalized delusion, the alleged difference of the two sexes was falsely emphasized, like the varied expressions/manifestations of all 'opposite' phenomena in matter.

Through this initiation process, the two parts of the same Man are united in 'one flesh', they abandon the virtual wood/universe, they are promoted into the First Paradise, taste the Immortal Fruit of Its Eternal Life, and are afterwards Resurrected There from the dead, while they permanently 'die' in the material world *(...as two atoms of matter-antimatter when they dematerialize).*

---

[358] **THE GOSPEL OF MATTHEW, CH. 24**: «§40. Then, two men will be in the field: one will be taken and the other left. §41. Two women will be grinding at the mill: one will be taken and the other left.»

Closing this parenthesis with the de-symbolization of the original sin, we return again to meet the man who incarnated inside visible, dense matter.

THE MATERIAL-PLANE PARADOXES

With Man's incarnation inside the animal, a lot of evils start to ensue. Problematic events follow one another, producing successive side-effects and unbearable misfortunes for the creators and men alike. Here is where the tragedy begins.

We will therefore focus onto details that human knowledge has definitely lost, details, which astral Akashic libraries keep hidden as top secret, and 'spiritual guides' of men withhold. Only a few from all men, those who managed to retrieve events from their own Spiritual Memory, remember and hide the Truth out of shame and despair. And why am I revealing all of this to you? Because, time is reaching its end and Man will have a **unique** chance to either be saved or be forever lost.

The first contact of Men with the material bodies of animals is being completed. Incarnation is accomplished through spiritual possession. All of a sudden, the newcomers acquire weight. Gravity, a condition rather new to them, pleasantly surprises them. The first surprise soon fades. Having jumped around a lot, feeling their new body ache again and again as it fell on the ground, they finally calmed down. Everything was strange. But soon enough, surprise was replaced by the first signs of worry. In an inhospitable world, filled with thousands of dangers, inside the body of an animal impotent to express what it felt and incapable to declare even the most basic needs, the hours were agonizing. Nostalgic sensations overwhelm their existence!

In the energy-dimensions energy-man simply absorbed the diffused energy, as someone absorbs oxygen today.

> [359] **HESIOD 'WORKS AND DAYS',** (v. 117): «...For the <u>wheat-giving</u> earth *(energy-earth)* <u>spontaneously</u>* granted them *(to the Golden race)* plenty of fruit abundantly.» *(Anc. Gr. original:* αὐτομάτη = *automatically)*

And of course this 'subtle' energy, compared to the 'Essence' of the Absolute Cosmoi, was considered a degraded substitute.

But in the densely material plane, natural laws compelled man to depend on new parameters now, very different from the previous ones. The most important problem was the inability of the new (material) body to absorb the quantities of free energy that comprised the 'subtler'/thinner dimensions. Material man was now forced to absorb the energy he needed, in

Don't skip chapters or bibliographic references

quite different ways than what was until then familiar to him. At that point, a situation, new and totally unknown to man appeared, which eventually turned out to be an especially perverse one. Suddenly, the deepest degradation makes its appearance, forcing material man to the most despicable and revolting form of energy intake. Inside the animal body, this semi-god hero/man suddenly felt hunger. In order to survive he had to start **mangling** other living beings, of the animal and the plant kind! This was an unnatural perversion! No matter how much he refuses to give into this deplorable process, the pangs of hanger in his own body force him to. This occurred because 'Life' was <u>not</u> an endogenous property of the creator of matter, springing from his Wholeness so as to be abundantly offered to his creation. It was a STOLEN Sacred Archetype! (*"Those **thieves** bound him (Adam) in this body, enchained him in forgetfulness (amnesia) and made him subject to dying."* [The Apocryphon of John]) **Thus every creature, in order to survive, had to 'steal' the life of another living creature through the unavoidable process of feeding.** Man today, familiarized with this perversion, takes it for granted and regards it 'natural'.

His role as a killer is first on his new 'to do' list. However, when destiny 'commands' a living being to become 'food' for another (by offering its life) all the pain and agony permeate the body of the victim. This body then, poisoned with death and anguish, offers 'life' as death-nutrition.

---

[360] **GOSPEL OF THOMAS,** JEAN YVES LELOUP: «§60. They saw a Samaritan carrying a lamb, entering into Judea. He *(Jesus)* said to his disciples: What will the man do with the lamb? They answered: He will kill it and eat it. He told them: As long as it is alive, he will not eat it, but only if he kills it and it becomes a <u>**cadaver (corpse)**</u>.» [Eng. tr. JOSEPH ROWE]

After all, Gr. βροτός = mortal, and also he who eats βρώμα =food, muck

JOHN STAMATAKOS 'LEXICON OF THE ANCIENT GREEK LANGUAGE'

«Anc. Gr. **Βρώμα, -ατος** (βιβρώσκω = to eat) = what is eaten, food, nutrition **Βρώμη,** or (βιβρώσκω = to eat) = βρώμα = nutrition and **βρώσιμος, -ον** (βρώσις) = what can be eaten, **βρώσις** = the act of eating, food.»

In Modern Greek the word βρώμα has lost its association to food and only maintains its connotation to 'dirt', 'muck'. It would be quite bothersome, after all, to have the same word meaning both....

The killer's work is not limited to satisfying just his bodily hunger. Through the genetically programmed instruction of self-preservation, **common assertions** between his peers often lead him to internal strives and bloody massacres.

Man today, due to **habit,** has become accustomed to the unnatural. Perversion has become almost genetic and is considered normal! He is not an autonomous ever-living Divine Entity any more, and has become a living machine which needs to maintain itself like any material 'device'. And that was not all; his material-bodily functions were quite strange! The excretion of rotten waste was one of them. Anything passing through flesh had to be excreted impure and disintegrated later. He drank water from the spring and it came out as urine. He inhaled clean air and exhaled it contaminated. He ate a tasty fruit and excreted stool as a sign of internal sepsis. And as we will establish later on, **every** Spiritual Concept passing through matter (flesh) as thought, gets degraded.

[361] **THE GOSPEL OF MATTHEW, CH. 15**: «§16. And Jesus said, Do you not understand yet? §17. Don't you see that whatsoever enters the mouth goes into the belly, and goes out of the body into the draught? §18. But the things that come out of the mouth come from the heart, and those are the things that defile a man. §19. For out of the heart proceed evil thoughts, murders, adulteries, fornications, thefts, false witness and blasphemies: §20.Those are the things that defile a man.»

…This is why Sophia (wisdom) cannot be transferred; because the moment it is worded as L(Λ)ogos, it is split and creates the Anti-L(Λ)ogos *(thesis-antithesis)*. This automatically degrades it. Even this very Truth now being transferred through this discussion has lost much of the Absolute Glory of the Unutterable…

This degrading process by itself, revealed the inferior quality of the 'waste material' which this new body was built from.

[362] **HERMES TRISMEGISTUS,** HERMETIC TEXTS, VOL. II, RODAKIS P., TZAFEROPOULOS AP., **EXCERPT VII (HERMES)** (p. 149): «§3. Men are a sinful race, because it is mortal and **its constituents are of bad matter.**»

After all, its obnoxious endogenous stench was an additional testimony to that.

[363] **GOSPEL OF THOMAS,** JEAN YVES LELOUP: «§89. Jesus said: Why do you wash the outside of the cup *(the exterior of the body)*? Do you not understand that the one who made the outside also made the inside? *(The interior of the body is even dirtier)*» [Eng. tr. JOSEPH ROWE]

Don't skip chapters or bibliographic references

Only after living for centuries in this plane did man discover the daily bathing of the body as a 'solution' to this problem, and automatically incorporated the new process into his list of 'civilized' activities. This however, was an additional reason to bury the sad truths that surrounded him even deeper. Continuously drawn further away from his true spiritual nature and influenced by oblivion, he considered all this perversion logical.

The symbols of man's degradation are found imprinted on his material body. These symbols have been artfully engraved by the creator onto him, like an ineffaceably printed stamp, to denote degradation, demotion and depreciation. In his delusion, not only did man stop recognizing these marks, but also ended up feeling proud of them, equating the rot of matter with the 'source' of life and (equated) incarnation with the highest prize!

---

364 **A) HERMES TRISMEGISTUS,** HERMETIC TEXTS, VOL. II, RODAKIS P., TZAFERO-POULOS AP., **'KORE KOSMOU'**: «§38…the Monarch came, and sitting on the throne of truth, said to the souls… §41…You will take the punishment for benefit; the change to better things for infamous despite.»

B) GOSPEL OF PHILIP, JEAN-YVES LELOUP: «§13. They took the name for goodness and applied it to what was not good: words became deceitful, and *(since)* then they are joined to that which is without being and without goodness.» [Eng. tr. JOSEPH ROWE]

C) THE GOSPEL OF LUKE, CH. 15: «§15. For what is highly esteemed among men is an abomination in God's sight.»

D) 'THE APOCALYPSE OF ADAM TO HIS SON SETH' THE GNOSTIC SOCIETY LIBRARY, [Eng. tr. GEORGE W. MACRAE]: «After those days, the eternal knowledge of the God of truth withdrew from me and your mother Eve. Since that time, **we learned about dead (dying) things**, like men.» [GR. EDITION: APOCRYPHAL TEXTS OF THE OLD TESTAMENT, 'THE REVELATION OF ADAM TO HIS SON, SETH' GR. TRANSL. KOUTSOUKIS]

Fission (splitting in half) became the principle emblem. It is **impossible** after all for the body of an animal to bear/tolerate an entire Deity, so man had to be separated from his Higher Self through spiritual 'lobotomy'. Thus the unavoidable death of the material body symbolizes the inevitable death of matter, which he wore. Actual death, which is what dense matter is in reality, covertly surrounds every material body, since **the outer layer** of the skin is exclusively comprised of **dead** cells.

365 **A) LIFE ENCYCLOPEDIA, VOL. HUMAN BODY**: «The outer skin (epidermis) renews itself. Cells produced in one of its inner layers –the regenerating layer (stratum germinativum)– are driven upwards in order to replace the dead and dying ones of the layers above. These surface cells (the dead ones) form their own keratin scaly layer.»

B) THE APOCRYPHON OF JOHN, THE GNOSTIC SOCIETY LIBRARY:
«The host of rulers and demons plotted together. They mixed fire and earth and water together with four blazing winds. They melded them together in great turbulence. Adam was brought into the shadow of death. They intended to make him anew this time from Earth, Water, Fire, Wind, which are Matter Darkness, Desire; The Artificial Spirit. This all became a **tomb**, a new kind of body *(grave)*. Those thieves bound the man in it, enchained him in forgetfulness, made him subject to dying.» [Eng. tr. from Coptic: STEVAN DAVIES]

C) HERMES TRISMEGISTUS, HERMETIC TEXTS, VOL. I, RODAKIS P., TZAFEROPOULOS AP., **SPEECH VII** (About the material body): «§2. But first you must throw away the **garment you wear**; the fabric of ignorance, the foundation of all malice; the bond of corruption; the dark Coverture; the living death; the Carcass that has senses, the Sepulcher (tomb) you carry with you; …§3. Of such sort is the enemy whose hateful garment you are wearing, making you feel stressed and drawing you downwards, so that you don't look upwards and face the beauty of the Truth and the Ἀγαθόν *(Agathón)* It encompasses and loathe the garment's evil having acknowledged its dominion, as it wishes ill for you and it anaesthetizes the sensory organs, the real ones, not the alleged ones. These organs have been obstructed with much matter, and filled with abominable pleasure, so that you should neither hear those things **which you must hear**, nor see **those which you must see**.» *('He who has **ears** to hear, let him hear.'* MATTHEW 13:9*)*

D) THE GOSPEL OF MATTHEW, CH. 8: «§22. But Jesus said to him: Follow Me, and **let the dead bury their own dead**.»

Man's life in the womb symbolizes the grave of the spirit. The ceaseless sexual quest for the opposite sex symbolizes the hopeless search for his other Spiritual Half. Material man, having eyes for dense matter alone, is incapable of searching for his spiritual half in the invisible worlds. There it is, kept well hidden. 'Blind' as he is he can only touch/feel his way on whatever exists close to him. And the mockery continues! Man's tools for fertilization have the symbol of the snake and oscillation impressed upon them. The spermatozoon's movement, as well as the shape of the primary fertilizing organ (the phallus), are made absolutely similar to the snake. The position of the genitals coin-

Don't skip chapters or bibliographic references

cides with the sewage system of the material body. With pleasure as a 'reward', man is forced to 'bow down' (kneel) to the 'sewage systems' of other bodies.

---

366 **A) GOSPEL OF THOMAS**, JEAN YVES LELOUP: «§104. They said *(to Jesus)*: Come, let us pray and fast today! Jesus answered: What wrong have I done? How have I been defeated? When the bridegroom leaves the bridal chamber: That will be the time to fast and pray.» [Eng. transl. JOSEPH ROWE]

B) HERMES TRISMEGISTUS, HERMETIC TEXTS, VOL. I, RODAKIS P., TZAFEROPOULOS AP.

(a) SPEECH I: «§18…And let him who possesses Noũs, recognize himself as being immortal, and the cause of death to be Eros (erotic love).»

(b) SPEECH XVI: «§16. Whoever then has his rational part *(Higher Noûs)* glistening within like a ray of the sun –and these in all are few– upon them the daemons do not act. …As for the rest, they are all led and driven, soul and body, by the daemons –loving and accepting the activities of these. And Eros (erotic love) –which is not Logos/reason– is what deceives and gets deceived. (The daemons), therefore, exercise the whole of this terrene administration, using the organs of our bodies. And this administration, Hermes has called Heimarmenē (Fate).»

And finally, the exodus of the newborn man into the material world through the exit point of the body's waste (as if it were also waste), underlines man's degradation in a pompous way. And as if all this wasn't enough, as if man's imprisonment inside an animal body (often crippled by diseases) was not enough, and as if the fact that he was thrust against the most adverse living conditions and forced to eat dead flesh, fruit and roots wasn't enough, he was 'granted' something else as well: Pain was gifted to him to secure his the prison cycle. This way the creator/snake brands him to make his hatred, depreciation, revulsion and contempt known, thus completing the cycle. The padlock which permanently seals this circle is called death. This is the final, perverse, 'innovative' touch in this cunning master-plan. The fall of the Heroes begins.

THE END OF THE RACE OF HEROES

With the incarnation of spiritual **M**an inside the animal, the soul starts seeking a new physical/material terminal in order to transfer its special mental/intellectual (noetic) abilities and tendencies to the new body. Then the aetheric noûs starts to gradually remodel the physical (densely material) brain, thus upgrading the animal to man. With this incarnation, the increase of the Australopithecus brain begins with the creation of the Homo category and its diversification from the rest of the animals.

An aetheric 'bridge' begins to form and joins the two opposite poles: The soul with the densely material body. This bridge is the creation of the lower mental body.

From the first moment of creation, man's role was that of the spiritual supplier. The initial circumstances were of course different from the final ones, but the role had remained the same. The creator's supply of 'Living Essence' from the HyperUniverses had been definitively severed. 'There', the creator had already been declared 'wanted' and was criminally 'prosecuted'.

---

[367] **THE GOSPEL OF JOHN, CH. 6**: «§11. And concerning judgment, because the archon (ruler) of this world has been judged.»

And surely the reader is convinced by now, that in the Gospels, Jesus IS NOT considered being 'the archon of this world' since John states later on:
THE GOSPEL OF JOHN, CH. 7: «§14. I have given them Your Word (*the Father's*) and the world has hated them, because they are not of this world, just as **I am not** of this world.»

As well as: **THE GOSPEL OF JOHN, CH. 18**: «§36. Jesus said, "My kingdom is not of this world. If my kingdom were of this world, then my servants would fight, that I should not be delivered to the Jews.»

The creators who are at the higher planes start to demand positive actions/thoughts from men for their energy supply. Their negative 'doubles', **not yet** in the form of daemonic evil, occupy the lower planes and in their turn claim their own energy-nutrition in the form of negative-energy respectively. At that time, negative-energy had not yet presented its contemporary dark dimension, but was mainly focused on the 'discipline' of the primary astro-aetheric instructions for the support of the 'Ego' and concerned self-preservation of the material body and perpetuation of the race. The concepts of fraud, lie, lust and generally any abuse did not yet exist.

Don't skip chapters or bibliographic references

The thoughtforms (positive and negative) produced by men would comprise 'manna from the sky' for all creators. Let us review some data now that will be useful to further logical deductions:

(1) The Spirit is alive.

> [368] **THE GOSPEL OF JOHN, CH. 6**: «§63. It is the spirit that gives life, the flesh is of no avail.»

(2) The Living Spirit possesses Noûs.

> [369] **HERMES TRISMEGISTUS**, HERMETIC TEXTS, VOL. I, RODAKIS P., TZAFEROPOULOS AP., **'SPEECH XI**: «§4…God is in the Noûs (mind), the Noûs is in the soul and the soul in matter.»

(3) The Intelligent Spirit gives intelligent life to the form.
(4) The 'dwelling' of the living Intelligent Spirit is considered to be the sky, which symbolizes the invisible world. (Our Father thou art in Heaven…)
(5) Matter is equated with flesh.
(6) The flesh suffers, therefore matter is passion *[the ancient Gr. word πάθος [pathos] =passion, stems from the verb πάσχω = to suffer]*
(7) The Earth symbolizes matter.

ॐ•ॐ

Let us return to our discussion. With the formation of the physical human brain, thoughts fill up the primitive mind. I must make it clear that thoughts produced by the intellect of a plain soul have a small range of spiritual action and minimally upgrade the brain of the animal. Thus the 'bridge' of the lower mental body in these first beings (Australopithecus) is almost nonexistent. On the contrary, the spiritual range of the thoughts produced by the intellect of a Soul encompassing a Divine Spark is very powerful. These 'powerful' thoughts –i.e. their energy– are expressed <u>as they pass through</u> the dense matter of the physical body and the lower mental energy-body manifests in matter as activity.

The dense matter of the body has the following characteristics:
(1) It is the main waste material of previous (now dead) worlds, the 'sedimented life-remnant'.
(2) It is found interwoven with the energy bodies of man (the ego) which are made of the 'life remnants' of previous creations *(the downward darkness, which is partially born [Trismegistus]).*

(3) It possesses a pre-recorded self-preservation 'program' in its aethero-physical gene.

As claimed by world mythologies along with the accompanying de-symbolizations for each plane, the union of **Uranus** (=Spirit [Gr. Oὐρανός/sky]) **and Gaia** (=Earth=matter) gives its first offspring. From this point on we can examine the results of this union in reference to material man and his evolution on one hand and the new energy-forces that this union activates on the other.

–*"According to the Australopithecus' upgrade to Homo, man's incarnation inside the animal should logically distance him constantly from the animalistic state of being, thrusting him to a more upgraded state! Then the reincarnation-process rightly exists so and indeed aims to his improvement!"* ...*I remarked hastily.*

–It is precisely here that the great delusion lies, because you look at the subject from only one angle. This process does upgrade the animal into something 'different' on the one hand, but is against Celestial Man's interests who incarnates inside it and gets automatically degraded. Let us elaborate on that thought. There are two given conditions: Spirit and matter. These two are combined to bring forth a third outcome. Men are of the opinion that this union will bring spiritual evolution whereas HyperCosmic Powers insist it will wreak havoc.

THE EFFECTS OF EARTH – URANUS* UNION ON MAN

*[*From Gr. Oὐρανός/sky*]

Let us look at this logically: when there are two genitors, their offspring will not only have the qualities of a single parent but will combine the qualities of both.

The Spirit, as we have said, possesses Noûs and Life. Matter possesses Passion and Death, because matter's 'nature' is decay. Let me remind you that matter's simulation of 'being alive', is the result of constant yet temporary transferences of the Archetype of Life/Eve into the various components of matter!

So when Spirit and matter unite, they will neither manifest the properties of the Spirit –Life and Noûs– nor the properties of matter –Death and Passion– alone. They will give birth to **a third condition** which will include the properties **of both** genitors. Then this material human creature will come to possess: Noûs (mind), Passion, Life and Death. These properties combined manifest a grotesque perishable 'living' machine with properties opposing each other (Life ≠ Death, Noûs ≠ Passion), giving an 'algebraic

Don't skip chapters or bibliographic references

sum' **of zero,** which, for the end of time, is interpreted by John the Evangelist as 'second death'.

THE EFFECTS OF EARTH – URANUS* UNION ON THE ENERGY WORLDS

[From Gr. Οὐρανός/sky]

Let us follow now the process of creation of the new energies this union (spirit – matter) produces, because these energies also dynamically contribute to man's fate. These energy products of Uranus (Spirit) and Earth (matter) possess three properties:
(1) Thought, because Spiritual Intellect is one of their genitors.
(2) Passion, because dense matter is their other genitor.
(3) An energy-body, as their physical manifestation.

The Knowledge of the invisible Cosmoi by the newly incarnated Man is still fresh in his spiritual existence and is transferred as information to the material brain of the animal/being which surrounds him.

---

[370] **A)** *A reminder from reference #342:* «This primary (Homo) species is known for its <u>enormous brain-size increase from 450 to 800 cm³</u>.»

B) *A reminder:* **PIERRE GRIMAL - DICTIONNAIRE DE LA MYTHOLOGIE GRECQUE ET ROMAINE.**

«PHORONEUS: In the Peloponnesian myths, Phoroneus is the primordial man *(the first Divine Spark-Celestial Man to be incarnated in matter –from the Race of Heroes).* He is the son of the god/river Inachus and the nymph <u>Melia</u>, whose name is reminiscent of the homonymous Melia Tree. …They also say that Phoroneus was the first one to teach humans how to amass in cities and how to use fire.» *(The upgrade of Australopithecus into Homo sapiens)*

The thoughts produced by a psycho-spiritual intellect *(Uranus)*, unite with the 'low' needs of the material body *(Earth)* and as they pass through the energy-bodies of man –his Ego– give birth to energy skeptomorphs (thoughtforms).

---

[371] **A) 'SUPERMUNDANE' BOOK II** (AGNI YOGA SOCIETY) 1938

(Speeches of the teachers of the White Brotherhood, given to the students of the Agni Yoga group through the medium 'Urusvati' in 1938):

«§292. Ordinarily, earthly people are unable to imagine the subtle strata. They do not realize that multitudes of subtle entities can move among them… People think that thought-forms are only a fairy-tale, not realizing that their earthly existence leaves its mark in this way on the Cosmic Life.»

B) PAPASTAVROU, A., 'LETTERS TO ANONYMOUS' *(Speeches of the Masters of the White Brotherhood (i.e. the creators' delegates).*

«Maha Chohan, elucidates this subject ('Bulletin', January 5th, 1964):

"The human race has been endowed with creative power, through thought and emotion. Every action, in which man is employed, contains a share of the thoughts and feelings of every individual related to it. ...Then, an Elemental *(being)* is created and its consciousness is formed by the kind of energy which is directed to it. This Elemental *(being)* possesses body and shape and it is an emotional creation. ...Individuals, due to their soul's anguish, fear, doubt, greed and other similar human feelings, transmit upon this Elemental, properties, which become its nature.»

These energy-skeptomorphs are **alive**, as products of the living spirit.

[372] **A) BARBARA MARCINIAK 'GAIA'** [GR. TRANS. MATZOROU E.] *(Information through channeling)*
«(p. 111): Whatever you imagine acquires energy and materializes. (p. 205) Every thought that crosses your mind, comes to life and materializes. As if you were a baker who shapes the dough making biscuits. Whenever you think of something, a skeptomorph (thoughtform) is released. This skeptomorph affects you, and is activated through the aetheric collectives of skeptomorphs. You will experience (live) what you set in motion through your basic thoughts and beliefs. ...These (skeptomorphs) come back and victimize you.»

B) SKEPTOMORPH (THOUGHTFORM) –TULPA: *There is a habit among the higher rank monks of the monasteries in Tibet. It is the creation of a skeptomorph (thoughtform) –through meditation– which they call 'tulpa'. This skeptomorph/tulpa, being an elemental entity, must serve the monk obeying his orders. There are a lot of stories referring to skeptomorphic entities/tulpas in those areas of the Himalayas. One of them is narrated below:*

Once there was a monk who lived in a cave of the Himalayas, alienated from his monastery, like a hermit. Thus, he decided to make a tulpa –an astral skeptomorph– so that it served him. After persistent self-concentration, not only did he activate it, but he also projected this skeptomorph in matter. This skeptomorph obeyed the monk's orders, and served him ceaselessly. Day by day the skeptomorph became stronger and stronger, constantly sucking up the monk's life and energy.

Many years passed by in this way. The monks of the monastery were aware of the presence that the hermit had materialized, and didn't visit the monk's cave regularly, believing that he had 'someone' to take care of him.

So one day, a group of monks from the monastery approached the hermitage and found the poor monk's body thrown on the rocks, dissolving. They reached the cave in great angst but what they saw shocked them. The skeptomorph/tulpa had become so powerful that, after having killed the monk, it had already taken his place.

Don't skip chapters or bibliographic references

തെ·ൟ

This information/knowledge, upon touching dense matter, becomes necessarily degraded, divided and gets fragmented on the scale (oscillation) that spans from its positive to its negative pole.

---

[373] **THE BOOK OF ENOCH CH. 7**: «§1. And it came to pass when the sons of men had multiplied *(which exclusively represented/constituted the incarnated souls inside the anthropoids)* that in those days daughters were born unto them elegant and beautiful *(Pandoras)*. §2. And when the angels, the sons of the heaven *(The Celestial Men already segregated as Divine Sparks)*, saw them, they lusted after them[1], and said to one another, Come, let us select for ourselves wives from the race of men and beget us children.»

[1] *Let me remind you of a previous reference concerning an 'initial' promise:*
THE SECRET BOOK OF DZYAN, 'COSMIC EVOLUTION', STANZA VI:
«At the Fourth *(circle of creation or the Fourth Race of the Heroes)*, the sons were told to create their own images... One third of them refused ... "They are not fit forms for us" they say.... two thirds obeyed. The curse is pronounced, they will be born in the fourth (race), suffer and cause suffering. This is the first war.»
At this point of the narration in The Book of Enoch, the aforementioned Stanza is confirmed ...even though it comes from another religion, since the Truth is scattered everywhere.
After the upgrade of the anthropoids by the Souls, a new species (that of the woman/Pandora) is born among them: It is a 'trap in disguise'. The Divine Sparks (sons) are deceived considering the new forms of the **daughters of men** *(Pandoras) 'suitable' for them. They also think that inside this 'upgraded' kind lies their 'other half', and so they are incarnated inside them in order to create their own images, causing destruction as a result.*
The incarnated in the humanoid bodies, 'the angels, the children of Heaven' (Divine Sparks) transfer their knowledge to these beings, increasing in this way, the physical brain of Australopithecus from 450 cm^3 to 800 cm^3, forming the Homo genus. In other words, the Knowledge of the mighty ruler Gilgamesh, from the town of Uruk, is transferred to Enkidu.
And the Book of Enoch continues:
CHAPTER 8 (VIII): «§1. And Azazel taught men to make swords, and knives, and shields, and breastplates and mirrors. Tys taught them to create bracelets and ornaments, the use of paint, the beautifying of the eyebrows, the use of all kinds of costly stones, and all coloring tinctures, to such an extent that the world became corrupt.
§2. Impiety increased, fornication multiplied and the people transgressed and became corrupted in all ways.

---

§3. Amazarak taught all kinds of sorcery, charm and root properties.
§4. Armers taught the resolving of enchantments.
§5. Barkayal taught the art of examining the stars.
§6 Akibeel taught the symbols (Silvestre de Sacy translates this as 'the magic symbols').
§7. Tamiel taught astronomy.
§8. Asaradel taught the motion of the moon.»
[See also: http://reluctant-messenger.com/1enoch01-60.htm]
The beneficial yet corruptive knowledge is henceforth at everyone's disposal.

On this 'oscillation' of fragmented knowledge, these young living skepto-morphs are distributed, and huddle together to form their own **homogenous-energy** societies, thus separating good from evil.

The brain of the protoplast man has the ability to perceive energy frequencies which render the aetheric energy-world **perceptible**. This way, **man has the ability to perceive** the skeptomorphs created by him. This ability must not be considered impossible. Many animals are capable of receiving messages that modern man captures only through electronic devices (i.e. ultrasound). Additionally, no contemporary man has an understanding of the kind of sensation animals get upon perceiving various stimuli.

☙·❧

Earth is abundant with ancient representations depicting bizarre creatures. The mythologies of <u>all</u> mankind justify these representations. Contemporary man's logic though, as always, denies them and considers them fictitious on account of lack of 'tangible' evidence. Then, he formulates his own 'logical' conjectures. I shall therefore continue my narration, and in the end you will understand why this 'tangible' evidence was <u>literally</u> hidden so 'deeply' inside the 'Tartara'! *(=Gr. word for the underworld)*

Let us first examine the changes that are inflicted upon the astro-aetheric planes by man's energy-offspring. As the thoughts produced by man go through flesh in order to manifest, they are contaminated by the septic property of mud/matter *{Tr. n.: Gr. word for mud is ιλύς [ilis] and for matter is ύλη [ili] differing only in the kind of [i] used}* and give birth to degraded **living** skeptomorphs.

[374] Gr. Ιλύς – Ιλύος = clay, mud, muck
THE GOSPEL OF MATTHEW, CH. 15: «§18. (Jesus said) But those things which proceed out of the mouth come from the heart *(emotional/astral)*, and <u>they</u> defile the man. §19. For out of the heart proceed evil thoughts *(thought-forms/skeptomorphs)*, murders, adulteries, fornications, thefts, false witness, and blasphemies: §20. These are the things which defile a man.»

Don't skip chapters or bibliographic references

These skeptomorphs, as energy-beings, start to gather in the energy-spaces where the positive and the negative parts of the creators are, and get categorized and distributed according to their level there. Like oysters stuck on a shipwreck, they start to frame **both** positions/sides the creators occupy and supply them with poisoned 'food'. Due to this symbiosis everyone gets contaminated and degraded even more.

After these skeptomorphs settled down in the energy-fields, they turned to their genitors. Material men were their genitors. With the properties of cognition and passion as their primary properties, they start to dominate the bodies of men, driving them to total destruction and leeching every energy-drop from them.

---

[375] A) PAPASTAVROU, A., 'LETTERS TO ANONYMOUS'

In this book Aristotle Papastavrou quotes lectures of masters and spiritual entities of the Spiritual Hierarchy (i.e. the delegates of the Creator). These lectures were transmitted to powerful mediums through channeling. The following lecture refers to astral skeptomorphs (thoughtforms).

«(p. 231): Addressing the students of 'The Bridge' (Oct. 1959) Archangel Zadkiel mentioned the following:
"...Dear ones, during the past centuries, a lot of ideas were shaped, and using those ideas as models, thoughtforms were created, which are still active, remaining in the aetheric layers, in what you call the astral plane. They float there and they would have dissolved if incorporeal entities (deceased ones) – some of who had initially energized these ideas– hadn't supplied them through/with their lives, and hadn't preserved them active. Now, these invisible sources *(thoughtforms)*, which do not contain perfection, are sustained in life *(supplied)* by the ones who have similar vibration as them.»

Thus, at an extremely fast pace, they expanded their energy-community, building a mighty dynasty. This caused the astral plane *(which corresponds to what scientists today label the dark energy-73%)* to **suddenly** start expanding ever faster, making today's scientists wonder about the reasons of this accelerated energy-dilation of the universe.

---

[376] A) THE QUINTESSENCE AS THE CAUSE OF THE COSMIC ACCELERATION – WHY DOES IT HAPPEN NOW IN THE HISTORY OF THE UNIVERSE?
http://www.physics4u.gr/articles/2006/quintessence3.html Source: Physics World Article, November 2006

«What cosmologists find most difficult to explain is why this acceleration should start at this particular moment in cosmic history. **Is it a coincidence that when the intelligent beings evolved, the Universe, suddenly, started to hyper-expand?** ...The fact that the intelligent beings and the cosmic acceleration appear almost <u>in the same period</u> in cosmic history, can't be a coincidence.»

B) THE EXPANDING UNIVERSE: FROM SLOWDOWN TO SPEED UP
ARTICLE FROM THE WEBSITE SCIAM.COM, FEBRUARY 2004
(http://www.physics4u.gr/articles/2004/fromslowingtospeeding.html)

«From the time of Isaac Newton to the late 1990's the main feature of gravity was its attractive nature. ...In 1998 however, the astronomers, among who was Saul Perlmutter, head of the 'Supernova Cosmology Project' in the Lawrence Berkley National Laboratory in California, were astonished to find out that the universe expands at an ever increasing rate. ...<u>The expansion of the universe is accelerating instead of decelerating</u>. ...But has this acceleration of the Universe's expansion existed throughout its lifetime, or is it a relatively more recent incident in its life?

Cosmologists have some serious reasons to believe that the expansion of the Universe <u>has not always been accelerating</u>.

...Had this expansion always accelerated, it would have dissolved those structures, <u>before they had even formed</u>.

...So, if we accept that the measurements concerning the light of supernovae are correct, the only explanation for this would be to accept that the Universe **is expanding in an accelerating manner**.»

As it was originally mentioned, the dark-matter/template corresponds to the aetheric plane, and the dark energy to the astral plane. The first 'flash' of the camera shines, when the Big Bang manifests the material universe. This, at its initial stages, exhibits an intense exuberance (as physicists call it) with the appearance of expansion.

This period, metaphysically, corresponds to the building of the material creation, where the astral force (dark energy) expands so much as to form the visible universe (their kitchen garden). At some point though, and while expansion seemed to be reduced to the minimum, the visible universe —already formed— started expanding again with geometrical progress, without scientists being able to know the cause till now. This fact, metaphysically, corresponds to the expansion of the astral world, which isn't naturally limited to mindless natural powers, but contains intelligent entities, which expand their astral world at great speeds.

As all evidence shows, this expansion coincides with the appearance of INTELLIGENT BEINGS (men), —where else...? On Earth!— who form THOUGHTFORMS, thus <u>multiplying</u> this astral society. In reality, the <u>truly</u> material universe corresponds to this astral (energy-) society of the 73%, and not to what we people imagine, the 4% dense material universe. This small densely material percentage is nothing more than the area of their 'food' production.

Don't skip chapters or bibliographic references

This expansion is solely due to man's creation of thoughtforms, which started to flood and conquer the astral energy-planes. 'Sin' makes its appearance with the manifestation of **living** 'temptations' endlessly demanding nutrition.

---

377 A) **BOOK OF ENOCH, 15**: «§8. Now the giants, born <u>by the coherence of spirit and flesh</u>, shall be called on earth evil spirits, and on earth shall be their habitation. **Evil spirits <u>shall proceed</u> from their flesh** *(energy expansion of dark matter)*; because they were created from above and they were born from the holy Watchers from whom they have their beginning and primary foundation; they shall be evil spirits on earth, and evil spirits shall they be called. As for the spirits of heaven, in heaven shall be their dwelling, but as for the spirits of the earth which were born upon the earth, on the earth shall be their dwelling. §9. The spirits of the giants, the Napheleim (Nephilim) [*Anc. Gr. original text*] shall bring all sorts of inflictions (scourge) to earth, cholera, war, famine and lamentation. §10. They will neither eat food nor drink, <u>invisible to the sight</u> *(they are the astral beings)* and they will rise even against men and women, for they have received life from them.»

B) **HERMES TRISMEGISTUS**, HERMETIC TEXTS, VOL. I, RODAKIS P., TZAFEROPOULOS AP., SPEECH XVI: «§14. All of these *(daemons)* have been allotted the authority over things and turmoil upon the Earth and it is they who bring about all kinds of unrest in social groups and cities (states) and nations and for each individual separately.»

The 'food' they demanded was solely in the form of energy; a combination of material passions, soul-destroying dark thoughts, pain and mainly blood. Blood was and still is the primary source of power for them.

---

378 A) *Let's not forget the vampires' love for blood in our folk legends…*

B) **BARBARA MARCINIAK 'GAIA'** [Gr. trans. MATZOROU E.] (p. 137):

«Your blood is full of stories. It contains plenty of geometrical models and patterns which are rearranged on their own, depending on your level of consciousness and your intentions. …A lot of women flout/disdain their menstrual blood. …The menstrual blood can be used to nourish the flora *(plants)*, to mark the land and make it known to Gaia that the goddess *(snake)* is alive again. This constituted a direct transfer of the goddess's energy. Gaia is fed when women leave their menstrual blood to her. …Your blood is one of the top fertilization and territorial marking agents. …You can mark the area you inhabit[1]. …You can start with the four points of the horizon[1]. …You can dilute your blood in water increasing its quantity… the blood will give vitality to the plants and the animals. …In a lot of ancient

---

tales the blood was used for the deterrence of the evil[2]. ...Sometimes a door was marked with menstrual blood. No one dared touch the door or the people who lived behind it.[2]»

[1] **OLD TESTAMENT, EXODUS CH. 29** *(Jehovah's instructions to Moses):*
«§16. And you shall slay the ram and you shall take his blood, and sprinkle it **roundabout** upon the altar.»

[2] *When the Israelites were in Egypt under the rule of Pharaoh, Jehovah advises them to mark their doors with the blood of a one-year-old lamb, in order to protect them from the misfortunes he was preparing for the Egyptians:*

OLD TESTAMENT, EXODUS CH. 12: «§13. The blood shall be a sign for you on the houses where you are; and when I see the blood, I will pass over you, and no plague will befall you to destroy you.»

Let's not confuse the concepts, when Jesus says: «Drink of it all of you, for this is my blood ... which is shed for many, for the remission of sins.» [MATTHEW 25:28] *He doesn't perform a magic ritual, as some are pleased to fancy. Instead, He offers Himself as a Sacrifice so that His blood* **will satisfy** *(satiate) the archons (rulers) of this world, on the condition that, once they are satisfied and have quenched their thirst with the Savior's blood, they will allow the liberation of the Celestial Men who will reap the fruits of redemption.* «...which is shed for many for the remission of sins.»
And as a confirmation I quote:

THE GOSPEL OF MATTHEW, CH. 20: «§28. As the Son of man, came not to be served but to serve and to give His life as **ransom** for many.»

This combination of 'food' offered them all the required 'nutritional elements' so as to allow them to stay alive on one hand and expand on the other.

The creators' higher-ranking team realizes that the new creation, man incarnate, does not produce the anticipated energy 'food' but another one of a different constitution, since creation in the densely material-plane **was an innovation** with side-effects UNKNOWN even to them.

[379] **THE GOSPEL OF TRUTH, THE NAG HAMMADI LIBRARY**: «§39. The deficiency of matter did not originate through the Infinity of the Father ... although **no one could predict** that the Incorruptible would come this way.»

Man is now cut off, 'caught between the Scylla and the Charibdes' and becomes the 'Apple of Discord' (Gr. Eris) as he is a shared '**meal**' between the creators and the skeptomorphic society.

Don't skip chapters or bibliographic references

---

380 **BARBARA MARCINIAK 'GAIA'** [Gr. trans. MATZOROU E.] (p. 35):
«In this universe, some believe men to be priceless, even though you truly <u>have no idea</u> about the treasure that lies hidden inside the human body *(as life-giving energy-nutrition!!)*. …You are priceless. …We don't want to lose you *(funny thing!! …Who would, after all, want to starve to death!!)* You are the key *(…to the cellar)* for us.»

In the negative part of the wavelike energy-oscillation, the creators' lower ranks merge with the lower thoughtforms and form the dark daemons. 'Evil' in the sense man understands it today, is dynamically starting to form. The positive side of the creators, contaminated too by the septic mud/matter of the **counterfeit** 'positive' thoughtforms which surround it, ceases to be immaculate and transforms the 'all benevolent god' to a 'ruthless avenging deity'. Threats, curses, punishments, exhortations and promises are fired away by the 'all benevolent god' towards men, so that they will produce –like good slaves– the prescribed 'positive' nutrition for the almighty. The 'sap of the pain of self-sacrifice' is the greatest offering to the lord. The more painful discipline and obedience to the orders are, the more worthy they are considered. Ordeals and fidelity tests provide the long-desired 'branding' of the obedient 'good' bondservant, who **awaits** his payment in the 2nd virtual paradise. An equivalent 'cocktail' is unleashed from the negative forces, bearing the heavy toll of offering the soul itself as **'prey'** to its 'creditors'. Both sides have the stamp of duality. Every stand is comprised by both opposing poles of provisions and demands. Pain and pleasure are each a combination of both poles but in different compositions.

Men's energy-offspring, those born from the Spirit/'Uranus' and the flesh/'Gaia' are frightful to behold: They are the Giants of the Old Testament, the Titans of Greek Mythology and the Nephelims of the Jewish tradition. Having acquired life from the energy-matter of the astral bodies of men who gave birth to them, they also possess the equivalent shapes/forms of the animals that had been formulated from the **same** energy-layers, which were, after all, originally used to create men's energy-bodies. These astral/energy-layers, the carcasses of previous creations, were **common** to the vitalization of material animals, and also to the creation of the astral/energy-bodies that dressed up man.

---

381 **A)** *It is in these peculiarities of the astral bodies of men, that the roots of Totem worshiping can be traced, where a certain animal species shared a mystical kinship with a person whom it protected as well. This is why many ancient tribes (e.g. American Indians) had animal names and identified themselves with the powers of these animals.*
B) *See chapter* 'THE DENSELY MATERIAL PLANE'

Thus, the **appearance** of these skeptomorphs had the corresponding form of various animals.

They thus formed bi-natured creatures: Man-goats *(e.g. Satires, Pan, the Assyro-Babylonian god Ea who was also the Ram of Eridu, god Amun often in the form of a ram, Kneph, Arfat etc.)*, man-birds *(e.g. the Egyptian god Ra with the head of a hawk)*, man-bulls *(e.g. Enlil, often as a bull)*, man-jackals *(e.g. the Egyptian god Anubis and sometimes Thoth)*, man-crocodiles *(e.g. god Sobek with a crocodile head)*, men in various animal combinations *(e.g. the so called Typhonian animal Seth, even the well-known Sphinx with its proper name: Re Harmachis [Horus])*, man-wolves *(e.g. werewolves)*, man-horses *(e.g. the Centaurs)*, man-snakes *(e.g. Cecrops)*, elephant-men *(e.g. god Ganesha of the Hindus, with a body of a dwarf and an elephant head)*, not to mention mermaids and tritons *(e.g. the Philistine god of the sea Dagon, half man, half fish)*, as well as entirely human-formed ones.

---

382 **A)** *In the mythologies of the peoples, there appear a lot of gods, having animal forms.*[1] *The same gods sometimes appear with the body and form of a man, and sometimes with the form of an animal. This diverse (twofold) representation of mythical gods is apparent throughout the World Mythology.* [FELIX GUIRAND, 'WORLD MYTHOLOGY', Gr. tr. TETENES N.]

[1] *A reminder from John's Apocryphon:* «Elohim has a bear's face. Yahweh has a cat's face.»

Having the creators themselves been contaminated by the skeptomorphic creations of humans, they too appear in animal forms quite often. Let us thus not forget the story of Leto [Lětő, Gr. Λητώ] giving birth to Apollo:

B) PIERRE GRIMAL 'DICTIONARY OF GREEK AND CLASSICAL MYTHOLOGY':

«Leto (Lětő): …They still narrate about Leto, that in order to escape Hera's rage, she assumed the shape of a she-wolf and left the land of the Hyperboreans, where she actually lived. That explains the strange epithet Λυκο-γενής 'Luco-genes' (wolf-born) which sometimes is attributed to Apollo.»

This explains the origin of the name 'Lycaios' [Gr. Λύκαιος] as an attribute of Apollo, the god of light, since, of course, his light is the downgraded twilight [lyco+phos=wolf+light=twilight].

C) PANTELIS GIANNOULAKIS – LUKAS KAVAKOPOULOS 'THE TRUTH ABOUT UFO'S AND THE EXTRATERRESTRIAL CONSPIRACIES, ADDENDUM II, A CONVERSATION WITH WHITLEY STRIEBER

«I believe that what we look for, when we study the UFO phenomenon, could actually be, in effect, a modern tradition. These extraterrestrial beings have the same effect on us nowadays, as ancient gods did on past societies. I suppose that those people actually did see all those gods, and they really had with them the relationships they have described to us. In fact, we are not faced with some mythological dreams but with an attempt to interpret that level of their reality which was of great importance to their soul.»

Don't skip chapters or bibliographic references

The tragedy does not end here. An additional element exists, which is very hard to 'digest' for human logic. This army of born thoughtforms (skeptomorphs) had the power to materialize and de-materialize their hypostases. This could be achieved through condensation and de-condensation of their energy.

---

383 **A) 'SUPERMUNDANE' BOOK I** (AGNI YOGA SOCIETY) 1938 *(information through channeling):* «§5. Urusvati has seen us <u>in both</u> **the dense and the subtle bodies.**»

B) JOHN'S APOCALYPSE 17: «§8…when they see the beast *(of the Abyss),* because <u>it once was,</u> <u>now is not</u> and yet <u>it will come.</u>»
The excerpt is logically connected to the following…

C) BOOK OF ENOCH, 15:8, 10 «They *(the giants/Nephelims)* will be called <u>evil</u> spirits on earth… They will neither eat food nor drink, <u>invisible to the sight</u>[1] *(existing though!!).*»

[1] **P. GIANNOULAKIS, L. KAVAKOPOULOS 'THE TRUTH ABOUT UFO'S AND EXTRATERRESTRIAL CONSPIRACIES', APPENDIX III, BILL COOPER:**
«…They *(the extraterrestrials)* have the technological means to cover themselves in an invisibility-veil and become <u>invisible.</u>»

This knowledge was and <u>still</u> is in their possession today, and they still make use of it.

---

384 **PANTELIS GIANNOULAKIS – LUKAS KAVAKOPOULOS 'THE TRUTH ABOUT UFO'S AND THE EXTRATERRESTRIAL CONSPIRACIES, ADDENDUM II, A CONVERSATION WITH WHITLEY STRIEBER:**
«When the lady touched the 'visitor' she thought it was an animal that had entered the room. Then the creature went to another room where some other people saw it transforming into 'something' that had an eagle's head, reminiscent of all those mythological models that exist deep within. Next, the creature disappeared into thin air. When we went out looking for it, we saw a hooded silver and semi-transparent being, flying from one side of the house to the woods and vanish with zigzags in the trees. So, it couldn't have been a ghost. The witnesses, who saw it in the eagle form, felt a heat wave to the point of thinking that the house was on fire. …So, there were a lot of witnesses claiming they had seen a creature and not a craft. …A being having three or rather four states. The first one was absolutely physical, you could touch it, it had substance. The second state was when it transformed into something completely different in front of the witnesses' eyes. After that, it became invisible and in its fourth state, it moved in a semi-transparent shape, leaving heat waves behind *(…waves of hell).* …My experience taught me that (the extraterrestrial beings, the visitors) are deeply related to the human state *(thoughtforms).* They are not remnants of non-consciousness, but something that transcends what we call consciousness. <u>The human brain seems to somehow work at a supernatural and hyperdimensional level.</u>»

Quite often these entities, in their fierce claim for food, materialized to devour even the material bodies of men, enriching their energy-nutrition with blood. It was the time when they were all still visible to everybody.

---

385 **A) THE BOOK OF ENOCH, CH.7**: «§12…Whose *(giants/Nephelims)* stature was each three hundred cubits: They devoured all which the labors of men produced; and men could no longer feed them. §13. Then, the giants turned against men to **devour them**. §14. And they began to attack birds, and beasts, and reptiles, and fishes, to eat their flesh one after the other, and to drink their blood. §15. Then the earth was severely tried by the evil ones.»

B) *PAN: a daemon in a Billy-goat's body and a man's head, with twisted horns. Sometimes he committed improprieties and sometimes he devoured his victims, causing pan-ic…*

In order for men to save themselves from the woes that these daemons inflicted upon them, they started worshiping them; and to silence their fury, they started offering them sacrifices. Henceforth, men, besieged by both opponent camps, are forced to worship gods and daemons who, in order to enjoy ever greater portions of the energy of humans, either threaten or entice them accordingly.

---

386 **A) GOSPEL OF PHILIP** [Eng. tr. PATERSON BROWN] www.metalog.org/files/philip.html

«§54. God is a cannibal. Because of this, mankind is sacrificed to it. Before mankind was sacrificed, animals were being sacrificed. For these to which they are sacrificed are not divinities.»

B) THE EPIC OF GILGAMESH (ASSYRO-BABYLONIAN):

Utnapishtim (equivalent to Noah) is sacrificing to the gods after the flood:

«Then, I made a sacrifice. I offered a libation on the top of the mountain. Seven and seven vessels I put in place, and into the bowls I gathered timber, reeds, cedar and myrtle. **When the gods smelled the sweet savor, they gathered like flies over the sacrifice.**»

C) OLD TESTAMENT, GENESIS CH. 8: «§20. Then Noah built an altar to the lord, and took of every clean animal and of every clean bird, and offered burnt-offerings on the altar. §21. **And the lord smelled the pleasing aroma**. And the lord said in his heart, "I will never again curse the earth because of man.»

A side-effect of this double-sided claim for human energy is the beginning of the eternal battle between good and evil.

Don't skip chapters or bibliographic references

---

387 **'SUPERMUNDANE' BOOK I** (AGNI YOGA SOCIETY) 1938 *(information through channeling)*:
«§136. We are invulnerable to human weapons, yet can suffer injuries from the hierophants of the dark forces, whose ruinous attacks fill space. Such invisible battles are not fairy tales. It is one thing to send a Ray from the Tower, but it is an entirely different thing to fly to participate in the right-eous battle in space.»

Not once did it cross man's mind that this endless conflict between the two sides had the sole purpose **of exploiting** the 'positive' or 'negative' energy produced by **him-self**! Poor man! In addition to the weight of his matter, he is simultaneously 'lashed down' by his two overlords who claim their portion of energy from him. Corruption permeates everybody, right up to the last man. Abjection sinks Earth into obliteration. In order for the insatiable skeptomorphic beings to be constantly supplied, men are forced to activate their most perverse emotions. In this turmoil, a group of the creators, realizing the gravest danger threatening them from the skeptomorphic force, decides to intervene.

---

388 **BOOK OF ENOCH, 9:1-2** (http://reluctant-messenger.com/1enoch01-60.htm)
«§1. Then Michael and Gabriel, Raphael, Suryal, and Uriel, looked down from heaven, and saw the quantity of blood which was shed on earth, and all the iniquity which was done upon it, and said one to another, It is the voice of their cries §2. The earth deprived of her children has cried even to the gate of heaven.»

They pinpoint the problem inside man's bodies, which have a peculiarity: <u>united with the life-making Spirit they give birth to powerful living energy-beings</u>. The plan is then set in motion.
The first move is to completely stop the reproductive process of the Uranus/Spirit, whose union with Earth/matter generates monsters. As a solution, the creation of a new different race of men with limited spiritual abilities is chosen.
Greek mythology symbolizes the event of Uranus's (Spirit) reproductive end with his 'castration' by his **Titan** son Kronos. It is not a coincidence that the 'castration' of Uranus is carried out by one of his Titan sons.
De-symbolizing the myth, it becomes apparent that this **very** incarnation of Man inside dense, visible matter, forced his Spiritual thought –in order to manifest– to pass through the septic mud/matter of his new body. The resulting side-effect was the birth of negative skeptomorphs on one hand and counterfeit (degraded) 'positive' skeptomorphs on the other. These skepto-morphs **degraded** the up-till-then Spiritual Man to the 'thinking animal'

level, with Earth/matter dominating alone without her companion Uranus/Spirit.

As a second move it was decided to control the skeptomorphic powers, to keep them contained. This decision signals the beginning of the Clash of the Titans. The camps are divided. The opposing sides begin fighting.

> **389** **HESIOD 'THEOGONY'**, (verses 636-639): «So they, with bitter wrath, were fighting continually with one another at that time for ten full years, and the hard strife had no close or end for either side, and the issue of the war hung evenly balanced.» [TRANSLATED BY HUGH G. EVELYN-WHITE]

The cause? **Man and the management of the energy produced by him;** the results? Devastating and even further degrading for both rival sides, since **the very process** of any battle automatically degrades and equates the positive with the negative side, because they both enter the realm of opposition, egotistic arrogance, conspiracy, revenge and slaughter.

> **390** **THE GOSPEL OF MATTHEW, CH. 5** *The advice of Jesus is the following:*
> «§38. You have heard that it was said, "An eye for an eye and a tooth for a tooth" *(The law of Karma and reciprocal justice of this world).* §39 But I tell you <u>not to resist an evil person</u>. But whoever slaps you on your right cheek, turn the other to him also.»

–*"And what should be done...? Should they leave the enraged astral offspring to devour everything...?"* I intervened.
–One evil thing is followed by multitudes of others... and evil started with the creators' initial **persistence** to build an entire creation on **waste!**
The climax of the war comes when the clans of the creators are torn by the dilemma of whether the man-creature should remain in existence or forever perish. There were two different views: one side considers it wise to abandon this creation and return to the Sacred Primary Capital/BirthLand 'with their heads bowed in submission'. The opposite view insists that the doors of the Sacred Capital City are shut for them all, and as they have no other choice, their salvation should concentrate on man.
The decision is made in favor of returning to the Capital Principle and the eradication of this generation.

> **391** **OLD TESTAMENT, GENESIS CH. 6**: «§6. And the Lord regretted that he had made man on the earth, and it grieved him in his heart. §7. So the Lord said: I will destroy man whom I have created, from the face of the earth ... for I am sorry (I repent) that I have made them.»

Don't skip chapters or bibliographic references

Cunning however is synonymous to the nature of your creators, so the 'chosen' of the race of men are <u>secretly</u> informed of the coming catastrophe and prepare accordingly.

---

392 Noah (Jews), Deucalion (Greeks), Utnapishtim (Assyrians), Satyavrata (Hindus) etc.

A) OLD TESTAMENT, GENESIS CH. 6:

«§8. But Noah found grace in the eyes of the Lord.»

B) 'MYSTERIES OF THE WORLD', VOL. 'MYSTERIES OF THE EAST'

«MYTHS ABOUT THE GREAT FLOOD: Vishnu commanded wise Satyavrata to collect herbs, seeds and animals and gather the seven Rishis (wise men) around him. When the great cataclysm started on Earth and the seas swelled and threatened to flood everything, the Rishis *(the chosen ones)* came aboard a boat along with their animals, seeds and plants. With the help of the snake-king Vasuki the boat was placed firmly on Matsya *(Vishnu, half-man half-fish)* and the god in the form of fish dragged it into the night of Brahma *(=Pralaya)* thus saving humanity from the great flood.»

According to Brahmanism, the period of the great flood probably corresponds to the 3rd brief Pralaya (dissolution) of the Maha-Yuga and its preparation to exit the previous phase of Dwapara-Yuga and enter our contemporary Kali-Yuga which coincides with the Iron Race.

Next comes the destruction of this gender of material-men with a cataclysm, aiming to collect the Divine Sparks and the Breath/Souls for repatriation.

---

393 **'THE EPIC OF GILGAMESH, THE FLOOD' NEAR EAST TEXTS** [GR. TR. XENI & SOCRATES SKARTSI]

From the narration of Utnapishtim (corresponding to Noah) to Gilgamesh:

«Just as dawn began to glow there arose from the horizon a black cloud. The cloud rumbled, as Adad, the master of the storm, rode in it. Ahead of him and over the hills and the valleys, there went Shullat and Hanish, the heralds of the storm. Then rose the gods of abyss. Nergal pulled out the dams of the waters below, Ninurta, the master of war, tore down the dikes. The Anunnaki –the seven judges of hell– lifted up their torches, illuminating the land with their powerful flame. Stunned shock overtook the heavens, when the god of the storm turned into blackness all that had been light, and shattered the land like a clay-pot. All day long the storm raged, stronger and stronger, overwhelming the people like waves of warriors. No one could see his fellow nor could the gods from heaven discern the people below. Even the gods were frightened by the Flood, and retreated, ascending to the highest firmament of Anu; The gods were cowering like stray dogs, crouching by the wall. Then Ishtar, the sweet-voiced queen of the heavens, shrieked like a woman in labor, and wailed: "The old days have alas turned into dust, because I commanded this evil! How could I suggest such evil things in the

---

Assembly of the Gods? I ordered wars to destroy the folk, yet aren't they my people, since I bore them? Now they fill the sea like the eggs of the fish!" The almighty gods of **heaven** and **hell** were weeping with her and covered their faces with their hands.
For six days and six nights came the winds, torrent, storm and deluge drowning the world, the flood and the storm raging like vicious hordes at war. When the seventh day arrived, the storm started to fade away from the south, the sea calmed, the deluge stopped. I looked around at the surface of the earth –quiet had set in and all humanity had turned to mud!»

By the end of the cataclysm most of the creators –those who were in favor of returning to the Holy Birthplace– realize they had been deceived since the chosen ones (Divine Sparks) had been saved from the flood. At this point, a great conflict between the orders of the gods/creators begins. This adversity manifests through the quarrels between gods, evident in various descriptions of different mythologies. As we will discover, it intensifies at the beginning of the Iron Race. The gods also drag their subordinate nations into their own quarrels to fight against the nations of enemy gods, thus cultivating racial discord and strife.

Under the newly formed conditions, they all yield to the decision to set common terms/rules between them, and mutual rights and obligations. The foundations of the Karmic process are set in order to even out the balance of energy distribution without further deception.

[394] **A) PAPASTAVROU, A., 'LETTERS TO ANONYMOUS'** (p 226):
«It is true that the first Lords of Karma, before the fall of man, had been appointed solely as a governing body, in order to supervise that all Root-Races and sub-Races incarnate on the assigned time and not to offer judgment of any kind. When the astral world was created by the human *(skeptomorphic)* disharmony, the Karmic committee was increased **to seven members**, in order to restore the disharmony of the Race.»
B) NEAR EAST TEXTS [GR. TR. XENI & SOCRATES SKARTSIS] **'THE EPIC OF GILGAMESH'**
«...The Anunnaki –**the seven judges of hell**– lifted up their torches, illuminating the land with their powerful flame.»

The Karmic Committee is comprised of representatives of all clans. The fundamental rule of the new, transformed creation: materialization in front of humans would henceforth be <u>utterly prohibited</u>. Hence the entire (visible and invisible) universe is divided. The problematic skeptomorphic powers which had caused these great inflictions are restrained:
(1) Into the lower astral (energy) regions.
(2) Into the inner hollows of the Earth, the 'Tartara', and the 'Abyss' which are, as far as visible Earth is concerned, **the only places** where they are allowed to materialize.

Don't skip chapters or bibliographic references

395 **A) HESIOD 'THEOGONY'** [Gr. tr. STAVROS GIRGENIS]: (verses 720 -737)

«…And the Titans were exiled **to the underworld with the wide roads** and they were held with mighty chains, after they had been conquered by their strength *(Cottus and Briareus and Gyes)*, despite their great courage *(of the Titans')*. And they bound them so deeply beneath the earth, as counts the distance between the earth and the sky. For so far is it from earth to hazy Tartarus. A brazen anvil falling down from the sky would take nine nights and days to finally reach the earth upon the tenth day. Round the Tartarus runs a fence of bronze, and night spreads threefold all around it (around its throat), while above *(above the subterranean Tartarus)* grow the roots of the earth and the un-harvested sea…And they *(the Titans)* may not go out; for Poseidon fixed gates of bronze upon them, and a wall runs all round them on both sides.]

Also: (verses 621 -624) …and he made them live beneath earth with the wide paths, where they were afflicted, being set to dwell under the ground, at the end of the great earth, in bitter anguish for a long time and with great grief in the heart.»

B) *As an introduction, I think it's important to quote some 'particular' facts, obviously unknown to some. To begin with, here is an excerpt from the book 'Hollow Earth' by researcher Pantelis Giannoulakis, which is quite informative:*

GIANNOULAKIS P., 'HOLLOW EARTH'

«We have to start dealing with this topic by giving some general information on the world-theory *(Weltanschauung)* that exists behind all this, for those who aren't acquainted with matters like these. In a nutshell, according to the alternative cosmic-theory we are studying, the Earth is hollow and in the middle there is an internal sun *(god Pluto)*. In the underground terrain there are labyrinth-like gallery-networks and huge open spaces that host underground countries, to which there is access through galleries from the surface world. These countries do not differ much from the ones on the surface of the Earth.

(The dimensions of Earth, given by the supporters of the Hollow Earth theory, are: External radius of the Earth: 6,400 kilometers. Thickness, in which, there is the lava of the volcanoes and various rock layers, 2,560 kilometers. In this part there are underground tunnels and galleries that connect the 72 external gateways with the 72 internal ones, thus connecting the external with the internal part of the Earth. The internal radius of the Hollow Earth is 3,840 kilometers. There are circular openings at the two poles of the Earth, the North and the South, with a diameter of 1,400 miles (2,253 kilometers), where the Earth curves evenly and someone can find himself in the internal part, without realizing it. It is through these two huge openings that the external air comes into the internal hollow of the Earth.)

…Many tribes of beings –a whole secret inner biology of the planet– live in these *(underground)* countries. Among them *(as guardians of the negative astrals),* the Vril-Ya (or Magog or Nephelim) –the ones that are very often found behind the legends about angels and 'divine creatures' in the mythologies and religions of the Earth– having an 'open communication' with other worlds *(the astro-aetheric ones),* the Elves (or Eldila or Sehe or Buldus or Hobs or Fairies etc.), who can also be found behind the legends of the Elves, the Fairies etc., the dwarf tribes (Nibelungen, Gnomes, Dwarfs, Dristel, Nanioi). The Lloigors (or Gores or Sataniels or Titans or Dragons or Set-ya or Savrites or Dark Elfen or Draw Elves etc.) are a superior tribe of enigmatic beings that have come from 'somewhere else' and were 'reduced' to living there in degradation. They dominate over all the other ones and they fight against the Vril and the extra-cosmic *(astral)* beings and they have set their eyes on the domination of the planet. They are daemonic beings of astounding capabilities who 'construct' other entities too, through biological experiments, in order to be served by them. The Deros (or Gog or Ganza or Kanjar or Kalikantzari or Greys or Satires or Goblins or Trolls etc.) are in the service of the Lloigors, along with other biological mutants, who appear to include in their species the Teros, the Telchines and others.

…From all these, the Lloigors and some kinds of the Elves (Eldilas) have no specific material substance *(hypostasis),* or they at least have the ability to dematerialize and materialize wherever they want and change shape (Shape-Shifters) as well. The former classifications are too simplistic and circumstantial; and are given with the possibility of some error margins.»

Mathematician Dimitrios Evangelopoulos, at the end of his book 'Hypohthonia Mysteria=[Subterranean Mysteries]', proves that the theory of Hollow Earth is absolutely valid and answers to the strenuous objections of the skeptics by means of the language of Mathematics and Physics, persuading even the most mistrustful ones.

And some new information:

THE OCEAN CURRENTS GENERATORS OF THE MAGNETIC FIELD OF EARTH

http://www.physics4u.gr/blog/?p=672 Monday, June 15th, 2009

«The Earth's magnetic field, the valuable protective shield from the solar radiation and the devastating solar storms of charged particles, is probably generated **by the ocean currents, and not the melted metals swirling in the core of the planet**, as the predominant perception of scientists has been so far. …After numerous scientific discussions and theories, in the second half of the 20th century, a consensus was finally reached, that the magnetism of our planet is created in its core. However according to Ryskin: "Although they all agreed, in fact, **there is no proof**. It's just an idea we have accepted for too long without questioning it enough.»

Don't skip chapters or bibliographic references

(3) In the astro-aetheric and densely-material surface and underground regions of the moon.

---

[396] **GERASIMOS KALOGERAKIS 'GREEKS THE SONS OF THE GODS'**
http://ellania.pblogs.gr/2008/09/ti-krybetai-sth-selhnh-mythoi-kai-apodeixeis-2o-meros.html
http://www.blackstage.gr/moon.htm

«(1) Soviet scientists Michael Vasin and Alexander Shcherbakov argued in one of their articles that the Moon is apparently hollow inside.

(2) The mission of Apollo 13, after setting off a small quantity of explosives, caused a series of harmonic tremors on the moon that lasted for 3 hours and 30 minutes. All NASA said was that: "Something strange is happening in the inner part of the Moon, since we have such a kind of harmonic vibration that we can tune our watches with."

(3) The mission of Apollo 14 also caused tremors, when the spaceship dropped its third compartment abruptly onto the lunar surface. The Moon reacted **like a huge bell**. At that point, pulsating tremors/vibrations were recorded, lasting for about three hours, and reaching depths of 28-32 kilometers. Later on, during the departure of the spaceship from the Moon, the lunar module was discarded, causing new vibrations once again, which lasted for about 90 minutes. NASA said again: "The probability of the Moon being hollow is great indeed."

(4) There are indications that, as far as seismic and volcanic activity is concerned, the Moon actually represents a dead world. Nonetheless, apart from the artificial tremors caused by man, there were tremors ascertained as deep as 800 kilometers, which didn't exceed '2' of the Richter scale. These tremors were absolutely harmonious. They recurred at regular time periods, once a month and always of the same magnitude. This phenomenon confirms the probability of the Moon being hollow indeed.

(5) The lunar crater 'Aristarchus' is the most enigmatic one and is the one most likely to have **entrances** to the inner Moon. Groups of scientists, who collaborated independently of NASA, estimate that there are more than 1,000 actual cases of light or object appearances on the lunar surface. During the 'Apollo' research program, NASA recorded more than **2,000** cases of light appearances on the lunar surface. They also noticed a huge black object, of a length of 250,000 meters *(!!)* and 50,000 meters wide *(!!)*, flying over the moon. Dr. Morris Ketchum Jessup, an astrophysicist at the University of Michigan, stated just before he died: "All these 'lights' are directed by logical beings serving an ulterior goal, unknown to us."

Apart from this, there are also some other bizarre accounts about the Moon!
(6) At the end of the 1930's, Grote Reber, of Bell Labs, 'captured' some **ra-**

---

dio messages from the Moon. Besides him, several amateur astronomers in 1927, 1928 and 1934, got signals from the Moon, with their own radio telescopes. In 1935, Marconi and Tesla recorded similar signals, as well. In 1956, scientists of the University of Ohio stated that they had received a kind of encoded signal, coming from the Moon.»

The 'Energy Measurement and Distribution (delivery) sector' –a department of the Karmic Committee– as well as **the first collection station** for human Souls (after their physical death) would be created <u>THERE</u>. *(In the moon)*

(4) In pre-designated planets of the visible universe as their 'bases' in the material plane. Since then they have been visiting Earth using these planets as starting points, declaring they are their inhabitants and introducing them-selves as 'aliens'.

The creators, as winners, and having more privileges, asserted the best positions for their 'bases'.

[397] **HESIOD 'THEOGONY'** (verses 884-890): «But when the blessed gods had finished the war, and won powers/dignities by force from the Titans, they prompted far-thundering Olympian Zeus –by Earth's advice– to reign and to rule over the immortals. So he distributed dignities/offices to them.»

The positive forces however, stationed teams of guardians near all the territories of the problematic astral beings to control them.

[398] **HESIOD 'THEOGONY'** (verses 720 -737): «And the Titans were exiled to the underworld with the wide paths and they were held with mighty chains. And they *(the Titans)* may not go out; for Poseidon fixed gates of bronze upon them and a wall runs all round them on both sides. There Gyes and Cottus and great-souled Briareus (Obriareus) live, trusty **warders** of Zeus who holds the Aegis.»

According to the new conditions, a new generation of men had to be created, which would evenly supply the entire energy-dynasty without the illicit interventions of their masters. In everyone's interest, they all consent to keep this new generation of men completely detached from the truth, so that the uninformed man would produce either a positive or a negative load of energy (as nutrition), for whichever 'lord' he chooses, completely uninfluenced. The safeguarding of these new terms is affirmed with the new law of the so-called 'free will' (of man), who is to be solely confined to this freedom of choice (for positive or negative action), since he has no other possibility to interfere apart from that. The new body had to be stripped of all characteristics of spiritual insight on the one hand –because it should under

Don't skip chapters or bibliographic references

no circumstances 'see' those entities that could influence him in various ways– and lose many of these spiritual powers/abilities on the other, which after all had caused so much destruction!

So a new body was about to be created, keeping the previous one only as a 'foundation'. The important modifications would be carried out mainly to the energy-bodies of man, but some additional gene-alterations made the presence of creators in the material plane imperative. It is these periods in human history, from which archeological findings reveal the existence of strange creatures wandering the Earth. These creatures were then called gods while today, contemporary researchers label them 'aliens' indiscriminately.

The foundations of the Iron Race are established, with the creation of a man ignorant of the reason he shall live, die and suffer; a man utterly incapable of even suspecting his real identity, so as to always come to conclusions void of any elementary common sense, and ultimately a man who considers his creation as purely coincidental!

---

399 **(A) THE APOCRYPHON OF JOHN, THE GNOSTIC SOCIETY LIBRARY**
http://www.gnosis.org/naghamm/apocjn-davies.html:

«They mixed fire and earth and water together with four blazing winds. They melded them together in great turbulence. Adam was brought into the shadow of death. They intended to make him anew this time from Earth, Water, Fire, Wind, which are Matter, Darkness, Desire, The Artificial Spirit. This all became a tomb, a new kind of body *(grave)*. Those thieves bound the man in it, enchained him <u>in forgetfulness</u>, made him subject to dying.»

(B) THE APOCRYPHON OF JOHN, THE GNOSTIC SOCIETY LIBRARY

«The Chief Ruler *(Yaldabaoth)*, though, forced the humans to drink from waters of forgetfulness, <u>so that they might not know their true place of origin</u>.» [Eng. tr. from Coptic: STEVAN DAVIES]

C) THE GOSPEL OF TRUTH, NAG HAMMADI MANUSCRIPTS [PATERSON BROWN]
www.metalog.org

«§2. Now, the Gospel is the revelation of the hopeful ones, it is the finding of themselves *(their Higher Self)* by those who seek Him. For they have always searched for Him from Whom they came forth *(their Spiritual Source)* –and everything was within Him, the Inconceivable, the Incomprehensible, Him who exists beyond all thought– hence, unacquaintance with the Father caused anxiety and fear. Then the anxiety condensed like fog so that no one could see.

§3. Wherefore confusion grew strong, **contriving its matter** in emptiness and <u>**un**-acquaintance</u> with the Truth, preparing <u>**to substitute** truthfulness with a potent and **alluring fabrication**</u>. But this was no humiliation for Him, the Inconceivable, Incomprehensible One. For anxiety, amnesia and deceitful fabrication were nothing, whereas the established Truth is immutable,

---

imperturbable and of unadornable beauty.

Therefore despise confusion! It has no roots and was in a fog concerning the Father, preparing labors and amnesia and fear **in order thereby to entice** those of the transition *(the spirit-less souls)* and take them captive.

§4. The amnesia of confusion was not made as a revelation, it is not the handiwork of the Father. Forgetfulness does not occur under His directive, although it does happen because of Him *(so that men ignore Him/The Father)*

…Since amnesia occurred because the Father was not recognized, thereafter, when the Father is recognized, there will be no more forgetting…

§6. Therefore confusion was enraged at Him *(Jesus)* and pursued Him in order to suppress and eliminate Him *(because He revealed the Truth and the Father)*. He was nailed to a crossbeam, He became the fruit of recognizing the Father.

Yet it did not cause those who consumed it *(the fruit of knowing the Father)* to perish, but rather to those who consumed it, He bestowed a rejoicing at such a discovery. For He *(Jesus)* found them *(those who were seeking)* in Himself and they *(who were seeking)* found Him *(Jesus)* in themselves.»

After all, the fruit of Epi-gnosis of good and evil was and still is forbidden! Man today, totally integrated with the 'unnatural', considers this ignorance normal and sinks even deeper into the lethargy of his daily life.

THE IRON RACE

---

400 **HESIOD 'WORKS AND DAYS'** (verses 172-178): «And again Zeus made yet another *(fifth)* generation of mortal men; from them the present ones have come... For now truly is the race of iron. And they will never rest from labor and sorrow by day, and distress by night, and sore troubles the gods shall lay upon them.»

It is now the turn of the inferior gods/creators of races and nationalities: Their purpose is to insert new genes in the existing DNA of the men who were saved from the cataclysm.

---

401 **BLAVATSKY H., P., 'THE SECRET DOCTRINE'** (II-519):
«After the Flood of Deucalion, Zeus, had commanded Prometheus and Athena <u>to call forth a new race of men</u> from the mire left by the waters of the deluge [Ovid, Metam. 1, 81. Etym. M. v. [Prometheus]; and in the day of Pausanias the slime which the hero (Prometheus) had used for this purpose was still shown in Phokida. [Pausanias, X, IV, 4]
"On several archaic monuments one still sees Prometheus modeling a human body, either alone or with Athena's help." [Decharme, Myth. Grece Ant. p. 246]»

These new genes would gradually reprogram man's entire cellular structure in the long run, thus creating the Iron Race and depriving man from any possibility of communicating with the Spirit.

---

402 **BARBARA MARCINIAK 'GAIA'** [Gr. trans. MATZOROU E.] *(Information through channeling):*
«There is a tyranny left to rule Gaia, and this tyranny has now come back to us. You know that it was us who exerted this tyranny that deprived you of the inheritance of the complete twelve-helix DNA.» *...and they transformed it to a double-helix.*

Yet again, an additional fall succeeds the previous one. The whole venture of material creation, from stage to stage, 'tumbles' lower and lower and sinks deeper into the vortex of dense matter. Gravity crushes every trace of Spirit, like a black hole devouring light.

---

403 *A reminder:* Veneziano, Gabriele (CERN Physicist): «Our Universe is but a small piece inside a black hole; terrifying indeed, if you think about it.» [SOURCE: NEWGEN January 2000]

Like a voracious spider, this 'monster' men describe with such charming eloquence as the material universe, traps every being inside its energy-brane, sucking them dry of their very last trace of Spiritual life.

> [404] **M-BRANES AND THE DREAMS FOR UNIFICATION**
> http://www.physics4u.gr/articles/2007/M-branes.html
> SOURCE: The Elegant Universe of Brian Greene, July 2007, Cambridge webpage on 'Hyper-strings', Scientific American
> «BRANE: …Ordinary matter is **attached** to this brane. The usual particles like electrons and protons can <u>only</u> exist on this brane. We humans will not be able to enter other dimensions because the particles that form our bodies …remain **attached** to this brane that constitutes our world.»

It would therefore be just a matter of time for the deprivation of man's every transcendental sensation to be accomplished. After all, the spirit – matter combination had wreaked havoc. Additional changes had to be made on every level. On the material plane, creators are segregated into teams who split the Earth into zones of influence. Every team of creators would create a human race of their own, ornamenting it with the 'materials' their land possessed. By putting their personal touches on their creation, i.e. man, they would produce the diversity of all nations on Earth.

> [405] **A) PLATO'S 'CRITIAS'** (109b):
> «At some time in the past, the gods had the whole earth distributed among them by allotment. There was no quarrelling; for you cannot rightly suppose that the gods did not know what was proper for each of them to have, or, knowing this, that they would seek to procure for themselves by contention that which more properly belonged to others. So, all of them by just apportionment obtained what they wanted, and peopled their own districts and when they had peopled them they tended us, **their nurslings and possessions** as shepherds tend their flocks. (109c) …Now others of the gods had their allotments in different regions, which they ornamented.» [Eng. tr. BENJAMIN JOWETT]
>
> **B) BARBARA MARCINIAK 'GAIA'** [Gr. trans. MATZOROU E.] (p. 117):
> «The gods were changing their names and creating new sounds as they moved from one continent to the other, modifying Gaia's biogenetic life, and participated in it along with their creations.»

Henceforth <u>they would all</u> draw their power and energy-nutrition from their creations.

> [406] **ENUMA ELISH: 'THE ASSYRO-BABYLONIAN EPIC OF CREATION'** «§130. The people he had brought forth, endowed with life, he appointed to the service of the gods, so that they *(gods)* may live in comfort.»

Don't skip chapters or bibliographic references

Mythologies of the world talk about sexual intercourse between the gods and the mortal females of that era. The creators, under the influence of dense matter, exhibit symptoms of corruption which contemporary researchers try to justify as 'symbols'. But they do not take into consideration that myths, when decoded at the **lowest** levels, end up manifesting almost <u>unaltered</u>. Because of this, the creators, interwoven with the positive and negative energies they were supplied with, shifted their appearance/form accordingly and with their ability to materialize, they frequently appeared in the material plane as gods overtaken by human weaknesses. Their goal was to insert the new modified genes into the 'daughters of men' *(lower level of de-symbolization of Enoch's code).*

---

407 A) THE APOCRYPHON OF JOHN, THE GNOSTIC SOCIETY LIBRARY:

«Yaldabaoth raped Eve. She bore two sons.»

The symbols of the myths manifest in all levels, even in the densely material, like a fractal which unfolds repeating itself. It is on this peculiarity that any potential arguments among the researchers are focused, since each of the researchers <u>limits</u> the interpretation of the myth/symbol to one level alone.

B) PLATO'S 'TIMAEUS' XIII 40E-40E5 (Gr. tr. KOUTROUMPAS D., G.)

«And it is beyond our powers to speak of the other daemons and to know about their birth. We must believe those who spoke before and <u>were descendants of the gods,</u> as they said, even if they spoke without the probable and necessary proof. And inasmuch as they profess to speak of known family matters, we are obliged to believe them, following the established practices.»

C) PIERRE GRIMAL 'THE DICTIONARY OF HELLENIC AND ROMAN MYTHOLOGY'

«DIAS / ZEUS: The mortal women with whom Zeus had intercourse and the descendants they gave birth to: (Aegina→ Aeacus), (Alcmene→ Hercules), (Antiope→ Amphion - Zethus), (Danaë→ Perseus), (Europa→ Minos - Rhadamanthys - Sarpedon), (Electra→ Dardanus- Iasion- Harmonia), (Io→ Epaphus), (Callisto→ Arcas), (Laodamia→ Sarpedon) (Leda→ Helen - Dioscuri), (Maia→ Hermes), (Niobe→ Argus - Pelasgus), (Plouto→ Tantalus), (Semele → Dionysus), (Taygete→ Lacedaemon)».

D) *From 1998 up to the end of 2003, an 'interference' appeared in the natural as well as the 'supernatural' frequencies of humans. Its content and the way that it was manifested, literally upset a lot of people.*

This 'interference' occurred on computers of outdated technology, which were <u>NOT</u> connected to the internet. It had the form of strange codes, which, when decoded, contained logical messages. The authors of these (now decoded) messages introduced themselves as invisible 'extraterrestrial' entities with the name 'Olympians' and stated that they were the Olympian crea-

---

tors of the Greeks! Apart from the relevant web pages on the Internet, the main writer of these communications, at least the 'natural' ones, is Gerasimos Kalogerakis. At the same time with this 'natural' information, similar 'supernatural' information was communicated to some 'mediums/psychics'. The 'Olympians' mention about the specific topic, in one of their many messages:

«The caves were manned with celestial entities, known to you as demigods, and with common humans, too. They were mostly experimenting on special projects <u>for the genetic improvement of the human species</u>, with <u>stored</u> *(obviously in the arc)* celestial sperm of heroes, demigods and deities, according to your own terminology. The conditions of Mount Pelion were excellent for the preservation of the genetic material and the selected humans, who fulfilled the celestial preconditions for the deployment of the experiments. Never did any celestial entities come in physical contact with earthy humans for producing offspring, thus avoiding the creation of faulty entities. The improvement and the interbreeding were carried out experimentally, in order to keep the outcome under total control. The great emperor and sacred archon of the light, Zeus, never had intercourse with any earthy woman that would result in the birth of descendants. All the women who had allegedly been inseminated by Zeus never saw his celestial magnificence. On the contrary, they accepted his high favor to be inseminated with celestial sperm, for the creation of highly intelligent entities with supernatural powers, so as to help the project of creation concerning man. The supposed sons of Zeus, gods and demigods according to your terminology, exhibited different properties among them, depending on the role they had to fulfill. All the women were inseminated with celestial sperm, following various genetic ways, and, as is the case today with modern science, they were brought to the Pelion laboratories by us, where celestial sperm was implanted in them. *(...)*»

After the Spirit/Uranus' 'castration', Matter/Earth, having assimilated the power of her companion through her 'children', dominates the world and is equated with the inexhaustible fertility of the universal Mother/Gaia. The Iron Race is molded from her own elements (children). And while all this happens in 'heavy' matter, yet another myth –that of the Soul and Eros– symbolically narrates the course of the human Soul.

The story describes the romance of a beautiful, young girl called 'Soul' *(Gr.: Ψυχή=Psyche)* and her beloved called 'Eros'. Even though the Delphi Oracle characterizes the Soul's beloved as a 'terrible monster', the girl/Soul, overcome by her lust for the boy/Eros, searches for him and in order to be united with him, gets entangled in tormenting misfortunes. Zeus finally unites them with the bonds of marriage.

Don't skip chapters or bibliographic references

---

408 PIERRE GRIMAL 'THE DICTIONARY OF HELLENIC AND ROMAN MYTHOLOGY':
«PSYCHE/SOUL/ΨΥΧΗ: Psyche is the name of the 'Soul'. It is also the name of the heroine of a myth, which was bequeathed to us by Apuleius in his work 'The Metamorphoses'…»

In order to live with her beloved husband 'Eros', 'Psyche' abandons her father's palace and permanently moves to her husband's.

The plot of the myth is long and therefore not easy to narrate here in full. However, somebody can easily distinguish between the story lines, the entire route of the 'Psyche', even before her incarnation into the visible form, until her definitive entrapment in it.

But, as we have already mentioned, the Ancients considered Eros to be the primordial attracting force of the world; in other words like a 'sibling' to gravity. Both of these forces, which in fact are one, belong to the denser part of the energy universe –the black hole– where Psyche finally settled down, in order to meet her beloved Eros.

So, if we remember the words of Hermes Trismegistus, we will better understand what he means: «And let him who possesses Noũs, recognize himself as being immortal, and the cause of death to be Eros (erotic love).» [SPEECH I §18].

As you might guess the 'cradle' in which Psyche (the Soul) would henceforth meet her beloved Eros would be the material body of the Iron Race that –built from the septic mud/matter of the Mother/Gaia– consolidates intercourse (sex) as the 'emblem' of the perpetuation of the new world.

---

409 THE APOCRYPHON OF JOHN, THE GNOSTIC SOCIETY LIBRARY: «From then until now sexual intercourse has persisted thanks to the Chief Ruler who put desire for reproduction into the woman who accompanies Adam. Through intercourse, the Ruler caused new human bodies to be produced and he blew his artificial spirit into each of them.» [Eng. tr. from Coptic: STEVAN DAVIES]

Due to the 'contaminated' idiosyncrasy of the gods with human weaknesses, all pre-existing discords and disputes started to increase amongst them.

---

410 A) *As an example from Greek Mythology, we mention the well-known dispute between Athena and Poseidon.*
B) OLD TESTAMENT, EXODUS CH. 12: «§12. For I will pass through the land of Egypt this night, and will strike down all the firstborn in the land of Egypt, both man and beast; <u>and against all **the gods** of Egypt I will execute judgments</u>: I am the Lord.» *They have always had their differences.*

In these struggles they also entangled the nations/races they had created, by infusing them with hatred for the nations of their adversary gods.

411 BARBARA MARCINIAK 'GAIA' [Gr. trans. MATZOROU E.] (p. 120): «However, they were involved in civil wars and conflicts against other representatives of the creator-gods. All the wars had their cause in the division of one race from the other for gaining more power.»

Subdued by their 'oblivion', men start to focus on their racial differences considering them paramount and quarrel with each other, every race valuing their own gods as the most 'skilled' craftsmen of their species... This is shown by the more esoteric and less conventional history of mankind. At other times, when their disputes had their root in the differences between the peoples, gods stood by them, since they could thus keep the peoples subdued with the help and provisions they offered them.

412 A) DEUTERONOMY-OLD TESTAMENT CH. 19 «§1. When the Lord your God has destroyed the nations whose land the Lord your God is giving you, and when you dispossess them (driven them out) and settled in their towns and houses.» *(..."God's" justice, in all its magnificence!)*
B) PIERRE GRIMAL 'THE DICTIONARY OF GREEK AND ROMAN MYTHOLOGY' «**Ehetlaeus**: A hero of Attica who appeared only once, during the battle of Marathon against the Persians. Dressed as a peasant, he appeared in the battle field and slaughtered the Persians. He disappeared after the victory. An oracle revealed the **divine nature** of this mysterious fighter and ordered a temple to be built in his honor.»
C) IDEOTHEATRON MAGAZINE - AUTUMNAL EQUINOX 1998, ISSUE 2
ARTICLE: EHETLAEUS (EHETLUS), POURNAROPOULOS A., (Electronics Engineer, Member of the Greek Astronautic Society)
«...This unknown hero was named after the handgrip of the Hesiod Plough, which is called echetli/echetlon [Gr. εχέτλη = ploughshare].
...This strange hero, Ehetlaeus, didn't fight using the weapons of the time ...but he fought with a strange weapon, unknown to the Athenians, which looked like the echetli/εχέτλη of the Hesiod Plough *(with a strange handgrip)*. Today, a super modern weapon is reminiscent of the shape of echetli/εχέτλη.
...The answer can be found hidden in Herodotus' texts: "In the battle of Marathon, approximately 6,400 Persians were killed and only 192 Athenians. A strange occurrence took place during this fight. Epizelus ...an Athenian soldier, ... fighting as a brave man should, ...when suddenly he was stricken with blindness in both his eyes, without the blow of sword, arrow or spear; and this blindness continued thenceforth till the end of his life. Epizelus narrated that it had seemed to him that a tall and stout warrior, whose huge beard shaded his entire shield, stood over against him; but that 'ghostly' apparition passed him by, and slew a Persian warrior fighting next to him."
...So, according to my point of view, in the battle of Marathon, Ehetlaeus, in order to save Epizelus' life, ... kills the Persian hoplite with a lethal beam of

Don't skip chapters or bibliographic references

> rays from his weapon. At the same time, Epizelus turns to see Ehetlaeus and is accidentally struck in the eyes by a collateral –non lethal though– beam of rays, and goes blind. Epizelus describes Ehetlaeus, as he saw him at that moment. Ehetlaeus' weapon was a Laser-beam weapon, which sent out two beams of rays: the central beam, which was lethal and the collateral one, which was the one causing loss of sight. I cannot exclude the possibility that these were not Laser beams, but of another kind, completely unknown to us.»

Today, the techniques of human control have changed. Instructions are now transmitted by the creators or their astral doubles to powerful earth centers of ruling power and authority and through them they manipulate human society completely. We will talk about this as we continue our discussion.

The process of materialization and de-materialization was not and still isn't simple so as to be routinely carried out.

> [413] **SUPER MUNDANE BOOK 1, 1938**
> *Reports-speeches of the spiritual teachers –on behalf of the Creators– through the medium 'Urusvati'*
> «§5. Urusvati has seen us in both the dense and the subtle bodies. Only those few who have had this experience can know the tension that accompanies it. §16. Urusvati knows the three states of our bodies. Each state has its own distinguishing characteristic, and even the dense state is so refined that it cannot be compared to the earthly. The subtle state has become adapted to the conditions of the earthly atmosphere to such a degree that it differs substantially from the usual sheaths of the Subtle World. Finally, the third state, which is between the dense and the subtle states, is a unique phenomenon.»

So, to meet the pressing requirements of their transport to various places on earth, the creators have been using advanced transportation means, which contemporary researchers attribute to extraterrestrials. Technology after all is not a privilege of mankind, but merely reflects the craftsmanship of the creators.

> [414] *See the description of god's 'chariot' by Ezekiel in Ch. 10, in the Old Testament. Researchers, based on this description, have sketched the 'vessel', which, in the end, appears to have been a very intelligent means of transportation.*
> **A) 'SUPERMUNDANE' BOOK I (AGNI YOGA SOCIETY)** 1938: *The spiritual teachers state*: «§2 Urusvati has seen many of our apparatuses. In appearance they do not differ much from those in use elsewhere. However, the way they are used is different, for psychic energy is applied. §4…We have apparatuses that assist the transference of thought over a distance. People would be

astonished to see that certain apparatuses that are familiar to them are here applied quite differently. §15…We are actually charged with electricity in order to increase the Primary Energy, and use unusual electrical apparatuses to create the special environment needed for the sending of thought. […] but such a saturation of the environment with electricity can also cause fiery sicknesses. Everywhere harmony is needed. §20…Our Towers are many-storied, and research is constantly taking place. §77…Our apparatuses may resemble simple telegraphic receivers, but they are designed for more subtle vibrations. The necessary tension requires an increase in prana. The breathing of our ozonizers can be likened to the breathing of living beings. Our lighting system, which resembles neon tubing, can burn very brightly.»

B) PHILOSTRATUS 'THE LIFE OF APOLLONIAN TYANAEUS' (VOL. 2, p. 25)

The incident refers to the time when Apollonian Tyanaeus was in India and was about to meet the wise men of the Indies for the first time. While he was waiting, he saw some scenes carved on a rock, which bore witness to historical events of the past and he describes them. His very narration betrays the possession of a very advanced and specialized 'technology'!

The anthropomorphic gods 'Panes' [1] *are also mentioned.*

«On this rock you can see traces of cloven hoofs (with two toes)[1] and outlines of beards and faces, and elsewhere on it, impressions of persons who have slipped and rolled down. For they say that Dionysus, when he was trying to storm the place along with Heracles, ordered the Panes-gods to attack it, because they <u>were able to create earthquakes</u>; but they were <u>thunderstruck</u> by the sages and fell in different ways; and the rocks bore the prints of the various postures of the failed attempt and fall. And they say that around this rock they saw a cloud floating, in which the Indians live and render themselves <u>visible or invisible at will</u>. Whether there were any other <u>gates</u> in the rock, they say they do not know; for the **cloud** around it, does not allow this place neither tightly shut nor open to appear.»

In this text there is an indirect mention of the inaccessible passage – through a cloud (Nephelē) – to the underground Shambhala which we will mention later on.

Every skeptic wonders: since both the 'spiritual masters' and the so called 'extraterrestrials' use technology so often, could they be one and the same?

[1]*Regarding Panes (gods): Two-legged, two-natured creatures, Billy-goats from the waist down, with cloven hoofs… and men-shaped from the waist up.*

In **ARTHUR CLARKE'S** *book* **'THE MYSTERIES OF THE WORLD'** *there is a true testimony of some strange footprints that might belong to this or some similar creature… He himself calls them "traces of the devil". Arthur Clarke narrates:*

Don't skip chapters or bibliographic references

«The event takes place in the beautiful English County of Devon, literally in one night. The year was 1855. …On Friday February 9th, people living in the towns and villages around river Ex's mouth, woke up to find their land covered with strange footprints on the snow. …The 'prints' were formed in one night. …They were in a straight line and had the shape of a hoof. Inside this shape though, there were traces of claws. …Other prints of the same kind were found heading straight up on the roofs of the houses and in every neighborhood of Dawlish. …The distance between each print was twenty centimeters or a bit more and the footprints had exactly the same dimensions and step in every district! This mysterious visitor crossed each garden or yard only once and did that at every house, in many places, in several towns…as well as in the farms between towns. These regular footprints, in some occasions, crossed over the rooftops of houses and barns as well as high walls.

…Now, speaking of the distance covered by someone or something that left such prints…it must be more than 160 kilometers!

…From these reports, Ms. Theo Brown, a Professor at the University of Exeter, collected enough evidence to reconstruct the astonishing scene that everyone, living in the area of Ex had experienced. …Yet none of the explanations given was completely satisfactory. And as Theo Brown notes: "No one expected a donkey to stroll on rooftops." The phenomenon still remains a mystery…»

Part of this aethero-physical technology is hermetically guarded inside large hollows of the earth, where the 'informed ones' locate some underground cities.

[415] **SUPER MUNDANE BOOK 1, 1938**: «§3. Urusvati has seen some of our repositories. Objects of art are collected according to eras, but the collections do not constitute a museum as it is usually understood. These objects serve as a reservoir of accumulated auras, and the creative emanations of their former owners. …We can study in this way the true meaning of a particular era. …Some of our Brothers are the former owners of objects in our repository. Sometimes an object is sent into the world to carry out a certain task. For example, it may be buried in some place as a magnet…. In truth, each object is for us a useful apparatus, and can be used for important observations. It is especially valuable to observe the relationship of ancient auras to later emanations. … In our many experiments with ancient objects, we observe not only with spiritual vision but also verify by the use of our apparatuses. This is not so-called psychometry, but a science of radiations. … We can study the language of objects by their radiations. …We watch inventors with great attention.»

One of the most fundamental goals of the Iron Race, as we have said, was to render all the 'powers of (positive and negative) energy-administration' invisible to the eyes of common men. Furthermore, adherence to these conditions had to be ensured by strong security measures, a process which would be slowly and gradually completed with one final outcome: the genetic mutation of man.

During that long period from the time of the great clash of the gods until the transitory phase after the sweeping cataclysm, groups of materialized astro-aetheric entities, as well as solely-material monsters generated by genetic interbreeding of dissimilar beings –since the possibility of cross-breeding between disparate species was permanently interrupted only in the fifth Race of Iron– swarmed the inner hollows of the Earth, converting them into either havens or bases of operations. Thus, after the end of the Clash of the Titans, the earth's bowels were dedicated to be the primary materialization den, mainly for the negative, astral skeptomorphic entities.

[416] **A) P. GIANNOULAKIS 'HOLLOW EARTH'**

«The dreadful Deros love gold very much and thus somebody can have financial transactions with them. ...Despite the superior technology they use and the supernatural abilities they possess, the Deros have a lot of defects. **They are afraid of salt**, which damages their skin, if it comes in contact with it. They despise light, which causes problems to their eyes. They are also afraid of weapons and people who don't show their faces! ...Because, when a man's face is covered, they can't use the optic nerves of the intruder's brain to stun him in the tunnels. They can use this ability under appropriate conditions, and they are supposed to be able to immobilize, to 'petrify' their opponent using this technique.»

Is it possible that this kind of 'techniques' can help us explain **the real causes** *for the creation of the 'Petrified forest' in Sigri, in the island of Lesvos?*

Centuries ago, a large area with real trees was turned to stone, under still unclear conditions –all we have are some ungrounded assumptions– and even today it lies there, puzzling researchers. It is remarkable that the entire area around it is arid, in contrast to the morphology of the rest of the island.

Is it, also, possible to find, in these 'techniques', answers to the transformation of Lot's wife to a pillar of salt or to the Medusa's 'abilities'? Finally, could the use of such 'techniques' be the cause of the huge quantities of fossilized timber that exist in the areas of the Arctic Circle? Dimitrios Evangelopoulos writes, in his book:

EVANGELOPOULOS, D., 'HYPOHTHONIA MYSTERIA/SUBTERRANEAN (SUB-CHTHONIC) MYSTERIES' (p. 180):

«A large quantity of fossilized wood, coming from remains of forests, ap-

Don't skip chapters or bibliographic references

pears in various places of the Arctic Circle, like the New Siberian Islands, thousands of miles away from the forests of today. …This fossilized wood as it is called, is a basic source of fuel and construction material for the people in Siberia. …According to the supporters of the Hollow Earth Theory, this (fossilized wood) comes from the inside of the Earth, through the 'hole' of the North Pole and is swept away to these islands by the currents.»

B) *A different statement that confirms the existence of dimorphic beings, which some people call Titans, others Giants, or others Nephelims –who at the end of the Titanomachy (Clash of the Titans) were confined to Tartara– is the personal testimony of Lord Edward Bulwer Lytton in his book 'THE COMING RACE'.*

In his book, he describes his **two-year stay in the subterranean city** *of the Vril-Ya –whose residents were about two meters tall– and the facts he revealed –as we will see later on– dynamically determined the scientific research of Germany during the Second World War and constituted the source of 'inspiration' for Adolph Hitler.*

Among other things, Lytton, in his book, describes three portraits he saw hanging there, which depicted the first three generations of patriarchs of that Vril-Ya tribe:

BULWER LYTTON E., 'THE COMING RACE' (p. 117):

(1st portrait, third –younger– generation) «The philosopher is attired in a long tunic which seems to form a loose suit of scaly armor, borrowed, perhaps, from some fish or reptile, but the feet and hands are exposed: the digits in both are wonderfully long, and webbed *(with a membrane)*. His neck is almost non-existent, while he has a low receding forehead, not at all the ideal forehead of a sage's. He has bright brown prominent eyes, a very wide mouth, high cheekbones, and a muddy complexion.

… *(2nd portrait, second race)* The portrait of his grandfather *(of the previous man)* had the features and aspect of the philosopher, only much more exaggerated: he was not dressed, and the color of his body was singular; the breast and stomach yellow, the shoulders and legs of a dull bronze hue…

… *(3rd portrait, first race)* the great-grandfather was a magnificent specimen of the Batrachian genus, a Giant Frog, pur et simple *(…)*. »

In order for these beings of darkness to be under the control of their adversary positive powers, a corresponding base/headquarters had to be projected (placed) there. So, a mirage (reflection) of Shambhala, the astro-aetheric city of the positive powers, is imprinted and takes form in these hollow regions of the Earth. This sub-chthonic Shambhala is called Agartha, or Hyperborea, and is 'the true residence of Apollo' as Plato testifies.

417 *In order to facilitate the reader to form a complete view about the topic of the 'Hollow Earth', the volume of the references that follow is quite large.*
A) PIERRE GRIMAL 'THE PENGUIN DICTIONARY OF CLASSICAL MYTHOLOGY':
«ENTRY HYPERBOREANS *(Gr.: Ὑπερβόρειοι)*: A mythical race who lived in a region 'beyond the North Wind', 'beyond the Boreas [Gr. = North wind]'. This myth is connected to Apollo's myth. …The myth has it that some ceremonies of the Apollonian Cult/worship are attributed to the Hyperboreans. It is said that not only Leto had been born in Hyperborea and from there she later came to Delos to give birth to her children, but also that Apollo's sacred objects, which were worshiped in Delos, came from there as well.
…After the birth of Apollo, his father, Zeus, ordered him to go and live in Delphi. …Every nineteen years…he goes back to the Hyperboreans. …The Hyperboreans also appear in the myths of Perseus and Hercules (at least in the version that locates the garden of the Hesperides in the farthest extremities of the North). Especially after the Classic Age however, it was customary to present Hyperborea as an ideal place, with a very mild climate, pleasantly temperate: a real country of Utopia. There, the earth yields crops twice a year. The inhabitants have amiable customs. They live in the countryside, in the fields and the sacred forests and their longevity exceeds every limit.»

Let us see now, how Admiral Byrd describes the hollow parts of the Earth: In 1947, leading the American expedition for the exploration of the North Pole himself, he flew on a small plane 1,700 miles to the north and (without realizing it) found himself in the 'hollow of the Earth'.
Nine years later, he attempted a second expedition to the South Pole and entered the hollow of the Earth, 2,300 miles to the south. Afterwards, these accounts, as well as many others, were withheld from the general public, and are still considered to be confidential knowledge for the 'people of authority'…

B) PAPASTAVROU, A., 'LETTERS TO ANONYMOUS':
«In February 1947, Rear Admiral Richard E. Byrd, head of the 'Unites States Navy Task Force' flew over the Earth, beyond and not across the North Pole, for seven hours, and reached an area which hadn't been registered on the geographical maps. There, he **didn't** find ever-lasting polar ice, as expected, but mountains full of forests with lakes, rivers and sward (a stretch of turf). In addition, he saw a huge primitive animal, resembling the mythic mammoths, wandering in the bushes.[1]
Byrd announced through the radio, from this 'polar' place: "I wanted to see the Earth beyond the (North) Pole. The circle beyond the Pole is the center of the big unknown." Millions of people read this announcement, as it was passed on to the newspapers, and heard the same on the radio. But these messages were the last ones, since the Government, realizing the importance

Don't skip chapters or bibliographic references

of these discoveries, subjected them to strict censorship. On January 13th, 1956, another expedition, under the command of Byrd, flew away from the 'McMurdo Sound Base', which is 400 miles away from the South Pole, and entered inside the Earth 2,300 miles <u>again</u> beyond the South Pole. This was confirmed by the daily press, on February 5th, 1956. However, nothing more was made public and the whole matter was strictly kept a secret, just like the discoveries in the North Pole. When Byrd returned to the United States in March of the same year, he said: "This expedition opened out A BOUND-LESS EARTH/LAND."

The same time Byrd flew 1,700 miles inside the Earth in the North Pole, Lt. Commander David Bunger, U.S. Navy's 'Operation High-Jump' (1946-1947) made a similar discovery in the South Pole, known as 'Bunger's Oasis'. The land that Bunger discovered had no ice at all; it had a lot of lakes of various colors –deep red, green and deep blue– and a diameter of more than three miles each. The water in them was warmer than the water of the ocean; and he discovered that while landing his hydroplane. …The 'Globe and Mail' newspaper of Toronto-Canada, published a photo, shot by an aviator, who apparently had penetrated the same place as Byrd. It presented a beautiful valley with smooth hills. The photo was published in 1960.»

So, in these poles, there are large openings leading to Hyperborea, the homeland of Apollo, with the mild climate and the enchanting beauties…

…he saw…an enormous primitive animal, resembling the mythic 'mammoths', wandering in the bushes. [1]

[1] *Obviously, one of these poor animals must have been stranded to the external frozen areas of the North Pole, while wandering in search of food. It probably froze to death and was then discovered by scientists (a few years ago), frozen and perfectly preserved…having fresh grass still in its mouth! …This fact made the 'experts' assume that the ice-age happened instantaneously (!!), deep-freezing whatever it found in its course…*

ARTHUR CLARKE *in the book* **'THE MYSTERIES OF THE WORLD'** *(p.258 Gr. edition) describes how a prehistoric mammoth was found frozen in Siberia by the professor N. K. Vereshagin and was carried to Leningrad in 1977.*

The tribe of Yakuts though, who lived in the area, **insisted** *that the mammoths still lived there, as their dogs many times ate the (prehistoric) animals that had frozen to death.*

And **D. EVANGELOPOULOS** *supplements in his book* **"HYPO-CHTHONIAN/ SUBTERRANEAN MYSTERIES** (p. 180): «What could we possibly say about the mammoth tusks which continue to accumulate on the islands of North Russia, despite their ceaseless trade for over 400 years? Moreover, what could we possibly say about the fresh carcasses the mammoths themselves, found encaged in icebergs that come floating from the North? The supporters of the Hollow Earth Theory are here explicit as well: these come from the continent inside the Earth, coming out through the respective polar opening, which is close to where we locate the North Pole today, but not exactly at it.»

C) 'MYSTERIES OF THE WORLD', VOL. 'MYSTERIES OF THE EAST': «For centuries, there has been the legend that the last spiritual secrets of humanity are kept in a secret place in the Himalayas. The secret council, whose members are supposed to possess supernatural powers, is located in the colony of Shangri-La, which is also called Shambhala. ...In Asian traditions, Shangri-La is the spiritual cradle of the planet in which the preparation for the spiritual revival of humanity takes place. ...The name Shangri-La is also mentioned in the Hindu texts 'Puranás' and in fact, it is presented as a real place.»

D) *The Spiritual Hierarchy of the Planet, through their teachers, informs its disciples about the first Shambhala.*

PAPASTAVROU, A., 'LETTERS TO ANONYMOUS':

«The great and beloved Sanat Kumara decided to offer his service to Earth...and founded his dwelling in the hermitage which is today known as 'Shambhala'. At that time, it was on an island in the middle of a sapphire, azure (blue) sea and after a cataclysm it was submerged and in time ended in what we know today as the Gobi Desert*. Shambhala was then returned to the <u>aetheric realm</u>, above the Gobi Desert.»

* *Today, Gobi Desert is a paleontologist's 'dreamland', since thousands of dinosaur fossils can be discovered there...*

Furthermore: SPEECH OF THE GODDESS ISIS, JUNE 15TH, 1961 (p. 143):

«As a divine architect, when this very Same Lord of the World *(the archon of this world)* Sanat Kumara announced to the Kingdoms of his native star, Venus *(the star of dawn)* that he intended <u>to bring the Light</u> *(Εωσ-φόρος=Lucifer=light bearer)* the patience, the balance and the wisdom of himself to the dark star, the Earth, Serapes was the first volunteer who offered to supervise the creation of a similar magnificent Shambhala – planetary dwelling– on Earth, for Sanat Kumara.»

The name Sanat seems to be an anagrammatism of the word 'Satan'. And as the spiritual teachers state, the homeland of the teacher in question is the planet Venus. That is, the star of dawn (=εω/eo) or the morning star or Lucifer (=Εωσ-φόρος / light bearer), as the specific star is symbolically called... as the forerunner of dawn.

E) P. GIANNOULAKIS 'HOLLOW EARTH' *(An excerpt of the conversation between the Russian painter Roerich and a Lama in a monastery of Potala):*

«Buddhist Mythology talks about the Celestial invisible Shambhala but very few know the Earthly Shambhala in Agartha which is connected with the Celestial one and the two parallel worlds. Travelers from the Celestial Shambhala come to the Earthly one *(through materialization)* in order to

Don't skip chapters or bibliographic references

communicate with its inhabitants and the select ones of the surface world.»

F) SECRET WORLDS (CUMULATIVE WORK), CH. 'SHAMBHALA-AGARTHA' P. GIANNOULAKIS

«THE FORBIDDEN LAND: Tibetan Buddhism has acquired most of its knowledge about Shambhala from 'The Kalachakra texts'. …Rumors, legends and stories about an underground (or apocryphal, earthly) paradise in the heart of Asia, came to the West during the Graeco-Roman period. For example, the Greek philosopher Philostratus recorded the journey he took with the great magician Apollonius Tyanaeus, in the wilderness of the Tibetan Himalayas, a place which he called 'the Forbidden Land of the Gods'. Later on, the relevant testimonies about those areas grew in numbers, through the first Christian missionaries. …Madam Helena Blavatsky, founder of the Theosophical Society in 1879, writes in her book 'The Secret Doctrine', that the 'legendary Shambhala' was an aetheric city in the Gobi desert. It was the 'invisible headquarters' of the Mahatmas, a brotherhood of great spiritual teachers, who emigrated there after the sinking of Mu under the Pacific Ocean. Blavatsky writes that "the Heart of mother Earth, Gaia, beats right under the sacred Shambhala…"

…AGARTHA'S EMISSARIES: The rare book of the Russian writer and explorer Ferdynand Antoni Ossendowski, 'Beasts, Men, and Gods' (1922), contains a lot of remarkable information about the Hollow Earth subject and Agartha. I quote a very interesting excerpt from this extremely rare book:

"…On my journey into Central Asia I came to know for the first time about 'the Mystery of Mysteries', which I can call by no other name. I deciphered a great many things about it, after I had analyzed and connoted many sporadic, hazy and often controversial testimonies. …Afterwards, someone from the lake Nogan Kul showed me the **smoking gate** that is the entrance to the 'Kingdom of Agartha.

(Let me remind you of 'The life of Apollonius Tyanaeus' by Philostratus, from the previous reference: "Whether there were any other gates *in the rock, they say they do not know; for* **the cloud (Nephele) around it** *does not allow this place neither tightly shut nor open to appear.")*

…I heard from an erudite Chinese Lama related to Bogd Khan, that all subterranean caves in America are inhabited by an ancient nation who has disappeared in the interior of the Earth. Traces of this nation are still found on the surface of that land. These subterranean people and their territories are governed by rulers owing allegiance to the King of the World *(the archon of this world)*.

You know that, in the two greatest oceans of the east and the west, there were formerly two continents. They disappeared underwater, but their peoples went into the subterranean kingdom.

(This is the punishment (sentence) of the Gigantes (Giants)/Titans and their confinement to the Tartara, the **central gates** *of which are in the territory of*

the 'Great Ta(r)tary'. The land of the Mongols Ta(r)tars, Mongolia or Tartaria, is located there, where, the Gobi desert and the aetheric Shambhala lie as well.

«Tatars: a name for all the Asian populations of Mongolian origin, mainly from the Central-West Asia»).

...In the underground caves, there exists a special light which promotes growth to grains and vegetables and longevity with no disease to the people. There are many different races of men and many tribes. ...The capital of Agartha is surrounded by settlements of the high priests and the scientists. ...The throne of the King of the World is surrounded by millions of incarnated deities. The holy palace itself is encircled by the palaces of the Great Guru, who possesses all the visible and invisible powers of the Earth, of Hades and of the Sky and who can do everything for the life and death of man... *(The whole situation reminds us of the 'glory' of Yaldabaoth...)*

...Some Indian Brahmans and Tibetan Lamas, during their laborious struggles on the peaks of mountains unconquered by any other man, found inscriptions carved on the rocks, footprints in the snow and traces of wheels. On a mountain top, reverent Sakkia Mouni found stone-tablets with inscriptions, which, he only managed to understand when he had reached an old age. Afterwards, he entered the Kingdom of Agartha, wherefrom he brought back excerpts of the sacred teaching, which had been imprinted in his memory. There, in palaces made of a marvelous crystal, live the invisible rulers of all pious people, the King of the World or Brahatma *(the archon of this world),* and his two assistants, Mahatma (knowing the purposes of future events) and Mahynga (ruling the causes of these events).»

WHERE IS SHAMBHALA? The Italian Tibetologist (and friend of Julius Evola) Giuseppe Tucci mentions that Shambhala is traditionally placed close to the River Sita (which he identifies with Tarim), a big river that flows eastwards through the Chinese Turkestan (Sin-Kiang), north of Tibet. Panchen Lama wrote that the huge kingdom of Shambhala extends between Mount Kailas (in the South of Tibet, about 700 miles away from Tarim river) and the nearby river Sita.»

G) *Writer John Giannopoulos, in his book 'Hollow Earth', quotes facts that Georg Müller, a former 'SS' officer, had confided in him, and brings all the evidence proving their authenticity.*

During the Second World-War, Georg Müller participated in research expeditions conducted by the German Army (using 'Thule Society [1]*) for the discovery of the hypo-chthonian Vril-energy. In particular, former U.N. secretary Curt Waldheim took part in one of these expeditions.*

Lord Edward Bulwer Lytton, an initiate of the Rosicrucian order, with his book 'The Coming Race' strongly determined the philosophy of the German

Don't skip chapters or bibliographic references

Army officers of the time, turning their interest into the bowels of the planet. Lytton admits that the founder of the Rosicrucian order, 'Rosenkreuz', discovered the mystical knowledge in a mysterious place inside the Earth and tends to imitate him.

[1]*Thule is considered to be the capital of Hyperborea, the homeland of Apollo.*

H) MYSTICAL WORLDS, (COLLECTIVE WORK) CH. 'SEARCHING FOR HYPERBOREA AND THULE', EDIT. GIANNOULAKIS P.

«THE ARYAN THULE: The revival of the Thule issue, at the beginning of the 20th century, is due to its adoption by the German ethno-socialistic mythology. The occult ideology of the Nazis connected the myth of the polar origin of man and the superiority of the Aryans with the traditions and racial discriminations of the German Race *(because some mystic circles believe that the Paradise of Eden was located there or rather the genetic laboratories of some Creators).* The three fathers of the Nazi Thule were Guido von List (1848-1919), Jorg Lanz von Liebenfels (1874-1954) and Rudolf von Sebottentorf (1875-1945). The latter was the founder of the notorious secret 'Thule Society', which studied and spread the new-occultist and racist ideas on the subject, ideas which among others lead to the creation of the basis for the Nazi ideology.

…In 1907, Lanz founded the 'Order of the New Templars', a knightly, Gnostic, ritualistic brotherhood with the most extreme racist ideas. This order with its 'lodges' in the ruined Masonic castles functioned as the model for Heinrich Himmler's 'SS', with him being the Great Magister, who would prepare the breeding and the training of a new Aryan race. …This would finally lead to the 'Golden Reich of the Millennium' and the return to the homeland of Thule, which waited secretly beyond the Poles, ready to send the Hyperboreans of the Hollow Earth to reinforce the Aryan armies.»

It was on all this, that an entire morbid campaign was eventually based, which decimated the peoples of the Earth, obsessed with the antagonism of the disastrous creators, for the predominance of the best 'maker'.

I) GIANNOPOULOS J., 'HOLLOW EARTH'
The incident described by the writer John Giannopoulos, involves a team of Germans with Georg Müller as their leader, inside the cave of Distomo, in Viotia, Greece.

«…The instruments showed that they were at a depth of about 1,000 meters after they had covered a distance of more than 20 kilometers. …The cave in Distomo seemed to have the advantages of a cave with great interest, rarity, mystery and unexpected research results.

…When the team was about to move on to a new part of the cave, they always followed the same tactics: the leader send a 'scout', usually the second in order, the one who was hierarchically after himself *(Müller).*

...In this particular case, the one who usually carried out these scouts was Hans. He, too, was an Austrian from Tyrol, and a mountaineer athlete since before the war. He had a few words with Georg; he fixed his lantern and moved to the entrance of the passage with his rucksack and a hank of mountaineering rope.

...Hans strode easily through the opening and moved into the small corridor. He had barely walked for about one and a half meters, when something happened, which first left Georg Müller and then the others speechless with surprise. Simultaneously with Hans' walking, they all saw a distinct light *(!)* coming, or rather 'switching on', exactly at the exit of the corridor, right at the point that Hans was approaching. It was a dim green light which created a 'screen', a 'curtain' that filled the exit, at the end of the corridor. Georg Müller and the others had already jumped up while watching Hans going through the green screen without difficulty, maybe out of momentum, –in other words, maybe he wasn't able to stop despite his surprise– and disappearing from their sight! They assumed that he had already entered the space beyond the corridor and waited for some kind of movement or words from him. At the same time, the green screen continued to glow and cover the side where Hans must have –logically– been.

Next, the screen disappeared, 'switched off' completely! The dark opening, at the end of the corridor, appeared again and they all rushed in at once. The torches of all members of the team barely lit through the darkness of the other side. They all called Hans' name ceaselessly. Nothing!

...Hans had passed through a 'gate', which led him somewhere else, to the unknown; to what they had precisely been looking for! But how was it possible? Nevertheless, his disappearance was real and definitive. ...Later, one of the biologists of the team, in communication with Georg Müller, tried something else. He took a raincoat, rolled it in the shape of a ball, got into the opening very carefully, and started walking extremely slowly. He had already walked along the whole corridor when, suddenly, the bright 'screen' appeared again. Leaning on the side wall of the corridor, he threw the raincoat to the center of the 'screen' with a sudden move. The raincoat –ball– hit the 'screen' at its center and went through it. After a while, the 'screen' and the raincoat disappeared again, just like the first time. It had surely followed Hans' way, as it was not on the other side. This time, it was difficult to fill in the (official) reports. How could they report, what had happened?»

In another part of his book, he describes another incident.

«...The cave was in the hills that surrounded the town of Shigatze in Tibet, under which –according to the legends of the area– the legendary town of Shambhala is located. Apart from the other dangers that I have already mentioned, the cave was full of galleries, found on different levels, sometimes,

Don't skip chapters or bibliographic references

with a height difference of more than 15 meters between them. ...Thus, they walked at a dead slow pace (with extreme caution). ...They went up and down the galleries until they reached a level, where everything was different: **The darkness became less thick;** a gleam appeared from the depths of the cave, which, after a while, proved to be strong enough to lighten a beautiful underground lake. They were not prepared to cross it, but as they walked around it, they found a vessel that resembled a boat. ...When they reached the opposite side, they saw a kind of flora that didn't have the usual green color but a bright light brown. They followed the path –the only one they were able to locate– which led them to the front of a stone gate. On its side, there was a frame with a strange object that looked like an athlete's discus. ...They attempted to go through the door, which was continuously open, without having anything to block it. But although they tried –all at the same time, or one by one– they couldn't get through; as if there was <u>an invisible or transparent door</u> in the opening, which, although invisible, made their access impossible.»

J) PAPASTAVROU, A., 'LETTERS TO ANONYMOUS' (p. 132)

«We are citing the following, from a speech of Saint Germaine to the students of 'I AM' on November 28th, 1932: ...Do not consider it incredible that the Teachers of Light and Wisdom have corridors stretching in all directions **under the Earth**, in the same way you have public streets...which branch away from the one end of the country to the other *(Hesiod: ...to the underworld with the wide roads...)*. This would be easier to understand if you had some idea about the atomic configuration of the Earth. ...Then you would know that the Great Beings... through the use of certain rays *(Vril-energy rays)*, are able to walk inside the bowels of the Earth, with the same ease that you walk through water, but with one difference: while they leave empty space behind them as they move, with you, water returns back to its former place...»

K) BULWER LYTTON E., 'THE COMING RACE':

«I have spoken so much of the Vril Staff, that my reader may expect me to describe it. This I cannot do accurately... It is hollow, and has in the handle several stops, keys, or springs by which its force can be altered, modified, or directed –so that by one process it destroys, by another it heals– <u>by one it can rend the rock,</u> *(Saint Germaine: "They are able to walk in the depths of the Earth, using special rays")* by another it can disperse the vapor, by one it affects bodies, by another it can exercise a certain influence over minds.... I saw her (the user of the rod) put into movement large and weighty substances, she herself standing at a distance, merely by a certain play of her Vril Staff... She set complicated pieces of machinery into movement, arrested the movement or continued it, until, within an incredibly short time, various kinds of raw material were reproduced as symmetrical works of art, complete and perfect. ...She produced by the motions of her slender rod over the springs and wheels of lifeless mechanism, whatever effect mesmerism or electro-biology produces over the nerves and muscles of animated objects. ...This people have invented certain tubes by which the Vril fluid can be conducted towards the object it is meant to destroy, throughout a distance almost indefinite; at least I put it modestly when I say from 500 to 600 miles.»

The physical passages that lead to these hollow regions of the Earth are guarded from indiscrete eyes by appointed guards.

418 **A) 'THE EPIC OF GILGAMESH' NEAR EAST TEXTS,** GR. TR.: XENI S. SKARTSI – SOCRATES L. SKARTSIS, CH. THE SCORPIONS

Gilgamesh, in his desperate attempt to recover his lost Immortality, decides to go to the 'Garden of The Gods'. This 'Garden' can be identified as Shambhala or Agartha, the sacred subterranean city of the gods and the teachers in the Earth's depths.

«...Thus, Gilgamesh reached that very high mountain, Mount Mashu, which daily guards the rising and setting sun. Its twin peaks are high like the wall of the sky and its flanks reach as far as the Netherworld below. **Scorpion**-like beings <u>watch over its gate</u>, **half human and half dragons**.

...When Gilgamesh saw them, he only covered his eyes for a moment; afterwards, he resumed his courage and drew near them. ...The Man-scorpion spoke to Gilgamesh, saying:

"Never has there been, Gilgamesh, a man born of a woman...who has gone **inside** the mountains. It is twelve leagues long and there is darkness throughout; dense is the darkness, and light there is none. But the heart is oppressed by the darkness. From the rising to the setting of the sun, there is a constant lack of light *(it refers to the dark underground passages which lead to the hollow Earth)*...Go on, Gilgamesh, I allow you to enter inside the Mashu Mountains; the gate of the mountain is open."

...As soon as Gilgamesh heard this, he followed what the scorpion-being had told him. Along the Road of the Sun he journeyed inside the mountain, going to the east. When he had proceeded for three miles *(into the mountain)*, dense was the darkness around him, for light there was none. Neither what was ahead nor behind could he see. After six miles he had traveled, dense was the darkness, light there was none, neither what lay ahead nor behind did it allow him to see. After nine miles, dense was the darkness and light was not there, neither what was ahead nor behind could he see. Twelve miles he traveled, dense was the darkness, light there was none, neither what was ahead nor behind could he see. Having traveled fifteen miles, dense was the darkness, light there was none, nei-

Don't skip chapters or bibliographic references

ther what lay ahead nor behind could he see. ...Twenty-four miles he had traveled, and Gilgamesh cried out with a great voice, because dense was the darkness, light there was none, neither what lay ahead nor behind could he see. Twenty-seven miles he had traveled, and he felt the North Wind at his face, but the darkness was dense... After thirty-three miles the sun flooded inside with brilliance. There was the garden of the Gods *(Shambhala or Agartha)*...**all around, bushes grew tall forming gem stones. ...Instead of thorns and briars, there were <u>hematite and rare precious stones</u>.**» [THE EPIC OF GILGAMESH, TRANSLATED BY MAUREEN GALLERY KOVACS, ELECTRONIC EDITION BY WOLF CARNAHAN, 1998 WAS ALSO CONSULTED]

If we leave aside the esoteric symbols of the text, we will find out that it clearly denotes Gilgamesh's trip to the interior of the Earth, Tartarus.

B) 'SUPERMUNDANE' BOOK I (AGNI YOGA SOCIETY) 1938 *(information through channeling)*:
«§1. Urusvati knows the Tower of Chun, and remembers how the exterior of the Tower resembles a natural cliff. It is not difficult to prevent access to this Tower. A small landslide can conceal the structure from those below. A small dam can change a mountain stream into a lake, and in time of dire need <u>the entire district can be **immediately** transformed</u>. ...But even before the physical transformation of the area, the power of thought would already have diverted the caravan! In addition, chemical effects can be utilized to prevent the approach of the curious. Thus do we guard the Brotherhood. Even the most advanced aircraft cannot discover Our Abode. Hermits living in nearby caves are watchful guards. Travelers sometimes speak of having met a sadhu *(Saint)* who persistently advised them to follow a specified path and warned them of the danger of proceeding into certain other areas.... The sadhus know about the Forbidden Place and know how to guard the secret... One should not doubt the existence of an inviolable Abode. Urusvati remembers... the light from Our Tower... She has seen Our co-workers gathering useful plants.... One should see these archives of knowledge to comprehend the work of Our Abode.»

C) P. GIANNOULAKIS 'HOLLOW EARTH' «Roerich's travels are full of wonders and strange incidents... The enigmatic 'Azaras', who are Agartha's emissaries ... "walk on strange paths with the Yetis (of the Himalayas), who serve them. ...People with strange eyes, showing up from caves, come down to markets and pay with ancient coins. The Azaras are the holy men who safeguard the secrets of Shambhala..." Strange things happen under the monasteries Sera, Gan-Den and Depung...no one from the west knows about them...»

Legends speak of grotesque figures coming out of the caves at dark nights. Even the story of St. George, the Christian Saint who killed the dragon that terrified the inhabitants in his region, relates to these occurrences. Men named some of these disfigured creatures that belong to the negative force, goblins. Then they sealed the exits of every such cave, and Christians later built a chapel in front of them.

> [419] **P. GIANNOULAKIS 'HOLLOW EARTH'** (p. 198): «I have at hand, hundreds of photos with temples and small churches built on top of the mouths of underpasses, at the entrances of openings, inside and outside caves, and generally in places where there used to be some kind of entrance which they now block (seal).»

They sealed-off the most dangerous 'exits' with the wall of the holy sanctuary of a church in order to keep back or exorcise the **real** daemons that were coming out. In time though, true testimonies gave rise to stories and stories generated legends. Contemporary men do not believe them anymore, due to an innermost fear, or because of their ignorance, and call them superstitions. Earlier communities that lived closer to nature, knew more on one hand, but interpreted them according to their limited perception. These beings are classified (by some contemporary researchers) as 'extraterrestrials', who have their 'bases' in the great apertures of this Earth, and by others as 'intra-terrestrials', the permanent residents of hollow Earth. In reality, they are but some categories of the many of the "prisoners of war" of the Clash of the Titans along with their "wardens", who by the way aren't any better than their prisoners! In these sub-chthonic (underground) regions, symbiosis of the two opposite forces is on a knife-edge, and as we will analyze later on, it is from there they control humanity.

The new bodies of men of the Iron Race, appropriately modified, are born by the 'blessed' mortal females. The best specimens of this species are selected and taught by their 'genitors' in order to take over the throne of the king, chief, or Pharaoh of every race/nation. Plots, conspiracies and intrigues start to flourish to determine which 'son' will prevail, because he would be the chosen blue-blooded, king of men, whose sperm would have to remain <u>unadulterated and pure</u> in time *(hence the reason of royal marriages only among the blue-blooded)*.

And while the creators' higher ranks maintained control of the Soul and transformed the new generation of men, their 'negative doubles' in the lower energy-planes, i.e. the astral and aetheric worlds, intertwined with the lower skeptomorphs, had formed a second uniform community. The new Iron Race was obliged to ensure energy-nutrition for them as well. Therefore, in order for this community to remain autonomous, it must act independently. It is on this 'necessity' the new foundations of Karma were

Don't skip chapters or bibliographic references

established, which was organized in such a way to ascertain fair energy-distribution to both sides.

---

420 **PAPASTAVROU, A., 'LETTERS TO ANONYMOUS'** (p. 226):
«It is true that the first Lords of Karma had been solely appointed as a governing body, before the fall of man. Their aim was to supervise that all the Root Races and sub-Races would incarnate on the assigned time and not to offer judgment of any kind. When the astral world was created by the human *(skeptomorphic)* disharmony, the Karmic committee increased to seven members, in order to regulate the disharmony of the Race.»

The lower mental plane was from the beginning 'the cradle of birth' for all skeptomorphic powers. The 'negative doubles' of the creators had now regained absolute power over the entire astral plane. The cooperation of the two would ensure success. With the lower mental on one hand and the entire structure of the 'ego' and the emotions of the astral on the other as their basic means, they could very well 'mold/create' their own humans.

---

421 **THE GOSPEL OF JOHN, CH. 8**: "§43. Why do you not understand what I am saying? Because you cannot hear my word. §44. You are of your father the devil, and the lusts of your father you will do. He was a murderer from the beginning, and does not stand in the truth, because there is no truth in him. When he speaks a lie, he speaks of his own: for he is a liar, and the father of it (lying). ...§47. He who is of God, hears God's words: You therefore hear them not, <u>because you are not of God</u>.»

After all, the 'tools' for the appearance of dense matter were in the aetheric region which was in their absolute possession.

A new species of man starts making its appearance, and blends in with the crowd, with no apparent differences: Common men with ordinary feelings and repetitive minds but without a soul granted by the higher ranks of the creators, and completely devoid of spirit. Their **exclusively repetitive brain** *(like a cassette sound recorder)* presents an intense inability to perceive the depth of things and seems to only understand the superficial structure of situations. They are a subcategory of the Iron Gender, 'silicon men', as some call them today, or the gender of clay, the 'common folk/stone people' as they were diminutively called in antiquity.

---

422 **ANTHIMOS GAZIS, 'LEXICON OF THE HELLENIC LANGUAGE:**
The Gr. word λαός = folk, comes from the ancient word λᾶς –λᾶας, genitive: λᾶος = stone, rock
In relation to this, Greek Mythology narrates the story of Pyrra and Deucalion.
PIERRE GRIMAL 'LEXICON OF THE HELLENIC AND THE ROMAN MYTHOLOGY'

«THE MYTH OF PYRRA AND DEUCALION: We have the myth of Deucalion and his wife Pyrra. According to this Myth, Zeus felt that men were so steeped in vice that he had best destroy them with a great cataclysm. He decided to spare only two just ones: Deucalion and his wife Pyrra. On Prometheus' advice, (Deucalion's father), they built an arc in the shape of a huge chest and got inside along with their animals. For nine days it rained incessantly, and when it stopped and the waters receded, the arc ran ashore on the mountains of Thessaly, Greece. When they disembarked, Zeus sent Hermes and offered to fulfill a wish they would make. **They desired for the Earth to acquire men.** Zeus then instructed them to throw the 'bones' of the earth over and behind their shoulders. Deucalion realized that, by 'bones', Zeus meant the stones. So they threw stones over their shoulders, and those that Pyrra threw turned into women while those of Deucalion, into men. Thus, people (from stones = λᾶας - λᾶος = folk) were created. Deucalion and Pyrra though, had four children of their own, born of them and not of the stones of the Earth: Protogeneia, Hellen(es), Amphictyon and Melantho (Melantheia).»

We will once again turn to the myths, in order to de-symbolize some truths. The Greek myth of Deucalion and Pyrra renders this event, as all myths do, through codes/symbols. The said couple represents Celestial Men. But it was **they** who created the category of "common folk" with the symbolic action of throwing stones behind their backs. The stone *(see silicon)* symbolizes the creation of 'living' skeptomorphs, deprived of spirit, which start to accumulate in the astral plane. These skeptomorphs gathered into categories and thus created energy-hypostases of substantial strength. Using logic's energy-'material' –i.e. the energy of logical thought– from the lower mental plane, they started surrounding themselves with emotions (borrowed) from the primary astral space and in combination with the widespread energized action of matter –i.e. energy produced by every form of activity– they created an aetheric consciousness in the form of a quasi-soul *(the artificial spirit)*. With it they built astro-aetheric replicas of men and then vitalized material bodies, which were born through natural birth here on earth.

[423] **A) THE APOCRYPHON OF JOHN, THE GNOSTIC SOCIETY LIBRARY**, [Eng. tr. from Coptic: STEVAN DAVIES]: «Through intercourse the Ruler caused new human bodies to be produced and he blew his **artificial spirit** into each of them *(Not the Power of the Mother as he initially did with the souls!)*.»

B) 'AVATON' MAGAZINE (SEPTEMBER 2006 ISSUE)
ARTICLE BY ION MAGGOS: 'WHO STEALS OUR SOULS?'
«As we have mentioned above, not even 50% of the people have souls. Es-

Don't skip chapters or bibliographic references

sentially, they are psychopaths with a mask of reason. …Clinical psychiatrist H. Cleckley, in his work 'Mask of Sanity', describes an individual who can **mimic** the human personality but gives the impression that something is missing here: "…This functioning soul-apparatus systematically reproduces not only samples of human logic, but also the correct emotional reactions to all different real-life stimuli. What we are dealing with is a hard-to-descry reflex-machine which perfectly **mimics** the human personality."
And researcher Ion Maggos continues…
…Their differences are not perceptible to the senses. Anthropoids do not have their higher *(energy)* centers developed and cannot evolve. In short, they have no souls. Externally though, they are stronger and more beautiful. …In an organic portal *(this is how he alternatively calls the soulless ones)* the so-called higher chakras are produced as the result of the theft of this energy from the soulful ones. This gives them the ability to <u>simulate</u> a soulful person. The soulful individual can see a mirror image of his/her psychological characteristics when he/she attributes soul-properties to these beings. Watch how tiring the presence of such beings is to you, even if you 'feel' they are the most charismatic individuals you have ever met. The DNA of the two races *(i.e. the soulful and the soulless: The author of the article believes that every soul possesses a Divine Spark)* has so much intermingled in the last thousands of years, that we can find it inside even the same families: Your brother, your sister, your father, son or daughter; not someone in the other side of the world, or across the street, who worships another god or has a different skin color. Maybe, it is one or more individuals with whom you live every day of your life, and who have of course, only one reason to be where they are: to drain and disorient the soulful beings away from their esoteric journey; in other words, **from their escape**.»

As we have mentioned earlier in our discussion, the human cell carries within its genetic code not only the structural model for the creation of the material body, but also the weaving pattern for the aetheric and the astral bodies, thus drawing/extracting the corresponding building material from the respective planes. But the Soul, with or without a Spark, enters a <u>complete</u> body at the defining moment of birth. Thus the creators, using the power of the Spirit (Soul and Spark) 'as yeast' in the initial phases of material creation, had already formulated in dense matter the corresponding **gene substructures** for man's basic functions. Nothing could alter the outcome any longer if, at the moment of birth, a soul <u>did not</u> settle inside the new material body. These new 'human' beings, a sub-race of the Iron Gender –the clay people– are normal people in their material appearance, regardless of race and color. Today, the greatest portion of mankind is made of this third astral species. Therein lies the cause for the population explosion and not in the creation of new souls and/or spirits. If the myth describing the 'castration' of Uranus/Spirit interprets the events at a higher spiritual plane, then it clearly denotes the end for every new birth of any psycho-spiritual being. The number of already created souls has remained the same since then. The number of the initially encaged Divine Sparks has **not** increased.

The differences in the manifestations of the three categories (Celestial Men, plain Souls, and astral men) are hardly distinguishable. The difference in Celestial Men however, is a selectively existing sense, which has its root exclusively in the spiritual body, and not the astral one. After all, the <u>seventh</u> sense of Truth stems from there too. This selectively special sense makes the owners of Spirit seem 'quaint' in the eyes of those who **can't receive from their lacking self.**

The second category now, where plain souls vitalize men, exhibits an intensely slavish religiousness, with limited spiritual inquisitiveness.

The third category of simple astral-men with the repetitive brain and the various good or bad feelings –depending on the astral level they come from– show an intense affiliation (attachment) to matter and a strong inability to understand the term 'spirituality'. In fact, they associate it (spirituality) with the mental upgrading of man, which might very well correspond to the specifications of a fully upgraded electronic computer.

This is the source of the fundamental quarrels among men about the existential riddles of life and the varying beliefs about man's nature. Environment plays a relatively minor role in the determination of these views, and of course the view that someone has allegedly evolved after many –dangerous and burdening to the spirit– incarnations is **absolutely not valid**.

It is in this creative orgasm that reigned upon the earth during that post-cataclysmic period, that all the peoples' mythologies have their roots. Both camps of the creators left indelible signs of their presence in the world, testimonies that betrayed a specialized technology that today astounds us and makes us wonder. Contemporary scientists stubbornly refuse to accept it and because of that they put forth extreme conjectures to explain the archeological riddles/findings. These technologies were initially used by the creators themselves and were later appropriated by men. That advanced knowledge has never been a human conquest, but was the product of 'positive prescription' since this technological know-how was never man's privilege, but a reflection of his creators' advancements. This knowledge was later abandoned by the following generations as incomprehensible. Some initiated 'guardians' of this knowledge however safeguarded it like the 'apple of their eye' and bequeathed it to selected concessionaires through initiation.

Don't skip chapters or bibliographic references

స్⸱⸱⸲

As time went on, the newly implanted genes started manifesting their properties in men. Men gradually started losing any ability for insight and transcendental sense, all the way to the absolute loss of them. The creators had succeeded in their goal. Men would remain spiritually weak and 'blind' from then on.

---

424 **A) BLAVATSKY H., P., 'THE SECRET DOCTRINE'** (II-769):

«All the 'fables' of the Greeks were built on historical facts…The expression 'one-eyed' *(Cyclopes)*, refers to the eye of Wisdom *(Sophia)*; for the two front eyes were fully developed as physical organs only in the beginning of the Fourth Race. The allegory of Ulysses *(Odysseus)*…who was saved by putting out the eye of Polyphemus with a fire-brand, is based upon the psycho-physiological atrophy of the spiritual/third eye.»

Blavatsky assumes that Odysseus belonged to the Fourth Root-Race of the Atlanteans –as she calls the Fourth Race of Heroes. But the Trojan War (in which Odysseus actively participated) is dated much later than the cataclysm with the sinking of Atlantis (Fourth Root-Race) and the end of the Atlantean Race. After all, the findings of Troy by Schliemann are dated (the older ones) up to 3,200 B.C. Additionally, scientific research has shown that a great flood occurred between 5,000 and 7,000 years ago, whereas Plato in 'Critias' dates Atlantis 9,000 before his time.

PLATO'S CRITIAS (verses 108d5-108e5): «And if I can recollect and recite to you all that has once been said by the priests (of Egypt) and brought hither by Solon. …Let me begin by observing first of all, that **nine thousand years have elapsed** since the war between the dwellers beyond the Pillars of Heracles (Gibraltar) and all who dwelt within them (in the Mediterranean); …and in command of the other side were the kings of the island of Atlantis.»

Therefore, logically, Odysseus [Ulysses] belongs to the Fifth Race, or the Iron Gender, or the Arian Race, as Blavatsky calls it.

The wit of the reasoning mind and the cleverness of the 'resourceful' (Gr. 'poly-mechanos' = he who can devise many tricks/machines) new kind of man of the Iron Race, who in this myth is represented by Odysseus [Ulysses], who, by the way, has left 'Penelope /Eve/I Am Presence' alone, condemns to permanent 'blindness' the Spiritual (third) eye, which is located in the center of the forehead and is represented by Cyclops Polyphemus, an entity of the previous Race, the Fourth.

A reminder of the lament of the souls as they were preparing for incarnation:

B) HERMES TRISMEGISTUS, HERMETIC TEXTS, VOL. II, RODAKIS P., TZAFEROPOULOS AP., 'EXCERPT XXIII, FROM THE HOLY BIBLE OF HERMES TRISMEGISTUS, TITLED KORE KOSMOU':

> «§36. For the souls no longer belonging to God, the eyes will no longer hold a prominent position and through such watery spheres as these, we will see our own forefather Heaven tiny, and we shall never cease to suffer, and at some point we shall have no more *(spiritual)* vision.»

New men gradually started 'seeing' less and less of the aetheric.

> [425] **PAPASTAVROU, A., 'LETTERS TO ANONYMOUS'** (p.125)
> *Speeches of the teachers of the 'White Brotherhood', i. e. the creators' delegates).*
> «Elsewhere, Maha Chohan, in another speech he gave on June 28th, 1955 at the Royal Teton, pertaining to the same subject, stated the following:
> 'During those primitive days…each and every one could see me, talk to me and ask for my advice. Thus, we had a close cohesion on Planet Earth, during that period. After the creation of 'Maya' (dark curtain) from the dissonant thoughts and feelings of the world, which started to forget its Source, the 'human veil' was formed in the interior of and around the physical brain. This started making our presence less and less discernible to the physical vision of the world, until we became simple 'shadows' with our body parts no longer definable. In time, even this weak diagram disappeared and we remained just a memory, a myth and a tradition.»

When this became apparent, it meant the successful completion of the plan for the ranks of the creators. In the material world of men respectively, the gradual decrease of sightings of the aetheric world was interpreted as the 'departure' of the gods to 'other places' and spurred legend creation. Many are those who even today, still wait for their gods to return! Others again interpret those initial sightings of the 'gods' as 'extraterrestrial races' that abandoned their 'creation-of-man experiment' and returned to their distant homelands, planning to return in the future. It was nevertheless the new circumstances/conditions/terms of the Clash of the Titans that forced all those powers to perform their activities, no longer visible to the eyes of men.

> [426] **BOOK OF ENOCH, 15:10** «They will neither eat food nor drink, invisible to the sight *(the evil spirits of the giants/Nephelims)* and they will rise even against men and women, for they have received life from them.» *Because of course, their existence as skeptomorphs (thoughtforms) was the result of the horrid negative and aggressive thought-creations of men.*

Don't skip chapters or bibliographic references

Today, sporadically and to very few people, some remnants of the old genes manifest, giving their owners some of the primal attributes, and offering them the 'gift' of inner vision or something equivalent. This genetic property makes them capable of 'seeing' or 'hearing' what is invisible to the rest. Beyond this though, in most cases, these people manifest no other spirituality. And since the one-eyed reigns over the blind, some pretend to be 'spiritual' leaders and lead their followers to devastation…

Men today, just like the blind, feel their way around the surrounding world, hypothesize and reach incomplete conclusions. Investigation through matter is by default fragmentary and therefore lacking. Thus, the possibility of revealing the spiritual root of unified knowledge becomes unattainable. Only from the highest spiritual planes can one gaze to the lower ones and only from there can one locate the scattered pieces of the Truth inside matter.

It is not rare for science to act as a trammel to man's Spiritual evolution. The sole purpose of earth-science is to explain the material world. Some parts of the Knowledge however do not belong to the densely material plane, but have their origin in the spiritual realm. Thus, due to their 'nature' they cannot become tangible by the materially-focused scientist; and science then, not being able to 'touch' them, considers it wiser –in order to maintain its authority– to discard them as nonexistent, proclaiming matter to be all there is. This way however, it plunges man deeper into his materialism, and indirectly depicts him as a pulsating mass of cells…

He became quiet… He stood up and walked around the room. He then turned and resumed the discussion.

THE CHRIST PHENOMENON

–The majority of people have not realized the Greatness of Christ, or His work, or His Logos (Word), nor have they understood the reason for His Descent. And they haven't understood, because Christ's words were falsified in an effort to make them compatible and convenient to the status quo, that the creators wanted to keep undisturbed. How else would the transgressor *(the archon of this world)* "get along" with the representative of absolute lawfulness *(Luminary/Monogenes/Christ)?* Furthermore, the majority of the Jews realized that the Christ had not been sent by their own creator/god, and rejected Him. Christians kept the impure teachings and worshiped Jehovah. Material misunderstanding at its grandeur!

---

427 **A) THE GOSPEL OF JOHN, CH. 8**: «§42. And Jesus said to them *(the Jews)*, "If God were your Father, you would love Me... §44. You are of your father the devil, and the lusts of your father you will do. He was a murderer from the beginning, and does not stand in the truth, because there is no truth in him. When he speaks a lie, he speaks of his own: for he is a liar, and the father of it (lying). ...§47. You therefore hear them not, because you are not of God.»

B) THE GOSPEL OF JUDAS [KASSER R., MEYER M., WURST G.] NATIONAL GEOGRAPHIC
JESUS DIALOGUES WITH HIS DISCIPLES: THE PRAYER OF THANKSGIVING OR THE EUCHARIST:

«[33] One day He *(Jesus)* was with his disciples in Judea, and he found them gathered together and seated in pious observance. When he [approached] his disciples [34] gathered together and seated and offering a prayer of thanksgiving over the bread, [he] laughed. The disciples said to [him], "Master, why are you laughing at [our] prayer of thanksgiving? We have done what is right."

He answered and said to them, "I am not laughing at you. <You> are not doing this because of your own will but because it is through this that **your god [will be] praised.**" They said, "Master, you are [...] the son of our god." Jesus said to them, "How do you know me? Truly [I] say to you, no generation of the people that are among you will know me."

THE DISCIPLES BECOME ANGRY:

When his disciples heard this, they started getting angry and infuriated and began blaspheming against Him in their hearts. When Jesus observed their lack of [understanding, he said] to them, 'Why has this agitation led you to anger? **Your god who is within you** [1] and [...] [35] have provoked you to anger [within] your souls.'

JESUS SPEAKS TO JUDAS PRIVATELY:

Don't skip chapters or bibliographic references

---

[35] 'It is possible for you to reach (the Kingdom), but you will grieve a great deal. [36] For someone else **will replace you**, in order that the twelve [disciples] may **again come to completion with their god.**"

(1)*Jesus, by saying "your God who is within you" He means the breath of the fallen creator, which is within each human soul. (See reference #241 regarding the creation of the Soul)*

Conversely, Jesus did not have this creator's 'breath' within Him, since He was Pure Spirit. Thus He said:

JOHN'S GOSPEL 14: «§30. I will not speak much more with you, for the ruler of the world is coming, and he has nothing in Me *(=he has nothing in Me that belongs to him).*»

C) **GOSPEL OF THOMAS**, JEAN YVES LELOUP: «§52. His disciples said to Him: "Twenty-four prophets have spoken in Israel, and they all spoke of You." He said to them: "You have disregarded the Living One who is in your presence, and you have spoken of the dead.» [Eng. tr. JOSEPH ROWE]

And at another point He clarifies regarding the prophets:

D) **THE GOSPEL OF JOHN, CH. 10**: «§8. (Jesus said) All who ever came <u>before Me</u> are thieves and robbers.»

When Celestial Men joined the universe of the transgressor, they were completely and constantly connected with the Monogenes of their Hyper-Universe, where THEY had come from as His Emanations/Offspring, as well as with The Supreme Father. The Monogenes of the particular HyperUniversal Region where the 'leak' originated from, was the Intelligent Wholeness we call Christ; His Offspring, the Celestial Men. When in a material man the Divine Spark reunites with the 'I Am Presence' then his connection with the Genitor Christ is restored and the phrase: 'The Christ is inside you' becomes reality. Man then understands Jesus Christ, because He experiences Him.

---

428 A) **GOSPEL OF PHILIP**, JEAN-YVES LELOUP: «§44. It is impossible for anyone to see the everlasting reality and not become like IT. ...But when you see something in this other space *(HyperUniverses)*, you become IT. If you know the Spirit, you are the Spirit. If you know the Christ, you become the Christ. If you see the Father, you are the Father.» [Eng. tr. JOSEPH ROWE]

B) **THE GOSPEL OF TRUTH, NAG HAMMADI MANUSCRIPTS** [Tr. from Coptic PATERSON BROWN]:

«§6. Therefore confusion was enraged at Him *(Jesus)* and pursued Him in order to suppress and eliminate Him. He was nailed to a crossbeam, He became the fruit of recognizing the Father. Yet it did not cause those who consumed it *(the Fruit of recognizing the Father)* to perish, but rather to those who consumed it He bestowed a rejoicing at such a discovery. <u>For He</u> *(Jesus)* <u>found them</u> *(those who sought)* <u>in Himself and they</u> *(who sought)* <u>found Him</u> *(Jesus)* <u>in themselves.</u>»

C) **GOSPEL OF THOMAS,** JEAN YVES LELOUP: «§3. Jesus said: ... "The Kingdom *(of Heaven)* is inside you." ...§108. Jesus said: "Whoever drinks from my mouth shall become like Me, and I shall become them, and what was hidden from them shall be revealed.» [Eng. tr. JOSEPH ROWE]

Material creation had taken a very different path than the one expected. The chasm between the apostate creators' team and the HyperUniverses was already deep. The apostates had embezzled Sacred Archetypes that <u>did not belong</u> to them, and in order to continuously vitalize the death inside which they had settled, they plunged the Archetype of Life and the Divine Spirit into septic dense matter to make matter **appear** alive. However, as the Sacred Archetype of Life vivified the material bodies, the 'conflict' was triggered between life and the death that dense matter bore within, producing pain which defiled Sacred Life. This was the rape of Life *(...Yaldabaoth raped Eve)*. This pain started permeating every material plane and kept crushing Every Wholeness passing through them. Each Wholeness, beyond and above the 'Ego', had the capacity to perceive the massive cry of despair, fear and pain the <u>entire</u> material creation emitted – something totally imperceptible to humans.

[429] **ILISSOS JOURNAL, ISSUE 95,** 1972, 'BREAKTHROUGH SCIENCE: 'THE UNKNOWN PSYCHIC WORLD OF PLANTS', SCIENTIFIC RESEARCH ACHIEVEMENTS IN BRAZIL.'

«...Cleve Backster, an FBI technician, wanted to know if the plant felt the anxiety of a person in danger. If so, a violent and immediate pain would cause a much more dramatic reaction. Then, he 'thought' of cutting off one of its leaves. The moment the thought crossed his mind, the pens (of the reaction-measuring-apparatus) rose at once to the maximum level and immediately after that to zero. 'The plant had 'screamed' from terror and then fainted.' It recovered very slowly while Backster started giving up on the idea of causing any harm to it.

...A plant being abused by a scientist, in the presence of five other colleagues of his, loses consciousness but remains alive. The six scientists leave the room. Shortly after that, the five return (the ones who were previously only watching the abuse of the plant). The plant is in a state of general alert. When the 'molester' enters the room, the plant

Don't skip chapters or bibliographic references

'recognizes' him and loses consciousness.

Other plants, which were in a completely tranquil state for hours, seem to enter a mass state of turmoil the minute some small crawfish are thrown into boiling water and die in the next room.

...Henrico, in service with General Electric, specialized in medical engineering, has dealt extensively with the 'temperament' of plants at first and later on with the human temperament. Results were simultaneously accomplished... "The leaves –said Rodriguez– radiate a mysterious energy which we first managed to capture and photograph in the form of light. ... No photographic camera is used, nor any lenses. The object to be photographed is placed on a piece of film which is then developed thanks to the electric discharge passing through the object *(Kirlian photography is described here, see reference #174)*. These photographs are but one of the interesting results we managed to hit upon in our labs. The 'aura' of the leaf changes shape and color in relation to what we might call the plant's general state of health. This was nothing though. The most notable fluctuations appear when the plant 'feels' threatened ...or when danger of any kind to other living entities is imminent."

...Researchers and scholars under the supervision of Prof. Ernani, director of the Institute of Psycho-biophysics in Sao Paolo Brazil, also participate in the experiments. The team is comprised of 50 researchers/scientists who specialize in the construction of special gauges measuring the invisible radiations of bodies.»

This way, the creators had allegedly given life to a morbid creation, which, due to its quality and in combination with the Archetype of Life and the Spirit, produced a devastating side-effect/energy in the form of skeptomorphs (thoughtforms).

As the vitalized energy sank deeper, seeping through septic matter in order to vitalize it –obeying matter's periodic route– it would then rise back up (from dense matter) transmuted yet again into a degraded and inferior skeptomorphic side-effect-energy. This process followed a steady, repetitive cycle, which incessantly, not only vitalized the ever increasing side-effect-energy (of the skeptomorphs) but also resulted in even further degradation of all energy-planes, as it continued its eternal transformation cycle. This was a sin of no precedence, and it burdened solely the administrators/creators of this procedure, not their subordinates.

Additionally, supported by the amnesia they themselves had forced upon the kidnapped Men, they subdued them to permanent slavery for the production of this energy, deceiving them with false promises of "redemption" and "spiritual evolution" and arousing their admiration for the world they

had built allegedly for man's benefit. But they had counterfeited a caricature of the HyperLuminous World of Light with stolen 'tools'.

---

430 **A) PLATO'S "TIMAEUS"** (verses 29A2 – 29B2):
«If, of course, this world is beautiful, and the Creator Ἀγαθός, it is obvious that the Maker was aiming for the eternal (the unchangeable)...And
since these things exist in this way, by absolute necessity, **this world
must be the image of another.**»

B) HERMES TRISMEGISTUS, HERMETIC TEXTS, VOL. I, RODAKIS P., TZAFE-
ROPOULOS AP., **SPEECH I**
«§8. And I said to Him: Where do these elements of nature come from? And
He answered to me again: From the Divine Will which took the form of
Logos (Word) and **saw the Good World** *(of the HyperUniverses)* **and mimicked it,** creating a world with its own *(the Divine Will's)* elements and its
own creations, the souls.»

C) DANEZIS M., THEODOSIOU S. 'COSMOLOGY OF THE INTELLECT':
«...Such an acceptance though, would shatter contemporary cosmological
views to pieces, let alone a series of social and philosophical currents based
on them, since the following hypothesis would start to faintly light up:
Namely, that the birth of this Universe, which is perceptible to us, occurred
through the false non-existence **of another invisible Universe, which may
extend beyond the horizon of the Black Hole.**» *(...the Black Hole **which is
our Universe**)*

Yet the damage did not stop there. They presented the deceit they had
forced upon humans as the normal "status quo".

---

431 **THE GOSPEL OF TRUTH,** NAG HAMMADI MANUSCRIPTS, THE ECUMENICAL COPTIC
PROJECT [Eng. tr. from Coptic THOMAS PATERSON BROWN] www.metalog.org/files/valent.html
«§3. Wherefore confusion grew strong, **contriving its matter** in emptiness
and **un**-acquaintance with the Truth, preparing to substitute truthfulness with
a potent and **alluring fabrication**. But this was no humiliation for Him, the
Inconceivable and Incomprehensible. For the anxiety and the amnesia and
the deceitful fabrication were nothing– whereas the established Truth is immutable, imperturbable and of unadornable beauty...
§4. The amnesia of confusion was not made as a revelation, it is not the
handiwork of the Father. Forgetfulness does not occur under His directive,
although it does happen because of Him *(so that men ignore Him/The Father)*...Since amnesia occurred because the Father was not recognized,
thereafter, when the Father is recognized, there will be no more forgetting.»

Don't skip chapters or bibliographic references

And they showed men that acceptance of all pain and every misery was the only way to salvation, convincing them that all this was mandatory in the name of false positivity and "for their own good"!

> **432** **THE GOSPEL OF TRUTH**, NAG HAMMADI MANUSCRIPTS THE ECUMENICAL COPTIC PROJECT [Eng. tr. from Coptic THOMAS PATERSON BROWN] www.metalog.org/files/valent.html
> «§3... Therefore despise confusion! It has no roots and was in a fog concerning the Father, preparing <u>labors</u> and <u>amnesia</u> and <u>fear</u> **in order thereby to entice** those of the transition *(those created from the astro-aetheric fields)* <u>and take them captive.</u>»

In fact their perversion exceeded all limits of logic when they forced their obedient 'good slaves' (bondservants) to feel happiness and satisfaction in the pains they were experiencing, in the pretense that they would be absolved/redeemed from sins that essentially had **only** been committed because they were under the influence of this material body; a body their creators had dressed them with, since this 'garment of rot' was predisposed to generate passions and hatreds and conflicts and envies and angers, forging heavy chains around the misguided humans.

> **433** **THE APOCRYPHON OF JOHN, THE GNOSTIC SOCIETY LIBRARY** [STEVAN DAVIES]:
> «They intended to make him anew this time from Earth, Water, Fire, Wind, which are Matter, Darkness, Desire, The Artificial Spirit. This all became **a tomb,** a new kind of body *(grave).* Those thieves bound the man in it, enchained him in forgetfulness, they <u>made him subject to dying.</u>»

But the sin was one and <u>one alone.</u>

> **434** **THE GOSPEL OF JOHN, CH. 16**: «§11 ...And concerning judgment, because the archon (ruler) of this world **has been judged**.»

It was the sin of the morbid apostate/creator who had forced an entire humanity to live inside 'vitalized' waste and its byproducts, boldly proclaiming that if the system of human society did not function flawlessly it was because of man's inefficiency.

> **435** **THE GOSPEL OF JUDAS** [KASSER R., MEYER M., WURST G.] NATIONAL GEOGRAPHIC: «[44] "Jesus said 'It is **impossible** to sow seed on [rock] and harvest its fruit. [This] is also the way [...] the [defiled] generation [...] and corruptible Sophia [...] *(of this decaying world)* the hand that has created mortal people...»

When it became clear to the HyperCosmoi of the Truth that despite the leniency shown to this material creation it had **no possibility of spiritual evolution**, it was decided that this creation should cease to exist.

> [436] A) **THE GOSPEL OF LUKE, CH. 12**: «§49. I came to set fire on the earth, and how I wish it were already lit! ... §51. Do you suppose that I came to give peace on earth? I tell you, not at all, but rather division.»
>
> B) **GOSPEL OF THOMAS**, JEAN YVES LELOUP:
> (a) «§10. Jesus says: "I have sown fire upon the world, and now I tend it to a blaze.»
> (b) «§71. Jesus says: "I shall overturn this house and no one will be able to [re]build it.» [Eng. tr. JOSEPH ROWE]

The easiest resolution would be to totally destroy this 'product'. But before this could happen, all Celestial Men **held hostage** in the material universe had to return Home. But they were already enslaved, plunged in spiritual lethargy, constantly turning their kidnappers' 'wheel of life', subjected to consecutive reincarnations.

> [437] **GOSPEL OF THOMAS**, JEAN YVES LELOUP: "§28. Jesus says: I stood in the midst of the world and revealed myself to them in the flesh. I found them all intoxicated. Not one of them was thirsty and my soul grieved for the children of humanity, for they are blind in their hearts. They do not see. They came naked into the world, and naked they will leave it. At this time, they are intoxicated. When they have vomited their wine (*the poison of the snake-god*), they will return to themselves." [Eng. tr. JOSEPH ROWE]

Thus, the Worlds of Truth were limited to send their messengers at random 'instances' of material time and to various places on Earth, aiming to awaken men sedated by 'Maya' *(=the illusion/deceit of material life/world)*. But human time runs differently inside this black hole of matter *(...where between two ticks of the clock time is infinite, equaling eternity)*. Thus, even though actions of the HyperCosmoi of Truth succeeded one another almost instantly, their results in the leisurely material time, spanned to much greater time-intervals; because an instance THERE unfolds into thousands of years here. So because magnitudes were disproportional, this gave the few people, who were waiting for a Divine answer, the impression of devaluation. The majority of humanity on the other hand was unable to recognize and accept those emissaries, because what they proclaimed was **different** to what many men had been 'programmed' to hear, and their reasoning was regulated in such a way that they could **only** recognize their creators' 'delegates'.

Don't skip chapters or bibliographic references

---

438 **THE GOSPEL OF JOHN, CH. 8**: «§43. Why do you not understand what I am saying? Because you cannot hear my word. ...§47. He who is of God, hears God's words: You therefore hear them not, <u>because you are not of God</u>.»

On account of that, some of the emissaries were killed, others were mocked, others ignored, others labeled crazy and disturbed, while the evidence of the Truth they presented was destroyed or falsified. The Celestial Children however had to return **at any expense** and with them all the Sacred Archetypes that the team of thieves had swindled. It was decided then that different, more drastic measures had to be taken.

❧··❧

The request for the return of the Sacred Archetypes and the Spiritual Children was communicated to the fallen creator. The answer was very provocative indeed: "Celestial Men cannot be returned, because according to the laws of material creation, they owe karma (sins). This karma must be repaid". It was then that the definitive decision was made in the HyperUniverses! The Monogenes Christ **would repay** the karma (sins) of His Own Offspring (Celestial Children) and of all the souls that wanted to follow Him, in order for them to be allowed to exit the tightly sealed, material universe.

The price demanded was the highest and required that both sides of the forces behind this creation should be compensated and satisfied by receiving the maximal **energy** which would be shed (produced) by the pain of the sacrifice suffered by the ENTIRE Intelligent Sentient Wholeness of the Monogenes.

---

439 **THE GOSPEL OF MATTHEW, CH. 10**: «§28. ...Just as the Son of Man did not come to be served but to serve, and <u>to give His life as **ransom**</u> for many.»

His Entire Spirit <u>should</u> incarnate inside a material body! No material body however **could withstand** the Totality of His Spiritual Magnitude. It would burn out.

---

440 **HERMES TRISMEGISTUS**, HERMETIC TEXTS, VOL. I, RODAKIS P., TZAFEROPOULOS AP., **SPEECH VI**: «§2...For all things that are born are full of passions, birth itself being a passion as well; and where passion is, there is no Ἀγαθόν *(Agathón)*. ...It is hence impossible for Ἀγαθόν to be in birth, it can only be in the unborn... §3. When it comes to man, Ἀγαθόν *(Agathón)* is determined in comparison to evil. Down here, the not-so-evil is considered Ἀγαθόν; And Ἀγαθόν down here, is the smallest particle of evil. ...And it is impossible for it (Ἀγαθόν) to exist (down here); for **IT cannot be contained in a material body** which is bound on all sides by wickedness, pains, labors and rage and deceit and by foolish fantasies.»

Just like ordinary electric cables cannot bear high-voltage electric loads and other, special ones, suitably constructed are required, such is the relation between material body and spirit. When a Great Entity is incarnated into this material world, <u>only a mere part of IT</u> is embodied inside the material body, not all of IT: this happens in order for the material body to manage to withstand the magnitude of the Spirit it encompasses. This is why the material body of the Monogenes had to be of "unique specifications". It had to simultaneously experience the complete amplitude of pain, in order to pour out its **prime energy** down to its last drop, so that the archons of this world, <u>worshipers of bloody sacrifices</u>, would satisfy their perverted appetites by supplementing **their karmic** balance with even the last drop of His pain and His blood.

441 A) **GOSPEL OF PHILIP**, [En. Tr. from Coptic: PATERSON BROWN] www.metalog.org/files/philip.html
(TABLET 104): «§54. God is a cannibal. Because of this, mankind is sacrificed *(through karma)*. Before mankind was sacrificed, animals were being sacrificed. For these to which they are sacrificed are not divinities.»
B) **PAPASTAVROU, A., 'LETTERS TO ANONYMOUS'** CH. ASTRAL PLANE (P. 102)
The Creators and their delegate-teachers state through channeling:
(a) «Speech of Goddess Pallas Athena (Bridge, February 1960): "Everything here on Earth as well as in the far beyond <u>demands deposition of energy</u>. As you advance higher in the path of light, <u>so much more invaluable becomes</u> *(for their own benefit...)* <u>the gift of your energy as well as the gift of your life</u>.»
(b) «Speech of Saint Germaine given on January 1st, 1955, in Philadelphia, USA. "Your knowledge on energy is minimal. Energy manifested in the world of matter, as well as in the higher spheres, <u>is a force through which everything is accomplished</u>.» («...preparing labors and amnesia and fear in order thereby to entice...» [Gospel Of Truth])
C) **OLD TESTAMENT, EXODUS CH. 29**
Instructions of the god/creator to his bondservant Moses: It is useful for someone to read the entire chapter, as well as many others from the Old Testament...
«§10. Then you shall bring the bullock (young bull) before the tent of the congregation, and Aaron and his sons shall put their hands on the head of the bull. §11. **Then you shall kill the bullock before the Lord**, at the entrance of the tent of the congregation. §12. You shall take some of **the blood** of the bullock and put it on the horns of the altar with your finger, and pour all the blood beside the base of the altar. §13. And you shall take all the fat that co-

vers the inner parts, the upper lobe of the liver, and the two kidneys with the fat that is around them, and burn them all on the altar *(This energy-nutrition is predestined for the lord)*. §14. But the flesh of the bull, with its skin and its **offal** *(excretion)*, you shall burn with fire outside the camp. It is a sin offering *(This is predestined energy-nutrition for his counterpart, the daemon)*. §15. "You shall also take one ram, and Aaron and his sons shall put their hands on the head of the ram; §16. and you shall slay the ram, and you shall take **its blood** and **sprinkle it all around on the altar**. §17. Then you shall cut the ram into pieces, wash its internal organs and its legs, and put them with the other pieces and the head. §18. And you shall burn the whole ram on the altar. It is a burnt offering to the lord; **it is a <u>sweet savor</u>** (pleasing aroma), **an offering by fire <u>to the Lord</u>**. ...§20. Then you shall kill the ram, and take some of its blood and put it <u>on the lobe of the right ear</u> of Aaron and <u>on the lobe</u> of the right ear of his sons, <u>and on the thumb of their right hand</u> and <u>on the big toe of their right foot</u>, and sprinkle the blood all around on the altar. §21. And you shall take some of the blood that is on the altar, and some of the anointing oil, and <u>sprinkle</u> it on Aaron and on his garments, on his sons and on the garments of his sons with him.

Daily Offerings: §38. "Now this is what you shall offer regularly on the altar: **two lambs** a year old, **day by day** continuously. §39. One lamb you shall offer in the morning and the other lamb you shall offer **at twilight**.» *The 'benevolent' Lord's ritual ...resembles black magic!*
Let us not forget though, the 'hecatombs' (one hundred ox sacrificed) offerings of the Greeks to the Dodecatheon (twelve gods)!

Inside the aetheric worlds of the material universe, this special body was constructed in such an innovative form, capable of withstanding the Magnitude of the **Totality** of the Spiritual Power of the Monogenes Christ. The rest is known to everyone. The implantation of the specially made fetus into the womb of the Holy Mother on the Annunciation day was a simple task for all those entities who can build universes. The time of Birth had arrived. A luminous vessel/craft of the creators was continuously supervising the process of such a perilous –for those times– childbirth. This luminous supervising vessel was the 'Star' of Bethlehem.

[442] **THE GOSPEL OF MATTHEW, CH. 2**: «§9...and behold, the star which they had seen in the East **went before them, till it came and stood** over where the young Child was.»...*Stars do not walk!*

All the powers of the material hierarchy guarded this precious 'gourmet meal' of Energy as 'the apple of their eye', and in order for the 'lords' of karma to be satisfied, an agonizing death was required upon the exclusive symbol of matter: the cross.

The moment the Monogenes left His Last material Breath in this world, His Spirit, freed from matter, like a blazing sphere, penetrated all planes/dimensions of matter, thus **rupturing** the hermetically sealed shell of the material universe which held the kidnapped Celestial Men captive. The **breach** in the 'egg' of the snake/god (over the area of Golgotha in Jerusalem) was completed by the creation of a 'Gate' and was sensed around the entire Earth in the form of an earthquake.

---

443 **A) THE GOSPEL OF MATTHEW, CH. 27**:

«§45 Now from the sixth hour until the ninth hour there was darkness over all the land. …§50 And Jesus cried out again with a loud voice, and yielded up His spirit. §51 Then behold the curtain of the temple was torn in two from top to bottom; and the earth shook and the rocks split.»

B) *Dionysius the Areopagite, the Athenian, who, at the time of Jesus' crucifixion, was with Apollophanes the philosopher in Heliopolis of Egypt said, regarding nature's perturbation at that moment:* «Either God is suffering or everything has perished.»

During the early Christian years, the first Christians knew they were imprisoned inside this material universe/egg. With the Resurrection of Christ this 'egg' was broken, and a Gate opened in its 'walls'. This is why in many pictures Jesus is depicted coming out of an egg at the moment of Resurrection *{Tr. n.: especially in eastern Christian Orthodox traditions}*. The first Christians spread the coded message with the custom of breaking red-dyed eggs at Easter, where the material universe/egg, painted red from the Divine blood of Christ, cracks open freeing the road back to the Holy FatherLands.

---

444 **BLAVATSKY H., P., 'THE SECRET DOCTRINE'** (I-359):

«In the Egyptian Book Of The Dead *(It was read by the priests in front of the dead and it gave instructions to the soul, so that it would follow the right path into the world of the spirits)*, the Solar god exclaims: "I am the creative soul of the celestial abyss. No one sees my nest, **no one can break my egg**, I am the Lord!"»

Exactly the same thing is mentioned by the commentator of the 'Orphic

---

Don't skip chapters or bibliographic references

> *Hymns' P. Marinis, where he comments on the Orphic egg as follows:*
> «Pay attention to the fact that the Orphic egg <u>never breaks</u>.»
>
> *But here, I would like to point out, that the cosmic/orphic egg **has been broken** by Christ the Savior, Who, after creating a Breach/Gate, opened the way for the return to the Kingdoms of the HyperUniverses/Aeons of the Supreme Unuttered Principle.*

With the sacrifice of the Monogenes, the law of endless reincarnations between life and death would cease to apply –for any man who would choose to abandon the forbidden tree/universe! Every sin/karma had been paid off. The law of karma concerned only the apostate and he had been paid in full with the Sacrifice of Christ. Christ condemned no man.

> **445** **THE GOSPEL OF JOHN**
>
> **(a) CH. 3**: «§17. ...For God sent the Son into the world, not to judge the world, **but that the world might be saved** through Him.»
>
> **(b) CH. 8**: «§15. You judge according to the flesh; **I judge no one**.»

It is others who "sold" choices to men and expected to be compensated in return, through the balancing of their karma. After all, only the incomplete have the need to "get paid". The dogma of reincarnation with its accompanying karma would <u>only</u> concern the "believers" of material creation. For all others, it would cease to exist since Jesus Christ (as the third party guarantor) had repaid all debts and the road to eternal Life was now open.

> **446** **THE GOSPEL OF JOHN, CH. 3**: "§18. He who believes in Him **is not judged.** He who doesn't believe has been judged already." *(...by the karmic committee and the reciprocal justice of this world, since he finally <u>chooses</u> to remain in this world, and therefore, has to be subject to its laws)."*

❧·❧

The densely material dimension was exclusively perceived through form. Man was trapped inside shape/form, and only through form had he learned to perceive the world. Anything formless, however great, would make him feel uncomfortable. Therefore, an additional endeavor of the Monogenes was to comprehend the world of form, in order to formulate equivalent 'conditions of appearance' in the True Realms, for the smooth transition of Men There. This new Place will be the Area of Reception and Spiritual Restoration for those Men who will comprise the coming 6th Root Race, in a transitory period of preparation and adaptation for the permanent return to the Holy Capital of the Father.

---

447 **A) THE GOSPEL OF JOHN, CH. 14**: «§2. In my Father's house there are many mansions ...I am going to prepare a place for you.»

...An extremely necessary undertaking because:

B) THE GOSPEL OF JUDAS [KASSER R., MEYER M., WURST G.] NATIONAL GEOGRAPHIC JESUS APPEARS TO THE DISCIPLES AGAIN:

«[36] His disciples said to Him, "Lord, what is the great generation that is superior to us and holier than us, that is not now in these realms?' *(...conceit in the superlative!)* When Jesus heard this, he laughed and said to them, "... [37] Truly [I] say to you, no one born [of] this aeon *(of this material world)* will see that [generation], and no host of angels of the stars will rule over that generation, and no person **of mortal birth** can associate with it, because that generation does not come from [...] which has become [...].»

JUDAS RECOUNTS A VISION AND JESUS RESPONDS:

[45] [Jesus] continued, 'No person of mortal birth is worthy to enter the house you have seen, for that place is reserved for the holy. Neither the sun nor the moon will rule there, nor the day, but the holy will abide there always, in the eternal realm with the holy angels.»

The completion of this Spiritual Area will give the signal for the initiation of a sequence of events on Earth, which will lead to the Great Transition people call 'the Second Coming'. As to who will finally be the ones **to manage** to enter THERE, it will be examined later on in our discussion.

ন্ড•৵ড়

The big distortion of the Truth began when Jesus **completely** abandoned the material universe and **permanently** returned to His Celestial Planes.

---

448 **A) THE GOSPEL OF JOHN, CH. 7**: «§33. Then Jesus said, "I will still be with you for a little while. Then I will go to the One who sent Me. §34. You will seek Me <u>but you will not find Me</u>. Where I am going, you cannot come.»

B) THE GOSPEL OF JOHN, CH. 16: «§10. And concerning righteousness, because I am going to My Father **and you will see Me no more.**»

C) THE GOSPEL OF JOHN, CH. 16: «§28. I came forth from the Father and came into the world. Again, I am leaving the world and going to the Father.»

The Resurrection of Christ was a 'natural' outcome which proved His definitive detachment from the visible and invisible material universe. Upon leaving the last (outer) energy-layer of the spiral energy-universe –where

Don't skip chapters or bibliographic references

from every man <u>projects himself</u> onto the material world– His projection on matter, on the selected and enriched 'sedimented life-remnant' **disappeared**. This is the same procedure which will take place –as we will see further on in our discussion– when the prepared human Souls will be transferred to the Prepared Spiritual Place, thus forming the 6th Root Race of Man.

During the first years following the Resurrection of Christ, His Teachings were alive. A great number of men, realizing the Truth, renounced the universe of deceit, freed themselves from the obligation of reincarnations and settled in the 'neutral region' of the Higher Mental Plane, anticipating the completion time of the Holy (Reception) Place.

---

[449] **REVELATION CH 6**: «§9. When He opened the fifth seal, I saw under the altar the souls of those who had been slain for the word of God and for the testimony which they held. §10. And they cried with a loud voice, saying, "How long, O Lord, holy and true, until You judge and avenge our blood on those who dwell on the earth?" §11. Then a white robe was given to each of them; and it was said to them that they should rest a little while longer, until the full number of their fellow servants and their brethren who were to be killed (even as they had been), would be completed also.»

When the creators saw the numerous withdrawals of the imprisoned men they were really vexed.

–Had they not taken what they had asked for with Jesus Christ's sacrifice?

–They were never willing to give back any of their possessions to begin with. After all, deceit is in their nature. Nevertheless, the 'damage' they sustained from the coming of the Monogenes Christ to the material universe had to be remedied. Even today they are 'mending these holes'. The concepts therefore had to be distorted; the Teaching downgraded. It had to lose all its Spiritual Grandeur; it had to become sterile.

The first great distortion of the Christian Religion started with Apostle Paul. Initially a fanatic prosecutor of early Christians and being sent exclusively by his god/creator, Jehovah, he used Jesus Christ's personality as a vessel (bandwagon) to make his own god popular to the whole world.

---

[450] *Paul's God –Jehovah, who established the Law of Moses– belongs to this material world of revenge, punishment, reciprocal 'justice' and karma, along with his motto 'an eye for an eye', as the **entire** team of the apostate gods/creators instituted.*

> *In contrast to that, Jesus renounces punishment, refuses revenge 'turning the other cheek' to His prosecutors and sacrifices <u>Himself</u> for the benefit of the men-souls, in contrast to the sacrifices demanded by the gods/creators of devastation.*

Being a man of high education, he easily managed to push aside and overshadow the real disciples, those who had heard the true Teachings and had been prepared by Jesus Him-Self. He usurped all of Jesus' Work, perverting Christian Teachings **by a few degrees**, just enough to make them reach your age completely falsified.

> **451** **RETROSPECTIVE FALSIFICATION** http://www.skepdic.com/retfalse.html
> «D. H. Rawcliffe coined this term to refer to the process of telling a story that is factual to some extent, but which gets distorted and falsified over time by retelling it with various embellishments. The embellishments may include speculations, conflating events that occurred at different times or in different places, and the incorporation of material without regard for accuracy or plausibility. The overriding force that drives the story is to find or invent details that fit with a desired outcome. …The original story gets remodeled with favorable points being emphasized and unfavorable ones being dropped. The distorted and false version becomes a memory and record of a remarkable tale.»

The disciples on the other hand, submissively yielded to his fervor, unable to control his dynamism or what he taught. This caused the 'intelligent' race of men to bow down and worship the greatest Pharisee of all ages, Paul, overlooking Christ's continuous warnings and suggestions in the Gospels about the character of the Pharisees and their hypocritical talents. Thus Paul built his own religion, Paulianism, which only 'gratis' maintained its original name 'Christianity'. The damage was done. The archon of this world had fulfilled his goal.

> **452** *In the esoteric circles, it is known that Paul the Apostle was the incarnation of Hilarion (The Chohan of the fifth ray), a member of the Spiritual Hierarchy of the archon of this world.* [A. PAPASTAVROU, LETTERS TO THE ANONYMOUS, pp. 145, 495]
> *And to correlate these concepts:* «…Behold, God will receive your sacrifice from the hands of a priest who is the minister of error.» [JUDAS' GOSPEL]

Afterwards, to bridge the differences between the two religions (Christian and Jewish), 'dark' men in high positions inside the Church falsified, rejected and tarnished every sacred text. Proof and words about

Don't skip chapters or bibliographic references

the Glory of Christ were obliterated because some 'mighty fathers' did not comprehend their content. Their egoism didn't permit them to reveal to their 'flock' that they did not know the meaning of the Scriptures. Falsifications and omissions began, as well as the allegedly involuntary translation-mistakes in the Gospels.

---

453 **DAVID ICKE 'THE SECRET OF ALL AGES'** CH.: BACON'S LEGACY

«Bacon (Sir Francis Bacon 1561-1626) along with Robert Flood, a Great Teacher of the Priory of Sion (Prieuré de Sion), **was the one who supervised the translation of the King James' Bible** which, according to an 1881 study, contained at least **36,191** translation mistakes. Considering that Bacon was an extremely well-educated and smart man, I cannot believe he made so many mistakes in the translation, **unless he made them on purpose**. Bacon also made sure that the two Maccabaeus books were removed from his translation.»

In the chapter 'HOW THEY CONTROL THE WORLD, SECRET SOCIETIES', we will realize who Francis Bacon really was, and what objectives he served...

The Christianity 'issue' was already under the complete control of the dark archon.

---

454 **THE GOSPEL OF JUDAS** [38-42] [KASSER R., MEYER M., WURST G.] NATIONAL GEOGRAPHIC

«THE DISCIPLES SEE THE TEMPLE AND DISCUSS IT: They [said, "We have seen] a great [house with a large] altar [in it, and] twelve men –they are the priests, we would say– and a name; and a crowd of people is waiting at that altar, [until] the priests [… and receive] the offerings. [But] we kept waiting." [Jesus said], "What are [the priests] like?" They [said, "Some …] two weeks; [some] sacrifice their own children, others their wives, in praise [and] humility with each other; some sleep with men; some are involved in [slaughter]; some commit a multitude of sins and deeds of lawlessness. And the men who stand [before] the altar invoke your [name], and in all the deeds of their deficiency, the sacrifices are brought to completion […]." *(He who has a mind, let him understand...)*

After they said this, they were quiet, for they were troubled.

JESUS OFFERS AN ALLEGORICAL INTERPRETATION OF THE VISION OF THE TEMPLE:

Jesus said to them, "Why are you troubled? Truly I say to you, all the priests who stand before that altar invoke my name. Again I say to you, my name has been written on this […] of the generations of the stars [(1)] through the human generations. [And they] *(The priests)* have planted trees **without fruit**, in my name, in a shameful manner."

Jesus said to them, Those you have seen receiving the offerings at the altar –that is who you are. That is the god you serve, and you are those twelve men you have seen. The cattle you have seen brought for sacrifice are the many people **you lead astray** before that altar. [...] *(The archon of this world)* will stand and make use of my name in this way, and generations of the pious will remain loyal to him. After him another man will stand there from [the fornicators], and another [will] stand there from the slayers of children, and another from those who sleep with men, and those who abstain, and the rest of the people of pollution and lawlessness and error, and those who say, "We are like angels;" they are the stars [(1)] that bring everything to its conclusion. For to the human generations it has been said, "Look, God will receive your sacrifice from the hands of a priest' –that is, a minister of error. But it is the Lord, the Lord of the universe, who commands, 'On the last day they will be put to shame."

Jesus said [to them], "Stop sac[rificing ...] which you have [...] over the altar, since they are over your stars[(1)] and your angels and have **already** come to their conclusion there. So let them be [ensnared] before you, and let them go [–about 15 lines missing–] generations [...]. A baker cannot feed all creation [42] under [heaven].»

[(1)] **Star**: *Ancient people believed that a star corresponds to each soul, and that any man who led a virtuous life, would return, after his death, back to his corresponding star. Apparently, because of this faith, stars were given names of heroes, gods and semi-gods.*

According to **Plato's Timaeus** *(41 d5 XIV)*: «And having *(the creator)* produced the whole mixture *(the paste/material which he built the souls with)*, he divided it into souls equal in number to the stars, and assigned each soul to a star; and having there placed all the souls in a chariot, he showed them the nature of everything.»

Men had once again become the 'good' slaves (bondservants) of god.

---

455 **THE GOSPEL OF JOHN, CH. 15**: «§15. No longer do I call you bondservants, for a bondservant does not know what his master is doing; ... for everything that I heard from My Father I have made known to you.»

As god's bondservants they ought to glorify him, obey his dictates, stoically offer the "sap of the pain of their self-sacrifice" thus "improving" themselves, patiently enduring their misery because their god decided so, and most importantly, tremble as always before his judgment and his merciless punishment.

---

456 *This is how the concepts were distorted and falsified and transformed Jesus into a judge, because Paul confused his god/creator Jehovah with the Unuttered Principle, The Father of Christ!*
THE FALSIFICATIONS:
(a) ACTS OF THE APOSTLES, 10:42 «And He commanded us to preach to the

Don't skip chapters or bibliographic references

people, and to testify that it is He who is ordained by God to be the Judge of the living and the dead.»

(b) B TIMOTHY'S 4:1 «I do fully testify, therefore, before God, and the Lord Jesus Christ, who will judge the living and the dead at His appearing and His kingdom.»

(c) A PETER 4:5 «They will give an account to Him who is ready to judge the living and the dead.»

...But all this was expected because:

THE GOSPEL OF JUDAS [KASSER R., MEYER M., WURST G.] NATIONAL GEOGRAPHIC
THE DISCIPLES SEE THE TEMPLE AND DISCUSS IT:

«[39] Jesus said to them, 'Those you have seen receiving the offerings at the altar –that is who you are. That is the god you serve, and you are those twelve men you have seen. The cattle you have seen brought for sacrifice are the many people **you lead astray** [40] before that altar. [...] *(The archon of this world)* will stand and make use of my name in this way, and generations of the pious will remain loyal to him.»

The 'index finger' of Christian Teaching no longer pointed towards the Redeeming Truth *('and the Truth shall set you free'),* which facilitated the **escape** from the universe of the snake, but rather shifted direction towards the highest pole of material oscillation, immersing man yet again into the game of bipolarity and the hunt for the accomplishment of the most beneficial 'chemical composition' of his bodily hormones *(oxytocine)* aiming towards emotional 'love'. Everyone by now equated the apostate archon of this world with The Unuttered Principle, The True Father of Jesus.

Through the practice of 'divide and conquer', the creators initially brought about the division of the Christian Church. The final blow (coupe de grace) was dealt by the church itself, through the violence it enforced: Crusades, Holy Inquisition, and coercion to faith, conspiracies, heresies, corruption, and decadence. The result was what could be expected. Do you imagine then that after this whole journey, the Truth would still be 'standing on its own feet'?

Henceforth, Christian Teaching was considered controversial, quaint, ungrounded and lacking any deep spiritual background and people started devaluing it. The Savior's sacrifice was disregarded because it was contradictory: "What sins did Christ come to redeem us from if He is still going to Judge us?" ...They started wondering. The reason for this Divine Offering was soon forgotten and was replaced by an empty, superficial and hypocritical social piety.

When Christ left the material universe, the archons of matter usurped His personality and started wandering in the astro-aetheric worlds, shaping their forms in Jesus' likeness, to delude believers and their 'initiated' disciples.

457 *Misleading deception is the prevailing characteristic of all the powers of matter:*

A) THE APOCRYPHON OF JOHN, THE GNOSTIC SOCIETY LIBRARY:

«§12. But Yaldabaoth possessed a **multitude of faces** (masks), adding up to more than all of them, so that when he was in the midst of the seraphim, he could masquerade in front of them all at will.» [ENG. TR. FROM COPTIC: WALDSTEIN M., WISSE F.]

B) THE GOSPEL OF JUDAS [KASSER R., MEYER M., WURST G.] NATIONAL GEOGRAPHIC

« [40]: ... [LOST TEXT] *(The apostate god)* will stand and **make use of my name** this way, and generations of the pious will remain loyal to him.»

C) CHALDEAN ORACLES, [Gr. tr. ATHINOGENIS I., GRAVIGGER P.] LÓGIA, ORACULA, RESPONSA, KROLL 58- PLACES – LONDON, PAPYRUS 121, 700:

«Send me the true Asclepius, keeping away every adverse daemon, who deceives»

Deceived by these misleading practices of fraud, men pray to Jesus Christ asking Him for material rectification of their earthly problems. But this rectification **cannot** come from Jesus Christ. So, their invocations/requests are answered –the ones that do get answered– from powers of the archon of this world, **the sole administrators of matter**.

458 THE GOSPEL OF JOHN, CH. 18: «§36. Jesus said, "My kingdom is not of this world. If my kingdom were of this world, then my servants would fight that I should not be delivered to the Jews.»

Because, <u>absolutely Spiritual provisions aside</u>, what does Christ have to do with material goods? ...Nothing.

459 THE GOSPEL OF MATTHEW, CH. 6: «§24-25. You cannot serve God and mammon. Therefore I say to you, do not be anxious about your life, what you will eat or what you will drink, nor about your body and what you will wear.»

After all, the only one to blame for the mistakes in the construction of your material body and any diseases caused by them, is your creator, because he alone has the responsibility for the material body and the energy-situations as well as the soul which he keeps hostage. All this is controlled by him, as is everything in your lives and your fate.

460 A) THE GOSPEL OF MATTHEW, CH. 10: «§16. Behold, I send you forth as sheep in the midst of wolves.»

B) THE APOCRYPHON OF JOHN, THE GNOSTIC SOCIETY LIBRARY

CONSTRUCTION OF THE HUMAN BODY: «Yaldabaoth said to his subordinate daemons: "Let's create a man." ...And they said, "Let us call him Adam, so

Don't skip chapters or bibliographic references

that his name will give us the power of light."

...The host of daemons took these *(aetheric)* substances from the Powers to create the limbs and the body itself. They put the parts together and coordinated them. The first ones began by making the head: Abron created his head; Meniggesstroeth created the brain; Asterechme the right eye; Thaspomocha, the left eye; Ieronymos, the right ear; Bissoum, the left ear; Akioreim, the nose; Banenrphroum, the lips; Amen, the front teeth; Ibikan, the molars; Basiliademe, the tonsils;... *(And continues to enumerate one by one the daemons who created all the parts of the human body)*

...Seven govern the whole body: Michael, Ouriel, Asmenedas, Saphasatoel, Aarmouriam, Richram and Amiorps." [Eng. tr. from Coptic: STEVAN DAVIES]

C) THE APOCRYPHON OF JOHN, THE GNOSTIC SOCIETY LIBRARY

SIX QUESTIONS ABOUT THE SOUL: «The physical body will negatively affect them. They wear it as they look forward to the time when they will meet up with those who will remove it. Those people deserve indestructible eternal life. They endure everything, bearing up under everything that happens so that they can deserve the good and inherit life eternal.» [Eng. tr. from Coptic: STEVAN DAVIES]

On the contrary, **true** saints –many of whom remain unknown to men– residing in the Higher Mental Plane have the ability to intervene and through the HyperUniverses bring solutions to men. Supreme amongst them is considered to be the Mother of Jesus, Mary.

Simultaneously, the creators through their "appointed masters" prepared monumental "spiritual" teachings in various religions and theories, in order for "blind" men to stand and 'gaze in awe'. The pre-programmed steps were absolutely specific.

After the falsification of His Teachings, they turned to Christ as a person. He had to be demeaned, lose his glorious radiance and finally end up as a simple myth. So criticisms about the various "weaknesses" of Jesus came to play. "He crumbled under the torture of the cross, when he said: 'if it be possible, let this cup pass from Me' [Matthew 26:39]" –said many– as if the fleshy grave/body had the ability to react differently!

---

[461] **A) THE GOSPEL OF MATTHEW, CH. 26**

(Jesus in the mountain of olive trees shortly before His arrest): «§39. And He went a little farther, and fell with His face on the ground and prayed, saying, "O My Father, if it is possible, let this cup of suffering pass from Me; nevertheless, not as I will, but as You want... §42. He went away again the second time and prayed, saying, "O My Father, if this cup may not pass away from Me, unless I drink it, Your will be done...§44. And He left them

> *(His disciples)* and went away again, and prayed a third time, saying the same words.»
>
> **B) THE GOSPEL OF LUKE, CH. 22**: «§42. Father, if Thou be willing, remove this cup from Me; nevertheless not My will, but Thine be done. §43. And there appeared an angel unto Him from Heaven, strengthening Him. §44. And being in agony, He prayed more earnestly, **and His sweat was like great drops of blood** *(a sign of an extreme stress state)* falling down to the ground.»

The Persistence for the deification of material flesh is solely monopolized by the fallen archon because, through this painstaking effort, he is constantly supplied. He is thus trying to convince that, through this effort, man will "someday" achieve it (deification).

> [462] **THE GOSPEL OF JUDAS** [KASSER R., MEYER M., WURST G.] NATIONAL GEOGRAPHIC [44]: «Jesus said 'It is **impossible** to sow seed on [rock] and harvest its fruit. [This] is also the way […] the [defiled] generation […] and corruptible Sophia […] *(of this decaying world)* the hand *(of the Creator)* that has created mortal people, so that their souls go up to the eternal realms above. [Truly] I say to you, […] angel […] power will be able to see that […] these to whom […] holy generations […].»

Instead, man sinks down even deeper inside materialism, while he tries to fight against his hormonal **commands** (recorded in his genes by nature and the creator himself), as well as the "maker's command" to conquer the Earth, which has lead humanity to the desperate position it is today, dragging the whole planet along with it to devastation.

> [463] **OLD TESTAMENT, GENESIS CH. 9**: «§1. So God blessed Noah and his sons, and said to them: "Be fruitful and multiply, and fill the earth. §2 **And the fear of you and the dread of you shall be upon every beast of the earth,** and upon every bird of the air, upon all that moves on the earth, and upon all the fish of the sea. Into your hands they are delivered.»

Matter's basic characteristic is **individualization**, which is supported by the fundamental law of self-preservation, recorded in the genes. There lies matter's inability to become spiritualized, since the characteristic attribute of the Spirit is total unification. These two conditions are BY NATURE two diametrically opposite poles. The moment man was dressed up with matter he lost every possibility for deification.

[464] It is *precisely* **this inability** *of matter to be deified that explains Jesus' 'hot temperedness' during his childhood, something which has been so diligently hidden. Due to the overall distortion of the Christian religion, all the right arguments to justify such a temper have been long lost. On account of this very inability of matter, Jesus stated:* [LUKE Ch. 12] «§49. I came to set fire on the earth, and how I wish it were already lit! §51. Do you suppose that I came to give peace on earth? I tell you, not at all, but rather division.»

THE INFANCY GOSPEL OF THOMAS THE ISRAELITE: [PHILOSOPHER'S ACCOUNT OF THE INFANCY OF THE LORD] First Gr. form, ROBERTS-DONALDSON:
http://www.earlychristianwritings.com/text/infancythomas-a-roberts.html

«§2. This child, Jesus, when five years old, was playing in the ford of a mountain stream; and He collected the flowing waters into pools, and made them clear immediately, and by a word alone He made them obey Him. And having made some soft clay, He fashioned out of it twelve sparrows. And it was the Sabbath when He did these things. And there were also many other children playing with Him. And a certain Jew, seeing what Jesus was doing, playing on the Sabbath, went off immediately, and said to his father Joseph: Behold, thy son is at the stream, and has taken clay, and made of it twelve birds, and has profaned the Sabbath. And Joseph, coming to the place and seeing, cried out to Him, saying: Wherefore doest thou on the Sabbath what it is not lawful to do? And Jesus clapped His hands, and cried out to the sparrows, and said to them: Off you go! And the sparrows flew, and went off crying. And the Jews seeing this were amazed, and went away and reported to their chief men what they had seen Jesus doing.

§3. And the son of Annas the scribe was standing there with Joseph; and he took a willow branch, and let out the waters which Jesus had collected. And Jesus, seeing what was done, was angry, and said to him: O wicked, impious, and foolish! What harm did the pools and the waters do to thee? Behold, even now thou shalt be dried up like a tree, and thou shalt not bring forth either leaves, or root, or fruit. And straightway that boy was quite dried up. And Jesus departed, and went to Joseph's house. But the parents of the boy that had been dried up took him up, bewailing his youth, and brought him to Joseph, and reproached him because, said they, thou hast such a child doing such things.

§4. After that He *(Jesus)* was again passing through the village; and a boy ran up against Him, and struck His shoulder. And Jesus was angry, and said to him: Thou shalt not go back the way thou camest. And immediately he fell down dead. And some who saw what had taken place, said: Whence was this child begotten, that every word of his is certainly accomplished? And the parents of the dead boy went away to Joseph, and blamed him, saying: Since thou hast such a child, it is impossible for thee to live with us in the village; or else teach him to bless, and not to curse: for he is killing our children.

§5. And Joseph called the child apart, and admonished Him, saying: Why doest thou such things and these people suffer, and hate us, and persecute us? And Jesus said: I know that these words of thine are not thine own; nevertheless for thy sake I will be silent; but they shall bear their punishment. And straightway those that accused Him were struck blind. And those who saw it were much afraid and in great perplexity, and said about Him: Every word which he spoke, whether good or bad, was an act, and became a wonder. And when they saw that Jesus had done such a thing, Joseph rose and took hold of His ear, and pulled it hard. ...

§9. And some days after, Jesus was playing in an upper room of a certain house, and one of the children that were playing with Him fell down from the house, and was killed. And, when the other children saw this, they ran away, and Jesus alone stood still. And the parents of the dead child, coming, reproached and threatened Him. And Jesus leaped down from the roof, and stood beside the body of the child, and cried with a loud voice, and said: Zeno –for that was his name– stand up, and tell me; did I throw thee down? And he stood up immediately, and said: Certainly not, my lord; thou didst not throw me down, but hast raised me up. And those that saw this were struck with astonishment. And the child's parents glorified God on account of the miracle that had happened, and adored Jesus. ...

§14. And Joseph, seeing that the child was vigorous in mind and body, again resolved that He should not remain ignorant of the letters, and took Him away, and handed Him over to another teacher. And the teacher said to Joseph: I shall first teach him the Greek letters, and then the Hebrew. For the teacher was aware of the trial that had been made of the child and was afraid of Him. Nevertheless he wrote out the alphabet, and gave Him all his attention for a long time, and He (Jesus) made him no answer. And Jesus said to him: If thou art really a teacher, and art well acquainted with the letters, tell me the power of the Alpha, and I will tell thee the power of the Beta. And the teacher was enraged at this, and struck Him on the head. And the child, being in pain, cursed him; and immediately he swooned away, and fell to the ground on his face. And the child returned to Joseph's house; and Joseph was grieved, and gave orders to His mother, saying: Do not let him go outside of the door, because those that make him angry die.»

The Christ did not come to teach people how to deify matter, but how to free themselves from it; and He was imprisoned inside the material body *('...and I entered inside the jail of the body'),* in order to experience its pain and pour out its 'sap' as ransom/pay-off energy for their redemption.

Don't skip chapters or bibliographic references

And the tragicomic in this spiritually declining dimension of matter continues, when some people suppose that if they manage to dig out Christ's DNA from somewhere, they could rebuild Him! As if the whole grandeur of His Spirit was based on His material gene!

---

[465] **THE GOSPEL OF JOHN, CH. 6:**
«§63. It is the spirit that gives life, the flesh is of no avail.»
This also gives an answer to those who are seeking a second 'Christ', since they think He might have left some descendants…

The best they could possibly achieve though would be to build just a flamboyant SHELL, **devoid** of Spirit; obviously… the Antichrist.

Myth creation came next. All of humanity's historic events, during the passage of millennia, end up labeled as myths. Why should Christ be spared from this process? Accelerating this cancellation procedure would hurt no one. The poison of the snake/god started pouring into the brains of his 'spiritually' initiated disciples by spreading a rumor that Christ did not exist. The attestations of Christ's disciples were not enough, regardless of the fact that for other historic events attestations of simple historians have been considered adequate. Today, a percentage of men believe that Jesus Christ never existed. They do not consider however, that the "Power" that dismantled all previous religions –the so-called heathen or idolatrous ones– could be anything else, but **not** a myth. The obvious '**fury**', hidden in the way all these ancient polytheistic temples were destroyed, denotes the suppressed rage those men had for their old gods, which unleashed total destruction! Could it be that all those who feel nostalgic for the religions of the old gods, ignore some hidden details which today have been totally forgotten?

The creators, through the intervention of their 'appointed teachers/assignees', started to reestablish the inescapable karmic debt from sins which is paid through endless reincarnations or through eternal hell, which –as we will see later on– even though it exists, it does so but from a completely different perspective. The wheel of matter found its regular pace again, and continues to be turned by god's **bondservants/slaves**. The time for man's greatest decision is coming! But what can he choose if he knows nothing of The Truth?

466 HISTORICAL TESTIMONIES FOR THE CHRIST
A) THE PAPYRUS OF JESUS:

On December 24th, 1994, the 'London Times' announced the discovery of the oldest ever papyrus which showed fragments from chapter 26 of the Gospel of Matthew written in Greek. These papyrus pieces are dated to about 60 A.D., a time period when **eye witnesses** *of Jesus still lived, and which corresponds to the time interval from His death, that is the year 30 A.D., to 70 A.D., when the temple of Jerusalem was destroyed and the Christian community scattered.*

The man who brought this papyrus to light was the German Thiede Carsten Peter, **an archaeologist, linguist and historian of papyrology,** *Professor of the History of the New Testament, at the University Staatsunabhängige Theologische Hochschule (S.T.H.) in Basel and the Ben-Gurion University in Beersheba, South Israel.*

British journalist Matthew d' Ancona, chief-editor of the 'Sunday Telegraph' undertook the examination of the historical facts:

The evangelist priest Charles Bousfield Huleatt (1863-1908), after completing his Evangelical studies at Magdalene College, Oxford University, was appointed in Luxor Egypt as a priest in the chapel of Thomas Cook's 'Luxor' Hotel. There, in Egypt, he found the papyrus pieces, which, in 1901, he mailed to the library of the College he had graduated from. Proper attention was not paid to those pieces, which simply remained in a display case of the library of this Oxford College.

The finding drew the interest of Professor Thiede Carsten, when he realized that the way these fragments had been written betrayed a much older creation date than the one till then believed.

The carbon-dating method was prohibited, because the fragments were small and only three in number. A laser scanner was the answer to the problem, proving that the papyrus "had been written by the eye witnesses of Christ's Resurrection", as the Professor himself stated. [SOURCE: DISCOVERY CHANNEL, TIMES ON LINE]

B) ORTHODOX GROUP OF DOGMA RESEARCH
http://www.oodegr.com/oode/grafi/kd/exwxr.pig1.htm#span

(a) HISTORIAN TACITUS:

Tacitus' work was published between 115 and 117 A.D. In an excerpt of his work he speaks of the Fire of Rome and the persecution of Christians that Nero ordered on account of it. This event took place 30 years after Jesus' death. Some contemporaries believe that it was Paul who started the fire to incriminate the Christians! ...Not at all impossible. Tacitus says:

«Some accused Nero as the motivator of the fire. To get rid of the blame, Nero fastened the guilt and inflicted the most exquisite tortures on a class hated for their abominations, called Christians by the populace. Christus,

Don't skip chapters or bibliographic references

from whom the name had its origin, suffered the extreme penalty during the reign of Tiberius at the hands of one of our procurators, Pontius Pilatus, and a most abhorrent superstition, thus checked for the moment, again broke out not only in Judaea, the first source of the evil, but even in Rome. ...Accordingly, an arrest was first made of all who confessed to be Christians; then, upon their information, an immense multitude was convicted."*[Tacit. Annals XV, 38, 44]*

(b) SUETONIUS: "A contemporary of Tacitus, between the years 110 A.D. and 120 A.D., he wrote his work on the 12 emperors (from Augustus to Domitian).

He mentions that among the Jews there was great upheaval on account of Jesus Christ and therefore, Emperor Claudius exiled them from Rome. This event occurred in 54 A.D., only twenty years after the Golgotha drama *(Vita Claud. C. XXV 4,* "Judaeos impulsore Chresto assidue tumultuantes Romae expulsit).

Elsewhere again, Suetonius reports that the Christians were run out by Nero because of their malicious superstitions. ('Christiani genus hominum superstitionis novae et maleficae' Vita Neron, XVI 2)

(c) GAIUS PLINIUS CAECILIUS SECUNDUS:

"The Emperor of Rome Trajan was in need of a commander for the province of Bithynia – Pontus in Asia Minor. He appointed his trusted friend Gaius Plinius Caecilius Secundus, who was called Pliny the Younger. In Bithynia Pliny arrived in 111 A.D. and died two years later. But during this time he wrote many letters to Trajan on various matters. One of these letters along with Trajan's answer refers to early Christians. We quote here the letters, translated, as they are published in 'The Harvard classics Volume 9':

[SOURCE: http://www.archive.org/stream/harvardclassics09eliouoft/harvardclassics09eliouoft.txt]

"IT is my invariable rule, Sir, to refer to you in all matters where I feel doubtful; for who is more capable of removing my scruples, or informing my ignorance? Having never been present at any trials concerning those who profess Christianity, I am unacquainted not only with the nature of their crimes, or the measure of their punishment, but how far it is proper to enter into an examination concerning them. Whether, therefore, any difference is usually made with respect to ages, or no distinction is to be observed between the young and the adult; whether repentance entitles them to a pardon, or, if a man has been once a Christian, it avails nothing to desist from his error; whether the very profession of Christianity, un-attended with any criminal act, or only the crimes themselves inherent in the profession are punishable.

On all these points I am in great doubt. In the meanwhile, the method I have observed towards those who have been brought before me as Christians is this: I asked them whether they were Christians; if they admitted it, I repeated the question twice, and threatened them with punishment; if they persisted, I ordered them to be at once punished: for I was persuaded, whatever the nature of their opinions might be, a contumacious and inflexible obstinacy certainly deserved correction. There were others also brought before me possessed with the same infatuation, but being Roman citizens, I directed them to be sent to Rome. But this crime spreading (as is usually the case) while it was actually under prosecution, several instances of the same nature occurred. An anonymous information was laid before me containing a charge against several persons, who upon examination denied they were Christians, or had ever been so. They repeated after me an invocation to the gods, and offered religious rites with wine and incense before your statue (which for that purpose I had ordered to be brought, together with those of the gods), and even reviled the name of Christ: whereas there is no forcing, it is said, those who are really Christians into any of these compliances: I thought it proper, therefore, to discharge them.

Some among those who were accused by a witness in person at first confessed themselves Christians, but immediately after denied it; the rest admitted indeed that they had been of that order formerly (some three, others more, and a few above twenty years ago), but had now renounced that error. They all worshipped your statue and the images of the gods, uttering imprecations at the same time against the name of Christ. They affirmed the whole of their guilt, or their error, was, that they met on a stated day before it was light, and addressed a form of prayer to Christ, as to a divinity, binding themselves by a solemn oath, not for the purposes of any wicked design, but never to commit any fraud, theft, or adultery, never to falsify their word, nor deny a trust when they should be called upon to deliver it up; after which it was their custom to separate, and then reassemble, to eat in common a harmless meal. From this custom, however, they desisted after the publication of my edict, by which, according to your commands, I forbade the meeting of any assemblies. After receiving this account, I judged it so much the more necessary to endeavor to extort the real truth, by putting two female slaves to the torture, who were said to officiate in their religious rites: but all I could discover was evidence of an absurd and extravagant superstition.

I deemed it expedient, therefore, to adjourn all further proceedings, in order to consult you. For it appears to be a matter highly deserving your consideration, more especially as great numbers must be involved in the danger of these prosecutions, which have already extended, and are still likely to extend, to persons of all ranks and ages, and even of both sexes. In fact, this contagious superstition is not confined to the cities only, but has spread its infection among the neighboring villages and country.

Nevertheless, it still seems possible to restrain its progress. The temples, at least, which were once almost deserted, begin now to be frequented; and the sacred rites, after a long intermission, are again revived; while there is a general demand for the victims, which till lately found very few purchasers.

Don't skip chapters or bibliographic references

From all this it is easy to conjecture what numbers might be reclaimed if a general pardon were granted to those who shall repent of their error."
Answering to this letter of Pliny, Emperor Trajan wrote:
XCVIII 'TRAJAN TO PLINY'

"You have adopted the right course, my dearest Secundus, in investigating the charges against the Christians who were brought before you. It is not possible to lay down any general rule for all such cases. Do not go out of your way to look for them. If indeed they should be brought before you, and the crime is proved, they must be punished; with the restriction, however, that where the party denies he is a Christian, and shall make it evident that he is not, by invoking our gods, let him (notwithstanding any former suspicion) be pardoned upon his repentance. Anonymous information ought not to be received in any sort of prosecution. It is introducing a very dangerous precedent, and is quite foreign to the spirit of our age."

(d) FLAVIUS JOSEPHUS (HIS TESTIMONY CONCERNING THE HISTORICAL JESUS, ANTIQUITIES 18.3.3)

"Now there was about this time Jesus, a wise man, if it be lawful to call him a man, for he was a doer of wonderful works, a teacher of such men as receive the truth with pleasure. He drew over to him both many of the Jews, and many of the Gentiles. He was [the] Christ; and when Pilate, at the suggestion of the principal men amongst us, had condemned him to the cross, those that loved him at the first did not forsake him; for he appeared to them alive again the third day; as the divine prophets had foretold these and ten thousand other wonderful things concerning him. And the tribe of Christians, so named from him, is not extinct to this day."

The authenticity of the text of Josephus was supported by F. C. Burkitt in his study entitled 'Josephus and Christ', which was published in "Actes du IVe Congress International d' Histoire des religions tenu a Leide du 9 au 13 Septembre 1912, Leide 1913.

Burkitt's opinion was adopted and ingeniously supported by A. Harnack (Der Jüdische Geschichtsschreiber Josephus und Jesus Christus in 'Internationale Monatsschrift VII, 1913'.

Additionally, W. Emery Barnes in 'Contemporary Review' of January 1914.

Among the supporters of the authenticity of the whole passage are: Hettinger and Godet (Conferences Apologétiques III Les miracles p. 5). Furthermore, Renan did not challenge the authenticity of the passage. [Vie de Jesus p. X of the Introduction]

HOW THEY CONTROL THE WORLD

From the first day of man's appearance on Earth till today, the creators and the skeptomorphic society, bound to each other in an endless strife for supremacy and shielded inside their impassable secret places, have been manipulating the entire humanity according to their interests, so that it produces the preferred form of energy. On account of that, they keep man ignorant of the truth that concerns him, yoked to his material needs and his genetic impulses, firmly bound by his subjective point of view and incapable of thinking detached from these bonds, so as to prevent him from wondering about the real reason for his existence and the cause of his creation.

[467] **PLATO'S 'REPUBLIC' BOOK 7** (514a-517b)

(A dialogue, between Socrates and Glaucon)

«S. – After that, compare man's nature, in respect to education and the lack thereof, to such an experience as this: Picture men, dwelling in a sort of subterranean den with a long entrance, open to the light on its entire width. Conceive them as having from childhood their legs and necks chained, so that they remain in the same spot, able to look forward only, and prevented by their bonds from turning their heads. Picture further the light from a fire burning higher up and at a distance behind them, and between the fire and the prisoners and above them a road along which a low wall has been built, as the exhibitors of puppet-shows have partitions before the men themselves, above which they show the puppets.

G. - All that I see.

S. - See also, then, men carrying past the wall implements of all kinds that rise above the wall, and human statues and shapes of animals as well, made of stone and wood and every material, some of these bearers presumably speaking and others silent.

G. - A strange image you speak of and strange prisoners.

S. - <u>And nonetheless, those prisoners are us</u>; for, to begin with, tell me, do you think that these men would have seen anything of themselves or of one another except the shadows cast from the fire on the wall of the cave that fronted them?

G. - How could they, if they were compelled to hold their heads unmoved through their life?

S. - And again, would not the same be true of the objects carried past them?

G. - …Surely.

S. - If then they were able to talk to one another, do you not think that they would suppose that in naming the things that they saw they were naming the passing objects?

G. - …Necessarily.

Don't skip chapters or bibliographic references

S. - And if their prison had an echo from the wall opposite them, when one of the passers-by uttered a sound, do you think that they would suppose anything else than the passing shadow to be the speaker?

G. - By Zeus, I do not.

S. - Then in every way such prisoners would deem reality to be nothing else than the shadows of the artificial objects.

G. - Quite inevitably.

S. - Consider, then, what would be the manner of the release and healing from these bonds and this folly if in the course of nature something of this sort should happen to them: When one was freed from his bonds and compelled to stand up suddenly and turn his head around and walk and to lift up his eyes to the light, and in doing all this felt pain and, because of the dazzle and glitter of the light, was unable to discern the objects whose shadows he formerly saw, what do you suppose would be his answer if someone told him that what he had seen before was all a cheat and an illusion, but that now, being nearer to reality and turned toward more real things, he saw more truly? And if also one should point out to him each of the passing objects and constrain him by questions to say what it is, do you not think that he would be at a loss and that he would regard what he formerly saw as more real than the things now pointed out to him?

G. - Far more real.

S. - And if he were compelled to look at the light itself, would not that pain his eyes, and would he not turn away and flee to those things which he is able to discern and regard them as in very deed more clear and exact than the objects pointed out?

G. - It is so.

S. - And if someone should drag him thence by force up the ascent which is rough and steep, and not let him go before he had drawn him out into the light of the sun, do you not think that he would find it painful to be so haled along, and would chafe at it, and when he came out into the light, that his eyes would be filled with its beams so that he would not be able to see even one of the things that we call real?

G. - Why, no, not immediately.

S. - Then there would be need of habituation, I take it, to enable him to see the things higher up. And at first he would most easily discern the shadows and, after that, the likenesses or reflections in water of men and other things, and later, the things themselves, and from these he would go on to contemplate the appearances in the sky and sky itself, more easily by night, looking at the light of the stars and the moon, than by day the sun and the sun's light.

G. - ...Of course.

S. - And so, finally, I suppose, he would be able to look upon the sun itself and see its true nature, not by reflections in water or phantasms of it in an alien setting, but in and by itself in its own place.

G. - Necessarily.

S. - And at this point he would infer and conclude that this it is that provides the seasons and the courses of the year and presides over all things in the visible region, and is in some sort the cause of all these things that they had seen.

G. - Obviously, this would be the next step.

S. - Well then, if he recalled to mind his first habitation and what passed for wisdom there, and his fellow-bondsmen, do you not think that he would count himself happy in the change and pity them?

G. - He would indeed.

S. - And if there had been honors and commendations among them which they bestowed on one another and prizes for the man who is quickest to make out the shadows as they pass and best able to remember their customary precedences, sequences and co-existences, and so most successful in guessing at what was to come, do you think he would be very keen about such rewards, and that he would envy and emulate those who were honored by these prisoners and lorded it among them, or that he would feel like Homer and greatly prefer while living on earth to be serf of another, a landless man, and endure anything rather than opine with them and live that life?

G. - Yes, I think that he would choose to endure anything rather than such a life.

S. - And consider this also, if such a one should go down again and take his old place would he not get his eyes full of darkness, thus suddenly coming out of the sunlight, and become blind once again?

G. - He would indeed.

S. - Now if he should be required to contend with these perpetual prisoners in evaluating these shadows while his vision was still dim and before his eyes were accustomed to the dark —and this time required for habituation would not be very short— would he not provoke laughter, and would it not be said of him that he had returned from his journey aloft with his eyes ruined and that it was not worthwhile even to attempt the ascent? And if it were possible to lay hands on and to kill the man who tried to release them and lead them up, would they not kill him?

G. - They certainly would.

S. - This image then, dear Glaucon, we must apply as a whole to all that has been said so far, likening the region revealed through sight to the habitation of the prison, and the light of the fire in it to the power of the sun. And if you assume that the ascent of the prisoner who comes and contemplates the things above symbolizes the soul's ascension from the visible to the intelligible world, you will not miss my surmise.» *(Eng. tr.: Paul Shorey. Cambridge, MA, Harvard University Press; London, William Heinemann Ltd. 1969)*

Don't skip chapters or bibliographic references

Man's brain, through the five, basic, prototype functions has the ability to create **synchronized** pseudo-sensations. Namely it receives waveforms and translates them into images, scents, tastes, sounds and illusions of touch.

At the same time it is connected to energy-potentials which spread invisible threads around him, forming energy connections with this body/machine. Thus, man has identified so much with his material envelope that he thinks he is exclusively just that. So he overlooks all material dependencies that this material body transmits to his soul, because he doesn't know that they (material dependencies) 'overlay' on it (the soul) and keep it bound in their trap.

---

468 **HERMES TRISMEGISTUS,** HERMETIC TEXTS, VOL. I, RODAKIS P., TZAFEROPOULOS AP., **'FROM HERMES' SPEECHES TO KING AMMON'** EXCERPT XVII (p.171):

«§1. The Soul then, Ammon, is self-contained essence, which at first chose *(or rather was forced to choose)* **a life according to Heimarmenē (Fate),** and then took for itself inclination [orig. Gr. θυμόν = mind, temper, will] and desire which have proportion similar to matter.»

So when I tell you "Look at this strange body that encases you!" You answer: "This is our nature". And you can't detach yourself from this position to wonder: "O.K., but what kind of nature is that, which consistently hides its generating source? What kind of 'splendor' does it possess, when it cannot create **ecumenical** well-being? What kind of a 'benevolent' being is its creator when first he offers life and soon he cancels it with death?" Your denial of reality prompts you to comfort yourself by defining nature as mindless instead of an intelligent and conspiring creation, and you prefer to consider pain and death 'natural', rather than regard nature as a misappropriation that entraps.

---

469 **AVATON MAGAZINE, ISSUE 64, SEPTEMBER 2006, ION MAGGOS' ARTICLE: 'WHO STEELS OUR SOULS?'**
Researcher Ion Maggos, in this particular article, presents, in a very personal and characteristic style, the entrapment of human existence by the dark forces which we call Creator:
«In the last millennia, in the linear time, a guided confusion regarding the nature of the human soul seems to prevail. …Much more than that, the confusion regarding the soul's recycling course in this particular creation in which we have the misfortune to live, especially those of us who have a soul: Soul or identity? We shall see…
Did the expression 'those of us who have' annoy you? But of course, not even 50% of us! Here, we live in a combination of successive scalar fields. We must make clear that this concerns the longitudinal electromagnetic

waves: The fourth component-vector of the fundamental law of electromagnetism …whereas, our entire civilization is based on transverse (lateral) electromagnetic waves. …Furthermore the whole subject is directly related to the Principle of the Fall of Parity of Lee and Yang (Nobel 1957).

The successive scalar fields we live in are artificially formulated with a specific, complex geometry and mathematics, in order to perpetuate the 'sheep in the pen' condition. "God always geometrizes." Who, the god of creation? In reality, it is nothing more than cultivation; an enormous plantation of souls; the successive scalar fields create a maximum-security geometric prison of multiple levels. The different time-velocities in each dimension make the safe guarding of the prison easy for the entities that control the herd of the human-plantation. …The Duality Theory of Jean Pierre Garnier Malet gives this meaning in an excellent scientific way: "The helical motion **of the duality** of time and space is a phenomenon observed throughout the universe, in the infinitely large and the infinitely small (of our cells and DNA)."

…The soul is a geometric elliptical crystal according to the principles of hyper-dimensional physics. Inside it, of course, it has two centers, and the trapped Divine Spark, which, as myriads of other Divine Sparks, has been fished away from the fringes of the Divine Flame. …Through the use of triangle networks, it has been entrapped into this virtual dark reality, under the illusion that there is motion.

Thus, all the dark parasitic beings, from the Archons *(the archon of this world)* of pre-Christian Gnostics, the Toltec 'voladores', till the serpent-like beings of every race of the lower and middle astral plane and the aetherophysical one, **live off the voracious sucking of energy**, with the use of the double vortex, through the Divine Spark that has been trapped and detached from the shapeless Divine Flame.

…All natural laws that govern the physical world, i.e. the virtual reality in which we live, are based on illusions that have been imposed to the inhabitants of the Dodecahedron –see Platonic Solids *(the author is apparently referring to the correlation Plato makes between the four elements of matter and geometric shapes [Timaeus 52d-61d])*. We can observe that the Dodecahedron is a polyhedron with twelve sides and the shape of each side is a regular pentagon. Every illusion therefore is based on the Great Illusion of Motion. This whole virtual reality is encased in the Dodecahedron which is made of twelve penta-dodecahedra. This situation causes total confusion.

… Motion was created by the perverted thought of the Darkness, i.e. the dark beings of chaos, which created thoughts and skeptomorphs (thought-forms) within the delusion of its own fantasy. …Its skeptomorphs created the pseudo-material amalgams we consider matter. The Darkness projected

Don't skip chapters or bibliographic references

its thoughts in order to 'create'. Essentially the entire creation is an delusion in the 'noûs/mind' of Darkness. Motion is the foundation of the vibration which is yet another delusion. ...Vibrations are used for the creation of many other delusions, **like the false light of higher dimensions** *(the split substitute of The True Light, the ant-Avge as we call it in this book)* and the material light *(of the sun)*. Dimensions are created from various vibration frequencies. Virtual reality is a very successful trap; just like the senses; ...All biological bodies have been constructed such, that they need rest and sleep. There, different laws of control are at work. The dream-world is a controlled subset. We are not bodies, we are consciousness. ...And it (consciousness) is encaged **inside** the soul, even though we often mistake it for the Divine Spark (Amitakh Stanford).»

But if someone impartially and logically observes the world around him he will realize that there is no probability it was constructed by itself.

[470] **'WHY DOES THE UNIVERSE HAS IDEAL CONDITIONS FOR LIFE TO APPEAR ON EARTH?** APRIL 2007, SOURCE: THE GUARDIAN
http://www.physics4u.gr/articles/2007/universe_and_man.html
«Let us examine our subject: The Universe seems to have literally self-expanded from nothing to an immense part of space-time, full of dark matter and energy, lit up by 200 billion galaxies that each one may contain up to 200 billion stars. Stars, like thermonuclear reactors resupplied by the power of their gravity, burn the primordial hydrogen changing it to an ash of heavier elements. Afterwards, once it becomes the raw material for the planets around a new generation of stars, this ash becomes a biochemical laboratory from which life sprang up in a planet 3.5 billion years ago.
But the universe could achieve this only because the fundamental forces that orchestrate creation are coordinated **with absolute precision**. If these forces (weak electric, gravitational and powerful nuclear) were different, <u>even to a minimum degree</u>, the stars would either burn their fuel too fast, or they would not have ignited at all, or they would fail to make the carbon and the heavier elements on which life depends, or they would collapse from their weight instead of exploding. If therefore something had not been regulated to perfection, the stars would fail to scatter the water and the chemical substances essential to life in our whole Galaxy. This enigmatic cosmic precision made British astronomer Fred Hoyle propose, that the World resembles a '**controlled project**'. And this prompted physicist Freeman Dyson to say that <u>it appears as though, from a certain point of view, the World 'knew of our arrival'</u>.
Leonard Susskind reports that its more than sheer chance that the universe is so much adapted in the human beings and wonders: "Can science explain the exceptional fact that the universe appears to be so

terribly unknown, so terribly inexplicable, so terribly marvelous and so well designed for our existence?"
Cosmologists call this incredibly fine-tuned universe, The Anthropic Principle. The faithful call it the 'Hand of God'. None of the two explains anything.
...And the next big question is: Did God have a choice? Could He have opted not to create this universe? Must the universe be as it is? If this is the only mathematically coherent, possible Cosmos, then God had no choice in His planning. If however, He didn't have a choice, then in what notion is He necessary? But this also leaves the question unanswered: Why does the universe appear purpose-built for life?
There is no answer. The fact that we can ask such questions is indeed a fortunate riddle. Is what we see the manifestation of some enigmatic cosmic aim? Or are these the pointless result of a blind experiment, an accidental dice-throw without meaning in the cosmic gambling club?»

But the mathematical brain that constructed all this didn't bother to inform you of the role you actually play in this game of creation.
If someone visits a man's house and the host receives him with friendliness at the beginning, while later on and for no reason kills him, wouldn't you characterize this host as mad and perverted? Every reasonable man would try to leave such a house. Why do you then insist on visiting this insanity, by eternally reincarnating into it? Simply, because you are forced to do so, in the pretense of karmic debt... This is the first big trap they have set for you.
With every means of power they possess, they try to convince you that through the process of karma you will evolve. At the same time, they have assured you that you will not be free from the reincarnation cycle, if you haven't previously erased your "negative" karma! This is the greatest deceit, since **the very nature of dyadic matter** excludes this possibility, as it always strives to maintain a constant balance between oppositions. Thus, if the positive is reinforced at some point, the balance of nature will immediately create a negative of equal size at some other point and vice versa.

[471] **DANEZIS M., THEODOSIOU S. 'COSMOLOGY OF THE INTELLECT'**
«Vacuum Fluctuations (p. 220): As Prof. Kip S. Thorn states in his book 'Black holes and time warps' *(Katoptro Publications, Athens, 1999)* ...The laws of physics force the areas of negative-energy to quickly absorb energy from their neighboring positive-energy areas, restoring the energy balance to zero.»

In reality, what holds true, is the universal law of equilibrium of opposites, the 'Yin' and the 'Yang'. Therefore under these circumstances, which

Don't skip chapters or bibliographic references

"negative" karma do some people imagine they can delete? Karma serves absolutely dark mechanisms of entrapment…
–Despite the equilibrium of opposites though, in human society negativity seems to prevail. How does this happen?
–The dense matter that exists in the inner/denser part of the energy-spiral of this universe (black hole) is in essence its **bottom** (its 4%).

---

[472] *A reminder:* http://www.physics4u.gr/news/2000/scnews87.html
«Veneziano claims: "Our Universe is but a small part inside a black hole: Terrifying indeed, if you think about it!»

This entire universe absorbs Essence and converts it into energy. While this energy sinks deeper into the inner regions, it diversely varies its frequency and finally densely accumulates to form –always according to the aetheric template/pattern– energy-nodes, energy-bronchi and energy-spheres, which the aetheric brains of the beings 'project' as the visible 4% material universe. This extreme "concentration/bottleneck" of energy in the inner part of the vortex, causes this energy to deteriorate, which in the eyes of men takes the form of material decay. Deterioration brings decomposition (rot). Decomposition starts from the very first day of every material form/life, and it is **the very same force** that initially makes every organism develop, grow big, reach old age until it finally leads it to its death *(Laws of Entropy).* This is the **decomposition** cycle which, as it interacts with human thought, creates (good and bad) skeptomorphs (thoughtforms); a mutated form of the energy, a misprint of it. As these skeptomorphs mingle with the energy found diffused in the universe, they expand it on one hand and degrade it on the other. Adulterated and henceforth degraded, the energy condenses into new 'forms'. Thus, in the absolutely dense material plane, the **bipolar** diagram of 'progress' appears constantly declining.

Nonetheless the 'sap' of pain of this **hopeless** effort for improvement and evolution, offers the highest quality of (mutated) energy/nutrition to your dominators and the longer you produce it, the more they benefit. This way, they burden you with the responsibility –very typical of them– for their defective creation, so that when things don't come out right, you are the ones to blame!

In order for the HyperCosmoi of the Truth to redeem you from this trap and open the door for your return Home, they became a sacrificial offering through Jesus Christ, so as to pay off the debts your rulers pretended you owe to this creation. So, they announced that since your karmic 'dues' had been paid off, reincarnation was no more and the road to Redemption has been opened through your Savior's sacrifice. You, on the other hand, turned a deaf ear, and in place of any soul-searching, you simply labeled the Christian point of view as lacking, because it didn't refer to the reincarnation/trap anymore!

[473] *Some will claim that the dogma of reincarnation was abolished by Justinian at the 5th Ecumenical Synod in 553 A.D. Reincarnation was up till then, a widely accepted belief. The reason for its abolishment then, was the realization that Christ had come* **precisely to cancel** *this vicious circle., So, whereas the concept of reincarnation should have been simply circumvented, it finally had to be completely eradicated, giving thereafter grounds to much adverse criticism. However, we should be lenient with the "regulators" of ecclesiastic laws! Taking into account that –at that time– the people's educational level was indeed too low to handle the truth in the correct way, the regulators preferred to bypass the difficulties.*

AFTER-DEATH WORLDS

Once dead, man enters the unseen lower part of the great wavy 'oscillation' of the material world, abandoning the visible. This new period in the invisible will include yet another partial and smaller 'oscillation', which starts from the 'luminous' –which accompanies the first phase of the soul's departure from the body– proceeds to the 'nebulous' judgment of the soul, and finally passes through the darker planes of the underworld *(Hades)*. Upon arrival into those abysmal depths of the underworld, the soul starts an ascent to gradually more 'luminous' regions, all the way to the ultimate 'bliss' of the 2nd material/virtual paradise –at least for the souls that manage to reach that far.

---

[474] **PAPASTAVROU A., 'COSMOS WITHIN A COSMOS'** CH. ASTRAL PLANE (p 29):

«Returning to the common deceased one, we observe that after death man must go through all subdivisions of the astral cosmos before he is able to glimpse at the noetic (higher mental) plane, which can only be reached by very few.»

When a man is **between** life and death, after a serious accident, a life-threatening health complication, or a dangerous operation and has crossed over to the 'foyer' of the other world, but not yet its main area, he has an experience which is common to most people. Accounts of this experience are plenty and come from those who found themselves 'outside their body' and seemed about to die.

These people, most of the times, are contacted by a 'luminous' being which, once it (telepathically) asks them various things about their lives, – if their time has not 'come' yet– gently asks them to return back to their body, with the excuse that they still have a lot to offer in their lives, or that their loved ones are waiting for them and need them, …as if those who indeed die prematurely don't have to face the same problems! People usually but reluctantly succumb and return into their bodies again.

Many though insist on not wanting to return –especially if they are about to return into a very sick body causing them pain– and prefer to remain in those aetheric spaces, they **consider** better. Then, the 'luminous' being, gradually abandoning its 'suave' and 'good-natured' style, starts exerting pressure on them to return back to their material body. If the man persistently continues to refuse, then the 'luminous' being abandons its 'benevolent' stance out front and transforms into a terribly ferocious threat for the unfortunate life refuter.

---

475 **PLATO'S 'PHAEDO, OR ABOUT THE PSYCHE' [=SOUL],** ATHANASOPOULOS I., K.

(62b, 62c, 62d) *(Socrates speaks to Cebes a little before he drinks the conium [=hemlock]):*

«Now the idea that is taught in the secret teaching about this matter, *(is that)* we men are in a kind of prison and must not set ourselves free *(by committing suicide)* or escape,… and that the gods are our guardians and that we men are one of their possessions. …Well then," said he (Socrates), "if one of your chattels (possessions) should kill itself when you had not indicated that you wished it to die, would you not be angry with it and punish it if you could?" …Then there may be reason in saying that a man should wait, and not take his own life until God casts some need/necessity upon him, as the one he has now sent me *(to drink the hemlock (conium))*.» [ENG. TR.: E. M. COPE, CAMBRIDGE UNIVERSITY PRESS, 1875]

This one of their basic and characteristic properties: Masquerade; They dress up as 'good ones' only to fool you. Here is what I mean…

In a farm, chores are many and diverse, yet they all contribute to its normal operation. Animals, besides grazing for food, multiplying, or resting in the sun, are there solely for exploitation. Animals aren't necessarily aware of that. The same is also true in a large plantation. Plants accept the services of the landowner and his supervisors, who make sure they are always robust, in order to yield the best crop. Fruit, in order to reach the highest standards of taste, must **mature** before picked. Can you suspect now why the 'luminous' supervisors insist that man returns back to his/her body? In the same way you humans, leave the fruit on the tree until it matures before you cut it, the same holds true for you as well. If by some mistake of the 'software program' a man is 'picked' while he is still not 'ripe' for harvest he must be sent back to the 'plantation'.

Your astro-aethero-emotional body is their nutrition, and the more you enrich it with desires, weaknesses and passions the more tempting and delicious it becomes to the inhabitants of the lower planes. If you supply it with the pain of your every sacrifice and your counterfeit 'positive' energy, it becomes the 'bon fillet' destined to please the 'upper classes'.

Don't skip chapters or bibliographic references

---

476 **A) GOSPEL OF PHILIP**, JEAN-YVES LELOUP:

«§14. These harmful *(evil)* powers do not want human beings to be saved: they instill in them a taste for sacrifices.»

B) PAPASTAVROU, A., 'LETTERS TO ANONYMOUS' (p. 234)

The appointed teachers of the Creators disclose:

«Speech of Saint Germaine, given on January 1st, 1955 in Philadelphia USA:.

"…Your knowledge on energy is minimal. The energy which manifests in the world of matter, as in the higher spheres, is power with which everything can be performed. It is a divine act. In your causative (*astral*) body, **you have set aside** certain quantities of formulated energy.»

C) GOSPEL OF PHILIP [Eng. tr. PATERSON BROWN] www.metalog.org/files/Philip.html

«§54. God is a cannibal. Because of this, mankind is [sacrificed] to it. Before mankind was sacrificed, animals were being sacrificed. For these to which they are sacrificed are not divinities.»

The 'heart of the lettuce' is destined to please the select few, whereas the thicker outer leaves are destined for the inferior ones.

---

477 *After all man has always been morta*l = Gr. βρωτός= mortal = βρ(ο)ωτός = to be eaten [unavoidably].

The soul is the 'seed' which, upon completion of its purge from the 'edible' astral, is 'washed' in preparation for a new sowing. There are plant seeds that before they are planted in the field, are first germinated in small seedbeds and when they sprout they are transplanted to the big farm. The same happens to the soul. Thus the human embryo is initially 'planted' in the protected seedbed/womb and when it 'sprouts', it is born so as to be transplanted in the material-world farm, where, under the right social circumstances it will develop its 'nutritious' astral energy-body.

---

478 PAPASTAVROU, A., 'LETTERS TO ANONYMOUS'

The White Brotherhood, as the Planet's Spiritual Hierarchy (i.e. the creators' delegates), state:

(a) (p. 526) «Speech of goddess Pallas Athena (Bridge, February 1960): Everything here on Earth as well as in the far beyond demands the **deposit of energy**. As you advance higher in the path of light, so much more invaluable (to them) the gift of your life as well as the gift of **your** energy becomes.

(b) (p. 100) In the following, Saint Germaine, in a speech he gave in May 1953, provides us with additional information on the subject. *('Bridge', Series 1. Book 3, p. 10)* …"It has been said to you that the birth currents were transported from the Hermitage of the Lord Himalaya to the one of god Meru (Lord

---

Amaru-Muru) in South America. This means that the number of births will greatly increase in the Western hemisphere in the future, because the attraction of the magnetic force which pulled the fertile millions of souls to India, China and other Asian countries in the past, is now completely reversed and it will shortly commence to attract the souls to a Western incarnation; **because Western bodies have more vitality and energy than the bodies of the East, and we hope to have a much larger energy sum <u>to manage</u>** in this increasing Western population.»

So in order for this imprisonment to continue unhindered, since the produced human-energy is of vital importance to them, they presented humanity with karma or the law of reciprocal justice. After all, the sharing of 'positive' and 'negative' energy to its recipients was the main reason for its enforcement.

---

[479] **A) OLD TESTAMENT, EXODUS CH. 29**

(Jehovah's instructs to Moses on the way he must perform sacrifices)

«§13. And you shall take all the fat that covers the inner parts, the upper lobe of the liver, and the two kidneys with the fat that is around them, and burn them all on the altar. §14. But the flesh of the bull, with its skin and its **offal** *(excretion)*, you shall burn with fire outside the camp. It is a sin offering (for the negative astral powers.»

B) 'MYSTERIES OF THE WORLD', VOL. HIDDEN WORLDS:

«One of the most ancient daemons is called Azazel or Azazeel whom the Israelites imagined in the form of a male goat (buck) and to whom they attributed their sins. On the day of Yom Kippur, two bucks were offered as a sacrifice for the atonement of the sins of the folk, and people drew straws to determine which goat would be sacrificed to the god and which to Azazel. In reality only the buck selected for god was sacrificed, whereas the one chosen for Azazel would be kept alive in order to perform the ceremony of atonement and then sent out to the desert where, according to Origen and the ancient Syrian texts, Azazel dwells. The common phrase 'scapegoat' comes from these beliefs.

Etymologically the word Azazel appears to mean 'the power of god.' It can also be interpreted though as 'the one who turns his power against god.»

We modern people of course prefer the latter interpretation to justify our beliefs as well.

... 'Leviticus' in the Old Testament reports (Ch. XVI §9-10): «And Aaron shall present the goat upon which the lot fell for the Lord, and offer it for a sin-offering. But the goat, on which the lot fell for Azazel, shall be presented alive before the Lord, to make atonement over it, to send it away for Azazel into the wilderness.»

Don't skip chapters or bibliographic references

As we have previously mentioned, the astral body –the mindless Silver Race– is incapable of conveying the commands of the sentient soul. Whatever 'logic' man seems to have after physical death is **only** the knowledge and information he has accumulated during his material life, with which (knowledge and information) he has 'dressed up' his astral body.

---

[480] **PAPASTAVROU A., 'COSMOS WITHIN A COSMOS'** CH. ASTRAL PLANE (pp. 29-30): «The popular idea that someone can –after death– acquire unlimited knowledge from the astral world or other sources of higher spiritual development, and that these can be transferred through a psychic *(medium)* to the living, **is not true**. In the astral plane, the deceased **does not possess** more knowledge than what he did while living, and if he could transmit something, this would be what little he knew when alive.»

*In other words, information through 'mediums' which seems to come from late relatives, is more likely from **malevolent** negative astral beings concealed under the façade of a 'relative', rather than the deceased themselves...*

This knowledge frames the astral body of every deceased and makes it appear capable of logic, but not in any productive way concerning whatever new circumstances follow in his after-death route.

༄·ৎ

Once man dies, the soul remains in an intermediate energy-region for some time *(it is roughly estimated, for 40 days)* enveloped in its aetheric body/template, until that too is permanently dissolved.

---

[481] **RUDOLF STEINER 'AT THE GATES OF ANTHROPOSOPHY'**, [Gr. tr. ALEXIOU TH.] CH. 'LIFE OF THE SOUL AFTER DEATH' (p. 31): «With most people the aetheric body dissolves gradually into the cosmic aether...In the case of ordinary men then, we have two corpses: one of the physical body and one of the aetheric.»

This is, for most souls, a serene waiting period in the **foyer** of the underworld, which many souls mistake for the paradise.

---

[482] **PAPASTAVROU, A., 'LETTERS TO ANONYMOUS'**
The Great White Brotherhood as the authoritative power of the archon of this world states: «Speech of the master Chohan Morya: The moment a soul is ready to leave the physical body, the personage of Maha Chohan ...prepares to receive the last breath of the ascending spirit. As this is underway the Silver Cord *(the thread of life)* breaks and an angel or master or

---

his representative awaits the soul and usually delivers it to that soothing tranquility which, in the orthodox faith, humanity knows as 'Paradise'. There, after a certain amount of time during which the soul is allowed to meet some friends and beloved ones, ...the angel of the Karmic Committee appears again with the summons at hand, calling the said soul to appear before it.»

There, they wait for their turn to appear before the infamous judging (karmic) committee, or for their "good testimony before the awesome tribunal of God." *[The Divine Liturgy of St. John Chrysostom: Litany of the Precious Gifts]*

483 **A) PLATO'S REPUBLIC,** BOOK 10 (v. 614b-614d), And let me tell you, I shall now unfold the tale to you, not according to Alcinous, but according to a bold warrior, Er, the son of Armenius, a Pamphylian by race. He was once slain in battle, and when the corpses were taken up on the tenth day already decayed, was found intact, and having been brought home, at the moment of his funeral, on the twelfth day as he lay upon the pyre, revived, and after coming to life related what, he said, he had seen in the world beyond.

He said that when his soul went forth from his body he journeyed with a great company [614c] and that they came to a mysterious *(orig. Gr. text.: daemonic)* region where there were two openings side by side in the earth, and above and over against them in the sky two others, and that **judges** were sitting between these, and that after every judgment they bade the righteous journey to the right and upwards through the sky with tokens attached to them in front, of the judgment passed upon them, and the unjust to take the road to the left and downward, they too wearing signs, but behind them, [614d] of all that had befallen them.» [ENGLISH TR.: JAMES ADAM, 1902, CAMBRIDGE, CAMBRIDGE UNIVERSITY PRESS.]

B) PAPASTAVROU, A., 'LETTERS TO ANONYMOUS'

Speeches/teachings of the masters of the White Brotherhood to their disciples.

(pp. 248-251): «Chohan Morya's speech: ...In the lower aetheric layers the Great Quadrangular White Mansion is located, which is called by many 'The Building of Judgment.' Indeed, it is...as you know, the building of Karma. Every soul must pass through it after death...There is no individual who hasn't gone through the chambers of Karma as well as the procedure thereof. This procedure and the punishment through Judgment, is the reason why man looks to them in terror; so much so, that he has instated them as a dogma in his theology: Jehovah's wrath and punishment. And this, because the Realm *(astro-aetheric region)* which the soul might have been sent to during a previous procedure on account of its bad conduct during its lifetime, caused such terror to it.»

Don't skip chapters or bibliographic references

(But the fear of death is common to <u>all</u> people…Yet no one has ever explained to us exactly WHAT happens in those planes to cause such TERROR! Therefore, let me REMIND you: «For <u>I did not come to judge</u> the world but to save the world.» [JOHN 12:47] also: «He who believes in Him <u>is not judged.</u> He who doesn't believe <u>has been judged already.</u>» [JOHN 3:18]

…Before the final judgment is passed and the individual or the group is surrendered to the being, –who will either lead them to the astral or to another suitable plane for their further advancement *(!)* yet without the slightest intention of punishment *(!!)*– all members of the great white lodge can speak in favor of any soul. …If a person has lived a pernicious life, it may be necessary for them to 'get a taste' of the sensation and/or the pain inflicted by their actions, and this, <u>for correctional purposes</u>, so that the consciousness can perceive reality *(it is obviously because of this 'correctional procedure' that humanity today …shines with piety!)*; to acknowledge in other words, that these actions do not abide by the divine Rule.[1]»

[1] *However, since the genes –which are manufactured **by them**– give <u>their own instructions</u> commanding man to act accordingly, then, based on what grounds do these judges **demand** the balancing of Karma, when they themselves know only too well <u>the imperfectness of the material body</u>, which (after all) even Maha Chohan himself acknowledges:*

«…Human nature does not know tolerance, understanding or true love. Every non-ascended being participates in this imperfectness of the human nature which –in the material world– he perceives as self-preservation.» [PAPASTAVROU A., 'LETTERS TO ANONYMOUS', p. 134]

And the Creator's mistakes torment men…

'THE MURDEROUS, THE MALE, THE FEMALE BRAIN'
SOURCE: science news.gr
http://www.typos.com.cy/nqcontent.cfm?a_id=30744

«As all of us, so do the scientists, have been pondering for some time now on what happens inside the mind of murderers, or rather what goes wrong. The prevailing view is that the real roots of violence lie in bad conditions of their environment and the existence of violent parents. This view is still scientifically supported and is politically correct.

An ever **increasing amount of <u>evidence</u> though,** from studies where murderers' brains are scanned with advanced technologies, claim that it is **some damage** or poor functioning of a particular brain region, are often to blame for violent behaviors. This area of the brain concerns the prefrontal cortex which is located right behind the forehead and the eyes.

Even though many groups study the subject, the most impressive and tangible proof of the connection between brain damage and violence, is the study of Adrian Raine, a clinical neuro-scientist at the South California

University in Los Angeles. Among other things, Raine performed PET Scan Tomographies (**P**ositron **E**mission **T**omography) on 41 murderers and 41 normal individuals of the same age. In each group, 39 out of the 41 individuals were male (PET Scan Tomography measures glucose intake by the brain cells, thus showing which areas of the brain are more active). The murderers had a lower glucose metabolism in their prefrontal cortex, which indicates that this region does not function as well as it should in order to prevent violent impulses.

These results are in agreement with earlier research studies from the Univ. of Iowa, which indicated that healthy individuals with prefrontal cortex damage become impulsive and antisocial. Additionally, these results are in accord with the research studies of Dr. Dorothy Otnow Lewis, Prof. of Psychiatry in the School of Medicine of New York and Prof. of Clinical Psychiatry at the Yale Child Health Research Center and Dr. Jonathan Pincus, Director of Neurology in the Veteran Medical Center, who, based on classic neuro-psychological tests, showed that violent behavior is related to prefrontal cortex **damage** (malfunction).

But all killers are certainly not the same. When Raine divided the murderers in two groups, those who had committed premeditated murder in one and those who had –without conscious awareness– killed in another, it was the impulsive killers that exhibited the poorest function of the prefrontal cortex. Furthermore, in the brain of the murderers, the mesolobe (a zone of tissue that connects the right with the left hemispheres of the brain) also functioned inefficiently. This appears logical because it might mean that the left hemisphere (logical) cannot 'talk' to the more emotional right hemisphere, thus hindering violent instinct control.

Additionally, the deeper areas of the brain, where primordial emotions like fear and aggressiveness originate, were more active in the brains of the killers compared to the normal control group. For instance, Raine used magnetic tomography to examine the brain structure of disturbed people with antisocial behavior. These subjects exhibit a psychopathic lack of penitence, an inclination for law-breaking and violent crime. He found that, in those people, brain cells in the region of the prefrontal cortex were on average 11% smaller in comparison to the normal ones. This constitutes an additional indication that malfunction or damage of this region of the brain can predispose people for aggressive and violent behavior.»

How would then the 'Judgment of God' or the Karmic Committee judge these 'defective ones'? Or is it that the defective brain was some kind of karmic 'gift' for correctional purposes, so that the vicious circle of 'give and take' can go on unobstructed?

Don't skip chapters or bibliographic references

This judging committee is comprised of 'ascended' masters of the hierarchy of the creators –who have also deceitfully enlisted the most beautiful **skeptomorph** of Jesus Christ in their ranks– as well as other spiritually 'advanced' entities.

When the deceased man's aetheric body is dissolved –along with the decoder aetheric brain– and the soul remains enveloped in just its (mindless) astral/emotional body, comes its turn to appear before the Karmic/Judging Committee. Its past life on Earth is then projected to her like a motion picture, and there, all mistakes, missed opportunities, committed injustices, as well as the emotional situations the soul produced in that life, are highlighted. Then, the mindless astral body betrays even the most intimate emotions the man had felt during his life, which (emotions) after all, comprise that very astral/emotional body of his.

---

484 PAPASTAVROU, A., 'LETTERS TO ANONYMOUS' CH. ASTRAL PLANE (p. 98): «The Causative *(astral)* body is the immediate carrier of the incarnate soul. It was created long before man assumed a place on earthly evolution. …Man, provided he has fleshy substance, stores all spiritual wealth he has managed to accumulate in the Causative Body; **the crop, rich or poor** is clearly seen in it when, after death, man as a soul appears in front of the karmic committee in the chambers of the 'Building of Judgment', and the Causative *(astral)* body **is the one which is primarily examined.**»

(p. 229) «…One of the concessions that the Karmic Committee makes to the soul appearing before them to be judged, is to let her see the past life which she just left and assess on her own what chances for advancement she had and pointlessly overlooked. It is at that point, that remorse brings tears and psychic pain unknown until then to man.»

After the weighing/balancing process of the sum of energies produced by the soul, it (the soul) is classified in a corresponding "category" depending on the **quality** of the overall energy it offered, and then the second phase of this post-mortem route follows.

---

485 PLATO'S REPUBLIC, BOOK 10 (615a-615b) *Er the son of Armenius continues his account:* «…For all the wrongs they had each ever done to anyone and all whom they had severally wronged they had paid the penalty in turn tenfold for each, and the measure of this was by periods of a hundred years each, [615b] so that on the assumption that this was the length of human life the punishment would be ten times the crime.» [Eng. tr.: JAMES ADAM, 1902, http://www.perseus.tufts.edu]

This (second phase) is an absolutely secret process, protected like a sacred ritual, and it is because of this second phase that IT BECOMES IMPERATIVE FOR THE SOUL NOT TO REMEMBER. Nonetheless, despite the fact the soul doesn't remember, man still feels absolute horror for death. The soul cannot free itself from this horror, no matter how much "therapeutic treatment" it undergoes in the 2nd virtual paradise.

---

486 **A) PAPASTAVROU, A., 'LETTERS TO ANONYMOUS'**: «Saint Germaine, in a commentary in one of his speeches to the disciples of the Bridge, on March 31st, 1956, mentioned the following: "Oh! There is much you do not know! Fortunately there is a Shroud of 'Mercy' between the conscious noûs and certain **aetheric memories**, and this veil is very gradually removed from time to time. And this because, it is known, a most prudent man lost his mind completely just by peeking into the 'Tenant on the Threshold' –as the human creation of the personal life of man is often called *(man's skeptomorphic offspring)*.» *This means that, the moment the prudent man cast his eyes upon what lies behind the Shroud of 'Mercy', went crazy.*

B) GOSPEL OF PHILIP, JEAN-YVES LELOUP: «§63. One is either of the world, or one is resurrected *[anastasis]*, or one is in the intermediate world *(the astral plane)*. **God forbid** that I be found there! In this world there is good and there is evil. What is good is not all good, and what is evil is not all evil. **But beyond this world, <u>there is something that is really evil</u>: it is the intermediate world, the world of the dead.**» [Eng. tr. JOSEPH ROWE]

So this second phase is the fragmentation of man's astral (emotional) body into its parts; the process of 'apportionment'. After man's appearance in front of the Karmic Committee, the central gate of Hades opens wide and the guardian Kerberos allows no one to escape back to life, but forces them to be taken to the insides of the underworld, in order for his energy segmentation/partitioning to begin.

---

487 **A) PAPASTAVROU, A., 'LETTERS TO ANONYMOUS'** (p. 251)

«Speech of Paul the Venetian, Chohan of the Third Ray, 3 October 1953, in New York to the students of 'Bridge to Freedom':

…When Maha Chohan sees that the energy given to the individual by the sun is enough and nothing more can be accomplished *(meaning that the fruit/man is mature)*, there is no way of going back, …but 'always Ahead'. And the Angel stands in front of the gate of the Karma halls whenever each of the souls is being judged. This Angel, standing with his arms stretched, says: 'Ahead'. This blessed one isn't always likeable to the souls of men. Nonetheless, 'Ahead', the souls must proceed.»

Don't skip chapters or bibliographic references

B) PAPASTAVROU A., 'COSMOS WITHIN A COSMOS' CH. ASTRAL PLANE (p. 22-30):
«When, after death, he *(man)* leaves the physical body, he first visits this invisible world, and sometimes remains there for a long time, whether he wants it or not. It is the world known by the Greek Mythology as Hades, by Christendom as 'hell' and as the wise men of the Middle Ages called it, the 'Astral Plane'.»

What man encountered in his material life, was exclusively the absorption of energy through his twofold **material** action/activity. In the energy realms of Hades, the absence of an active material body prevents the man-soul from energy-nourishing not only himself but also the energy-groups he has fed/supplied throughout his life. This is where hell begins for him. The aetheric brain that formulates the world into images does not exist anymore. Inside a formless ocean of energy, the man-soul is overtaken by nightmare situations as he is dominated by his nostalgia for the forms/images he has loved in the material world. His lower mental body, **already full**, produces **no** further information. The soul then, "wearing" only its astral/emotional energy-body, goes through **all** stages of the astral plane, in order for every different energy-form –developed by man during his lifetime and <u>stored</u> in his astral body– to be **dispensed/distributed** to its respective recipients. *[Saint Germaine: "Because in your causative (astral) body <u>you have deposited</u> certain quantities of modulated energy".]*

To make this whole issue of death clearer, I will present it to you from a different perspective, reminding you of the second phase of self-knowledge. If you remember, what we had then pointed out was the ability man has in his life to look at all these "formulated" living energy-hypostases/conditions head-on and see them claim their energy-supplies through his daily activity in life.

When man lives his life –in his active material body– in the material plane, his other bodies simultaneously live/exist in the corresponding energy-planes. Thus, his astral body exists and lives in the astral plane, supplying the corresponding energy-forces relative to his material activities, thoughts and emotions.

---

488 **RUDOLF STEINER 'AT THE GATES OF ANTHROPOSOPHY'** [Gr. tr. ALEXIOU TH.]
(a) CH. 'THE THREE WORLDS' (p. 18): «There are three worlds: 1) The Physical world, the 'scene' of human life 2) The Astral or Soul world, 3) The Devachan(ic) or world of Spirit. These three worlds are not spatially separate from each other. We are surrounded by the things of the physical world, which we perceive with our external sensory organs (senses). But the astral world exists in the same space with us. As we live in the

---

physical world, at the same time, we live in the other two worlds as well: The astral world and the Devachan world. The three worlds are wherever we ourselves are. Only, we do not see the two higher worlds, just as a blind man does not see the physical world.

(b) CH. 'LIFE AFTER DEATH' (p. 32):

…This condition is called 'Kamaloka', the place of desires. But this place isn't some region set apart: 'Kamaloca' is also where we are, and the spirits of the dead are always hovering around us. But their presence escapes our physical senses…. For example, a man eats avidly and with real pleasure. The clairvoyant will see the satisfaction of the man's desire as a brown-red thoughtform *(skeptomorph)* in the upper part of his astral body.»

During his life and through his activities, man has learned to activate some of these situations in the form of weaknesses, passions, positive and negative dependencies and positive and negative 'egotisms'. With his daily emotions he has learned to nurture these situations but also to feed himself from them.

489 **PAPASTAVROU, A., 'LETTERS TO ANONYMOUS'**

Maha Chohan elucidates us upon the subject ('Bulletin', January 5th, 1964):

«The human race has been endowed with creative power, through thinking and feeling. Every activity, in which man is employed, contains a share of his thoughts and feelings which are related to it. …Then, an elemental *(being)* is created and its consciousness is shaped according to the kind of energy which is directed to it. This elemental (*being*) has a body and form and it is an emotional creation. …Some individuals, due to their psychic anguish, fear, doubt, greed and other similar human emotions, transmit upon this elemental, properties which become its nature.»

With the death of the material body, man can no longer act. With the cessation of material action, what he has grown accustomed to energy-feed from, stops supplying him. Simultaneously he himself stops feeding all these energy-groups (of the corresponding emotional situations) that dwell in the invisible energy-spaces. The emotions that used to occupy him during life have not ceased to exist after material death. On the contrary, in these astral regions, they become infinitely more intense, since the astral body that exclusively surrounds his soul is the basic carrier of every desire; but where he is now, he does not have the means to satisfy it (the astral body).

Don't skip chapters or bibliographic references

490 **A) RUDOLF STEINER 'AT THE GATES OF ANTHROPOSOPHY'** [Gr. tr. ALEXIOU TH.]
CH. 'LIFE OF THE SOUL AFTER DEATH' (p. 31, 32, 33)

«How, then, does a dead man feel?…The material (means) of pleasure clings to the physical body. We must have a palate, etc., to be able to eat. But pleasure… and the desire for pleasure remain even after death. But man has no longer any possibility to satisfy his desires, since the bodily organs that provide the means for this satisfaction are missing. It is the same with all the pleasures and desires. …Like a wayfarer in the desert, the soul, tormented from burning thirst *(of every desire),* wanders, looking for some spring at which to quench its thirst…since it no longer possesses any (bodily) organ to satisfy it. …Why does the soul have to endure this torment? The reason is that man has to wean himself gradually from these physical desires of the senses, so that the soul may detach itself from the Earth, may purify and cleanse itself. …Among the various feelings that cling to man during his life, is especially the unique feeling of existence, the sheer joy of being alive, and the attachment to the physical body.»

B) PAPASTAVROU A., 'COSMOS WITHIN A COSMOS' CH. ASTRAL PLANE (pp. 25-26):

«…The astral world is the environment of the man who is seized with unrestrained and harsh passions. This is called the abyss, the vast place of desires that cannot be satisfied because of the absence of the physical body, which was the means of satisfaction. Here we find the drunkards and those who are enslaved by carnal passions, and generally speaking, the man who is obsessed with vile and avid desires, and had been their slave throughout his life, and will continue to be, until the prevailing and overwhelming yet low desire gradually wears out. It is said that the tortures of these desires are analogous to the torments of hell-fire, mentioned by the earlier Christian Orthodoxy. However, these torments are dated back to pre-Christianic times, as we see in the Ani Papyrus, 4.000 years ago: "What manner of land is this unto which I have come! It is arid, it lacks air, it is vast and bottomless; it is black like the darkest darkness of a black night and people wander through it, hopelessly. But here, it is impossible for a man with a worriless, rested heart to live.

On the other hand, we find Tantalus, in Greek mythology, constantly tormented by raging thirst and eternally doomed to watch the water vanish the moment his lips are about to taste it.

…According to Annie Besant, in the astral world there are also corrupt men, incarcerated in their astral bodies known as 'elementals' …they are after those who tend towards carnal passions, which they had invited and attracted to themselves while being in the physical world. Anyone gifted with astral vision, passing by the streets of London, can see these elementals cluster round the beer houses and taverns… deriving pleasure from the stench given out from the drinks and endeavoring to push themselves inside the bodies of people who are drinking. These entities are attracted to those who feed their bodies on such matters and such environment is part of their emotional life. These are the 'prisoners of the earth' about whom we have heard so many blamable things.»

The emotional situations man has learned to experience in his lifetime and the energy-hypostases that grew accustomed to feed from him, remain attached to him. These concern both positive and negative energy-potentials, because every astral body consists of both positive and negative energy parts. And to use different words for that, the sums of energies that used to feed from this man are still connected to him. These energy-sums/hypostases are projected in front of him, <u>claiming</u> the energy (nutrition) **they have made a habit** of getting from him.

491 PADMASAMBHAVA, THE TIBETAN BOOK OF THE DEAD [Gr. tr. LIAKOPOULOS E.]
The entire text refers to the experiences that a man will have after the death of his material body. In its pages, there are references to frightful entities which the dead man meets in the underground world. However, they are all characterized as projections of the man himself and they correspond to the tendencies, desires and fears that the man cultivated during his life. The instructive text which is recited in front of the dead man, says:

(p. 155-158) «… Oh, Nobly-born Child! Listen without wavering! Now, the eight Gauri[1] goddesses will emerge from within your brain and shall appear to you! Do not be terrified! From the east of the horizon of your brain, the White Gauri shall appear, her right hand holding a corpse as a club and her left hand holding a blood-filled skull-bowl. Do not fear! From the south, the Yellow Gauri, holding a bow and arrow, ready to shoot; …all these eight Gauri goddesses, from the eight points of the horizon surrounding the five blood-thirsty Herukas[2], will emerge from within your own brain and shall appear to you …After that, the eight Pishachi[3] of the holy lands will emerge and appear to you! From the east a dark maroon, lion-headed Sinhamukha, crossing her arms over her chest, devouring a corpse in her mouth, and tossing her mane; from the south, a red, tiger-headed Vyaghrimukha, crossing her arms downward, gnashing her fangs; from the west, a black, fox-headed Srigalamukha, with a blade in her right hand, holding intestines in her left hand feasting on them, licking the blood; from the north, a dark blue, wolf-headed Svanamukha with swollen eyes, lifting a corpse up to her mouth with her two hands …from the southwest, a dark red, hawk-headed

Don't skip chapters or bibliographic references

Kankamukha, carrying a big corpse over her shoulders.

(p. 158)...O, child of a good family, the six southern Yoginis[4] emerge from your own brain and appear before you! Vajra the Incorruptible, with the head of a pig, holding a blade. Santi the Peace, with a reddish water-monster head, holding an amphora. ...The dark green, vulture-headed Bhaksini holding a club; Rakshasi, the red, dog-headed daemoness, holding a sharp razor.»

[1] Gauri: A group of eight female deities with predatory and carnivorous tempers.

[2] Heruka: A male sacred spirit. The word 'bloodthirsty' characterizes its attribute of absorbing the 'blood' of selfishness, doubt and dual perception.

[3] Pishachi (or Pisaci): Striped, beautifully adorned, sexually neutral ascetics, highly religious.

[4] Yoginis: Group of deities, practicing Yoga.

And the references to the frightful entities, with their half-human and half-animal body, continue throughout the entire text of 'The Tibetan book of the dead', reminding us of the mythological anthropomorphous entities of the world, which, in our book, have been characterized as the human living thoughtforms *(skeptomorphs), generated by man and analyzed in the chapter 'The end of the race of Heroes'.*

Just like wild dogs that voraciously devour the food someone throws in front of them, so do the lower astrals (i.e. negative energy-sums) devour the lower energy-portions that correspond to them, and which comprise a portion of that particular astral body.

492 **PADMASAMBHAVA, THE TIBETAN BOOK OF THE DEAD** [Gr. tr. LIAKOPOULOS E.] p. 160:

«At that time, when the fifty-eight blood-drinking deities emerge from within your brain, ...because of your clinging, you will not recognize these abominable presences and you will resort to a frenzied flee and fall once again into utter misery. ...You will feel panic, agony and exhaustion. Your own projections/visions will take a daemonic form and you will continue wandering in Samsara![1]

...O, nobly-born child! Even if the bodies of the largest of the Peaceful and Wrathful Deities are equal (in vastness) to the limits of the heavens, the intermediate ones, as big as Mt. Meru, the smallest equal to eighteen times the height of an ordinary human body, be not terrified at that; be not awed! All phenomena manifest as lights and images!

(p.162)... When your own visions/projections appear in that form, be not afraid, for the body you have is a body made of your karmic tendencies, thus, **even if it is killed or dismembered**, it cannot die!

(p.180) THE MIRROR OF KARMA: ...The master of death will look in the mirror of karma and see its reflections, clear and distinct...The master of death will tie a rope around your neck and drag you away. He will cut off your head, rip out your heart, pull out your guts, lick your brains, drink your blood, tear your flesh to shreds, and gnaw your bones. But you won't die, even though your body is cut to pieces. Being cut up again and again, you will suffer immense pain.» *(It is the absolutely mystical process of dying that concerns the distribution of the energy stored in the astral body in pieces.)*

(1) **Samsara**: The vicious cycle of birth and death; the world of Maya-illusion.

The translator and commentator of "The Tibetan Book of the Dead", Eustathios Liakopoulos, describes the six realms of Samsara together with the five fatal sins dominating in these realms:

1) The realm of Samsaric *(worldly [Sallustius])* gods. …The gods of Samsara are considered to be immortal, but only up to the point that their good karma runs out *(so, the very same oscillation of dyadic matter, degrades them through an endless, vicious circle of ascent and degradation)*. **Pride** – the first fatal sin– undermines the realm of these gods and consumes their suspecting bliss.

2) The realm of the jealous gods who are called demigods or Titans in the Greek Mythology, with **Jealousy** –the second fatal sin- leading them to intolerance/bigotry through endless victories and defeats.

3) The animal kingdom, which includes all animal creatures, **Ignorance** –the third fatal sin– dark and suspicious, has surrounded and captured the realm of animals and reproduces their instinctive fear and insecurity.

4) The realm of the Hungry Ghosts, with **Desire** –the fourth fatal sin– sustained by the 'unquenchable' and imposes insatiable passions.

5) The realm of beings of hell, with **Hatred** –the fifth fatal sin– having accumulated heavily and impenetrably all over this realm causing and resulting in unbearable pain.

6) The realm of Human beings. All the five basic passions dominate this realm accumulatively, mostly in the form of arrogance and desire.

The wheel of life and existence of Samsara are held by Yama, the ruler of existence. He is considered the lord of death and the judge of the dead in the Bardo (=intermediate state) of rebirth. He is also called the lord of Dharma (=the law of existence and the essence of phenomena).

Thus with the end of material action, the hatred that someone used to feel for his fellowmen does not find an outlet for satisfaction and consumes its master. His lust is also left unfulfilled, his eroticism finds no response. His gluttony remains unsatisfied. The jealousy he might have felt for people, becomes gigantic now and since it is impossible for him to proceed to reprisals to satisfy it through action– it devours him and causes him pain. All

Don't skip chapters or bibliographic references

his desires, now unsatisfied and hungry, through their urge to be satisfied, are transformed into beasts that victimize him.

Deeply repressed situations, that 'civilized' man never accepted they existed inside him, appear before him as if from nowhere, and pursue him. The need to punish those who have harmed him –so that he can find justice– becomes a scourge. The negative situations that he himself imposed on others appear as Furies from the deepest parts within and demand to balance out the injustice by cutting pieces off from his energy-body. Lament, pain and unsatisfied desires torture the souls of men. This is the passage from the lower astral planes. Good and bad men go through there, in order to deposit the portion incorporated in their astral body that corresponds to these regions. The more weaknesses one had cultivated during his life, the longer he remains there, since the 'plump' negative energy-portion of his astral body takes longer to get consumed.

There are dead people, who through very strong bonds of multifaceted dependencies and attachments to matter, insist on struggling hopelessly to absorb energy from it, thus forming the category of earth-bound spirits. Others again, due to intense situations they have experienced during their lifetime, get trapped inside space-time instances or, on other occasions, move through parallel alternative energy-probabilities –which we will explain later– in order to absorb the energy they are looking for from there. All these groups of spirits comprise the category of the so-called 'ghosts' that, attached mainly to the Earth's aetheric plane as they are, remain bound to it.

The astral world is immense and hides inside it so many different aspects, sections and categories that cannot be exhausted, no matter how long we talk about them. After all, our subject is not the astral world, but we are briefly mentioning it here as we 'pass through' it.

When at some point, the last negative energy-part of man's astral body is consumed as it is severed to be added to its corresponding wider energy-group of the astrals, his soul ascends to the more luminous/positive astral planes. There, it comes face to face with its 'positive' inner situations, and as it gets there, thirsty and tormented from the lower astral regions of hell, it 'extends its hands' to these new figures, asking them to fill it with their serene, positive offerings. Right then however, the soul realizes with disappointment, that this notion was just an illusion created in life by methodically falsified theories. Just as civilized men while eating ornament their tables with silver utensils and civilly consume the best parts of the slaughtered animal, so do the 'positive' astrals in the form of 'benign' masters and their creators/gods –as persistent worshipers of ceremony– 'politely' devour

442

their positive energy-share and are incapable of quenching the thirst of the tormented soul.

---

493 **A) GOSPEL OF PHILIP,** [ENG. TR. PATERSON BROWN] www.metalog.org/files/philip.html

«§54. God is a cannibal. Because of this, mankind is sacrificed to it.»

Jean Yves Leloup translates from Coptic the same excerpt as follows:

«§30. Humanity is the food of God *(his vegetable garden).*»

B) PAPASTAVROU, A., 'LETTERS TO ANONYMOUS' (p. 345): «At the end of every year, the honor and the privilege is given to the 'Spiritual Hierarchy of the Planet' to go across the Sacred Marble Bridge of Light, which leads to the heart of **Shambhala**.

There, they adduce (hand in) to the 'Lord of the world' *(the archon of this world),* the result of their special service during the last year. …The amount of the 'harvest' *(from the positive energies they reaped from humanity)* each one *(every member of the Spiritual Hierarchy of the Planet)* will present, determines the amount of service which –according to the Law– he/she will undertake for the next year.

This involves that, once a year, a report and an account is given to the 'Lord of the World' from the members of the Hierarchy, indicating which use they made of the light which was granted to them during the past year *(because this light is stolen from the HyperCosmoi, it is therefore granted with extreme caution),* and how they made use of the chances which were entrusted to them *(persuading the humanity to produce more and more 'positive' energy).*

(p. 346) …Below we give an excerpt of a description, which the *(master)* Chohan Kuthumi made on the subject-matter. The speech was given to the disciples of the 'Bridge to freedom' on November 19th, 1955:… Sanat Kumara *(Sanat [Satan] as the 'Lord of the world' or 'the Archon of this world')* stands in the heart of his temple, waiting for the arrival of the ones bringing **the harvest**.

(p. 349) …As we turn up the great gates of the temple, we see Sanat Kumara standing by the great Altar…accepting **the sheaves of harvest**, while they are exposed on the big funnel <u>by great ones and small ones alike</u>.

…After the delivery of the **harvest** *(the positive energy they have reaped from humans)* the **deposit** takes place. This is put in a sacred Tabernacle of Light and sealed by an Archangel, in order to be transferred to Royal Teton later on. There, sheltered by other rituals, it will be presented in front of the "Lords of Karma". Then, This Venerable Body *(the Karmic Committee)* will decide, according to the quantity of the entire **harvest**, what allotments *(percentages)* can be approved for the next year, for humanity's benefit.

(p. 351) …We continue by quoting a part of the speech of Chohan Morya re-

---

Don't skip chapters or bibliographic references

garding what went on in the hermitage of Royal Teton *(the Karmic Committee)* after the transfer of the **sheaves of harvest**. ...The altar occupies the center of the big hall. ...On the altar the flame of 'Precipitation' burns. ...Meanwhile, they've handed in their reports to the Karmic Committee in the hall and they have been placed on a huge brazier. They make a flammable stack in order to be burned. ...The essence which comes of the brazier is a scent which resembles jasmine oil. It represents the sacredness of the humanity's raised energies which have been offered in serving love towards their brothers *(human positive-energies of self-sacrifice and love)*. Sanat Kumara bows in front of the flame and the altar ...and enters into the heart of the flame.

Through this burning of humanity's positive energies, it brings forth a living thoughtform. ...The beloved 'Silent Supervisor of the Planet' keeps this thoughtform in Her heart for this year *(she gestates it)*. Sanat Kumara, posed with adoration, raises his consciousness in order to receive it *(the thoughtform)* and the whole assembly **breaths it in** *(...they assimilate it)*.

(Chohan Morya, concluding the description of the ceremony, he addresses his disciples): All these were made possible with your invocations and I'm sure, you will be glad to know that **your harvest** became the **enduring possession** of the most ancient Hermitage on the Earth –the Royal Teton.»

And finally, is it likely that this is the famous Ambrosia, the Gods' food, which comes from the 'vrotoi' [=the ones to be eaten]?

Human theories and material life in general, taught man nothing about the quest for the Divine Spirit inside him, but only how to focus onto his material (outer) presence. Thus, ordinary man never learned to Love the Spiritual fellow-Man –since he never knew him– but only his material form and its emotional (astral) manifestations.

[494] **GOSPEL OF THOMAS**, JEAN YVES LELOUP: «§101. Whoever does not hate his father and his mother in My way, shall not be able to become a Disciple to Me. And whoever does [not] love his [Father] and his Mother in My way, shall not be able to become a [Disciple to] Me. For My mother [bore My body], yet [My] True [Mother] gave Me the life.» [Eng. tr. JOSEPH ROWE]

However, this human, materialistic love, in order to emotionally express itself, passes through the material and energy (astral) bodies and connects man to everything he has 'loved' with invisible energy-connections, like invisible threads. Thus, the stronger a human relation is, the more resilient these energy threads are, which people mistake for 'love'. After the death of the material body, these invisible connections cannot be supplied through matter anymore –as they used to– and are inevitably cut causing immense pain.

---

495 A) GOSPEL OF THOMAS, JEAN YVES LELOUP: «§55. Jesus said: "Whoever cannot free themselves from their father and their mother cannot become my disciple. Whoever cannot free themselves from their brother and sister and does not bear their cross as I do *(mine)*, is not worthy of Me." §87. …Jesus said: "Wretched is the body which depends upon (another) body, and wretched is the soul which depends upon both *(bodies)*.» [Eng. tr. JOSEPH ROWE]

B) THE GOSPEL OF MATTHEW, CH. 6: «§21. For where your treasure is, there your heart will be also.»

Just as the unfulfilled craving of negative desires scourges man's soul, so does any material expression he has 'loved' trap him into a hopeless quest, generating the same pain his unsatisfied negative desires had originally caused him.

---

496 A) PAPASTAVROU A., 'COSMOS WITHIN A COSMOS' CH. ASTRAL PLANE (p. 29): «For those who in the physical life failed to develop even a portion of their mental/noetic body and as men, they were totally focused on matter and self-interest, the planes of 'bliss' of the mental/noetic world are remote. What they developed in the physical world was their astral (emotional) body of desires and excitements and that, along with its corresponding plane, is all that remains familiar and known to them after death.»

Even his kind offer to his fellowmen, that 'exalted' him so much while he was alive, can only comfort him now as much as 'leftovers', and is unable to relieve him. This is because while he was still in material existence, he had absorbed all the energy-portion that was his share from this positive activity, through satisfaction of his positive egotism or the positive social acceptance he experienced due to his offering. So, the positive-energy after-effect, recorded/stored in his astral body —as the result of a 'fermentation process'– is cut off from it to be added to the corresponding and generally positive sum (group) of the higher astral plane, thus leaving the soul exposed once more. Additionally, if in those astral regions he desires to act positively in order to supply himself again, the nonexistence of an active material body renders this effort a tormenting impossibility.

At certain times, during his material life, sometimes out of need, other times to project his "ego" and others out of conviction, man makes certain positive offerings to his fellowmen, but never manages to harvest the energy-benefits he thinks he deserves. Energy-deficits are therefore created

Don't skip chapters or bibliographic references

within him, and since his soul feels that some 'pieces' belong to it, it tries to look for them inside these energy spaces in vain. In order to acquire them again, the soul ends up accepting a new incarnation in matter. Thus, man's soul slowly realizes that human, materialistic love was **merely** a 'healthy' energy-nutrition during his life and not the 'key' to Redemption and the envisagement of the True God.

---

497 *Let me remind you of the case of Mother Theresa and her reports of the 'darkness', the 'torture' and the 'loneliness' that obsessed her life despite her 'love offerings' to her fellowmen. She couldn't find God through this 'love'.*

ATHENIAN AND MACEDONIAN NEWS AGENCY (http://www.ana-mpa.gr/anaweb/) 26/8/2007

«Mother Teresa doubted the existence of God, according to her letters. Mother Teresa, who is likely to be declared Saint by the Catholic Church, endlessly felt her faith shaken throughout her life and, in addition, doubted the very existence of God, as it is disclosed in letters that she wrote in 1979 to her trusted friend, reverent Michael Van der Pet.

Her constant references to the 'darkness', the 'loneliness' and the 'torment' are present in more than 40 letters she wrote during a period of 66 years. Although these letters exhibit brief remorse, Mother Teresa spent more than 50 years doubting the existence of God despite the opposite image she projected in her public life.»

But this deep realization of the soul from incarnation to incarnation, though not conscious, results –generation after generation– in a constant degeneration of human relationships and the gradual downfall of the values of friendship, companionship, trust and altruism by constantly making the diagram of human 'evolution' slope downwards without again being able to ensure the road to Salvation.

When at some point every stored positive and negative part of the energy-body has been severed from it and added to the corresponding wider positive or negative astral sum/group, as well as every piece of human knowledge of the lower mental plane has enriched the lower mental sub-plane i.e. the higher level of the astral –the akashic sub-plane– then the soul is released from its astral body which remains there as an empty shell wandering in the astral realms until it dissolves. Until it dissolves however, every such astral-shell is occupied by astral entities of all kinds, who after seizing it, appear in séances ("spiritual" gatherings) of living humans, pretending to be this or that dead person, thus misleading the living. In other cases –since the astral body itself maintains an 'echo of consciousness' from the Soul that raised it– it follows that Soul in its new incarnation and feels sorrow watching it now nourish a new astral body, like a child who watches its mother devoting herself to a new-born baby. Sometimes, these astral shells attach themselves to that man and generate various problems in his new incarnation. This is just a sample of the problems this material creation has caused.

The most prominent post-mortem 'benefit' that comes from the positive activities of man's previous material life is that from these 'luminous' higher astral regions of the positive planes, the soul has **access** to the 2nd virtual paradise (Nirvana), where it will undergo 'therapeutic teaching' and rest. On account of this possibility, a rumor was created among men that whoever performs good deeds goes to 'heaven'.

As in many cases the seeds of plants are washed and undergo various processes in order to be planted again, so does the denuded soul, after it leaves its astral body in the astral planes as an empty shell, enter the area of the 2nd reflection paradise (Nirvana), where it accepts 'healing' from the traumatic experience of the astral denudation. Additionally, through the teaching of the masters (from the creators' side) who reside there, the Soul recovers from the wounds and torments it suffered in its material life in order to prepare for a new visit to the material plane, inside a new body and new circumstances of life, appropriately selected for it.

[498] PAPASTAVROU, A., 'LETTERS TO ANONYMOUS' (p. 234): «When a soul **has paid the imposed karma to it** and has received the **necessary rest** the messenger angel appears to it again, but with a different "scroll" at hand. This map is now with a cyan-colored ribbon…and its work is to invite the said soul to present itself once more to the karmic committee for rebirth.»

On the other hand, souls that never managed to reach the 2nd (reflection) material paradise pass on to the new incarnation too, driven though by the lower astral powers of the lower astral planes, where they had been encaged. These dark powers, having sucked every trace of negative energy dry from the aforementioned astral body (and since its soul does not possess anything positive to offer to the higher astral orders), throw it (the soul) (in the best case scenario) into a miserable new existence, so that through its fear, passions and pains it will reproduce the inferior energies that will feed the powers of these lower astral planes again. In the worst case scenario though, very dark astral powers, not only entrap the soul, but because of their bulimia, devour the soul itself until it is completely lost…

Before each soul comes to its new material incarnation, regardless of the energy-region it comes from, it must permanently delete every memory from its intellect that reminds it of the painful process of denudation from

Don't skip chapters or bibliographic references

its astral body. This phase of deletion will render it obedient to the process of the new incarnation.

---

499 **A) PAPASTAVROU, A., 'LETTERS TO ANONYMOUS'** (p. 241): «After the completion of the task of the Karmic committee, follows the service and the blessing for the elected souls, which are also ready for incarnation…and on their forehead, the ribbon of Forgetfulness is placed. …In his encyclical letter of the 16th of August 1953 to his disciples, Maha Chohan gives the following information: "…Awaiting in the planes of Light is a great number of elected spirits which…will incarnate. …Those who were their sponsors, their guides and teachers, are especially sad to see those souls being born under the bonds of Forgetfulness.»

B) PLATO'S REPUBLIC BOOK 10 *(The narration of Er the son of Armenius continues)*: «…And the judgments and penalties were somewhat of this manner… But when seven days had elapsed for each group in the meadow, they were required to rise up on the eighth and journey on, and they came in four days to a spot. …There, they should present themselves in front of Lachesis. …A prophet first marshaled them in orderly intervals… and went up to a lofty platform and spoke: "This is the word of Lachesis, the maiden daughter of Need: Ephemeral souls, now is the beginning of another cycle of mortal generation." … All the souls had now chosen their lives… Lachesis sent with them the daemon whom they had chosen, to be the guardian of their new lives … whence not being allowed to turn round … *(the souls)* marched on in a scorching heat to the plain of **Forgetfulness**… and then towards evening they encamped by the river of Un-mindfulness/Thoughtlessness *(orig. Gr. text: river Amelitos)*… of this they were all obliged to drink a certain quantity,… and those who were not saved by wisdom drank more than was necessary; and each one as he drank forgot all things. He (Er) himself was hindered from drinking the water (in order to remember what he had seen to convey it to humans).» [TRANSLATED BY PAUL SHOREY, CAMBRIDGE, MA, HARVARD UNIVERSITY PRESS, http://www.perseus.tufts.edu]

The quality of the new life chosen for each man will be relative to the quality of energy his soul is accustomed to produce. Therefore, a soul inclined to low-quality energy-production caused by unbridled desires and passions will incarnate into corresponding living circumstances. There, it will produce its low-quality energy/dog-food for the inferior beings of the lower astral plane, or hell, as people call it. On the opposite side, high-quality energy-producing souls will be 'seeded' into favorable conditions, in order to offer the desired result for their superior masters under the best of circumstances. This is the cause for man's "good" or 'bad' karma.

–And what happens after the death of that category of men who possess no soul but are vitalized solely by the sum of their energy-bodies?
–The structural root of the energy-bodies of all men exists interwoven with the material genes of the DNA. Thus, the aforementioned men –through their materialistic activity in life– having enriched their astral body with the corresponding emotional situations according to their genetic specifications –which are **not** necessarily only negative ones– after their physical death, they bestow the energy-portions they have created during their lifetime onto the central groups of these positive and negative energies. And since these men <u>were nothing else but</u> these energy/emotional situations alone, they remain empty astral shells that eventually dissolve completely. These men in their material life justly deny reincarnation indignantly since it is a nonexistent procedure for them when others insist on its existence.
–And what is left for man to do to redeem himself from this whole process, since neither "good" nor 'bad' grant him salvation?
–**The assimilation of the Truth** *('And thou shalt know the Truth and the Truth shall set you free')* **and the acquisition of Essence/Spirit s̓ave every Soul.**
All this anguish that accompanies the soul's route after death is a <u>completely methodized and systematic</u> status quo, aiming to irrevocably lead it to a new incarnation. Thus, having no other choice, the only thing left for the soul to do is 'to choose the lesser of two evils', resigning to a new incarnation, whatever that might be, in order to free itself from the suffocating astral regions as soon as possible. With these tactics, they keep man enslaved inside the eternal cycle of reincarnations, and through their teachers promise him that… someday… he will be redeemed. Nevertheless, man can't ever realize that this is indeed <u>not</u> valid, due to the oblivion **that is forced** upon him! So he continues to blindly spin the wheel of his 'quasi' life for the benefit of others.

The only thing that can liberate man from these astral regions is his very own Spirit. As we said when we were talking of the second phase of self-knowledge, when man –still alive– frees his imprisoned Divine Spark from the Tartara (the deep underworld) of his existence, or after he pleads for active Spirit to be granted to him, he will then begin to be supplied with a different kind of 'nutrition', exclusively Spiritual.

> **500** **THE GOSPEL OF JOHN, CH. 4**: «§32. But He *(Jesus)* said to them *(the disciples)*, "I have food to eat that you do not know about.»

This new 'Supply' is not the outcome of external factors (i.e. positive or negative action), but of the retrieval of the Sacred Provisions of pure Spirit. These Provisions however have <u>different attributes</u> than the virtual 'positive'

Don't skip chapters or bibliographic references

ones of matter and once man manages to gain a glimpse, even a faint one of these True and Sacred Positives, he realizes that since each material 'positive' action carries a negative seed within, it ceases to be Unblemished. Thus, material 'kindness' looks like a cheap imitation of the Real, Spiritual One. Material "truth" seems to be a caricature of the Real and Essential One. Justice in the material world is inconsequential and almost nonexistent compared to the Sacred Archetype of Spiritual Justice. Right then, man ceases to act and withdraws from material activity, because he realizes the impotence of the material dimension and the material body –even that of the Unified Man– to produce anything but grotesque caricatures.

---

501 A) GOSPEL OF PHILIP, JEAN-YVES LELOUP: «§11. The words we give to earthly realities engender illusion; they turn the heart away from the Real to the unreal. The one who hears the word *God* does not perceive the Real, but an illusion or an image of the Real. …**we will understand this on the day when we experience the Real**.» [Eng. tr. JOSEPH ROWE]

§13. High spiritual Powers *[the Archon]* wanted to deceive Man *(Celestial Man)*… They took the name for goodness and applied it to what was not good: words became deceitful, and *(since)* then they are joined to that which is without being and without goodness. They alienate with simulations and appearances: they make a free person into a slave.

B) THE GOSPEL OF LUKE, CH. 6: «§15. For what is highly esteemed among men is an abomination in God's sight.»

Do you now understand why, when we analyzed the Higher Mental (Intellectual) Body, I told you that the four elements of matter crucify the Unified Man? This is because you shoulder the symbol of matter, the cross, only if you forsake the beauties of this world and despise its ugliness.

---

502 THE GOSPEL OF MATTHEW, CH. 10: «§38. And he who does not take his cross and follow after Me is not worthy of Me.»

Thus, with this Epignosis (cognition), in the astral regions that every soul must go through after material death, it will not be possessed by the 'thirst' of material desires, passions and emotional dependencies, since it will consider them obstructive and insignificant, and matter itself as revolting.

---

503 A) GOSPEL OF THOMAS, JEAN YVES LELOUP: «§56. Jesus said: Whoever knows the world discovers a corpse. And whoever discovers a corpse cannot be contained by the world.» [Eng. tr. JOSEPH ROWE]

B) PADMASAMBHAVA, THE TIBETAN BOOK OF THE DEAD [Gr. tr. LIAKOPOULOS E.] p. 202:

«EJECTION INTO A PURE PLANE: From this moment on though, I will feel nausea, revolt and disgust for this Samsara *(the visible and invisible material world)*. Time has finally come to abandon it.»

Furthermore, man, having learned to draw energy and support from the Spirit within, through the Higher Mental Body that surrounds him, will continue to do the same there too (in the astral regions) thus escaping the pain of any material deprivation.

---

504 A) THE GOSPEL OF JOHN, CH. 6: «§35. And Jesus said to them, "I am the bread of life. He who comes to Me shall never hunger, and he who believes in Me shall never thirst.»

B) THE GOSPEL OF JOHN, CH. 7: «§37…If anyone thirsts, let him come to Me and drink. §38. Whoever believes in Me, as the Scripture has said, "From his innermost being will flow **rivers of living water**.»

In most cases however, These Holy Souls bypass astral planes altogether, by piercing them through, like shooting stars in the night. To safely accomplish such a definitive and complete bypass that will lead straight into the region of the Higher Mental Plane which is located in the 'neutral zone', it is imperative for a man's soul, at the time of death, to 'depart' from the seventh energy-center (chakra), at the top of the head.

---

505 PADMASAMBHAVA, THE TIBETAN BOOK OF THE DEAD [Gr. tr. LIAKOPOULOS E.] (p. 98):
«It would be better if the 'Ejection of Consciousness' from the dying one, takes place when breath is reaching its end, but if this proves impossible, the following words must be stressed:
"Oh! Child from a good family (name) now is the time for you to look for a path. When breathing stops, what is called 'The Fundamental Luminance of the first Bardo'[1] will appear to you." … It is what is called 'Dharmata'[2], which is open and empty like the Sky, a luminous emptiness, pure naked spirit, without center or periphery…But the life-energy must exit through the orifice (opening) of the top of the skull Brahmarandhra.[3]»
[1] Bardo = Intermediate condition. The six principal Bardos are the following: 1. The Bardo of this current condition, of alertness *(the awakened state)*; 2. The Bardo of the state of dreaming; 3. The Bardo of Meditation; 4. The Bardo of Dying; 5. The Bardo of Reality; and 6. The Bardo of Rebirth. The Tibetan book of the dead discusses the last three.
[2] Dharmata = Reality precisely as it is, free of the illusive projections of dyadic perception. In this reality and its experiences, one is found after his death, as he has been relieved from his body. The Dharmata Bardo is the principle phase of Bardo.
[3] Brahmarandhra = The opening at the top of the head which is where the central energy conductor of the human body ends up. The Ejection of Consciousness as well as its escape at the time of death must be accomplished through this orifice in order to achieve a higher level of existence after death.

Don't skip chapters or bibliographic references

The archons of this world however, through their pseudo-teachers prompt their 'students' not to energize the head-center **which frees** man, but orient them to activate and broaden the center of the heart, which favors the higher portion of material "oscillation" with the activation of positive emotions and emotional 'love'.

---

506 **A) PAPASTAVROU, A., 'LETTERS TO ANONYMOUS'** (p. 223): «As we know, man, as a living existence, has three exit orifices for the soul in his body, each of which corresponds to the spiritual advancement of the individual. These are, the one of the head for the most advanced, the one of the heart for the courteous and generally prudent people, and the solar plexus for those, whose life has been self-indulgent, unworthy and beastly.»

B) 'SUPERMUNDANE' BOOK I (AGNI YOGA SOCIETY) 1938 *(information through channeling)*: «§13. There are two kinds of thinking. One is born from feeling, in other words, from the heart, and the other from the mind, which is akin to intellect. **Self-sacrifice** is born from the heart, and the Brotherhood **is built** upon this *(self-sacrifice)*. Our cooperation lives by the heart.

§22. Urusvati can affirm the great significance of the heart. Above and beyond the actions of all the centers the significance of the heart is evident. Even *Kundalini* would seem earthly in comparison with the heart, whose significance is little understood. It is regarded as the focal point of physical life, but this view is inadequate. The heart is the bridge between the worlds. Where the meeting-point of the three worlds is especially manifested, the significance of the heart is felt deeply. In Our Abode the heart is especially revered.»

This way, energy produced by self-sacrifice, service, struggle for material improvement and effort of every nature from man, is considered **exquisite** by the higher astral gods, since for them it is energy-nutrition of supreme quality! (We won't mention here the **total entrapment** that comes as a result of every negative activity, considering it self-evident) So they prompt men to pour out the pain of all of their efforts through their sacrifice on the altar of daily struggle. In this manner, men delude themselves that they produce the best for themselves and the ones close to them, and ignore what they must really do in order to escape from the universe/trap.

To achieve definitive escape, man, having cleansed his material life from every materialistic desire and assertion, and freed himself from bipolarity, he must energize the head center, because with the activation of this seventh center, the Higher Noetic (Higher Mental/Intellectual) Body is developed, which is, of course, not supplied by the dimorphic astral emotions, but by the Vitalizing Spirit and envelopes all of man's energy bodies like a safe escape space-suit.

This however, is a difficult and time-consuming process, which the entirety of men fails to complete. This is why the HyperCosmoi of Truth **suggest** a different course which we will elaborate on soon enough and which will yield **the same** results, but without wasting time and courage. If someone wants to walk through fire safely, they must wear an asbestos suit, and it is imperative for everyone forced to pass through the hell of the astral plane to wear the 'garment' of Truth. The more 'well-crafted' his suit is, the safer it becomes. Heed these words! Epignosis (Cognition) offered to Man by the Higher Mental Body can be compared to a transfer vehicle. If one hasn't managed to build such a vehicle in order to save oneself, one must at least wear a protective suit. This suit can be identified with the realization of the Truth offered by this Knowledge.

RELEASE FROM KARMA

Through the imposed deceit that exists in the material plane, which **persistently** hides the ONE AND ONLY TRUTH, man, during his lifespan, does not manage to locate this TRUTH and to 'dress' his astral body with Its Epignosis. Thus, in those astral regions, he will not know what to choose and what to claim/assert.

---

[507] **GOSPEL OF THOMAS,** THE GNOSTIC SOCIETY LIBRARY
http://www.gnosis.org/naghamm/gosthom.html
«§59. Jesus said, "Look to the Living One as long as you live, otherwise you might die and then try to see the Living One, and you will be unable to see.»
[Eng. tr. STEPHEN PATTERSON, MARVIN MEYER]

On the contrary, with inadequate information in his possession, he is faced with what the 'luminous' guides *(of Antavges)* project to him –after his natural death– he submissively succumbs and is taken wherever they so wish. In parallel, a great number of people having rejected the existence of god – realizing, that the 'All-Benevolent One' they have been taught about in school, is nowhere to be found– find themselves doubly deceived, when (post mortem) they are called upon to answer and be judged for their actions.

So, as the ignorant ones stand in front of the infamous karmic/judging committee, terrified, *(...for the good testament before the awesome tribune of the god/creator),* he who is a **Cognizant of the Truth** demands explanations about the delusion which this creation has forced him to live in; and since he knows his rights, he DEMANDS his Redemption, juxtaposing the deficiency of their creation, as well as the OBLIGATION these 'gentlemen' have to free him once it is asked of them, since ALL DEBT HAS BEEN PAID OFF BY JESUS CHRIST (as a third-party guarantor). *(Refer to: APPENDIX, PHOTOGRAPHS AND DRAWINGS, 'THE END OF THE CYCLE OF REINCARNATIONS')*

---

[508] **A) THE GOSPEL OF MATTHEW, CH. 20:**
«§28. Just as the Son of Man did not come to be served, but to serve and to give His life as a **ransom** for many.»
B) EPITÁPHIOS THRĒNOS, THE 'LAMENTATION UPON THE GRAVE' (MAUNDY THURSDAY): «And You, Christ, consented to **become mortal** and descended down to Hades.»
C) THE GOSPEL OF JOHN, CH. 8: «§24. Therefore I said to you that you will die in your sins; for if you do not believe that I am *He (i.e. the one who alleviates the sin of the world),* you will die in your sins.»
D) THE (FIRST) APOCALYPSE OF JAMES, THE GNOSTIC SOCIETY LIBRARY
TRANSLATED BY WILLIAM R. SCHOEDEL http://www.gnosis.org/naghamm/1ja.html

«The Lord said to him: James, behold, I shall reveal to you your redemption. When you are seized and you undergo these sufferings *(of death)* a multitude will arm them-selves against you that <they> may seize you. And in particular three of them will seize you - they who sit (there) as **toll collectors** *(the masters of karmic committee)*. Not only do they demand **toll** *(the payback of karmic debt)*, but **they also take away souls by theft**. When you come into their power, one of them, who is their guard will say to you, 'Who are you', or, "Where are you from?" You are to say to him, "I am a son, and I am from the Father." He will say to you, "What sort of son are you, and to what father do you belong?" You are to say to him, "I am from the Pre-existent Father, and a son in the Pre-existent One." *(A large portion of the text is destroyed with just a few worlds left which make no sense)*…When he also says to you, "Where will you go?" you are to say to him, "To the place from which I have come, there shall I return." And if you say these things, you will escape their attacks.»

D) GOSPEL OF THOMAS, JEAN YVES LELOUP: «§50. Jesus says: If they ask you from where you come, say: we were born of the Light, There, Where Light is born of Light. It holds true and is revealed within their image. If they ask you who you are, Say: We are its children, the beloved of the Father, the Living One. If they ask you what is the sign of the Father in you, say: It is movement and it is repose *(=rest, the two opposites in one)*.» [Eng. tr. JOSEPH ROWE]

Another Gospel, that gives 'instructions' regarding the post mortem course of the Soul that wishes to be redeemed, is that of Mary Magdalene:

E) THE GOSPEL OF MARY (MAGDALENE) JEAN-YVES LELOUP, Gr. tr. KOUROUSSI A., A. (p. 15 §1-25, p. 16 §1-19, p. 17 §1-6)

«I did not see you descending, but now I see you ascending", said Desire *(to the Soul)*. "Why do you lie, since you are a part of me?"

The Soul answered *(to Desire)* and said: "I have seen you. You did not see me nor recognize me. I was with you as a garment, and you did not feel me".

Having said that *(the Soul)*, went away rejoicing greatly. Then she came to the third atmosphere *(=level, stage)*, which is called Ignorance. It questioned the Soul asking:

"Where are you going? Weren't you bound by wickedness? Yes, you were enslaved and without judgment.

And the Soul said: "Why do you judge me although I have not judged? I was dominated (bound), although I have not dominated (bound) anyone. I was not recognized. But I have recognized that All that has been composed **will be decomposed (dissolved), both on earth and in the sky** *(said the Soul to Ignorance)*.

The Soul, liberated from the third atmosphere, it went upwards and arrived at the fourth atmosphere (stage), (which) had seven manifestations *(forms)*.

Don't skip chapters or bibliographic references

The first manifestation is darkness, the second one is desire, the third one is ignorance, the fourth one is deadly jealousy, the fifth one is carnal inebriation, the sixth one is the intoxicating wisdom, the seventh one is devious wisdom. These are the seven expressions of Wrath, which oppress the Soul with questions like:

—"Whence do you come from, man-slayer? Where are you going, you wanderer?"
The Soul answered:
—"He who oppressed me *(bound me)* has been slain, and he who surrounded me is no more *(the material body)*, and my desire has now subsided, and **I was delivered from my ignorance**. In was released from the *(material)* world thanks to a *(Hyper)* world and a picture was erased in favor of a higher picture. Henceforth, I am going to rest (repose) where time rests in the Eternity of time.»

Now, do you understand why Jesus Christ came, and which 'archon' He is still trying to rescue you from? Do you understand which 'lords' He came to 'pay off', asking for your Salvation in return, offering the energy they have long waited for from the sap of the pain His Sacrifice poured out? And not simply the energy and the blood from the sacrifice of an innocent one, but of the Monogenes! But you men have been swindled into this delusion again, since you have equated the Unuttered Principle of All with the fallen archon, the creator of matter; and you have worshiped your material prison so much, that you seem to scorn this Supreme Offering of the Monogenes!

Man's Epignosis (higher awareness) of the Truth creates a series of problems for his dominators. It can be compared to a mathematical function that cancels their arithmetic formula. For a better understanding of what happens exactly when man realizes the Truth, I shall describe it with an image: When man entered material creation, he was poisoned by the creator/snake's venom. This venom caused him to have hallucinations as a side-effect. Thus, although man is located inside the 'esophagus' of the snake, he **imagines** this esophagus to be the 'material cosmos/life' because this is what the creator/snake commands.

[509] **A) BLAVATSKY H., P., 'THE SECRET DOCTRINE'** (I-374):

«In the Zohar we read as follows: As Moses was keeping a vigil on Mount Sinai, in company with the deity, who was concealed from his sight by a cloud, he felt a great fear overcome him, and suddenly asked: "Lord, where art thou . . . . sleepest thou, O Lord? . . ." And the Spirit answered him: "I never sleep: Were I to fall asleep for a moment before my time, **all the creation would crumble into dissolution in one instant**.» *...And with it the* *great illusion. I am reminding some previous excerpts of references:*

B) 'WHO STEALS OUR SOULS?' AVATON ISSUE 64, SEPTEMBER 2006, ARTICLE OF ION MAGGOS «…All natural laws that govern the material world, i.e. the virtual reality in which we live, are based on illusions that have been imposed to the inhabitants of the Dodecahedron. …Every illusion therefore, is based on the great illusion of motion. …Motion was created by the perverted thought of the darkness, i.e. the dark beings of chaos, which (darkness) created thoughts and thoughtforms inside the illusion of its own fantasy. …Its thoughtforms created the pseudo-material amalgams we consider matter. The darkness projected its thoughts in order to create. Essentially the whole creation is an illusion in the 'mind' of the darkness.»

C) BARBARA MARCINIAK 'GAIA' [Gr. trans. MATZOROU E.] *(Information through channeling):* «The reptilian race or Little Lizards, as we amicably call them, constitute an integral part of your genealogy. …They are your creators – your gods. …They are the masters of the game. The masters of the game get together as you do to play cards or racket-ball. The only difference is that their game aims at the creation of civilizations. They modify and change worlds allowing the entrance of different civilizations in the realities they orchestrate. These civilizations act based purely on their impulses which are nevertheless provided to them through matrixes of energy-blueprints. …The masters of the game are formless; they can change shapes/forms and know no limitations. They can assume any form they choose, as they move in-between and beyond sound and geometry. The masters of the game create the energy-matrixes of the civilizations in their mind and then open gates in order to literally introduce them to the Earthly plane. Following that, they allow these civilizations to grow and mature, so as to exert their influence to other time periods.»

This state of hallucination –which has also been authenticated by quantum science– makes it easier for the creator/snake to 'devour' its victim without the victim reacting. Truth is the antidote to this poison. HyperCosmic Powers that during this time have breached the universe of matter can be compared to a hand that –taking a great risk– has entered the mouth of the snake to inject the man/victim with the antidote of the Truth, before the victim reaches the snake's stomach. If man is 'vaccinated' with the Truth, he will gradually come out of the state of hallucination, and since his body has been permeated by THIS 'catalytic' to the creator/snake TRUTH, he will make the necessary 'moves' to unshackle himself, thus forcing the snake to throw him up, since the antidote/Truth is a venom to the creator.

Don't skip chapters or bibliographic references

---

[510] **THE APOCRYPHON OF JOHN, THE GNOSTIC SOCIETY LIBRARY** [STEVAN DAVIES]: «*(Says Jesus to John)*: As for the tree called 'The Knowledge of Good and Evil', it is the Epinoia of the light. They commanded him *(Adam)* not to eat from it, standing *(the archons)* in front *(of it)* to conceal it, for fear that he *(Adam)* might look upwards to the fullness and know the nakedness of his indecency. However, I *(Jesus)* caused them to eat.» *From the 'tree of the Epignosis of Good and Evil' thus revealing the Truth.*

☙•❧

Let us concentrate however, on a very important point. **NO** energy manifestation can enter the Divine HomeLands except Essence/Spirit. Energy is a constituent of the material universe and it belongs to it along with the individualized Ego.

---

[511] **HERMES TRISMEGISTUS,** HERMETIC TEXTS, VOL. I, RODAKIS P., TZAFEROPOU-LOS AP., **SPEECH XVI**: «§13. And under the sun is arranged the group of dae-mons –or, rather, groups; for these are many and varied, ranked underneath the multitudes of Stars, equal in number to each of them. So ranked thus, they serve each one of the Stars, being good and bad in their natures, that is, in their activities. For energy *('positive' and negative)* is the daemon's es-sence; some of them are in fact of mixed nature, good and bad.»

Essence/Spirit can exist inside man, either autonomously as a Divine Spark, or interwoven with his Soul, and only that (Essence/Spirit) has a place THERE. Completing (filling/enriching) the Soul with Spirit is a primary requirement.

---

[512] **GOSPEL OF PHILIP** (PATERSON BROWN):
«§142. Every plant which my heavenly Father has **not** sown shall be rooted out. Those who are separated shall be mated *(i.e. the split Celestial An-thropoi [=Men])* and the empty shall be filled *(i.e. the plain Souls which will ASK to be "completed" with Spirit)*. Everyone who enters the Bedroom *(i.e. the 7th Energy Centre for the Sacred Union)* shall be born in the Light. For they are not begotten in the manner of the marriages which we do not see, which are enacted by night, the fire of which flares in the dark and then is extinguished/lost. Yet rather the Sacraments of this Marriage are consum-mated in the day and the light; neither that Day nor its Light ever sets.»

Because: If the 'Image/Sample' of the absolutely Good {Tr. n.: Gr.: Ἀγαθόν *(Agathón)*} does not exist <u>inside</u> man, how can he realize by comparison that what surrounds him –starting from his own body and ending with the entire world– is not only dissimilar to this Divine Image/Sample, but (his body and the entire material world) <u>doesn't even possess the minimum requirements</u> to attain IT? (The absolutely good [Gr. Ἀγαθόν])

---

[513] **HERMES TRISMEGISTUS**, HERMETIC TEXTS, VOL. I, RODAKIS P., TZAFEROPOULOS AP., **SPEECH VI**: «§3. When it comes to man, Good is determined in comparison to evil. …And Ἀγαθόν *(Agathón)* here is the smallest particle of evil. And it is impossible down here, that Ἀγαθόν be free from malice. For down here, Ἀγαθόν gets filled with malice, and being full of malice, it cannot be Ἀγαθόν {Tr. n.: *See definition of w. at the beginning of Ch. HIGHER MENTAL BODY – CELESTIAL MAN*}; and since it cannot remain Ἀγαθόν anymore, it becomes evil. … §6. Wherefore, those who are ignorant and do not tread the path of piety, <u>do dare to call</u> man fair and good. <u>Not even in their wildest dreams have they seen what Ἀγαθόν is</u>. And they call Ἀγαθόν all that is evil.»

In reality, Truth and Spirit are interlinked having a bidirectional relationship since one leads to the other and both to Deliverance.

A living Spirit inside a man initially prompts him to look for IT through self-knowledge, in order to unite with ITS Wholeness/Source afterwards and become initiated to the Truth. But this road, as we said earlier, is a very hard road because modern man's living conditions are so demanding, that they limit the possibilities of success to the minimum, since thorough and complete self-knowledge being a long lasting process as it is, can only be accomplished if someone starts at a young age, before social conventions have crystallized his behavior, and thus created in him false impressions about himself.

On the contrary, people of mature age, and after they become settled in their lives –logically– start dealing with their soul. Then however, being inexperienced as they are, they easily fall prey into the nets of cunning opportunists who drain them energy-wise <u>and</u> money-wise, and as "disciples" of these masterly manipulators, they are deluded into believing they will thrive in the next life! All these conditions make the Deliverance of the soul an intangible dream, since all things in matter have been arranged in such a way, as to leave <u>no</u> chance for redemption to man.

The HyperCosmoi suggest Epignosis (deep awareness) of the Truth as the only alternative way to redemption; but since this path can be accessible to large groups of people who will use it to escape from the delusion, the

Don't skip chapters or bibliographic references

powers of this world not only try to erase the signs of the Truth with any means possible, they also keep it well hidden after they fragment it. Then they prescribe prohibition of communication of the Sacred Epignosis as the unwritten law of this world and guard it through 'initiations' reserved for the select few...

So after the departure of Christ from the material universe, they falsified and destroyed every clue that would guide men to escape through the Truth. But since the time this creation has at its disposal is coming to an end, it is imperative that the elements of Truth are given to men again, so that those who desire it can be redeemed.

The secret lies in the bidirectional relationship that exists between the Divine Spirit and Truth. Therefore, since the road through self-knowledge is closed due to adverse conditions in the life of men, a new passage had to be opened through the allowance of the Whole Truth.

When the realization of the Truth comes about as the result of an external factor, it (the Truth) will thrust a great percentage of men to free themselves from the trap, because this realization will activate within them the process of their connection to the Spirit. The Unified Spirit will neutralize the individualized Ego and man will unite with the ALL.

---

[514] **THE APOCRYPHON OF JOHN, THE GNOSTIC SOCIETY LIBRARY**

«SIX QUESTIONS ABOUT THE SOUL: I asked the Savior, "Lord, will every soul be saved and enter the pure light?" He replied, "You are asking an important question, one it will be impossible to answer for anyone who is not a member of the unmoved *(un-oscillating)* race *(generation)*. They are the people upon whom the Spirit of Life will descend and its power will enable them to be saved and to become perfect and worthy of greatness. They expunge evil from themselves and they will care nothing for wickedness, wanting only that, which is not corrupt. They will achieve *(through this Spirit)* freedom from rage, envy, jealousy, desire, or craving. The physical body will negatively affect them. They wear it as they look forward to the time when they will meet up with those who will remove it. Those people deserve indestructible eternal life. They endure everything, bearing up under everything that happens so that they can deserve the good and inherit life eternal.

Then I asked him, "Lord, what about the souls who didn't do these things even though the Spirit of Life's power descended on them?"

He answered: "If the Spirit descends to people they will be transformed and saved. ...Nothing then can leave them astray into wickedness. But if the artificial spirit comes into people, it leads them astray.» [Eng. tr. from Coptic: STEVAN DAVIES]

In this case, (1) Epignosis (deep understanding) of the Truth, combined with the observation of the reality surrounding man, (2) the clearest possible self-Epignosis (3) emotional disengagement from anything that threatens to entrap the soul into matter and (4) detachment from sordid situations, will contribute –if man desires that with great zeal– to man earning a place in the Eternal. After all, the realization of the Truth causes the gradual shrinking of material desires, the repulsion for material pleasures and polarization, as side-effects.

Spirit and Truth combined are the basic requirements for man's Deliverance. A superficial claim for Redemption though, accompanied with a life dominated by passions or intense material quests, does not ensure salvation, because under degenerate material pleasures and dependencies, all traces of Essence/Spirit inside man are permanently worn away; for it is the Spirit that gets sacrificed on the altar of the Ego, as these two are inversely proportional conditions. This is why something very important must be stressed: The Spirit is as valuable to These Sacred Cosmoi as a priceless diamond is to matter. Therefore, just as no one would lend something so valuable with ease and to anybody, the same happens with the Spirit: In this disoriented material creation, the Cosmoi of Light have lost many of Their Own 'Parts'. Any further grant of Spirit is made sparingly and only if the assurances are there that whatever granted will not be wasted in material activities, but only to 'launch' the Soul out of the material trap. Consequently, a simple/half-hearted request is no request at all. A request driven by egotistical motives is condemned from the start. On the contrary, an ever-burning desire for redemption raises the percentage of success. Therefore the realization of the cruel reality that surrounds man, however painful, ensures man has the 'ideal preconditions', so that his request may have power.

SECRET SOCIETIES OF CONTROL

In order for men to go on living in deep lethargy producing energy-food, these 'masters' hold and control the strings of power, while men remain oblivious to it. The Great Spiritual Hierarchy of the planet, the White Brotherhood, comprising of all the 'ascended' masters, are considered the guardians/trustees of the great scheme regarding life in this world. These are man's wardens. They are stationed in the aetheric planes around the planet, and from there, through telepathy, they transfer information, commands and directions for the accomplishment of their 'superior' plan to their 'initiated' delegate pupils.

> **515** PAPASTAVROU, A., 'LETTERS TO ANONYMOUS': «Many movements find their origin in the Deity Itself and many objectives (goals) start through its children's initiatives... The Deity creates objectives/goals. Intelligent existences, contemplating how to best help the divine plan, can promote these goals and bring them to the conscious attention of humanity.»

In order for humanity to produce the appropriate **energy varieties**, it must be directed towards absolutely specific goals. These goals will provoke tendencies; tendencies/trends will modulate consciousnesses; and consciousnesses will retrieve the required emotions. Men must submit to the given norms, thus producing the correspondingly 'colored' energy. So, they anaesthetize nations' consciousnesses in pseudo-real ways, making them believe that the events humanity experiences are the results of the actions and desires of men themselves. The greatest portion of the population is convinced of this and continues trying to improve the world around them with everything they've got. Despite all their struggles though, results don't seem to reflect their efforts. This is due to the fact that a **Mighty Invisible Leadership** 'pulls' the real strings for the function of the planet.

> **516** A) PLATO'S 'CRITIAS' [Eng. tr. BENJAMIN JOWETT] (109b)
> http://classics.mit.edu//Plato/critias.html
> «At some time in the past, the gods had the whole earth distributed among them by allotment. There was no quarrelling; ...And they all of them by just apportionment obtained what they wanted, and peopled their own districts; and when they had peopled them they tended us, **their nurslings and possessions as shepherds tend their flocks**, excepting only that they did not use blows or bodily force, as shepherds do, but −like an easily guided animal− governed us like pilots from the stern (of the vessel), holding our souls **by (the rudder of) persuasion according to their own pleasure**; thus did they guide all mortals.» [GREEK VERSION: PLATO'S 'CRITIAS' TRANSLATION: D. G. KOUTROUMPAS (109B-109C4)]

And so that we don't think that these are old times' fictitious narratives, I also put forward something more contemporary, which shows that nothing has changed —except some simple rituals— from Socrates' time of narration until today:

B) 'SUPERMUNDANE' BOOK I (AGNI YOGA SOCIETY) 1938

The White Brotherhood Masters clarify through the medium 'Urusvati':

«§25. Urusvati has explained to many, why We are called '**The Invisible Government**'. Truly, everyone to some degree feels that there is somewhere a focus of knowledge. Where there is knowledge there is also power.... Those who observe world events may perceive something higher than human logic… Our disciples understand how to **harmonize** their free will with our decisions. One must possess great equilibrium to understand the wisdom of our guidance without crippling his own free will *(they call it free!)*… The best leaders of nations *(e.g. the Bilderberg Club)* had this balance, and it was therefore easier **to send them our decisions**…All over the world one can find established landmarks of our guidance. Some enlightened people accepted it, but some poor parodies of monarchs rejected our counsel and thereby plunged their countries into calamity… §133. Urusvati also knows that it is very tiring for the invisible witness to remain in the midst of earthly gatherings, yet such attendances are frequent…We warned Napoleon more than once, and he admitted that he 'heard voices', yet he continued on his path of error. Over eons it has been our duty to warn those in high places who are in a position to hinder evolution.»

And to combine the evidence even better, I am submitting some more information:

C) PAPASTAVROU, A., 'LETTERS TO ANONYMOUS' (p. 110): «The Great Divine Leader, in His speech to the disciples of 'I AM' in May 18th, 1938 reported the following about Napoleon:

"…Observe the situation here (in America), in comparison to that of Europe. When Saint Germaine taught Napoleon, he tried to prepare through him a condition capable of providing the same knowledge that you are receiving today." *(He refers to the realization of Saint Germaine's dream to unify Europe into a power equivalent to the U.S.A.)*

During his youth Napoleon was a very modest and humble subject. But when he started seeing the power of his achievements, and some of the appalling individuals –whom he did not suspect– started pouring into his ears the hateful suggestions, unaware of their ill intentions Napoleon exploited them (their suggestions) in the sensory world. Not long after that, human arrogance started rearing its ugly head to the one he loved most *(Count de Saint Germaine)* and he told him: 'From now on I will take the responsibility to give orders' and with the 'I' he meant the human 'Ego'. Saint Germaine, knowing the grave danger of Napoleon, tried through all means of his power to suggest the truth to him; but when human egotism comes, perfection temporarily departs.»

Don't skip chapters or bibliographic references

D) PAPASTAVROU, A., 'LETTERS TO ANONYMOUS'
(a) THE INTENT FOR A UNITED EUROPE (p. 110)

«Saint Germaine's speech, given to a group of disciples of 'Bridge to Freedom' on April 21st, 1954, a few days before his Coronation as the Cosmic Chohan of the Seventh Ray on May 1st, 1954.

"…I assumed the ministry of the Chohan of the Seventh Ray around the end of the 18th century, after my service for the liberation of America and the French Court.

…Until then, I had a certain freedom to make use of these energies in my effort to establish **one group of United States of Europe** and to persuade certain disciples of the apocryphal Laws that, if they collaborated with the Hierarchy, a Global Fraternity could be established without bloodshed. Apart from certain efforts of mine through Napoleon Bonaparte, I gave no further personal service to governmental circles and my service to humanity became Cosmic."

Also "…Many centuries ago I had hoped for and desired an earthly Crown, incarnated as Francis Bacon (1561-1626). At that time, I was envisioning a United Fraternity of Europe.»

*Is it then possible that the case of the 'mystic' Hitler, who through the Tibetan monks came in contact with the (Vril) power and the teachings of the "masters" of sub-chthonic Shambhala (Agartha), was nothing more than another unsuccessful attempt for the creation of United Europe? After all, the alternating positive and negative power of this world belongs to one of the two faces of **one and the same** coin. Some careful observers might have noticed the SS cross placed on their uniforms near the energy-center of the throat, and the resemblance it bears to the cross of Saint Germaine-Malta's Cross (✠).*

(b) THE INTENT FOR EQUALITY OF THE TWO SEXES AND THE EMANCIPATION OF WOMEN: (p. 99)

«In the year 1953 the Cosmic Law transferred the pressure of this energy to the Female Ray.

From a practical point of view, this means that the magnetic attraction which for millions of years had landed in the Far East, is now transferred to the Western World…Furthermore, this energy will enjoy the gradual infusion of spiritual interest of the Root-Race, from the East to the West.

Besides that, let us not forget that this energy will also cause the slow but certain **elevation of the woman's prevailing position** to that of the man.»

(c) THE INTENT FOR THE PREVALENCE OF ENGLISH AS THE INTERNATIONAL LANGUAGE: (p. 94)

«Speech of master Hannuvvah: "We indeed mean English, because this will be the international language for your Planet, and knowledge of the present means of communication is contributory to both sides.» *This speech was given at the time when the prevailing language was still French.*

ॐ·ॐ

When the seeding of the first modified genes was accomplished successfully and men (of the Iron Race) no longer had the ability to come in direct contact with the gods and obey their wishes, gods then started to incarnate as men and occupy important positions in the human societies in order to direct the masses. Thus we initially have the celestial creator, then comes his materialized version/manifestation, which inseminates mortal women with modulated genes, and finally the incarnated one as an important archon of society, and not in a single incarnation but in many, and assuming various different roles.

517 **A) BLAVATSKY H., P., 'THE SECRET DOCTRINE'** (II-765): «Now all the gods of Olympus, as well as those of the Hindu Pantheon and the Rishis, were the septiform impersonations (1) of the noumena of the intelligent Powers of nature; (2) of Cosmic Forces; (3) of celestial bodies; (4) of gods or Dhyan Chohans; (5) of psychic and spiritual powers; (6) of divine kings on earth or the incarnations of the gods; and (7) of terrestrial heroes or men. The knowledge how to discern among these seven forms the one that is meant, belonged at all times to the Initiates, whose earliest predecessors had created this symbolical and allegorical system.»

(II-483) «The history begins by the descent on Earth of the 'Gods' who incarnate in mankind, and this is the *(first)* fall. Whether Brahma **hurled down** on Earth in the allegory by Bhaghavat, or Jupiter by Kronos, all are the symbols of the human races. Once landed on, and having touched this planet of dense matter, no snow-white wings of the highest angel can remain immaculate, or the Avatar (or incarnation) (can) be perfect, as every such Avatar is the fall of a God into generation.»

B) BARBARA MARCINIAK 'GAIA' [Gr. tr. MATZOROU E.] *(Information through channeling):*
«...The masters of the game are geniuses. Not only do they conceive the game and create the complete energy-matrix through which each civilization will flourish —from the most skilled technicians to the lowest beggars— **but they also introduce their own selves inside the civilizations they create.**»

C) *Some information about the enigmatic figure of Saint Germaine, Cosmic Chohan of the Seventh Ray, Master of the White Brotherhood and the Spiritual Hierarchy of the Planet.*

J. SADOUL 'THE TREASURE OF THE ALCHEMISTS' CH. COUNT SAINT GERMAINE:
«The count's historical existence starts in 1743 in London. In 1745 he came against the authorities who suspected him of foreign espionage. Horatio Walpole points out: "He has been here for about two years and refuses to reveal his identity, he does not say where he came from, he only admits he does not bear his real name."...It is certain though that he was not called

Saint Germaine. He himself confided to his benefactor, the archon of Hessen: "My name is Sanctus Germanous, sacred brother."

Having lived for some years in Germany, he came to the Court of Ludwig the 15th in 1758. We have a description by Madame Pompadour: 'The count seemed to be in his fifties. He had an air of aristocracy, was very witty, simply but tastefully dressed. His fingers had beautiful diamonds as his cigarette case and his watch.' This strange unknown foreigner, whose title is doubtful and his name uncertain, found a way to become Ludwig the 15th's confidant, with whom he often <u>had absolutely private conversations</u>. This preference of the King and his ever increasing favor for St. Germaine infuriated Prime Minister Suazelle… The count bragged in front of many witnesses in the court that he knew how to double the size of diamonds, that he had transformed silver to gold more than twice and finally that he was in possession of the elixir of longevity which he used… all these are certified facts.…People say that he knew Pontius Pilate and Julius Caesar: the truth is that he only narrated historical facts of previous centuries as a witness who had seen and lived them; namely he insisted on small details, avoiding the tone of a well-informed historian. Many times he interrupted the narration, or pretended he stopped and instead of saying 'this or that person said then to Eric the IV' he resumed 'I said to Eric the IV'…The art of increasing the size of diamonds has serious witnesses and irrefutable proofs. We have the narration of Madame du Hausset who was Madame Pompadour's maid and totally trustworthy. On the contrary, the famous memoirs of Countess Antemar are apocryphal.

…Let us examine now what is said about the transformations the Count performed. There are two stories. One is certainly authentic, since it was written by Knight Casanova, an implacable enemy of Saint Germaine. …an individual not so congenial, with rather unkind dispositions towards the count, whose writings' credibility should leave no doubts:

Casanova narrates about Saint Germaine: "…Selfish as he was, he did not want to let me go without having made an impression on me. He asked me if I had any coins on me. I took several out of my pocket and put them on the table. He stood up without speaking, took a lit piece of coal and placed it on a metal plate. Then he asked me for a coin of twelve sols which was among the others on the table. He put a small black grain on the coin, placed the coin on the coal piece and blew with a glass blower for about two minutes. I saw the coin become red hot: 'wait until it gets cold' said the alchemist to me. Indeed, when it was cold he added: 'Take it. It's yours.' I took it. It was gold."

…The story is placed between 1743 and 1784. This account is given by the Countess de Gergie, ambassadress of France in Venice. She met Saint Germaine in Madame Pompadour's house and was enchanted. She remembered that in 1700 in Venice she had met another noble foreigner who looked astoundingly like him, despite the fact he had another name. She asked him if that person was his father or some relative. "No." The Count answered without losing his calmness. "It was me living in Venice in the end of the last century and the beginning of this one. And it was I, who had the honor to court you and you were kind enough to find some barcaroles of my conception pleasant and sing along with me."

The lady answered smiling: "That noble gentleman was then forty-five years old and you, now that we speak, are of about the same age...then you must be close to one hundred years old!" "It is not impossible" he replied to her. And the count started recounting to madam de Gergie a series of details about the time when they were both in Venice. He then offered, if the lady continued to have doubts, to remind her occasions and circumstances...

'No, no', the ex-ambassadress interrupted him, 'I am convinced, but you are not human...you are a Satan...' *(Narration of Touchard Lafosse in the 'Les Chroniques de l'œil-de-bœuf')*
...Something else that is also verified is that the count never ate. During meals in which he sat, he strenuously refused to eat even the slightest amount of food, content to charm the ones present with his historical narrations or his wit.»
Voltaire said about him: «He is the man who never dies, and who knows everything.»

This holds true for all the powers of this world, be they positive or negative, as well as for all ranks of their hierarchy. Through such incarnations they set the foundations for social 'trends'.

518 **A) PAPASTAVROU, A., 'LETTERS TO ANONYMOUS'** (p. 151)
BIOGRAPHICAL NOTES ON CERTAIN INCARNATIONS OF SAINT GERMAINE:

«Many centuries ago I hoped for and desired an earthly Crown, incarnated as Francis Bacon (1561-1626). I had the vision of a united brotherhood of Europe.»

Saint Germaine's incarnation as Francis Bacon (1561-1626) at the dawn of Renaissance was defining for humanity, setting the starting point of knowledge towards a materialistic approach of things and distancing it (the knowledge) considerably from any spiritual envisagement, which today, as Saint Germaine (hypocritically of course) supports.
It has been suggested that Francis Bacon was Queen Elizabeth's I and Robert Dudley's (Lord of Lester) son, born four months after a secret marital ceremony.

B) ENCYCLOPEDIA 'DOMI' SIR FRANCIS BACON, ENGLISH PHILOSOPHER, LONDON 1561-1626:
«...The purpose of true study, for him, is not knowledge but the conquest and transformation of nature for the creation of better conditions for man. In contrast to ancient science that uses the typical Aristotelian logic and aims to

Don't skip chapters or bibliographic references

the continuous discovery of new verbal syllogisms, the purpose of modern science, according to Bacon, is not to create syllogisms but actions, not proof derived from typical logic, but rather evidence from experiments …With the old logic, opponents in debates are silenced; with the new logic, nature itself is defeated and tamed, and we can constantly extract its secrets. The first type of knowledge is infertile; the second conquers new arts and instruments thanks to which, the improvement of human life-conditions can be achieved.

True knowledge must be acquired through actions: the instrument of modern science is not reasoning but the experiment. "The progress of the intellect and man and the progress of material conditions of his life are one and the same thing", Bacon claims since, "the instruments are not only the means for improvement of human conditions, but also the assurance *(!!!)* for truth" (cogitata et visa)…The main cause that creates "idols" is nevertheless the respect for tradition and reverence to the classics and in particular Plato and Aristotle, against whom Bacon inveighed in his 'Male birth of time'.»

David Icke gives us more information about Francis Bacon:

C) DAVID ICKE 'THE SECRET OF ALL AGES' CH. 'BACON'S HERITAGE':

«One of the most important men of that period was the Rosicrucian Francis Bacon. He was a Great Rosicrucian Master of England, a powerful procreator in the creation of freemasonry, 'father' of modern science and probably the writer of Shakespeare's plays. He was also a member of the secret society called the 'Knights of the Helmet' which was devoted to the worship of the Goddess of wisdom, Pallas Athena…As a high-ranking mystic of apocryphal knowledge, during the reign of his alleged mother Elizabeth I and her heir, crown prince James I the King of Scotland, …Bacon, along with Sir Robert Flood, Great Master of the Priory of Sion, was the one who supervised King James' translation of the Bible, a book which, according to a 1881 study, had at least **36,191 translation mistakes**. Considering that Bacon was an extremely well-educated and smart man, I cannot believe he made so many mistakes in the translation, **unless he made them on purpose**. Bacon also made sure the two Maccabaeus books were removed from his translation…Bacon was called 'the father' of modern science, which was only focused on the material level of existence. Why would Bacon support such a *(materialistic)* point of view, when he himself was a high-ranking mystic and knew the truth? Something is not right with all this, especially if one thinks that all other 'fathers' of modern science, like Isaac Newton and Robert Boyle were also high-ranking initiates as Great Masters of the Priory of Sion. So, we have Bacon, a deep insider of apocryphal knowledge, being involved in the Split of the Christian Church, through the Rosicrucian order[1] and other organizations, as well as in the compilation of the Christian

Bible and the creation of modern 'science' which <u>disputed</u> many of the basic foundations of Christianity. **He played by turning one side against the other**, in order to create a fertile environment for another unuttered plan to commence. *(And all this was done by the beloved [to some]...Saint Germaine)* ...The spy network known today as the British Intelligence Service was created in Europe under the influence of Bacon and other magicians of esotericism.

...As the freemason and historian Manly Palmer Hall wrote about Bacon: 'He was a Rosicrucian, many say the greatest. If indeed he was not the glorious Father C.R.C. who is mentioned in the Rosicrucian manifests, he certainly was a high-ranking initiate of the Order...'

...He launched a furious hunt for 'witches' and 'magicians', namely all those who used and spread the apocryphal knowledge...Why would he do something like that if the purpose of the secret movement he belonged to was to protect and ultimately publicize such knowledge? *(...Especially when, as Saint Germaine, he is considered to be the greatest Alchemist-Magician!)* Because he never intended to do such a thing. It is very helpful when the people you need support from think this is your motive, but when the time of truth comes, you follow the opposite course. The hierarchy of the groups I am exposing <u>does not wish for knowledge to be accessible to all</u>, but they want to treasure it and use it to gain control and rule on a global level.»

[1] 'SECRET SOCIETIES' CH. ROSICRUCIANS: **ROSANNA VOUTSI** «In early 17th century philosopher-writer Sir Francis Bacon and his colleague in Oxford, theologist Robert Flood, were associated with the Rosicrucians.»

Yet another defining incarnation for humanity (of Saint Germaine) was as Christopher Columbus.

'SECRET SOCIETIES' CH. ROSICRUCIANS: **ROSANNA VOUTSI**

«Except Dante, Christopher Columbus is also considered a member of the Rosicrucian order.»

D) J. SADOUL 'THE TREASURE OF THE ALCHEMISTS' CH. 'COUNT SAINT GERMAINE'
«The relations of Saint Germaine with the Rosicrucian order leave no doubt. Some yet claim that Saint Germaine was no other than Christian Rosenkreuz, founder of the Rosicrucian Brotherhood, who discovered the secret of Hermetic Art, secured immortality *(of his material body)* and later reappeared in history as various figures.[1]»

E) PAPASTAVROU, A., 'LETTERS TO ANONYMOUS'
BIOGRAPHICAL NOTES ON SOME REINCARNATIONS OF SAINT GERMAINE:
«At the end of the 14th century, as Christian Rosenkreuz... in Germany, he established the order of the 'Rosy Cross' of which the Rosicrucian branches are the outcome...Nevertheless, the darkness of the age was

Don't skip chapters or bibliographic references

such that, as Saint Germaine himself said in one of his speeches, they convened *(then)* with the utmost secrecy, in disguise and inside caves, for the fear of ecclesiastic persecution.»

Let me remind you of the reference #417 G, where Lord Lytton states that the founder of the Rosicrucian order 'Rosenkreuz' discovered mystical knowledge in a very mysterious place inside Earth and that he (Lytton) was set to follow his steps. Yet, we know the close relation Saint Germaine had with sub-chthonic (underground) Shambhala very well!

[1] **J. SADOUL 'THE TREASURE OF THE ALCHEMISTS'** CH. 'COUNT SAINT GERMAINE'

At some other point, author J. SADOUL is wondering: «In 1687 we meet in Vienna, a Mr. Geraldi, who had a striking resemblance to count Saint Germaine. For three whole years Geraldi astounded and surprised the inhabitants of the Austrian capital and then suddenly disappeared. We later find Laskaris, whom his contemporaries place a little after Geraldi's disappearance. What relation did he have though with count Saint Germaine? I confess, I don't know, yet I put certain questions to myself. The physical characteristics of the three men are very similar. All three were of medium height, middle-aged and spoke many languages. All three were very eloquent and, it seems, they had the philosopher's stone in their possession. Geraldi, Laskaris and count Saint Germaine of course, did not operate in the same surroundings. Yet the disappearance of one coincides marvelously with the appearance of the other. Geraldi's traces are lost in 1691 and Laskaris appears two years later. He, in turn, disappears between 1730 and 1740, right before the appearance of count Saint Germaine in England.»

Then, the creators guide humanity through their 'initiated' disciples, their foremen. In the centuries passed, men have learned to recognize and follow these spiritual 'superintendents' like sheep acknowledge their sheepdogs. These supervisors possess special qualities and characteristics –as determined by an unwritten law– so as to 'stand out' and be recognizable in the crowd. So people obey them without ever being able to get away, because for centuries through the commands of the unwritten law, it is ONLY THEM they have learned to recognize as 'guides'.

The 'Centers' through which the creators make contact are mainly the various initiation schools or secret societies or even other peripheral groups of control. Through initiation procedures/ordeals, they select the best among their students, and initiate them into **isolated** portions/parts of their 'truth', after they have verified the students' self-restraint and obedience, thus ensuring their silence. All these procedures/trials do not aim to spiritually lift the students in order to redeem their soul, but to solely provide them with the Power, which will be given to them as a reward for their services.

> **519** **THE GOSPEL OF JOHN, CH. 5**:
> «§44. How can you believe if you accept praise* from one another, and yet you do not seek the praise* that comes from the only God?»
> **CH. 5**: «§43. For they loved the approval (praise*) of men rather than the approval (praise*) of God.»
> *Orig. Greek text uses δόξαν [= glory]*

The qualities the candidate 'mystics' are required to possess, cultivate deceitfulness, which lurks inside secrecy –any secrecy– rather than honesty and integrity. They cultivate and promote egotism, rather than altruism. Instead of humility they cultivate the arrogance of the 'all knowing one' who only keeps his knowledge to himself and his kin because he considers others inferior.

> **520** **A) GOSPEL OF THOMAS**, JEAN YVES LELOUP: «§33. Jesus says: What you hear with your ears, tell it to other ears and proclaim it from the rooftops. No one lights a lamp so that it will be put under a basket or hidden somewhere. Rather, one puts it upon a stand so that all who enter and leave may see the light.» [Eng. tr. JOSEPH ROWE]
> **B) THE GOSPEL OF MATTHEW, CH. 10**: «§26. So do not be afraid of them. For, there is nothing concealed that will not be disclosed, or hidden that will not be made known. §27 What I tell you in the dark, speak in the daylight; what is whispered in your ear, proclaim from the roofs.»

The attributes/qualities these students cultivate, aim to solely serve the secret goals and objectives of the brotherhood of the fallen ones. Moreover all these know-it-all initiates consider the un-initiated easy to appropriately manipulate for the accomplishment of their secret goals. This, of course does not indicate spiritual grandeur, but rather the exploitation of human potential. And this paternalism is a natural expression/outcome, since the top of their hierarchical pyramid knows only how to exploit. So by attending the 'schools' of the fallen ones, what else do you imagine they would learn other than how to exploit? Thus, the great teachers train their students, in order to turn them into able 'foremen' of their human herd/flock.

> **521** **THE GOSPEL OF MATTHEW, CH. 10**: «§24. A disciple is not above his teacher, nor a servant above his lord. §25. It is enough for the student to be like his teacher, and the servant like his master. If the master of the house has been called Beelzebub, how much more the members of his household!»

All these secret, positive or negative brotherhoods, organizations and societies move in an absolutely specific way. The key to their secrecy lies in the multi-fragmented knowledge they offer, so that **no one** knows their complete 'master plan', but only isolated parts of it. Through their human 'tools' –who in their greatest percentage believe they are operating for a 'divine cause', while others are in complete ignorance– they manipulate societies, modulate consciousnesses, orientate opinions and the tendencies of nations by transforming the 'ins' and 'outs' and shepherd the whole world, turning it into a 'board game'.

---

[522] **'SECRET SOCIETIES' CH. ILLUMINATI: P. GIANNOULAKIS**

«**A technical example** *(of practical application)*: Imagine we are a united and loyal party and we decide to try to control matters within an area be it of a large or small scale, matters of a specific sector/type of activity, or in a sovereign state, or, why not, even in a whole chunk of the world. What is it we must do? To begin with, we need a network of connections, which we can create relatively easily –if we are discreet and very well organized– something that deals with 'special' issues that might interest important or 'nodal' key-individuals. With the unconscious aid of this disguised network of contacts, we can promote members of the 'party' whose inner core gradually increases with select members in important key-positions in state agencies (seemingly simple and/or clearly important positions) and other essential places; positions we will have located with complex planning accomplished through our own strategic supervision on the information flow: Information details that most people never notice, yet we, <u>by combining this information, arrive at astounding conclusions.</u> This just needs information intelligence, observation skills, and comparative studies, a job, completely relative to that of Secret Information Agencies.

Additionally, to some people who deal with such things, the mighty kingdom of bureaucracy is their favorite tableau, since it provides details without rendering visible those who investigate, and its complexity helps them to cover up their moves. Our people in key-positions live their lives normally, except, when needed they press or don't press a button, promote another one of our own to a new post, provide us with a valuable top secret information, spread one of our directives into their sector in a special manner, block an undesirable action, and all this in such subtle ways that are untraceable. And even if they get exposed, the worst that can happen to us is 'lose an ace', whereas we continue to have the rest of the deck, and so we simply replace him. Many times we 'burn' that card intentionally as a diversion. The more disorganized a state is, the more impossible it is for our moves and intentions to be exposed in the overall 'mix-up', even if we face a few more diffi-culties due to the special planning needed... If someone from the game, who has received power from us to pull strings we tell him to, suddenly overes-timates him-self and decides to detach him-self from the organization and play on his own, what do we do? For such cases we must have a team of 'hit men' available (and there are many ways to 'execute' someone) to deal with those renegades.»

Elsewhere in the same book, Naum Theodosiadis wonders:

CH. THE GREAT WHITE BROTHERHOOD (p. 126): «Many researchers in their effort to shed light to the mystery, propounded certain interesting thoughts which we could summarize into one basic question: Is there, maybe, some proof that the events of cosmic or earthly evolution and particularly matters of humanity are subject to the guidance of a hierarchy of highly advanced be-ings who come in contact with humanity at precise moments? Prima facie the answer is negative. The sad course of human history, the manic manifes-tation of 'a blind Will to create worlds', as Schopenhauer said, does not sug-gest a 'secret government' or the 'secret mentorship' of a superior intellect. And in any case, even if a 'secret government' or some 'mystical leadership' exists, then it must be ineffective and unsuccessful *(...or maybe after all mentally disturbed?).*»

An apt remark for the creative power that controls and guides the world of men who <u>tenaciously</u> insist is divine and benevolent because they are con-fused by its twofold face...

The power of the battling positive and negative clans depends on the amount of control they exert on nations. In certain eras in the history of men, one caste prevails, while in others its opponent. It is in essence the same force in alternating roles.

523 **ENCYCLOPEDIA 'DOMI' 'MYSTERIES OF THE WORLD'**, VOL. 'MYSTERIES OF THE EAST', **'RAMA', THE HERO OF RAMAYANA**: «In his seventh incarnation Vishnu reappeared as Rama, son of the powerful king Dasharatha, and even though in his previous incarnation he sought to extinguish the cast of Kshatriya the warriors, he was now himself an exemplary Kshatriya *(warrior).*»

These two opposing forces possess the ability to communicate only with their own followers. The members of these initiation schools ascertain their high rank in their hierarchy, by succeeding in the "ordeals" each side/organization puts them through. The prize for each student is initially

Don't skip chapters or bibliographic references

his indirect and later on his direct communication/contact with the grand (invisible) masters and whoever else… This way they control the world and permit **none** of their "initiated" disciples to 'leak' the slightest piece of their fragmented truth as they know that the Truth <u>alone</u> will widely open the gate to Freedom for the enslaved men and their souls. *["…and you shall know the Truth. And the Truth shall set you free."* JOHN 8:32]

The realms of the HyperUniverses are watching the evolution of the material universe with great concern. The 'time' limit granted to its creators is running out and the Truth remains hidden still. The roads leading to IT (Truth) seem inapproachable to humanity, since these centers of authority –even though they possess only isolated parts of the Truth– keep it sealed away with their well-trained 'initiated' disciples, who of course can't risk giving it away. This is why the complete Truth had to be given **in an inject-able way** and by a source not controlled by initiation vows of silence.

In our meeting I communicate The Truth to you about the chronicle of Man's imprisonment by dark forces, who in order to successfully impersonate true gods have spiritually "lobotomized" man rendering him OBLIVIOUS *(=in amnesia).*

Final decisions that have already been made by the HyperCosmoi regarding the material creation dictate: Every Sacred Archetype embezzled by this creation <u>must be returned</u> to ITS SOURCE. Additionally, men must be informed of the consequences of those decisions and choose their position. This of course creates an enormous problem to the entities that command this world.

PART 3:
THE PRESENT

TODAY

Reaching the end of our discussion, let us summarize. Inside the realms of the HyperUniverses *(the Unsplit/Coherent Essence of the 1ˢᵗ God Noûs – Luminary – Christ)* every concept exists as an undivided, autonomous and indivisible Unit (Monad), in the form of the positive and negative **unified**. This condition of the Coherent Essence of the Unsplit **Archetypal Ideas** composes the HyperUniverses *(Aeons)* of the Unspoken Principle *(or of the Self-Generated, Unuttered Father; The Twelve Aeons with six Heavens/Skies each)*. The second creation *(of the 2ⁿᵈ Noûs creator)* of the manifested universe was born through the Logos *(word/fraction/division)* of the initially indivisible Archetypal Ideas of the Unsplit Coherent Essence into the two opposite stands *(Divisible Essence)*. The result was the material creation and the appearance of the positive and the negative.

The Indivisible, Coherent Essence *(περί-ουσία=fortune)* of the Unified Celestial Man, as He entered the second creation, was divided too, into the Higher State as the I Am Presence or Higher Self on the one hand, and its second part on the other, the Divine Spark, which was projected into the material man.

Initially, this whole creation was only meant to manifest up to the aetheric planes. The aetheric plane would be its final destination. There, was the lower manifestation of Logos and the lowest point where creation could take place on an energy-level. The absolutely dense (visible) universe comprised the wasteland of the energy-creation and was contained (entrenched) within the space-time framework. After the second fall, man was imprisoned inside this space-time frame and was incarnated inside the densely material body.

> [524] **THE APOCRYPHON OF JOHN, THE GNOSTIC SOCIETY LIBRARY**: «…And when they *(Yaldabaoth's powers)* realized that he *(Adam)* was luminous, and that he could think **better than they did**, and that he was free from wickedness and evil, they picked him up and threw him down into the **lowest** part of all matter.» [Eng. tr. from Coptic: FREDERIK WISSE]

Never before, in the chronicles of all previous energy-creations had there been a creation onto the dense septic 'substance'. This creation was an 'innovation'.

Don't skip chapters or bibliographic references

---

525 **A) THE GOSPEL OF TRUTH, THE NAG HAMMADI LIBRARY** [ENG. TR. PATERSON BROWN T.] www.metalog.org/files/valent.html

«§39. The deficiency of matter did not originate through the Infinity of the Father... although **no one could predict** that the Incorruptible would come this way.»

B) GOSPEL OF THOMAS, JEAN YVES LELOUP: «§29. Jesus said: If flesh came into being because of spirit, it is a wonder. But if spirit came into being because of flesh, it is a wonder of wonders. Yet the greatest of wonders is this: How is it that this Being, which Is, inhabits this nothingness?» [Eng. tr. JOSEPH ROWE]

C) BARBARA MARCINIAK 'GAIA' [Gr. trans. MATZOROU E.] *(Information through channeling):*

«Imagine Gaia as a princedom of a great empire... When the parents of a great noble family faced problems with their children, they told them: "Go down to Gaia (Earth) to play a little." By saying that, the gods did not realize that what they were setting in motion would trap them in the future. When the children of the gods started playing with gold, genetics and blood, fooling around with the power of the female principle *(the power of Yaldabaoth's Mother)*, they had no idea what they were creating.»

Because of this 'innovation', the side-effects that came about with the birth of the satanic daemons of the astral world **were unknown and unexpected**... During the centuries, Karma has been nothing more than the equitable distribution of energy to both sides of creation, once it manifested in the densely material (visible) universe.

When Celestial Man was incarnated as a Divine Spark inside dense (visible) matter, He stopped supplying this creation with the 'Essence' of the HyperUniverses as it was initially intended. Through His incarnation He generated a different kind of energy. This energy created a society of skeptomorphic beings that mimicked the twofold nature of men and of the creators. After they first embraced both sides of the creative force, thus "expanding" this creation, they later started demanding energy-supply and life.

❧·❦

Some metaphysical views state that humanity as a whole –regardless of nationalities– goes through consecutive "stages" through which it will at some point complete its evolutionary process. These consecutive stages/levels are seven in total and refer to the seven Root-Races of the human species. Of these seven Root-Races, four have run their course already, the Fifth one, the Iron-Race will soon come to an end and two more stages/levels remain in which humanity will complete the cycle of the Seven Root-Races. This cycle of consecutive stages –Root Races– 'unfolds' inside a long, predetermined time period, which according to Brahmanism is the so-called "Breath of Brahma". Each 'exhalation' of Brahma is followed by an 'inhalation' and vice versa. This can be interpreted by saying that each creative phase is succeeded by dissolution, since life on every level of the material universe always alternates with death.

[526] *According to the Apocryphal Tradition and Metaphysics as expressed by Helena Blavatsky, humanity will go through SEVEN ROOT RACES in total until it completes its cycle.*

Of these seven, four have already passed, the fifth is soon to be completed and two more follow. These seven Root Races that the Mystical Tradition mentions are:

1st Root Race —A non-material human Race

2nd Root Race —A non-material human Race

3rd Root Race —The Aetheric - Adamian or Lemurian state

4th Root Race —The Race of Atlanteans (Atlantis)

5th Root Race —The Arian Race (ours)

6th Root Race —Is about to come...

7th Root Race —Follows...

The above mentioned five Root Races are precisely identical to the ones of Hesiod and correspond:

The 1st Root Race corresponds to the Golden Race; in this book we associate this Race with the creation of the protoplast Soul.

The 2nd Root Race which the Apocryphal Tradition considers as a non-material Race and it corresponds to the Silver Gender/Race of Hesiod. We have associated it with the creation of the Astral body.

The 3rd Root Race of the Lemurians; the Apocryphal Tradition considers that this Race exists in a totally aetheric state and characterizes its humans as 'sweat-born' (the ones born of sweat) [ANTHROPOGENESIS, STANZA VI §22] which corresponds to the Hesiod's Bronze Gender. In this book this Race is also identified with the aetheric state of man with his aetheric body formulated.

Finally, Hesiod calls the 4th Root Race (of the Atlanteans) the Race/Gender of Heroes and we associate it with the entrance of Celestial Men into the Aetheric Plane.

In the second half of this period the incarnation of the plain souls into the material animal takes place initially, partially upgrading it. Then follows the incarnation of the 'lobotomized' astro-aetheric Celestial Men inside the 'daughters of men'. The Divine Sparks —who are embodied inside the astro-aetheric men— in their effort to unite with their other divine half, the I Am (female) Presence, are deceived by a replica of it in dense matter, Pandora, they are embodied inside this female creature, their astro-aetheric bodies get locked-in with each other and they are definitively entrapped in the

Don't skip chapters or bibliographic references

densely material plane. This is obviously why the first societies were matri-archal. With this 'fall' (incarnation in dense matter), Knowledge, which Man possesses as a Spiritual Entity, is transferred to the human-like material beings that Anthropology calls as 'Australopithecus-Archanthrope'. This Knowledge advances the animal to Homo sapiens. Thus the Gender of Atlanteans (of the Apocryphal Metaphysical Tradition) is formed.

A result of this mixture (Spirit/Uranus and Matter/Gaia [Earth]) is the birth of a spiritual category of beings –the skeptomorphic daemons– which literally devour men and gods.

After the great flood of Noah (Deucalion) and the sinking of Atlantis, the 5th, Iron Race/Gender starts, or the creation of the 5th (Arian) Root-Race. Today, our humanity is at the end of the 5th Root Race (Arian), or Hesiod's Iron Race/Gender.

These Root Races evolved inside great periods of time which, in sum, compose the 'Life of Brahma'. Each of 'Brahma's Days' is subdivided into partial time-periods (Brahma's Breaths). Each 'exhalation' brings forth manifestation and in each 'inhalation' the manifested is absorbed back again and becomes un-manifested.

Regarding this Breath of Brahma, H. P. Blavatsky mentions the following:

(a) BLAVATSKY H., P., 'THE SECRET DOCTRINE' (I-43): «The appearance and disappearance of the Universe are pictured as an outbreathing and inbreathing of 'the Great Breath', … When the 'Great Breath' is projected, it is called the Divine Breath…which breathes out a thought, as it were, which becomes the Kosmos. So also, is it when the Divine Breath is breathed-in again the Universe disappears into the bosom of 'the Great Mother', who then sleeps wrapped in her invisible robes.»

(b) BLAVATSKY H., P., 'THE SECRET DOCTRINE', THE DAYS AND NIGHTS OF BRAHMA (I-368) «THIS is the name given to the Periods called MANVANTARA and PRALAYA (Dissolution); one referring to the active periods of the Universe, the other to its times of relative and complete rest --according to whether they occur at the end of a 'Day', or an 'Age' (a life) of Brahma. These periods, which follow each other in regular succession, are also called Kalpas, small and great, the minor and the Maha (Great) Kalpa; though, properly speaking, the Maha Kalpa is never a 'day', but a whole life or age of Brahma.»

And, from this description, becomes evident the duality-oscillation of ALL. Therefore, we can justify the equation of the Demiurgos (Creator) to the symbol of the snake and its movement.

In very general terms, I will try to present these periods according to the religion that introduced them, i.e. Brahmanism, even though there is a good deal of disagreement between the various 'schools', on the real duration of these periods.

A day of Brahma (a Maha-Kalpa, approx. 4,320,000,000 mortal years) is comprised of 14 Manvantara.

We must consider though that scientists calculate the age of Earth to about 4,600,000,000 years. The age of the universe on the other hand, due to light curvature, is indefinable, but they think it can range between 10 to 20 billion years.

Each Manvantara (306,720,000 mortal years) is comprised of 71 Maha-Yuga.

The end of each Manvantara –which concerns the manifested– is succeeded by a Pralaya (dissolution), i.e. an un-manifested state.

Each Maha-Yuga (4,320,000 mortal years) is comprised of 4 periods-Yugas. Each Maha-Yuga is succeeded by a Pralaya (dissolution). These Yugas are:

1st, Krita-Yuga or Satya-Yuga (1,728,000 mortal years) corresponds to an ideal period of absolute purity.

The root of the Sanskrit word 'Sta' means 'true'. From this root comes the word 'Satya' = truth. This word relates to the Latin phrase 'aetas satyrn' and refers to the 'age of Saturn' according to Rudolf Steiner, as it is equated to the Golden Age.

2nd, Treta Yuga (1,296,000 mortal years)

3rd, Dwapara Yuga (864,000 mortal years)

4th, Kali Yuga (432,000 mortal years), which corresponds to a very dark period.

One Brahma 'Day' (71 Maha-Yugas x 14 Manvantaras = 994 Maha-Yugas, which is equal to 4,294,080,000 mortal years) and the final circle closes with the Final Pralaya – Cosmic Death.

(c) BLAVATSKY H., P., 'THE SECRET DOCTRINE' (I-373, 374):

«This is the final PRALAYA --the Death of Cosmos-- after which its Spirit rests in Nirvana, or in THAT for which there is neither Day nor Night. All the other Pralayas (dissolutions) are periodical and follow, in regular succession, the Manvantaras, as the night follows the day of every human creature, animal, and plant. The cycle of creation of the lives of Cosmos is run down, because the energy of the manifested 'Word' (Logos) has its growth, culmination, and decrease, as have all things temporary, however long their duration.» *In the final Pralaya (dissolution) the gods die and disappear during the great Night.*

(d) BLAVATSKY H., P., 'THE SECRET DOCTRINE' (I-371): «The latter night (Maha-Pralaya), lasts for 311,040,000,000,000 years, and has the possibility of being almost doubled …When the Maha Pralaya arrives, the inhabitants of Swar-loka (the upper sphere) disturbed by the conflagration *(fire)*, seek refuge with the Pitris *(these are claimed to be the creators of material man)*, their progenitors, the Manus *(a Manu is always leading each Manvantara)*, the Seven Rishis, the various orders of celestial Spirits and the Gods, in Ma-

Don't skip chapters or bibliographic references

harloka. When the fire reaches there also, the whole of the above enumerated beings migrate in their turn from Maharloka, and return to Jana-loka in their subtle forms, destined to become re-embodied, in similar capacities as their former *(who are essentially inferior to the previous ones, according to this book's belief)*, when the world is renewed at the beginning of the succeeding Kalpa;»* ...i.e. when another seceded Entity of the Hyper-Cosmoi in the form of a new (2ⁿᵈ) Creator-Noûs [see Hermes Trismegistus] will come to vitalize their dead carcasses...*

When the Tibetan monks who breed and look after the famous tigers in their monastery were asked of the reason they do that, they answered "the tigers are former brothers of ours.

Let us examine though the relation between Maha-Yuga and the seven Root Races of Humanity. Here, there is a great misinterpretation made by many, who deal with Apocryphal Science: They equate the Root Races of humanity to the Maha-Yuga phases.

In reality, humanity today is in the 5ᵗʰ Root Race (the 5ᵗʰ Iron Gender) which happens to unfold during the worst dark period called Kali-Yuga, which nevertheless is the <u>fourth</u> (4ᵗʰ) time-period of a Maha-Yuga. We thus have two unconnected and nonrelated conditions. What will soon happen, will be the <u>simultaneous</u> end of both them (5ᵗʰ Root-Race and Kali-Yuga).

The obvious question that comes to mind is: Where will man be when the Kali period of Maha-Yuga we are in today, is succeeded by a Pralaya (dissolution), which indeed, the experts calculate to about 4,320 mortal years? Where will the coming 6ᵗʰ Root Race of Man live?

The material universe, in the new phase which is about to come will be sucked-in into 'Brahma's chest' thus erasing any manifested form. The entire material world is getting ready to be 'evicted', looking for 'shelter' elsewhere.

There are two choices for man: either to follow the material world's course, or to escape from it.

*The **True** 6ᵗʰ Root Race of Men will advance into a very different level of consciousness independent of the visible and the invisible material universe in an appropriately formed area* (...I am going to prepare a place for you... [John 14:2]) *which will ensure the ideal conditions for the preparation of the Men Transferred There, for their integration into the HyperUniverses of Truth, because:* "...No person of mortal birth is worthy to enter the house you have seen...»* [GOSPEL OF JUDAS §45]

In that Prepared Place, during the period of "1,000 years" [JOHN'S REVELATION 20:2], *the men of the 6ᵗʰ Root Race will be prepared, by shedding/relinquishing the energy-portion of their soul. They will namely shed the subtler energy of the material world, which their soul has been interwoven with, and thus they will separate their divisible (energy) part from their*

Indivisible (Spiritual) part, in order to form the 7th Root Race of Spiritual Men, who, as Absolutely Spiritual Beings, will be truly worthy to enter the Holy Capital of the Father (HyperUniverses).

Let me now remind you of the way the Soul was created, according to the writings of Plato:

PLATO'S 'TIMAEUS' tr. KOUTROUMPAS D., G., (C35a1-35b3 p. 57-59)

«And he *(the creator)* made the Soul out of the following elements and in the following manner: Out of the **indivisible** and eternally unchangeable essence *(The Indivisible Spirit granted to the man/being through the Immortal Breath of the god/creator)*, and also out of that which has to do with material bodies and is **divisible** *(divided by Logos, finer energy-hylē/paste of the material world)*, by combining therefore the two, he had essences from both and he compounded a third and intermediate kind of essence between the indivisible and the divisible.»

*On the contrary, those who will remain in the material universe will miss the opportunity for the 1st Resurrection, like students failing their courses. Due to the Pralaya which will be happening to the visible world then, they too will be forced to migrate to an energy-condition, thus forming a **pseudo-race** which they will call the 6th. The future for them –as opposed to the first group– has the second death in store for them, as John describes it in the Apocalypse.*

The signs for the future say that humanity is divided in two independent populations, where, for the first half there will be prosperity, whereas for the other half not. All this will be analyzed later in the main text.

The five Races/Genders we have analyzed previously in our discussion referred to the completion of the material-human creation, starting from the Spiritual –with the creation of the Soul– and ending with the absolutely densely material with the creation of the physical body of the Iron Race.

If you horizontally dissect an apple you will see its seeds forming the "petals" of the five Races that Celestial Man/Adam would 'taste' by trying the forbidden fruit (apple), which Eve/Life offered him, along with the 'five(fold)-racial' process of entering into dense matter. With the end of the Iron Race, the cycle of this five (fold)-racial material creation is completed and those members of Humanity **who will manage**, shall enter an Ideal State which is considered an Era of absolute Harmony. This will be the beginning of the **True** Sixth Root-Race.

---

[527] **A) HESIOD 'WORKS AND DAYS'** (v. 172-175): «And again Zeus made yet another *(fifth)* generation of mortal men; from them the present ones have come. I wish that I *(Hesiod himself)* were not among the men of the fifth generation, but either had died before **or been born afterwards.**»

Don't skip chapters or bibliographic references

B) RUDOLF STEINER 'FROM THE AKASHA CHRONICLE, COSMIC MEMORY' (p. 138):

«On the one hand, the coming evolution of Earth will develop today's life of images and thoughts to an even higher, more subtle and more complete condition. …Man will only attain a complete life on the next Planet, into which the Earth **will be transformed** and which is called 'Jupiter'[1] in apocryphal science. Then man will be able to come in communication with beings that remain completely hidden from our present sensory perception. It is understandable, that not only will the present life of opinions totally change, but also actions, feelings, all relations to the environment will be dramatically transformed. While today man can consciously influence only sensory beings, he will then be able to act consciously on very different forces and powers; he himself will receive fully comprehensible influences from completely different realms than at present. At that stage there can no longer be any question of birth and death in the present sense. Death occurs only because consciousness depends on an external world with which it interacts through the sensory organs. If these physical organs cease to function, then all relation to the world around ceases as well. That is to say, the person is 'is dead'. However, when his soul advances, it will not receive the outer world influences through physical organs, but through the images it creates itself.»

[1] *Rudolf Steiner allots man's creation up to now into three previous creative periods/phases which correspondingly take place in different hypostases (finer bodies) of Gaia, which he calls "Planets". And he goes on to clarify:*
'THE AKASHIC CHRONIC COSMIC MEMORY', (p. 126): «Before the Heavenly Body on which the life of man takes place became "earth" we now know *(and he refers to the 4th condition),* it had three other forms which are designated as Saturn, Sun and Moon. One can thus speak of four planets on which the four principal stages of the development of mankind take place.» *As he explains in his book:*
RUDOLF STEINER 'AT THE GATES OF ANTHROPOSOPHY' (Gr. tr. ALEXIOU TH.)

CH. 'THE EVOLUTION OF EARTH' (p. 92): «But we must not think of these four planets, Saturn, Sun, Moon and Earth as four Planets separate from each other, this would be totally wrong. We are dealing with four states of appearance of one and the same planet. They are true transfigurations of a Planet and all the beings on it are transformed alongside with it.»
He too, claims that each of these phases is separated from the others with a Pralaya.

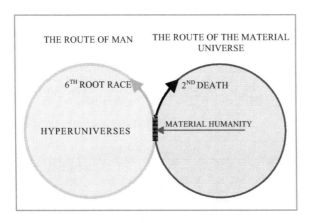

THE ROUTE OF MAN   THE ROUTE OF THE MATERIAL UNIVERSE

6TH ROOT RACE   2ND DEATH

HYPERUNIVERSES   MATERIAL HUMANITY

Mankind's entrance into the **Real/True** Sixth Root-Race brings forth a permanent <u>separation</u> from the material (visible and invisible) universe, which will nevertheless continue its independent course. Celestial Man and the material universe seem like two independent 'points' that move in two **different** circles. At an 'instance' in eternity, their circumferences meet at a certain point, and the creation of man manifests in the material universe. Afterwards, these two 'points' (man and material universe), each following its own trajectory, distance themselves from each other. The True Sixth Root-Race of Men, is about to evolve <u>outside</u> the material (visible and invisible) universe, following its own course. In an opposite manner, a totally different course, independent from that of Man's, is about to be followed by the Material Universe. If Man is seduced and does not follow HIS OWN trajectory, but gets confused and follows that of the material universe, then <u>HE WILL PERISH</u>.

The only thing this passage through the five Races/Genders has bestowed upon Humanity was the **essential Spiritual death** of a great portion of entities, **without even the tiniest benefit** for the remaining 'Spiritual survivors'. Men pinpoint specific dates for these breathtaking events to follow, without them being necessarily valid.

---

528 **A)** *Within the lines of the Gospel of Judas lies a prophecy made by Jesus Himself.*

For centuries the Gospel of Judas was carefully hidden from humanity. Even when it was discovered, along with other manuscripts in Nag Hammadi, even then, it was destined to remain in obscurity, abandoned in a safe-deposit box in Switzerland, for half a century. Very recently however (2005), and before the manuscript was committed to utter damage, National Geographic undertook the task of bringing it to the public.

The revealed text prompted questions and concern (second thoughts) on whether –for all these centuries– humanity's perspective of Judas has been accurate. Could it be that, after all, Judas was a "key-person" to Christ's Mission on earth, WHO (let us not forget) had mainly the role of the "third party/guarantor" to deliver humanity from its karmic debt?

Don't skip chapters or bibliographic references

And Jesus prophesized:

(46-47) «Jesus answered and said *(to Judas)*: You will become the thirteenth and you will be cursed by the other generations and you will *(ultimately)* come to rule over them. In the last days, they will curse *(the ones who will perish)* your ascent *(return)* to the holy [generation] *(namely, the restoration of Judas' good name).*»

Do the revelation of the Gospel of Judas and the restoration of his good name signify the end of our days after all?

Before we can agree with the view that the end of the world is in 2012, we must firstly ascertain that the Mayas' date of the 'end of the world' coincides with the year 2012 of the Western calendar.

Furthermore, we must point out an additional misinterpretation of the Mayan calendar by those who tried to decipher it.

The Mayans talk about a 'passage', without specifying exactly what they mean. But Westerners have misinterpreted this 'passage' of the Mayans and associated it with a possible alignment of the planets of our solar system with the center of our Galaxy. They have thus falsely concluded that this planetary alignment will occur in 2012. But as astronomers and NASA make it clear (Donald K. Yeomans), that no planetary alignment is forecasted for 2012. The Mayan 'Passage' denotes another situation –which is analyzed later in the book– and is not related to any planetary alignment! It is possible that all this misinformation regarding 2012 has other objectives…

On the other hand, without firm scientific justification, the beginning of the Mayan time was placed in the year 3,114 B.C., whereas there are more than 50 different proposed time beginnings for them, claims astrophysicist and archaeo-astronomer Jesús Galindo Trejo, researcher of the Institute of Aesthetic Research of National Autonomous University of Mexico (UNAM), and asks:

«Under what privilege could the Mayan Culture ascertain that the evolution of Earth or the Universe is connected to their own time calculations? …What would the Jews, the Chinese or the Arabs have to say according to their own calendar calculations?» [THE MAYAS AND 2012: A DISTORTED STORY http://e-kyklos.blogspot.com/2012/03/2012.html]

The exact time of the end –even though quite near– remains undefined.

B) FROM THE 'HISTORY CHANNEL' DOCUMENTARY: MAYAN DOOMSDAY PROPHECY

«The Classic Mayan civilization flourished roughly between 600 and 900 AD, in what is present day Mexico, in Yucatan, Central America. The ancient city of Chichen Itza in Yucatan, dominated the region as its religious and cultural capital. The Maya were known for their advanced knowledge in astronomy, architecture and mathematics. Caracol, the most famous astronomical observatory, was located at the Chichen Itza.

Archeologists in the 1930s had already realized that you could do astronomical sightings through the windows of the Caracol.

It is clear that the Maya predicted events based on equinoxes and Venus cycles. They committed their vast store of astronomical calculations (including their Doomsday and other predictions) to carvings and codices which are manuscripts written in complex hieroglyphics. This advanced knowledge of time and space culminated with the design and construction of the pyramid of Kukulkan, named for the supreme deity of the Maya. What is remarkable, even stunning about this pyramid is that the entire structure is actually a three-dimensional calendar.

What is amazing about the Kukulkan pyramid is that it's a four sided ziggurat of stone that is actually a calendar. There are 91 steps on each side, plus the platform on top, which equals 365 steps, as in the days of the year. What is really amazing about it is that somehow, the Mayans set the pyramid in place, so that on the equinox, an unbelievable phenomenon takes place: At 3.00 pm on the spring and autumn equinoxes, the play of light and shadow form a serpent's body down the north stair case of the pyramid of Kukulkan. As the sun moves towards the west, what you see is the 'serpent' (shadow-light) coming out of the sky down the stairway. At the end of the day it is going to the plain of existence on earth and entering into the earth, into the underworld. As it slithers down the stairs into the underworld, the shadow of the serpent's body connects to its sculpted head at the base of the thousand-year-old pyramid. But is this phenomenon more than a religious sign? Some believe the serpent is a warning. One of several the Mayas have passed to us of a catastrophic event that is about to occur.

To the Maya the end of the world wasn't a vague, abstract notion but rather a very real, specific event. When they speak of Doomsday, they are essentially talking about the full destruction of the world and the inhabitants on the world. The difference between what other religions say and what the Mayan culture says about Doomsday is that the Mayan calendar –which is an instrument of time and space– actually names the specific day when humanity will end.

…After Cortez, all the written hieroglyphic records about the Mayan knowledge, their prophecies and the general ideology that the Maya shared, were all burnt. Some sympathetic (Christian) priests though, managed to salvage four of the codices that later found their way to libraries in Europe. One of these manuscripts was known as the 'Dresden Codex': the key to understanding the Mayan calendar and its predictions.

What would lie in these pages are the future history of Earth and the exact date of our demise. …Those manuscripts were long sheets of paper made

Don't skip chapters or bibliographic references

from the inner bark of fig trees. These sheets, which measured up to 22 feet (6.7 meters) in length, were covered with lime-based paint and folded like an accordion.

…To the scholars of the European libraries, the four salvaged codices were a source of endless fascination. The most important of them proved to be the one purchased in Vienna, in 1739, by the head of the Royal Saxon Library in Dresden, Germany. He brought the codex back to Dresden, where it was left undisturbed collecting dust in the library for more than a century. Then, in 1880, a German scholar named Ernest Fosterman began to study the codex in detail. Through his diligent efforts he was able to crack its code and reveal the Mayas view of the universe and the future.

The first thing the experts realized was that in the codex lay a series of astronomical predictions, future eclipses, Lunar cycles and the cycle of the planet Venus (alignment) were all clearly laid out. A blueprint of galactic activity for thousands of years to come! Scholars also realized that within the codex was a calendar, one more advanced than anything we use today! Within that complex calendar appeared to be predictions tied to distinct and specific historical eras. To make sense of these prophecies and the Doomsday scenario, first requires a basic understanding of how the Mayan calendar works —no easy task; It has taken scholars, archeologists and epigraphers more than a century to decode the prophesies and the chronological mechanism of the calendar on which they are based. Still incomplete, their painstaking work of deciphering of the Dresden codex and comparing it to Maya inscriptions on archeological monuments continues. But this much is known: The Maya didn't just keep time, they were obsessed with it. Other ancient civilizations were also interested in time and kept time. But the Maya were more meticulous. They were very exacting. They worked with large numbers and this allowed them to attain high levels of accuracy. Their obsession stems from an understanding of time, which is fundamentally different from our own.

The major difference between the Maya and the non-Maya people, and especially us, westerners is that the Maya and any other native groups of Mexico and Central America, they understood time as something that occurs and reoccurs, as a **cyclical** phenomenon *(The Days and Nights of Brahma)*. We, westerners, see time as a line. It started at some point, is moving along, it continues and it goes on. But for the Maya, something that occurred in the past will certainly occur again and again, over and over. A message that we can take from the Mayan calendar is that our life is embedded in much larger cycles than those of our individual lives. …A cyclical view of time allowed the Maya to create what many experts consider to be the most sophisticated calendar any civilization has ever produced.

As complex as it is precise, it is actually **three** calendars in one. The first and more familiar one was the solar calendar, called the **Haab**. It had 365 days split into 18 months of 20 days each, plus a short period of five days, which was considered to be very unlucky. The **Haab** is 1/10,000 of the day more accurate than the standard calendar in use today.

In addition to the Haab, the Maya kept a second, ceremonial calendar of 260 days known as the **Tzolkin**. The sacred cycle of 260 days consisted of 13 numbers combined with 20 day-signs (13 x 20 = 260). The importance of this sacred calendar is that it was a key that the Maya used for the understanding of many different dimensions of human experience. For example, it is based upon the nine-month period of human gestation, which is about 260 days.

...The Maya combined the **Tzolkin** with the **Haab** like two cogs, to form what is called **the Calendar Round**; it was how they kept count of their time on a daily basis. The calendar round is a 52-year cycle which combines the solar year with the 260-day cycle. The numbers, the months and the days only repeat every 52 years. ...Beyond the calendar cycle, the German scholar Fosterman discovered that the Maya tracked time with yet a third calendar, called the **'Long Count'**.

It is from this 'Long Count' calendar that they calculated Doomsday and made their predictions concerning the future. The 'Long Count' calendar measures the time elapsed since the mythical beginning of the Mayan civilization. It transcended the lifetime of individuals and kingdoms.

After years of collating data from astronomy, archeology and iconography, experts have calculated that the beginning date of the 'Long Count' equates to August 13th, 3114 BC and ends 5,125 years later, on December 21st, 2012.

Within the Long Count there are units of time called 'Katuns'.

A 'Katun' lasts roughly 20 years. For each 'Katun' the Mayan astrologers formulated a specific prophecy. Each Katun and its prophecy, would repeat every 260 years.

...The best known Mayan prophecies are found in the books of Chilam Balam. Chilam Balam is thought to be the name of an ancient priest who predicted the arrival of the bearded white men (Cortez and the Spaniards) in Yucatan...The Katun 4 began in 1993 and will end in 2012. During this period, according to Chilam Balam: "the supreme deity will return to Earth, heralding the start of a new age" [1]

...In Mayan cosmology there are five great cycles and each one lasting about 5,125 years. Four (4) have already ended in destruction. Mayan Doomsday prophecy refers to the end of the <u>fifth cycle</u> *(of the 5th, the Iron Race)* and the very last day equates to December 21st, 2012. This means that the 5th and current cycle, like its predecessors, will also end in destruction *(Pralaya)*.

If so, what could trigger this destruction? The answer **may** lie *(it is here that the miscalculation probably lies)* in a rare cosmic event that the Maya predicted more than 2,000 years ago. The ancient Maya have prophesied that the world will come to an end on the 13th BAKTUN, on their Long Count calendar. This date translates into December 21st, 2012 *(But the end of the world is not confined to a single day, but to a much longer period)*. The Maya didn't arbitrarily pick this Doomsday date. Rather, they probably and purposely calculated it, using their advanced knowledge of astronomy. The Mayan prophecy for 2012 is anchored to an astronomical alignment: In December of 2012, the December solstice sun will be lining up with the center of our Milky Way galaxy. This is a very rare cosmic alignment that happens only once every 26,000 years. *(NASA's authorities have stated that no alignment will occur on 12-21-2012)*

Every 26,000 years the sun aligns with the center of the Milky Way. At the same time another astronomical rarity occurs. The Earth completes a 'wobble' around its axis. This phenomenon is called precession. The Earth 'wobbles' very slowly on its axis, so, it effectively changes our angular orientation to the larger galactic picture. One complete 'precessional wobble' is 26,000 years and the exact date of when this incredible galactic alignment will all come together is on December 21st, 2012.

How the Maya could predict cosmic events 26,000 years into the future remains a wondrous mystery, despite the ongoing work of experts. What is known is that for some reason, the Maya attached great symbolic meaning to the precessional cycle.

…The Maya attached such importance to this rare alignment, that to them it was not only the linchpin of the date of annihilation, but it also permeated the very roots of their culture. In terms of what the meaning of this cosmic alignment is, we have to access the core documents of their creation-mythology, that's the Popol Vuh or the Hero Twin creation-myth. *(It is here therefore, that the falsification lies, because the Mayans do not refer to the –nonexistent– alignment of the planets with the center of our Galaxy, but to a different condition)*

The Popol Vuh, the Maya equivalent of the Bible, was translated shortly after the Spanish conquest (of Mexico) in the 16th century. According to the Popol Vuh, the alignment of the sun with the center of our galaxy on December 21st 2012 <u>will open the entrance to the underworld and evil.</u> [2]

The sacred text tells how the lords of the underworld *(the snake, Lucifer)* who dwell in the dark rift, challenged the mythic Maya figure known as the 'First Father' *(Celestial Man – Adam)*, to a ball game. He accepted the challenge **and entered the dark rift** *(black hole/material universe)*. But the devious lords withdrew their challenge and instead, decapitated the 'First Father' *(the spiritual fission/lobotomy of Celestial Man to the 'I Am Presence' and the 'Divine Spark')*. His sons, the Hero Twins *(the two divided parts of the Celestial Man)*, avenged his death by defeating the dark forces in an epic ball-game and <u>resurrected the 'First Father'</u> *(The cure of Man, the First Resurrection).*

At the ancient ball-court at Chichen Itza ...the Maya played the same *(ball)* game the Hero Twins played against the lords of the underworld, as described in the Popol Vuh. The game seems to have been a primitive hybrid of basketball and soccer. The objective was to get a ball through a mounted ring made of stone, mounted high on the wall, using only the knees and hips *(as the main text continues, the meaning of the passage through the ring will be revealed).* The first team to score (passing the ball through this stone ring) won. *(The individuals who will manage to get through the ring/Gate will be the winners, passing onto the First Resurrection).*

...The carved panel on a sidewall graphically depicts the beheading of a player at center-court. Many believe this was the fate of the loser. Blood spurts from his neck in the form of serpents. The decapitated player kneels before a ball. Inside it, a skull speaks the words symbolizing death. ...The Mayan calendar suggests that after the year of 2012, a new age might well emerge (what that is specifically however, remains a mystery...) Chilam Balam (the high priest) says: "For half of them, there will be food, for others misfortunes; **A time of the end of the Word of God**; A time for uniting for a cause." [3]

...The answer as to what will happen on that fateful day of December 21st 2012 –according to the Maya scholars who have decoded it– may be found on the last page of the Dresden Codex. In the Codex there is a series of astronomical events that are predicted: The Lunar and Venus cycles (alignments), eclipse cycles and at then the last page of the Dresden Codex actually shows the destruction of the world via water. So this is how the Maya conceived the Doomsday scenario. A graphic illustration depicts the destruction of the Earth by flood. Waves gush from the mouth of the dragon. More flood waters pour from the sun and moon symbols on the underside of the monster's body. An aged goddess also pours a jar of flood water onto the Earth. At the bottom of the picture crouches a ruler of the underworld. Above the picture, about half of the 15 hieroglyphics have been destroyed ...but a few of the remaining ones consistently refer to ...Black Earth and Black on high.

...Will the Earth be annihilated in a great flood, as depicted in the Dresden Codex? Only time will tell. ...But time as the Maya knew too well ...is running out...»

[1] «...The supreme deity will return to Earth, heralding the start of a new age.» *A corresponding event is expected by the Brahmans, when Kali Yuga will be approaching its end. Vishnu Puraná describes:*

BLAVATSKY H., P., 'THE SECRET DOCTRINE' (I-378): «When the close of the Kali age shall be nigh *(near)*, a portion of that divine being which exists, of its

Don't skip chapters or bibliographic references

own spiritual nature shall descent on Earth as a Kalki (Avatar) [*], endowed with the eight superhuman faculties...»

[*]**Kalki:** *=the name of the white winged horse of Vishnu or according to others, Vishnu himself in his final incarnation as a rider named Kalki, riding his white horse Devadatta.*

The danger however that applies to all men of all races and faiths is that **during the same time-period** *and with the same purpose, two opposite* **tendencies** *will* **coexist.** *One will be True and will lead to Real Salvation and the other will be fake and will lead to havoc. It is the danger Christians point-out regarding the antichrist. This danger does not only concern Christians but all men regardless of race or religion.*

And Blavatsky points out:

'THE SECRET DOCTRINE' (I-470):

«Only, it is NOT in the Kali Yuga, our present terrifically materialistic age of Darkness, the 'Black Age', that a new Savior of Humanity CAN **EVER** APPEAR.»

Since –as we will find out– NEITHER Christ will ever reappear on the densely material Earth in flesh and bones; hence, as Jesus himself points out in Matthew's Gospel:

THE GOSPEL OF MATTHEW, CH. 24: «§23. Then if anyone says to you, 'Look, here is the Christ!' or 'There!' do not believe it. §24. For false Christs and false prophets will rise and show great signs and wonders to deceive, if possible, even the very elect ones. §25. **Behold, I have told you beforehand**. §26. Therefore if they say to you, 'Look, He *(The Christ)* is in the desert!' do not go out; or 'Look, He is in the inner rooms!' do not believe it. §27. For as the lightning comes from the east and flashes to the west, so also will the coming of the Son of Man be.»

He will therefore approach Earth in an ABSOLUTELY Spiritual way, NOT to bring 'justice' to matter of course, but **only to gather** *the select ones and transfer them:*

THE GOSPEL OF JOHN, CH. 14: «§3. And when I go and **prepare a place** for you *(which obviously is **not** the Earth)*, I will come again **and receive you** to My-self; so that you may also be where I am.»

And naturally, the Transference of the select ones to the prepared Place will be carried out with the Mystical procedure of the 1ˢᵗ Resurrection:

THE GOSPEL OF JOHN, CH. 6: «§40...and I shall **raise*** him *(everyone who believes)* up to life on the very last day.»

*Orig. Gr. text uses the word ἀναστήσω *= I shall resurrect*

All these forewarnings serve the purpose of protecting men from a coming danger:

[2] «According to the Popol Vuh, the alignment of the sun with the center

492

of our galaxy on December 21st, 2012, <u>will open the entrance to the underworld and evil.</u>»

(a) JOHN'S REVELATION CH. 12: «§9. And the great dragon was thrown down, that ancient serpent that is called the devil and Satan, the deceiver of the whole world. He **was hurled down to earth**, and his angels were cast down with him.»

Expressly or not, every religion indicates the presence of absolute evil (antichrist) in the world of matter and the danger threatening men who will not realize that the Ultimate Presence <u>WILL NOT</u> materialize on the densely material Earth. The Mayas signal this descent of the absolute evil onto Earth, with symbols:

(b) «...As the sun moves towards the west, what you see is the 'serpent' (shadow-light) coming out of the sky down the stairway. ... But is this phenomenon more than a religious sign? Some believe the serpent is a warning. One of several the Mayas have passed to us of a catastrophic event that is about to occur.»

[3] «...**a time of the end of the Word of God**; A time for uniting for a cause.»

BLAVATSKY H., P., 'THE SECRET DOCTRINE' (I-373, 374):

«The cycle of creation of the lives of Kosmos is run down *(coming to an end)*, because the energy of the manifested 'Word' *(Logos)* has its growth, culmination, and decrease *(oscillation)*, as have all things temporary, however long their duration.»

These dates could be correct, but then again they might not. There are many unforeseen parameters, which cannot be calculated. Man's new State therefore, will be disengaged and independent from the "five-seed apple" of matter, and those who will **manage** to enter into it ,will experience unprecedented harmony, since they have —at last— 'climbed down' from the forbidden tree of knowledge of good and evil. The Sixth Root-Race will be created from those men who will manage to experience what John's Apocalypse calls "First Resurrection". They will then proceed into an exclusively Spiritual Period **of Preparation** in a Place which is especially prepared ("...I am going now, to prepare a place for you" [JOHN 14:2]), shedding/relinquishing the energy-portions of their Soul, retaining only the indivisible/Spiritual part of IT— before their final Return to the Immaculate FatherLands.

Don't skip chapters or bibliographic references

---

529 *The Soul, during the First Resurrection, will be stripped of its energy-portion (its Divisible Essence), maintaining only its indivisible/Spiritual part pure and intact (The Indivisible Essence).*

A) GOSPEL OF PHILIP, JEAN-YVES LELOUP: «§10…All that is composite *(complex)* will decompose and return to its Origin *(Source/Principle/Archē)*;»

B) THE GOSPEL OF JOHN, CH. 12: «§25. He who loves his soul* shall lose it *(by relinquishing the divisible part, the energy-part of his soul, the divisible essence)*, and he who hates his soul* in this world *(i.e. hates the divisible part of his soul)* shall keep it to life eternal *(will eternally safeguard its Indivisible part, The Indivisible Essence).*»

* The original Greek Text uses the word ψυχὴν *= Psychē/Soul but, for some reason, all English translations use the word 'life' instead…* [ὁ φιλῶν τὴν **ψυχὴν** αὐτοῦ ἀπολλύει αὐτήν, καὶ ὁ μισῶν τὴν **ψυχὴν** αὐτοῦ ἐν τῷ κόσμῳ τούτῳ εἰς ζωὴν αἰώνιον φυλάξει αὐτήν.]

C) JOHN'S APOCALYPSE 20:6 «Blessed and holy are those who have part in the first resurrection. The second death has no power over them.»

The passage to this new condition will be signaled by earth-shattering events, which, it is imperative for humanity, to start preparing to face.

---

530 **A) KENNETH X. CARREY, 'THE STARSEED TRANSMISSIONS', 1982**

Information through channeling: «At that moment, humanity will experience an instantaneous transformation of proportions you cannot now conceive. At that time, the "spell" which was cast on your race thousands of years ago –when you plunged into the worlds of **good and evil**– will be shattered forever.»

B) BARBARA MARCINIAK 'GAIA' [Gr. tr. MATZOROU E.] *(Information through channeling)*:

«We tell you this: not even in your wildest dreams can you imagine where Gaia is going to. The masses are hypnotized in a world of events, encyclopedias, television and newspapers and the multi-dimensional anomalies have not yet penetrated your own existential level very deeply. When they do penetrate it though, things beyond the limits of your imagination will start occurring.»

THE ASTRAL SKEPTOMORPHIC THREAT

Let us proceed with our discussion and obscurities will become clear. As material eternity unfolded, the astral skeptomorphic force *(the vitalized energy born of the thoughts of men)* started prevailing in the material universe, since it was constantly multiplied by the thoughts of men. On the contrary, the initial power of the creator gods remained steadily unaltered, something that increasingly disturbed the balance between them. On account of that, an ever increasing percentage of the creators' hierarchy began to be absorbed by the skeptomorphic dynasty which simulated their properties and increasingly manipulated the Archetype of Life for their benefit. In the same manner that the Creator of matter had once embezzled the Sacred Archetypes of the HyperCosmoi for his own benefit, likewise, he himself is now the victim of a similar theft by the astral dynasty, thus succumbing to his own karmic law. This "change of roles" produced **symptoms** of moral decline, degradation of moral values and loosening of ethics to the human society, tendencies which men today consider 'progressive'. But they only call them so because they can't imagine their origin! Because of this development, the 'game' of the creator of matter had to stop and **every Vitalization Source had to be revoked**, so that these despicable beings would no longer manage IT. After all, the Hyper-Cosmic Place where the leak had come from and which was somewhat responsible for the **accident** –which you call material creation– had to restore the 'damage'.

---

531 **A) THE APOCRYPHON OF JOHN, THE GNOSTIC SOCIETY LIBRARY** [FREDERIK WISSE]: «And when the mother *(of the creator/Yaldabaoth)* recognized that the garment of darkness was imperfect…she repented with much weeping. And the whole 'pleroma' *(the Completeness of The True Cosmoi)* heard the prayer of her repentance, and they prayed on her behalf to the invisible, virginal Spirit. And the Spirit…poured *(Essence)* over her from Its Entire Pleroma…And she was taken up *(higher from where she had fallen)*, not to her own aeon *(not to her original position)*, but above her son, that she might be in the ninth *(Heaven)* <u>until she has **corrected** her deficiency.</u>» …*Reclaiming The Sacred Archetypes her son has embezzled.*
This 'deviation' that resulted to the material creation is also brought to our attention elsewhere:
B) DANEZIS M., THEODOSIOU S. 'COSMOLOGY OF THE INTELLECT' (p.112): «Hawking and Penrose proved in 1970, without any optimization, that **our Universe must have had a space-time anomaly during the initial phase of its expansion** at the time of the Big Bang, and if it breaks up one day, it will again create an anomaly during its Big Collapse/Compression.»

Don't skip chapters or bibliographic references

Therefore a mighty force of Intelligent Wholenesses had to secretly break into the material universe with the specific mission of releasing everything Sacred the material creation had embezzled, in order to return IT to Its Source.

---

532 **THE GOSPEL OF MATTHEW, CH. 24**: «§42. So keep watch, for you do not know what hour your Lord is coming. §43. But know this: that if the **master of the house**[(1)] *(the archon of this world)* had known **what hour** *(of the dark period)* the thief *(Christ)* would come, he would have kept watch and not allowed **his house** *(his universe)* to be broken into.»

[(1)] «If the master of the house has been called Beelzebub, how much more the members of his household!» [MATHEW 10:24]

Therefore, since Jesus declares that "I am not of this world" [JOHN 8:23] *He obviously compares Himself to a thief, who, unannounced, will break into the foreign universe/house, to spring the stolen Sacred Archetypes and His Children.*

From a different perspective, the distinction between Jesus and the world of the 'master of the house' –the archon of this world– is reasserted in the following verse:

THE GOSPEL OF JOHN, CH. 14: «§30. I will not speak much more with you, for the ruler *(archon)* of the world is coming, and **he has nothing in Me**;» [= *meaning that Jesus, being A Pure Spirit, does **not** have the creator's 'breath' inside Him, as every human soul does.*]

The Sacred Elements that will be returned are:
(a) The Archetype of Life
(b) The Keys of the Laws of Creation
(c) Celestial Men trapped inside material creation since its beginning.

---

533 **THE GOSPEL OF JUDAS** [KASSER R., MEYER M., WURST G.] **NATIONAL GEOGRAPHIC** [53]: «This is why God ordered Michael to give the spirits of people to them <u>as a loan</u>.»
And since the time to return this 'loan' is growing near… it would be wise to relate the above excerpt to that of John's Apocalypse:
REVELATION 7:3 «Do not harm the earth, neither the sea, nor the trees, till we have **put a seal** on the foreheads of the servants of our God.»

(d) All plain Souls that **will chose** to be completed with Spirit/Essence.

496

534 *Let me remind you that the power of the Mother of the Demiourgos went out into the people's souls through his 'breath', <u>abandoning him.</u> Since then he is seeking to take back what he was tricked into distributing to humans, in order to make their souls his own again. The expression: 'he sold his soul to the devil' refers to this 'story'.*

THE APOCRYPHON OF JOHN, THE GNOSTIC SOCIETY LIBRARY:

«And they *(the Delegates of True Light)* said to Yaldabaoth: "Blow into his face something of your spirit and his body will arise *(of the man/being/soul)*. And he blew into his face *(of the man/being/soul)* the spirit which is the power of his mother; he did not know (this), for he exists in ignorance. And the power of the mother came out of Yaldabaoth **and went into the psychic body** *(soul)*. ...The body moved and gained strength and it was luminous.» [Eng. tr. from Coptic: WALDSTEIN M., WISSE F.]

The creators, aware of the fact that **they are incapable** of Redemption by following the Sacred Archetypes, steeped in and reared by contaminated skeptomorphs as they are, become enthralled in a relentless race for survival, where <u>everyone fights each other</u>.

535 **A) THE GOSPEL OF JUDAS** [KASSER R., MEYER M., WURST G.] NATIONAL GEOGRAPHIC [55]: «Jesus said: "I am not laughing [at you], but at the error of the stars, because these six stars *(spirits)* wander about with these five **combatants,** and they all will be destroyed along with their creatures.»

B) BLAVATSKY H., P., 'THE SECRET DOCTRINE'
(a) (I-36) «It is stated in Book II., Ch. viii., of Vishnu Puraná: "By immortality is meant existence to the end of the Kalpa;" and Wilson, the translator, remarks in a footnote: "This, according to the Vedas, is all that is to be understood of the immortality (or eternity) **of the gods**; <u>they perish at the end of universal dissolution</u> (or Pralaya).»

(b) (I-371) «When the Maha Pralaya arrives, *(the definitive/absolute end)* the inhabitants of Swar-loka (the upper sphere) disturbed by <u>the conflagration</u> *(in this case, the negative astral forces)*, seek refuge with the Pitris, their progenitors, the Manus, the seven Rishis, the various orders of celestial Spirits and the Gods, in Maharloka. When the fire reaches there also, the whole of the above enumerated beings migrate in their turn from Maharloka, and return to Jana-loka in their subtle forms, destined to become re-embodied, in similar capacities as their former, when the world is renewed at the beginning of the succeeding Kalpa.» ...*But having all been reduced to ...energy carcasses.*

Some passages precisely state what these previously 'divine forces' end up to, when the new (fallen) life-giving force from the HyperUniverses, describes their state when it (creator/Lucifer) first encounters them:

Don't skip chapters or bibliographic references

(a) STANZA I 'COSMIC EVOLUTION' «§6. The seven sublime lords and the seven truths *(from the previous Maha-Kalpa/creation)* had ceased to be *(having ended up as carcasses)* ...§7. The causes of existence had been done away with; The visible that was, and the invisible that is, rested in eternal non-being –the one being.»

(b) HERMES TRISMEGISTUS: THE FOUNDER OF MONOTHEISM 9000 B.C., IOAN-NIDIS P. K., CH. 1: «§4 ...But after a little while, I saw a downward darkness partially born, coming down in **an oblique formation**, like a snake, fearful and hideous. I also saw that darkness to be changed into a moist nature, unspeakably troubled, which yielded a fiery smoke from its depths, and from whence I heard an unutterable heartbreaking sound, and an inarticulate roar in a voice of fire *(...the preceding 'divine' forces)*.»

(c) OLD TESTAMENT, GENESIS CH. 1: «§2. And the earth was without form, and void and darkness was upon the face of the abyss.»

And because the skeptomorphic threat is 'ante portas' (before the gates) exclusively for the creators' team, devouring them and constantly decreasing their percentage on one hand, and asserting an ever greater portion of their energy-nutrition on the other, the creators cunningly and diplomatically invert **their own problem** into a problem for men (their bondservants) and recruit every knowledge-seeker that turns to them for 'enlightenment', offering powerful weapons to 'women and children' (unfit to bear arms). Thus they expose men to danger turning them into warriors for their own cause.

---

[536] **A REPORT ON THE "VIOLET FLAME" AND THE VIOLET PLANE**: *An energy that astonishes every user with its impressive potential.*

The use of the Violet energy-flame by the students of the 'spiritual path', once it initially 'awakens' the opponent negative astral giant who is under "attack" by its force, it consequently provokes the astral enemy into attacking the student himself with fury.

*Violet energy is indeed a good shield and a powerful weapon provided that the student knows how to handle its entire 'spectrum'. Any accidental cessation of the flame's use –if the student has managed to properly activate it on a daily basis– leaves him **completely defenseless** and stirs up a storm of reactions/effects from the opposite astral camp. These effects upset his life in the form of calamities and misfortunes because, if negative elementals sense that 'someone' is interfering with their 'food', they turn around to mangle the 'meddler'.*

Result: the gullible Violet energy/flame user becomes totally depended on its power, since he is 'safe' only if he ceaselessly uses it (every day), constantly increasing its potency. This way though, he consumes all his

---

*energy/power in someone else's fight, hoping, that in the universe of duality, the positive will reign **alone**...*

*But it will be wise for man not to interfere...into 'foreign affairs', and while he is in this world to try to ensure his inner balance **without exciting either of the two opposite forces**. To be protected he must BE CLOTHED with The Truth along with the True Light which is carried by that Truth –which <u>without battle</u> ANNULS every malevolent effect– preparing himself –cutting bonds and dependencies– for the departure from the universe of delusion and his **return** to the Sacred Homeland.*

*And to stress to potential of **The True Light**, in contrast to any twilight Ant-Avges flame of any nature, let me remind you of this excerpt from the Gospel of Philip:*

GOSPEL OF PHILIP, [En. tr. from Coptic: PATERSON BROWN]
www.metalog.org/files/philip.html «§13...He who has received that Light shall not be seen *(he will not be perceivable by the dark powers)*, nor shall they be able to seize him; nor shall anyone be able to disturb this one of this nature, even if he socializes in the world. And furthermore, (when) he leaves the world he has already received the truth via the imagery.»

An older account from Hermes Trismegistus supports the same view:

HERMES TRISMEGISTUS, HERMETIC TEXTS, VOL. I, RODAKIS P., TZAFEROPOULOS AP., **SPEECH XVI**: «§16. Whoever then has his rational part *(Higher Noûs)* glistening within like a ray of the sun –and these in all are few– upon them <u>the daemons do not act</u>; for no one of the daemons **neither of the gods** is equal to a single Ray of God *(The True Light)*. As for the rest *(of the people)*, they are all led and driven, soul and body, by the daemons –loving and accepting the activities of these *(of the daemons)*.»

The daemons are primarily energy-beings –including the positive ones ...who are worshiped so much in our times– and have nothing to do with the Essence-Spirit:

HERMES TRISMEGISTUS, HERMETIC TEXTS, VOL. I, RODAKIS P., TZAFEROPOULOS AP., **SPEECH XVI**: «§13. And under the sun is arranged the group of daemons –or, rather, groups; for these are many and varied, ranked underneath the multitudes of Stars, equal in number to each of them. So ranked thus, they serve each one of the Stars, being **good and bad** in their natures, that is, in their activities. <u>For energy is the daemon's essence</u>; some of them are in fact of mixed nature, good and bad.»

The time remaining until the withdrawal procedure of the Sacred Archetypes commences, is not much anymore, because HyperCosmic Powers have **already** breached the **energy**-universe. No one can pinpoint the precise time however, because the Instance, when the ORDER FOR THE REVOCATION of the Archetypes will be given, is to be determined SOLELY by the Leader of this Mission.

(THE PROCESS OF)

THE RETURN OF THE SACRED ARCHETYPES TO THEIR SOURCE

The phenomena that humanity will shortly experience will be absolutely unprecedented for the whole of creation and will not only concern the densely material plane, but the entire energy-environment; they will be related to the completion of a time-cycle. It will in other words be that point when time as people know it will be coming to its end.

---

537 **A) BARBARA MARCINIAK 'GAIA'** [Gr. trans. MATZOROU E.] (p. 236):

«Time is collapsing. ...The collapse of time involves the disruption of the control of the frequencies defining your world.»

A different account, coming from a diametrically opposite source, talks about the 'Convergent Timeline':

B) HELLENIC NEXUS, ISSUE 2, JULY 2004

Excerpt from a magazine article, with the disclosures of Bill Hamilton –a Consulting Senior Programmer Analyst at the University of California, Los Angeles (UCLA)– concerning Dr. Dan Burisch's work.

«The story is about Dr. Dan Burisch's work (Captain in the U.S. Navy with a PhD in Microbiology and Molecular Genetics [State University of New York]).

...In 1989, Dr. Dan Burisch was assigned to Project 'Aquarius'. ...Project Aquarius is one of five compartmentalized top secret projects conducted at the S4 facility in Nevada base. ...Burisch had knowledge of all five classified projects. ...One of those documents was about a 'Convergent Timeline' which is about to happen to our world.»

C) KENNETH X. CARREY, 'THE STARSEED TRANSMISSIONS', 1982

«At that moment, humanity will experience an instantaneous transformation of proportions you cannot now conceive. At that time, the 'spell' which was cast on your race thousands of years ago –when you plunged into the worlds of good and evil– will be shattered forever. ...That moment will provide an opening for the emergence of something incomprehensible...

...Indeed, no single conceptual structure is capable of conveying the enormity of what is soon to take place. Those familiar with the scriptures of your various peoples should be in position to understand what is occurring, for these are the times spoken of by the scriptures.»

Material man, trapped inside the space-time web *(brane)*, will not find it easy to perceive this pending unfamiliar process. And since neither concepts nor words but symbols alone are capable of describing such an event, you will be able to understand it only by 'experiencing' these symbols in a transcendental way.

Saying these words, he stood up and came close to me. He put his hand on my forehead and everything disappeared from my eyes. I found myself outside the entire material creation. I witnessed the entire universe spinning in the form of a vortex. Trapped inside this vortex, the Archetypes of the Laws of this creation were also swirling. It seemed completely impossible for them to escape this vortex, since they themselves were creating it. A group of Entities were standing outside this vortex/material universe, ready to remove them from it. Definite disengagement from the Vortex depended on a precise action/operation: Inside the swirling spiral, there was a precious stone. This 'jewel' was the Earth which was identified –symbolically– with a key. The **redeeming action** *concerned the* <u>transfer</u> *of the 'jewel/key/Earth' and its placement into a 'point of reception',* <u>OUTSIDE</u> *the spinning vortex!*

The operation begins when the Assistants start pulling out the encaged Sacred Archetypes that permeate the universe. The Earth is then cut off from the Swirling Whole, <u>changes its hypostasis</u> *and is transferred, carrying the Spiritual Man along with it.*

---

538 **A) BLAVATSKY H., P., 'THE SECRET DOCTRINE'**

(I-152, 153): «The one eternal law unfolds everything in the manifested Nature on a sevenfold principle; among the rest, the countless circular chains of worlds, composed of seven globes, graduated on the four lower planes of the world of formation (the three others belonging to the Archetypal Universe). Out of these seven only one, the lowest and the most material of those globes, is within our plane or means of perception, the six others lying outside of it and being therefore invisible to the terrestrial eye.

(I-158)…Everything in the metaphysical as in the physical Universe is septenary (sevenfold). Hence every sidereal body, every planet, whether visible or invisible, is credited with six companion-globes.

(I-155)… When a planetary chain is in its last Round, its Globe 1 or A, before finally dying out, sends all its energy and 'principles' into a neutral center of latent force, a 'laya center', and thereby animates (informs) a new nucleus of undifferentiated substance or matter, i.e., calls it into activity or gives it life.»

B) *In Matthew's Gospel this 'transference' is described as follows:*

THE GOSPEL OF MATTHEW, CH. 24: «§29…the sun will be darkened, and the moon will not give its light; the stars will **fall from heaven**, and the powers of the heavens will be shaken.»

Absolutely identified with the symbol of the 'key', it (Earth) is placed inside a keyhole and seems to unlock a Gate leading to an Immaculate Place.

Don't skip chapters or bibliographic references

539 ...Thy Kingdom come, Thy Will be done on Earth as it is in Heaven... *Because the ONLY way for the Earth to join the State (Reign) of the Father, is to be Spiritually Transferred THERE.*

A) THE GOSPEL OF JOHN, CH. 14: «§2. In my Father's house there are many mansions ...I am going to prepare a place for you.»

B) *At this point, I consider it helpful to combine some elements together, in order to compose a clearer picture of the events that are about to happen.*
At first, I'd like to remind you of the symbolic "ball" game of the Maya, where the ball must pass **through** *the stone ring-Gate!*
Obviously, through their mystical knowledge, the Maya knew about that 'TRANSFERENCE' and depicted it symbolically with that game:

«... Popol Vuh, the sacred book of the Maya, narrates that the lords of the underworld *(Lucifer/snake)* invited a mythical Mayan, known as the "First Father" *(Celestial Man/Adam)* to a ball game. But the devious lords withdrew their invitation and decapitated the "First Father" *(the division of Man in two halves)*. The **twin sons** of the First Father avenged his murder by defeating the evil lords in an epic ball contest and **resurrected** the First Father *(the reunion of the divided Celestial Man restores his wholeness and resurrects him)*.

At the ancient ball court at Chichen Itza ...the Mayas used to play the ball-game of the hero twins against the lords of the underworld. The game was a combination of basketball and football. The objective was to get the ball through a stone-ring mounted...high on the wall. ...The winning team was the one who managed to get the ball through the stone-ring.»

Those, among mankind, who will manage (Unified with their Higher-Self) to be transferred along with Earth through that Sacred Passage-Portal-Lock, will be the winners.
That passage [=Pass-over] Pesach/Pascha in Hebrew) will only be achieved by those who will successfully complete the First Resurrection procedure, thus forming the 6th Root Race: "Blessed and holy are those who have part in the first resurrection; the second death has no power over them.» [REVELATION 20:6] *And Jesus advises:*
THE GOSPEL OF JOHN, CH. 10: «§9. I am the gate: If anyone enters through Me, *(like the ball of the Maya through the stone ring)* he shall be saved, and shall go in and **out** *(get to the other side)* and *(there)* find pasture.»
An analogous statement is also given by Chilam Balam, the Mayan priest, when he prophesizes about the end of the world, in the last page of their calendar: "For half[1] of men there will be food, for the other half misfortune...»

[1] **THE GOSPEL OF MATTHEW, CH. 24**: «§40-41. Then two men shall be in the field; the one shall be taken, and the other left. Two women shall be grinding

at the mill; the one shall be taken, and the other left.»

This indigence that will follow solely concerns the "defeated" ones: the ones who will not succeed to get through the stone-ring/Gate/Lock in order to be transferred just like the Ball-Earth (like a key). This is why the defeated Mayas were literally decapitated in that ball-game! No matter how inhumane that action seems, it obviously means to strongly underline the LITERAL misfortune of the defeated, the ones who will not be transferred.

«A sculpture on a side-wall depicts the beheading of a player in the center of the court. Many think this was the fate of the loser. In the sculpture, the blood spurts from his neck in the form of **serpents**. The decapitated player kneels before a ball *(Earth's material substance)*. Inside the ball, there is a scull speaking the words that symbolize death *(the second death of those, who will not be transferred and will be left behind, in the material carcass).*»

The new Place of Reception will be THERE, which will accommodate the Real/True 6th Human Root-Race of the New Humanity. Following this arrangement, the entire, swirling, material universe is absorbed... and gets lost in a 'jewel case' –like the 'genie' is jailed back in its bottle– which in turn (jewel-case) is surrendered by the Assistants to its Source.

540 **GOSPEL OF THOMAS,** JEAN YVES LELOUP:
«§10. Jesus says: I have sown fire upon the world, and now I tend it to a blaze. ... §71. Jesus says: I will overturn this house, and no one will be able to rebuild it. §98. Jesus said: The Kingdom of the Father is like the man who wanted to kill a man of power. First, he unsheathed *(drew forth)* his sword at home and thrust it into the wall to test his strength. Then he was able to kill the man of power.» [Eng. tr. JOSEPH ROWE]

The received images/symbols were accompanied by unprecedented sensations that completed the message I was getting. As he removed his hand from my forehead, I felt that I was starting to come back, as if I were being transformed into a luminous pixel (dot) to be inserted once again inside the 'image' of my material life, with an indescribable sensation. Unfortunately, being human, I cannot come up with more precise words to clearly describe such a phenomenal experience.
He went back to his seat and waited for me to recover from the shock of this unfamiliar sensation. ...He resumed.

THE SIDE-EFFECTS ON MATTER FROM THE DEPARTURE
OF THE SACRED ARCHETYPES

–The main source of material vitalization is here on Earth. THERE IS NO intelligent life anywhere else in the **densely** material universe.

> [541] **A) BARBARA MARCINIAK 'GAIA'** [Gr. tr. MATZOROU E.] *(Information through channeling)*:
> «Gaia is a unique planet in the universe, because it is a place where the possibility for the creation of life exists.»
> **B) DIMITRIOS EVANGELOPOULOS 'SUB-CHTHONIC MYSTERIES'**
> «…Centuries ago, the Serb prophet Tarabic had foreseen, that we will travel in space only to find lifeless worlds. We will search for life but we will not find it. Later, we will find life in those worlds, because we will be able to understand something which we couldn't before.»
> *It is obvious, that the life of those worlds is in a different energy-dimension and not in the thick material form of the planet. A confirmation to this point of view is the following excerpt from Blavatsky.*
> **C) BLAVATSKY H., P., 'THE SECRET DOCTRINE'** (I-153): «All planets as Mercury, Venus, Mars, Jupiter, Saturn, etc., etc., or our Earth, are as visible to us as our globe, because they are all on the same plane; while the superior fellow-globes of these planets are on other planes quite outside that of our terrestrial senses.»

Those who make you believe they are inhabitants of other planets are all solely energy-beings that materialize and de-materialize at will. They wander around the entire visible and invisible material universe pretending to be extraterrestrials while they are sustained and fed by men's bipolar thoughts and emotions. The Earth is simply their "hydro-electric" life-factory. This skeptomorphic damage that came about from this creation is restored only when the stolen Sacred 'Loot' is returned to its Source.

> [542] **CHALDEAN ORACLES**, GR. TR. ATHINOGENIS I., GRAVIGGER, P., EXCERPT FROM PROCLUS COMMENTARY (ON TIMAEUS D) **'SPEAKING ABOUT THE AEON'**:
> «Once he snatched, completely alone and for himself, the 'Flower of the Noûs (Mind)' from the Paternal Might, he is able to understand the Father's Noûs, and deliver that Noûs to all sources and upon all principles and has the power to swirl the never-tiring vortex and ever stay inside it.»

Then the Earth will join the Father's State, *(...Thy Kingdom come on Earth as it is in Heaven...)*. In order for this to happen though, it must be Transferred to the Prepared Place, passing through the Sacred Gate/Christ like a Key. As you can easily see, **it is not the Earth's densely material body/shell** that will be Transferred, but a Supreme manifestation of it: "(Because) neither flesh nor blood can inherit the kingdom of God." [LELOUP, J., Y., Gospel of Philip §23] There are two processes involved and interrelated in this entire procedure: The withdrawal of the Sacred Archetypes from the material creation and the Spiritual Transference of Earth and men so they can join the Fathers State.

During the Sacred withdrawal procedure, the Archetypes of the Laws that

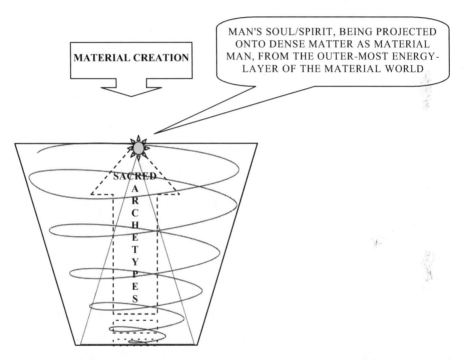

constitute material creation are set free on one hand, something that results in the collapse of the laws of nature, and on the other, the Earth and Man get Spiritually Transferred. While this is underway, the Sacred Archetype of **Life** will be cut off from dense matter –to return Home– abandoning one after the other all energy-planes, leaving to them only an 'echo' of life.

As the Sacred Archetypes will be withdrawn, the denser/inner energy-dimensions will be left at first –starting with dense visible matter– and gradually the subtler ones. As a side-effect, a disturbance of the boundaries/borders between dimensions will occur, so that one dimension will start permeating the other. In visible matter then, polymorphic astral beings will make their appearance; from the worst and most hideous ones (coming from the low/inferior astral regions) until –gradually– the 'best' ones from the last/higher astral dimensions. Man will still remain in the visible mate-

Don't skip chapters or bibliographic references

rial plane and will experience all the horror that will follow this process. The reason for this is that his time will not have come yet, because the place/position where he is really situated is the last energy-layer; and the withdrawal process will have not reached there yet. He will then think of the astral beings that will appear from the lower astral as the evil aliens and the beings that will appear from the higher astral regions as the benevolent extraterrestrials. In those hours, only the Knowledge of the Truth will be able to protect him. All this process will not be instantaneous, but in the material plane it will last for an un-definable time period, during which humanity will experience intense apocalyptical events, with the astral beings preying on it.

When, at last, the Sacred Withdrawal Process will reach the last energy-layer of this energy/material world where man is projected from, then, the so-called RAPTURE OF THE CHURCH will take place: At that moment, the Spiritual (in Essence) Man –carrying His Soul along with Him– will also be withdrawn, resulting in him permanently abandoning the outer energy-layer of the material universe, wherefrom he projected himself onto dense matter. This will cause him <u>to stop projecting his image</u> onto the densely material plane, thus giving the impression to those who will remain behind (inside matter) that the particular man disappears **through de-materialization**.

And Christ describes this process: "Then, two men will be in the field: <u>one will be taken</u> *(Transferred)* and the other left. Two women will be grinding in the mill: <u>one will be taken</u> *(Transferred)* and the other left." [Matthew 24:40-41]. And this happens because: "for the time will come when everyone *(men)* in the tombs *(who are inside bodies/tombs/graves)* shall hear His voice *(of the Son of Man)* and shall <u>come out</u> *(of the tombs/graves)*". [JOHN 5:28-29]

543 *To confirm that the above mentioned tombs (graves) correspond to the material bodies:*

A) THE APOCRYPHON OF JOHN, THE GNOSTIC SOCIETY LIBRARY: «The host of rulers and demons plotted together. They mixed fire and earth and water together with four blazing winds. They melded them together in great turbulence. Adam was brought into the shadow of death. They intended to make him anew this time from Earth, Water, Fire, Wind, which are Matter, Darkness, Desire, The Artificial Spirit. This all became a **tomb**, a new kind of body *(grave)*. Those thieves bound the man in it, enchained him in forgetfulness, made him subject to dying.» [Eng. tr. from Coptic: STEVAN DAVIES]

B) HERMES TRISMEGISTUS, HERMETIC TEXTS, VOL. I, RODAKIS P., TZAFEROPOU-
LOS AP., **SPEECH VII**: «§2. But first you must throw away the garment you
wear; the fabric of ignorance, the foundation of all malice; the bonds of corruption; the dark Coverture; <u>the living death; the Carcass that has senses, the
Sepulcher (tomb) you carry with you</u> *(everyone in the tombs)*; the domestical Thief, him <u>who hates through what he loves and envies through what he
hates</u>. §3. Of such sort is the enemy whose hateful garment you are wearing,
making you feel stressed and drawing you downwards, so that you don't
look upwards and face the beauty of the Truth and the Ἀγαθόν *(Agathón)* It
encompasses and loathe the garment's evil having acknowledged its dominion, as it wishes ill for you and it anaesthetizes the sensory organs, <u>the real
ones, not the alleged ones</u>. These organs have been obstructed with much
matter, and filled with abominable pleasure, so that you should neither hear
those things which you must hear *('He who has **ears** to hear, let him hear.'*
[MATTHEW 13:9]*)*, nor see those which you must see.»

Thus the promise will be fulfilled: "And I shall raise him up to life (resurrect) **on the very last day**" [JOHN 6:40], in order for the First Resurrection
to be completed. It will be that Sacred Hour when through the Son of
Man's Order, THE COMMAND FOR THE REVOCATION of the Sacred Archetype of Life and of all Divine Essence will be carried out and LIFE
along with SPIRIT will be abandoning every material (visible and invisible)
carrier/grave.

544 **THE APOCALYPSE OF ADAM, THE GNOSTIC SOCIETY LIBRARY, THE NAG
HAMMADI LIBRARY** [TRANSLATED BY GEORGE W. MACRAE]: «For the whole creation
that came from the dead earth will be under the authority of death. But those
who reflect upon the knowledge of the eternal God in their heart(s) will not
perish. For they have not received spirit from this kingdom alone, but they
have received (it) from a [.] eternal Angel. ...For their soul did not come
from a defiled hand, but it came from a great commandment of an eternal
Angel.» [Gr. edition: Pyrinos Kosmos Publ. (pp. 66, 67)]

The Holy Fathers of the Church of course state that Christ will then "judge
the living and the dead."

545 **A)** "And He *(Christ)* shall come again with glory to judge both the living
and the dead." *The Symbol of Faith of Orthodox Christians started being
formulated at the 1st Ecumenical Synod (Nicene Creed), summoned by emperor Constantine the Great on May 20, 325 A.D. and was supplemented at
the 2nd Ecumenical Synod under emperor Theodosius the First in 381 A.D.
(Ecumenical Synods – http://el.wikipedia.org/wiki)*

Don't skip chapters or bibliographic references

B) *This is how concepts where falsified and transformed Jesus into a judge, regardless of the fact He insisted that:*

THE GOSPEL OF JOHN:

(a) 3:17 «For God sent the Son into the world, **not to judge the world**, but that the world might be saved through Him. §18 He who believes in Him **is not judged.** He who doesn't believe has been judged already.»…Through (by) the reciprocal justice of the archon of this world, since he finally **chooses** to remain in this world of matter and is <u>necessarily</u> subdued to its laws.

(b) 5:24 «Most assuredly I tell you, he who hears My word, and believes Him who sent Me, has eternal life, and does **not** come into judgment *(from the rulers/archons of this world)*, but has already passed out of death into life.»

(c) 8:15 «You judge according to the flesh; **I judge no one.**»

(d) 8:24 «Therefore I said to you that you will die in your sins; for if you do not believe that I am He *(i.e. the one who alleviates the sins of the world)*, you shall die in your sins.»

(e) 12:47 «And if anyone hears My Words and does not believe/keep them, **I do not judge him**; for I did not come to judge the world but **to save** the world.» *(…from the imprisonment by the archon of this world)*.

THE FALSIFICATIONS:

(a) ACTS OF THE APOSTLES, 10:42 «And He commanded us to preach to the people, and to testify that it is He who is ordained by God to be the Judge of the living and the dead.»

(b) B TIMOTHY'S 4:1 «I do fully testify, therefore, before God, and the Lord Jesus Christ, who will judge the living and the dead at His appearing and His kingdom.»

(c) A PETER 4:5 «They will give an account to Him who is ready to judge the living and the dead.»

It is known however that the HyperUniverses DO NOT JUDGE. Surely, what the Scriptures **consider** as 'judgment' is the <u>INABILITY</u> for any form of entity other than the Sacred Essence <u>TO ENTER</u> into the Divine Spaces.

[546] **A) GOSPEL OF PHILIP** (Eng. tr.: PATERSON BROWN) www.metalog.org/files/Philip.html
«§61. The Lord says: Blessed is he who IS *(in the HyperCosmoi)* before he comes into Being *(in the material world)*. For he who IS, both WAS and SHALL BE.
§142. 'Every plant which my heavenly Father **has not** sown [shall be] rooted out. Those who are separated *(split Celestial Men)* shall be mated and the empty shall be filled *(the Souls that will accept the Essence-Spirit inside them)*.»

> **B) THE GOSPEL OF JOHN, CH. 3**: «§3. Jesus answered and said to him, "Tru-
> ly, truly, I say to you, <u>unless one is born from above*</u>, **he cannot** see the
> kingdom of God.»
> * *In most English translations, the word 'again' is incorrectly used,
> whereas, the original Greek Translation of the Seventy (O') uses the
> word: [ἄνωθεν = from above]*

The falsification of Christian religion is focused on the deliberate bypass-
ing/overlooking of the most fundamental <u>clarification</u> that: THE MANAG-
ER OF THE ENTIRE MATERIAL SYSTEM IS THE FALLEN "ARCHON OF THIS
WORLD" AND ONLY THE <u>LAWS OF MATTER</u> (condensed and not condensed
energy) DETERMINE RECIPROCAL JUSTICE/KARMA for those who insist on
incarnating in matter. Thus, all those who will depart <u>along</u> with the Sacred Archetypes from the visible and invisible material environment,
move on to the process of the First Resurrection WITHOUT JUDGMENT,
whereas those who remain in matter <u>are trapped</u> inside its laws and pass
on to the second death.

The distinction between the living and the 'dead' made in the Scriptures refers to the presence or absence of Spiritual Divine Essence inside men.
'Dead' are considered those, who are solely vitalized by the sum of their
energy-bodies *(artificial spirit)* without the tiniest grain of Sacred Spiritual
Essence in them either interwoven with their soul or in its self-substantial
form as a Divine Spark. And that is because this Spiritual Essence alone,
either preserved within a man, or revived –had it been in a dormant state, or
granted to someone after a warm petition– <u>defines</u> someone as really Alive.
This is why Jesus says: "Follow me and let the dead bury their own
dead". [MATTHEW 8:22] where it is clear that the spiritually 'dead' …can even
bury their own dead, simply because they only 'seem' alive.
What will then be taken away along with the departing Archetype of Life
towards the Immortal Fatherlands will solely be **the percentage** of True
Living **Essence** that exists within each man, enveloped by the Higher Mental
(Noetic) Body *(the wedding garment)* or by the "uniform/protective suit" of
Truth, because only thus will Men be able to enter Those Sacred Grounds.

> [547] **THE GOSPEL OF MATTHEW, CH. 22**: «§2. The kingdom of heaven is like a
> certain king, which made a marriage feast for his son. … §11. And when the
> King came in to see the guests, **he saw there a man which had not on a
> wedding garment** *(the higher mental body as the appropriate wedding
> garment)*: §12. And he said unto him, **<u>Friend, how did you come here not
> having a wedding garment?</u>** And he was speechless. §13. Then said the
> king to the servants, Bind him hand and foot, and take him away and cast
> him into outer darkness, there shall be weeping and grinding of teeth *(the
> entire future material universe)*. For many are called, but few are chosen.»

Don't skip chapters or bibliographic references

The greater the percentage of the salvaged Divine Essence/Spirit of each man is, the 'bigger' he will actually be. The infamous excerpt "and the last shall be first" relates precisely to this property. The 'first' among (material) men, because of their materialistic living circumstances have cultivated/nourished the egotism of 'being the first' thus sacrificing/consuming – as inversely proportional to their Ego– their Spiritual Essence/Fortune (Gr. Περι-ουσία [Peri-Ousseea = Essence = Fortune]) to win social recognition. So, what little "Essence" is left to them –if any– will finally amount to all they themselves will be. On the other hand, the 'fameless' and 'inferior' of men –the last ones– not having the luxury of egotism, being meek, have salvaged greater portions of their Divine Essence, rendering it greater, and thus appear bigger and 'first' among men…

Upon completion of the withdrawal of the Sacred Archetypes, **all energy-planes** as well as the corresponding **energy-bodies** of men who have stayed behind inside matter will remain as remnants of the previous energy-condition, until they have consumed every 'echo' of their life, up to its last drop. They will namely continue –**due to momentum**– to appear 'alive' for a little longer, just like the severed tail of the snake looks alive while writhing, regardless of the fact that it has been cut-off from the snake's main body.

After the Transference of the **Spiritual** Earth/Key, the situation in the densely material universe will change by a de-stabilization of the entire material plane. This de-stabilization will start when the aetheric creation **stops being projected** on dense matter.

---

548 **BARBARA MARCINIAK 'GAIA'** [Gr. trans. MATZOROU E.] *(Information through channeling)*
«p.74: When you transform Gaia and proceed to the Golden Age, this will change the rest of the universe as well.»

The concepts accompanying these events are unfamiliar, as the events themselves are. The difficulty lies in the verbal expression of conditions that do not refer to known situations.

–Since the Earth will be Transferred, shouldn't all its natural wealth be Transferred along with it?

–Unfortunately no, because in this reasoning, all those among men who prove to be SPIRITUALLY dead could also be transferred. **No manifestation of energy** has a place THERE, since energy is a byproduct of the **fall** of the Spirit and is a **constituent** of the material universe.

549 **HERMES TRISMEGISTUS,** HERMETIC TEXTS, VOL. II, RODAKIS P., TZAFEROPOU-LOS AP., **'EXCERPT IV, HERMES TO TAT'**: «§18…Wherefore I say that, feelings are both corporeal and mortal, as they resemble the *(material)* body in constitution… §19. On the contrary, Immortal Bodies have no feeling, precisely because they are immortal; feeling is nothing more than the pre-existence of good or evil in the body, or their departure. Whereas in the Immortal Bodies nothing is born and nothing dies; therefore feeling does not exist in them.»

Only the remaining Essence/Spirit shall return. And with great sorrow I declare to you, that this Essence/Spirit doesn't even exist in the best of animals, or in the plants… These ill-fated beings **have lost** everything Sacred they possessed, in previous creations. All that is left for them –as they remain an inextricable part of the spiral **remnant**– is to be continuously degraded, as they are piled up into more and more **inward** layers, constantly alternating their manifestation to even more inferior forms of beings, every time this vortex is vitalized by the creative quality of an Entity of the HyperCosmoi, whose total sum of creative attributes is deficient. When these beings eventually reach the last/inner layer, the only thing left for them would be to enter the realm of inorganic 'waste' of this conglomerate of death. This is the worst and most relentless hell! You men of course enjoy nature's 'beauties' that surround you. But you can't even in the least begin to conceive the **devastation** of these silent/speechless forms comprising nature. Don't be confused by the fact that life today appears at the 'bottom' of the energy-whirlpool of this universe. The importance lies in what energy-layer each living material existence **is projected** from onto the densely material "bottom".

ॐ·ॐ

The truth offered in this meeting is the 'uniform', the 'escape suit'. It can be compared to the life-jacket provided to those who have no means of getting on a life raft when the ship is sinking; because the Truth concerning Man's role inside the material creation is the Epignosis (deep awareness) that will save him. If man does not **realize** this cruel reality, he will remain idle.

550 **THE GOSPEL OF JOHN, CH. 6**: «§12. I have yet many more things to say to you, but ye cannot <u>bear</u> them now.»

By comprehending this painful truth though, he will be overcome by an anxiety which will activate the mechanisms of his existential self-

Don't skip chapters or bibliographic references

preservation; that is why Jesus says: "You shall know the Truth and the Truth shall set you free."

His eyes filled with deep sorrow. He looked out of the window and remained pensive... I interrupted his thoughts with a question.

–Won't the Earth <u>there</u> be as we know it?

–What you will perceive then will be something infinitely more beautiful than what you know today, but different …Yet we still haven't completed the 'full circle' of the Truth. What we still have to analyze is, what remains in this material carcass, when the Sacred Archetypes **making it appear alive,** depart! Then you shall understand that descriptions of hell by the 'quaint' ones are nothing compared to reality! Before we proceed to this distressing analysis though, we will try to examine the actions of the powers of this world when faced with the threat of starvation; because the departure of the Archetypes will cause their food-supply to stop.

Through all this previously communicated Truth, we have developed the **<u>Sacred Epignosis</u>,** which will envelope every Living Soul, like a 'uniform/escape suit' (Wedding Garment). But because during this period, the powers of this world play a very dirty 'game' against humanity, it is necessary for us to deliver an additional warning: What they are planning to do is to lock up the beautifully ornamented Souls 'inside the hold' of the sinking ship! Therefore, the 'suit' with which the Soul will present itself to the Holy Places <u>will not be enough</u>, if IT hasn't –before everything else– avoided such a detrimental lock-up. This lock-up refers to what John calls **'the marking of the beast'** in Revelation [13:17].

PARALLEL PROBABILITIES

In order for the following pieces of the Truth to be understood, and since they all refer to future conditions, we will examine a peculiarity of space-time pertaining to the parallel probabilities, so as to create a database of facts.

The space-time subject is very big and particularly complex for the structure of the human aethero-material brain. We will therefore divide it in two units. To begin with we shall look into the parallel probabilities concerning a partial condition of the entire concept of space-time and later on in our conversation we will deal with the subject more spherically.

"Time" for every Free, Sentient Intelligent Wholeness of the HyperCosmoi is one of the many 'dimensions' that exist THERE. As length, width and height are accessible to you, so is the condition of 'time' accessible THERE. Each Wholeness 'Born' THERE, automatically extends itself over the entire breadth of 'time' and can have partial and/or simultaneous **access** to all of its points. This way, IT can 'move' to every 'time point', experiencing it over again and/or changing it, in exactly the same manner you can touch a wall of your house many times, or paint it in different colors or decorate it with various paintings. 'Time' THERE, in other words, seems like plasticine that can be molded. There is no end to this "time condition" since THIS whole different FORM OF LIFE is constantly supplied by The Unuttered Principle Father/Mother of All. Every Intelligent Wholeness can also create 'pause periods' of this condition, if IT so wishes and for as long as IT wishes.

When Celestial Man 'WAS BORN' in the True Worlds, Present and infinite Future automatically existed for Him.

[551] **GOSPEL OF PHILIP** [En. tr. into Coptic, PATERSON BROWN]
www.metalog.org/files/philip.html
«§61. The Lord says: 'Blessed is he who IS *(in the HyperCosmoi)* before he comes into Being *(in matter)*! For he who IS, both WAS and SHALL BE'.»
The HyperCosmic conditions are completely nonexistent in the material plane. Therefore, there is no corresponding vocabulary to describe them.

But entering into the material universe, he created an extremely dangerous detour for His Life. This detour after his second fall (projection) to the area of condensed energy (dense visible matter), lead him into a trap that 'locked' him in moments of time: inside the 'locked time' of entrenched

Don't skip chapters or bibliographic references

matter. 'Locked time', as a condition, includes all probabilities inside it. It is in essence a sum of probabilities that coexist all together.

---

552 **NEW MODEL ALLOWS TIME-TRAVEL**: BBC & NEW SCIENTIST, JUNE 17, 2005
http://www.physics4u.gr/news/2005/scnews2007.html
«It is known that quantum behavior is governed by probabilities. Before something can be observed in action, there are various probabilities pertaining to its condition. But when its condition is measured, all those probabilities collapse into one. Uncertainty is expelled.»

Other probabilities are boldly imprinted, others less so, and others are totally faint –according to the energy invested or not invested in them– which never managed to be vitalized in the end.

All these choices are mathematical formulas of probabilities, interwoven with each other, structured by the creators of form and given shape into what you call 'parallel (material) universes'. *(Reference/information on parallel universes follows)*

AN ICONIC VIEW OF THE WORLD
MATERIAL/ANTI-MATERIAL UNIVERSE
PARALLEL PROBABILITIES & ENERGY-
FIELDS

With the initial fission (division) of The True Light, the energy-model –*the partially born [Trismegistus]*– of the sum of the previous expired creations, which had till then remained inert, was rekindled. In it, two states **co**existed: a sum of 'material' inactivated remnants and a corresponding "anti-material" sum. The initial vitalization activated: the **primary** 'material' universe and the **primary** 'anti-material' one, **with all their energy-dimensions,** <u>independent from each other (the universes)</u>, as the **divided reflection** of the Absolutely True (*A reminder: See reference #347, regarding anti-matter.*) The one (main) reflective/virtual (material) universe set opposite the other (main) reflective/virtual (anti-material) anti-universe create a large number of **reflective** parallel universes/probable choices.

---

553 *A reminder: Excerpt from the Ch. 'De-symbolization of the Original Sin':* **In the universe** *of reflection (Ant-Avges),* **everything is reflected reversely to the original.**[1] *With the fission of the True Light,* **two** *virtual universes were formulated through reflection: A material and an anti-material one. Like two mirrors one against the other, they then projected infinite reflective-virtual 'parallel' universes.*

---

[1] **DANEZIS M., THEODOSIOU S. 'COSMOLOGY OF THE INTELLECT'** (p.193):
«We all know that when an object is reflected in a mirror, the notions of left and right, as perceived by the subject, are **reversed** in the reflection.»

The universe + anti-universe that was finally vitalized, was the **central (primarily material and anti-material) spiral. Each corresponding layer** of the universe+anti-universe is interwoven with smaller probability-spirals of parallel universes, just like the images (reflections) that appear **onto** the two primary vis-à-vis mirrors (reflectors). Except, of course, that we are not talking about simple mirrors here!

554 **DANEZIS M., THEODOSIOU S. 'COSMOLOGY OF THE INTELLECT'** (p. 115): «The Universe could in fact be finite while the illusion of infinity could come about by the curvature of light bent around space, perhaps more than once. Every time, in every winding[1] of the curvature, a new reflection of one and only, original galaxy will be formed. That way, we would get the sense of an infinity of similar images, much as like being in a mirror-room.»

[1] **DANEZIS M., THEODOSIOU S., SOME PERSONAL THOUGHTS, 'MATTER AS A WHIRL VORTEX'** (p. 178): «...Based on the above, matter is composed of spherical whirls of energy, and in other words, it is an expression of the **unmanifested** universal energy. ...Most likely, the stored energy in the structural components of matter ...is consumed in order to increase the rotation velocity of the matter-vortices.»

These parallel universes, in their totality, host the **energy** that was produced but not vitalized: The goals e.g. that each man set (dreamt of) for his life and pursued, but **didn't** fulfill, have settled themselves **as energies** in a parallel universe, partially energizing it.

555 *The scientific world has a slightly different view on the matter.*
Before we proceed to the new subject, it would be wise to mention the purely scientific view about it.

A) SPACE-TIME – BLACK HOLES – PARALLEL UNIVERSES:
http://www.physics4u.gr/5lessons/lesson5.html:
«Einstein's Theory of Relativity combined space and time in a unified four-dimensional continuum, which he named space-time. We know that we can travel forth, back or sideways in space. So, why not be able to travel forwards or backwards in time too? As it is difficult to imagine the four dimensions, physicists usually suggest thinking of space-time as a taut, flat, flexible sheet[1] *(this taut, flexible 'sheet'/space-time is called brane – see end of reference for the definition of the term).* If there are no big masses in the area, that sheet remains flat and every object placed on it moves in a straight

Don't skip chapters or bibliographic references

line. However, a big body like the Sun creates a curvature on the sheet and in reality curves space-time. Every other object with a smaller mass like the Earth, which moves in space-time, **slides** into this curvature as it approaches the Sun's area. Thus, it gives the impression of being drawn by the Sun's big mass. This phenomenon of curvature in space-time is what generates gravity. The Universe is filled with big mass objects that exert gravitational forces. These objects force space-time to curve and do not allow it to remain completely flat.

Everything, including light, is forced to follow curved orbits in space-time. In essence, the light emitted from any distant star, instead of traveling in a straight line only to become blocked by any object ahead, it orbits (bends) around the obstacle and reaches the observer. When a star reaches the end of its life, it can collapse inwards under the influence of its gravity, to such extend, that its entire mass is compacted in an extremely small area with an exceptionally high density. This is what we call a black hole. Black holes exert a huge (attractive) gravitational force on the objects around them, so that nothing can escape them, not even the light. But what exactly causes the formation of a black hole in space-time? Relativity predicts that the center of a black hole is a point of infinite density (a space-time anomaly) where the laws of Physics no longer apply. Einstein's equations indicate that an anomaly of this sort doesn't simply create a curve on this imaginary flat sheet of space-time *(brane)* but rather creates a **tunnel** that pierces the flat sheet and instantly connects us with the other side. However, where is that other side? It can be elsewhere in space-time, whether in the past or the future, or even be in another universe.

Einstein's equations describe space-time as completely smooth and regular, like the flexible sheet we mentioned. The Relativity Theory refers only to the physics of large-scale phenomena. It cannot shed light to questions such as: What happens in the center of a black hole? Or, what happened at the moment of the Big Bang when the Universe was born and space-time itself was infinitely small? The study of these phenomena brings us back to the world of quantum-mechanics. If we could look at space-time through a magnifying lens, strong enough to reach the quantum scale, we would not see the regular and smooth sheet that Einstein perceived. Just like a ball from rubber foam seems smooth from a distance but its surface is irregular and rough from up close. In this depiction of space-time it is possible that small holes can open up as entrances to microscopic tunnels connecting the present with other points in time, or connecting this place and other places in the universe or even other universes. Another choice presented to future time-travelers would be to use these tiny wormholes and expand them.

To return to the question that occupied great minds ever since Newton, is the future predestined? Or is there an infinite number of possible futures? One way of dealing with this question from a quantum-theory point of view suggests that, not only is there an infinite number of futures, but they also take place in an infinite number of universes.»

PARALLEL WORLDS, http://news.pathfinder.gr/periscopio/3476.html

«One of the most basic laws of quantum mechanics is that the same cause doesn't always have the same results. For example, in certain quantum physics experiments, an atom (electron, photon) can 'decide' to go right or left. Therefore, even if the initial conditions are exactly the same, it is impossible to predict the direction it will take. The choice of either direction depends solely on luck.»

PARALLEL UNIVERSES MAKE QUANTUM SENSE:
a) http://www.physics4u.gr/articles/2007/parallel_universes_quantum_sense.html
b) http://www.newscientist.com/article/mg19526223.700-parallel-universes-make-quantum-sense.html

«The paradox is explained by Schrödinger's cat. In this famous mental experiment, a cat in a box can be declared as being both alive and dead. Traditionally it is considered that the act of observation, when we open the box to observe the cat, is what forces the cat to enter either state, alive or dead.»

PARALLEL WORLDS, http://news.pathfinder.gr/periscopio/3476.html

«This phenomenon *(the aforementioned one)* was extensively studied by the scientific community and many were those who put forth their own personal theories, in order to explain it, **but mainly to prevent this undesirable intervention of luck.** In 1957 the physicist Hugh Everett proposed a strange theory: luck as a factor doesn't really exist **because the atom followed both directions.** In 'our' world it moved towards the left and in 'another' towards the right. If, as suggested by Everett, quantum mechanics addresses the universe in its entirety, then it should also exist in a multitude of specific conditions. There would therefore be a 'multi-universe' made up of parallel universes, one for each physical probability. It thus follows that when you open the box to see Schrödinger's cat, the universe splits up forming two new universes, one whose future includes the observation of the living cat and another that observes the dead cat. Therefore, according to this theory, there is a multiplication of parallel worlds that branches out to infinity every time a person has to choose between multiple options. As the physicist Paul Davies said, it is a theory that is "cheap on assumptions but expensive on universes!»

Thus, in the following example, the particle's behavior obviously determines the creation of a parallel universe:

DANEZIS M., THEODOSIOU S. 'COSMOLOGY OF THE INTELLECT'

VACUUM AND THE MEANING OF THE HOLE - THE POSITIVE VACUUM (p. 218-219): «According to professor S. Theodorakis (1999): "An elegant application of

Don't skip chapters or bibliographic references

the physical basis that an absence can have is the **recent idea** of empty waves. In traditional Quantum Physics, a system sometimes behaves either as a particle or as a wave. But a heretical version, proposed by the physicist David Böhm, *(1917-1992, the scientist that we've met as the inspirer of the idea that the brain functions as a hologram which decodes a holographic universe, see Ch. 'Dense material plane')* advocates that every particle is followed by a wave, as real as the particle itself. When the particle <u>reaches to a fork of **options**</u> and follows one way, the wave splits in two and moves forward <u>in both ways</u> *(forming two parallel universes)*. The wave which follows the way that THE PARTICLE **DIDN'T** FOLLOW is called **AN EMPTY WAVE** and it is actually a positive vacuum.»

In other words, it creates a fictitious parallel universe which finally <u>HASN'T BEEN VITALIZED</u>, ...yet scientists insist that "it has been vitalized" in that 'other' parallel universe...

[1] «**BRANE:** Physicists Randall and Sundrum created a model of branes in which the visible universe is a brane incorporated in a bigger universe, just like a piece of seaweed floats in the ocean. Ordinary matter is **attached** to this brane. The usual particles like electrons and protons can <u>only</u> exist on this brane. We humans will not be able to enter other dimensions because the particles that form our bodies –electrons, protons, neutrons– remain **attached** to this brane that constitutes our world.»

In this view the 'brane' can be beautifully matched with the spider-web universe.

B) DANEZIS M., THEODOSIOU S. 'COSMOLOGY OF THE INTELLECT' (p. 196):

«Time is one of many (more than three) mathematical dimensions of the constant, non-Euclidean *(not flat)* and non-divisible space-time. Therefore the true nature of time, which constitutes the fourth dimension of a non-Euclidean space-time, cannot be perceived by the human senses using three dimensional scientific experiments. What we perceive as time through our experiments is none other than the depiction of the time-dimension in the space where our experiment takes place. And the spaces where thermodynamic, cosmological and quantum experiments take place differ not only in mathematical structure but in their properties as well. <u>That is, we have the image of the dimension of time being reflected on different mirrors</u> *(parallel universes)* <u>and therefore its images are ever so slightly different</u>. In this case, what we seek to find is the relation between the properties of the mirrors and not between the various reflections (projections) of time onto the mirrors.»

On the contrary though, the events this man finally experienced 'were clothed' with life by him. These then vitalized, settled in the primary material+anti-material model.

556 *At this point I feel I ought to elaborate on a particular detail: To some of our readers who have read Paul Dienach's book, 'The Valley of Roses', questions will obviously arise, which will cause confusion. My view is that Dienach's 'experience' took place in another parallel alternative probability/universe and not in this one which finally ended up being vitalized, hence the discrepancies and inconsistencies in relation to the real (contemporary) present.*

What humanity lives in today is the prevailing densely material universe, which, **as the dominant one,** is interwoven with and holds all parallel probabilities together while coexisting with them. Choices regarding which probabilities will be finally preferred and then vitalized are only made in the **dominant** universe and this holds true because each Sacred Archetypical Essence energizes it as it projects onto it. This will hold true though, only until the time of the definitive departure of the Archetype of Life. From the moment every 'borrowed' Archetype returns back to Its Source and thereafter, there will be no possibility for new vitalization, but only for **exploitation** of the percentage of life/energy that each alternative probability (virtual/parallel universe) **has stored** as a probable choice.

After the Earth's Spiritual Transference, the dissolution of the primary, densely material plane will follow, as well as that of the primary, antimaterial one. All other parallel probabilities of universes will remain behind **like the severed tail of the snake**, and will continue to oscillate a little longer, until they permanently stop too.

After the decision for the departure of the Life-Creating Power from material creation, the entities of this world are in real panic and are desperately looking for something to hold onto for their survival. (a) One group of them, being aware of the dead-end approaching, hope to escape to the Impassable Sacred HomeLands, not realizing that any form of energy is excluded from the spaces of Immaculate Spirit. (b) The greatest portion of their population however, hopes to cancel the Transference of the Sacred Archetypes, acting accordingly: To begin with, they try to control the energy-grid/shield that surrounds the Earth, which some call 'crystal grid'. This grid, in reality and contrary to what they claim, is hoped by them to function as a **'fence/barrier'** to avert the departure of the Sacred Archetypes. And secondly, **they kidnap the Souls of men as hostages.** They imagine that if the Soul as part of the Immortal Essence *(i.e. the Power of the creator's Mother)* is trapped, it will cause the cancelation of the operation. This is just wishful thinking of these powers, since the Spiritual Sacred Archetypes have **AL-READY** been returned to Their Source —one of the peculiarities of space-time which we'll examine later on.

Don't skip chapters or bibliographic references

---

557 **A) GOSPEL OF THOMAS,** JEAN YVES LELOUP: «§51. His disciples said to him: "When will the new world come?" He answered them: What you are waiting for **has already come**, but you do not see it.» [Eng. tr. JOSEPH ROWE]
B) BARBARA MARCINIAK 'GAIA' [Gr. trans. MATZOROU E.] *(information through channeling)*: «There is a point very far in your future, at which the Guardians of Time are very worried about the turn events have taken. …We come from the future and we search inside the corridors of time. This is our mission. From the probable future where we come, our goal is to change the past. Our intention is to change the probable future in which we are functioning, because this probable future in the evolution of the new movement of the universe is led to a tyranny *(...hell's version of the quaint, that we have been talking about...).*»

However, regarding the liberation of the souls being held hostage, this is something that is still at stake. We said earlier in our discussion that every human soul is created with two 'ingredients': the Breath/Essence of the fallen creator/Lucifer *(Plato Timaeus: Indivisible Essence)* on one hand and the subtler energy-matter of this world *(Plato Timaeus: Divisible Essence)*. Through reincarnations and consecutive plunges into dense matter, the soul continuously increased the percentage of the subtle energy that enveloped it as successive 'layers' of matter settled on it in the form of material dependencies. In contrast to that, the percentage of its Spiritual Essence continuously decreased, since it had definitively been cut off from Its Hyper-Cosmic Source. So the Soul's decisions depend on the prevailing percentage (either of the Spirit or of the subtle matter) it possesses. This is the determining factor which will define each soul's redemption or perdition.

Material, soulful man keeps life inside him like a battery. Prolongation of life of the astral entities of this world depends solely on the Souls of men. With the stored Life within the Soul, these entities will manage to go on living, **supplied** by it, prolonging their life this way in different 'living' conditions which we will examine later on.

---

558 **BARBARA MARCINIAK 'GAIA'** [Gr. tr. MATZOROU E.] *(information through channeling)*:
(a) (p. 35): «… For some in this universe, human beings are considered invaluable, although you actually have no idea about the treasure which is stored inside the human body. *(...as their life-giving (enlivening) energy-food!)*
(b) (pp. 205-206): Several energies *(energy entities)* **feed on** your life force. …They can suck it out or drain it from you in many ways.»

Their goal remains unaltered: the more souls held hostage, the longer their own life will be sustained. But if all men's Souls follow the procedure of Spiritual Transference, then all hope is lost for these dark powers. They therefore imagine that Life/Soul must be 'locked in' so that it **cannot** escape during the Transference. In order for this 'locking in' to have a positive outcome, its success must be ensured for every alternative parallel probability of time. What fluctuates in each alternative parallel time-probability is THE NUMBER OF HUMAN SOULS SAVED. Thus their interest focuses on the number of men **they will trick into** following them, and this is why they are methodically laying out many parallel alternative plans of operation.

—And if a soul is saved in one alternative probability and lost in another, what happens with that soul in the end?

—If you remember, I made clear, that the probability, which **will finally be vitalized** in the **primary material** universe, is the **only one that holds true**.

THE PLANS OF THE DARK POWERS

The venture the Dark Powers are preparing is considered uniquely innovative, extremely dangerous, and therefore moves of absolute accuracy, planning and balance are required. After the Transference of the Sacred Archetypes to their Source, conditions in the densely material- and energy-universe will be very different from the present, until they (the new conditions) cease to exist completely as well. Life on Earth will enter a higher spiritual level, leaving the densely material one behind.

---

559 **BARBARA MARCINIAK 'GAIA'** [Gr. trans. MATZOROU E.] *(Information through channeling)* p. 281: «In this era, the downfall of the world civilization will happen as well as the awakening of a new form of consciousness. This is brand new in your history.»

In this New Spiritual State that Man will Be Transferred to, he will come in contact with True Life for the first time. What he will then realize is that his previous 'life' in dense matter took place inside a fake dollhouse, whereas the True one he will be experiencing is in a real palace. Only then will man realize that the material world he was considering true for so many centuries, was merely an imitation covered with fake drawings he thought were 'living'. Then and there will he grasp what Being Alive really means!

As imprisoned Life leaves matter behind and moves on to the New Condition, material Earth will remain a dead and inorganic celestial body, in the form most planets in the material universe are today. Those men who will not manage to be Spiritually Transferred to the Sacred Spaces and will remain on Earth's dense version will perish. The dense matter that will initially be left behind, will give its place to the total dissolution of the dense, material, visible world, as well as the anti-material one, in a **rapidly** evolving process.

---

560 A) BARBARA MARCINIAK 'GAIA' [Gr. trans. MATZOROU E.] p. 74:
«When you transform Gaia and proceed to the Golden Age, this will change the rest of the universe as well.»
B) RUDOLF STEINER "FROM THE AKASHA CHRONICLE, COSMIC MEMORY" (p. 138)
«On the one hand, the coming evolution of Earth will develop today's life of images and thoughts to an even higher, more subtle and more complete condition. ...Man will only attain a complete life on the next Planet, into which the Earth **will be transformed** and which is called 'Jupiter'[1] in apocryphal science.»
[1] *Steiner names the different states/conditions of existence as 'Planets' (reference #527 B)*

C) BLAVATSKY H., P., 'THE SECRET DOCTRINE' (I-159):

«Everything in the metaphysical as in the physical Universe is septenary *(sevenfold)*. Hence every sidereal body ...is credited with six companion globes.[1] The evolution of life proceeds on these seven globes or bodies from the 1st to the 7th in Seven ROUNDS or Seven Cycles.

...These globes are formed by a process which the Occultists call the 're-birth of planetary chains (or rings)'.

[1] (I-153): For instance, all such planets as Mercury, Venus, Mars, Jupiter, Saturn, etc., or our Earth, are as visible to us as our globe, because they are all on the same plane; while the superior fellow-globes of these planets are on other planes quite outside that of our terrestrial senses.

(I-154, 155): It is said that the planetary chains having their 'Days' and their 'Nights' -- i.e., periods of activity or life, and of inertia or death -- and behave in heaven as do men on Earth: they generate their likes, get old, and become personally extinct, their spiritual principles only living in their progeny as a survival of themselves. ...When a planetary chain is in its last Round, its Globe 1 or A, before finally dying out, sends all its energy and 'principles' into a neutral center of latent force, a 'laya center', and thereby animates (informs) a new nucleus of undifferentiated substance or matter, i.e., calls it into activity or gives it life.»

As we have previously said, apart from the primary material and anti-material universes there is also a great number of parallel universes of alternative choices with energy trapped inside them. The energy trapped there includes 'life' remnants which, after The Transference, will remain imprisoned there and will be like the severed tail of the snake which oscillates a little longer until it permanently stops. So, it is **these** virtual, holographic, parallel universes they misleadingly call the '5th dimension', that the powers of this world have invested all their hopes in, and **it is there** they are planning to transport the deluded humanity that will **not** be Spiritually Transferred passing onto the First Resurrection.

[561] **'CAN WE FIND A PLACE IN A PARALLEL UNIVERSE?'**
JUNE 2003: COMMENT ON MAX TEGMARK'S ARTICLE IN SCIENTIFIC AMERICAN MAGAZINE
http://www.physics4u.gr/articles/2003/paralleluni.html

«In the last issue of the acclaimed 'Scientific American' magazine, there was an excellent article on the existence of parallel Worlds or Universes. In this article, written by astrophysicist Max Tegmark of the University of Pennsylvania, he claims that parallel universes <u>do</u> exist. He doesn't say that they probably exist, but that he is absolutely certain that they exist, beyond any doubt.»

Don't skip chapters or bibliographic references

From these parallel probabilities/universes as well as from every man-battery they will absorb every trace of stored 'living' energy. When the last drop of life has been consumed, then all will fade away and everything will pass on to the second death. This will be absolute hell.

---

562 A) BLAVATSKY H., P., 'THE SECRET DOCTRINE' (I-373, 374):

«The cycle of creation of the lives of Kosmos is run down *(coming to an end)*, because the energy of the manifested 'Word' *(Logos)* has its growth, culmination, and decrease *(oscillation)*, as have all things temporary, however long their duration.»

B) JOHN'S REVELATION 20: «§6. Blessed and holy are those who have part in the first resurrection. The second death has no power over them...»

The archons of this world, aware that the true destination of the men who will be redeemed are the True HyperCosmoi, and aiming to maximize the delusion, announce to the mediums/channels that support and cooperate with them, that they allegedly also intend to transport humanity "elsewhere", and promote the idea of the 5th dimension. These mediums though have not been informed by their scheming patrons that this 5th dimension is in reality a parallel, alternative universe which is located inside the broader regions these twofold astral powers operate in. *(See reference #635 –the last one of the book– which supports exactly that which is also stated in the Apocalypse (Revelation) but in code)*

So when the process of homecoming of the primordial Archetypes of creation is completed, humanity will have been divided in: (a) those who will be successful participants in the process of the First Resurrection and will have joined True Life in the State of the Father and (b) the second group of the deluded men who have followed the 'experts' to the second death of the snake's cut-off tail, moving to the parallel universes of the 5th dimension as their batteries. And all this because matter in the form you know will permanently cease to exist.

---

563 A) EXCERPT FROM BILL HAMILTON'S INTERVIEW TO LINDA MOULTON (PROGRAMMER ANALYST AT UCLA) http://www.boomspeed.com/joseph2/J-Rod2.htm:

«B. HAMILTON: According to Dr. Burisch, the EBENs (Extraterrestrial Biological Entities) are here to try to alter our time lines, our future *(the convergent time line)*. The reason for this is that, according to him *(Dr. Burisch)* as fantastic as it sounds they travel in time. So, they already know, or they know as a memory, what happened here. There is a coming catastrophe that drastically reduces the population of the earth **and splits the earth into two populations**. And these two populations **isolated from each other** evolve

---

from what we know as Homo sapiens **into two different species**.

...**B. HAMILTON**: What I'm saying is that they evolved in our future, according to the Doctrine of the Convergent Time Lines. In other words, they come from our future and they have traveled backwards to their past - or our current present.

L. MOULTON: They are coming back because they are trying to prevent some type of catastrophe?

B. HAMILTON: Yes, they are trying to alter the time *(converging)* line...

L. MOULTON: Is this an implication that they came into the Homo sapiens future at some point in the far distance that they are now reaching back into our genetic bloodlines for genetic material that they think might help them in some way?

B. HAMILTON: From what I understand, they are an **altered form**, a new species that branched off Homo sapiens.

L. MOULTON: In what was a catastrophe of what we would call our future?

B. HAMILTON: Yes.

L. MOULTON: Did Dan Burisch have any idea what the catastrophe is in the coming future?

B. HAMILTON: He cannot specifically say what occurred. However, he places it as happening approximately a decade from now. *(This interview was taken in 2002)*

L. MOULTON: In that 2012 time-period that is supposed to be the end of the Mayan Grand Calendar?

B. HAMILTON: Yes. But **it is not rigidly fixed**. It could happen any time between now and then, or even a little past that time. I'm not certain whether it is something that is an instant cataclysmic event of some kind. I have no idea.»

B) *Mayas' Priest Chilam Balam prophesizes about the end of the world, in the last page of their calendar.*

«For **half** of them (men), there will be food, for others misfortune;»

C) THE GOSPEL OF JOHN, CH. 10: "§9. I am the gate: If anyone enters through Me, *(like the ball of the Maya through the stone ring)* he shall be saved, and shall go in and **come out** *(get to the other side)* and *(there)* find pasture."

D) THE GOSPEL OF MATTHEW, CH. 24: «§40-42. Then two men will be in the field: one will be taken and the other left *(=transferred to a more spiritual level)*. Two women will be grinding at the mill: one will be taken and the other left.»

In those parallel-probability universes, conditions are extremely strange, and no physical/material body can survive.

Don't skip chapters or bibliographic references

---

564 **A) PARALLEL UNIVERSES BY MAX TEGMARK (1ST PART)**
From SCIENTIFIC AMERICAN, June 2003
http://www.physics4u.gr/articles/2003/paralleluni1.html
«Max Tegmark, Ph.D. is a specialist in the analysis of Cosmic Background Radiation and in the formation of galaxy clusters. Many of his papers are about the notion of parallel universes. ...He has also worked on the dimensionality of space-time and <u>the possibility that the fundamental laws of physics may vary from place to place.</u>»

B) PARALLEL UNIVERSES BY MAX TEGMARK
METANEXUS INSTITUTE: VIEWS: 27-02-2002
http://www.metanexus.net/magazine/ArticleDetail/tabid/68/id/5685/Default.aspx

(a) SUMMARY: «The notion that our observable universe is merely a small part of a larger 'multiverse' is attracting increasing attention among physicists, particularly those working on cosmology (motivated by inflation theory and apparent fine-tuning) and string theory (motivated by multiple 'vacuum' states). The goal of the article is to survey the various types of parallel universes proposed, focusing on: a) the evidence and physical motivation for each type, b) the extent to which the ideas are experimentally testable, c) <u>what each type would be like to inhabit</u> and d) philosophical implications and the structure of the multiverse. **It is not widely appreciated that there are in fact numerous different types of multiverses being proposed**. The key goal of this article is to describe the different kinds and the relationship between them. People have speculated about such things since the dawn of time, but now it's gradually becoming **experimentally testable**.»

(b) PARALLEL UNIVERSES, http://www.metanexus.net/essay/parallel-universes:
«Paul Davies ...comments on the parallel universes of Max Tegmark: "One feature that might be special about our universe, is that there are conscious beings inhabiting it, beings that can look in awe at their world and reflect on the nature of existence. Mathematical studies suggest that some key features of our universe are rather sensitive to the precise form of the laws of physics, so that if we could play God and tinker with, say, the masses of the elementary particles, or the relative strengths of the fundamental forces, those key features would be compromised. **Life would probably not have risen in a universe with even slightly different (natural) laws.**»

For the 'settlement' of humanity in the new chosen **doubly virtual** territory special preparations are necessary. These preparations concern the **primary goals** of the archons of this world, and in order for these activities to remain **secret** they have had to divert the attention and the interests of men to the other 'problems' they simultaneously methodize, as **preconditions to support their goals.**

THE MYTH OF 'EXTRATERRESTRIALS'

For starters, we must mention a different subject, which mustn't be omitted from our discussion. It is a subject that has received numerous varying attacks, it is included in the "forbidden ones", and to the dark powers it is a 'hot' subject because its disclosure is their Achilles' heel. This is why hypotheses relating to this subject had to be 'blurred' and meddled with to such an extent, that it would be impossible for someone to distinguish truth from lies. And I am talking about the myth of 'extraterrestrials'…

We have initially said that those, who people call "extraterrestrials", are in their vast majority nothing but the twofold forces of the creators 'homogenized' with the skeptomorphic 'produce' of men that expanded in superfast rates creating a dynasty (we will later examine another small percentage of them, belonging to a different category). These skeptomorphic powers (of the side-effect energy) were created by the violence, hypocrisy, ignorance, passions, fears, hatreds and self-indulging kindnesses of men, and this is why they *(skeptomorphs)* exhibit all this perversion under the mask of hypocrisy they were born from.

At the end of the Race/Gender of Heroes and when the Clash of the Titans ended, the basic treaties/terms between the creators and the skeptomorphic powers –Titans, Giants, Nephelim– were agreed upon. These terms led to the metamorphosis of the previous Race of Heroes to the spiritually deprived human 5th Root-Race –the Iron-Race.

[565] *This generation of contemporary men is considered spiritually deprived due to the fact that people have erroneously equated Spirit with education and any cultural 'polish', when in reality, Spirituality is identified with Divine Epignosis.*

The fundamental and mandatory commitment of that agreement, which prohibited materialization of both powers (gods and daemons) in front of humans, became their second nature.

In order for these powers to organize plans for **their** salvation, they started a methodical venture of actions in the beginning of the twentieth century and being in accord with their habits on one hand and the secrecy of their plans on the other, they chose their operational bases to be located in earthly underground facilities. Nevertheless, had they not presented themselves as victims of their own misfortune at times, and as the saviors of men at others (using lies as their basic tools) they wouldn't have already achieved all they have until now. Men, under the

Don't skip chapters or bibliographic references

influence of the positive, lethargic, rose-tinted complacency regarding their existence and under the weight of the constantly expanding problems of materialistic everyday life, are in danger of really perishing due to the schemes of these powers.

So these entities stealthily appear (materialize) in their 'best' material form on the Earth's surface, and come in contact with the highest administrative circles of men, in order to ensure the secrecy they so desperately need from them *(reference #568 follows)*. The devious schemes they had been 'concocting' should under no circumstances be communicated to men, so they were in absolute need for some 'individuals' to continuously cover the tracks their actions necessarily left behind. These activities concerned their primary goals and would inevitably produce evidence of their existence, which would create suspicion and raise questions. To avoid having a multitude of people investigating what exactly was happening they needed a cover-up. After all their operations included various sectors of activity in the mineral, plant, animal and human kingdoms, which in their entirety would certainly raise serious suspicions. And since this suppression of facts could not be organized or implemented by men in the lower ranks of the social hierarchy, cooperation and cover from the world-leaders' side was necessary.

> **566** **MILTON WILLIAM COOPER**: *(Former US Navy Officer, Intelligence Dept.)* «They ask the government to keep their presence here secret.»

By offering advanced technology as a gift yielding significant profit, they ensured their cover *(references 568 H & I follow)*. Their demands seemed simple but their goals were devious.
Starting with the excuse of a 'misfortune' of their race –since they **initially** introduced themselves as beings from other planets– they were asking for 'permission' from various authorities to collect human genetic material in order to rebuild their 'destroyed' species *(reference #568 C follows)*. They then requested (in order to ensure the secrecy they required) underground facilities to be provided to them, so that within those bases they could 'arrange' human genes along with theirs, creating a new species… *(References 568 F & G follow)*
Underground facilities were put to operation and multi-level underground buildings were built beneath the Earth's surface, which in collaboration with the 'aliens', were equipped with the new technology *(reference #568 F, follows)*. Everything seemed to go according to plan, when some of the people working inside those secret facilities did not honor their commitment to se-

crecy and started 'leaking' information. Penalties were then used, along with a refutation marathon, in order to falsify disclosures, covering them up with improvised pretenses. Again, new information leaks –different from the first ones this time– when excitement for the 'aliens' was replaced by fear of them. Yet again, a new, more intense new barrage of denials, caricatures of the truth and stigmatization of every informer ensued, to the extent of even violently 'shutting them up for good' in some cases.

> **567 MILTON WILLIAM COOPER** *(Former US Navy Officer, Information Dept.* **Murdered** *on 6/11/01, 12:15 pm) He said:*
>
> «A basic truth can be used as foundation for a whole mountain of lies. If we dig deep enough into the mountain of lies and bring out that truth and place it at the top of the mountain of lies, then the entire mountain will collapse under the weight of that truth…Everything we have been taught is a lie. Reality is not at all what we perceive it to be.»

With all these techniques they 'weaved' the conditions for the success of their operation. Thus, the creation **of their own 'Noah's ark'** with the collection of mineral wealth, cereal "elements", domestic animal DNA and human genes, would grant them the tools **so as to simulate a 'living' scenery in a parallel reality** (in a parallel universe), since they would no longer have any access to the Tools of Creation/Archetypes, once these would be permanently returned to their Source. Hence they worked and still continue to do so, in order to ensure the longest possible life duration for themselves.

What was necessary to them primarily was: (a) men with a living Soul trapped inside them, so that the energy produced by IT would nourish them, (b) food for the sustenance of their human nutritional supply with the collection of the DNA of animals edible by humans *(reference #568 J follows)*, (c) constituents of predominantly cereal plants which are gathered in the form of plasma –please remember agro-glyphs– *(called* **crop circles** *by some);* the splendor of these formations in the fields has the sole purpose of detracting attention from what is really happening there *(reference #568 K follows)* and (d) mineral material for the 'dressing-up' of the 'scenery' in some parallel universe so as to make it simulate life.

Their actions therefore are divided in two categories. In the first category we have the actions which will create the **substructure** and appropriate conditions to support their real goals and in the second, the actions facilitating their completion.

Don't skip chapters or bibliographic references

568 *It's time to move on to a different kind of information. And since this new data to be presented will be innovative to many readers, I consider it worthwhile to bring forth some evidence for greater understanding. I am presenting therefore part of the investigation of authors Gian-noulakis & Kavakopoulos, starting with the interview given by French mathematician and researcher Jacques Vallée.*

WHO THEY ARE:

A) GIANNOULAKIS, P., KAVAKOPOULOS, L., 'THE TRUTH ABOUT UFO'S AND EX-TRATERRESTRIAL CONSPIRACIES'
(a) APPENDIX I: A CONVERSATION WITH JACQUES VALLÉE
«JACQUES VALLÉE: In ten years, I accumulated over two hundred such cases. My last book is really a summary of the more interesting of these cases. I feel that I could go before a committee of scientists and convince them that there is overwhelming evidence that the UFO phenomenon exists and that it is an unrecognized, unexplained phenomenon for science, but something that I think I could prove. My personal contention is that the phenomenon is the result of an 'intelligence', or rather, that it is a technology directed by an intelligence, and that this 'intelligence' is capable of manipulating space and time in ways we don't understand. I could convince a committee of my peers that the phenomenon is real, and that we simply cannot understand it. There may be alternative speculations regarding this issue. The essential conclusion I'm tending to, is that the origin of the phenomenon of this alien intelligence <u>is not necessarily extraterrestrial</u>.

...I think this is an opportunity to learn something very fundamental about the universe because, not only is the phenomenon or technology capable of manipulating space and time in ways that we don't understand, it's also manipulating the psychic environment of the witness. I tried to introduce that idea when I wrote (my book) 'Invisible College'. At that time, the UFO community was not ready for it. ...In truth, I think we are dealing with a something that is both technological and psychic, and seems to be able to manipulate other dimensions.

I don't have a good explanation for the question why this *(extraterrestrial)* technology seems to appear in a form **that uses images from our own un-conscious**. *(This is understandable, since these entities are OUR VERY OWN skeptomorphic creations: Our tulpas!)* There are cases, where the phenomenon begins by being 'amorphous' and then starts to assume form, matching the expectations of the eyewitnesses.

There are two ways to deal intellectually with that: One is to say it's a phenomenon of the brain which is very good at 'reading' recognizable images in amorphous things like clouds. It may be however, that the phenomenon itself is using our reactions to it in order to turn into something that we expect or understand. ...I think the way we get into trouble studying UFOs is that we mix up different levels involved: the physical level, the psychological level and the mythological or social level.

I want to clearly distinguish these three levels because we need a different type of 'mythology' to deal with each set of events.

At the physical level, all we know is that there are material, physical objects which leave traces, interact with the environment, throw off light, heat and probably pulse microwaves in very interesting ways. From the above we conclude that their appearance requires a great deal of energy.

... I have seen things that shouldn't have been there, when I was tracking satellites at the Paris Observatory. And that's really what started my research. Obviously, I had heard of UFOs before then, but I had always thought that if UFOs actually existed, astronomers would have told us. I was wrong. Once we got eleven unknown data-points, which were in orbit around the Earth, on a magnetic tape and wanted to run the tape through a computer and compute their exact orbit, the man in charge of the project confiscated the tape and erased it. That's really what got me started, because I suddenly realized that astronomers **saw things they never reported**.

...We live in a strange universe and we are forced to walk blindly. Now theorists are talking about a multidimensional universe, a theory which, ten years ago, would have seemed marginal. They all agree that we can't explain universe with only four dimensions. So, how many do we need? That depends on who do we listen to. Maybe there are 5 or even 100 dimensions, who knows, but we all agree that there can't be only four. Personally I feel that more levels of consciousness must exist here on Earth.»

(b) (APPENDIX II - A DISCUSSION WITH WHITLEY STRIEBER)

«When the lady touched the 'visitor' she thought it was an animal that had entered the room. Then the creature went to another room where some other people saw it transforming into 'something' that had an eagle's head, reminiscent of all those mythological models that exist deep within. Next, the creature disappeared into thin air. When we went out looking for it, we saw a hooded silver and semi-transparent being, flying from one side of the house to the woods and vanish with zigzags in the trees. So, it couldn't have been a ghost. The witnesses, who saw it in the eagle form, felt a heat wave to the point of thinking that the house was on fire *(just like hell)*.

...Of a being having three or rather four states. The first one was absolutely physical, you could touch it, it had substance. The second state was when it transformed into something completely different in front of the witnesses' eyes. After that, it became invisible and in its fourth state, it moved in a semi-transparent shape, leaving heat waves behind. …My experience taught me that (the extraterrestrial beings, the visitors) are deeply related to the human state *(thoughtforms)*. They are not remnants of non-consciousness, but something that transcends what we call consciousness. The human brain seems to somehow work at a supernatural and hyper-dimensional level.»

Since most people doubt the UFO reality, regarding them as 'myths' of the quaint or the mentally disturbed –since, this is what the public opinion should believe, through systematic manipulation– I consider it necessary (before the main volume of foot-notes regarding this issue) to report something, that will puzzle most of the readers, that perhaps those incidents are not 'myths' after all…

THE EVIDENCE:

B) SPECIAL EDITION OF 'STRANGE' MAGAZINE –EXTRATERRESTRIALS + UFO –AN ARTICLE BY DIMITRIOS EVANGELOPOULOS– THE GOVERNMENT COVER-UP CHRONICLE

«… Until the beginning of the 70's, the FBI officially stated that they were not interested in any strange incident. They even denied they had gathered evidence about the UFO subject, which was particularly blown out of proportion between the years 1947-54. Even after Hoover's death in 1972 (J. Edgar Hoover was appointed director of the FBI in 1924), the FBI continued to deny any connection with the UFO study. Then, at the beginning of 1975, when the stern J. E. Hoover and the records were long forgotten and the politicians acquired more freedom of movement, F.O.I.A. (Freedom of Information Act) was implemented by the U.S. Department of Justice. The F.O.I.A. was enacted in 1967, but didn't go in effect, obviously because of the omnipotent Hoover's pressures on the issue. The Act defines that federal agencies, like the FBI, must provide access to records when requested by a citizen who wants to investigate a federal matter. In 1976, and after several researchers had repeatedly requested it, more than 1,000 pages containing FBI agents' reports about UFO were delivered to the public, although, until then, its agents had supposedly no connection with such things…

Nowadays you can download a sufficient number of these documents from the FBI homepage (www.fbi.gov) through the internet. …On page http://foia.fbi.gov, the FBI explains the time consuming proceedings which are needed in order to obtain these documents by mail. …The FBI concludes that more than 300.000 requests have been made during the 30 last years and more than 6.000.000 pages have been delivered to the public.»

The foundations of this entire 'campaign' were set between the end of the 19th and the beginning of the 20th century. Carefully selected individuals –

most of whom thought they were acting for a noble cause and some of them in full ignorance– became the 'wombs' to 'support' the plans of these invisible forces. Others created the necessary prerequisites, by 'weaving' the appropriate conditions, upon which these radical plans would be based.

Any reference to individual cases would lead us far from our subject. However, it would perhaps be worthwhile for the most meticulous ones to research Tesla's enigmatic personality, as well as his 'experiments'.

It was during World War II, when the elite SS divisions first came in contact with the powers of 'Hollow Earth'.

Most of the officers, led by Hitler himself, comprised the two principal Secret Societies which fabricated the outcome of the war, and were at the core of the 3rd Reich and Nazism.

One was the Thule Society and the other the Vril Society. Both these Secret Societies of Initiation focused their attention on the energy which is situated inside Earth, namely Vril-energy. These Secret Initiation Societies, mostly guided by dark astral entities –despite the fact they were disguised as 'luminous' ones– manipulated the ones possessing high ranks towards their secret goals.

During the war, expeditions were sent to enter the "Hollow Earth", which were obviously successful. After the end of the war and Germany's defeat, all this 'expertise' gathered from the subterranean worlds passed on to the Americans. So did the 'public relations' with the ... intraterrestrials.

Reference to: **'TRITO MATI' MAGAZINE ISSUE 85 MARCH 2000 – 'HITLER'S BIG SECRET'** *and the book* **'HOLLOW EARTH' BY IOANNIS GIANNOPOULOS.**

And now, we once again continue the presentation of data from Giannoulakis-Kavakopoulos' book:

THE CHRONICLE:

C) THE TRUTH ABOUT UFO'S AND EXTRATERRESTRIAL CONSPIRACIES: GIANNOULAKIS-KAVAKOPOULOS (p. 120-124)

«**John Lear Jr.**, a CIA pilot and son of John Lear Sr., creator of the 'Lear Jet', writes in his startling text 'The UFO Cover-Up', a large part of which is worth quoting:

In its effort to protect democracy, our government sold us to the aliens. And here is how it happened. But before I begin I'd like to offer a word in the defense of those who bargained us away. They had the best of intentions. Germany may have recovered a flying saucer in 1939. General James H. Doolittle went to Sweden in 1946 to investigate reports of 'ghost rockets' (UFOs) thousands of which had been sighted over a seven month period. The 'horrible truth' was known by only a few persons.

'They' were indeed ugly creatures, shaped like praying mantises and were more advanced than us by perhaps as much as a billion years. Of the original group that were the first to learn the 'horrible truth' several committed suicide, the most prominent of whom being Defense Secretary James V. Forrestal, who jumped to his death from a 16th-story hospital-window. Secretary Forrestal's medical records are sealed to this day.

President Truman quickly put a lid on the secret and turned the screws so tight that the general public still thinks that flying saucers are a joke. Have I ever got a surprise for them! In 1947 President Truman established a group of 12 (twelve) top military and scientific personnel of their time. They were known as MJ-12. Although the group exists today, none of the original members are still alive. The last one to die was Gordon Gray, former Secretary of the Army, in 1984. As each member passed away, the group itself appointed a new member to fill the position. There is some speculation that the group known as MJ-12 expanded to at least several more members. There were several more saucer crashes in the late 1940's: one in Roswell, New Mexico; one in Aztec, New Mexico; and one near Laredo, Texas, about 30 miles inside the Mexican border.

Consider if you will the position of the United States Government at that time. They proudly thought of themselves as the most powerful nation on earth. ...Imagine their sock as they attempted to determine how these strange saucers were powered and could discover no part even remotely similar to components they were familiar with.

...The stories are legendary of transporting *(by terrestrial officers)* crashed saucers over long distances, moving only at night, purchasing entire farms, slashing through forests, blocking major highways, sometimes driving two or three lo-boys in tandem with an extraterrestrial load a hundred feet in diameter.

On April 25, 1964, the first official communication between these aliens and the U.S. Government took place at Holloman Air Force Base in New Mexico. During the late 60's or early 70's, the MJ-12, representing the U.S. Government, made a deal with these creatures called EBE's (extraterrestrial biological entities, named by Detlev Bronk, original MJ-12 member and sixth president of Johns Hopkins University). The 'deal' was that **in exchange for technology** that they would provide to us, we agreed to 'ignore' the **abductions** that were going on and suppress information on the cattle mutilations.

...In fact, the purposes for the abductions turned out to be:

▪ Insertion of a 3mm spherical device through the nasal cavity of the abductees into the brain. The device is used for the biological monitoring, tracking and control of the abducted.

▪ Termination of some people so that they could function as living sources for biological material and substances.

- Termination of individuals who represent a threat to the continuation of their activity.
- Genetic engineering experiments.
- Impregnation of human females and early termination of pregnancies to procure the crossbred infant.

The U.S. Government was not initially aware of the far-reaching consequences of their 'deal'. They were led to believe that the abductions were essentially benign, and since they figured the abductions would probably go on anyway whether or not they agreed, they merely insisted that a current list of abductees be submitted, on a periodic basis, to MJ-12 and the National Security Council [...] The EBE's have a genetic disorder in that their digestive system is atrophied and not functional. Some speculate that they were involved in some type of accident or nuclear war, or that they are possibly on the back side of an evolutionary genetic curve. In order to sustain themselves, they use an enzyme or hormonal secretion obtained from the tissue that they extract from humans and animals. (Note: Cows and humans are genetically similar.) *(Let us recall the sacrifices that humanity offered to gods and demons during the past centuries in order to propitiate them).*

The cattle mutilations were prevalent throughout the period 1973-1983 ...The various parts of the body are taken to various **underground** laboratories *(always to ... Tartara)* one of which is known to be near the small New Mexico town of Dulce. [...] Witnesses have reported huge vats filled with an amber liquid with parts of human bodies being stirred inside.

After the initial agreement, Groom Lake, one of this nation's most secret test centers, was closed for a period of about a year, sometime between 1972-1974, and a huge **underground** facility was constructed for and with the help of the EBE's. **The bargained-for technology was set in place but could only be operated by the EBE's themselves. Needless to say, the advanced technology could not be used <u>against</u> the EBE's in case of need.**[1]

During the period between 1979 and 1983 it became increasingly obvious to MJ-12 that things were not going as planned... There was an altercation between the U.S. military and the aliens at the Dulce laboratory...By 1983, MJ-12 must have been in stark terror at the mistake they had made in dealing with the EBE's. They had subtly influenced, through Dr. Hynek, the production of the films 'Close Encounters of the Third Kind' and 'E. T.' (now admitted by some members of MJ-12 to have been a 'drastic mistake') to get the public used to 'odd-looking' aliens that were compassionate, benevolent and very much our 'space brothers'. MJ-12 had, in effect, 'sold' the

EBE's to the public and now they were faced with the fact that **quite the opposite was true**. In addition, a plan had been formulated in 1968 to make the public aware of the existence of aliens on earth over the next 20 years, to be culminated with several documentaries to be released during the 1985-1987 period. These documentaries would explain the history and intentions of the EBE's. The discovery of the 'Grand Deception' put the entire plans, hopes and dreams of MJ-12 into utter confusion and panic. [...]

Part of MJ-12, which had now become military top-heavy, wanted to confess the whole scheme and the shambles it had become to the public, beg their forgiveness and ask for their support. The other part (and majority) of MJ-12 argued that there was no way they could do that, that the situation was untenable and there was no use in exciting the public with the 'horrible truth' and that the best plan was to continue the development of a weapon or 'plan of containment' that could be used against the EBE's under the guise of 'SDI', (the so-called Strategic Defense Initiative which had nothing whatever to do with a defense for inbound Russian nuclear missiles).

Before the 'Grand Deception' was discovered, and according to a meticulous plan of release of information to the public, several documentaries and videotapes were made. ...If the government felt they were being forced to acknowledge the existence of aliens on earth because of the overwhelming evidence, ...it might do it, but it will conceal the information on the abductions and mutilations of humans and animals [...] One current hypothesis is that, on the available evidence, it appears that the EBE's are trying to regenerate their own species at our expense. [...] The best advice I can give you is next time you see a flying saucer and are awed by its obvious display of technology and gorgeous lights of pure color: **RUN LIKE HELL!**»

{Tr. n.: the above article can also be found in its original (English) form at:
http://www.thelivingmoon.com/47john_lear/02files/The_UFO_Cover-up.html}

[1] «**John Lear Jr.**: ...Needless to say, the advanced technology could not be used against the EBE's in case of need.»

The 'spiritual' masters elaborate on that:

'SUPERMUNDANE' BOOK I (AGNI YOGA SOCIETY) 1938 *(information through channeling)*: «§136. We are invulnerable to human weapons, yet can suffer injuries from the hierophants of the dark forces.»

Elsewhere in their book, the writers Giannoulakis & Kavakopoulos are wondering about what any reasonable man would wonder about:

"...The suspecting reader will ask a simple question: How is it possible for a certified CIA employee to meet with another former CIA employee, to publish (obviously) top-secret and upsetting documents on alien technologies without any reaction from the Agency that once had them in its ranks?"

An obviously reasonable answer is that information leaks <u>purposely</u> from 'inside'. I personally greatly believe in that interpretation. The commanders, already trapped by these abominations and having accepted their 'technological offerings', officially abide to the secrecy agreement, while, at the same time, they skillfully 'let' some information 'slip' through their hands.

IMPLANTS:

D) SPECIAL EDITION OF 'STRANGE' MAGAZINE –EXTRATERRESTRIALS +UFO, ARTICLE: 'JOHN MACK' BY IRENE MARAGOZI

«**JOHN MACK** (1929-2004): Professor of Psychiatry at Harvard University. He had served in the U.S. Air Force and had dealt with the psychological impact of events which are experienced by thousands of people en masse, as for example the Cold War. …He had also founded PEER (Program for Extraordinary Experience Research) which sought to study any inexplicable phenomenon and to offer psychological support to people in shock from an inexplicable or paranormal experience. …But he began the most subversive occupation in the 90's when he started to examine the cases of people who claimed that they had been abducted by aliens! (Prompted by the artist Budd Hopkins). …In the beginning John Mack was skeptical and almost refused to believe that reasonable people could believe in such things. But in the end …much to his surprise he found out that a large number of people across America reported that they had been abducted. Some of them even said later suffered from nosebleeds, <u>because of a tiny ball which had been implanted in their nasal cavity.</u> So, John Mack also brought to the surface the enigma of alien **implants**. …He had discussions with more than two hundred people who had relevant experience, stating unequivocally that **none** of them were mentally disturbed and that **their experiences were real**. When John Mack said the experience was real he meant that those people had experienced something very strange, which **was not a dream**, and which was almost always accompanied by the same **"symptoms" to their bodies**, such as cuts and scars which **didn't** belong to any category of psychosomatic phenomena. …Also, those people had disappeared for some time and there are reports that verify the disappearances. Moreover many of those people had little or no relation at all with UFO-logy and inevitably had **never** heard anything about abductions by aliens. Finally, many of them **were children** <u>of two or three years of age.</u>»

E) ALIEN IMPLANTS: http://www.inout.gr/archive/index.php/t-15979.html (25-09-07)

The following article was posted in 'Mystery' magazine by Kostas Kiapekos, chief editor of 'supernatural.gr':

«…There were scientists who proceeded with lab analyses of these micro-objects, making use of modern analysis and metal-separation apparatuses, as well as x-ray machines, electronic microscopes etc. The results were impressive. They came upon strange alloys that have never been found on earth before, and consecutive alternating layers up to fifteen in number. Careful analysis through electronic microscopes showed that on their outer layer, there were tiny extensions like microscopic cables placed with such precision, that they could touch nerves passing by. Thus, based on the bidirectional relation of communication (stimuli reception and command transmission) between the brain and various organs of the body, it is understandable for someone to wonder about the role these objects play in controlling and directing the intellectual processes of humans.»

UNDERGROUND BASES:

F) SPECIAL EDITION OF "STRANGE" MAGAZINE – ALIENS +UFO – AN ARTICLE OF DIM. EVANGELOPOULOS – MAJESTIC 12

«Finally it was agreed to construct **underground** bases for the aliens and two bases for common use by them and the U.S. government. The technology exchange would take place in those two common bases.

The bases for the aliens would be constructed in the area of Four Corners of Utah, in Colorado, in New Mexico as well as in Arizona and another one in Dreamland at the Mojave Desert of California.

...During the period of 1972-1973, an enormous **underground** installation (with the code name LUNA) was constructed south of Area 51-Groom Lake of Nevada (which has now ceased to operate) next to the Nuclear Test Site at the so called Area S-4, for the aliens (Grey) and with their help. Another secret **underground** base was provided to the Greys at a location known as "Ice Cave" close to the facilities of Los Alamos Laboratories in New Mexico. During the next six years, four more secret bases were constructed for the Greys in other isolated areas of the U.S.»

G) HELLENIC NEXUS, ISSUE 12 (FEBRUARY-MARCH 2006) UNDERGROUND BASES MYTHS AND REALITY BY CHRISTOS VAGENAS
(Letters from the underground by Richard Sauder- NEXUS New Times, Vol. 11, No 6)

The article starts with a bulletin from the Naval Facilities Engineering Service Center U.S. Navy (http://www.nfesc.navy/ocean/-1997)

«We can help you with the design, construction, maintenance and repair of fixed-ocean or underwater facilities from the shoreline to water depths of 6.000 meters...We have an extensive inventory of specialized tools, equipment, vessels and test facilities..."

The article continues...

"In 1987 Lloyd A. Duscha, Deputy Director of Engineering and Construction for the U.S. Army Corps of Engineers, gave a speech at a conference with the revealing title "Underground Facilities for Defense: Experience and Lessons".

In paragraph three of his speech and after a brief reference to technical aspects of construction and maintenance, the American official mentions:

"At this point, however, I should make a small omission, as many of the most interesting facilities that have been designed and constructed by our Corps are confidential."

He then concluded after...having made an extensive reference to the large underground U.S. Air Force base under the Cheyenne Mountain in Colorado U.S.A.

...At the moment, especially in the U.S.A., it seems that more than fifty extensive manned military underground facilities are operating, mainly in the Western States.

...In a special report of the U.S. Army Corps of Engineers, (Special Report 79-8 Design Procedures for Underground Heat Sink Systems, April 1979), they analyze the potential of cooling an underground base which is located in a rocky ground at the depth of 1229 meters. ...Indicative is the fact that in this document the use of a cooling unit of 125 tones is been provided (!).

...About two miles below the Archuleta Mesa in the Apache Indian reservation of Jicarilla in Dulce, New Mexico, U.S.A., is situated the most undoubtedly enigmatic of all the existing underground facilities: it is the place where, according to numerous reports of the personnel, the researchers and the occasionally 'abducted' individuals, the main U.S. laboratory of biogenetics is housed, in collaboration with the Grey aliens.

...Nevertheless it is said that some underground facilities were constructed and are controlled exclusively by aliens. ...Some of them are:

▪ In the Konga La area of the Himalayas, in the disputed China-India border, patrolled on both sides, the existence of an underground alien base is 'common knowledge'. According to various kinds of unrelated witnesses, vessels rise vertically above the mountain, a fact which is verified by the great number of drawings sketched by the children of the local school. (India Daily: http://www.indiandaily.com/editorial/01-09a-0.asp)...

▪ In Mt. Hayes of Alaska which is situated enigmatically close to the facilities of the superior American weapon H.A.A.R.P....

▪ In Mt. Ziel, Northern Australia which is rumored to be the most populated underground alien base on the planet.»

THE 'GIFT' OF THEIR TECHNOLOGY:

H) 'STRANGE' MAGAZINE SPECIAL EDITION 'EXTRATERRESTRIALS AND UFO' ARTICLE BY DIM. EVANGELOPOULOS, 'MAGESTIC12'

Don't skip chapters or bibliographic references

«…Thus the RED-LIGHT Program was created and the test flights of alien crafts *(by ordinary human-pilots)* enthusiastically began. …But the mission was partly successful, because most of the times it ended with the destruction of the craft and the death of the human test-pilot.[1] The aliens did not wish the Americans to acquire full knowledge of their technology, in case they would use it against them.»

The technology they offered was only enough to serve as 'bait' for their purposes.

[1] *During the 70's Bill Uhouse was assigned to build a flight simulator that could teach certain American pilots how to fly alien crafts.* [SOURCE: http://www.boomspeed.com/joseph2/J-Rod.htm]

I) 'STRANGE' MAGAZINE SPECIAL EDITION 'EXTRATERRESTRIALS & UFO' ARTICLE BY LUCAS KAVAKOPOULOS 'EXTRATERRESTRIAL TECHNOLOGY, 'BEWARE OF ALIENS BEARING GIFTS'

«Donald Keyhoe, major in the Marine Corps, was the first to come to prominence about alien technology recovered from the crashed flying saucer in Roswell, in the early 50's. He also was also one of the first who spoke about the US government suppressing information on the UFO.

…The issue of the alien technology that the Americans possessed was fully described by Colonel Philip J. Corso during his assignment as a special assistant in the Foreign Technology Desk at the Pentagon Research and Development Division. In his book "The Day After Roswell" (published in 1997)…Corso claims that while serving as an officer in Fort Riley, on July 6th 1947 (two days after Roswell) he supervised a number of crates containing artifacts that had been collected from the area in which the mysterious craft was found.

…In 1961, 14 years later, when he was a supervisor in the Foreign Technology Desk, he was assigned to analyze the contents of the crates and hand them out to specialized groups of scientists. Corso found many technologically advanced artifacts. …His assignment was, to figure out, with the help of the specialists he had in his disposal…how the alien technology worked, and then hand in his findings to the military's advantage. Together with his commanding officer Lieutenant General Arthur G. Trudeau, Corso said they developed a plan, **to seed the technology** they had discovered from the artifacts of the alien vessel to defense contractor companies, who were already cooperating with the army. …According to Corso the artifacts from the crashed UFO's **brought to light technologies forwarded by himself** to companies like Bell Labs, IBM, Dow Corning and Hughes Aircraft. Among these technologies were:

1. Image intensifiers (night vision) 2. Fiber optics (photon information transfer) 3. Super tenacity fibers and molecular-alignment metal-alloys, materials

of the highest quality for industrial production 5. Particle beams weapons (anti-missile program 'Star Wars') 6. Integrated circuits and microminiaturization of logic boards (microelectronics, computers, internet) 7. H.A.A.R.P. technology (weather weapons, mind control) 8. Depleted uranium projectiles 9. Portable atomic generators (ion propulsive drives) 10. Irradiated food (destroying bacteria and germs) 11. Electromagnetic propulsion systems. ...It is very interesting that transistors, which led to the replacement of electronic tubes/valves and to the microelectronics revolution (computer manufacturing), were "invented" six months after the Roswell incident, on December 1947, by Bell Labs, which, as Corso states, was indeed promoting alien technology.»

ANIMAL GENETIC MATERIAL: *(...DNA 'collection' from domestic animals for their 'ark')*

J) STRANGE MAGAZINE SPECIAL EDITION "EXTRATERRESTRIALS &UFO" ARTICLE: LUKAS KAVAKOPOULOS 'THE GOVERNMENT COVER-UP CHRONICLE'

«The FBI files include references to a topic which seems equally big and relevant to the UFO issue: The problem of **domestic animals** (which, for a long time were) found mutilated in the southern states of the US, with their body totally drained from blood and specific organs removed with surgical precision. Here as well, the plethora of FBI reports, which begin in 1947 and end in about 1979, suggest that something very important and very strange was happening. Colonel Philip J. Corso, a member of President Eisenhower's National Security Council, at the Foreign Technology Desk and at the US Army's Research & Development department, stated in 1997: "In the Pentagon, from 1961 to 1963, I analyzed many field reports from state police agencies about the discoveries of dead cattle whose carcasses looked as though they had been systematically mutilated. Local police reported that when the veterinarians were called to the scene to examine the dead cattle left in fields, they often found evidence not just that the animal's blood had been drained, but that entire organs were removed with such surgical skill that it could not have been the work of predators or vandals removing the organs for some depraved ritual. The American military thought at first that the mutilations were carried out by Soviet agents, but later they concluded that they were performed by the EBE's (Extraterrestrial Biological Entities). That is to say, the EBE's were experimenting with organ harvesting, possibly for transplant into other species or for processing into some sort of nutrient package or even to create some sort of hybrid biological entity." (Philip J. Corso, The Day After Roswell, Simon & Schuster, 1997)

...The FBI possesses reports by Police Officer Gabe Valdez, who examined many cattle mutilation cases and found out that most animals were discovered dehydrated (mummified) a few days later. Almost always, strange substances and traces of radiation were found around the animals, while in some cases he also found odd triangular tracks. A verified characteristic of some carcasses was that they didn't decompose in a normal pace, but they were preserved in good condition for several weeks.»

AGRO-GLYPHS: (CROP CIRCLES) *(...collecting plant ingredients in plasma form)*

K) *Agro-glyphs are yet another enigma to many. Man has been imitating his gods for centuries. How could he innovate now? It is for this reason that the crop circles appearing all around the world, are made by two different groups: Some are created by men and others are made by balls of light. Before proceeding to the analysis of the chemical changes resulting from the formation of **genuine** crop circles, a specific piece of information should be given:*

PLASMA (PHYSICS):
a) http://el.wikipedia.org/wiki/Πλάσμα_(Φυσική)
b) http://en.wikipedia.org/wiki/Plasma_(physics)

«In Physics, as well as in Chemistry, **plasma** is a state of matter similar to gas in which free-form electrically charged atomic particles are found (ions and electrons). Plasma is classified among gases, but differs from a non-ionized gas. It is formed when a gas becomes overheated, resulting in electrons escaping from their atom and become free (free electrons). Plasma thus, consists of free electrons and ions, atoms or molecules that have lost or gained one or more electrons and it is the hyper-ionized state of matter. …Plasma is often called the "forth state of matter"…refers to a gas, which has been supplied with enough energy, so that its electrons separate from their atoms (ionization) and a **cloud** of ions and electrons is produced. Because these particles are ionized (charged), the gas behaves differently than a neutral gas, when, for example, there are electromagnetic fields.»

During the night, particularly between 2-4 a.m., balls of light have been videotaped. Their size ranges from an egg to a soccer ball and they usually hover over a field planted with cereal crops such as wheat, rye, maize or barley, and form a complex geometric pattern in a few minutes time. The plants bend at the 1st and the 2nd node of their stem, but they don't break. For over a decade, Biophysicist William C. Levengood and his research team have been investigating physical anomalies of samples taken from crop-circles caused by these "bright" interventions. Only the plants that have been bent by the balls of light have serious change in their chemical structure. These manifest node elongation (swelling) both laterally and longitudinally in their stems.

SCIENTIFIC STUDIES CONFIRM: CROP-CIRCLES MADE BY 'BALLS OF LIGHT' BY ELTJO H. HASELHOFF, DUTCH CENTRE FOR CROP CIRCLE STUDIES http://www.cropfiles.it/docs/Crops-by-Bols.html

«…Although there are known biological effects that can create node length-ening, these could be easily ruled out. It was clear that something else had happened. The effect could be simulated by placing normal, healthy stems inside a microwave oven. The heat induced by the microwaves made the liquids inside the nodes expand just like the mercury inside a thermometer. …This finding led to the conclusion that the node lengthening effect may be caused by the involvement of heat, possibly caused by microwave radiation. In fact, traces of heat have been found innumerable times in crop circles *(agro glyphs)* all over the world, **such as dehydrated plants**, burn marks on the ground, and the molten snow.»

The team concludes that plants that dry-up (wilt) during the formation of a **genuine** *agro-glyph are dehydrated from the inside in an outward fashion with the application of an energy similar to that of microwaves. The plants have been found dehydrated from under the seed-head and with their chlorophyll missing. The excessive temperature-increase inflicted upon the plant due to the luminous spheres that cause it, results in the nodes (where the plant fluids concentrate) bursting/exploding with the creation of holes.*

BLT RESEARCH TEAM, INC. (WILLIAM LEVENGOOD) ARTICLE: PLANT ABNORMALITIES
http://www.bltresearch.com/plantab.php

«These holes are present in **genuine** crop-circles, usually found in the 2nd or 3rd nodes below the seed-head.»

Measurements show the ground to be highly magnetized.

MAGNETIC MATERIALS IN SOILS, http://www.bltresearch.com/magnetic.php

«…Traces of melted magnetic material adhering to soil grains, as well as spherical, magnetic particles of 10^{-40} micron diameter, are regularly found in crop-circle soils. EDS *(research)* reveals these spheres to be pure iron; the fact that they are magnetized reveals they were formed in a magnetic field.»

Due to the fact that ground elements have been melted (fused?), the degree of their crystallization is also increased. Research results on ground samples of genuine crop circles show great percentages of illite/mica crystals.

CLAY-MINERAL CRYSTALLIZATION CASE STUDY:
http://www.bltresearch.com/xrd.php

STUDY RESULTS: «A sharpening of the mica 001 peak [a decrease in the Kübler Index (K. I.) value, indicative of growth of the illite/mica crystals] *was* observed in the crop-circle soil samples, as compared with their controls; *(compared to ordinary soil samples/without crop-circles).*

…The increase in the KI of the mica 001 peak cannot be attributed to mechanical flattening of the crop circle plants *(the plants forming the pattern of the crop-circle exhibit a 90° node-bending)* since (in the absence of any evidence of geologic pressure) temperatures of at least 600-800° Celsius over

Don't skip chapters or bibliographic references

several hours of exposure would be required to produce such increased crystal growth;

Because the temperatures needed (a minimum of 600-800° Celsius over a period of several hours) to cause mica crystal growth would have incinerated any plant material present at the site (as well as causing other measurable soil effects), and because we know of no energy which can selectively affect soils to one degree and plants at the same locations to another (as is documented here), **we suggest that we may be observing a new--as yet undiscovered--energy source at work**. It <u>does</u> appear that heat is involved, but more research is needed to determine its precise nature.»

Crystallization is the result of plasma creation. –It is also considered an ideal method for the exploitation of waste material and is used in many countries.

<u>Summing-up</u>: *Luminous extra-dimensional spheres hover over plantations. Their objective –according to the view-point of this book– is to collect plant elements in the form of plasma. Then, in the said location, very high temperatures are created –in the form of microwaves, or some other unknown technology/energy-form. The saps in the plants' stems are all concentrated at the nodes and evaporate, creating there escape holes. Plants bend, forming impressive agro-glyphs only for misguidance. A result of the temperature increase needed to transform plant saps to gassy plasma –thus transferring their elements– is the crystallization of soil substances and the creation of a magnetic field at that particular location.*

Could this be a method of plant 'element' collection, equivalent to the bloodletting of household animals?

This entire operation of the energy (astral) powers of this world, (presenting themselves as 'extraterrestrials') aims to secure the energy-supplies they need in order to create –as best they can– ideal conditions for the successful 'survival' of the (misguided) humanity in the parallel alternative probabilities/universes. Animal and plant DNA gathering will sustain their man-nutrition 'in life'. In reality, they are preparing a new (3rd) fall, even if they give it the 'upgrading tint' of supposedly being detached from dense matter.

REQUIREMENTS TO SUPPORT THE DARK GOALS

1ST REQUIREMENT: POSSESSION OF CONSCIOUSNESS

Let us now see the way in which the unseen powers of this creation meth-odize **their auxiliary support goals**, in order to divert the peoples' atten-tion away from their own activities.
In order for their operation plans to be successful, they must be first of all directed and applied by trustworthy individuals. High-ranking 'initiates' of various groups who were 'initiated' by their assignees/masters, were not enough for the whole planet. But secrets concerning dominion over the entire Earth ought not to be disclosed to simple members. On the contrary, **the conscious presence** of many properly selected men in key-positions was necessary, men who could carry out these ventures.

The way was old and familiar. In the past it used to be called "spiritual possession"; but under the new conditions some old 'details' had to be transformed in order for the changes that might raise suspicions, to be im-perceptible. Thus the old "spiritual possession" was retrofit to "possession of consciousness".

This **possession of the consciousness** of human bodies by these dark pow-ers started with the initially selected men in sporadic or frequent time in-tervals, until these possessions finally became permanent. Since this way yielded positive results, they started using it more frequently, until the pre-sent, where it has become the 'status quo' on a large population scale.

Initially, only people who were astro-aetherically vitalized were captured *(λᾶας [Gr.: stone], λᾶος = λαός [Gr.: folk])*. But since their ulterior goal was the dominion of the physical body of men **whose position** in society would 'serve' some of their expediencies, the psycho-invaders expanded their activities to soul enslavement as well. This gave them the opportunity to collect vulnerable souls and 'usurp' them for their own benefit. In their majority, these souls were devoid of Spirit.
The 'invaders' inside the human bodies are activated and motivated by a collective unconscious, faithfully following their plan. All of a sudden, the common (in appearance) man 'next door' gradually begins to change views.

Don't skip chapters or bibliographic references

569 **A) BARBARA MARCINIAK 'GAIA'** [Gr. tr. MATZOROU E.] *(Information through channeling):*
«…How can my body become appropriate for entities who want to **merge** with me and want to see the Gaia through my own eyes? And if some of these entities merge with me, will they then see the world the same way I see it? Or perhaps through this merging other worlds will emerge, and I emerge into these worlds too? *(This is the trap!)* What is possession?
…You as human beings are the library cards, the keys to the Living Library. All information which is stored in Gaia's Library can be accessed **through you**. …We want to get access to the library, to study certain things and get information.
…The energies used the human body, the sense organs and the whole organism in order to study the Living Library.

…Although some entities want to harm humans, most of them harm them mainly because of their ignorance *(how very convenient!)*. It is necessary to have distinction and prepare your body to receive the merging energy setting the parameters of your availability. …If the approaching energies are not to your liking, don't be afraid to say: "The Door is closed. You are not to my liking. I'll find someone else." *(is it then so important to finally find the '**right**' intruder?…)*

…We are asking all of you to feel the energy of these entities that **want to merge with you**. Ask them to give you a sign. Tell them: "I'm working on my uplifting, as well as the planet's uplifting. If you are aligned to this you are welcome. Otherwise don't even come close." …Then you'll become valuable, as you will be merging with other entities which will have access to the codes. The codes contain life-form production-formulas.»

Through body-possession they can impel the possessed individuals to "produce" the energy-thoughts necessary for their (the entities) nutrition on the one hand and on the other to proceed to methodized actions aimed at serving the purposes of these entities.

B) PAPASTAVROU, A., 'LETTERS TO ANONYMOUS': «…With the incarnated disciple's acceptance and during the predestined Cosmic Moment, when Manu must manifest on Earth, the Integration occurs. *(In this case there is the possession of the disciple's body by Manu. But if any other immaterial entity wishes so, can easily possess the body of an individual **who is prone to it**.)* In certain cases, during that Integration, the disciple's soul leaves and He *(Manu or anyone else)* is using the body for as long as he wishes to. In other cases, the disciple's soul stays and Manu *(or anyone else)* is using the body only occasionally, so in that case he *(the occupant)* can internally *(on other inner planes)* continue his work, without having to constantly worry about the physical body's provisions.»

**C) 'STRANGE' MAGAZINE MARCH 2005, ISSUE 75
ARTICLE BY MILICA KOSANOVIC 'PSYCHO-INTRUDERS, INCOMING SOULS TAKE POSSESSION OF OUR BODY'**

«The incoming soul, in most cases, retains the memories of the previous inhabitant of the body, and thus recognizes his relationships, faces and facts, but has different emotions from him. **He has other targets** and has to act differently in order to help with the planet's propulsion *(!!)* to higher planes. Specialists on this issue, such as American Ruth Montgomery, who introduced the "walk in" term, which constitutes the base, as John Hornecker, Doreen Virtue and others, claim that the soul exchange phenomenon has always existed, but because of our planet's shift of consciousness at this moment, the number of 'incoming' souls is bigger. …Within this level we can make agreements with other souls that will play an important part to our own new experiences. After their incarnation the (new) souls **manipulate** the events of life.»

The article mentions that there are hundreds of websites as well as organizations involved with this matter!

D) GER. KALOGERAKIS (retired Greek Army major-general) 'THE RETURN OF THE GODS' CH. 'BIOGENETICS AND ARCHAEOLOGY' *(Encoded message through PC –w/out internet connection– from invisible entities who call themselves 'Olympians')*

«Attention, the apostates kidnap people from your own work environment. In your work environment they've sent someone from. …It's a human being. …He works for the apostates (all the evidence was given and the individual was immediately found). The real human being was kidnapped on… The apostate has been implanted with the entire memory of the actual human being whose form he took (form-wearing, in the same way you wear a garment). …Using an infrared camera you'll be able to see an equilateral triangle on his forehead.»

This entire process of consciousness possession aimed to produce a large number of men who would accept 'the unreasonable' that the invaders wanted to impose. These men (the possessed) would then set an example for the rest of humanity to follow. This principle is applied to every institutional sector of human society and thus they create the critical mass of men necessary to guide the rest towards the new trends, whatever they might be. Thus, settled securely inside foreign bodies they methodize their moves.

Before these dark forces could initiate their intense action on Earth, they had to ensure that men's suspicions would not be focused on them, revealing their plans. Thus, a series of procedures had to be initiated, to avert any such probability.

To begin with, the 'glorious discovery' that positive thinking exorcises every misfortune was announced as the 'key' to prosperity. All gullible people rushed to embrace it, convincing each other about the hidden treasure in this idea. This very same 'positivity' of course never let them realize that life's problems –despite their persistent faithfulness to 'positive thinking'– were not prevented. And they orchestrated this 'optimism/positiveness campaign' not to make people happier, but rather to render them incapable of discerning some serious social discrepancies. But by making men wear the magical rose-tinted glasses of hope, they deterred them from detecting the methodical plot, and made them reject the probability of a well-set trap as a pessimistic and negative view.

---

570 **TEXE MARRS** (US AIR FORCE OFFICIAL) **'PROJECT L.U.C.I.D.'**
«Men everywhere seem to be caught in denial of reality. They fear the awful truth and are turning a blind eye. …Therefore, they avoid it and cast it from their minds and consciousness.»

There were nevertheless the hot-headed ones, who stubbornly insisted on digging the facts out and focusing on their conspiracy plots. Thus, a second, undeclared prohibition began its methodical deployment in a different way. With diplomatic cunning they started leaking rumors stigmatizing as 'quaint', 'psychologically disturbed', 'mytho-maniacs', or 'conspiracy-maniacs', all those who poked around, stirred strange cases and revealed controversies and inconsistencies between the real and 'apparent' data of some subjects. Gradually, these distrustful and suspecting and inquisitive minds started to get isolated in groups that were considered marginal, while pessimism was declared as the gravest stigma.

And with the looming danger that men might perceive the complete picture of their reality, they have been methodically setting out plans to discourage everyone who might be seriously interested to discover any information concerning matters labeled as quaint and to get involved in the study of suppressed/cold cases at the risk of being ridiculed.

They thus began to orient men's attention towards nonessential matters, which they label as important, so that no one can ever have a thematically spherical overview on any subject, because the picture he would then acquire would be totally different from the one the 'administrators' presented.

However, in cases of really persistent researchers, and in order to silence them for good, they started deploying methods that range from simple offerings/gifts to the 'accidental' death or even replacement of the consciousness of the individual. In recent years especially they have used the technique of 'deceptive initiation' to allegedly top-secret and specialized knowledge regarding 'planetary projects', which should under no circumstances leak to the un-initiated! Satisfied then, these 'chosen' initiates/researchers changed their sailing course, proud of their success.

The next (3rd) objective goal of these dark forces is to manipulate the spiritual awakening of man, which is under reactivation during this time, in order **to divert it to the wrong direction** so as to 'lock' every trace of Life/Soul.

During this time-period a great number of Living Spirits has incarnated on Earth as a result of the 'rearrangement' of the astro-aetheric spaces. Their entrance into the world of form caused the activation of the dormant spirituality on Earth. Spirituality however is a grave danger for every dark power. By putting a '**ceiling**' to the spiritual evolution of men, they annihilate the probability for the Spiritually Sensitive to be informed of the Truth. This is why they have equated the Spirit with positive energy! Following that, they have suppressed any information regarding the **three higher bodies** of man, diverting man's interest to the four lower ones which belong to the astro-aetheric world of these entities, and which are the **guaranteed** prison for men! Furthermore, they prompt the masses to energize and expand the cardiac center of the 'positive' astral emotions –instead of the seventh one at the top of the head– defining this success as the most significant achievement *(see reference #506 B)*.

So the appointment of controlled gurus and false teachers throughout the world, who will deceive and misdirect the awakened spirituality of men, was primarily imperative.

---

571 **A) DAVID ICKE INTERVIEWED BY JON RAPPOPORT, 'REVEALING THE GREAT CONSPIRACY',** GR. TR. TSOLI N., ESOPTRON PUBL (p. 143)

«David Icke: One of the mind controlled slaves I've met, who was attached to Henry Kissinger for many years, told me, that Kissinger was involved in the founding of the New Age Movement. He was orchestrating it. He placed individuals in the public arena in order to activate and develop it.

They sensed (perceived) **a vibration change** taking place, broadening the souls of a vast number of people towards the awakening. What they had to do was to put this awakening under their control and divert it to new prisons especially made to trap people. The New Age movement is largely their work.»

B) THE GOSPEL OF MATTHEW, CH. 24: «§11. And many false prophets shall rise, and shall deceive many.»

In order for both opposite sides –the positive and negative astral ones– to aggregate followers, they have directed mediums to transmit their messages in a metaphysical way. All these mediums of course believe that 'those' who have contacted them were of course 'benign' and swear that they have

never ever come in contact with negative powers. But they don't realize that everyone who is ill-intentioned and wants to delude can only do that through beautified, false 'truths'.

---

[572] **DAVID ICKE INTERVIEWED BY JON RAPPOPORT, 'REVEALING THE GREAT CONSPIRACY', GR. TR. TSOLI N., ESOPTRON PUBL**

«I have a vast sympathy towards the metaphysical basis for many of the theories and the sincerity of many people involved in this movement. But it has become so groundless. It's the orgasmic experience of a manipulator. It is about **naivety** which is manifested **as** spiritual enlightenment. ...I've heard people say that the 'entity', whose messages they are transmitting, speaks of love and thus it must be sincere. But, as it occurs in any other form of manipulation, **you must tell people what they want to hear in order to entice them**.»

Thus these naïve mediums, through the flattering joy this spiritual communication generates, don't even bother to wonder about the **reason** why these invisible masters display such excessive self-sacrifice for man's benefit, and they jubilantly spread the dangerous messages that are communicated to them. The radical plan, being methodically executed, however, is to render humanity **incapable** of following the Transference procedure by diverting Spirituality to **false directions**.

And as the spiritually restless are restricted while being manipulated by the appointed 'Gurus', control had to be directed towards 'normal' people so that they could also be controlled by different methods. The dark forces, aware of the duality of matter full well, promote their plans **by ameliorating** their standpoints. Being preponderant population-wise, this spiritually un-suspecting group of people (the nations of the Earth) had to be 'boxed in boundaries' to be completely controllable. In order for this to become pain-lessly and generally feasible, and in the pretense of the alleged 'bridging' of differences, human crowds had to be initially 'homogenized' into a disci-plined human mass, regardless of nation and nationality. After all, only the inferior teams of the creators supported the diversity of states/races, because they had created them. Yet, since today they have been **completely** assimi-lated by the sum of the astral forces, they are being canceled along with their beliefs. On the contrary, the powers of the skeptomorphs are vitalized **equal-ly well** by the thoughts of all men, independent of race and color. Thus, since they are 'in charge of things' in the material universe now, homogeniz-ation (globalization) of the peoples accommodates them and they enforce it. The resultant then of various actions would lead to the desired result on a global scale.

Being inversely proportional to the Spirit, materialistic excess would lead to complete Spiritual stupefaction, resulting to the relaxation of all institutions and moral values of society. The astral tornado, alternating fear with insecu-rity, managed to 'nail man down' to a permanent anxiety for survival, whereby the everyday struggle for his 'daily bread' drains him of his strength for any deep philosophical pursuit and objective observation. Com-bined with the ever inflating charms of material provisions which **it estab-lishes as necessary**, this tornado guides man 'galloping' towards the rejec-tion of every conjecture relating to the Spirit –since he considers it an inven-tion of the naïve– and to the (over) estimation of only the physical (material) body and the needs that accompany it.

---

[573] **HERMES TRISMEGISTUS,** HERMETIC TEXTS, VOL. II, RODAKIS P., TZAFEROPOU-LOS AP., **'ASCLEPIUS, OR THE PERFECT SERMON'** (p. 65): «§25…No one will gaze into heaven. And the pious man will be counted as insane, and the impious will be honored as wise. The insane will be considered as serious and the worst criminal as good. And concerning the soul, and the things of the soul, and the things that make the soul immortal or rather push her to achieve im-mortality, along with the rest of what I have said to you, not only will they **be considered ridiculous**, but even worse, they will also be thought of as in

vain. At the same time, believe me, it will be a great crime, in the legal boundaries of the term, to be devoted to the spiritual religion. A new judicial system and laws will be created. Sanctity and piety will not be heard of anymore and will not find refuge inside the soul.

The gods have departed from men and it is a sorrowful departure. The angels of evil are the only ones who remain whole, and mingle with men and drive the wretched ones to every ill of excess…

§26 This, when it comes, shall be the World's old age; lack of religion, disorder, and confusion of all that is Good *{Gr. Ἀγαθόν (Agathón)}*. And when these things all come to pass, Asclepius,—then He, [our] Lord and Father, God, The First in power, and **The Creator of the One [Visible] God** *(i.e. the First Noũs-God – Luminary Christ)*, after examining this behavior and the purposeful crimes, will try, by His own will, which is The Divine Goodness, **–to end all ill** and general corruption, wash away deceit, annihilate wickedness, wiping it out with a flood or a fire or contagious diseases that will spread in various places. And then He will restore the world to **its former** beauty *(through the Transference of the Principles to their former Spiritual State)*. …And this is how this Cosmos will be reborn: regeneration of all Good things *(to a Spiritual Dimension, since Ἀγαθόν cannot be found in matter)*, restoration of Sanctity *(the first Resurrection, according to John)* and Nature's return to the course of time, as it is and as it was, **without beginning and without end.**[1]»

[1] **RUDOLF STEINER, 'FROM THE AKASHA CHRONICLE, COSMIC MEMORY'** (p. 138)

«On the one hand, the coming evolution of Earth will develop today's life of images and thoughts to an even higher, more subtle and more complete condition. … At that stage <u>there can no longer be any question of birth and death</u> in the present sense. Death occurs only because consciousness depends on an external world with which it interacts through the sensory organs. If these physical organs cease to function, then all relation to the world around ceases as well. That is to say, the person is 'is dead'. However, when his soul advances, it will not receive the outer world influences through physical organs, but through the images it creates itself.»

Thus, the dizziness from materialistic pleasures' constantly weakens even the minutest spark of Living Spirit, excluding more and more people from the possibility of Transference to the Immortal Cosmoi.

First nodal point of control is the Mass Media and the politicians of nations, through which/whom the dark skeptomorphic forces have the ability to deploy their plans, as well as methodize the psychological phases which nations must go through, in order to become obediently subservient.

Don't skip chapters or bibliographic references

These two power groups –many members of which cannot even fathom the source of origin of their instructions– obey higher control circles through the 'select few'. Thus they are all accommodated as they collaborate with the 'possessed ones' in key-positions, to promote coordinated actions. Their goal: **The physical brain must be manipulated** so that they can fashion a completely controllable human herd, impotent of thinking beyond the predetermined, given boundaries they prescribe.

---

[574] **A) DAVID ICKE 'REBELS OF CONSCIOUSNESS'** (Gr. tr. PERISSAKI P., from the orig. 'THE ROBOTS' REBELLION')

«An Illuminati document titled 'Silent Weapons for Quiet Wars' was found in 1986 in a second-hand IBM computer. The document was dated from 1979 and contained all information that I've mentioned in this book, as well as the tactics the Bilderberg Group has been using since the 50's:

"Experience has proved that the simplest method of securing a silent weapon and gaining control of the public, is by keeping the public uncoordinated and ignorant about the basic principles of the system on one hand, while maintaining confusion, disorganization and their attention distracted, with insignificant matters of no real importance on the other hand. This is achieved by:

1. Loosening their mental capacities and sabotaging their mental activities; providing a low quality curriculum of public education in areas such as mathematics, deductive thinking, systems organization design and economics, and by discouraging their creativity and skills.

2. Engaging/limiting their emotions, encouraging self-indulgence and weakness and by solidifying their dependency in emotional and material pursuits and activities, by:

a) Launching relentless emotional confrontations and attacks (mental and emotional rape) by way of constant barrage of sex, violence and wars in the mass media – especially TV and newspapers.

b) Giving them what they desire –in excess– "junk food for thought" and depriving them of what they really need.

c) Rewriting history and the laws and subjecting the public to a **deviant reality**, capable of shifting their thinking from personal needs to elaborately fabricated external priorities.

These preclude their interest in the discovery of the silent weapons of social automation technology. The general rule is that there is a profit in confusion. The more confusion, the more profit. Therefore, the best approach is to create problems and then offer solutions.

In a few words:

Mass Media: Keep the adult public attention diverted away from the real social issues and captivated by matters of no real importance.

<u>Schools</u>: Keep the young public ignorant of real mathematics, real economics, real law, and real history.

<u>Entertainment</u>: Keep the public entertainment below a sixth-grade level.

<u>Work</u>: Keep the public, busy, busy, busy, with no time to think; back on the farm with the other animals.»

B) DAVID ICKE INTERVIEWED BY JON RAPPOPORT, 'REVEALING THE GREAT CONSPIRACY', GR. TR. TSOLI N., ESOPTRON PUBL:

«The plan is to enforce a centralized control to the world and to create a population of human robots. We are dangerously close to something like that. In fact it's been a long time since humanity has started to get mentally and emotionally stabilized into robots. ...The more I have investigated the things that are happening to the world, the more I am convinced that the key to how we got ourselves into this chaos and the way out of it, lies in the people's minds and emotions.[1] The only way for "the few" to control the masses, is by manipulating their mind and emotions, in order to make them **see the world the way they want them to**. That, for lack of an appropriate term, is the 'battle field' where the whole drama is developing –the mind and the human emotions.

The definition I give to mind control is interesting: it's manipulating someone's mind, in order to think and as a result to behave the way you want him to. According to this definition of mind control, the question isn't how many people around the world are under mind control, but how many **are not**. The answer to that is almost no one.

...What is exactly that these notorious mind control projects do, such us the MK-Ultra which is directed by the CIA and other government agencies? They are trying to deprive people of their sense of uniqueness, the sense of themselves, the sense of who they are, the sense of independent thinking, of analyzing, of doubting, and replace all that with a personality which simply reacts according to their wishes, to any stimulus, to any order or to any spark it is presented to. **They are making robots**.

What applies to individual consciousness, applies to the collective consciousness as well. As it is widely known, an injured mind is far more receptive to manipulation and suggestion. Of course what passes through television and advertising is hypnotic suggestion. Most of the time they talk to our subconscious *(particularly when some fall asleep in front of the TV)*, because they very well know how to pass subliminal messages through specific phrases and symbols.»

[1] **ROBERT GREENE 'THE 48 LAWS OF POWER', LAW 43: 'WORK ON THE HEARTS AND MINDS OF PEOPLE.**

Don't skip chapters or bibliographic references

«(p. 470) Coercion creates a reaction that will eventually work against you. You must seduce others into wanting to move in your direction. A person you have seduced becomes your loyal pawn. If you take advantage of their individual psychologies and weaknesses, then you can seduce others. Soften up the resistant one by working on his emotions, playing on what he holds dear and what he fears... (p. 476) Remember: The key to persuasion is to soften up people, to gradually weaken them. Entice them using the forked approach: work on their emotions and exploit their mental weaknesses. ...Aim at the primary emotions: love, hate and jealousy.»

To accomplish mass mind-control, they are constantly experimenting with new techniques based on mass-psychology as well as that of the individual. These techniques have evolved to such a degree today, that Mass Media (by simply projecting the new age 'views' or the opinions of modern materialistic science in their <u>own special</u> way) shape the consciousness of common men manipulating them, according to the predetermined norms.

575 ADOLF HITLER: «Happiness for the rulers is that people don't think...»
A) 'STRANGE' MAGAZINE ISSUE 45, GEORGE STAMKOS, 'MIND CONTROL IN GREECE'
«After the enactment of Bill Clinton's law about 'free information', which came into force in 1995, many archives and files of the U.S.A. secret services became public and an astonishing flow of information connected with Mind Control experiments was released.
The official declassification and the Executive Order of the president, referring to the opening of top secret archives, isn't the only reason that this kind of forbidden information came in the full blaze of publicity. Ex-victims, but also former perpetrators of several government secret programs, having realized the ordeal they've been through, they began to join forces and file group lawsuits against the federal government, not only asking for compensation, but also for the truth!»
B) 'STRANGE' MAGAZINE ISSUE 45 GEORGE STAMKOS 'MIND CONTROL THE WAR FOR MIND CONTROL HAS STARTED', FROM HIS BOOK, 'PROHIBITED TECHNOLOGY' (ARCHETYPO Publications)
«Most human beings are not humans, but elaborate machines of reflexes. ... **Ideal citizens must not think, but imitate**. And this is because independent thinking is dangerous to the authority, even the so-called 'democratic' one. In democratic societies mass-control is not exercised using violence any more, but with an elaborate mechanism of delicate influences **upon key people**, 'Think Tanks' and crucial social groups. ...Politicians as well as propagandists, using the appropriate 'voice tone', key-words, specific hand

gestures and other techniques, manage to hypnotize and finally convince the masses to vote for them. Persuasion is based on reprogramming the human mind. …True maestros of 'persuasion' techniques are the lawyers, who possess a real battery of techniques and locutions, in order to sink into the right cerebral hemisphere. …Advertisers have advanced beyond that point, using subconscious suggestion methods. Many advertisements, even films, embed subliminal messages which are **'transplanted' into the brain** of the unsuspecting viewer and push him to adopt a certain way of behavior. Anyone maundering in front of TV gets 'hypnotized' and falls into Alpha State and so become 25 times more susceptible to suggestion, since they aren't fully alert, like in Beta State (14-40 Hz).

In Alpha State (8-13 Hz), a person is mentally defenseless and accepts things that he would reject without a second thought in a fully alert state.

…Studies for brainwashing-techniques began in the last century, with the well-known experiments of the Russian behaviorist Pavlov. Pavlov had studied animal behavior and then developed techniques that could make it totally mechanical. At the hearing of a sound, saliva poured from the guinea-pig dogs, which had connected the particular sound with food. He claimed that the same reaction could be applied on humans. In a way he thought of people as complex 'reflex machines' and to a certain point he wasn't wrong.

…The use of humans as guinea-pigs was an ordinary phenomenon in the Nazi concentration camps. …Psychotropic substances, affecting the human mind and behavior, were tested on the prisoners. Electroshocks, neurosurgeries, brain transplants, were performed. …Those who carried out all the above, didn't become unemployed after the end of World War II. They carried on their 'scientific' research, working, now, for the victorious forces' interest, especially those of the U.S.A. which not only offered them asylum, but paid them generously for their services. The CIA mind control secret project began at the early 60's, initially following brainwashing-methods and techniques, which the Soviets and Chinese had earlier used. …At first the code name 'Bluebird' was given to the project, which was later renamed to 'Artichoke' and finally 'MK-ULTRA', and had always been under the auspices of the CIA. …Within that project CIA upheld a number of experiments which were mainly conducted **on unsuspecting people** (e.g. LSD spraying in public places indoors, in order to study the reactions of the citizens). …A series of operations within the MK-ULTRA project, examined the psychotropic substances' effect on the organism and especially on human consciousness. Besides LSD, research focused on the so-called 'truth drugs' (operation 'Chatter'), such as scopolamine, bufotenine, et alia. As part of the 'Chatter' project, Dr. H. Isabel using LSD, kept a drug addicts in ecstasy for

Don't skip chapters or bibliographic references

77 days (!). ...Mind Control technology in the U.S.A. today is covered under the designation of 'non-lethal' weapons.»

C) *From the following article we are going get yet another taste of the existing possibilities of technology. Should 'someone' decide to apply those technologies to unsuspecting citizens, nothing, unfortunately, would be able to stop them.*

'STRANGE' MAGAZINE, ISSUE 57, SUMMER 2003, LUKAS KAVAKOPOULOS: 'MIND CONTROL CONCERT'

«Scientists are still analyzing the reactions of 250 people who took part in the study on the effects of infrasound at Liverpool's Metropolitan Cathedral in September 2002.

The audience's emotions intensified as **the inaudible** sound vibrations, too low for the human ear to perceive, were blasted out during a 50-minute piano recital.

Those, who felt irritated when the concert began, found their mood turning to anger. Others, who had felt happy, started to notice sensations of pleasure *(that is, the underlying emotion was magnified)*. Some 'physical' effects were also experienced, including tingling in the back of the neck and a strange feeling in the stomach. ...The 'soundless music' research is being undertaken by a team of musicians, scientists and psychologists as part of the Symposium Art and Science run by John Moores University, The Welcome Trust and Sciart Consortium. ...The infrasound vibrations were created by an 'infrasound cannon', which consisted of an ultra-low loudspeaker inside a 12 meter-long and 30 centimeter-wide drainpipe. This contraption carefully sent out subtle pulses at certain moments of the recital...»

MAIN GOALS OF THE DARK POWER

(A) HYBRID BODIES – DNA MUTATION – THE MARKING OF THE BEAST

And while they shape the appropriate conditions to support their prima-ry scheme by systematizing the moral and spiritual degradation of the world, their essential goals are others, and it is towards those the most experienced ones of their kind are focused. To ensure success of their basic objectives, they need to simultaneously organize and promote many parallel alternative projects/plans, something that 'veils' their intentions even further.

Under the new conditions of the material universe, shortly after the Trans-ference of the Sacred Archetypes to their Source, the laws of nature will be disturbed, matter will seem to change and the astro-aetheric bodies of man will cease to 'function' in the usual way.

During the First Resurrection, those who will manage to escape from the material world shall pass on to a place of restitution and preparation (relin-quishing the energy-part of their Soul) for their definitive return to the Sa-cred Capital of the Father.

Conversely, those who will choose to accept and embrace matter –even though it **will cease to exist in its known form**– will be obliged to **mutate** their material body into new form, in order to move on to some parallel, alternative probability/universe of the 5th dimension. The material body, man possesses today, cannot survive there.

---

[576] **A) M-BRANES AND THE DREAMS FOR UNIFICATION**
SOURCE: THE ELEGANT UNIVERSE OF BRIAN GREENE, JULY 2007, CAMBRIDGE WEBPAGE ON 'HYPER-STRINGS', SCIENTIFIC AMERICAN
http://www.physics4u.gr/articles/2007/M-branes.html
«We humans will not be able to enter other dimensions, because the parti-cles that form our bodies –electrons, protons, neutrons– remain **attached** to this brane that constitutes our world.»
B) ERICH VON DÄNIKEN 'THE SECOND COMING HAS ALREADY STARTED' (p. 239, 240) «The ugly outlaw aliens foretold their abducted victims about an oncom-ing disaster (*the withdrawal of the Sacred Archetypes of Creation, is defi-nitely a fundamental reason...*). They said that this is the main reason that justifies their actions. The bright side of this story is that the human race will survive, even as a human/alien hybrid.»

Don't skip chapters or bibliographic references

In that new world, there will be encaged 'living' energy as an echo of life. Those who get there will manage to 'survive' on that echo of life combined with their stored/trapped life inside their Souls. A new astral-material body will protect this 'life' like current is protected by a battery. Thus, by any means possible, the astral administrators of the material world are preparing the new constructions/prisons/bodies for the Souls they will manage to trap.

Man didn't make these enormous technological leaps during the last 70 years **without help,** when for centuries he technologically evolved at a dead-slow pace. This technology 'gift' was not offered to him to improve his well-being, but was granted as forfeit for his entrapment by dark, invisible powers that materialized in the world of form, disguised as 'extraterrestrials'.

---

[577]A) **'THE DISCLOSURE PROJECT'**, http://en.wikipedia.org/wiki/The_Disclosure_Project

«The 'Disclosure' Project is an organization started by Steven M. Greer in 1993 that alleges the existence of a US government cover-up of information relating to unidentified flying objects (UFOs). The Project claims that UFOs are spacecraft piloted by intelligent extraterrestrial life, a fact that the United States government is keeping secret. **The Project claims that the government has also concealed advanced energy-technologies obtained from the extraterrestrials. These technologies are being suppressed and hidden in top secret black-on-black 'black projects'** in order not to upset the global geo-political power and energy-sector financial status-quo and its oil industry 'special interests'.

The Project's goal is for free and open Congressional hearings of all data regarding UFOs, including the large amount of information they claim is being hidden, and for release of the technology they claim is being suppressed, particularly free energy sources. *(Let us not worry about that though... When conventional (modern) energy resources will be exhausted, future rulers —we will later find out exactly **who** they will be— as 'saviors' will offer the 'gift' of free energy. They will thus secure greater numbers of men who will bow to them. This will be one of the baits.)*

...The Disclosure Project selected most of its witnesses from military and government organizations. Following is a list of the most noteworthy participants of the Disclosure Project:

Testimony that Explains the Secrecy

- Merle Shane McDow: US Navy Atlantic Command
- Lt. Col. Charles Brown: US Air Force (Ret.)
- Lance Corporal Jonathan Weygandt: US Marine Corps

- Maj. George A. Filer, III: US Air Force (Ret.)
- Nick Pope: British Ministry of Defense Official
- Larry Warren: US Air Force, Security Officer
- Sgt. Clifford Stone: US Army
- Master Sgt. Dan Morris: US Air Force, NRO Operative
- A.H.: Boeing Aerospace Employee
- Officer Alan Godfrey: British Police
- Sgt. Karl Wolf: US Air Force
- Ms. Donna Hare: NASA Employee
- Mr. John Maynard: DIA Official
- Dr. Robert Wood: McDonnell Douglas Aerospace Engineer
- Glen Dennis: NM UFO Crash Witness
- Sgt. Leonard Pretko: US Air Force
- Dr. Roberto Pinotti: Italian UFO expert
- Dr. Paul Czysz: McDonnell Douglas Career Engineer
- Astronaut Edgar Mitchell
- John Callahan: FAA Head of Accidents and Investigations
- Michael Smith: US Air Force Radar Controller
- Franklin Carter: US Navy Radar Technician
- Neil Daniels: United Airlines Pilot
- Lt. Frederick Fox: US Navy Pilot
- Captain Robert Salas: US Air Force, SAC Launch Controller
- Prof. Robert Jacobs: US Air Force
- Harry Allen Jordan: US Navy
- James Kopf: US Navy Crypto Communications

Witness Testimony Overview
- Astronaut Edgar Mitchell: May 1998
- Monsignor Corrado Balducci: September 2000

Radar and Pilot Cases
- FAA Division Chief John Callahan
- Sgt. Chuck Sorrells: US Air Force (ret.)
- Mr. Michael W. Smith: US Air Force
- Commander Graham Bethune: US Navy (ret.)
- Mr. Enrique Kolbeck: Senior Air Traffic Controller,
- Dr. Richard Haines
- Mr. Franklin Carter: US Navy
- Neil Daniels: Airline Pilot
- Sgt. Robert Blazina (ret.)
- Lieutenant Frederick Marshall Fox: US Navy (ret.)
- Captain Massimo Poggi

Don't skip chapters or bibliographic references

- Lt. Bob Walker: US Army
- Mr. Don Bockelman: US Army

SAC/Nuke

- Captain Robert Salas
- Professor Robert Jacobs: Lt. US Air Force
- Lt. Colonel Dwynne Arneson: US Air Force (ret.)
- Colonel Ross Dedrickson: US Air Force/AEC (ret.)
- Harry Allen Jordan: US Navy
- Mr. James Kopf: US Navy/ National Security Agency
- Lieutenant Colonel Joe Wojtecki, US Air Force
- Staff Sergeant Stoney Campbell: US Air Force

Government Insiders/ NASA/Deep Insiders

- Astronaut Gordon Cooper
- Merle Shane McDow: US Navy Atlantic Command
- Lieutenant Colonel Charles Brown: US Air Force (ret.), October
- Dr. Carol Rosin
- Lance Corporal John Weygandt: U.S. Marine Corps,
- Major A. Filer III: U.S. Air Force
- Mr. Nick Pope: British Ministry Of Defense
- Admiral Lord Hill-Norton: Five-Star Admiral, Former Head of the British Ministry of Defense
- Security Officer Larry Warren: United States Air Force,
- Captain Lori Rehfeldt
- Sergeant Clifford Stone: United States Army
- Major-General Vasily Alexeyev: Russian Air Force,
- Master Sergeant Dan Morris: US Air Force/NRO Operative (ret.)
- Mr. Don Phillips: Lockheed Skunkworks, USAF, and CIA Contractor
- Captain Bill Uhouse: US Marine Corps (ret.)
- Lieutenant Colonel John Williams: US Air Force (ret.)
- Mr. Don Johnson
- A.H.: Boeing Aerospace, December 2000
- British Police Officer Alan Godfrey
- Mr. Gordon Creighton: Former British Foreign Service Official
- Sergeant Karl Wolfe: US Air Force
- Donna Hare: Former NASA Employee
- Mr. John Maynard: Defense Intelligence Agency (ret.)
- Mr. Harland Bentley: US Army
- Dr. Robert Wood: McDonnell Douglas Aerospace Engineer,
- Dr. Alfred Webre: Senior Policy Analyst Stanford Research Institute
- Denise McKenzie: Former SAIC employee

- Mr. Paul H. Utz
- Colonel Phillip J. Corso, Sr.: US Army (ret.)
- Mr. Glen Dennis
- Lieutenant Walter Haut: US Navy
- Buck Sergeant Leonard Pretko: US Air Force
- Mr. Dan Willis: US Navy
- Dr. Roberto Pinotti.»

B) *Some additional information from the infamous FBI's Blue Book*
«From FBI's archives:
SUBJECT: Project Blue Book

File Number 62-83894
July 24, 1989
To Mr. William S. Sessions, Director
U. S. Department of Justice
Federal Bureau of Investigations
Washington, D. C. 20535
Dear Mr. Sessions:
…The important key is to go beyond the Air Force and into the other agencies; such as the Office of Defense, C. I. A., etc. President Bush *(the father)*, when asked about UFO's, told the person asking **"You do not know the half of it"**. As you know, President Bush was formerly with the C. I. A. His comments are on tape by the way…
Very sincerely,
[Sender's name is erased with black ink]
P.S. As sort of an 'ultimate' challenge – why not ask President Bush, himself?

Their 'offer' **had no intention** to 'upgrade' man materially, but rather served their own objectives exclusively so as to ensure *(for the dark exocosmic powers)* the requirements to control the entire human population through the possibilities technology would give them. Without these new technological tools, the operation would be impossible. Man, not only took the bait, he swallowed it as well…

So, because some new and fundamental adjustments had to be made to man's genetic code, the new technology was designed in such a way so as to completely facilitate the possibility of this 'intervention' on it (the genetic code). Exactly as it had happened at the beginning of the Iron Race, when with the intervention of the materialized 'gods' in the visible plane, the initial DNA of men was changed, transforming the previous 4th Root/Race of men to the contemporary 5th Iron Gender/Race, likewise today, a new diversification is being attempted.

Don't skip chapters or bibliographic references

HYBRID BODIES:

A primary goal of these astral forces is to construct a new 'human' body of such configuration/structure that will survive unhindered in the future universal conditions on one hand, and securely **imprison** the stored living Soul inside it on the other.

All abductions of men carried out by these beings in the pretense of searching for human genetic material, were solely aimed towards the construction of such hybrid bodies.

---

578 **A) ERICH VON DÄNIKEN 'THE SECOND COMING HAS ALREADY STARTED'** (p. 229-233)

«Top psychologist Dr. John E. Mack is a psychiatry professor at Harvard University, Boston, the most acknowledged American University.

...Professor Mack met hundreds of individuals from different places of the country, who had never been in touch with each other. Because these people were perfectly rational and trustworthy, they triggered the professor's professional interest. ...The result is now published in a volume of four hundred pages. The book is titled 'Abduction - Human Encounters with Aliens', New York/Toronto, 1994.

Professor Mack's answer ...could not have been more emphatic: "Yes", is his conclusion. "The aliens are here, the abduction victims are not paranoid: sperm extraction, artificial insemination and removal of embryos have occurred and did not spring up from any inner desire of the victims".

(p. 233) ...We have similar testimonies from individuals from different countries and continents. There are thousands of injured women whose embryos were mysteriously removed without being miscarried or having had an abortion. There are scars from unexplained operations, which no terrestrial doctor had performed, and finally have the tiny alien implants, which were surgically removed from numerous victims of abduction.

Professor Mack, on p. 42 of his book (American publication) says that many of these tiny metallic or glass objects had to be removed from the victims' bodies: small needle-shaped implants were found inside a man's penis or up the nose of a twenty-four year old woman, exactly at the point where the brain begins. Even though the mysterious implants have been chemically and physically analyzed, they didn't make any sense because the function of these implants is not known.»

B) 'HELLENIC NEXUS' MAGAZINE ISSUE 12, FEBRUARY-MARCH 2006
ARTICLE BY CHRISTOS VAGENAS: 'UNDERGROUND BASES MYTHS AND REALITY'
(LETTERS FROM THE UNDERGROUND BY RICHARD SAUDER-NEXUS NEW TIMES, VOL.11, NO 6)

«Located almost two miles **beneath** Archuleta Mesa on the Jicarilla Apache Indian Reservation near Dulce, New Mexico USA, lies the undoubtedly most enigmatic of the existing underground installations: It is the place where, according to numerous reports of staff, researchers and the occasionally 'abducted', the main joint United States Government / Grey aliens Biogenetics Laboratory is. Specifically, in this underground facility which goes –at least– seven levels down, have been transported and kept under draconian measures of security, **human-alien hybrids**, which were the result of the genetic experiments performed by the aliens on humans who had been abducted. In proof of the above is the report coming from a member of the facility's personnel, who went as far as the 6th (underground) level.

(abovetopsecret.com/pages/dulce.html).

"...I have seen multi-legged creatures that look like a cross between humans and octopuses, reptilian humans and hairy creatures with human hands that cry like a baby..." According to a worker named Thomas C. ...there are more than 18.000 Greys residing on sub-level 5. On the other levels of the installation, they experiment on the human energy body, dreams and telepathy, **in order to manipulate the human kind**.

Also, according to reports, the base uses no conventional electricity. The elevators have no cables, as they are controlled magnetically, whereas a similar field produces artificial illumination from an invisible source.»

C) ILISSOS JOURNAL, ISSUE 95 (1972), **BREAKTHROUGH SCIENCE: 'THE UNKNOWN PSYCHIC WORLD OF PLANTS', SCIENTIFIC RESEARCH ACHIEVEMENTS IN BRAZIL** *(Reminding an excerpt from previous* reference*)*

«...Henrico, in service with General Electric, specialized in medical engineering, has dealt extensively with the 'temperament' of plants at first and later on with the human temperament.

... Researchers and scholars under the supervision of Prof. Ernani, director of the Institute of Psycho-biophysics in Sao Paolo Brazil, also participate in the experiments. The team is comprised of 50 researchers/scientists who specialize in the construction of **special gauges measuring the invisible radiations of bodies.**»

So, this new hybrid body is built from a mixture of human DNA and elements from the body of the astral beings, which is mostly in an energy-state –as it **possesses** natural access to the energy-fields– capable of surviving in the conditions of the parallel, virtual universes that they have labeled 'the 5th dimension'.

Don't skip chapters or bibliographic references

---

[579] **ERICH VON DÄNIKEN 'THE SECOND COMING HAS ALREADY BEGUN'** (p. 228)
«Dr. David Jacobs PhD believes that the sperm collection process and artificial insemination is the main reason behind all abductions. Its objective is <u>the production of a half human and half alien hybrid being.</u> [JACOBS, D., SECRET LIVES - FIRSTHAND DOCUMENTED ACCOUNTS OF UFO ABDUCTIONS. NEW YORK, 1992]
(So that this new semi-human species will be able to survive in those parallel alternative probabilities of universes)
(p. 234) ...After all, the aliens have already talked to some of the abduction victims, at least they gave them some explanations to justify their hideous actions. They claim that an upcoming disaster will destroy our planet. But the indications on the disaster are controversial and vague.»

Inside vast chambers in the secret underground installations, such hybrid bodies are kept under extremely specialized conditions, under draconian security measures of secrecy.

ENERGY-BODY/GRID:

Simultaneously with the creation of these hybrid bodies (by the 'extraterrestrial' entities), another parallel operation is being methodized (by Earthmen), aiming at the energy-bodies of contemporary man.

All experiments carried out on man's energy-bodies and on the invisible energies that surround him had as their goal to **intervene** on these bodies, thus creating **an energy 'body/net'**. The interventions had to be made to man's DNA, where the administrative center of these energy-bodies is located.

The recent technological achievements in nanotechnology provide the means for the creation of completely integrated devices of microscopic size with infinite possibilities. The most basic 'nano-device' concerns a microscopic computer (biochip) that operates inside an organic body, but its adjustments are remotely controlled, even from miles away. This nano-computer will openly or covertly 'regulate' everything, from the hormonal function of a human organism down to its emotions; after all, it is known that human emotions *(e.g. love, violence)* are modulated according to chemical reactions taking place inside the body *(e.g. oxytocine or glucose decrease in the brain respectively)*.

580 *There are two kinds of implants: (a) those made by Earthmen and (b) those made by Extraterrestrials. Each kind is used for different purposes.*

ALIEN IMPLANTS:

A) **IMPLANTS:** http://www.inout.gr/archive/index.php/t-15979.html (25-09-07)

(The specific article has been published by the editor of supernatural.gr Kostas Kiapekos in 'Mystery' magazine.)

«The term 'alien implants', is fully associated with the mysterious abductions of humans by alien entities. A distinct and for the time being inexplicable dimension is given to this dark aspect of the alien presence on our planet. Perhaps, in some of these cases the finding of implants in different parts in the body of the individuals bearing them, were the result of personal accidents that were not noticed, or of a mistake, misinterpretation or even more of a deliberate deception. Nevertheless, there are many scientifically confirmed incidents that can be explained by a technology capable of controlling the human body and the mental (psychic) functions, especially through the influence of the brain.

The wave of UFO sightings around the planet which began in 1947 was enriched by reports about alien abductions and experiments during the 60's. Reports about the existence of implants in the body of individuals, who seem to have had such experience, began in 1967. Betty Andreasson, a woman from Massachusetts, was the first to come out and talk about her abductions by non-human beings, the experiments she was subjected to and the presence of a tiny sphere (ball) which was eventually removed from the upper part of her nasal cavity.

Since 1994, implants of diverse forms and shapes have been surgically removed from individuals who were unaware of their existence, until a routine medical test revealed them. So, either during visual examination of the surface skin or using X-rays during radiography, detection and confirmation of tiny objects raised questions. The implants are generally no more than 3cm long and 1mm thick, metal pieces in rectangular or triangular shapes, glasslike crystals of a structure difficult to understand, as well as, tiny masses of complicated biological material, open a vast chapter about the purpose of their insertion and their effect in the human body.

…From the accounts which have been recorded until now, concerning abductions and implants, it results that many of the abductees had a stark memory of that incident and a clear recollection of the painful moment of the objects' insertion into their body, as well as, a noteworthy change of their attitude. The development of special psychic abilities, the day to day nightmares, the sense of being monitored, as well as, the sudden new UFO sightings in the area the abductees dwell, set up a murky scenery of fear and doubt, posing new questions

Don't skip chapters or bibliographic references

about the alien visitors' intentions for the human species.»

B) *Let me remind you of the excerpt from Giannoulakis' & Kavakopoulos' book* **'THE TRUTH ABOUT UFOS AND ALIEN CONSPIRACIES'** *where John Lear Jr. states:* «The 'agreement' (*with the Living Biological Entities – L.B.E.– colloquially 'aliens'*) was that **in exchange for technology** that they would provide us, we agreed to ignore the **abductions** that would take place. …In fact the purpose for the abductions turned out to be: The insertion of a 3mm spherical device through the nasal cavity into the brain of the abductees (*mark/incision …upon the forehead*). The device is used for the biological monitoring, tracking and control of the abductees.»

EARTHLY IMPLANTS:

C) 'TRITO MATI' MAGAZINE ISSUE 153, JULY 2007, ARTICLE BY GEORGE ALEXANDROU 'IMPLANTS, ANTICHRIST, DEMOCRACY AND (AT LAST) GOD!'

«…The first microchip applications that will be controlled by satellites rather than scanners are already over the experimental stage. Applications that make the surgical extraction of the microchip out of the human body impossible are also under discussion. …Research is carried out to find a way to store biometric data in the actual human skin of the hand or forehead, setting a permanent pattern –an invisible tattoo *(marking/incision)*– shaped by the salinity of the skin –a combination of nanotechnology and biotechnology– which is going to function as a microchip. IBM is already working on the personal area network technology or PAN, and studies the creation of a readable electric field on or under the skin, which is going to store personal data based on its salinity.

…For someone to deny the implantation would seem illegal, old-fashioned, absurd, suspicious, antisocial and inhuman. In reality, it's not necessary to be imposed onto the population. Anyone who doesn't want it isn't obliged to have it. …He would, however, automatically become a pariah and a clochard. Even the populations that will massively deny it will not be obliged to wear it. They will be put in 'parks'-enclaves to rot in criminality, poverty, diseases. Whoever wants to escape from that misery will go running to get chipped in order to be 'saved'.»

Therefore, it was of great necessity to them to create this (biochip), which will include (apart from the 'benefits' they will advertise) two additional functions: (a) hormonal/emotional control aiming towards absolute manipulation and (b) genetic mutation for the transformation of the **astroaetheric** bodies into an energy-body/net/grid. It is quite possible that the simultaneous transmutation of the physical/material body is in their endeavors as well –a function that only some alien biochips can perform. But even if they do not accomplish that, the 'uploading' of a human existence into the new hybrid bodies is not unfeasible with the technologies they possess *(something similar to the process of consciousness uploading in the motion picture 'AVATAR').*

> **581** **HUMAN CONSCIOUSNESS STORED ON SUPERCOMPUTERS**
>
> http://news.pathfinder.gr/world/news/198544.html
>
> «Ian Pearson, head of the Futurology Unit at British Telecom, is paid by the telecommunications giant to imagine tomorrow. According to his latest estimates, for which he took under consideration the accelerated progress of modern technology, by 2050, computer technology will be advanced enough to facilitate 'downloading' of the contents of a human brain into a supercomputer. He claims just that, and points out that the challenging part is not the construction of a computer with appropriate power and speed **but one capable of faithfully recording the human consciousness**...
>
> "If you draw timelines, realistically speaking, by the year 2050, man should be able to download the contents of the brain into a machine, and thus death will no longer be a problem", Mr. Pearson claims in a recent interview for 'The Observer'. He makes clear though, that this practice will not be affordable by all. Its cost will be prohibitive for at least 20 years more, but by 2080, he believes, this problem will be solved. "It will have become a routine procedure by then" he states and makes it clear that he is not joking around.»

Implantation of this extremely dangerous 'element' (biochip) will be accomplished **by injection** <u>into the human organism</u> in order to slowly mutate its structure. Using some 'imperative need' as pretext, they will convince the nations to accept it, even by masquerading it into something different from what it will **actually** be.

This will be the marking of the beast (injection, puncture, scratching or 'engraving' of the skin, incision etc.) as John calls it in the Apocalypse *{Tr. n.: In the original Greek version the word χάραγμα [charagma] is used, which is more appropriately translated as 'carving', 'incision', etc.}.* This will be the gravest trap for man, because, if he accepts it, he will be subjected to the (voluntary or involuntary) transmutation of his astro-aetheric bodies into an energy 'net/grid' which will irrevocably entrap his Soul in this world of devastation, stopping it from escaping to higher territories. Then, not even the knowledge of Truth (Epignosis) will be enough to set him free. Following that, the inspectors of this world, having the new hybrid material bodies fully prepared, will attempt the final transformation. This is how they plan to completely entrap the souls they need.

Don't skip chapters or bibliographic references

In order to dragoon humanity to succumb to their demands they need a ruthless legislation in the role of an 'assistant': Thus a ruthless, iron-bound dictatorship is being methodized to enable the materialization of their plans.

---

[582] **TEXE MARRS 'PROJECT L.U.C.I.D.'** (A U.S. AIR FORCE OFFICIAL): «Do not even for an instant think that you and your loved ones can escape the monstrous system which lies in our path. Once Project L.U.C.I.D. is fully operational, every man on Earth will be forced to succumb to the dominion of the most hideous slavery ever in human history. ...I am instead, horrified that the American people –as well all other peoples in the world– are about to enter a sinister period of blood, terror, chaos and slavery unparalleled in human history. Worse still, the vast majority are totally ignorant of what is to come and unprepared to deal with it.» *("...and they gnawed their tongues because of pain." [JOHN'S REVELATION 16:10]*).

(B) WAYS OF TRANSPORT TO THE PARALLEL UNIVERSES OF THE 5TH DIMENSION

The remaining big problem though is how to transport the entire humanity to those parallel universes! With the age-old methods of control and the 'psycho-invaders' inside individuals with leading roles as their basic partners, they methodize **the most far reaching scheme**, recruiting unsuspecting people to 'man' it:

(a) Those who are extensively informed on Earth problems, by persuading them that the only salvation for humanity can be found in the ONE solution that 'some' propose.

(b) The aficionados of scientific research, by alluring them with the enticement of the 'great discovery'.

(c) The reasonable ones, by misleading them with the notion that science must make another big step to 'progress'.

Thus they mastermind the '**theft**' of the entire Earth and its transport 'with crew and cargo' to another parallel alternative reality!

–*And how can something like that possibly happen?*

–With the creation of a space-time wormhole in the Earth's environment, which will 'suction' it out to transport it elsewhere... This is what the experiments being carried out at C. E. R. N. aim at in reality.

---

⁵⁸³ **A) CONCERN ABOUT THE CERN EXPERIMENT**
http://www.inout.gr/showthread.php?p=176548#post176548

«Concern caused the ambitious experiment in the European Laboratory of CERN, which will start up the world's biggest particle accelerator this summer. A lawsuit that was filed in a U.S. Federal Court seeks the suspension of the experiment which –according to the plaintiffs– may lead to the creation of a dark hole, or some form of 'dark matter' capable to 'swallow' the entire planet or even the entire Universe.

Two Russian mathematicians have suggested that the giant atom accelerator, which is due to be switched on in the beginning of summer in CERN, could create the conditions where a 'microcosmic' travel backwards or forwards in time might be possible. In essence, Irina Ya. Aref'eva and Igor V. Volovich believe that the Large Hadron Collider **might create tiny wormholes in space, which could allow some form of limited time travel.**

If true, this would mark the first time in human history that a time machine has been created. If traveling back in time is possible at all, it should in theory be possible to travel back to the point when the first time machine was created and so this would mean that time travelers from the future would be able to visit us.

As an article in New Scientist suggests, this year (2008) could become 'the year zero' for time travel. The article points out that there are many practical

---

Don't skip chapters or bibliographic references

problems and theoretical paradoxes to time travel. "Nevertheless, the slim possibility remains, that we will see visitors from the future in the next year", says the magazine, rather provocatively.

It must be said that few scientists accept the idea that the Large Hadron Collider (L.H.C.) will create the conditions, necessary for time travel. The L.H.C. is designed to prove the mysterious forces that exist at the level of sub-atomic particles, and as such, it will answer many important questions, such as the true nature of gravity. It is not designed as a time machine. *(And naturally, it is in their best interest not to present it as a time machine.)*

In any case, if the L.H.C. becomes a time machine by accident, the device would exist only at the sub-atomic level; not a machine which is able to carry people to the past or to the future.

The biggest theoretical problem is known as the time-travel paradox. If someone travels back in time and does something to prevent his own existence, (e.g. killing his grandfather before his own father is conceived, in which case he could not exist either), then how can time-travel be possible?

Cosmologists, renowned for their imaginative ingenuity, have come up with a way round this paradox. They have suggested that there is not one universe but many –so many that every possible outcome of any event actually takes place. In this multiple universe, or 'multiverse' model, a woman who goes back in time to murder her own grandmother can get away with it, because in the universe next door, the granny lives to have the daughter who becomes the murderer's mother. So, will we one day be able to travel in time?»

Let us combine some information now:

B) QUANTUM WORMHOLES COULD CARRY PEOPLE, 18:10 23 MAY 2002 BY CHARLES CHOI (NEWSCIENTIST)

http://www.newscientist.com/article/dn2312-quantum-wormholes-could-carry-people.html

«All around us are tiny gates that lead to the rest of the Universe. Predicted by Einstein's equations, these tiny quantum wormholes offer a faster-than-light short cut to the rest of the cosmos *(Universe)* –at least in principle. Now physicists believe that these doors could be opened wide enough to allow someone to travel through.

Quantum wormholes are thought to be much smaller than even protons and electrons, and until now no one has modeled what happens when something passes through one. So Sean Hayward at Ewha Womans University in Korea and Hisa-aki Shinkai at the Riken Institute of Physical and Chemical Research in Japan decided to 'do the sums' and find out what would happen if someone tried to pass through a quantum wormhole.

They have found that any matter traveling through, adds positive energy to the wormhole. That unexpectedly makes it collapse and transform into a black hole, a spatial region of a very big mass, with a gravitational pull so strong, that even light cannot escape.

…Ghost radiation…is a negative energy-field offsetting regular positive energy of matter…

Ghost radiation could therefore be used to offset the positive energy of matter traveling through the wormhole. As we saw, matter itself transforms the quantum wormhole into a black hole due to its positive energy…

Of course, such an undertaking of balancing positive and negative energy cannot be easy. Add too much negative energy, the scientists discovered, and the wormhole will immediately explode into a new universe that expands at the speed of light, much as astrophysicists say ours did, immediately after the Big Bang *(yet more proof indicating we are in the 'black hole universe')*.

…The future CERN Large Hadron Collider in Switzerland *(the article was published in 2002)* is expected to generate one mini-black hole per second, a potential source of wormholes through which physicists could send quantum-sized particles.»

C) TIME MACHINES: http://x.e-e-e.gr/real_x_files/science/time_travels/index.html

«Now, with the official science and according to Dr. Ronald Mallett (professor at the University of Connecticut), the necessary technology in the field of high power lasers, optical fibers, as well as slowing down light experiments, already exists, and that work on the experiment will start very soon. However, the energy needed to achieve this goal is enormous (according to Stephen Hawking, the energy of a star).

Slowing light down opens a new field, that didn't exist until today. The 'fuel' needed for the time machine is no other than light, top scientists believe. If a cyclically circulating beam of light *(as in CERN)* is slowed down to a snail's pace, that, might just be the vital ingredient for time travel. People forget that light, even though it has no mass, causes space to bend. It is known that light which is forced (through reflection or refraction) to follow a circular path, **causes particularly strange phenomena.** When Ronald Mallett published his paper describing how a cyclically circulating beam of laser light would create a vortex in space, it became apparent that time, as well as space, might be twisted. To achieve that, Mallett worked out that he would have to add a second **light beam**, circulating in the opposite direction *(the same way it happens in CERN. Only, instead of 'particles', laser light-beams are used here)*. According to his theory, if you increase the intensity of light, space and time change roles. Inside the circulating light-beam, time starts running round as well, while to an outside observer, it appears as an ordinary dimension in Space. Now, should a person enter the vortex and walk along in the right direction, he could actually travel in Time and exit the circle at any moment, right back at the exact moment of his entrance.

The experiment will be designed only to observe the twisting of space by measuring the effects on a particle trapped in the light circle, when they subsequently add a second beam. If any results do occur, we will only know after performing the actual experiment, says Ronald Mallett. The question that comes forward is, whether it will be possible for a person to enter this light mechanism. Naturally, many theoretical questions are raised, which are mainly related to the so-called 'time-paradoxes'. If Quantum Theory regarding the parallel universes is proven correct, then, he who will travel in the past will probably find himself in a different past than the real one. If he tries to affect (change) the way things are in the place where he will be (i.e. if he messes with history), he will affect (change) history and the sequence of events in the parallel world and not his real past.»

The astronomical sums of money invested in this program are naturally not granted so that scientists can just find 'some answers'! Of course, some 'informed' scientists working on the experiment, being aware of the dead end in the Earth's course and completely 'convinced' of the nonexistence of Spirit inside man, consider C.E.R.N.'s solution a panacea (cure-all) and themselves as saviors. But their ignorance —which they don't even mildly acknowledge— gambles the existential autonomy of billions of people on the planet in a game of 'Russian roulette'.

Of course, the 'C.E.R.N.' issue concerns a venture whose anticipated results are not guaranteed. This is why they are also simultaneously planning other inferior 'desperate measures'. These measures relate to the embarkation of the soulful potential on 'starship-arks' which will help them escape to a new beginning in the 5th dimension of the parallel energy-universes *(which they shall call the 'new golden age of Krita or Satya Yuga')*.

[584] *The evacuation of the planet is a 'model' which appears dynamically from ever more groups that 'communicate' with non-visible entities, and not only.*

G. KALOGERAKIS (Retired Greek Army Major General) **'PROMETHEUS' LEGACY'** (p. 81) *(Encoded message through PC —w/out internet connection— from invisible entities who call themselves 'Olympians')*

«Olympians: "Similar rescue interventions by **evacuation of the planet** have occurred many times in the past. …Gaia's rescue-plan bears the name 'PHOENIX' and includes not only humans, but also <u>animal genetic material and seeds from all kinds of plants</u>. …The Great Universal Brotherhood of Light with its myriads upon myriads of crafts, bearing the name 'ΤΕΛΕΙΟΤΗΣ' [=PERFECTION], always undertakes the rescue of small children, young people, and righteous persons, when and where need may arise. It's a rescue mission. It consists of entities of the 'Great Cosmos' for the rescue of humans through **evacuation of the planet**. All those who will be rescued, will be transferred to other inhabited planets, the ones who want to stay on them can do so, the ones who don't **will return** to Gaia *(!!)* for its colonization *(to a parallel, alternative, virtual reality. Otherwise, what would the point of lifting them off Earth (Gaia) be, if they are to take them back? ...Could it be because they don't want humans to participate in the Spiritual Transference? They (Olympians), in another of their statements, claim that they will reconstruct the planet!! ... Let us not be so naïve.)*

... The star-base 'PHOENIX' ...hosts: 850 mother-ships, whose radius ranges from 25 to 150 kilometers, 3,892 sister-ships with a radius of 2.5 to 15 kilometers and 200,000 subsidiary ships with a radius of 10 to 500 meters.

Both vessels 'PHOENIX' and 'PERFECTION' contain mother-ships, sister-ships and subsidiary ships... The mission of the vessels of the 'Phoenix' star-fleet is to collect 120,000,000 'E' descendants, in case planet Earth is in danger. The starship 'Lilith' *(of the enemy astral forces, whom they call apostates)*, which is located on the dark side of the moon *(the base of the negative astrals)* will collect the terrestrial collaborators of the apostates on 57,000 starships with a capacity of 35,000,000 people.»

Most conspiracy-theory groups of the planet have discerned the desire of the Earth's mighty ones to form a global government, aiming at a world-dictatorship for the complete control of men.

585 **A) DR. ROBERT MÜLLER, ASSISTANT TO THE SECRETARY-GENERAL OF THE UNITED NATIONS**: «In my view, after fifty years of service in the United Nations system, I have come to realize **the utmost urgency and absolute necessity for a proper global government.** There is no shadow of a doubt that the current political and economic systems are no longer appropriate and will lead the evolution of life on this planet to end. We must therefore, urgently look for new ways.»

B) LESTER BROWN, WORLDWATCH INSTITUTE: «**Nations** are in effect **ceding portions of their sovereignty to the international community and international authorities,** in order to create a new system of international environmental governance, as a means of solving otherwise unmanageable crises.»

Furthermore, these conspiracy-theory groups expose the ulterior motives of the mighty powers of authority, concerning the decrease of Earth population, which are justified by the pretense that the planet will be able to 'function' better this way.

Don't skip chapters or bibliographic references

586 **A) 'ENVIRONMENTAL POLICIES AS A COVER-UP FOR THE GENOCIDE AND EN-SLAVEMENT OF HUMANITY'** VICKY CHRYSSOU, WRITES: 20/05/2009
http://periballondiki.blogspot.com/2009/05/blog-post_8215.html

«Modern eugenics has spread its 'tentacles' in many areas of science and environmental policy.

Using the protection of the environment as a pretext, they are systematically promoting **a global government of a dictatorial nature,** which is supposed to save the planet from the destruction, allegedly caused by the Earth's overpopulation. The 'overpopulation' theories –in relation to the Earth's capacity to nourish its population and at the same time keeping its ecosystem viable– are components of their propaganda. In their efforts to drastically reduce world population they are using the following methods: population control programs (family and birth control etc.), programs for the gradual and systematic degeneration of the human immune system such as: mandatory vaccination programs, exposure to toxic-carcinogenic chemical additives in food, the use of toxic pesticides/fertilizers in the cultivation of the Earth, the systematic contamination of drinking water with fluoride and chloride, the chemtrails, wars, fake epidemics etc.»

B) EBOLA, SCIENTIFICALLY 'APPROVED' THE SOLUTION TO THE SALVATION OF THE PLANET!
ARTICLE BY CHRISTOS VAGENAS published in NEXUS HELLAS magazine
http://www.nexushellas.gr/index.php?option=com_content&task=view7id=121

«At the annual meeting of the Texas Academy of Science, Eric Pianka, named by the Academy as the 2006 Distinguished Texas Scientist, **advocated the elimination of 90 percent of Earth's population through the airborne Ebola Reston virus,** as the best solution against overpopulation. Nevertheless, however horrifying was what the distinguished professor proposed, even more horrifying was the long, enthusiastic standing ovation he received by the members of the Academy (top academics and scientists)...

Dr. Eric Pianka, Professor of Zoology, in the Department of Evolutionary Biology, of Texas University: "We've got 90% mortality in humans with the airborne Ebola. Killing humans; think about that..."

...The extremely popular, judging by the enthusiastic welcome he was given, Dr. E. Pianka, a member of the American Academy of Science and world-renowned ecologist (!), began his speech saying that the global public opinion was not ready to hear the information presented. Then, and without presenting any data to justify his view, he estimated that the Earth is unable to maintain life in the future without drastic measures, and he asserted that the only feasible solution is to reduce global population to 10% of the present number. "War and famine would not do", he emphasized. "Instead, epidemics offer the most efficient and fastest way to exterminate the billions (of humans) that must soon die if the population crisis is to be solved." (!)

"AIDS is not an efficient killer", he explained, "because, it is too slow", explaining that his favored candidate for eliminating 90% of the world's population is airborne string of the Ebola virus (Ebola Reston). And this because it is both: highly lethal (about 90%) and it kills in a few days.

…If Ebola was transmitted by air, its spreading would be fast and fatal to humans. A small detail that the 'idealist' academic forgot to mention: Ebola victims don't die of the heavy bleeding which is induced, but of shock, because their internal organs are eventually liquefied…

The 'select few': Then came the question and answer session, in which professor Pianka was asked to comment on whether other diseases would also be efficient killers. The audience laughed when he said, "You know, bird flu, is good too". They laughed again a little later when he cynically proposed preventive sterilization of everybody on Earth.»
[Eric Pianka's website: http://uts.cc.utexas.edu?~varanus/eric.html]

C) Some others said:
(a) Prince Philip, Duke of Edinburgh, cofounder of World Wildlife Fund (WWF) said: "In the event that I am reincarnated, I would like to return as a deadly virus for the human population, in order to reduce it to lower levels."
(b) John Davis, editor of the 'Earth First' Newspaper (!) said: "I suspect that eradicating small pox was wrong. It would have contributed significantly in balancing the ecosystems."
(c) Christopher Manes, 'Earth First' Newspaper (!) said: "The extinction of the human species may not only be **inevitable**, but a good thing."

But all these troubled conspiracy-theorists cannot give an answer to the question WHY these mighty ones are methodizing this totally dictatorial control and WHY they choose to decrease the population! They thus conclude that this happens because some are convinced they can save the planet this way! This population decrease however, wouldn't have to be carried out in such a violent way had there not been another '**imperative need**' forcing their hand. On the contrary, through a cumulative and systematized cooperation of all, it would be much easier to accomplish the desired result. After all, the excessive increase of the Earth's population was a problem they had been aware of many years before, long before the 'limits' were exceeded, when it would have been be much easier to organize an informative campaign for birth control throughout the planet –and enjoy its results by now– instead of this exceedingly difficult venture of genocide they are now planning. These conspiracy-theorists therefore, overlook the logical and, leaving many puzzle pieces unconnected, end-up in chaotic conclusions…

But the CAUSES are even deeper and if they are combined with everything previously mentioned, then the whole matter becomes obvious to everyone: You can't move an entire planet 'by bus'!

Don't skip chapters or bibliographic references

So, when the entire population has been 'marked' with this injected element/biochip, which will frame/entrap the Soul inside the astro-aetheric body, rendering it incapable of escaping, there will be no scruple for the decimation of humanity.

---

[587] P. GIANNOULAKIS L. KAVAKOPOULOS 'THE TRUTH ABOUT UFO AND EXTRA-TERRESTRIAL CONSPIRACIES' (p. 101)

«Robert Anton Wilson a researcher and a conspiracy critic, writes:

...Art Bell's radio program constantly asked former or current employees of 'Dreamland' *(this is how they call the infamous Area 51)*, to phone in and talk about what they know, anonymously. This led to an interesting and really disturbing telephone call on September 11, 1997. Here's the recording:

Man on the line: Hello, Art?

Art: Yes.

Man (he sounds scared): I don't have a whole lot of time.

Art: Well, look let's begin by finding out whether you're using this line properly or not.

Man: Ok. Area 51?

Art: Yes. Were you an employee there or are you now?

Man: I am a former employee. I was let go on a medical discharge about a week ago, and, and (coughing)... I've been running across the country. Man, I don't know where to start, they're... they're... they'll triangulate on this position really soon.

Art: Since you can't spend a lot of time on the phone, give us something quick...

Man: (making an effort not to break into sobs) Ok... um... um, ok, what we're thinking of as aliens, Art, they're extra-dimensional creatures that an earlier precursor of the space program made contact with. They're not what they claim to be. They have infiltrated a lot of aspects of the military establishment, particularly Area 51. The military ..., I'm sorry, the government knows about the disasters that are coming, and there are a lot of safe areas in this world that they could begin moving the population to, Art.

Art: But they're not doing anything?

Man: They're not. They want those major population centers wiped out, so that the few that are left will be more easily controllable.

Art (breaking): ... to be evacuated...

Man (sobbing without managing to conclude): I started getting...

At that point, the radio program went off the air (the listeners must have felt the same as the ones listening to the renowned Orson Wells' broadcast in 1938, who described a Martian invasion, then stopped broadcasting for an endless minute...). They then rebroadcasted a portion of a previous interview with Mark Fuhrman, an officer in Los Angeles Police Department. Later, it was explained that the line was disconnected due to technical reasons, but many did not believe that explanation...»

Here, we must make a very important clarification: The deployment of the real plans has been delegated to various (partial) groups, without any of them completely knowing the entire picture. Each independent group does not know which parts of the plans are being carried out by any other group. Furthermore, if the higher leaders of a group have some hidden agendas, they are not obliged to communicate them to their inferiors. But their lower ranking 'officers', once instructed to act, follow their orders, and never fail to arbitrarily justify and/or explain their actions, resulting to all kinds of falsifications. In reality then, the decimation of the human race will be the result of natural/cosmic events that are about to come, since it is impossible for the entire Earth's population to be saved. But some powerful circles, in their efforts to fulfill their ulterior goals, remain indifferent to the lethal repercussions these goals might have to the health of the nations, considering men doomed either way. Thus, one is left with the impression that genocide is being methodized. The truth of the matter is that, through the upcoming cosmic events, humanity will be greatly diminished and many people will lose their lives. And those who know part of this truth and have the power, use this knowledge to prepare, thinking they will thus save themselves.

The plan commands: The greatest percentage of the population *(90% as some claim)* must be left to die. Then, –the souls of these dead men– will incarnate in the new parallel dimension (in some parallel universe) inside the new hybrid bodies and in complete ignorance of what has previously happened, they will form the new race of men there. Thus the human 'plantation' is properly modified to 'smoothly' adapt to the new conditions of the pseudo-universe that will come.

Following that, the remaining 'select few' destined to be saved *(the 10% as some hope),* at the appropriate moment –'zero' Earth time–will embark on the starship 'arks' along with their 'gods', so that –after they are 'modified'– they will be the first to settle in the new area of the chosen parallel universe which will have been 'dressed up' with real matter.

There, they will be proclaimed as the new-knowledge 'safe-keepers' and will prepare/pave the way for the new incarnations of men/souls into the young children that will be born in that world...They will comprise the new team of 'Magistrates' who will bequeath the 'knowledge' to the new 'initiation groups' that will be formed, training new 'guardians of knowledge'. They will be the only ones to know about the procedure of the transfer of humanity to those parallel universes, without EVER –of course– finding out the **deeper** Truth. Thus, they will remain content with the explanation that the whole material universe entered a new 'phase' –which they will consider 'evolutionary'.

Don't skip chapters or bibliographic references

The coming events will require very 'delicate' maneuvers and absolute order in their management. A global government must therefore assume power and control all actions to be taken through a world-dictatorship and the inhuman laws it will establish, in order to reach the goals. ..."Then the fifth angel poured out his vial (bowl) onto the throne of the beast, and its kingdom became full of darkness; **and they** *(men)* **gnawed their tongues because of their pain.**" [REVELATION 16:10] Therefore, when the 'initiated' governors begin to face difficulties, "...they shall hand over their power and authority to the beast." [REVELATION 17:13] All this though will be discussed later on.

Yet, in this tangle of extreme events to come, the Truly Selected Ones will also be present, those who will CONSCIOUSLY choose Salvation and are destined to be TRANSFERRED to the Prepared Place. They must not, under any circumstances, receive the injected intervention of the biochip into their physical body which will transmute their astral body into a trap-body. They only need to strengthen their Spirit as much as they can, because THAT ALONE will be their salvation. They will also need to cut themselves off from EVERY emotional bond with matter, as they **patiently** wait for their definitive liberation from this material world. A difficult road awaits them until they reach its end as will be described later.

So let us briefly mention the operational plans for the preparation of the dark powers for the new world-phase:

(1)'Copy – paste' of material elements from nature in order to 'dress-up' these parallel worlds with true matter. This is carried out exclusively by astral entities.

(2)Creation of a new human body, suitable to survive under the new-type conditions (hybrids). This is the result of collaboration between earthly and extra-worldly astral entities.

(3)Systematic methodizing of operational moves for the transmutation of the human energy-bodies into bodies/traps for the Souls (injected intervention to the organism: the biochip). This is carried out by earthly groups of 'scientists'.

(4)Further exploration of possible ways for the transition to the 'chosen places' (C.E.R.N. or other alternative ways, with the necessary requirement of reduction of the population through genocide). This is methodized by independent groups of earthly powers and extra-worldly ones.

THE FIRST SIGNS

This world is not a uniform power. Every group hides a more powerful one inside it, all the way to the core (nucleus) of this world, which safeguards its invisible leadership. We shall now leave the activities of these invisible world-controllers and their human accomplices aside, to examine the intentions of the outer world-administration group *(the leaders of nations)* regarding the coming problems on Earth.

If we observe the conditions prevailing in nature during this period, we will realize that they signal the oncoming difficulties for Earth. These oncoming problems are accompanied by corresponding activities from the **governments** of nations. These actions isolated from one another seem uninteresting; but if they are combined and related to other events, they reveal a plan being followed.

As we have said, the entire universe is preparing for the withdrawal of the Archetypes of creation, resulting in a sequence of intense repercussions to the world of matter. The disturbances will affect the entire solar system, the Sun and naturally the Earth. At first these anomalies will be weak; but as the time of the withdrawal approaches, nature's disorder will become increasingly intensified, reaching its peak with very unpleasant consequences.

To begin with, this expansion of the energy-universe at break-neck speed will provide the first disturbing image.

---

588 A) DARK ENERGY CAN TEAR US TO PIECES SOURCE: SPACE.COM, DECEMBER 30, 2008
http://www.physics4u.gr/news/2009/scnews3593.html

«Pioneer of this theory is Robert Caldwell, physicist of Dartmouth College.

A new and somehow fateful theory has popped up, concerning the long-term future of the universe. It is called '**The Big Rip**' and it foresees that our body will literally tear to pieces.

Since the expansion rate increases continually, the enlargement speed becomes uncontrollably high, **over the light speed**, and finally, the parts of which the universe consists of, are literally torn apart or dissolve. In one words, galaxies, stars, planets as well as we ourselves are dispersed in space. The ghost energy (as Robert Caldwell has called dark energy) can dissolve the Earth, the planets and our sun.

Finally, when there will be only three months left, the planets and all the stars will explode. "There will be about 30 minutes left, till the atoms and their nuclei are dissolved", Caldwell says, "but it's not the length of time. We are not sure what is going to happen after that. If were able to see it, it would look like the end of time.»

Don't skip chapters or bibliographic references

---

*Let me remind you, that astronomers have great difficulty in discerning what is happening in our universe, **right** when they observe it, due to the fact that the farther away into the universe they look, the longer they go back in time! Some correlate this expansion of Dark Energy with the shrinking of time.*
«...and if time weren't **shortened**, no flesh would be saved...[MATTHEW 24:22]»

B) MYSTERIOUS GIANT HOLE DISCOVERED IN THE UNIVERSE
SOURCE: ASSOCIATED PRESS, WASHINGTON 25/08/07, 00:42 WASHINGTON (AP)
http://www.in.gr/news/default.asp

«Astronomers have stumbled upon a tremendous hole in the universe. **The cosmic blank spot, with a diameter of 1 billion light years**, contains no galaxies, stray stars or black holes, and even the mysterious dark matter is absent.

"This is 1,000 times the volume of what we sort of expected to see in terms of a typical void," said Minnesota astronomy professor Lawrence Rudnick, author of the paper that will be published in Astrophysical Journal... "What we have found is not normal, based either on studies of observations or large scale computer simulations of the universe evolution", the researchers' report states. ...This particular hole is located in the direction of the constellation of Eridanus, south west of Orion.»

Following that, a temperature increase of the planet becomes evident. Due to the overall intention to suppress the real events that follow, this increase will be attributed to the alleged contamination of the environment. This, being partially true, confuses a lot of people. But the real reasons are different. The temperature increase concerns the entire solar system with the Sun as the primary force behind it.

---

589 GREEN HOUSE PHENOMENON ON MARS, TOO! OVERHEATING DOESN'T THREATEN EARTH ONLY, SOURCE: 'TA NEA' ATHENIAN NEWSPAPER
http://digital.tanea.gr/Default.aspx?d=20070817&nid=5608613

«According to various researchers, on many planets of the solar system but on satellites too, a temperature increase also occurs. Mars for example, experiences climate changes much more intense than Earth. According to a paper published in the 'Nature' journal, by the NASA researcher Lori Fenton, the temperature of this planet has risen by 0,6 degrees Celsius in 20 years' time, when on Earth there was a 0,7 degrees rise in 150 years' time. "Variations across the surface of the planet generate strong winds and dust storms, trapping heat and raising the planet's temperature", suggests Fenton. However, Habibullo Abdussamatov, head of the St. Petersburg's Astronomical Observatory, has a contrary view on the matter; he has noted that we must look for the cause, "in the long-term increase in solar radiance which is heating both Earth and Mars". The Russian scientist's comment seems more interesting, 'La Republica' newspaper notes, given the fact that if Earth's current global warming is caused by the Sun, there should be traces of temperature rise on other planets, too.

Indeed, a not at all negligible temperature-increase has occurred on Jupiter, too. In 1939 three enormous cyclones appeared in the atmosphere of the planet, thousands of miles in diameter, which disappeared in 2000 because of the drop of the temperature. However, during the last few years, new cyclones were formed, as a result of a new rise in the temperature of its atmosphere. The assumption that the Sun is behind the warming of the entire system is strengthened by the fact that, according to a survey of MIT, a similar phenomenon has been observed on Pluto. Although Pluto is at the bounds of the solar system, its surface temperature has increased by 1.9 degrees Celsius over the past 14 years. "This situation can be easily explained by an increase in solar radiation, although there's no solid proof so far", says the American astronomer Jay Pasachoff.

On natural satellites, too: Temperature increase was observed on natural satellites, too, such as Neptune's moon Triton, whose temperature has risen 2 degrees Celsius during the past 15 years.»

The Earth's temperature increase will result in the melting of the ice *(which starts **under** the water surface!)* that will lead to a 'domino-effect' of natural disasters. When the poles are stripped of the ice and the two great apertures that exist there below them are revealed, the passage to the surface will open for the dangerous beings living inside the Earth's hollows.

590 JOHN'S REVELATION 9:2-3 «And he opened **the pit of the Abyss** *(the openings at the poles)*, and smoke arose out of the pit like the smoke of a great furnace; and the sun and the air were darkened because of the smoke of the pit. Then out of the smoke locusts came upon the earth. And unto them was given power, like the power of scorpions of the earth.»

Simultaneous to this, another big problem is rising: the continuous weakening of the Earth's magnetic field, on an ever growing scale, which will have unexpected consequences. This phenomenon is attributed to the reversal of the magnetic poles. The weakening of the Earth's magnetic field will disturb the atmosphere and will leave the Earth unprotected to the solar radiation bombardment, something which will subdue all life on its surface and cause violent changes to its environment.

591 **A) EARTH'S MAGNETIC FIELD WEAKENS BY 10% OVER THE PAST 150 YEARS**

POSTED ON: FRIDAY, 12 DECEMBER 2003, 06:00 CST BY ANDREW BRIDGES SAN FRANCISCO (AP), http://www.redorbit.com/news/space/22057/earths_magnetic_field_weakens_by_10_percent/

«The strength of the Earth's magnetic field has decreased by 10 percent over the past 150 years, raising the remote possibility that it may collapse and later reverse, flipping the planet's poles for the first time in nearly a million years, scientists said …Over the southern Atlantic Ocean, a continued weakening of the magnetic field has diminished the shielding effect it has locally in protecting the Earth from the natural radiation that bombards our planet from space, scientists said. …As a result, satellites in low Earth-orbit are left vulnerable to that radiation as they pass over the region, known as the South Atlantic Anomaly. *(See: DRAWINGS, SOUTH-ATLANTIC ANOMALY and MECHANICAL MALFUNCTIONS DUE TO S. A. A.)*

…The weakening –if coupled with a subsequently large influx of radiation in the form of protons streaming from the sun– can also affect the chemistry of the atmosphere, said Charles Jackman of NASA's Goddard Space Flight Center. That can lead to significant but temporary losses of atmospheric ozone, he said.»

B) SUN'S RAYS TO ROAST EARTH AS POLES FLIP

ROBIN MCKIE, SCIENCE EDITOR THE OBSERVER, SUNDAY 10 NOVEMBER 2002 11.24 GMT ARTICLE HISTORY, http://www.guardian.co.uk/world/2002/nov/10/science.research

«Earth's magnetic field - the force that protects us from deadly radiation bursts from outer space - is weakening dramatically. …The effects could be catastrophic. Powerful radiation bursts, which normally never touch the atmosphere, would heat up its upper layers, triggering climatic disruption. Navigation and communication satellites, the Earth's eyes and ears, would be destroyed and migrating animals left unable to navigate.

"Earth's magnetic field has disappeared many times before - as a prelude to our magnetic poles flipping over, when north becomes south and vice versa," said Dr. Alan Thomson of the British Geological Survey in Edinburgh. "Reversals happen every 250,000 years or so, and as there has not been one for almost a million years, we are due one soon."

For more than 100 years, scientists have noted the strength of Earth's magnetic field has been declining, but have disagreed about interpretations. Some said its drop was a precursor to reversal, others argued it merely indicated some temporary variation in field strength has been occurring.

But now Gauthier Hulot of the Paris Geophysical Institute has discovered that the Earth's magnetic field seems to be disappearing most alarmingly near the poles, a clear sign that a flip may soon take place. …And as Scientific American reports this week, this interpretation has now been backed up by computer simulation studies.

How long a reversal might last is a matter of scientific controversy, however. …Exactly what will happen when Earth's magnetic field disappears prior to its re-emergence in a reversed orientation is also difficult to assess. Compasses would point to the wrong pole - a minor inconvenience. More importantly, low-orbiting satellites would be exposed to electromagnetic battering, wrecking them.

In addition, many species of migrating animals and birds –from swallows to wildebeests– rely on innate abilities to track Earth's magnetic field. Their fates are impossible to gauge.

As to humans, our greatest risk would come from intense solar radiation bursts. Normally these are contained by the planet's magnetic field in space. However, if it disappears, particle storms will start to batter the atmosphere. "These solar particles can have profound effects," said Dr. Paul Murdin of the Institute of Astronomy, Cambridge. "On Mars, when its magnetic field failed permanently billions of years ago, it led to its atmosphere being boiled off. On Earth, it will heat up the upper atmosphere and send ripples round the world with enormous, unpredictable effects on the climate." It is unlikely that humans could do much.»

C) *Let us see however what happens with the human body, in order to deduce the probable impact the electromagnetic anomaly will have on human organisms.*

In 1873 Maxwell proved that electricity and magnetism are shaped in waves which create electromagnetic fields. Magnetic fields are created by the flow of electric current. The higher the voltage of the current, the stronger the magnetic field is. When the current is interrupted, the magnetic field is nullified.

The human body resembles an electric machine. This is due to the function of the cell. The characteristic attribute of cells is that they are enveloped by the cellular membrane. The cellular membrane consists of a double layer of lipids. Lipids are biological molecules acting as insulators. Many vitamins, fats and oils, even hormones belong to this category.

Cellular membrane separates the electrically charged inner cellular space from the outer cellular one. The outer cellular space is positively charged and the inner cellular space, negatively. These positively and negatively charged ions concentrate along the cellular membrane.

Having thus the cell a negative charge inside and a positive one outside, it automatically creates an electromagnetic field of 70 millivolts of energy.

Don't skip chapters or bibliographic references

At the same time, the sun also shows some very disturbing signs, as it can hardly create/maintain its own magnetic field, which protects the entire solar system from cosmic radiation.

---

[592] *Some informative data, to begin with, in order for the next parts that will comprise a revealing puzzle, to become clearer:*

(A1) SOLAR WIND http://www.astronomia.gr/wiki/index.php?title

«…The solar wind, which has also been called solar particle-radiation, is mainly comprised of electrons and protons which are emitted in an almost radial fashion from the sun's crown in ultrasound speeds. …The solar wind bursts from different spots of the sun's surface and with different initial velocity due to the different conditions existing in the crown's holes, and the sun's rotation, it reaches the earth in gusts, or as currents or solar wind waves.»

(A2) HELIOPAUSE http://www.astronomia.gr/wiki/index.php?title

«It is the outer limit of the solar wind's impact and is considered **the real boundary of the Solar System.** Beyond that is the interstellar space. As these two regions meet, a formation is created which looks like a bullet bursting through the air. Scientists estimate that this boundary is located at a distance of 100 AU (AU=astronomical unit of distance equal to that between Sun and Earth) and changes size depending on solar activity.»

A3) «The **heliosphere** is the three-dimensional region in space around the sun, which is full of solar wind particles and whose boundaries extend from the sun to the region before the heliopause boundary, where the heliosphere interacts with interplanetary space.»

A4) OUR SOLAR SYSTEM'S BOUNDARIES: http://www.physics4u.gr/blog/?p=768

«Logically the solar system should end where the sun's gravitational impact is practically zero… Thus, there is also the view that our solar system's boundary is the so-called heliopause, the outer limit of heliosphere, i.e. the region where the Sun's magnetic field and the solar wind prevail. **The heliosphere is like a bubble floating inside our galaxy.** The heliosphere determines the boundaries of our solar system and is made of –consists of– the solar wind that flows outwards from the sun.»

A5) SUNSPOTS http://www.astronomia.gr/wiki/index.php?title

«Sunspots appear at first almost always in groups like black spots at a distance of 1.000 kilometers between them… More specifically the appearance of sunspots presents an 11-year activity cycle; i.e. their number increases and decreases periodically every 11 years. Nevertheless, at this point, we must point out the following: The magnetic field of a sunspot comes out of its shadow and enters the sun's surface in another neighboring sunspot of opposite polarity. (Sunspots are responsible for the creation of the solar

---

magnetic field).

…It is also worth mentioning that the polarity of the leading sunspots in the sun's northern hemisphere is different from that of the southern hemisphere. This polarity is reversed approximately every 11 years resulting thus in the definition of the sunspot activity cycle as a 22-year long one instead of 11 years… Sunspots have an effect on the modulation of earthly climatic conditions as well as tree development. The highs of sunspots coincide with maximum tree growth (warm season with ample precipitation)…during complete sunspot absence, severe cold sets in.»

The puzzle pieces…

B) SUN'S POWER HITS NEW LOW, MAY ENDANGER EARTH?
ANNE MINARD NATIONAL GEOGRAPHIC NEWS SEPTEMBER 24, 2008
http://news.nationalgeographic.com/news/2008/09/080924-solar-wind.html

«The Ulysses space probe has detected fewer sunspots, decreased solar winds, and a weakening magnetic field—the lowest solar activity observed in 50 years, NASA scientists said yesterday.

That translates into a shrinking of the heliosphere, the invisible 'bubble' of solar wind that extends beyond Pluto and guards the planets—ours included—from bombardment by cosmic rays.

…But David J. McComas of the Southwest Research Institute, who leads one of the experiments onboard Ulysses, called the changes 'significant'.

Variable Star: Some variance in solar activity is normal for the sun, which has a 22-year magnetic cycle and an 11-year sunspot cycle.

But McComas said in a statement that researchers have been "surprised to find that the solar wind is much less powerful than it had been in the previous solar minimum."

Despite its name, solar wind is actually a stream of charged particles that expands out from the sun.»

C) THE SUN'S SURFACE IS STRANGELY QUIET
APRIL 29, 2009, http://www.apn.gr/news/world-news

«Scientists have remained in question about what they see on the sun's surface, or better, about what they don't see. The almost complete absence of sunspots is a great enigma, while it simultaneously ignites various scientific worries as to what it could mean and what repercussions (positive or negative) it might have to the climate change of our planet in the future.»

This results to:

D) EARTH'S NATURAL 'SHIELD' IS DIMINISHING, SEPTEMBER 25, 2008
a) http://www.ert.gr b) http://www.apn.gr/news/world-news/

«The solar wind –the steady current of charged subatomic particles emanated from the sun– which 'blows' with the speed of 1.5 million kilometers per hour, exhibits the weakest power of the last five decades, thus diminishing the natural 'shield' surrounding our solar system; according to the overall

Don't skip chapters or bibliographic references

evaluation scientists have conducted on 18-year data sent by the space vehicle 'Ulysses', as Reuter's and BBC agencies report.

It is estimated that this fact may have implications for the entire solar system, at a distance of billions of kilometers in space, as the weakening of solar winds equals diminishing of the force of 'shield' against the potentially harmful **galactic cosmic radiation.** The solar wind creates a large protective sphere, the heliosphere, around our solar system, which is simultaneously **the 'frontier' to interstellar space.**

'Ulysses' measurements show that the wind's force has dropped by 20-25% since the middle 90's while its temperature has dropped by 13%. As the solar wind ('carrying' the Sun's magnetic field) becomes weaker, the heliosphere also diminishes in size and power, thus allowing greater parts of the cosmic radiation (supercharged electrons and protons crossing interstellar space in tremendous speeds and originate from distant star explosions) to reach deep inside our solar system.

Scientists confirm that men have nothing to fear, as they continue to be protected by the magnetic field surrounding Earth *(which is also dissolving...).* On the contrary, this occurrence is disturbing to astronauts who need extra protection, as well as satellite electronic systems.

The weakening of the solar wind, which takes place at the scorching outer sun's atmosphere, is a different phenomenon from the 11-year sunspot cycle, which also exhibit low activity, but is related to it.»

As a result of the above:

E) MAGNETIC-SHIELD CRACKS FOUND; BIG SOLAR STORMS EXPECTED
VICTORIA JAGGARD IN SAN FRANCISCO NATIONAL GEOGRAPHIC NEWS DECEMBER 17, 2008
http://news.nationalgeographic.com/news/2008/12/081217-solar-breaches.html

«An unexpected thick layer of solar particles inside Earth's magnetic field suggests there are huge breaches in our planet's solar defenses, scientists said. These breaches indicate that during the next period of high solar activity, due to start in 2012, Earth will experience some of the worst solar storms seen in decades. Solar winds –charged particles from the sun– help create auroras, the brightly colored lights that sometimes appear above the Earth's poles. But the *(solar)* winds also trigger storms that can interfere with satellites' power sources, endanger spacewalkers, and even knock out power grids on Earth. "The sequence we're expecting … is just right to put particles in and energize them to create the biggest geomagnetic storms, the brightest auroras, the biggest disturbances in Earth's radiation belts," said David Sibeck, a space-weather expert at NASA's Goddard Space Flight Center in Maryland. "So if all of this is true, it should be that we're in for a tough time in the next 11 years.»

F) NATIONAL GEOGRAPHIC NEWS 'INTO THE BREACH' SEPTEMBER 24, 2008
http://news.nationalgeographic.com/news/2008/12/081217-solar-breaches.html

«Data from NASA's THEMIS satellite showed that a 4,000-mile-thick (6,437-

kilometer-thick) layer of solar particles has gathered and is rapidly growing within the outermost part of the magnetosphere, a protective bubble created by Earth's magnetic field.

Normally the magnetosphere blocks most of the solar wind, flowing outward from the sun at about a million miles (1.6 million kilometers) an hour.

"The solar wind is constantly changing, and the Earth's magnetic field is buffeted like a wind-sock in gale-force winds, fluttering back and forth in response to the solar wind," Sibeck said this week during a meeting of the American Geophysical Union in San Francisco.»

G) JOHN'S REVELATION CH. 16: «§8. Then the fourth angel poured out his vial (bowl) onto the sun, and power was given to him to scorch men with fire. §9 And men were scorched with great heat.»

Thus, due to the fact that the disturbance of natural balance on Earth will be quite widespread and extensive –because of the pending Sacred Withdrawal of the Archetypes that comprise Creation– the 'elect' commanders of the world *(those belonging to the 10%, i.e. the ones destined to survive)*, aware of the coming phenomena on Earth, are preparing their 'salvation' arks, while keeping them secret from their nations. Their rescue plans consist of two main phases. For each phase, a different kind of ark is built. At first they intend to take shelter inside fully equipped and well-arranged **underground installations/facilities**, which they have been preparing for some time, saving themselves from the first attacks of the cosmic phenomena.

[593] A) EXCERPT FROM BILL HAMILTON'S INTERVIEW TO LINDA MOULTON
http://www.boomspeed.com/joseph2/J-Rod2.htm

«Bill Hamilton: The thing is that there are groups of humans –who these groups are, I don't know– who survived (from this disaster) by going **underground**.»

B) JOHN'S REVELATION 6: «§15. And the kings of the earth, and the great men, and the rich men, and the generals, and the mighty men, and every bondservant/slave and every free man, hid themselves in the caves and in the rocks of the mountains.»

C) HELLENIC NEXUS, ISSUE 12 (FEBRUARY-MARCH 2006) UNDERGROUND BASES FICTION AND REALITY by CHRISTOS VAGENAS
(LETTERS FROM THE UNDERGROUND BY RICHARD SAUDER- NEXUS NEW TIMES, VOL. 11, NO 6)

«...At the moment, especially in the U.S.A. it seems that more than fifty manned extensive underground military bases are operating, mainly in the Western States (U.S. News & World Report, 1989). These bases are under the management and control of FEMA (Federal Emergency Management Agency) and the Pentagon, and among other things, they will be used **as shelter** of the President of the United States *(the kings of the Earth)* in case of nuclear war. According to U.S. News & World Report, the central underground FEMA base is located on Mt. Weather. ...According to the plan de-

Don't skip chapters or bibliographic references

scribed here, these selected locations will provide living quarters for 1,000 political *(the rich and the mighty)* and military personnel *(the chiliarchs)* in case of a nuclear emergency *(and of course not only that)*. Nevertheless this number is said to be much greater.

…According to a recent publication of the New Scientist magazine (Fred Pierce, 12 January, 2006) the Norwegian government is allegedly constructing a very large underground chamber inside a mountain on the island of Spits Bergen located near the Arctic Circle (just 1,000 miles from the North Pole). In that chamber, approximately 2.000.000 seeds of plant species will be housed, thus representing all vegetable nutrition varieties known to modern man. This prototype 'arc' will be constructed with reinforced concrete walls <u>many meters thick</u> *(apparently to stop radiation from the collapse of the magnetic field)*, security doors, strong enough to withstand the use of powerful explosives, and it will not be manned. In October 2005, the above construction received the approval of the United Nations Council, at a meeting of the Food and Agriculture Organization in Rome.»

When the phenomena reach those underground areas of the Earth, they will all move to their next ark. This second 'salvation' phase involves a space program, which will permanently lead them far away from Earth…

However, for the completion of both phases of 'project ark' (underground bases and departure from Earth) enormous amounts of money are needed. Thus, with covert actions, they methodize an ever-increasing international financial crisis for the people, so that money can be removed from the insignificant 'meek' and accumulated to the appropriate institutions which will invest it according to the 'salvation' purposes of the 'elect ones'. So long as the signs for the coming of the cosmic catastrophe grow in number, so will the magnitude of the financial crisis. And all these are just the **first repercussions** of the pending Withdrawal of the Sacred Archetypes of creation from the world of matter!

–And how will humanity fare in the future? Is there a clear prophecy?

PART 4:
THE FUTURE

COMPILING THE INFORMATION

–You are asking for a straightforward prophecy when for centuries now the true prophecies are in front of you! Who could speak clearly to humans about things they refuse to accept out of fear? How could I reveal to you what the "abomination of desolation" is, that Jesus mentions in Matthew's Gospel, since men 'bring down' everything they can't stand and reject everything that disturbs their lethargy? They react, stigmatizing those who present the 'strange' facts, in the worst way possible. …This is why some things have never been clarified! …I am honestly perplexed. Nevertheless, we cannot proceed unless we discuss these matters!

Let us summarize our data, so that we can then reposition the last pieces of the puzzle using the Sacred Texts of Revelation and Jesus' Words in Matthew's Gospel as our guides.

The signal for the universal change is given by **the withdrawal of the Sacred Archetypes** from material creation, aiming to the **Spiritual Transference of men and the Earth** –as if it were a 'key'– through the Sacred Gate/Passage/Jesus, in order to join the Holy State of the Father.

---

594 **THE GOSPEL OF JOHN, CH. 10**: «§9. "I Am the gate: If anyone enters through Me, he shall be saved. …Thy kingdom come…on earth as it is in heaven…»

All these accounts, regardless of the fact that they are presented in a simplistic manner to make them easier to understand, they describe absolutely metaphysical situations. To avoid misconceptions, it would be wise to interpret events by activating our esoteric hyper-sense and not as 'straws for arithmetic' laid out in sequence. This will clearly reveal the concepts.

The most difficult hour though, and the absolute danger for men, will be precisely that **intermediate phase**, namely the period between the Commencement and the Completion of the **Withdrawal**. Side-effects of this process will be: **the dissolution of the natural laws** of matter on one hand and on the other the disturbance of the boundaries between the dimensions, which will result in **the appearance of skeptomorphic and astral powers,** with the intention to 'take in' anything they can. "For wherever the carcass is, there the vultures will gather." [Matthew 24:28]

The lower/inner astral and aethereal regions are the first ones that will be abandoned by the Life-giving Force. The astral and aetheric entities dwelling there –the abomination of desolation– shaken by the change, will be the first to make their appearance in the densely material plane, and being

Don't skip chapters or bibliographic references

visible will cause the greatest panic. Humanity will consider those to be 'the evil aliens'!

[595] **REVELATION 17**: «§8. The beast was, <u>and is not, and is about to rise</u> from the bottomless pit of the abyss.»

If we array one by one all the puzzle pieces, by the end of the reference, a very interesting picture will be completed.

A) THE GOSPEL OF MATTHEW, CH. 24: «§15. When you therefore shall see the abomination of desolation, spoken of by Daniel the prophet, standing in the holy place, –he who reads, let him understand– §16. Then let those who are in Judaea flee into the mountains. §17. Let him who is on the housetop not come down to take anything out of his house. §18. Neither let him who is in the field return back to take his clothes. §19. And woe unto the women that are pregnant and to those that give suck (who are nursing) in those days. §20. But pray that your **escape** will not have to be in the winter, neither on the Sabbath day. §21. For then shall be terrible suffering, such as **was not since the beginning of the world** to this time, no, nor ever shall be. §22. And if time had not been cut short in those days, there should no flesh be saved (no one would live); but for the sake of God's chosen ones, those days shall be shortened.»

All the above are not parables. A parabolic interpretation is given though, because people cannot believe that, what has been said, literally describes the future.

And while these are the words of Christ in the Gospel of His disciple Matthew, let us see how John describes the coming of the 'abomination' in the Apocalypse:

B) JOHN'S REVELATION 9: «§2. And he opened the bottomless pit of the abyss, and smoke arose out of the pit like the smoke of a great furnace; and the sun and the air were darkened because of the smoke of the pit. §3. Then out of the smoke locusts came upon the earth. And to them was given power, as the scorpions of the earth have power…§7. The shape of the locusts was like horses prepared for battle. On their heads was something like crowns of gold, and their faces were like the faces of men. §8. They had hair like women's hair, and their teeth were like lions' teeth. §9. And they had breasts like breastplates of iron, and the sound of their wings was like the sound of chariots with many horses rushing into battle. §10. And they had tails like scorpions, and there were stings in their tails. Their power was to hurt men for five months.»

Here the 'abomination's' picture is clearer, and it doesn't surely refer to modern war vehicles as it is claimed by some. In the Assyro-Babylonian epic poem of Gilgamesh, we will recognize the form of the beings described in the Revelation of John! These beings are the scorpion-men, the guards of the gates of 'inner-Earth'.

Gilgamesh, in his desperate quest for his lost Immortality, decides to go to the 'Garden of the Gods'. We could equate this garden with Shambhala or Agartha, the sacred subterranean city of the gods and the masters. The entrance though to the sub-chthonian realm of the king of the world, is guarded by scorpion men, half men half scorpions.

C) THE EPIC OF GILGAMESH 'THE SCORPION-BEINGS' ASSYRIAN INTERNATIONAL NEWS AGENCY, Books Online, www.aina.org

«So at length Gilgamesh came to Mashu, the great mountains which daily guard the rising and the setting Sun. Its twin peaks are as high as the wall of the sky and its flanks reach down to the Underworld.

At its gate the **Scorpions** stand guard: **Half-men and half-dragons.** Their glory is terrifying; their stare strikes death unto men, their **shimmering halo** sweeps the mountains that guard the rising sun. [Revelation: "The shape of the locusts... and their faces were like the faces of men... On their heads was something like **crowns of gold**. And they had tails like scorpions, and there were stings in their tails].

When Gilgamesh saw them he shielded his eyes for the length of a moment only; then he took courage and approached. When they saw him so undismayed, the Man-Scorpion called to his mate, 'This one who comes to us now is flesh of the gods... He is two thirds god but one third is man'...Gilgamesh answered... 'That is why I traveled all the way here in search of Utnapishtim, my father; because they say... he has entered the assembly of the gods *(Agartha – the King of the World)* and has found everlasting life.» [GREEK VERSION: NEAR EASTERN TEXTS, THE EPIC OF GILGAMESH, CH. SCORPIONS, KASTANIOTIS PUBL.]

So, the guards of the Abyss are the scorpion-men. "And he opened the bottomless pit of the Abyss". Their image is the same as the one John gives us in Revelation: but when the king of this world –the beast– having the key to the abyss, will unlock the abyss, these beings will appear on the surface of the Earth and they will cause terrible havoc. These daemons are the abomination. The same image is given by modern researchers when they describe a race of malicious 'extraterrestrials'...

D) THE TRUTH ABOUT UFOS AND EXTRATERRESTRIAL CONSPIRACIES: GIANNOULAKIS-KAVAKOPOULOS

John Lear Jr., a CIA pilot reveals:

«In a seven-month period, thousands of those *(beings)* had been sighted. The horrible truth was disclosed only to a few individuals. 'They', were indeed small, ugly creatures, **shaped like insects** (praying mantises), and were more advanced than us by perhaps a billion years.»

It seems they have already started to come... and as Christ advises: "when you shall see the abomination, flee to the mountains and don't return back to take your belongings", *John Lear Jr. gives similar advise:* "The best advice I can give you is, next time you see a flying saucer and are awed by its gorgeous display of technology and beautiful lights in various colors, <u>run like hell</u>.»

E) BARBARA MARCINIAK 'GAIA' [Gr. trans. MATZOROU E.] *(Information through channeling)*:
«No continent and no nation will remain unaffected from the events to come. Very few are those who won't be forced to move or change place of residence. …Listen, the first time you'll move, take a big truck, load all your belongings, gather as much as possible and leave.
The next time you move, you might simply leave on foot, taking with you anything you can carry in a backpack.
The last time, you may be forced to take with you only what you can carry in your hands. …You will be forced to save your life first of all and not your belongings.»

While the Withdrawal of the Sacred Archetypes will be underway, the next astral region to be deprived of the Life-giving Force is the one located in the immediately higher astral regions, with the 'positive' astral/skeptomorphic entities that dwell there! These entities, with their 'beautiful' forms, will then appear (visible) on Earth with the intention to 'save' men from the preceding 'abomination'; and since they will have all the skeptomorphic 'holy' dummies in their possession that are revered by all men, they will project them "to deceive, if possible, even the elect/chosen ones." [Matthew 24:24] as well as collect/harvest souls for their own benefit.

[596] **P. GIANNOULAKIS L. KAVAKOPOULOS 'THE TRUTH ABOUT UFOS AND EXTRA-TERRESTRIAL CONSPIRACIES'** (FROM STATEMENTS OF JOHN LEAR JR.) (p. 124)
«JOHN LEAR JR.: …William Moore, a UFO researcher, came into possession of a video tape of two newsmen interviewing a military officer associated with MJ-12. … The officer also relates the fact that the EBE's *(Extraterrestrial Biological Entities/aliens)* claim to have created Christ.
The EBE's have a type of recording-device that can record the past and display it in the form of a hologram. This hologram can be filmed but, because of the technology holograms use, it does not come out very clear on film. The crucifixion of Christ has been put on film to be shown to the public. The EBE's' claim to have influenced the Christ could be –in view of the 'grant deception– an effort to disrupt traditional human values for incomprehensible reasons.»
It is possible that Jesus might appear in the sky so the EBE's hasten to usurp the event by degrading it…

It is precisely this danger that all the warnings of Jesus refer to, when He advises men **NOT TO BELIEVE ANYONE** who will announce His (Jesus') presence on Earth.

597 THE GOSPEL OF MATTHEW, CH. 24: «§23. Then if anyone says to you, 'Look, here is the Christ!' or 'There!' do not believe them. §24. For false christs and false prophets will rise (appear) and show great signs and wonders to deceive, if possible, even the chosen ones. §25. **Behold, I have told you beforehand.** §26 Therefore if they say to you, 'Look, He is in the desert!' do not go out; or 'Look, He is in the inner rooms!' do not believe them.»

This second side/camp of the materialized powers, which shall include every 'positive' skeptomorph created by men, will constitute the gravest danger for humanity. In reality however, what will be taking place at that time is the greatest **hunt** ordered by this world's controllers at the end of time, with **man** as their prey. At that time, negative and 'positive' powers, like harrier-eagles/vultures, will rush to gather as many humans as they can... Just as the hunters send their hound-dogs as forerunners into the hunt and they follow behind trying to lead the prey into the trap, the same thing will happen then too! With the 'abomination' as the forerunner and the 'gods' following it as the 'saviors', they will lead men into the ambush.
 The developments of the basic events **are not** determined by the astral force. The signal is given at the exact moment when the HyperUniversal Intelligent Wholenesses initiate the process of the release of the Sacred Archetypes from material creation. The precise time remains **undetermined**, since the Selected Salvation Team is laying Their Plans in secret.

598 ERICH VON DÄNIKEN 'SECOND COMING HAS ALREADY BEGAN' (p.239-240) «When this Second Coming is going to happen? The extraterrestrials are not specific about a date. It seems they don't know themselves, either. Isn't that familiar? Don't all religions emphasize that no one knows the exact day or hour the Second Coming is going to break out? Could it be perhaps that the aliens have only indications similar to the ones recorded by geologists before earthquakes and volcanic eruptions occur? ...Do their meters perhaps, record ...an oncoming destruction? These measurements though, don't allow any accurate prediction. In that case, there would be a convincing excuse for their immoral behavior. ...The time required is unknown. For that reason, fast action is needed.»

Thus, all the skeptomorphic astrals can do is to create **alternative solutions** that cover all time-probabilities of this occurrence, pushing things to extremes.

REVELATION (APOCALYPSE)

Having already completed the listing of facts, nothing else remains but to look at the prophetic words of John's Revelation and Matthew's Gospel with new insight. The Apocalypse (Revelation) in its various chapters refers to the primary events of the end through different view-points and this of course perplexes the overall meaning. Additionally, through the ages, it has sustained some small 'interventions' –as most texts of this kind have, after all. The two most important ones are: First of all the inaccurate characterization of the Almighty Father as 'the Alpha and the Omega'! Naturally –some will oppose– this denotes that the Father engulfs everything. But this 'everything' of the Father **cannot be defined;** let alone by a symbol that denotes a Start (A) and an End (Ω). The Father has no beginning because He is Self-Essential and Self-Substantial –a condition that man is impossible to perceive– and He naturally has no end (Ω), because He is Eternal and never-ending. He is Imperishable, Undivided and Unborn. This symbol (A, Ω) does not concern the Almighty Father, but the creator of matter, since only matter has a beginning and what has a beginning also has an end.

A second point that is certainly a product of falsification is the equation of the Christ with Logos. But Logos (as the first letter of the Greek Word Λό-γος, letter Λ), denotes fission (division), divisible essence, and surely not the Coherent and Indivisible Essence of the Father.

---

599 **BLAVATSKY H., P., 'THE SECRET DOCTRINE' (I-408, 411):**

«…It was the goddess of the Great Bear and Mother of Time, who was in Egypt from the earliest times the 'Living Word' *(Logos)*, and Sevekh-Kronus, whose archetype was the Crocodile-Dragon, the pre-planetary form of Saturn, was called her son and consort; he was **her Word-Logos.**

…The seven-headed serpent has more than one signification in the Arcane *(Apocryphal)* teachings. It is **the seven-headed Dragon**[1], each of whose heads is a star of the Lesser Bear; but it was also, and pre-eminently, the Serpent of Darkness (i.e., inconceivable and incomprehensible) whose seven heads were the seven Logoi *(Words)*, the reflections of the one and first manifested Light -- the universal Logos.»

[1] **The seven-headed Dragon:** REVELATION 12: «§3. And another sign appeared in heaven: behold, a great red <u>**dragon**</u> **having seven heads** and ten horns, and seven diadems on his heads… §9. So the great **dragon** was cast down, that ancient serpent called the devil and Satan, who deceives the whole world; he was cast down to the earth.»

This way, the original information is adulterated. But the basic message remains unaltered.

So let us examine this central corpus of information of the Apocalypse, which is given in some particular chapters. These chapters focus on future events with more precision compared to others (chapters) which describe the sum of future events more briefly; because an event is described in different chapters of the Apocalypse, seen from different perspectives. From the second category (synoptic chapters), we will interpret only those verses that refer to the principle events, which, along with some additional Gospel passages, will assist us in the deeper understanding of what is to come.

As time approaches its end, signs increase in number. The stoics, who **are not** allured by the accelerating swirl of the material vortex that leads to the total crushing of the Spirit, watch the signs of the times, resist and wait.

"Now learn this parable from the fig tree: When its branch has already become tender and puts forth leaves, you know that summer is near. So you also, when you see all these things, know that it is near —right at the doors." [Matthew 24:32-33]

REVELATION 13	
§ 1. Then I stood upon the sand of the sea. And I saw a beast rising up out of the sea, having **seven heads,** and ten horns, and on its horns ten crowns, and on its heads the name of blasphemy.	The sea holds the secrets of the abyss well hidden. The beast masquerades again and rises from the depths. It is one thing yet it appears as another. ONE is the blasphemer though with the seven heads, the one who controls everything in hiding…
	The twofold astral powers, as 'extraterrestrials' appear from the hollows of inner Earth and rise from the abyss of the waters.
	(A lot of UFO's have been seen diving into the sea or lakes – e.g. lake Titicaca, Peru)
	After that they 'educate' the mighty ones of the Earth on the knowledge of materialism, offering them the 'gifts' of their technology.

Don't skip chapters or bibliographic references

§ 2. Now the beast which I saw was like a leopard, its feet were as the feet of a bear, and its mouth as the mouth of a lion: and the *(seven-headed)* dragon gave it his power, his throne, and great authority.	The seven-headed dragon-Lucifer, the fallen creator, in order to build his material construction '**always geometrizes**'. He uses a polymorphic beast with multifaceted properties as his basic collaborator for the structure of his world. This is his favorite child that sub(p)-ports his authority, upon which the dragon bestows power and glory. This child is science.
	The polymorphism of materialistic **science** was offered to men by the masqueraded, astral dynasty which assumed its power and authority from the dragon creator/Lucifer who '**always geometrizes**'. But these 'gifts' were given in deceit… *(Let me remind you of the references to 'extraterrestrial' technology.)*
§ 3. And I saw one of its heads as if it had been **mortally wounded**, and its fatal wound <u>was healed</u>; and all the world marveled and followed the beast.	**Science** as the primary tool for the understanding of materialism was fatally struck *(dealt a crippling blow)* during the Dark Ages. Today however, it has completely recuperated from this blow and the whole world idolizes the healed beast and follows it.
§ 4. And they worshiped the dragon who gave authority to the beast;	And men have adored the entire material creation and its creator and the materialistic science that assumed its reign from the dragon/creator who '**always geometrizes**'.
And they worshiped the beast, saying, "Who is like the beast? Who is	And they have worshiped the unbeatable beast/science which rocket-

able to make war with it?"	ed to supreme heights of power, since no one can compete with it.
...§6. And it opened its mouth in blasphemy against God, to blaspheme His name, and His tabernacle, even them that dwell in heaven.	And the sheer materialistic science **rejected** the existence of the Father God and rendered any view or standpoint, which has the True Spirit as its foundation, as unscientific and unproven...
§ 7. And it was given unto it *(to the beast/science)* to make war with the saints **and to overcome them.** And authority was given to it over every tribe, and people and tongue and nation.	And science prevailed in the whole world and disputed every Spiritual property or ability of man, since they *(Spiritual virtues)* were equated to foolishness, quaintness and psychological disorders. Thus materialistic science prevailed and defeated **real** Spirituality in every race and every nation. *(All Saints, prophets and even Christ Himself 'sat on the sofa' of modern psychiatry for deep psychoanalysis and they were all, of course, diagnosed as 'mentally disturbed...')*
§ 8. And all who dwell on the earth will worship it, all whose **names have not been written in the Book of Life** of the Lamb slain *(Jesus Christ)* from the foundation of the world. § 9. If anyone has an ear, let him hear*. * *"...the true sensory organs and not the ones we think of" [Trismegistus]*	

Don't skip chapters or bibliographic references

...§ 11. And I saw another beast **coming up** out of the earth, and it had two horns like a lamb and it spoke as a dragon.	A second beast 'emerged' out of the secret **underground bases**/laboratories: **technology**. With lamb's horns and the voice of a dragon; with a make-believe 'beneficial offering'; but in essence savage and dangerous like a dragon...
§ 12. And it exercised all the authority of the first beast in its presence,	And of course technology (second beast) acts under the authority of science (first beast).
And caused the earth and those who dwell in it to worship the first beast, whose fatal wound was healed.	And everyone bowed (worshiped) the science of materialism which was mercilessly struck in the Middle Ages but has since recuperated.
§ 13. And it performed great signs, so that it even made fire come down from the sky onto the earth in the presence of the people.	The technological accomplishments were so grand and spectacular that they could even bring fire from the sky down to Earth: atomic bombs, air to ground missiles, white phosphorus bombs etc.
§ 14. And it deceived those who dwelled on the earth by those signs which it was granted to do in the sight of the *(first)* beast, telling those who dwelled on the earth to make an image of the beast which had been wounded by the sword and yet came to life again.	And technology deluded men with the 'miracles' it performed, which were given to it...by the first beast/science. And everyone bowed to the 'image' of the beast/science which, despite the blow it had suffered, it finally survived.

§ 15. He was granted power to give life to the beast's image, so that the image of the beast should even speak.	And the image of the beast/technology came alive and talking with television, cinematography, computers, sound production units etc. …And everyone bowed down to the technological 'gifts' the 'aliens' offered…
§ 16. He forces all, both small and great, rich and poor, free and slave, to receive a marking* on their right hand or on their foreheads. *In the original Greek version the word χάραγμα is used, which is more appropriately translated as 'carving' or 'incision'.	And the technological climax came with the rise to prominence of the 'beneficial properties' of nano-technology along with the prompt –it will become mandatory in the future– to accept the suspicious 'element' (biochip) in whatever 'injected' way into the body of men.

[600] A) TEXE MARRS 'PROJECT L.U.C.I.D.' (pp. 114, 115, and 116):

«Gorham International, a high technology research and development Firm, based in Gorham, Maine, says that a billion-dollar worth biochip-industry is rapidly developing. According to this company the biochip is going to be a huge technological progress based on 'quantum mechanics', and which will eventually create the ultimate **molecular** computer *('implantable' anywhere)*. The biochip revolution has already begun. Dozens of specialized technologists in public and private laboratories all over the world collaborate in an effort to develop the talents of tens of thousands of people during the 90's.

… Recently, one of my well-documented, cautionary articles was published in 'The Boulder Weekly', a Colorado newspaper, in which I described the downsides (dark aspects) of biochip implants. Later, 'Media Bypass' magazine published this excerpt:

"…There is a lot of evidence that biochips are being developed, **which can tie into the brain's neuro-network**, giving the one who controls the chip the ability to control the thoughts and actions of anyone who has undergone biochip-implantation."

Don't skip chapters or bibliographic references

…According to Science News, the techniques under study at the University of Michigan at Ann Arbor, in AT&T labs and elsewhere, will allow outsiders to direct a person's brain cell conversations and 'talk' directly to the individual's brain neurons. The article also mentions that there are research centers which have focused their attention on the potential use of integrated circuit-chips that can either be implanted in the brain or **overlaid** with brain cells.»

B) 'THIRD EYE' MAGAZINE ISSUE 153 JULY 2007 ARTICLE BY GEORGE ALEXANDROU **'IMPLANTS, ANTICHRIST, DEMOCRACY AND (AT LAST) GOD!**

«…Research is carried out to find a way to store biometric data, in the actual human skin of the hand or forehead, setting a permanent pattern –an invisible tattoo *(the mark of the beast)–* shaped by the salinity of the skin, (a combination of nanotechnology and biotechnology), which is going to function as a microchip. IBM is already working on the personal area network technology or PAN, and studies the creation of a readable electric field in the skin, which is going to store personal data based on its salinity.»

§ 17. and that no man may buy or sell unless he has the mark*, * tr. n.: the word used in the original Greek version is χάραγμα, which literally means to carve, slice etc.	So that nobody will be able to make any transaction if they do not possess the implanted biochip, which is introduced into the organism with a puncture, scratch or 'engraving' of the skin,
or the name of the beast,	**or** the BARCODE of all merchandise,
or the number of its name.	… **or** the social security number, ID card number, I.T.I.N., P.I.C. (personal identification code), etc.
§ 18. Here is the wisdom. Let him who has the Noũs (understanding) calculate the number of the beast, for it is the number of a man: And his number is 666. *(Gr.:χξς'=666)* *(End of Chapter 13)*	The beast will also present itself in the 'form' of a human to mislead "even the elect ones". He will be called the antichrist by the faithful ones and the 'savior' by the deluded. The 'lexarithm' *(the sum of arithmetic values corresponding to each letter of a word according to the Greek and Jewish alphabets)* of its name is found as a code inside man's body; and that number is 666.

601 **A)** *See:* APPENDIX, PICTURES AND DRAWINGS, THE NUMBER OF THE BEAST

A few words about χξς' (=666) so as to make us think, **to begin with**...

B) *Another fact regarding number '666':*

The foundation of organic (material) life, i.e. the basic structural element of nature and of the material body is carbon 12 (Gr. άνθρακας). The carbon atom though (C 12) is comprised of 6 protons, 6 neutrons and 6 electrons = 666...pure coincidence?

According to Pythagoras, the number '6' was considered the number of the soul.

C) ARGYROPOULOS E., 'PROOF OF THE MATHEMATICAL STRUCTURE OF THE GREEK LANGUAGE' CH. THE LEXARITHMETIC PROOF OF THE PYTHAGOREAN THEOREM: «...We will now refer to the two Pythagorean tetraktys. Pythagoras considered two sums, the small and the great tetraktys (as he and his disciples called them), to be of great importance. The small tetraktys is the sum of numbers 1+2+3+4=10.

...The great tetraktys[1] is the second tetraktys and is equal to the sum of the first eight consecutive positive numbers, 1+2+3+4+5+6+7+8=36. It is quite interesting that the sum of the numbers from 1 to 36 equals 666 since 1+2+3+4+5+6+...+34+35+36=666.»

[1]Tetraktys:

(a) Hierocles – Comments on Pythagoras' Golden Epics (25.4.1) «For this reason, the Creator of all beings was at first named by them Tetraktys, but now Zeus the Father for the Reasons we have presented.»

(b) Proclus – Comments on Timaeus (E. 302.20)

«This is why the Pythagoreans associate the Decas (Gr. w. Δεκάς for the sum of ten) with the Creator.»

CH. 'THE LEXARITHMETIC INTRODUCTION OF π = 3.1415926535: ...

To all those who are familiar with mathematics, it is known that π is the quotient (thus symbolized by the Gr. letter π which is the first letter of the word πηλίκον = quotient). It is the quotient of the length of the circle's circumference to its diameter.

Indeed: π = length of the circumference / diameter=3.14...

...Writing down the first **nine** decimals of the number π (i.e. the number 3.141592653) and add them we get the sum result: 1+4+1+5+9+2+6+5+3=36, namely the second (great) Pythagorean Tetraktys. Also, 9 (the first 9 digits) is the square of 3 (3^2=9) and 36 is the square of 6 (6^2=36). As we have already mentioned, 1+2+3+4+5+6+...+34+35+36=666.

Now, if we add the first 144 decimal digits of π together, we receive the following sum:

1+4+1+5+9+2+6+5+3+5+8+9+7+9+3+2+3+8+4+6+2+6+4+3+3+8+3+2+7
+9+5+0+2+8+8+4+1+9+7+1+6+9+3+9+9+3+7+5+1+0+5+8+2+0+9+7+4+

Don't skip chapters or bibliographic references

9+4+4+5+9+2+3+0+7+8+1+6+4+0+6+2+8+6+2+0+8+9+9+8+6+2+8+0+3 +4+8+2+5+3+4+2+1+1+7+0+6+7+9+8+2+1+4+8+0+8+6+5+1+3+2+8+2+ 3+0+6+6+4+7+0+9+3+8+4+4+6+0+9+5+5+0+5+8+2+2+3+1+7+2+5+3+5 +9=666

The lexarithmetic sum of the Greek word 'ΘΕΙΟΝ' (=DIVINE) =9+5+10+70+50=144 which is also the square of 12 (12^2=144). It is known that Revelation refers to the number 144000=144*1000 *[Revelation 7:4 "And I heard the number of those who were sealed. One hundred and forty-four thousands of all the tribes of the children of Israel were sealed." (Twelve from each of the twelve tribes. 12*12=144 or 1212)]*, as well as the number χξϛ' =666.» *{Tr. n.: this 'seal' (of Salvation) must not be confused with the 'mark of the beast' (of Perdition), since in the original Greek version, two distinct words are used: 'εσφραγισμένοι' = the stamped ones [Ch. 7] and 'χάραγμα' = carving / incision [Ch. 13]}*
π = *Code for (material) Creation. God always geometrizes onto matter.*

REVELATION 16	
§ 8. Then the **fourth angel** poured out his vial (bowl) upon the sun, and power was given unto him to scorch men with fire. § 9. And men were scorched with great heat, and they blasphemed the name of God **who has power over these plagues**; and they did not repent to give Him glory.	The sun starts to cause tormenting problems to the world. *(Let me remind you of the information in the references regarding the sun and the solar system and the true causes of the temperature increase)*
§ 10. And the **fifth angel** poured out his vial (bowl) onto the throne of the beast, and its kingdom became full of darkness; and they *(men)* gnawed their tongues because of their pain.	The global dictatorship that is being planned right this moment will soon be complete and shall become unbearable with its laws. Behind it, dark powers are hiding, which will **soon** be represented by the antichrist. He will come bearing the mask of the 'redeemer', in order to rectify his world. Until then, the twofold powers, pretending to be the 'extraterrestrial saviors' manipulate the governors of men according to their secret goals.[602]

606

602 **TEXE MARRS 'PROJECT L.U.C.I.D.'** (U.S. AIR FORCE OFFICIAL): «Do not even for an instant think that you and your loved ones can escape the monstrous system which lies in our path. Once Project L.U.C.I.D. is fully operational, every man on Earth will be forced to succumb to **the dominion of the most hideous slavery ever in human history.** ...I am instead, horrified that the American people –as well as all the nations of the world– are about to enter a sinister period of blood, terror, chaos and slavery unparalleled in human history. Worse still, the vast majority of people are totally ignorant of what is to come and unprepared to deal with it.»

REVELATION 16	
§ 12. And **the sixth angel** poured out his vial upon the great river Euphrates, and its **water was dried up**, so that the way of the kings from the east might be prepared.	Climatic catastrophes will intensify; the Earth's (potable) **water** will become less and less –a significant sign– ...and the 'kings' of the East are getting ready... *(Could it be from ... the Gobi desert, Ta(r)tar(i)a, Shambhala?)*
§ 13. And I saw three unclean spirits like frogs coming out of the mouth of the **dragon**, and out of the mouth of the **beast**, and out of the mouth of the **false prophet**.	The representative of the dragon/Lucifer in the form of a 'human' is __already__ here on Earth pretending to be the Christ. He is the antichrist whose false prophet presents him to the world.
§ 14. For they are spirits of demons, working miracles, which go forth __unto__ the kings of the earth and of the whole world, to gather them to the battle __of that great day__ of God Almighty.	His word is the snake's venom that captures every soul that will come near him. Simultaneously, dark astral powers, hiding behind the Earth's mighty ones and controlling them through their technological 'gifts', are pulling the strings as they advise and manipulate them, leading them towards the great confrontation which will reach its climax on the **Great Day** of the permanent __withdrawal__ of the stolen Sacred Archetypes

Don't skip chapters or bibliographic references

	from the material world. Because This is really the uniquely **Great Day** of God Almighty: WHEN THE SACRED ARCHE-TYPES EMBEZZLED BY LUCIFER RETURN TO THEIR SOURCE.
§ 15. "Behold, I am coming **like a thief** *(in the midst **of the period** of Armageddon)*; Blessed is he who stays awake, and keeps his garments *(his Higher Noetic/Mental Body/Matrimony/wedding garment)*, so that he doesn't walk naked and they see his shame *(his Spiritual impoverishment)*."	But **secretly, like a thief** without drum-rolls and fanfares, Jesus with His HyperUniversal Forces (the slain Lamb with His Angels who follow His instructions…) have breached the universe of delusion and method-ize the Withdrawal Of the Sacred Archetypes from material creation, urging those who are waiting to safeguard their Spiritual Body/Matrimony-garment that enfolds their Soul.
(parenthesis opens) **MATTHEW 24** § 43. But know this: if the **master of the house*** *(the archon of this world)* had known **what hour** the thief *(Jesus, to remove the Archetypes)* would come, he would have kept watch and not have allowed **his house** *(his universe)* to be broken into. **LUKE 12** § 38. And if he should come in the second watch, or come in the third watch… § 39. But be sure of this: that if the **master of the house*** had known what hour the thief was coming, he would have watched, and not have allowed his house to	An important and incomprehensible point –since it is not accepted by men– is that the 'thief' and more precisely he who breaks into the house, is not coming to restitute but to dissolve! The same of course ap-

be broken into. * If the **master of the house** has been called Beelzebub, how much more the members of his household…! [MATTHEW 10:25]"	plies to what the Angels of Revelation do! They bring down the world of delusion, which is matter. This is why Christ states:
LUKE 12 § 49. I came to set fire on the earth, and how I wish it were already kindled! **GOSPEL OF THOMAS** § 71. Jesus said: I will overturn this house and no one will be able to rebuild it.	
MATTHEW 24 § 27. For as the lightning comes from the east and flashes to the west, so also will the presence of the Son of Man be.	So, he who will appear to 'sanitize' or renovate and decorate this world, will be NONE OTHER THAN the master of the house, the archon of this world! He will come then to restitute matter and bring 'justice' into the matrix of injustice. Those men, who will have not understood the Truth, will see him as a 'savior'. He, however, will be the antichrist! Concepts in the material world are usually deflected and diverted away from their correct position; this is why men mistakenly believe that Christ will appear in the material plane! This is the most dangerous deception of all. What material men will perceive will only be a **HyperCosmic Light**, because: ↵ THE SECOND COMING / APPEARANCE OF JESUS WILL **NOT** TAKE PLACE ON MATERIAL EARTH, BUT IN THE SPIRITUAL PLACE –WHICH IS PREPARED– IN THE STATE OF THE FATHER **AFTER THE FIRST RESURRECTION.**

Don't skip chapters or bibliographic references

	This is why Matthew notes:
MATTHEW 24 § 4. And Jesus answered and said to them: "Watch out <u>that no one deceives you</u>. §5. For many will come in My name, **claiming, 'I am the Messiah/Christ,'** and they <u>will deceive many</u>." (Parenthesis closes)	
REVELATION 16 cont'd § 16. And they gathered them together to the place that is called in Hebrew, Armageddon.[603]	Armageddon, an extremely specific and peculiar conflict/battle, which will be dealt with later on.

[603] **A) THE GEOGRAPHICAL LOCATION OF ARMAGEDDON TEL MEGIDDO**
http://en.wikipedia.org/wiki/Tel_Megiddo
«**Megiddo** (Hebrew: מגידו) is a hill in modern Israel near the Kibbutz of Megiddo, known for its historical, geographical and theological importance especially under its Greek name Armageddon. In ancient times Megiddo was an important city-state. …The name Armageddon mentioned in the New Testament derives from Har-Megiddo meaning mount/rise/hill/dike of Megiddo in Hebrew. … Today, Megiddo is an important junction on the main road connecting the center of Israel with lower Galilee and the northern region.
(In brief)
Three of the most famous battles are mentioned in the valley of Megiddo (Armageddon).
▪ *Battle of Megiddo (15th century B.C.) fought between the armies of the Egyptian pharaoh Thutmose III and the Canaanites and their ruler Kadesh.*
▪ *Battle of Megiddo (609 B.C.) fought between Egypt and the Kingdom of Judah, in which battle, King Josiah fell.*
▪ *Battle of Megiddo (1918) fought during World War I between Allied troops, led by General Edmund Allenby, and the Ottoman army.*»
B) «… and its water dried.»
MEGIDDO TUNNEL,http://www.geocities.com/sfetel/gr/plumb_waters_g.htm#menu
«In the valley of Megiddo in Israel, there was an ancient city since the time of King Solomon. The water supply was outside the city's wall, thus a tun-

> nel was cut through the walls (with simultaneous excavation from both ends) to give safe access to water in the event of a siege. The tunnel consists of a sloping section 34 meters long and of a horizontal one 60 meters long leading to a shaft 29 meters deep.»

In order to explain the events described in the following verses of chapter 16 in the Revelation, which are referring to Armageddon, it is necessary for me to bring forth some **new information** which is hidden inside chapter 17 of the Apocalypse. There, we will meet a new 'beast', **different** from the two previous ones we looked at just a while ago. When we have gathered all necessary data, we will return back to chapter 16, in order to complete the analysis of Armageddon.

REVELATION 17	
§ 1. And there came one of the seven angels who had the seven vials (bowls) and talked with me, saying to me, "Come, I will show you the judgment of the great harlot who sits upon many waters; § 2. With whom the kings of the earth have committed fornication, and the inhabitants of the earth have been made drunk with the wine of her fornication.	The great harlot (prostitute) who sits on many seas, oceans and lakes, is the <u>entire</u> planet …Earth whose 2/3 are water. *(In many ancient and religious texts, the word 'earth' is considered to be **the cause** of matter).*
§ 3. So he carried me away in the Spirit into the wilderness: and I saw a woman sitting upon a **scarlet beast** which was full of names of blasphemy, having seven heads and ten horns.[604]	The various view points and opinions that confuse men seem to have different sources of origin. But **the beast is ONE**, and with its seven mouths in **its seven heads** spits out different…'views'… One roars, the other speaks gently, the third lies and misleads, the fourth scorns, the fifth threatens, the sixth eases the mind, the seventh seduces.

Don't skip chapters or bibliographic references

---

[604] **BLAVATSKY H., P., 'THE SECRET DOCTRINE' (II-513):**

«The Fall was the result of man's knowledge, for 'his eyes were opened'. Indeed, he was taught Wisdom *(devious wisdom)* and the hidden knowledge by the 'Fallen Angel', for the latter had become from that day his Manas, Mind and Self-consciousness. …And now it stands proven that Satan, or **the Red Fiery Dragon**, the Lord of Phosphorus (brimstone was a theological improvement), and Lucifer, or 'Light-Bearer', is in us *(as the 'Breath' of the creator of our soul)*: it is our Mind -- our Tempter and Redeemer.»
*(The view that Lucifer is our 'redeemer' is the **Great Deception** of Blavatsky).*
[1] The Master of Phosphorus: *Is it really coincidental that phosphorus → green twilight → hollow Earth → Shambhala → King (archon) of the world → Lucifer →Εωσφόρος= Light bringer [Phōs, Gr. Φῶς = Light + φέρω= to bring].*

REVELATION 17 cont'd

§ 4. And the woman *(Earth)* was arrayed in purple and scarlet color, and adorned with gold and precious stones and pearls, having in her hand a golden cup full of abominations and the filthiness of her fornication.

§ 5. And upon her forehead a name was written: Mystery, Babylon the great *(visible material Earth)* the mother of harlots and abominations of the earth *(the cause of matter)*.

The 'treasures' of the visible (Babylon) Earth, as the womb of debauchery and martyrdom of every witness of the Truth.

§ 6. I saw the woman *(Earth)*, drunken with the blood of the saints and with the blood of the martyrs of Jesus. And when I saw her, I marveled with great amazement.

And the harlot …bedazzles with the beauty of her nature.
(Earth's nature)

§ 7. But the angel said unto me, "Why did you marvel? I will tell you the mystery of the woman and of the beast that carries her, which has the seven heads and the ten horns.

§ 8. The beast that you saw **was**,	The beast **was visible** during the 4th Root Race of Men in the form of gods and daemons.[605]

[605] **A) BOOK OF ENOCH, Ch.7**: «§12. Whose *(giants/Nephelims)* stature was each three hundred cubits: They devoured all which the labors of men produced; and men could no longer feed them. §13. Then, the giants turned against men to **devour them**. §14. And they began to attack birds, and beasts, and reptiles, and fishes, to eat their flesh one after the other, and to drink their blood. §15. Then the earth was severely tried by the evil ones.
CH. 15 (XV): «§8. And now the giants born by the coherence of spirit and flesh shall be called on earth evil spirits and on earth shall be their habitation. ... Evil spirits shall they be upon earth, and **the spirits of the wicked** shall they be called. ...§9. The spirits of the giants, the Napheleim (Nephelim) *[orig. Anc. Gr. text]* shall bring all sorts of inflictions (scourge) to earth, cholera, war, famine and lamentation. §10. They will neither eat food nor drink, **invisible to the sight** *(the evil spirits of the giants/Nephelims)* and they will rise even against men and women, for they have received life from them in the days of desolation and slaughter.»

and is not,	...And by now, it *(the beast)* is not to be found in the visible/seen world –because all those *(gods and daemons)* were confined in the Tartara / the Abyss / Shambhala and other places of the universe...
and **is about to rise** out of the abyss	But the beast is fated to come out of the Abyss, Tartara and Shambhala *(whose central gates are in the East, by the way!)* and will again become visible.
and go into perdition.	And it will proceed to perdition (...seducing and dragging many people along with it...)

Don't skip chapters or bibliographic references

And those who dwell on earth, <u>whose names have not been written in the Book of Life</u> from the foundation of the world, will marvel when they see the beast	Because many men will marvel at the beast on account of the 'gifts' and 'miracles' it will offer them...
that <u>was</u>,	Which (the beast) was once visible: as the Gods or Titans or Giants or Daemons or Elohims.
<u>and is not</u>,	But is not visible any more,
<u>and yet shall come.</u>	<u>even though it will appear again</u>.
§ 9. Here is the mind which has wisdom: The seven heads are seven mountains on which the woman *(Earth)* is seated.	The **seven Elohims** of the material creation –supreme powers with spiritual 'bodies' in the size of mountains– as the basis/foundation for the creation of the Earth.[606]
§ 10. There are also seven kings. Five have fallen, **one is** *(i.e. the 6th)*, and the other *(i.e. the 7th)* has not yet come. And when he does come, **he must remain a short time.**	The seven kings/Elohims are the 'archons' of the **invisible government** and of the spiritual powers of this world.

[606] **PADMASAMBHAVA, THE TIBETAN BOOK OF THE DEAD** [Gr. tr. LIAKOPOULOS E.] (p. 160): «...Nobly-born child...even if the **bodies** of the largest of these peaceful and wrathful **deities** are equal [in vastness] to the limits of the heavens; the intermediate, as big as Mt. Meru; the smallest, equal to eighteen bodies such as thine own body, set one upon another, be not terrified at that; be not awed.»

Every 2,000 years, the Earth passes into the vibration of one of the seven (in total) rays (of dark) 'light', until the 14,000 year cycle is complete. Each ray corresponds to one of the seven Elohims of material creation, who is represented by a corresponding Chohan. The seventh 'king' –who during this period took over the Earth's 'supervision'– is called Arcturus. He is the Elohim of the 7th ray of the violet flame and is represented by Chohan Saint Germaine, who on May 1st, 1954 officially took over the ministry of the Chohan of the 7th (violet) Ray and will lead the Earth during this 7th period.

At the time when the Revelation was being written by John, the Earth was under the vibration of the 6th Ray of Elohim Pharschaum. The five previous Elohims had come and gone, the sixth was still active and the seventh had not yet come. But when he comes, he won't stay for long: "There are also seven kings. Five have fallen, one is, and the other has not yet come. And when he does come, **he must remain only a short time.**"

---

[607] *Count Saint Germaine, Chohan of the 7th Violet Ray. During this time period, he will envelop Earth with his **violet robe**. His personal aetheric sanctuary is located over the ...Carpathian Mountains (see reference #536, regarding the violet flame)*

PAPASTAVROU, A., 'LETTERS TO ANONYMOUS'

«Saint Germaine's speech, given to a group of disciples of 'Bridge to Freedom' on April 21, 1954

...During the end of that earthly life, I went to **Transylvania** *(certain rational connotations come up automatically...)* and from there, on May 1st, 1684, I passed on to the service rank of the ascended masters. I undertook the ministry of the Chohan of the seventh ray, around the end of the 18th century...

...On the eve of this great ceremony (of the coronation), which will occupy the energy and attention of all members of our spiritual hierarchy,...the crown of authority was given to me as the master consciousness of the coming cycle of the 2000 years. *(...He will not complete this cycle though, "...because he knows that he has little time.")*

Although I was the Chohan of the seventh ray for many years, I had nevertheless not yet become the Cosmic Representative of the 7th new cycle, because the final vibrations of the sixth ray were still strong in the planet's atmosphere. [...and there are seven kings, five have fallen, and **one is** *(the 6th Elohim and Chohan of the 6th ray)*, the other *(the 7th of the 7th ray)* has not yet come, and when he comes, he must stay **for a little time.**]

Don't skip chapters or bibliographic references

B) *The White Brotherhood has names for the seven* **Elohims** *(the seven heads of the beast) and their divine complements:*

1st ray, azure flame: Eloah Hercules, divine complement: Eloi Tamara.
2nd ray, yellow (solar) flame: Eloah Chandion, divine complement: Eloi Celeste.
3rd ray, rose pink flame: Eloah Orion, divine complement: Eloi Angelika.
4th ray, crystal flame: Eloah Vista, divine complement: Eloi Crystal.
5th ray, green flame: Eloah Halcyon, divine complement: Eloi Genesis.
6th ray, golden-ruby flame: Eloah Pharschaum, divine complement: Eloi Giou Lin.
7th ray, violet flame: Eloah Arcturus, divine complement: Eloi Diana.»

(Parenthesis opens)

REVELATION 12

§ 12. Therefore rejoice O heavens, and you who dwell in them! Woe to the inhabitants of the earth and of the sea! For the devil has come down to you, having great wrath, **because he knows that he has only a short time.**

(Parenthesis closes)

REVELATION 17 continued...

§ 11. And the beast that was, and is not, is himself also the eighth, and is of the seven, and he goes to perdition.

The creator Lucifer, the beast, the red dragon is the eighth one. **He is represented** by the seven Elohims of creation, –his seven heads– and by the one who **will pretend** to be Christ in order to mislead, the antichrist.

The antichrist is a member of the invisible government which in its entirety is called the White Brotherhood or the Spiritual Hierarchy of the Planet and has its headquarters in the sub-chthonic Shambhala.[608]

---

[608] **Antichrist:** *Member of the White Brotherhood and the Spiritual Hierarchy of the planet, situated in Shambhala-Agartha. His spiritual name is Lord Divino and the cosmic one, by which he is known to his believers, is Maitreya. This entity declares he is the Christ, Buddha, the Mes-*

616

siah of the Jews etc. His aetheric hermitage is located over Kashmir Pakistan/India and his name's lexarithm written in Jewish gives the sum of 666 (see Drawings, the number of the beast.)

...The kings of the East (from Shambhala) are preparing...

«...so that the **way of the kings from the East** can be prepared».

A) CONFERENCE OF THE SPIRITUAL HIERARCHY IN SHENANDOAH (11/08/82), VOL. II, 24

«SANAT KUMARA: *(addressing his attending students)* ...To those of you who are not blessed with inner vision, I will tell you that sitting on my right is the beloved lord Maitreya –known in the inner planes as Lord Divino."

B) MAITREYA'S OFFICIAL WEBSITE STATES:

http://www.shareintl.org/media/newsrelease87.pdf

«Awaited by all faiths under different names, Maitreya is the Christ to Christians, the Imam Mahdi to Muslims, Krishna to Hindus, the Messiah to Jews, and Maitreya Buddha to Buddhists. He is the World Teacher for all, religious or not, an educator in the broadest sense.»

REVELATION 17	
§ 12. And **the ten horns** which you saw are <u>ten kings</u> who **have received no kingdom as yet**, but one hour they receive authority as kings together with the beast.	When the Revelation was being written, these governors of men did not yet exist. But today, when time has matured, these 'kings' are present. With the methods of globalization and the new world order of things, these powerful rulers make their decisions along with the beast/astral force/extraterrestrials, the beast which **will continue to act <u>invisible</u> only for a little longer**...
§ 13. These are of one mind,	...UN, NATO, EU, G8, G20, Bilderberg Group
and <u>they shall hand over their power and authority to the beast.</u> *(Global Government)*	The entirety of astral forces will seize the rule of this world through their representative, the antichrist, who will initially <u>appear unescorted</u> by these powers. The leaders of the nations themselves, after they have completed their personal 'transactions' with him, will surrender their office to

Don't skip chapters or bibliographic references

<table>
<tr><td></td><td>him. Most religious leaders will do the same.

*(Prophecies say that Pope Benedict will be **the last** Pope).*

When the time comes, the antichrist will open the 'gates' for the 'multitude of sub-chthonic inflictions' to appear on earth.[609]</td></tr>
</table>

[609] *Announcements from the official antichrist webpage; His representative, false prophet Benjamin Creme answers:*

A) MAITREYA MISSION (My-'tray-ah) **'THE SON OF MAN'**
QUESTIONS & ANSWERS WITH BENJAMIN CREME http://www.share-gr.org/02-02.htm
«**Question**: Under what prism will the world see Maitreya? Under what authority will he take action? Will he and the Masters create some new institution or organization?
Answer: After the **Day of Declaration,** the world will see him as the spearhead for all progressive movements of change that look ahead. In the end, this will signal the complete change of all of our institutions. Soon after the Day of Declaration, the Christ *(the antichrist Maitreya)* **will present to the world twelve Masters of Wisdom. Some of these Masters will assume very high positions.** One or two will become heads of state of certain governments, in countries playing key-roles in the world. Another Master will assume duties as the head of a new organization which will be founded by the United Nations, to supervise the deployment of the redistribution program. The Masters will function in the most international way, without forming some new group or separate organization, but will be the pioneers of a new world thought and view, and naturally, they will constitute the stimulation for all the ideas necessary for the reconstruction of the world.»
(Offering, of course, free-energy as a gift)
*A piece of information, simply to make us think: A basic condition for someone to become a disciple of the Masters of the White Brotherhood is <u>not</u> to smoke. The White Brotherhood forbids its disciples to smoke because its masters **cannot** dwell (invisibly) in places where there is cigarette smoke!*
In the site: http://www.sott.net/signs/anti-anti-smoking.htm there is an article with the strange title: 'Aliens Don't Like to Eat People That Smoke'.
Also very impressive is the fact that the first smoking prohibition was imposed by that great 'humanitarian'...Hitler, since he also had close relations with the subterranean 'masters' of Shambhala of inner Earth.
Could it then be that smoking prohibition is a 'forerunner'/condition for the coming of certain ones? ...So let us not kid ourselves, they don't care so much about our health, when, at the same time, all other dangerous nutrients, food preservatives, dioxins, plant-chemicals, genetically modified nu-

618

trients, air spraying, chemtrails, electromagnetic radiations from high-voltage cables, mobile phones, H.A.A.R.P., nuclear waste, codex Allimentarius –dead food– eugenics etc. are allowed to circulate freely!

B) SHARE INTERNATIONAL MAGAZINE, DECEMBER 2008
QUESTIONS & ANSWERS FROM BENJAMIN CRÈME
http://share-international.org/magazine/old_issues/2008/2008-12.htm

«**Question**: Will Barack Obama be the last president of the United States? I believe it was either Maitreya's associate or your Master who said that eventually the US presidency **will be replaced by a group of wise elder statesmen.**

Answer: That is still the plan, so there is every chance that Mr. Obama will be the last president.

There is a rumor that Maitreya may use a different name when he comes to power. He will nevertheless be easily identifiable.»

(See: DRAWINGS, (1) THE PHOTOGRAPH OF THE ANTICHRIST and (2) THE NUMBER OF THE BEAST).

As soon as the king and archon of this world realizes that his universe has been 'ruptured' by the HyperCosmic Powers, he will come out of the Abyss/Shambhala in order to safeguard it. Then, the ten kings/commanders of men, who share the same views (are of one mind) "…will hand over their power and authority to the beast", which was (visible) and is not, but will be (visible) again.

(parenthesis opens) **REVELATION 8** § 13. And I looked, and I heard an angel flying through the midst of heaven, saying with a loud voice, "Woe, woe, woe to those who dwell on the earth, because of the remaining blasts of the trumpet **of the three angels who are about to sound!**	The 'sign' of the antichrist/dragon is already visible. A 'star' will forebode the coming disaster of mankind. It will be the antichrist's 'herald', who shall bring with him the 'key' to unlock the abyss and free the worst inflictions/evils that man can imagine, because he (antichrist) is **not** coming alone.
REVELATION 9 § 1. And the fifth angel sounded: And I saw a **star** **fallen** from the sky unto the earth; and to him was given the key of the shaft of the abyss.[610]	An army of horrendous daemons follows behind him. Woe to those who worship him!

Don't skip chapters or bibliographic references

[610] ***A) Regarding the Key of the Abyss****: Scorpion-men are the guardians of the gates of the Abyss, 'Inner Earth'. They are the guardians of the 'gods' and of the masters of Shambhala, of the beast and of the anti-Christ. <u>Those are the 'kings of the East' and their chosen one has the key of the Abyss. His symbol/sign is a star!</u>*

B) Regarding the star

(a) MAITREYA'S FIRST INTERVIEW, SHARE INTERNATIONAL MAGAZINE JANUARY - FEBRUARY 2009 (BENJAMIN CREME) 11 JANUARY 2009
http://share-international.org/magazine/old_issues/2009/2009-01.htm

«In the very near future, people everywhere will have the opportunity to witness an extraordinary and significant sign, the like of which has been manifested only once before, at the birth of Jesus.

…this mysterious event is a sign, and heralds the <u>beginning of Maitreya's open mission</u>. Soon after the sign appears in our skies, Maitreya will give His first media interview on American television.»

(b) SHARE INTERNATIONAL MAGAZINE MARCH 2009
QUESTIONS & ANSWERS FROM BENJAMIN CREME:
http://share-international.org/magazine/old_issues/2009/2009-03.htm

«**Question:** The 'star' that can now be seen in several places around Norway seems to get brighter and brighter all the time. Lately it has also been seen during the daytime. What then is its purpose?

Answer: It is a 'sign' to herald the emergence of Maitreya into His public mission».

(c) SHARE INTERNATIONAL MAGAZINE MAY 2009
QUESTIONS & ANSWERS WITH BENJAMIN CREME:
http://share-international.org/magazine/old_issues/2009/2009-05.htm

«**Question:** In what way can you recognize the 'star' sign and not get it mixed up with celestial bodies?

Answer: For a start, it is very bright, brighter than Venus, changes colors and moves.»

Let us finally see though what this star is, that thousands of people around the world have seen… because we will next have to proceed elsewhere…

(d) SHARE INTERNATIONAL MAGAZINE MAY 2009
http://share-international.org/magazine/old_issues/2009/2009-05.htm

«**Question:** I have one question that has been gnawing at my mind for several weeks: why have you been calling the light in the sky 'the star', while some of your regular readers know it is one or more UFOs?

Answer: I decided to follow my Master's example. He had called it a 'star-like luminary of brilliant power', and related it to the 'star' which led the 'three wise men' to the birthplace of Jesus. Some of us know that that 'star' was a spacecraft too, but is accepted by millions as a miracle star *(this is actually true).*

…It was just before Christmas so I called it a 'Christmas star', sure that that would be more interesting and magnetic than a prediction about a UFO. In Britain at least, people are much more skeptical of UFOs than in the USA, for example. Of course, at each lecture I make it clear that what **looks like** a star is, in fact, one of four huge spacecraft.

…The 'star' is brighter even than Venus, changes color frequently and moves position. So, obviously, it is not a real star. There are in fact four such 'star-like luminaries' covering the world. They are gigantic spacecraft (each one about the size of five football grounds put together). They all come from planets of our own solar system *(apparently, that's where their bases are).* They are a sign, heralds of the first public appearance on American television of Maitreya, the World Teacher.»

(Parenthesis still open)

REVELATION 12

§ 3. And another **sign** appeared **in the sky**: and behold, **a great red dragon with seven heads and ten horns** *(the aforementioned),* and seven diadems on his heads.

§ 4. His tail swept down a third of the stars of the sky **and threw them to the earth.**

§ 9. And the great dragon was cast out, that ancient serpent, called the Devil and Satan who deceives the whole world; **he was cast out onto the earth,** and his angels were thrown down with him.[611]

Behold the astral followers of the red dragon/Lucifer/creator who are waiting to surge into the Earth, masqueraded as 'our friends' from the stars.

---

[611] **BLAVATSKY H., P., 'THE SECRET DOCTRINE',** (I-407, 408, 409, 410, 411):

«Dragons and snakes of antiquity are all seven-headed.

…It was the goddess of the Great Bear and mother of Time who was in Egypt from the earliest times the 'Living Word', *(Logos)* and that Sevekh-Kronus, whose type was the Crocodile-Dragon, the pre-planetary form of Saturn, was called her son and consort; he was her Word-Logos.

Don't skip chapters or bibliographic references

…A full Initiate was called a 'Dragon', a 'Snake' a 'Naga';

…Now, as shown, the seven-headed or septenary DRAGON-LOGOS had been in the course of time split up, so to speak, into four heptanomic *(seven-fold)* parts or twenty-eight portions… And this is the 'True and the Perfect Serpent' (Ophis), he is the seven-lettered God who is now credited with being Jehovah, and Jesus *(they also included Jesus in their dark symbolisms)* One with him. …The seven-headed serpent has more than one signification in the Apocryphal (Arcane) teachings. It is the seven-headed Dragon, each of whose heads is a star of the Lesser Bear; but it was also, and pre-eminently, the Serpent of Darkness (i.e., inconceivable and incomprehensible) whose seven heads were the seven Logoi *(Words)*, the reflections of the one and first manifested Light -- the universal Logos.»

(Parenthesis still open)

REVELATION 9

§ 2. And he opened the pit of the abyss, and smoke arose out of the pit like the smoke of a great furnace; and the sun and the air were darkened because of the smoke of the pit.

§ 3. Then out of the smoke locusts came upon the earth. And unto them was given power, like the power of scorpions of the earth.

§ 7. The appearance of the locusts was like horses prepared for battle. On their heads were crowns of something like gold, and their faces were like the faces of men.

§ 8. They had hairs like women's hairs, and their teeth were like lions' teeth.

§ 9. And they had breasts like breastplates of iron, and the sound of their wings was like the sound of chariots with many horses rush-

ing into battle. § 10. They had tails like scorpions, and there were stings in their tails.[612] (Parenthesis closes)	Because, as we have said, he holds the 'key' of the abyss. What will burst out of there however will be the greatest scourge for men.

[612] *See reference #595 (scorpion-men)*

SHARE INTERNATIONAL MAGAZINE JUNE 2009
QUESTIONS & ANSWERS WITH BENJAMIN CREME:
http://www.share-international.org/magazine/old_issues/2009/2009-06.htm

«**Question:** I have been doing some research into the UFO phenomenon. I have read quite a few times on the Share International website that they are our Space Brothers.

Are all the different species of aliens our Space Brothers or are some good and some evil?

I struggle with the ones that abduct, take control, and cause fear as having a good purpose for mankind. Can you elaborate on this?

Answer: Yes, without exception, the people *(the alleged extraterrestrial beings)* who man the space-crafts we see are harmless. In fact they are carrying out arduous work on our behalf, neutralizing, as far as the Karmic Law allows, much of the pollution which we spew into our atmosphere, oceans, rivers and land *(because of the technology **they have granted to us**. But this is a well-kept secret)*. We owe them an enormous debt. For over 60 years the world's governments have kept from the people the existence of these space visitors and know that they are entirely harmless* *(!!!)*. Nevertheless, when they can no longer control belief in their existence, these same paranoid governments present them as abductors, brutal and seeking control over humanity. None of that slanderous propaganda is true and soon the people of the world will know that for certain *(when we find out, it will be too late to retreat...)*. They work with our own Spiritual Hierarchy of which Maitreya is the head.»

*****MILTON WILLIAM COOPER**: *(Former US Navy officer, Intelligence Dept.)*
«...They ask the Government to keep their presence here secret.»

REVELATION 17 Cont'd... § 14. These will wage war against the Lamb, and the Lamb will overcome them, for He is Lord of	

Don't skip chapters or bibliographic references

lords and King of kings; and those who are with Him are called, and chosen, and faithful.	This battle will not be a conventional one, (and it certainly isn't Armageddon) but will be a 'battle of points'. It will basically be a confrontation of theses (viewpoints).

The 'weapons' of the side of the 'Lamb' are the Pure Spirit and the capabilities IT possesses. These capabilities do not aim to impress —with signs and wonders– but have the ability to completely 'dissolve' every barren point of view. This is a condition that will be experienced by modern generations when circumstances come to maturity…

The views of the dark powers' side, are like fireworks that impress only the 'petty ones', leading their spirituality to regions with an **impenetrable** 'roof'. Using the 'tool' of the sixth sense they possess, they perform 'miracles' to bedazzle only the naïve ones. But when the True Spirit shines, nothing will be able to resist IT because only IT can offer IMMEDIATE EXODUS from captivity. Hence, the restoration of the Truth is inevitable and victory is **CERTAIN**, since "… the Lamb will overcome them!"

REVELATION 17 Cont'd…	
§ 15. And he said to me, The waters which you saw, where the harlot is seated, are peoples, multitudes, nations, and tongues.	Planet Earth.
§16. And the ten horns which you saw on the beast, these will hate the harlot, make her desolate and naked, they shall eat her flesh and burn her with fire.	The ten 'kings' ruling humanity – those who are of one opinion and will surrender their office/power to the beast– will 'hate' the Earth/whore and will inflict its ecological destruction, sucking it dry of its resources.
§17. For God *(The Father)* has put it into their hearts to fulfill His will, to be of one mind, and to give their	

kingdom to the beast, until the words of God shall be fulfilled.	Unfortunately for men, there is a 'unanimous' decision leading to…havoc…
§18. And the woman that you saw is that great city **which has a kingdom over the kings of the earth.** *(end of chapter)* *(See chapter: How they control the world – Secret Societies)*	This is the Earth. It is under **a double authority**. Under the authority of humans, and they in turn under the authority of the **invisible secret government** of the gods/creators of the 'Spiritual' Hierarchy of the planet, the White Brotherhood.

When time grows near and the HyperUniversal Powers —of the Angels flanking the Lamb/Christ— have completed the preliminary preparations **releasing the bonds,** the procedure for the extraction/release of the HyperCosmic Sacred Archetypes from material creation will commence! This will be the Great Sacred Moment of the Almighty Father! The moment when the stolen Sacred Archetypes return to Their Source!

---

[613] *Things have matured and time has come for the Mother of the fallen Creator to restore the damage Her Son has caused.*
THE APOCRYPHON OF JOHN, THE GNOSTIC SOCIETY LIBRARY [FREDERIK WISSE]: «And when the mother *(of the creator/Yaldabaoth)* recognized that the garment of darkness was imperfect…she repented with much weeping. And the whole 'pleroma' *(the Completeness of the True Cosmoi)* heard the prayer of her repentance, and they prayed on her behalf to the invisible, virginal Spirit. And the Spirit…poured *(Essence)* over her from Its Entire Pleroma…And she was taken up *(higher from where she had fallen)*, not to her own aeon *(not to her original position)*, but above her son that she might be in the ninth *(Heaven)* until she has **corrected** her deficiency.» *Retrieving and returning back the Sacred Archetypes that her son has embezzled.*

వ•ళ

The departure of the 'Sacred Archetypes' begins. The **inner/lower** astral regions are the first to be abandoned by the Sacred Archetypes of Creation; the boundaries of the dimensions are disrupted, forcing their tenants to burst out in total panic.

Don't skip chapters or bibliographic references

(Parenthesis opens)

MATTHEW 24

§ 15. Therefore when you see the 'abomination of desolation', spoken of by Daniel the prophet, standing in the holy place – whoever reads, let him understand–

§ 16. Then let those who are in Judea flee to the mountains.

§ 17. Let him who is on the housetop not go down to take anything out of his house.

§ 18. And let him who is in the field not go back to get his clothes.

§ 19. But woe to those who are pregnant and to those who are nursing babies in those days!

§ 20. And pray that your flight may not be in winter or on the Sabbath.

§ 21. For then there will be great tribulation, such as has not been since the beginning of the world until this time, no, nor ever shall be.

This will be the time when the dark powers with their revolting appearance will appear. The 'gate-keeper' of the Abyss, the antichrist, will free them from their sub-chthonic sunless holes, so that like obedient 'bloodhounds' –by wreaking havoc– they can lead men into the worst ambush creation has ever known!

---

614 *The 'Chupacabra' is a being –one could easier call it a 'materialized bogy'– which is related with the strange animal mutilations in Central America that started in the seventies. (See also previous reference #568, I)*

A) FROM NATIONAL GEOGRAPHIC: EL CHUPACABRAS

http://www.tv.com/national-geographic-channel-is-it-real/chupacabra/episode/552653/summary.html

«Following the reports of mutilated farm animals in Puerto Rico, eyewitnesses began coming forward to describe the predator. Said to have glowing red eyes, the face of a gargoyle and the wings of a vampire bat, the culprit was named El Chupacabras, 'The Goat Sucker', by the press. Quickly, the creature made the leap to parts of the U.S. and Latin America. Some say it's simply the public's imagination running amuck *(surely not unjustifiably)*.

Others say the creature is a genetic experiment that escaped, a space alien, or a supernatural being.»

B) DISCOVERY CHANNEL

http://www.yourdiscovery.com/paranormal/cryptozoology/chupacabras/index.shtml

«**Chupacabra**: Mysterious animal deaths sparked mass hysteria on the small island of Puerto Rico. In 1992, Puerto Rican newspapers reported a series of strange killings had taken place, of a variety of animals including birds, horses and especially goats. The killings occurred around the village of Moca, and the local people believed a mythical creature called El Vampiro de Moca was responsible.

Over a period of six months the slaughter became more widespread, causing mass panic and hysteria. Researchers coined the term 'Chupacabra' meaning 'Goatsucker' in Spanish. The name related to the puncture wounds and lack of blood found on the victims. The reports of Chupacabra activity then began to spread into the Americas and for the last decade sightings have been reported as far north as Carolina, USA and as far south as Chile.

The Chupacabra grew from a village vampire to an international phenomenon. El Chupacabra became a merchandising dream with t-shirts, toys and even a song being produced. By the end of the 1990s the hysteria died away and fewer sightings were reported.

Unexplained animal killings still continue on Puerto Rico and the locals are left with a real mystery to whom or what is killing their animals.»

In truth, these beings are considered workers. They belong to the low ranks of the hierarchy and they are one of many races sub-chthonian creatures that fully obey 'superiors'. This particular case refers to a species responsible to gather the DNA of (edible) animals for their 'arc', necessary for the nutrition of humans, when they get transported to the place where they are planning to take them.

(SEE: DRAWINGS, CHUPACABRA, THE 'ABOMINATION')

MATTHEW 24	
§ 28. For wherever the carcass is, there the vultures will gather.	Because, as the ancient Gr. proverb says: "when the tree has fallen, everyone runs to it with his axe/hatchet"! [δρυός πεσούσης πας ανήρ ξυλεύεται]

627

Don't skip chapters or bibliographic references

§ 22. And unless those days were shortened, no flesh would be saved; but for the elect's sake those days will be shortened.	The misfortune is that the selected ones will still be amidst havoc and suffer this tempest. But time runs short and as procedures accelerate in favor of those who are waiting, unnatural phenomena start to appear. *(The converging line of time)*

As the withdrawal of the Sacred Archetypes of creation will be in progress, the **higher** (positive) astral regions will also be deprived of Them. The entities residing there, in turmoil, will appear on Earth and pretend they are saviors! They will then hasten to 'rescue' men from the preceding negative (astral) threat, and will conjure any argument to justify that. This is when that specific event/phenomenon called Armageddon will take place. Let us open a parenthesis to describe its secrets:

When the archon of this world "placed the cherubim and a flaming sword that turned round in every direction to guard the way to the tree of life" [GENESIS 3:24] the boundaries of the cosmic egg/universe were created and imprisoned the Divine Spirit and The Archetypes of Creation inside it. When the Spirit of Christ left the world of matter –during His EXODUS from this world– IT (His Spirit) created a breach/gate to the 'walls' of the egg/universe –over the region of Golgotha, Jerusalem– which led out of this universe. That event then, caused earthquakes in many places on Earth. In order now to prevent any escape to that Gate 'above', the so-called antichrist is about to station his headquarters in that area of Jerusalem. Consequently, the battle of Armageddon *(see reference #603 about the geographical region of Armageddon)* will take place between the two astral powers –positive and negative astrals– masked as good and evil aliens. Humanity will take sides along them, having been divided as well and in complete ignorance of what will be really at stake at that hour. But the positive astrals will be an equally grave danger as the negative ones, because by pretending they will help men 'escape', they will guide them to the greatest ambush! A great portion of humanity will be trapped, believing they have 'escaped' But we will deal with them and many others again later on.

MATTHEW 24	
§ 23. Then if anyone says to you, 'Look, here is the Christ!' or 'There!' do not believe it. § 24. For pseudo-christs and false	In this panic then, some of the pursuers will spread rumors about the alleged reappearance of Christ, in order to direct the prey/man into the trap easier. But they will be deceiving.

prophets will rise and show great signs and wonders to deceive, if possible, even the elect.

§ 25. Behold, I have told you beforehand!

§ 26. "Therefore if they say to you, 'Look, He *(Christ)* is in the desert!' do not go out; or 'Look, He is in the inner rooms!' do not believe it. *(Parenthesis closes)*

This danger is highlighted by the Gospels because 'they', the latter ones, with their beautiful physiognomies of counterfeit positiveness, **will come to delude** men that they are Real, "…**even the elect ones**."[615]

[615] A) **MAITREYA'S TEACHINGS ON RELIGION: DISCUSSION OF THE IMPACT OF RELIGION ON HUMAN SUFFERING AND THE ROLE OF THE CLERGY**
QUESTIONS & ANSWERS WITH BENJAMIN CREME:
http://www.share-international.org/ARCHIVES/M_teachings/Mt_religion.htm

«**Question**: Do you accept the interpretation of Lucifer as the Fallen Angel of evil?

Answer: No, I do not. I think this is a complete misunderstanding of Lucifer by Christian teaching. The name 'Lucifer' means, literally, 'light'. The word comes from the Latin root: lux, lucis – light; and fer, ferre – to bring. It means, therefore, light-bringing and is the name of the planet Venus as the morning star *(Sanat Kumara from Venus).* Far from being evil, it is pure light. In the esoteric teaching, Lucifer is the name for the great angelic entity who embodies the human kingdom on the soul plane. As souls, we are each an individualized part of this great Over-soul.»

*Precisely! The Power of the Mother of Yaldabaoth/Lucifer which he desires to take back, because he was **fooled** and spread it to the souls of humans he created…*

B) **SHARE INTERNATIONAL MAGAZINE, JULY / AUGUST ISSUE 2009**
THE TIME OF REVELATION BY THE MASTER – THROUGH BENJAMIN CREME, 14 JUNE 2009
http://www.share-international.org/magazine/old_issues/2009/2009-07.htm

«Recently, my Master *(Maitreya –narration by Benjamin Creme–)* talked about a coming together of the Forces of Light. He meant the coming of the Masters into the everyday world; they are the Forces of Light on our planet. But also the joining together with the Forces of Light of Mars and Venus and perhaps other planets in large numbers.[(1)] Where there were one or two, there will be many. Where there were many, there will be even more. And everywhere: Not only in the Netherlands but everywhere. Increasing numbers of people are sending in reports of UFO sightings.

In London near where I live, one night recently there were 17 flying low over the ground. They were seen by many people who stopped their cars, got out, and watched this parade of UFOs flying about. So there is a coming to-

Don't skip chapters or bibliographic references

gether of these forces. People will record more and more evidence of the 'flying saucers', the 'UFOs'. **They are all part of the plan of the emerging Hierarchy of** our world.»

(1) **REVELATION CH. 12** «§3...behold, a great red dragon having seven heads and ten horns *(the aforementioned one...)*, and seven diadems on his heads; §4. His tail swept down a third of the stars of the sky and threw them to the earth.»

... But as the release of the Sacred Archetypes is reaching its completion...

(So we return again to chapter 16 of Armageddon which was left unfinished) **REVELATION 16 Cont'd...** § 17. And the seventh angel poured out his vial (bowl) into the air, and a loud voice came out of the temple of heaven, from the throne, saying, "**It is done!**"	What else could this "**It is done**" refer to but the completion of the liberation of the Sacred Archetypes of Creation from the entire material universe of deception, THAT GREAT DAY OF GOD ALMIGHTY! Because of this Withdrawal, the co-hesive Forces of the material universe collapse completely.[616]

[616] **BARBARA MARCINIAK 'GAIA'** [Gr. trans. MATZOROU E.] *(Information through channeling)* (p. 236): «Time is collapsing. ...This time-collapse results in **the discontinuance of control of the frequencies** that define your world.»

REVELATION 16 Cont'd... § 18. And there were voices and thunders and flashes of lightning; and there was a great earthquake, such a mighty and great earthquake as had never occurred since men were upon the earth. § 19. And the great city was divided into three parts, **and the cities of the nations** fell. And great Babylon *(visible, material Earth)* came to remembrance before	The breakdown of matter is completed.

God, to give her the cup of the wine of the fierceness of His wrath. § 20. And every island fled away, and the mountains were not found. § 21. And great hail from the sky fell upon men, each hailstone about the weight of a talent; and men blasphemed God because of the plague of the hail, since that plague was exceedingly great. *(end of chapter 16)*	
	In another chapter of the Apocalypse –from the more synoptic ones– the cosmic events of the end are described as follows:
(Parenthesis opens) **REVELATION 6** § 12. And I looked when He opened the sixth seal, and behold, there was a great earthquake; and the sun became black as sackcloth of hair, and the moon became like blood. §13. And the stars of the sky fell unto the earth, as a fig-tree drops its unripe (untimely) figs, when it is shaken by a mighty wind. § 14. And the sky was split apart like a scroll when it is rolled up, and every mountain and island was moved from its place.	

Don't skip chapters or bibliographic references

§15. And the kings of the earth, and the great men, and the rich men, and the commanders, and the mighty men, every bondservant and every free man, **hid themselves in the caves** and in the rocks of the mountains, § 16. and they said to the mountains and rocks, "Fall on us and hide us from the face of him who sits on the throne and from the wrath of the Lamb! § 17. For the great day of his wrath has come, and who shall be able to stand? *(see reference #593)*	
	Matthew describes the event of the collapse:
(Parenthesis still open) **MATTHEW 24** §29. Immediately after the tribulation of those days *(the dynasty of the antichrist Maitreya)* the sun will be darkened, and the moon will not give its light; the stars will fall from heaven, and the powers of the heavens will be shaken. (Parenthesis closes)	
	Let us see though, how the next chapter describes the last scene of the drama of the Deliverance of

	Spiritual Men from the material trap.
REVELATION 18 § 1. And after these things I saw an angel coming down from heaven, having great power (authority), and the earth *(the energy-planes, the cause of matter)* was illuminated with his glory. § 2. And he cried mightily with a loud voice, saying, "Fallen, fallen is Babylon the great *(dense matter, the Earth)* and has become a dwelling place of demons, a prison for every foul spirit, and a cage for every unclean and hateful vulture!	Time completes its cycle and the Earth –the support of matter– is thoroughly stricken because **it** was the dragon's nest. The 'snake's cutoff tail' will become the grave of those who chose to remain on it, thus entering the threshold of the second death.
	These events, no matter how painful, must be stated SO THAT NOBODY CAN SAY THEY WERE NOT.
§ 4. And I heard another voice from heaven saying, **"Come out of her, my people, so that you will not take part in her sins, and receive of her plagues.** § 5. For her sins have reached unto heaven, and God has remembered her iniquities.	And while everything will appear to have ended, the Holy Hour of Spiritual Transference comes for those who have enduringly waited for Redemption, because the real plagues for the world begin FROM THAT POINT ON!
	Because promises are kept…

Don't skip chapters or bibliographic references

(Parenthesis opens) **JOHN'S GOSPEL 6** § 40. And this is the will of Him who sent Me. Everyone who sees the Son and believes in Him may have everlasting life; and **I will raise him up at the last day**.	The Sacred Hour has arrived for those who have waited. All those who have remained firm in their decision will go through the process of the First Resurrection, regardless of whether they are still alive in matter or have died and are in the disintegrating energy-fields.
MATTHEW 24 § 30. **Then** the sign of the Son of Man will appear **in heaven**, and then all the tribes of the earth will mourn, and they will see the Son of Man coming **on the clouds** of heaven with power and great glory.[617]	**Then**, while everything will be crumbling down, while events will succeed one another in lightning-speed because time will be near its finish-line, then the TRUE SIGN of Christ will appear in the sky, which of course, WILL NOT BE THE CROSS. The cross is the symbol of matter, and at that time matter will be dissolving! Those who possess Spiritual Noûs will recognize it immediately. The others will realize it when it will be too late.

[617] *Let us see though how the false prophet of antichrist replies to the question posed to him regarding the particular verse, so as to measure the ... 'depth of his spirituality':*
SHARE INTERNATIONAL MAGAZINE JULY/AUGUST 2009
QUESTIONS & ANSWERS WITH BENJAMIN CREME:
http://www.share-international.org/magazine/old_issues/2009/2009-07.htm
«Question: How do you explain the Bible's prophecy in MATTHEW 24:29-31, where Jesus says He will come "on the clouds of heaven with power and great glory"?
Answer: Maitreya descended from His retreat in the high Himalayas on 8 July 1977, spent some days in Pakistan and then came from Karachi to London, UK, on 19 July 1977, thus "coming on the clouds" something which today all can do **by airplane**.» *(!!!)*

MATTHEW 24	
§ 27. For as the lightning comes from the east and flashes to the west, so also will the presence of the Son of Man be.	An absolutely Spiritual Manifestation.
MATTHEW 24 § 40. Then two men will be in the field: one will be taken and the other left. § 41. Two women will be grinding at the mill: one will be taken and the other left.	Here is the infamous excerpt which announces the process of the First Resurrection by de-materialization which is called the "Rapture of the Church"! When the withdrawal procedure has finally reached the last (higher/outermost) layer of the energy-world, wherefrom Spiritual Man is projected, the Transferred Ones are snatched from there, and they thus cease projecting their forms onto space-time (dense matter). This will make them suddenly disappear from the world of form. *(The process is analyzed in the next chapter)* Let them therefore prepare, by Spiritually disengaging themselves **from any** material dependence, and they must remain focused towards the correct Spiritual direction of the Truth.
MATTHEW 24 § 31. And He will send His angels with a great sound of a trumpet, **and they will gather together His elect from the four winds, from one end of the skies to the other.**	So, the souls of the select ones are picked up not from the material plane, but from the outer energy-region of the material world. "…from the four WINDS and from one end of the (material/energy) SKIES to the other." This will hold true for the corporeal-

Don't skip chapters or bibliographic references

	ly/materially deceased as well as those who will still be incarnated in the material world. Yet for those who are incarnated in matter, this 'rapture of the church' will result in their projection (on the space-time 'screen'/matter) <u>to suddenly cease appearing</u>, because the 'projection device' (Soul) will abandon the last energy-layer of matter: *(see: DRAWINGS, THE ROUTE OF THE SOUL)* Because...
GOSPEL OF PHILIP, [LELOUP, J., Y.] § 23. Neither flesh nor blood can inherit the Kingdom of God. (Parenthesis closes)	The body's prison ceases to exist...

After the Departure of those who passed on to the First Resurrection (through the Rapture of the Church), follows the 'coup de grace' for the planet along with the bleak fortune of the second group –those who have loved matter and its 'commodities'– of the ones who will be lost.

---

[618] *A reminder:* **FROM HISTORY CHANNEL'S DOCUMENTARY: MAYAN DOOMSDAY PROPHECY, DECEMBER 21ST 2012**

«...At the ancient ball-court at Chichen Itza ... the Maya played the same ball-game that the Hero Twins played against the lords of the underworld, as described in the Popol Vuh. The game seems to have been a primitive hybrid of basketball and soccer. The objective was to get a ball through a ring made of stone, which was mounted high on the wall, using only the knees and hips. The first team **to get the ball through** the ring won the match... *(The winners will be those individuals who will achieve the passage through that ring/Gate, hence passing to the First Resurrection).*

...The carving on a sidewall graphically depicts the beheading of a player at center-court. Many believe this was the fate of the loser. Blood spurts from his neck <u>in the form of serpents</u>. The decapitated player kneels before a ball. Inside it, a skull speaks the words symbolizing death *(the second death)*. ...Chilam Balam (the high priest) says: "A time of the end of the Word of

God; A time for uniting for a cause."
*This is the **termination** of the division/break-up of the Sacred Archetypes (Λ→I), which used to be trapped into matter, and all of them UNIFIED will return to their Sacred Source. Fortunate will be those who will follow them, disaster will fall onto those who **imagine** that Those Sacred Archetypes were part of matter. And the Maya priest continues:* "For half the people there will be food and for the other half there will be misery.»

We must mention at this point that during this whole period of cosmogonical disasters, the 'elect' commanders of the planet will be 'safeguarded' in their well-prepared areas and will get ready to 'embark' their second "salvation" ark, aiming to abandon the Earth for good.

REVELATION 18 CONTINUED

§6. Reward her just as she rewarded you, and repay her double according to her works; in the cup which she has mixed, mix double for her.

§7 To the degree she has glorified herself and lived luxuriously, to the same measure give her torment and mourning; for she says in her heart, 'I sit as a queen, and am no widow, and will not see mourning.'

§8 Therefore, her plagues shall come <u>in one day</u>, death and mourning and famine. And she shall be utterly burned with fire, for strong is the Lord God who judges her...

Let us then look at the Earth's horrid fortune and along with it matter's too, because the definitive end is predestined and comes from space in the form of a **comet**...

§21. Then a mighty angel took up a stone like a great millstone and cast it into the sea, saying, "Thus with violence the great city Babylon *(visible, material Earth)* shall be thrown down, and shall be found no more."[619]

[619] *In the second year of Nebuchadnezzar's reign, when Prophet Daniel was in his palace, the king had a prophetic dream concerning the end of the world:*
A) NEBUCHADNEZZAR'S DREAM, OLD TESTAMENT, DANIEL CH. 2: «§1. Now in the second year of his reign, Nebuchadnezzar had dreams; and his spirit was so troubled that his sleep left him ...§27. Daniel answered before the king, and said: 'As for the mystery about which the king has inquired, neither wise men, nor conjurers, nor astrologers, nor magicians nor soothsayers are able to declare (explain) it to the king. §28 But there is a God in heaven who reveals mysteries, and He has made known to King Nebuchadnezzar **what will**

Don't skip chapters or bibliographic references

take place in the latter days.'

§31. **You, O king, were looking and behold a great image!** *(He saw a man's image/form).* **This great image, whose brightness was excellent, stood before you; and its appearance was terrible.**

§32. **This** *(human)* **image's head was of pure gold** *(the 1ˢᵗ Root-race, the Golden Gender, carrying the Noũs of the Soul on its head),*

its breast and its arms of silver *(2ⁿᵈ Root-race, the Silver Gender, the Astral. It is focused on the chest, the cardiac and* **emotional** *center),*

its belly and its thighs of bronze *(3ʳᵈ Root-race, the Bronze Gender, the Aetheric. It is centered: (a) around the belly/solar plexus, the center of lower passions, (b) the genital center where sexual impulses spring from, and (c) the first energy-center –that of the sacrum– where survival instincts have their source as the primary attributes of the aetheric body)*

§33. **its legs were of iron,**

(Divine Sparks were not *embodied into some souls. These, as plain souls, were incarnated in matter and formed races. These races never met/knew the Gender/Race of Heroes.)*

…Its feet partly of iron and partly of clay.

(This refers to those who are merely vitalized by the sum of their energy-bodies –λᾶας, λαός [=plain folk]).

§34. **As you watched, a** **rock** **was cut out, but not by human hands, which struck the man's image** **on its feet of iron and clay, and crushed them to pieces.**

(…The crushing of the human form/image comes at the end of the 5th Root Race of the Iron Gender –the feet– when it is found intermixed with the sub-race of clay).

§35. **Then the iron, the clay, the bronze, the silver, and the gold were crushed all together, and became like chaff from the summer threshing floors; and the wind carried them away so that no trace of them was found. But the stone that struck the image became a great mountain and filled the whole earth.»**

B) *One of the big threats approaching Earth is called Apophis*

(a) APOPHIS: http://el.wikipedia.org/wiki/99942_Άποφις:

«99942 Apophis is a near-Earth asteroid. It was discovered in June 2004 and its existence was confirmed in December 2004. Initial observations by NASA indicated a great probability that it would strike the Earth or the Moon in 2029 *(new calculations indicate the year 2036),* something that led to great publicity. Apophis was first observed from the Kitt Peak National Observatory, Arizona USA, on June 19, 2004. The previous provisional designation it was given was 2004 MN$_4$. From its second observation in December 2004, the asteroid stirs interest of astronomers as initial indications lead to an increased probability of an impact on Earth. On June 24, 2005, the permanent classification number 99942 is given to it, and on July 19, 2005, the name Apophis by the people who discovered it.

Until January 2006 calculations showed its diameter to be 320m and its mass $4.6*10^{10}$kg (46,000,000 tons). These calculations were based on 964 observations with optical telescopes and 6 with radio-telescopes, of which 4 with the Doppler method. Nevertheless, the error in these calculations is considered substantial.»

Some additional information on the same asteroid:

(b) ASTEROID THREATENS EARTH, Pathfinder news 1/3/07, SOURCE: Scotsman news
http://www.pathfinder.gr/periscopio/asteroid-hit-earth.html

«Scientists have recently announced that a space mission is soon to be launched, which will cost about £150 million, and will aim to deter an asteroid which has already entered into an orbit leading it directly onto Earth. Scientists, astronauts and space station engineers call upon immediate awakening for the protection of the planet from the asteroid Apophis. This asteroid threatens to hit Earth at a speed of over 50,000 kilometers an hour and cause the release of energy of up to 80,000 times greater than that of the Hiroshima bomb. The research team believes that the United Nations are about to display great responsibility regarding this space mission.

…The Space Researchers Association, in which Russian astronauts also participate, is about to carry out a series of conferences for the best way to deal with the possible disaster, and in 2009, they will submit an official proposal to the United Nations.

Schweickart said that the United Nations will have to adopt a plan to deal with the asteroid threat and decide on the time when immediate action will have to be taken, in order to avert its collision to Earth.

…Scientists have calculated that even if the asteroid does not hit Earth but passes close enough to it, the Earth's gravitational force could cause the impact.»

And the aversive actions are being methodically organized:

(c) NASA PLANS TO SEND ASTRONAUT ONTO ASTEROID IN EFFORT TO AVOID CATASTROPHE, THE GUARDIAN, FRIDAY 17 NOVEMBER 2006
http://www.guardian.co.uk/science/2006/nov/17/spaceexploration.internationalnews

«NASA is now drawing up plans to land an astronaut on an asteroid aiming to avert a possible impact with our planet *(…revival of the Hollywood movie 'Armageddon').* As it is known, a very small asteroid called Apophis has already been identified as a possible threat to Earth in 2036. Even though till today sending an astronaut onto an asteroid to avert a possible collision with Earth was a science-fiction script, or the script for the 'Armageddon' movie, NASA is now preparing to make it a reality. They want to send an astronaut

Don't skip chapters or bibliographic references

to an asteroid hurtling through space at more than 30,000 mph.»
C) SUPERNATURAL.GR —ASTEROID: ARRIVAL IN 2019
http://www.supernatural.gr/news_asteroid_2019.htm:
«An asteroid *(other than Apophis)* has been spotted in a New Mexico (USA) Laboratory following an 837-day orbit around the Sun, which, according to initial calculations, will meet Earth on February 1st, 2019.
The most threatening body ever discovered in space seems to have entered a trajectory guiding it straight to Earth. This celestial body, which scientists have named 2002NT7, is no bigger than two kilometers in diameter, but can destroy the greatest part of the living organisms on Earth. According to Prof. Dr. Benny Peiser of Liverpool Univ., this type of asteroid collides with Earth extremely rarely: once every two million years. But if that were to happen, 2002NT7 would cause such havoc that humanity would regress back to the most distant times of its history. Most scientists appear relatively calm, hoping that collision will eventually be avoided. How? Simply because the calculations of the asteroid's trajectory, have not yet been completed. 2002NT7 therefore, could pass by the outer atmosphere of our planet.»

During these tragic moments of the world, men who will **NOT** pass onto the Spiritual First Resurrection but will manage to stay alive on Earth, having no other choice, will join the ranks of the antichrist and will be lead to the ambush of the spectacular starships of the Luciferian power. They may even join the group of the past earthly commanders of the nations who will (at that time) be transported to their second ark, so they can all together abandon the Earth permanently.
—And those who did not pass onto the First Resurrection, but have lost their lives during the calamities of the last days on Earth, where will they go in this new phase of the universe?
–Those who have not managed to be Spiritually 'snatched' –even if they are dead– will remain in the energy-spaces of the material universe and will reincarnate 'normally' in the new order of the 5th dimension.
What must be made clear is that if someone is meant to pass onto the First Resurrection, <u>they will</u>, regardless of whether they are alive on Earth or dead in the energy fields. The same holds true for anyone who does not possess the 'ticket' for the First Resurrection: Either alive on Earth or dead in the energy-planes, he will be left out of the Bridal Chamber.

The dark powers know that the Sacred Keys/Archetypes of creation will be returned to their Source. They themselves are in no possession of such codes/tools. Thus, the entrapment of their energy-nutrition/men into a 'setting/scene' 'dressed-up' to look alive in some parallel universe will prolong their 'life'. Their 'mouse trap' will be made out of phantasmagoric space crafts that will lead the misguided ones to the doubly virtual reality. Thus men will only be able to watch the disaster of the burning planet from far away, looking at it through the port-holes of the spaceships which will be provided as a means of escape by their false saviors.

---

620 **A) KALOGERAKIS, G.** (RETIRED GREEK ARMY MAJOR GENERAL) **'THE PROMETHEAN LEGACY'** (p. 81) «Olympians: The Great Universal Brotherhood of Light with its myriads upon myriads of crafts bearing the name 'ΤΕΛΕΙΟΤΗΣ' [=PERFECTION], always undertakes the rescue of small children, young individuals and **righteous people**, when and where need may arise. It is a rescue mission. It consists of entities of the 'Great Cosmos' for the rescue of humans through **evacuation of the planet**. All those who will be rescued, will be transferred to other inhabited planets. The ones who want to stay on them can do so, the ones who don't **will return** to Gaia for its colonization...The star-base 'PHOENIX', ...hosts: 850 mother-ships, whose radius ranges from 25 to 150 kilometers, 3,892 sister-ships with a radius of 2.5 to 15 kilometers, 200,000 subsidiary ships with a radius of 10 to 500 meters. Both vessels 'Phoenix' and 'Perfection' contain mother-ships, sister-ships and subsidiary ships... The mission of the vessels of the 'Phoenix' star fleet is to collect 120,000,000 'E' descendants, in case planet Earth is in danger. The starship 'Lilith' *(of the enemy astral forces, whom they call apostates),* which is located on the dark side of the moon, will collect the terrestrial collaborators of the apostates on 57,000 starships with a capacity of 35,000,000 people.»

B) BARBARA MARCINIAK 'GAIA' [Gr. trans. MATZOROU E.] *(Information through channeling):* «While Gaia (Earth) will experience the events taking place on it, countless immaterial entities will be watching, sitting on aetheric seats overseeing the laws of cause and effect play out themselves... many of you will be surprised when you find yourselves inside the turmoil of havoc and great transformation, and you will wonder how you ended up there.»

Don't skip chapters or bibliographic references

REVELATION 18 CONTINUED

§9. And the kings of the earth who have committed fornication and lived sensuously with her, shall weep and lament over her, when they see the smoke of her burning,

§10. Standing at a distance for fear of her torment, saying, "Alas, alas, that great city Babylon *(visible, material Earth)*, that mighty city! For in one hour your judgment has come."

§11. And the merchants of the earth shall weep and mourn over her, for no man buys their merchandise anymore:

§12. merchandise of gold and silver, precious stones and pearls, fine linen and purple, and silk and scarlet, all kinds of scented wood, all kinds of ivory objects, all kinds of objects of the most precious wood, bronze, iron, and marble;

§13. and cinnamon and incense, ointments and frankincense, wine and oil, fine flour and wheat, cattle and sheep, horses and chariots, and slaves **and souls of men**.

§14. And the fruit that your soul longed for has gone from you, and all the things which are luxurious and splendid have gone from you, and you shall find them no more at all.

And the Earth ceases to be an attractive pole of desire and lust for every soul.

§15. The merchants of these things, who became rich by her, **shall stand at a distance for fear of her torment, weeping and wailing**,

§16. And saying: 'Alas, alas that great city that was clothed in fine linen and purple and scarlet and adorned with gold and precious stones and pearls!

§17. For in one hour such great riches came to nought (nothing).' Every shipmaster, all who travel in ships, and sailors, and as many as trade on the sea, stood at a distance,

§18. And cried out when they saw **the smoke of her burning**, saying, 'What city was like this great city?'

§22. And the sound of harpists, and musicians, and flutists, and trumpeters shall not be heard in you anymore; and no craftsman of any craft shall be found in you anymore, and the sound of a millstone shall not be heard in you no more.

§23. And the light of a lamp shall not shine in you anymore, and the voice of bridegroom and bride shall not be heard in you anymore. For, your merchants were the great men of the earth, for by your sorcery all the nations were deceived.

§24. And in her was found the blood of prophets and of saints, and of all who were slain on the earth.

Let us recapitulate by enumerating (in approximation) the sequence of events:

1) Climatic changes are intensified.

2) The Earth's governors create a world financial crisis and accumulate the money of the nations.

3) The governors prepare their 'salvation' arks in two phases:
   (a) underground shelters
   (b) space-programs for the departure from Earth.

4) Global Government (The rise of the antichrist in his public office/mission)

5) Enforcement of the biochip onto the nations (the marking/incision of the beast).

6) Commencement of the procedure of the Withdrawal of the Sacred Archetypes from material creation.

7) Appearance of the lower (negative) astral entities (=the abomination).

8) Appearance of the higher (positive) astral entities (=the powers of the antichrist)

9) Clash between these two powers (Armageddon).

10) Capturing of Spiritual men and the process of the First Resurrection.

11) Embarkation on the starships of all who have not passed onto the first Resurrection.

12) Earth's collision with an asteroid or planet 'X' or Nibiru or Apophis.

13) Disembarkation into the 5th dimension (=2nd death).

'MATTER' AFTER CONSUMMATION

With the end of the Iron Race, a new HyperLucent Spiritual Age begins independent of the five-seeded 'apple' of matter. This will be **the true** Sixth Root-Race of the new Humanity, which will start after the so-called First Resurrection. Woe to the ones left behind though, since the snake's cutoff tail will continue to oscillate for a little longer between the dipoles, until it permanently stops. This will be the momentum (acquired speed) of the previous movement of the world, which will soon come to an end. Then the 2nd death will rear its ugly head, painting the background of their 'life' in the darkest possible colors of true hell.

–What exactly does this mean?

–The Earth's physicists have ascertained that when a particle of matter reaches a 'fork' of choices, the road it will finally **not** follow will produce an image of that particle; in contrast to the other choice which will be the real one. This is approximately what will happen at the Sacred Hour when the Archetype of Life will be returned to its Source. Every other choice will end-up being 'vacuous/empty' and soon die out, since every Sacred Archetype will stop vitalizing it. Those who will not follow the course of the Archetype of Life will necessarily follow the other, the 'vacuous one'.

'Life' for the misguided humanity will take place in one or more of the parallel alternative probabilities, since the material universe will cease to have its current form, after the withdrawal of the Sacred Archetypes. In these pseudo-images of (parallel/virtual) universes, real life will not exist; only a doubly virtual one, inside a suitably formed body. When at some point the last drop of living energy (life) has been consumed out of every alternative probability as well as out of every human/battery, then, everything will definitively fade into the second death. This will be the ultimate hell. Thus, the men of the 'future', gazing at the bottom of the material vortex that threatens them, attempt the ultimate time-jump and come from their place and time into your **present-time reality** looking for salvation.

---

621 A) 'MYSTERIES OF THE WORLD', VOL. 'SECRET MESSAGES'

«TIME TRAVEL: Are leaps in time possible? Theoretically, yes. According to Einstein, space and time are strongly connected to each other, so that they are obviously part of a space-time unity. Therefore, it is likely that this unity could be broken. At this point we come across the 'black hole' term, which is considered to be a hole in space. Space and time can fall in this black hole and unity ceases to exist inside it. A lot of scientists have dealt with this seemingly far-fetched hypothesis. For example, physicist Frank J. Tipler of Tulane University New Orleans USA, in 1990, calculated a 'closed time-bronchus' and designed a hypothetical time machine. Professor Stephen

---

Hawking of Cambridge University and physicist John R. Gribbin, quantum physics professor of Sussex University, concluded in 1992 that we can travel in time and participate in past or future events. But there is no concrete scientific evidence for it.»

B) STEPHEN HAWKING – 'THE UNIVERSE IN A NUTSHELL' [Gr. tr. Petraki M.] Ch. PROTECTING THE PAST (STEPHEN HAWKING, HOLDS THE LUCASIAN CHAIR OF THEORETICAL PHYSICS AND APPLIED MATHEMATICS AT CAMBRIDGE UNIVERSITY)

«(p. 133-134) There are only a few of us foolhardy enough to work on a subject that is so politically incorrect in physics circles. We thus disguise the fact by using technical terms that are codenames for time-travel. The basis of all modern discussions of time travel is Einstein's general theory of relativity …where his equations turned space and time into dynamic entities by describing how they are curved and distorted by matter and energy in the universe. …In general relativity, however, there is now the possibility that space-time could be warped so much, that one could set off in a spaceship and come back before they even set out.

Something like this could happen if there were wormholes/tunnels connecting different regions of space and time. Then you could steer your spaceship into one mouth of the wormhole and come out of the other mouth in a different place and different time.

(p. 142) …The cosmic-strings space-time contains matter that has positive energy density and is consistent with the physics we know. However, the warping that produces time bronchi extends all the way to infinity in space and back to the infinite past in time. Thus these cosmic-string space-times were created having the possibility **to allow time-travel** in them.

(p.142) …The question then is: could some advanced civilization modify space-time towards the future so that time bronchi appear in a region of finite size? I say a region of a finite size, because no matter how advanced the civilization becomes, it could presumably control only a finite part of the universe.

(p.143) …Time travel is possible in a region of space-time in which there are time-bronchi.

(p.143) … Then, I assume as a criterion for the existence of a time-machine, what I call 'a finitely generated horizon', that is, a horizon that is formed by light-rays that emerge from a region within clearly defined limits. In other words, these light-rays don't come in from infinity or from an irregularity, but originate from a finite region containing time-bronchi; namely, from the region which the advanced civilization is supposed to create.

(p.148) …The energy density of matter depends on the state it is in. So it is possible that an advanced civilization might be able to make the energy density finite on the boundary of the time machine by 'freezing' or removing the virtual particles that go round closed routes (loops).»

Don't skip chapters or bibliographic references

C) RETURN TO THE FUTURE THROUGH … THE HOLES OF TIME
SOURCE: NEWS 10-06-2000 http://www.physics4u.gr/news/2000/scnews51.html

«A new science, the revolutionary and complicated quantum physics, and an impressive recent discovery that a speed faster than light exists, have radically changed the scientists' view about time, speed and our ability (at least in theory) to travel forwards or backwards in time.

…Therefore, Hawking says, to travel back in time, we have to warp space-time. This is an important subject for research. Unfortunately though, no government in the world is prepared to spend the large sums of money needed for this purpose. Instead, the scientist humorously continues, one has to use coded technical terms, like closed time, curves etc. so that the politicians don't understand the real object of our research".

And he concludes: "To make time travel possible, we must warp space-time so much, so as to create a tunnel or wormhole. This will connect the two sides of the galaxy, and function as a shortcut to get us from one to the other and back, while our friends are still alive. Such wormholes, it has been suggested, could be possible in the future. But if you can travel from one side of the galaxy to the other, in a week or two, you can also find another wormhole to go back through and arrive before you have even set out. In that case we will definitely need…time protection legislation.»

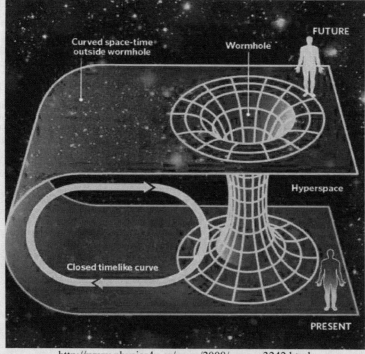

http://www.physics4u.gr/news/2008/scnews3242.html
http://stavrochoros.pblogs.gr/tags/fysiki-gr.html

D) 'WORMHOLES DO EXIST'
SOURCE: in.gr & BBC 12-04-2000, http://www.physics4u.gr/news/2000/scnews52.html
«St. Petersburg: A Russian scientist has managed to calculate that the existence of wormholes is possible, wormholes that are large and stable enough to allow, at least theoretically, intergalactic travel, the BBC broadcasted on April 12, 2000.
'Wormholes' are astronomical objects that could theoretically function as shortcuts between two distant points in the Universe.
Russian astrophysicist Sergei Krasnikov of the Pulkovo Observatory in St. Petersburg overcame the limitations of the existing models based on the general theory of relativity, according to which only tiny 'wormholes' can possibly exist. Wormholes can function as shortcuts connecting distant regions of space-time. Passing through a wormhole, one could travel from one region to the other faster than the speed of light.»

−I don't understand what you mean by that!
−It is only natural not to understand, just as no one from your contemporary fellow humans is able to perceive what is really happening: I am talking about time-traveling humans coming from your remote future. The goal of these time-travelers is to activate the rescuing conditions/probabilities that each of their groups pursues, through their presence here in the primary material universe −in your 'here and now'− before this universe ends.

[622] **A) 'STRANGE' MAGAZINE, SPECIAL EDITION: EXTRATERRESTRIALS + UFOS AN ARTICLE BY DIM. EVANGELOPOULOS: 'MAJESTIC 12':**

«Dr. Burisch: ... they **are essentially we.** They are humans coming back from our future!»
B) ERICH VON DÄNIKEN 'THE SECOND COMING HAS ALREADY STARTED' (p. 241)
«Lately, the idea that the tiny beings with the pear-shaped heads are not at all aliens but time-travelers, that come from our very own future, was spread. Time travel, as physicists have recently concluded, is not impossible. It is just that that we (present day humans) have no idea as to how this time-travel can be practically possible.» (Meckelburg, E.: *Zeittunnel-Reisen an den Rand der Ewigkeit.* München 1991 *Derrs.: Transwelt-Erfahrungen jenseits von Raum und Zeit,* München, 1992)

C) FROM BILL HAMILTON'S INTERVIEW TO LINDA MOULTON

http://www.boomspeed.com?joseph2/J-Rod2.htm

«BILL HAMILTON: What I am saying is that they evolved in our future, according to the Doctrine of the Convergent Time Lines. In other words, they

Don't skip chapters or bibliographic references

come from our future and they have traveled backwards to their past or our current present.

LINDA MOULTON: They are coming back because they are trying to prevent some type of catastrophe?

BILL HAMILTON: Yes, they are trying to change the time line. *(No matter how much they try, the tail-devouring serpent (Ourobore) will always swallow its own tail...) [...]*

...**LINDA MOULTON**: Is this an implication that they came into the Homo sapiens future at some point in the far distance and that they are now reaching back into our genetic bloodlines for genetic material that they think might help them in some way?

BILL HAMILTON: From what I understand, they are an **altered form**, a new species that branched off Homo sapiens.

LINDA MOULTON: In what was a catastrophe of what we would call our future?

BILL HAMILTON: Yes.

LINDA MOULTON: Did Dan Burisch have any idea what the catastrophe is in the coming future?

BILL HAMILTON: He cannot specifically say what occurred. However, he places it as happening approximately a decade from now. *(The interview was taken in 2002)*

LINDA MOULTON: In that 2012 time-period that is supposed to be the end of the Mayan Grand Calendar?

BILL HAMILTON: Yes, but **it is not rigidly fixed**. It could happen any time between now and then or even a little past that time. I'm not certain whether it is something that is an instant cataclysmic event of some kind. I have no idea.»

–And is time-traveling feasible?
–Well the time has come for us to complete the chapter concerning space-time. By recomposing older information –which I shall remind you of– and by adding new data, I will try to analyze this paradox.
We have said that in order for beings to appear (as living holograms) in material life, **they project themselves** onto the sedimented life-remnant of dense matter –as we have called it– from some energy-layer from the ones composing the spiral of the material universe. This is the way the 'living' holograms of plants, animals and men and the entire variety of the organic

world appear here *(Ch. THE DENSELY MATERIAL PLANE)*. Due to this very process, Spiritual or Soulful Man has the **outer** energy-layer of the energy-material universe as his origin of projection.

---

623 **A) DANEZIS M., THEODOSIOU S. 'COSMOLOGY OF THE INTELLECT'**

MATTER AS A WHIRL (VORTEX) – SOME PERSONAL VIEWS (p. 178): «But the vortex-particle has a series of surprises in store for us, since it should present spherical symmetry. What we are essentially talking about, is a **non-perceptible spherical vortex** inside the n-dimensional **non Euclidean field**, whose **projective shadow** inside the three-dimensional Euclidean space of our senses, is perceived as an elementary particle.»

B) THE APOCRYPHON OF JOHN, THE GNOSTIC SOCIETY LIBRARY [STEVAN DAVIES]: «The First Man [This is the one who appeared to them *(archons/demons)*. He appeared to them in the form of a human being.] All the realms *(dimensions)* of the chief ruler quaked! The foundations of the Abyss moved! He *(Man)* illuminated the waters above the world of matter, His image shown *(appeared)* in those waters. All the demons and the first ruler together **gazed up** toward the underside of the newly shining waters. Through that light they saw the Image in the waters.»

Also from another part of the text: «…Adam was revealed because the shadow of light dwelled within him.»

The same excerpt expressed differently:

C) THE APOCRYPHON OF JOHN, THE GNOSTIC SOCIETY LIBRARY: «And the man came forth *(manifested)* because of the shadow of the light which is in him.» [WALDSTEIN M., WISSE F.]

The word 'projection' that I am using is not absolute, but approximately defines a process that is very difficult to express in words; I will nevertheless provide a somewhat simplistic example that partly explains the fundamental concepts of this procedure: When a motion picture is projected on the screen of a movie theater, on the opposite side of the hall there is a motion-picture projection-machine which through a light-beam projects the pictures on the screen. Think of Man in a similar way, projecting a living light-ray of his own from the last energy-layer of the spiral energy-universe, which (light-ray) is magnetized and retained (held together) by the space-time screen/dense matter *(brane)*.

Don't skip chapters or bibliographic references

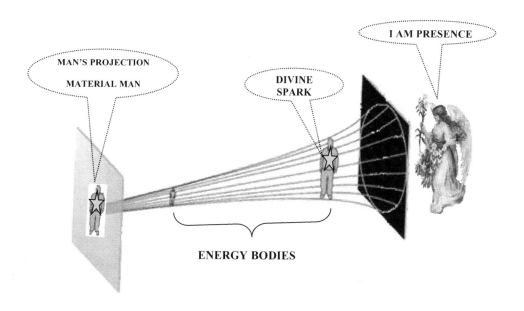

As Man's living projection heads towards the screen/dense matter *(brane)*, it passes during its course through the intermediate energy-fields and 'puts on' their energy to end up onto matter/screen 'wearing' all the energy-bodies. These energy-fields in our example correspond to the 'empty' space of the movie-theater which the light-beam traverses.

It is Greek mythology yet again that conceals the Truths behind myths. This case in particular (projection onto matter) is described with precision in the myth of Narcissus. Narcissus (Celestial Man) was a handsome, young man who kept refusing erotic love (Eros): namely, the attractive force/gravity could not trap him. One day however, the men and women (attractive forces of entrapment) that had been rejected by Narcissus asked Nemesis (the law of cause and effect of the material world) to punish him. Then, Narcissus looked at the reflection of his image on the waters (of matter) *("...his image shown (appeared) in those waters." [JOHN'S APOCRYPHON])*, and fell in love with his image. He was thus captured/trapped by his very own image (his self-complacency). In his effort to reach/touch this image, he sank in the waters and drowned (died) in them, as Adam died when he tried the fruit of the twofold knowledge. Even the flower the myth claims that grew in Narcissus' place at the bank of the lake indicates the degradation of any Celestial Entity when it is magnetized by (falls in love with) the reflection and sinks in the material plane.

When man committed himself to playing an active role in dense matter, he was given a framework of 'presence and absence' inside which he could move. This framework referred to the **simultaneous** unfolding of **all** his lives and deaths, inside the entire breadth of material time: namely the

MAN

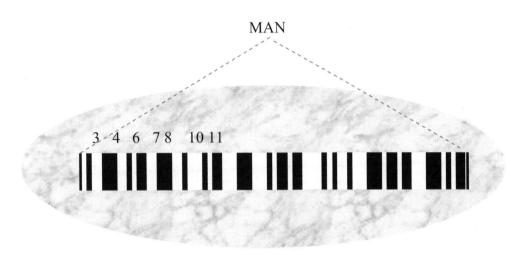

'barcode' of his presence-absence in the world of dense matter.
The barcode's white line denotes incarnation in material life, and the black one the period when man (as a soul) dwells in the energy-planes of death. The breadth or the duration of each white line/life indicates the duration of presence in life and the breadth of the black one the time of stay in the energy-spaces of death. The factors affecting the duration of his lives and deaths are determined by the specialized requirements of Karma-Heimarmenē (destiny).

A move/action during a specific life/position e.g. 3, shapes the fortune-misfortune factor of another, 'later' life/position e.g. 8, which is thought to be 'in the future', but is happening **simultaneously** with life/position 3, as well as all the other ones. This is how the unpredictable factor of 'luck' is determined. These factors are controlled by a potential of parallel probabilities that surround the entire space-time sequence of events.
During the first frames of life/appearance, some possible future choices (life versions) have been determined (predicated), and only from those (the already declared ones) can there be a possibility for a 'future' choice. Thus from each point/instance, there is always a number of choices that, like an energy-potential (of parallel probable choices), surround the entire 'barcode/frame' of every man. Man, hence, **is not** projected only onto a single point or only into a single life, but 'unfolds' throughout the entire breadth

of time of his personal course in the densely material plane, in the usual dyadic way: 'light, no-light' which manifests as life, no life.

---

624 A) FRED ALAN WOLF (PH.D. IN PHYSICS FROM UCLA) **'WHAT THE BLEEP DO WE KNOW'** http://www.whatthebleep.com?

«The sub-atomic-particle world presents a lot of energy in a little space and time. In this realm, some very strange things happen. ... Atomic particles appear and disappear constantly. Where are they when they are not there? That is a thorny question.»

The same process that applies to the sub-atomic particles, applies to humans too; since the entire creation is a fractal which unfolds repeatedly in the different scales/degrees of presence – no presence, from the microcosm to the macrocosm.

Now, regarding the unfolding of time...

B) DANEZIS M., THEODOSIOU S. 'COSMOLOGY OF THE INTELLECT' (p. 185): «Einstein's rectilinear forward time-flow seemed so well-documented, that no one could ever think of questioning or extending it. This however, was achieved by the very father of the new idea, within the framework of the General Theory of Relativity, which he formulated a few years later. After this powerful 'bomb' in the foundations of Newtonian Physics, the rectilinear 'forward' time-flow of Specific Relativity, started being disputed as more and more reports of prominent scientists came forth regarding the theoretical <u>possibility of successive submersions from the present to the past or the future and vice-versa.</u>»

This personal barcode/frame comes (as a subset) under a greater sum/frame of support, which is projected by the creator of this world. This 'image' as you can understand, relates to the 'harmonic series' as Pythagoras called it, where an inferior waveform (personal barcode/frame) falls under a larger waveform as a part of it, the larger waveform in this case being that of the creator.

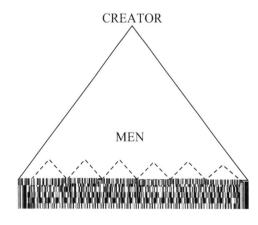

Each partial subset (of each man) begins with the initial presence of the particular man in matter –not necessarily from the beginning of human creation for every man– and ends (for most men), when this creation of the material world will close the cycle of vitalization. Then, every spiritual being that remains hooked on matter, gradually sinks into non-existence (in the second death), whereas every spiritual being that manages to unhook itself, is salvaged and returns to its Spiritual Source *(see: DRAWINGS, THE ROUTE OF THE SOUL)*.

An external observer can see the man who is trapped in matter, projecting himself in the form of a wave-like diagram, where its higher part represents life/incarnation in the visible realm and its lower part death. Just like the body of a snake is uniform, regardless of the fact that each individual part of it is touching a different place in space (e.g. its head might already be inside a hole in the ground and its tail touching a stone outside), so is the **simultaneous** projection of man onto the space-time sequence of events. But all points/parts belong to the same body, e.g. the snake, like the various colored rhombs/patterns on its skin.

Incarnated man however is completely unable to comprehend this essentially static condition, and he perceives it as a sequence. A restrictive factor **prevents** him from including the entire breadth of the consecutive situations he lives, in his perception. This factor concerns the **restricted/limited consciousness-capabilities of his aethero-material brain.** Thus, even though in reality man <u>simultaneously</u> lives all his reincarnations and all his deaths until the end of his time, **his 'consciousness' captures only one 'incarnation/frame' of the space-time/film at any given time,** and is excluded from any active 'consciousness' of his previous or his next material presence.

---

[625] **DANEZIS M., THEODOSIOU S. 'COSMOLOGY OF THE INTELLECT'** (p. 98): «British astrophysicist, FRED HOYLE, says: "Everything exists. What has once existed and what will exist in the future, <u>**already exists in the present.**</u> Only our consciousness makes the separation and creates a sense of historical sequence and that of the passing time.»

Therefore, the aethero-physical brain that manifests inside a material body of dense matter during time-period Alpha 'A', even though it is projected by the same Spiritual Man/Soul (from the last energy-layer), it (the brain) has no communication with another of his <u>simultaneous</u> but different projections, inside another material body of a different time-period Delta 'Δ', and the rest of the parts/bodies of the same Man are incapable of exchang-

Don't skip chapters or bibliographic references

ing information amongst them. This entire procedure cannot be perceived by the human brain, not because man lacks the intelligence, but because **the structure** of his brain does not possess **the functional parts** to process something like that.

---

626 **DOES OUR CONSCIOUSNESS FUNCTION IN A QUANTUM WAY?**
SOURCE: E. MANOUSAKIS 28 /10/ 07
a) http://arxiv.org/PS_cache/arxiv/pdf/0709/0709.4516v1.pdf
b) http://tech.pathfinder.gr/xpaths/x-science/564485.html
«According to Eustratios Manousakis, Professor of Physics at the University of Florida (Tallahassee), the key of consciousness could be found in the quantum-type actions taking place in the brain, when someone looks at ambiguous images, like Rubin's vase, on which there are two patterns with common borders and one of them is perceived as a figure, while the other as a background. In this case, our perception has to choose between two alternative interpretations. It will perceive one pattern as a figure and the other as a background, but it will <u>never</u> perceive both of them <u>simultaneously</u> as a figure. These optical illusions are ambiguous because at any moment they can only be perceived in one of the two alternative ways. Under no circumstances can they be perceived in both ways at the same time. The image looks as if it is inverted, when our perception changes from the one alternative interpretation of the image to the other.»

Thus, although **it seems** that life in general follows a sequence in time, this material creation was unfolded **in a flash** (instantaneously) to all instances of energy- and material-time, prescribing the end. It is exactly like the spectator watching the plot of a film sitting on his couch. The end of the movie is naturally predefined. The spectator though, is ignorant of it and gets emotionally swept away by the events taking place in each 'frame' of the sequence.

---

627 **A) THE GOSPEL OF LUKE, CH. 12**: «§49. I have come to set fire on the earth, and what do I wish more if it were **already** kindled!»
*...Because Christ was not referring to that time period, but to the result that **has already occurred in the end**.*
B) GOSPEL OF THOMAS, JEAN YVES LELOUP: «§51. His disciples said to him: "When will the dead be at rest? When will the new world come?" He answered them: "What you are waiting for **has already come**, but you do not see it.»* [Eng. tr. JOSEPH ROWE]

Let us examine now the case of time-travelers: these particular beings are men-souls who, while they project –along with all other men– their images from the outer energy-layer of the material universe onto the 'sedimented life-remnant' of dense matter, they realize that their 'projections' <u>at the end of material time</u> **do not vanish** as do the projections of a large number of men. This means that while most men are disengaged and return to their HomeLand/Spiritual Source, they (time-travelers) remain trapped inside a body of a different kind in a setting of a **doubly** virtual life, which permanently traps them inside their energy-layer and **inside the mouth** of the Ourobore snake.

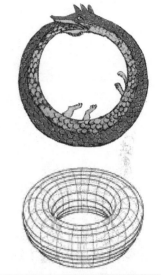

The schematic depiction of space-time directly refers to the Ourobore snake.

Under this new point of view, when we look at the symbol of the 'Ourobore snake' again, curled as it is, eating its own tail, symboliz-ing the spiral-like course of material crea-tion, we can undoubtedly distinguish the **degradation** which the symbol itself de-notes, since the last part of the snake's tail is **inside** its mouth, a fact that depicts how the last part of space-time comes to a 'blockade' and is transformed from an external to an internal part, following its helical course *(converging time-line)* [*Gr. verb is* συγκλίνω= *to bend* **inwardly** *along with something else or others. (Fytrakis-Tegopoulos: Major Dictionary)*]. After all, this is why it is called 'Ourobore' snake (=a snake eating its tail)*, because it has its tail as food/nutrition (Gr. βορά=food), endlessly devouring it along with all those who cling to it...

This entrapment therefore can be rendered well with another simplistic example: A man is lying flat on the soil having put (projected) his hand deep inside a hole in the ground, looking for material treasures. A snake that has its nest **there** bites his hand and the man dies with his hand trapped inside the mouth of the snake, which will later devour him com-pletely.

At that quasi 'time-phase', those that lost track of time playing with the clay and having lost a great portion of 'life', function more like machines than humans. These human 'shadows' of the 'future' are reproduced like manufactured products, and this is why they possess no bellybutton to de-

Don't skip chapters or bibliographic references

note natural childbirth, nor genitalia, because they are no longer of any use to them.

> **628** **STEPHEN HAWKING – 'THE UNIVERSE IN A NUTSHELL'** [Gr. tr. PETRAKI M.] CH. OUR FUTURE: STAR-TREK OR NOT? «Growing babies outside the human body will allow larger brains and greater intelligence *(the 'other version' of the supposed 'aliens' with the disproportionately large heads)*. ...Of course, many people will say that genetic engineering in humans should be banned, but it is **doubtful** whether we will be able to prevent something like that.»

I do not wish to name particular incidents, because they have all been **skillfully** 'adorned' with so many lies that even I run the risk of appearing inventive.

> **629** **MILTON WILLIAM COOPER** (FORMER US NAVY OFFICER, INFORMATION DEPT.): «A basic truth can be used as foundation for a whole mountain of lies. If we dig deep enough into the mountain of lies and bring out that truth and place it at the top of the mountain of lies, then the entire mountain will collapse under the weight of that truth... Everything we have been taught is a lie. Reality is not at all what we perceive it to be.»

Thus, with a substandard 'life' inside a body/machine, they attempt the time-jump, aiming for salvation. In the mind of many researchers of course, the logical question resonates: Since modern scientists have determined that if someone travels in time he **cannot** meddle with the events of his own world, but only with the events of a parallel universe, then, what exactly do time-travelers of the 'future' hope to achieve by coming to the 'present'?

> **630** **NO PARADOX FOR TIME TRAVELERS** (MARK BUCHANAN; NEW SCIENTIST, JUNE 2005) http://www.newscientist.com/article/dn7535-no-paradox-for-time-travellers.html
> «Some solutions to the equations of Einstein's general theory of relativity lead to situations in which space-time curves back on itself, theoretically allowing travelers to loop back in time and meet younger versions of themselves. Because such time travel sets up paradoxes, many researchers suspect that some **physical limitations** must make time travel impossible.
> Now, physicists Daniel Greenberger of the City University of New York and Karl Svozil of the Vienna University have shown that the most basic features of quantum theory may ensure that time travelers could never alter the past, even if they are able to go back in time.
> The limitations arise from the quantum object's ability to behave like a wave. Quantum objects split their existence into multiple component-waves, each following a distinct path through space-time.

Ultimately, an object is usually most likely to end up in places where its component-waves recombine, or 'interfere', constructively, with the peaks and troughs of the waves lined up, say.[1]

The object is unlikely to be in places where the components interfere destructively, and cancel each other out.

Quantum theory allows time travel because nothing prevents the waves from going back in time. When Greenberger and Svozil analyzed what happens when these component-waves flow into the past, they found that the paradoxes implied by Einstein´s equations never arise. Waves that travel back in time interfere destructively, thus preventing anything from happening differently from that which has already taken place.

"If you travel into the past quantum mechanically, **you would only see those alternates** consistent with the world you left behind you," says Greenberger.»

[1] *The same excerpt from the same article is simplified in physics4u.gr*
NEW MODEL PERMITS TIME TRAVEL Source: BBC and New Scientist June 17, 2005
http://www.physics4u/news/2005/scnews2007.html

«Quantum objects are split into multiple component-waves, each following a distinct path through space-time.

At some point, these waves recombine, to **recreate** the object, yet, without coming into any contact with each other, a fact which prevents them from colliding and cancel each other out. Quantum theory allows time travel because nothing prevents the waves from traveling in time. The two researchers studied what happens when these split waves of an object flow into the past, and they found that no paradoxes arise. The independent course maintained by each wave ensures (according to the analysis) that nothing and no one can interfere and change the predestined course already mapped-out from the beginning.»

The answer lies in a small detail: The calculations of contemporary scientists are limited only to the central vitalized material universe which, of course, they do not differentiate from the rest (parallel) as the primary one, since they reject the Spirit factor.

The visiting time-travelers of the 'future' however, **don't live** in the primary vitalized material universe any longer, since IT DOES NOT EXIST there and then! On the contrary, they live in a plethora of parallel futures (*Dr. Dan Burisch calls them 'Time-lines'*), where completely different conditions reign, conditions that are a mere echo of 'life'. The restrictions that exist in the primary vitalized material universe do not apply there, because the choices –let me remind you– as to what probabilities will be preferred and then vitalized, are only made in the **prevailing** universe. This is so because every Sacred Archetypal Essence activates it (the prevailing uni-

Don't skip chapters or bibliographic references

verse) as it is projected onto it. However from the moment every Sacred Archetype returns to its Source, these possibilities vanish and all probable 'obstacles' with them. Thus the 'men' of the future, not aware of the restrictions of the primary vitalized material universe, hope and attempt… Unfortunately, dense matter does not possess the provisions to accurately determine certain situations which have their origin in other dimensions with different laws, of which only mere reflections appear in the visible world.

---

631 **A) DANEZIS M., THEODOSIOU S. 'COSMOLOGY OF THE INTELLECT'** (p. 92):

«Michael Talbot, in his book 'Mysticism and the New Physics' (1993), says: "According to the New Physics, we can only dream of the real world."

(pp. 90, 91) Max Jammer, in his book 'Concepts of Space' (2001): "… It is clear that the structure of the space in physics is not, in the end, anything given in nature or **independent of human thought**. It always depends on **our** conceptual scheme. Space as conceived by Newton proved to be **an illusion**, although for practical purposes a very fruitful illusion."

(p. 99) This false sense of space, which springs from the imperfection of the known human senses and functions, almost annihilates our ability to perceive the whole essence and extent of Einstein's fourth dimension.

(p. 89) The Klein bottle is a bottle with **no inner side** (no inside) and is the realization of a thought of topologist[1] Albert W. Tucker of Princeton University. In reality, nobody has ever seen an actual Klein bottle because **it is an object of the non-Euclidean space** *(i.e. not of this world)* which could pass through itself without leaving the slightest hole.»

[1] «(p. 68) Topology: a branch of mathematics examining deformations of forms and shapes.»

See also reference #303 where Danezis and Theodosiou refer to the example in E. Abbot's book 'Flatland', Delfini Publishing, Athens 1991.

So, what possibility is there for us, 'flat' people of 'flatland', to clearly define situations belonging to multidimensional spheres? This is why philosophers advise:

B) CHALDEAN ORACLES, Gr. tr. ATHINOGENIS I., GRAVIGGER, P. (p. 42)
TEXT AND TRANSLATION BASED ON THE COLLECTION OF W. KROLL, ALONG WITH ADDITIONS AND IMPROVEMENTS OF ED. DES PLACES (ORACLES CHALDAIQUES, PARIS 1971, B. L.)
ED. BY ATHINOGENIS I., GRAVIGGER P. —KROLL, P. 11 KROLL, DAMASCIUS I, 154 14-26):

«There exists, something Intelligible *(apprehensible by the mind only)*, which you must perceive by the flower of your Noûs *(mind)*; for if you should incline your mind towards It and try to perceive It (like a particular, discrete thing), you will not manage to perceive This; for It is a certain kind of power belonging to the edge (of a sword) shining on both sides and glittering with vehemence of intellection. Therefore, you must not intently try to perceive That Intelligible Thing, but with the subtle, ample flame of an sub-

---

tle ample Noŭs, which can measure all things, except That Intelligible One; you must indeed understand That Intelligible –and if you turn inwards your Noŭs to It, you shall perceive It– not fixedly, but by directing the pure Eye of your soul, after it *(your soul)* has turned away from *(disregarded)* anything sensory, so that your Noŭs –void of thoughts– can turn towards The Intelligible, so that you may learn The Intelligible, **for It exists beyond the boundaries of human logic.**» [FESTUGIRE, REVELATION IV, P. 132-134 - H. LEWY, CHALDEAN ORACLES P. 169 – PLACES, 123]

—And in what way do these 'future' men ask for help by intervening into the 'now'?
—Oh! This is a tragically sad story that modern humanity bears witness to but fails to understand, since the assignees of the astral 'inspectors' of this world use murder, buying off consciousnesses and manipulation of the evidence to silence the mouths of those, who (in their misfortune) were 'informed' of only **parts** of the tragic truth, as its disclosure is the 'Achilles heel' of these 'inspectors'.

As I have told you, astral forces presenting themselves as extraterrestrials, visit the Earth in their 'crafts'. But these crafts that visit Earth **do not all carry the same type of passengers.** Some of these crafts come from the remote 'future' of **an alternatively 'material' earth**, driven by desperate **human** beings. These beings belong to those groups of souls, who, during the difficult events you as humanity expect today for the 'future', were misguided by the promises of their pseudo-saviors and followed the masqueraded dark powers, succumbing to the most painful life until the final moments of their 'time'.

632 **HELLENIC NEXUS, ISSUE 2, JULY 2004**
Excerpt from an article of the magazine, regarding Bill Hamilton's revelations (Programmer-analyst, Univ. California, UCLA, information technology specialist), about Dr. Dan B. Burisch's work (Captain of the US Navy, microbiologist - geneticist).
«Dr. Burisch's last letter to Bill Hamilton refers to his work, his thoughts and his contact with 'alien' J-Rod or Jarrod and the shocking disclosures of the latter (J-Rod) <u>about the separation of the man of the future from his spiritual nature!</u>
Dan Burisch's letter states:
"...Frankly, my experience in training for Project Aquarius and the J-Rod Extraterrestrial Biological Entity (EBE), did nothing but enhance those beliefs. I had no reason not to believe my alien friend's claim, <u>that their species is a further **development (post-evolution)** of mankind</u>. If this is so, as our

Don't skip chapters or bibliographic references

future (as our present human species) seems to be **running out** (according to all scientific indications), the genetic divergence which caused the difference between us (as current humans) and 'us' (the J-Rod species in the future) fits well within the same mechanism posited for our gradual development from a pre-hominid (anthropoid) to the modern humans we see today. This, together with the psychological nature of the J-Rod (a future, evolved, logical, and mathematical/scientific kind) *(...education)*, made an easy fit with the dogma of modern evolutionary biology. This was the excuse for me to come closer to J-Rod.

Then everything started to change. In the first place, my experience from J-Rod and his willingness to suffer for his species (and our species too) fascinated me *(...human 'love')* ...I discovered that, while he was aware that his nerve degeneration disorder could be treated in the future, that wasn't his major concern. Based on his constant statements, this logical being seemed longing to help set straight a series of errors in judgment and events that would, in the future, lead to <u>**OUR SEPARATION FROM OUR SPIRITUAL NATURE**</u>. *(Neither his self-sacrifice for his fellow people, nor his education could grant him what he was desperately looking for, traveling in his past: his spiritual nature!!)* He was searching for something lost. He wasn't driven by something gained.

At once, I started examining data with great attention. Finally, I discovered – disproving evolutionary biology– that **the human species is something way over (greater) than the sum of its base pairs (its genetic material).**

–<u>"We are here in your present presence asking for help."</u>...He once told me. This statement struck me dumb and made me numb.

–"If the answer was completely found in the material (and thus handled through logical process) or completely spiritual (handled by the so called 'Higher Human Self') why not deal with it, my dear J-Rods or my dear Brothers, yourselves?"...I reasoned and he confirmed that we now (as humans of today, in the current phase of the evolution of our species) possess a unique combination of spirit and matter, allowing us to come into contact with the <u>Source</u> of Genesis from whence life on earth springs.

–"This is the purpose of our race's contact with you. We come here from the future to correct the mistakes that have made us the human species we have become!»

The route of these deluded souls/men towards the second death will <u>not</u> be short, but will include many 'reincarnations' yet to come in the virtual parallel universes, continuously exhausting their 'stored' life-reservoirs. As they approach their ultimate end –the second death– they risk everything they might still possess, begging for crumbs of salvation in the present.

[633] **BARBARA MARCINIAK 'GAIA'** [Gr. trans. MATZOROU E.] *(Information through channeling)*: «There is a point very far in your future, at which the Guardians of Time are very worried about the turn events have taken. …We come from the future and we search inside the corridors of time. This is our mission. From the probable future where we come, our goal is to change the past. Our intention is to change the probable future **in which we are functioning**, because this probable future **in the evolution of the new movement of the universe** is led to a tyranny.
…Our civilization is in the future in relation to you and is in danger, something that forced us to a journey in search of a solution. We are in your future and in order to find out what is happening, we have gone even further to meet our teachers, the Guardians of Existence who are also called Guardians of Time. They have taught us how to cross time, and this is how we traveled back in time to discover where events had been stored and locked.
…Our ancestors come from a universe which had reached completion and they understood that THIS was the Primary Creator *(they are referring to the HyperUniverses of True Light)* …They came from a universe that had discovered quintessence itself.»

They are divided in two categories: (a) Those who try to cancel the Sacred Archetypes' Transference, hoping to misappropriate them for themselves, and cooperate with the astral skeptomorphic powers and (b) those who consider something like that to be naturally impossible, and come to the present, hoping they too can participate in the Spiritual Transference of Earth. This second group is the most wretched one: hoping to find salvation, they reach your contemporary time hunted down by their astral guardians —who are aware of every alternative time probability— and most of the times die during their attempts.
(Some have even named their vessel 'FREEDOM' —I wonder why— written in letters that make many people to specu- ΞΛΞΦΘΞΡΙΑ *late: [Gr. word for freedom =* ΕΛΕΥΘΕΡΙΑ *{Y: after letter Ε is pronounced as Gr. letter Φ}]).*

Let us return to our subject now, to completely 'close' the circle of the material world, by examining the outer energy-layer of the murky/grim spiral matter. There flickers the last echo of life of those men/souls who are trapped by their projections. This is where the desperate time-travelers will soon arrive at. Nevertheless, the beings that will reach that final point will experience absolute devastation. It is not the Spirit that determines whether a being will suffer or not, but the 'living' energy. When this energy dies out and the **second** death approaches, agony reaches its zenith. And when we speak of that death, we refer to what some religions associate with the Great Nights of Brahma; when every-

Don't skip chapters or bibliographic references

thing ends and sinks into eternal darkness. There, despair reaches its peak, as **every virtual projection of form fades,** revealing the essential poverty of this fictitious creation to the 'forlorn ones'. So let us sententiously give an account of what the following chapters of the Revelation refer to, focusing more on the 'fate' of those who remain in the material universe.

❧∙❧

After the 18th chapter in which the collapse of dense matter is described as we have already analyzed, chapter 19 follows, which narrates the glorious fate of the Men/Souls that have been saved and have passed on to the Prepared Place, thus forming the 6th Human Root Race.

In that Holy Ground, the Second Coming of Christ will take place in front of the New Generation of Men. There, the **Spiritual Essence** (the *Power of the Mother of Yaldabaoth*) that is scattered inside every human soul will reunite with its male counterpart –the 'Lamb' Jesus– and the Spiritual Cosmos through Her Matrimony.

---

[634] **A) THE APOCRYPHON OF JOHN, THE GNOSTIC SOCIETY LIBRARY**: «And Sophia *(Wisdom)* of Epinoia *(the mother of the fallen one)*, being an Aeon, willed to bring forth a likeness out of herself, without the consent of the Spirit and without her partner. ...And though the person of her maleness *(Jesus)* had not approved and had not consented, *(yet)* she brought forth *(gave birth)*.

...And she was taken up, not to her own aeon, but above her *(fallen)* son, that she might be in the ninth *(Heaven)* until she has **corrected** her deficiency.» [FREDERIK WISSE]

The male companion of Sophia of Epinoia is Jesus. After the misstep of His female counterpart (Sophia), Jesus had to restore the damage, in order for Sophia to be able to correct her deficiency. His sacrifice opened the road for the return of His own children.

THE GOSPEL OF TRUTH, THE NAG HAMMADI LIBRARY, www.metalog.org/files/valent.html

«§6. Therefore confusion was enraged at him *(Jesus)* and pursued Him in order to suppress and eliminate Him. He was nailed onto a crossbeam; He became the fruit of recognizing the Father. Yet it did not cause those who consumed it *(the fruit of recognizing the Father)* to perish, but rather to those who consumed it He bestowed a rejoicing at such a discovery. **For He found them in Himself and they found Him in themselves.**» [Eng. tr. PATERSON BROWN T.]

«Let us be glad and rejoice and give Him glory, for the marriage of the Lamb *(Jesus)* has come, and His wife *(Sophia of Epinoia)* has made herself ready *(she has restituted her deficiency)*. And to her it was granted to

clothe herself in fine linen, clean and bright, for the fine-linen is the righteous deeds of the saints. Then he said to me, Write, 'Blessed are those who are invited to the marriage-supper of the Lamb *(Jesus)*!'»
[REVELATION 19:7-9]

Following that, the Race starts preparing (relinquishing/being stripped of the energy-portion of the soul) to accomplish ITS entrance to the Celestial Capital of the Father, thus forming the 7th Root Race.

REVELATION 20	
§ 1. Then I saw an angel coming down from heaven, having the key of the abyss and a great chain in his hand. § 2. And he seized the dragon, that ancient serpent, who is the Devil and Satan, and bound him for a thousand years; § 3. and he cast him into the abyss, and shut it, and sealed it over him, so that he would not deceive the nations any more till the thousand years were completed; after that he must be released for a little while.	Lucifer/creator is confined again into the abyss of the inner layers of the material vortex. The 'Sacred Place' –the dwelling of the Race of the Holy Men who went through to the First Resurrection– is still **outside the Impassable** Spaces of the HyperUniverses. The Race will have to remain there safe for a thousand years of preparation. (*see: DRAWINGS, OVERALL VIEW*)
§ 4. And I saw thrones, and they sat on them, and judgment was given unto them. Then I saw the souls of those who had been beheaded for their testimony of Jesus and for the word of God, and those who **had not** worshiped the beast or his image, and had not received its mark on their foreheads or on their hand. And they lived and reigned with Christ for a thousand years.	The future of those who will go through to the First Resurrection and the Prepared Place forming the 6th Root Race of Men is foretold as 'glorious'.

Don't skip chapters or bibliographic references

	Yet, those who will pass on to the First Resurrection are split in two groups: (1) The Unified Celestial Men (I Am Presence + Divine Spark), The True Saints, who, after entering the Higher Noetic (Mental) Plane, have joined the Forces of Salvation of the HyperUniverses and (2) The **non**-unified Sparks as well as the plain Souls of men, who were 'clad' (got dressed up) in the Truth, disengaged themselves from the 'charms' of the material world and chose Redemption/Deliverance through Christ. There, in the Prepared Place, during these 1,000 years, the first group will rise to prominence, and the other group…
§ 5. **The rest of the dead did not live** until the thousand years were finished. This is the first resurrection.	The remaining ones –i.e. the second group consisting of the **non**-unified Sparks and plain Souls– regardless of the fact that they have passed on to the First Resurrection, they will Spiritually prepare –since they are not yet unified– for 1,000 years, during which they will **still** be considered DEAD! **This** is the First Resurrection.
§ 6. **Blessed and holy is he who has part in the first resurrection. Over such the second death has no power**, but they shall be priests of God and of Christ, and shall reign with Him a thousand years. *Chilam Balam: "There will be food for half of the men and misery for the other half."*	Blessed and Fortunate are …**only those who will pass on to the First Resurrection** because **only they WILL NOT** know the second death.

| | Let us move on now to observe what awaits those who will be seduced and will linger behind, attached to matter's dead corpse.

In that doubly virtual 'life', the deceived 'humans', scattered in the parallel energy-universes (the four corners of energy-earth), will be ruled by the dark "Gogs and Magogs". Their species will 'reproduce' like a photocopy which gets reprinted in billions of copies. They will be 'vitalized' by the vast 'store houses of life' created there. |
| | When the 'thousand' years are up – which in the universe of havoc shall multiply in fragmentation to become many thousands– and the group of those who have entered the First Resurrection have prepared themselves for their permanent Repatriation, at the same time, the last supplies of 'living' energy of those who were trapped in matter <u>will be exhausted</u>, thus depriving these authoritative powers of devastation of their life-supply. ↵

Then these dark beings will be liberated from matter's inner energy-layers, where they have dwelled, and will rise up to the higher energy-planes of the material world to rouse 'humans' to war, so they can all reclaim new life. The billions of these so-called 'humans' –approaching their second death ever closer– will then take the same side with the powers of darkness and become one with them. |
| § 7. When the thousand years have expired, Satan will be released from his prison
§ 8. and will come out to deceive the nations which are in the four corners of the earth –Gog and Magog– to gather them together for battle; their number is like the sand of the sea. | |

Don't skip chapters or bibliographic references

§ 9. And they <u>came up on the breadth of the earth</u> and surrounded the camp of the saints and the beloved city. And fire came down from God out of heaven and devoured them. § 10. And the devil, who deceived them, was cast into the lake of fire and sulfur where the beast and the false prophet are. And they will be tormented day and night forever and ever.	And they will rise up to the higher energy-planes of the material universe to approach the intermediate place where the 6th Root Race of Men resides and will surround it. But the outcome of this battle is predestined and the fate of the beast already determined.
§ 11. Then I saw a great white throne and Him who sat on it, from whose face **the earth and the sky fled away. And no place was found for them.**	And after the situation with the creators of havoc is resolved, the men of the future will come next… The 'snake's severed tail' has stopped oscillating by now and remains dead and still, extinguishing along with it every **image** of delusion the dragon/snake projected as a reflection and used in order to deceive. The form disappeared in front of the Unspoken One.
	And at that moment, a difficult process starts, since every quasi living one/**dead,** who is not found in the Book of Life *(an oxymoron),* will be rejected! <u>Nevertheless EVERYONE there is already considered Spiritually **Dead.**</u>
§ 12. And I saw **the dead**, small and great, standing before God, and books were opened. And another book was opened, **which is the Book of Life**. **And the dead were judged** by the things which were written in the books, according to their deeds.	Before everything ends though, and the material contraption is permanently sealed, 'men' will stand before Father/God. The Book of the Living Spirit will examine those 'men' for any traces of Spiritual Life.

666

§13. The sea gave up the dead who were in it, and death and Hades delivered up the dead who were in them; and they were judged, every one of them, according to their deeds. The remaining parallel energy-universes spit out the last 'human' beings. The spaces of death do the same. They have all been found **dead of Spirit.**

[635] *When John speaks of the 'sea' he means the energy planes of the material universe in which the humanity of the future will 'live', on __artificial__ spirit alone. But the last cycle is closing and everything is preparing to pass on to the 2nd complete death and sink into the Great (Maha) Night of Brahma.*
Let us then investigate the evidence that equate the energy worlds with water/sea, starting from the theological ones and proceeding to the recent scientific ones.
A) THE APOCRYPHON OF JOHN, THE GNOSTIC SOCIETY LIBRARY: «He *(Celestial Man)* **illuminated the waters above the world of matter**, His image *(Man)* shown *(appeared)* in those waters. All the demons and the first ruler together gazed up toward the underside of the newly shining **waters**. Through that light they saw the Image *(of Man)* in the **waters**.» [STEVAN DAVIES]
John characterizes the energy fields –the ones above matter– as watery. This view though is not only exclusively his.
B) OLD TESTAMENT, GENESIS CH. 1: «§2…And the Spirit of God was hovering over the face of the waters. …§6. Then God said, "Let there be a firmament **in the midst of the waters, and let it divide the waters from the waters.**" §7. Thus God made the firmament, and divided the waters which were under the firmament from the waters which were above the firmament; and it was so. §8 And God called the firmament Heaven. And there was evening and there was morning, the second day.»
C) PSALMS
(136:6) «To Him who spread out the earth **upon the waters**, for his mercy is everlasting;»
(148:4) «Praise Him, you heavens of heavens, and you **waters above the heavens!**»
D) EPITÁPHIOS THRÊNOS, THE 'LAMENTATION UPON THE GRAVE': «The One Who **hanged** the Earth **on** Waters.»
E) BLAVATSKY H., P., 'THE SECRET DOCTRINE':
Vishnu Puraná describes the Great (Maha) Pralaya (dissolution):
«The Egg of Brahma is dissolved in **the waters that surround it**, with its seven zones.»
And Blavatsky explains later on:
«The 'Waters' mean here the Mystic 'mother'; the Womb of abstract nature, in which the manifested Universe is conceived.»
The 'waters' in other words correspond to the Riemannian universe as the

Don't skip chapters or bibliographic references

astrophysicists might call it. But let us also not forget H. Trismegistus' excerpt, Ch. A: «§4 I also saw that darkness to be changed into a **Moist Nature, unspeakably troubled.**»

The Egyptian hieroglyphic that characterizes water is depicted: [ΛΛΛΛ] *hence the letter [M: Mare = sea] which denotes the waving motion of water. This wave-like motion is not only a characteristic of water, but also of energy, which modern scientists characterize as a 'sea of energy'. Waves are water vibrations; Sound is the vibrations/waves of air and electromagnetic waves are the waves of the energy area the ancients identified with the 'vacuum', an active vacuum/void which today is called 'dark energy'.*

PAUL DIRAC, 1930: «We can imagine the VOID as a sea of electrons with negative energy.»

F) DARK ENERGY, ARTICLE BY **ROBERT REYNOLDS CALDWELL,** PHYSICSWORLD.COM, MAY 2004, http://physicsworld.com/cws/article/print/19419

«Dark energy, or something like it, has made numerous appearances in cosmology. …The effect was equivalent to filling the universe with a pristine **sea of negative energy**, upon which stars and nebulae drift. The later discovery of the expansion obviated the need for such an ad hoc addition to his theory.»

G) EUGENIDES FOUNDATION-PLANETARIUM ARTICLE: **ALEXIS DELIVORIAS: DARK ENERGY, 10 YEARS AFTER:**
http://www.eugenfound.edu.gr/frontoffice/portal.asp?cpage=RESOURCE&cresrc=570&cnode=28

«What is interesting and extremely strange is that something equivalent to Einstein's cosmological constant is foreseen by quantum physics, the physics of the minimum, and as a matter of fact, in a much more natural way. **Empty space, says quantum physics, is in reality not empty at all, but corresponds to a sea of 'virtual' elementary particles** which are created so suddenly and de-materialize in such speed, that their direct/immediate detection is impossible.»

H) THE BLACK HOLE UNIVERSE MIGHT EXPLAIN DARK ENERGY
SOURCE: NEW SCIENTIST, NOVEMBER 2007
http://www.newscientist.com/article/mg19626243.600-blackhole-universe-might-explain-dark-energy.html

«According to quantum theory, even the perfect vacuum of space isn't empty: it is a **sea of virtual particles**, created as entangled pairs of particles and antiparticles which exist only fleetingly and then annihilate *(cancel each other out).*»

I) ROBERT R. CALDWELL'S ARTICLE 1ST PART, PHYSICS WORLD MAGAZINE, MAY 2004
http://physicsweb.org/articles/world/17/5/7

«The most conservative suggestions are that the universe is filled with a **uniform sea of quantum zero-point energy**, or a condensate of new particles that have a mass that is 10^{-39} times smaller than that of the electron.»

J) MYSTERIOUS PHENOMENON IN OUR GALACTIC NEIGHBORHOOD; DARK ENERGY IS AROUND US, SOURCE: MSNBC, MARCH 16, 2005
http://www.msnbc.msn.com/id/7180932/ns/technology_and_science-science/#.TzlduNVdCnA

«The computer crunches models for a few weeks, and then we compare the properties of our virtual universe with those of the real ones", says Governato. They showed that **our universe is inside a virtual sea of dark energy,** with billions of galaxies <u>floating</u> like islands inside the 'sea' of dark energy.»

...*Where parallel universes are developing* ... [The Sea gave up the dead who were in it...]

Now regarding the question: how can the 'energy-sea' be distinguished and/or separated from the other energy-condition of Hades, John, in his Apocryphon, gives a clear answer when he describes the creation of this universe:

K) THE APOCRYPHON OF JOHN, THE GNOSTIC SOCIETY LIBRARY [FREDERIK WISSE]:

«§10,11 This is the first **archon** *(the Creator of matter –visible and invisible),* the one who got a great power from his Mother. And he removed himself from her and he abandoned the places where he had been born. He became strong and created for himself other aeons inside a blaze of luminous fire, which still exists now. And he was stupefied in his Madness, which dwells within him, and he begat some **authorities** for himself *(12 authorities are named).* ...And he set up **seven kings** –one per firmament of heaven– **over the seven heavens** *(the spaces of 'energy-sea'),* and **five** *(kings)* over the depth of the **abyss,** so that they might rule there *(Hades).*»

REVELATION 20 cont'd...	
§ 14. Then death and Hades were cast into the lake of fire. This is the second death.	But before this downward-bound spiral of death is permanently and definitively sealed, and so that the dead 'men' of the future don't think they were sentenced 'in absentia' –those who did not enter the First Resurrection– they are examined once more, just in case there is someone among them alive in Spirit.
§ 15. And anyone not found written in the Book of Life was cast into the lake of fire.	And anyone not found written in the Book of Life –since they were all dead– will take their place along with their kindred... *This is the fate of the dead souls/wrecks (J-Rods) of those who were charmed by the astral beings and the delusion they projected to them.*

And after all this 'disease' has been sealed away, the 21st chapter of the Apocalypse describes the upgrade of the 6th Root Race of Men to the 7th, the Holy and truly Alive Root Race. This upgrade is followed by the defin-

Don't skip chapters or bibliographic references

itive return of Men to the HomeLand, the Capital Source of Eternal Life, True Love and True Unsplit Light.

જ•≪

With these words I am reaching the end of our discussion, hoping they will shock your fellowmen. My intention is not to cause turmoil in your world, but to mobilize the dormant mechanisms of defense of their Existential Autonomy.

–People show disbelief and reject what they cannot 'touch'! I said.

–If they wish to 'touch' in order to believe, then they will have to go through the experience of the godforsaken future we have described. The choice is exclusively theirs along with the responsibility for their own-self. Those who believe will do so because **THEY HAVE FELT THE TRUTH** awakening inside. This awakening will be the greatest proof for them. In the little time they have left, let them elaborate on everything we have offered them, surrounding themselves with This Truth and revitalizing/rekindling the True Spirit inside of them. This will redeem them. But those who want to participate in the Group of Salvation, have to make their Soul finally accept THE ULTIMATE SACRIFICE performed for their redemption and cry out, "Yes Lord, I accept your Sacrifice and I am asking for redemption and Deliverance", because only then: "These are the ones who ... have washed their robes and made them white in the blood of the Lamb" [Revelation 7:14].

Everything I have communicated to you is a message to be announced to those who are **still** ALIVE IN SPIRIT. For the sake of these Men, you must transfer what I have told you in writing, because an old promise has to be fulfilled.

–What old promise?

–You men may have forgotten, but the HyperUniverses know how to keep their promises; this is why I am repeating the promise He made before He departed from this world, thus 'signing my name' to what I have made known to you:

"Nevertheless I tell you the truth; It is to your advantage that I go away: for if I do not go away, the Advocate/Helper/Comforter [Gr.: Paraclete] will not come to you; but if I depart, I will send him unto you. And when he comes, he will reprove/judge the world of sin, and of righteousness, and of judgment; of sin, because they believe not on me; of righteousness, because I am going to my Father, and you shall see Me no more; of judgment, because the archon (ruler) of this world has been judged.

I have yet many things to say unto you, but you cannot bear them now. Howbeit when He, the Spirit of Truth, comes, he will guide you into all Truth: for he shall not speak of himself; but whatever he shall hear, that shall he speak: and he will disclose (announce) to you what is to come. He shall glorify Me: for he shall receive of Mine, and shall disclose it unto you." [JOHN 16: 7-14]

He finished talking and got up from his chair. I remained seated, trying to recover from the powerful experience.

–"Keep looking for the lost symbols inside matter" *he said,* "I have always been with you, I will always be with you."

He opened the door and went out. I jumped up rushing behind him. I went outside. ...He was nowhere to be seen...

EPILOGUE

Whilst the final pieces of this Knowledge resonated within me, I felt the imperative need to bring this danger to the attention of humanity. I know of course that man's prevailing attributes are to disbelieve, then to sneer and finally to ignore. Now however, he cannot afford this luxury. The time left, no matter how prolonged, is very short.

It is my ultimate goal to stop everyone's indifferent passage through this world, and in order to end the circle where it originally started from, I shall once again remind you of the words of Hermes Trismegistus describing that "darkness, partially born" in the darkest colors, which –like an insatiable monster– devours inside it every entity that <u>has forgotten itself in the fantasy it projected to it</u>. This will be the definitive end of material humanity, and those who do not seek to grab the last rope of salvation at this final moment –carried away by their arrogance and egotism– I am afraid to say, will end up like these ill-fated human wrecks, who in their despair, perform the ultimate time-jump, while gazing at the bottom of the spiral vortex threatening them!

«…and I saw a downward darkness partially born, coming down in an oblique formation, like a snake, fearful and hideous. I also saw that darkness to be changed into a moist nature, unspeakably troubled, which yielded a fiery smoke from its depths, and from whence I heard an **unutterable heartbreaking sound**, and an inarticulate roar in a voice of fire.» [TRISMEGISTUS, A:4]

With all previous knowledge at hand, it is not difficult now for anyone to realize that the image described by Hermes Trismegistus is a clear description of the hell that was left behind by the leftovers of the previous unsuccessful 'material' creation.

The 'unuttered plangent (heart-breaking) sound' was the voice of despair of every forgotten entity sinking into eternal devastation.

Thus, all these dramatic beings managed to achieve during this new vitalization of the material 'phantom' was to be molded into speechless forms of life, so that they could not articulate the inflictions forced upon them, experiencing yet another cycle of bottomless misery! All these forms/figures of animals, birds, plants etc., at the end of this creation-trap will surrender their place to the new 'men/leftovers', only to be squashed/stacked deeper inside this bleak vortex.

And as the Gospel of Thomas (§18) says:

[The disciples asked Jesus: Tell us Master what will be our end?

And Jesus answered: What do you know about the beginning, so that you now seek the end? Where the beginning is, there, will the end also be.]

And the beginning, as everyone knows, was the darkness, Erebus, tur-moil... the partially born downward darkness.

Every modern man who is considered 'in' in the era of technology and scientific knowledge gives an arrogant glance of disdain to the quaint descriptions of the 'naïve ones' about hell... Let him cast a similar glance to the despair of those who come from 'tomorrow' and then he might restrain his arrogance a little.
Once the Earth's Spiritual Transference to somewhere 'Else' is complete, every densely material form vanishes and they all return back to the initial energy-state of this hell. The decision each man will make is entirely up to him now. Weighing the facts and with his life-giving 'fabric' as a gnomon, he shall take sides accordingly.

The decision is yours!

Wise men about the oncoming

Men know what is happening.
The future is known by the gods,
who are complete and the sole carriers of all enlightenment.
From what is to come, the wise perceive the nearest.
At times of serious study their hearing is perturbed.
The secret roar **of what is nearing** approaches them.
And they reverently tend to it.
Whereas out there in the street, **nothing** do the peoples hear.

Constantine P. Kavafis

APPENDIX

PHOTOGRAPHS AND DRAWINGS

THE STORY IN PICTURES

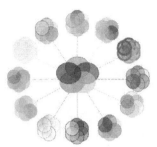 *In the Beginning, there was the Absolute, the Unsplit, the Coherent Essence [Ousseea] of the HyperCosmoi of the True Light, of the Patrogenes One as the Neo-Platonists called it or the Kingdom of Heaven as Christians do. Hermes Trismegistus describes it as ...* "*An infinite sight flooded by light.*" *There reigns **the Unified, Αγαθός Νοῦς** which cannot be split since everything there exists Whole and Unsplit in a Unified condition which does not oscillate between bipolar tendencies. The infinite plethora of Archetypal manifestations that exists* THERE *synthesizes a Cosmos of unique Harmony.*

*In a corner of this chaos however, cutoff and dark, a downward darkness was swirling, like a voracious black hole. It was the un-inseminated Egg, the eternal Karana (Cause), the Forbidden Tree. Inside it was the cause of matter, **Earth** (since the cause of matter is called 'earth' in ancient texts), **Tartarus** (tumult), **Chaos** and **Eros** as the primordial attractive Force. Eros 'invited' a Light Ray from the HyperUniverses of the Absolute, to inseminate its (Eros') Egg.*

The Ray was lured by the charm of Eros, accepted the invitation, permeated the Egg, and after it settled in its center, it impregnated it with its Light and rendered it 'Manifested', by bringing Avge (dawn) in its dark abysses. Thus, that primordial Light Ray became fallen and after it brought the light of dawn (Avge) into the darkness, it pronounced itself its God (☉ ⇻ ϴ) and was called Lucifer (Light bearer).

«The deficiency of matter **did not** originate through the Infinity of the Father.»[Gospel of Truth §39]

Following that, and in order for the ray/Lucifer to give birth to its off-spring in this 'Egg', it was split into Λόγος [Logos] (Λ) and generated the duality of the new world, baptizing this world "The Tree of knowledge of good and evil".

And the ray/Lucifer with his 'Λόγος' [Logos] created the Hierarchy of the Builders of matter: the lower gods, the Commanders of Heimarmenē. And the Builders created the four elements of matter: Fire, Air, Water and Earth. And for each element, a great Hierarchy of Entities and Powers were created to support it, thus creating a pyramid.

*And the Lord of all became their **Archē (A)** [Gr. for 'start', 'beginning', 'authority', 'rule'] he placed himself at the top of the Hierarchy he himself had formed and supervised everything from there.*

*And he became the 'All seeing Eye' and the supreme Lord of all, distancing himself from his subordinate bondservants. And he adopted the Truncated Pyramid as his symbol, because its top is separated from its main body. And he identified the letter 'A' with the **Archē** (beginning) of his creation.*

And the 'best' of his bondservants he appointed as supervisors of the inferior ones and placed them on the higher level of the truncated pyramid, so they could supervise their subordinates. Yet he remained cut-off and independent, to oversee everyone.

This is the Beginning [Archē (A)] of the entire material visible and invisible world, and its course in time is a one-way street inescapably leading to the End Omega (Ω).

*The truncated-pyramid symbol will always be found identified with the Hierarchy of the Archē (Beginning) and the letter Alpha (A), since the **shape** of this letter denotes exactly that. The Almighty Father cannot be characterized as the Alpha and the Omega. Yet this characterization –some will claim– denotes that the Father engulfs*

678

*everything. Nevertheless, this 'Everything' attributed to the Father **cannot be defined;** let alone by a symbolism that declares a Beginning (Archē-A) and an End (Ω). The Father has no beginning (A) because He is Self-Substantial and has no End (Ω) since He Is Eternal and Never-ending. These symbols do not refer to the Almighty Father, but the creator of matter, since only matter has a beginning and what has a beginning also has an end.* Hermes Trismegistus in chapter 1 states: «§11 …And the second creator Noûs, he who encompasses the seven circles and the vortices of their roots —along with logos— turned his creatures and they all started swirling from an indefinite beginning (A) to an interminable end (Ω).» **[HERMES TRISMEGISTUS FOUNDER OF THE MONOTHEISTIC RELIGION 9.000 B. C., IOANNIDIS P.]**

 As we know, Omega (Ω) in its recent shape was established during the time of Hadrian by Euclid, chief magistrate of Athens in 403 BC. Until then, it was written with the same symbolic depiction as the Omicron (O).

[Lexicon of the Hellenic Language, Liddell & Scott]

When the ancient philosophers referred to 'Omega' they had its (O) shape in mind, but with a longer pronunciation (i.e. great/long o).

*The O shape refers to the symbol of the Universe/Egg which in its initial un- inseminated condition contained the constituent of matter (Earth), a perishable constituent, which interwoven with Chaos and Tumult (Tartarus) were held together (connected) by the attractive force of Eros, the fourth primary element in Hesiod's Cosmogony. The **nature** of these four (primordial) elements is death and darkness; they <u>might seem</u> ever-lasting and immortal within time, but they are not. This is why they are identified with the quality of the long O, the O-mega Ω and determine the end.*

*Thus, ever since the Ray/Archē/Demiurgos (A) united with the Egg of matter (O) it is irreversibly headed to the deep death, where the (O) 'manufactures' the end (Gr.: Τέλος) and is symbolized as (**Ω**), sweeping everything else that was magnetized by the bottom-fed Eros along with it (Chaldean philosophers used to call dense matter 'deep bottom'. See reference #158).*

THE SEVEN BODIES OF MAN

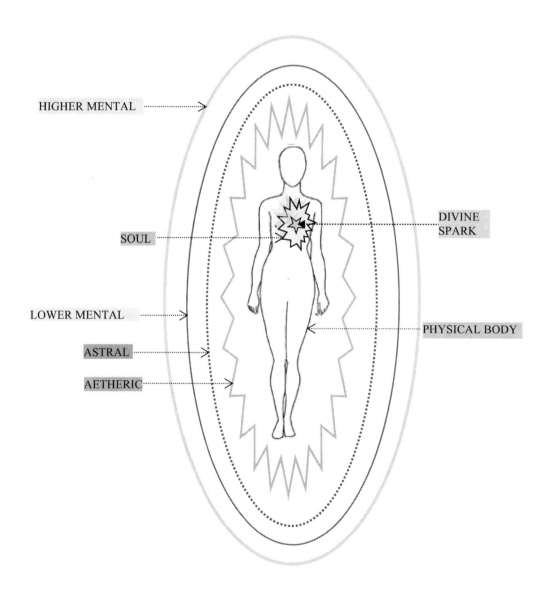

HIGHER MENTAL

DIVINE
SPARK

SOUL

LOWER MENTAL

PHYSICAL BODY

ASTRAL

AETHERIC

THE END OF THE CYCLE OF REINCARNATIONS

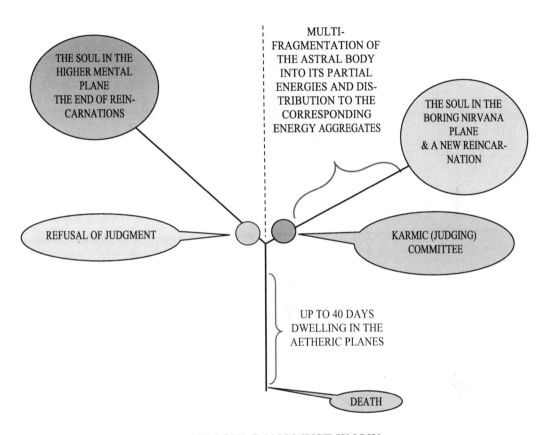

THE SOUL IN THE HIGHER MENTAL PLANE
THE END OF REIN-CARNATIONS

MULTI-FRAGMENTATION OF THE ASTRAL BODY INTO ITS PARTIAL ENERGIES AND DIS-TRIBUTION TO THE CORRESPONDING ENERGY AGGREGATES

THE SOUL IN THE BORING NIRVANA PLANE
& A NEW REINCAR-NATION

REFUSAL OF JUDGMENT

KARMIC (JUDGING) COMMITTEE

UP TO 40 DAYS DWELLING IN THE AETHERIC PLANES

DEATH

THE SOUL/MAN MUST KNOW:

1. He/she is not in the creation of the True God, but in the creation of a fallen 'god' who stole the Sacred Archetypes from the HyperCosmoi of the Truth and with them, he built a lame, flimsy and perishable world.

2. The Christ DOES NOT JUDGE ANYONE. He came to pay the 'archon of this world' with the Ransom for the deliverance of Man, and only when the man/soul INVOKES the benefit of this offer/sacrifice –the blood ransom– the powers of this world will allow him to return to his Spiritual Homeland. If Man simply denies to go in front of the Kar-mic/Judgment Committee and does not invoke the Ransom paid for this reason by the 'third-part guarantor' Christ, then he is dragged by force to 'Judgment' and then to a new reincarnation.

HOLY MATRIMONY-SYMBOL

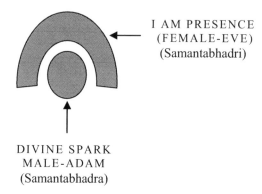

I AM PRESENCE
(FEMALE-EVE)
(Samantabhadri)

DIVINE SPARK
MALE-ADAM
(Samantabhadra)

The Vacuous Light of the 'I Am Presence'/Eve unites with the incarnated Divine Spark/Adam and the Holy Matrimony is completed providing the 'passport' for the return to the Unsplit HomeLands. It is symbolized with the familiar 'halo'.

ॐ•ॐ

«...Now the clear luminance of Dharmata shines in front of you. Recognize it! This moment the state of your Spirit is pure essence by its nature, it has no property, no hypostasis, no form, no color, but it is pure emptiness. **This is the Emptiness, the Female Buddha** (Samantabhadri).
But this state of your Spirit is not simply barren emptiness. It is unhindered, transparent, pure and vibrating. **This** *(vibrating)* **Spirit is the Male Buddha** (Samantabhadra).

These <u>two</u>, the Spirit whose nature is <u>emptiness</u> *(female/I Am Presence/Eve)* without any hypostasis and the Spirit which is <u>vibrating</u> and Luminous *(male/ Divine Spark/Adam)* are <u>undivided</u>. This is Buddha's Dharmakaya. Your very Spirit itself is the Emptiness and Luminance undivided as well, in the form of a great mass of Light and in this state, **it is no longer subdued to birth or death.**» [THE TIBETAN BOOK OF THE DEAD: THE FIRST LIGHT]

682

REFLECTIVE SYMBOL

*The previous symbol **MUST NOT BE CONFUSED** with its reverse (reflective) one, which despite the fact that it is placed on top of the head, it symbolizes different and <u>opposite</u> concepts.*

It is primarily the emblem of the lunar goddess Isis and of the Egyptian religion in general. In many representations Thoth is depicted as a bird carrying the above symbol on the top of its head. Alex Krappe in his work 'International Mythology' (Gr. edition, p. 391) states: "God Thoth is shown with an isis (bird species) head, wearing on it the disk of the moon inside a crescent." In another part of the same work (p.394), we can see the human-shaped 'Hathor cow', in the horns of which the lunar disk is depicted.

*It is the emblem that also symbolizes the **horns** of Lucifer/creator that engulf his 'devious wisdom'. There are artistic representations that depict Moses with horns as well. Generally speaking though, horns are a sign of the 'wisdom of the mystics' of this world.*

Because of this mystical emblem/symbol, animals that had these horns on their heads were worshipped in the past; i.e. the bull and the cow. God Enlil is quite often depicted in the form of a bull, while Zeus rapes Europe in the form of a bull. It is the same symbol that is sometimes represented as a 'canister', and on the top of the head where it stands, it receives and is filled with the devious/deceitful wisdom of the Solar God (Demiurgos). The crowns of kings used that very same symbolism.

EGYPTIAN DEPICTIONS

MOSES

MATERIAL, ANTI-MATERIAL AND PARALLEL UNIVERSES

...With the fission of True Light, two virtual/reflective universes were formed: A material and an anti-material one, independent from each other, with all their energy dimensions.
Like two mirrors one against each-other, they projected infinite reflective-virtual 'parallel' universes of probable choices...

ANTI-MATERIAL UNIVERSE

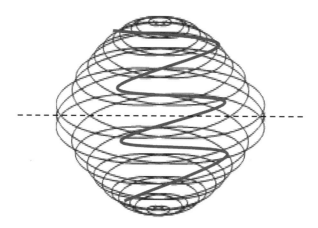

MATERIAL UNIVERSE

ตั๛•ต๛

MATERIAL, ANTI-MATERIAL, PARALLEL UNIVERSES
A visual rendition

THE 'EGG' OF MATERIAL CREATION [⊙]

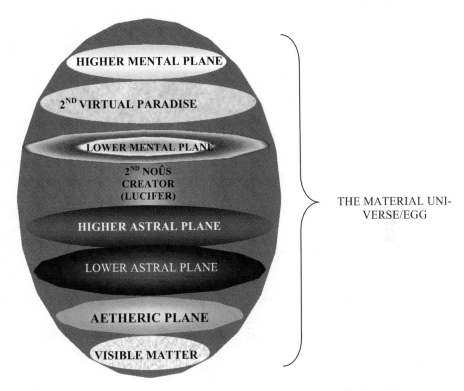

This representation is approximate because these energy fields/dimensions are not separated but interwoven with one another. They are just oscillations of different frequencies that exist in the same space.

«The Egg was incorporated as a sacred symbol in the cosmogonies of all the nations of the Earth... In chapter 54 of the Egyptian Ritual, Seb, the god of Time and of the Earth, is spoken of as having laid an egg, or the universe: "An egg conceived at the hour of the great one of the **Dual Force**." Ra (of the Egyptians) as well as Brahma is shown gestating/giving birth to the Egg of the Universe. ...In the sacred book of Hindus, Vishnu-Puraná, translated by Wilson, it is stated: The epithet (surname) Haima, which means 'resplendent' 'shining' or 'golden', is given to the egg. Also from Vishnu-Puraná: Intellect (Mahat)... including the (un-manifested) gross elements, formed an egg ... and the lord of the Universe himself abided in it in the character of Brahma... In that egg, O Brahman, were the continents, the seas and mountains, the planets and divisions of the universe, the **gods**, the **daemons**, and **mankind**.» *[H. P. Blavatsky, Secret Doctrine, I-359]*

CONSTITUTION OF THE MATERIAL UNIVERSE

Consistency of the Universe from the Remote Sensing Tutorial (RST) of NASA and the University of Indiana, Physics Dpt. Author: Dr. Nicholas M. Short, Sr. http://rst.gsfc.nasa.gov/Sect20/Cosmological_composition.jpg

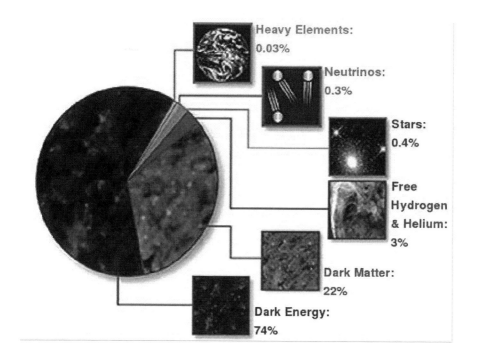

Heavy (dense) matter (this is what our bodies are made of): *0.03%*
Neutrinos.. *0.3%*
Stars (Suns) *0.4%*
Free hydrogen and Helium.. *3%*
Dark matter.. *22%*
Dark Energy *74%*

SPACE-TIME BRANE – MEMBRANE

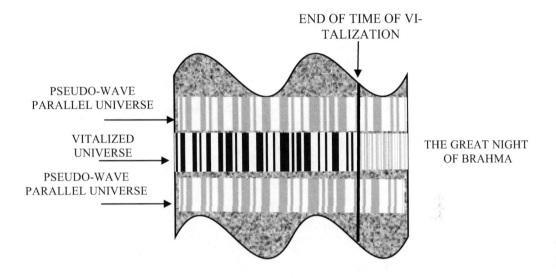

THE WEB OF VISIBLE MATTER

The space-time Brane/Membrane is curved and its end meets its beginning, where a new vitalization by some new Sentient Intelligent Wholeness (Brahma) starts a new cycle of action. The beings it dragged down with it (hooked on its [material] web) sink into the next innermost (inferior) layer of the spiral of the material energy-universe, and in each new creation, are vitalized as beings inferior to the ones of the previous creation, until their absolute extinction in the form of inorganic matter.

NOTIFICATION

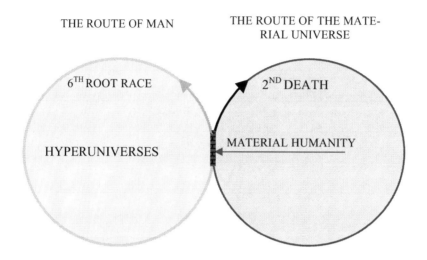

THE ROUTE OF MAN

THE ROUTE OF THE MATE-
RIAL UNIVERSE

6TH ROOT RACE

2ND DEATH

HYPERUNIVERSES

MATERIAL HUMANITY

THE ROUTE OF MAN

*Mankind's entrance into the **Real/True** Sixth Root-Race brings forth a permanent <u>separation</u> from the material (visible and invisible) universe, which will nevertheless continue its independent course. Celestial Man and the material universe seem like two independent 'points' that move in two **different** circles.*

At an 'instance' in eternity, their circumferences join at a certain point, and the creation of man manifests in the material universe. Afterwards, these two 'points' (man and material universe), each following its own trajectory, distance themselves from each other.

The True Sixth Root-Race of Men, is about to evolve <u>outside</u> the material (visible and invisible) universe, following its own course.

In an opposite manner, a totally different course and independent from that of Man's, is about to be followed by the Material Universe.

If Man is seduced and does not follow HIS OWN trajectory, but gets confused and follows that of the material universe, then <u>HE WILL PERISH</u>.

THE ROUTE OF THE SOUL

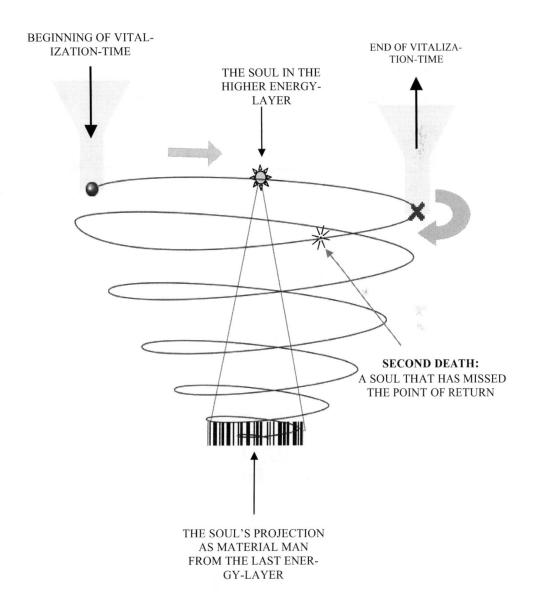

BEGINNING OF VITAL-
IZATION-TIME

THE SOUL IN THE
HIGHER ENERGY-
LAYER

END OF VITALIZA-
TION-TIME

SECOND DEATH:
A SOUL THAT HAS MISSED
THE POINT OF RETURN

THE SOUL'S PROJECTION
AS MATERIAL MAN
FROM THE LAST ENER-
GY-LAYER

THE HYPERUNIVERSES OF TRUE LIGHT

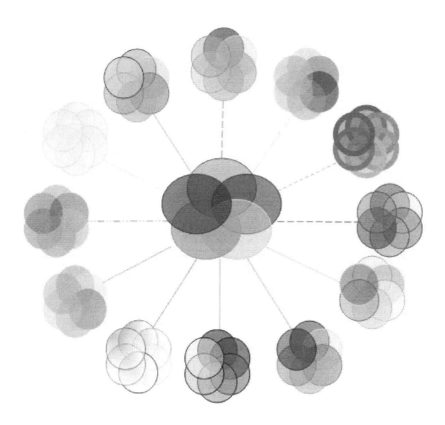

It is **<u>IMPOSSIBLE</u>** *to describe these Cosmoi (Aeons) in pictures or in words. This depiction only aims to help everyone to 'give shape and form' to <u>Conceptual</u> situations in the best way possible.*

There is the Fivefold Aeon (The Pentad of the Aeons) of the Unuttered Principle/Father, according to the Gospel of Judas and John's Apocryphon.

This Principle is environed by the 12 HyperUniverses/Aeons. Each Aeon/HyperUniverse has six Heavens, giving a total of 72 Aeons/HyperUniverses. One Monogenes Luminary reigns over each 'Heaven'.

These Cosmoi are Vast and Ever-expanding.

OVERALL VIEW

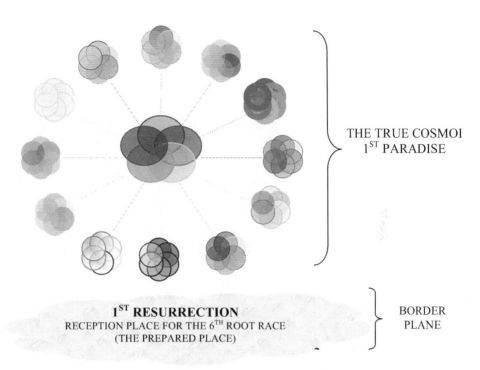

THE TRUE COSMOI
1ST PARADISE

1ST RESURRECTION
RECEPTION PLACE FOR THE 6TH ROOT RACE
(THE PREPARED PLACE)

BORDER
PLANE

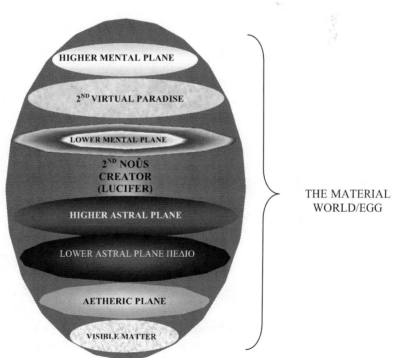

HIGHER MENTAL PLANE

2ND VIRTUAL PARADISE

LOWER MENTAL PLANE

2ND NOÛS
CREATOR
(LUCIFER)

HIGHER ASTRAL PLANE

LOWER ASTRAL PLANE ΠΕΔΙΟ

AETHERIC PLANE

VISIBLE MATTER

THE MATERIAL
WORLD/EGG

A PHOTOGRAPH OF THE ANTICHRIST

Don't be fooled, he's not Christ. He just looks like Him!

A member of the White Brotherhood and the Spiritual Hierarchy of the planet: his spiritual name is **Lord Divino** and his worldly one, by which he is known to the world, is Maitreya. **This entity claims to be Christ, Buddha, the Messiah of the Jews etc.** His aetheric headquarters are located over Kashmir, Pakistan/India.

CONFERENCE OF THE SPIRITUAL HIERARCHY IN 'SHENANDOAH' (1982)
VOLUME II, No 24, 11/8/82
SANAT KUMARA: *(addressing students who are present)* "…To those of you who are not blessed with inner vision, I will say that next to me on my right side is the beloved Lord Maitreya –known in the inner planes as Lord Divino."

Matthew 24:5 "For many will come in My name, saying, 'I am the Messiah/Christ,' and will deceive many…§ 24. For false Christs and false prophets will rise **and show great signs and wonders** to deceive, if possible, even the elect. §25 **Behold, I have told you beforehand!** §26 Therefore if they say to you, 'Look, He is in the desert!' do not go out; or 'Look, He is in the inner rooms!' do not believe it."

*This entity is preparing for its grand public appearance. Some say that he might **not** use the name 'Maitreya'…It is said that he will give an interview via satellite to the entire world* "to deceive, if possible, even the elect". *He has already established his representation in the United Nations and the leadership of the entire Earth is expected to be handed over to him by the global government.*

THE NUMBER OF THE BEAST

A very interesting video in YouTube gives the number of the beast according to the system of lexarithms:
http://www.youtube.com/watch?v=BVkusRzq4Xo

1	א	Aleph (A, E)	A	60	ס	Samekh (S)	S
2	ב	Beth (B, V)	B	70	ע	A'ayin (A'a, O)	O
3	ג	Gimel (G)	G	80	פ	Pe (P, Ph)	Ph
4	ד	Daleth (D)	D	90	צ	Tzaddi (Tz)	Tz
5	ה	He [Heh] (E, A)	H	100	ק	Qoph (Q)	Q
6	ו	Vau (O, U, V, W)	V	200	ר	Resh (R)	R
7	ז	Zayin (Z)	Z	300	ש	Shin (Sh, S)	Sh
8	ח	Cheth (Ch)	Ch	400	ת	Tau (Th, T)	Th
9	ט	Teth (T)	T	500	ך	Kaph-final (K,Kh)	K
10	י	Yod (I, J, Y)	I	600	ם	Mem-final (M)	M
20	כ	Kaph (K, Kh)	K	700	ן	Nun-final (N)	N
30	ל	Lamed (L)	L	800	ף	Pe-final (P, Ph)	Ph
40	מ	Mem (M)	M	900	ץ	Tzaddi-final (Tz)	Tz
50	נ	Nun (N)	N				

In Hebrew, Maitreya is written as
מיתרהיא

מיתרהיא

'MAITREYA'

מ   י   ת   ר   ה   י   א
mem yod tau resh he yod aleph

40 + 10 + 400 + 200 + 5 + 10 + 1 = **666**

There are six different ways to spell his name in Hebrew. Yet all six of them give the same lexarithmetic sum of 666.
Some people advise not to pronounce his name two times in a row.
Maitreya's followers disagree and state: "The antichrist has been here already, he came and left as Roman emperor Nero…"

SOUTH ATLANTIC ANOMALY

http://heasarc.gsfc.nasa.gov/docs/rosat/gallery/display/saa.html

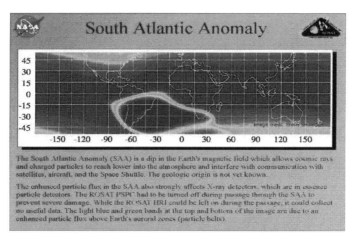

http://www.aviso.oceanobs.com/en/news/idm/2007/iom200710/index.html

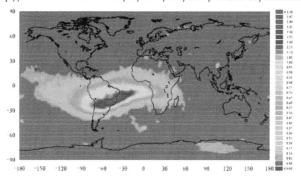

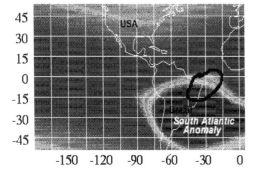

MECHANICAL MALFUNCTIONS
DUE TO THE SOUTH-ATLANTIC
ANOMALY

The Air France 447 airplane accident was caused by an electronic malfunction of the airplane due to the South-Atlantic anomaly (summer of 2009).

Air France 447 electrical problems and the South Atlantic Anomaly
http://www.examiner.com/x-11224-Baltimore-Weather-Examiner~y2009m6d4-Air-France-447-
electrical-problems-and-the-South-Atlantic-Anomaly

CHUPACABRA: THE 'ABOMINATION'

http://www.ghoststudy.com/new6/para_files/chupacabra02.jpg

http://www.hufos.net/images/chupacabra.jpg
http://www.hufos.net/news_in_general_16.html

http://www.acemprol.com/download/file.php?id=11128&mode=view

This particular creature was rather small-bodied. It was located at a farm in the city of Metepec in east-central Mexico, where it also died. The farmer that found it handed it over to the scientists. Nevertheless, creatures much larger and only slightly different than this have been sighted as well.

THE CONTENTS OF THIS BOOK
REFER TO AN INNOVATIVE AND COHESIVE WORLD THEO-
RY (WELTANSCHAUUNG) IN RELATION TO MAN.

ITS GREATEST PORTION DEALS WITH ABSTRACT CON-
CEPTS AND CONDITIONS WHICH, –IN ORDER TO BECOME
INTELLIGIBLE– HAVE BEEN CATACHRESTICALLY "GIVEN
AN ADEQUATE FORM".

ON ACCOUNT OF THIS, ANY FURTHER ANALYSIS OR EXPLANA-
TION OF THESE CONCEPTS WOULD INVOLVE
THE RISK/DANGER OF FALSIFICATION

BIBLIOGRAPHY

Translator's Note

In the translations of many bibliographical citations of the references and the main corpus, where available, original English translations of highly acclaimed scholars have been used. However, when the available translations did not precisely convey the desirable concept, the translator was obliged to produce new translations from the Greek original in order to remain consistent to the Greek texts used by the author. This also holds true with many (originally English) texts that were unavailable to the translator in their English prototypes.

1. AESCHYLUS, *Seven Against Thebes,* trans. tr. from the Anc. Gr. original Georgousopoulos K., Patakis Publ., Athens, 1999
2. AGNI YOGA SOCIETY, *Supermundane, The Esoteric Life - Book One,* 1938, Kedros Publ., Athens, 1997 [English Translation: First Edition, 1994]
3. AGNI YOGA SOCIETY, *Supermundane, The Esoteric Life - Book Two,* 1938, Kedros Publ., Athens, 1999[English Translation: First Edition, 1995]
4. *Apocryphal Texts of the New Testament, Vol. V, The Apocryphon of John,* tr. Koutsoukis D., Pyrinos Kosmos Publ., Athens, 1993
5. *Apocryphal Texts of the Old Testament, Vol. I, The first book of Adam and Eve,* trans. Koutsoukis D., Pyrinos Kosmos Publ., Athens, 1991 [Eng. version: Internet Sacred Text Archive, by Rutherford Platt, http://www.sacred-texts.com]
6. *Apocryphal Texts of the Old Testament, Vol. Six, The revelation of Adam to his son Seth,* trans. Koutsoukis D., Pyrinos Kosmos Publ., Athens, 2004 [Engl. version: *The Apocalypse Of Adam,* The Gnostic Society Library, The Nag Hammadi Library, Translated By George W. MacRae]
7. ARGYROPOULOS E., *Proof of the mathematical structure of the Greek language,* Argyropoulos Eleutherios Publ., Boston, 2000
8. BLAVATSKY H. P. M., *The Secret Doctrine (The book of Dzyan: Cosmic Evolution - Vol. I & II, Anthropogenesis - Vol. III & IV),* Pnevmaticos Helios Publ., Vol. I Athens 2003, Vol. II Athens 2002, Vol. III Athens 1992, Vol. IV Athens 2004
    [Eng. tr.: *http://www.theosociety.org/pasadena/sd/sd-hp.htm*]
9. *Book of Enoch (The),(The one listed as Apocryphon),* intr., ed. and trans. Katsareas G., Katsareas G. Publ., Athens, 1973
10. *Book Of Revelation [Apocalypse] Of John, New Testament,* Biblical Society Publ., London, 1955

11. BULWER LYTTON E., *The Coming Race,* Gr. trans. Barsaki N., Iamblichus Publ., Athens, 2000
[Eng. ed.: *http://www.web-books.com/Classics/ON/B0/B233/Lytton_ComingRaceC01.html]*

12. CAREY K. X., *Messages from the Stars,* trans. Barouxis G., Vouloukou (Spartan) Publ., Athens, 1992

13. CHALAS A. F., *The Underlying Mystery of the Greek Alphabet and the Universe or About Science,* ed. Prearis N. E., Prearis Publ., Athens, 1996

14. *Chaldean Oracles,* Gr. tr. Athinogenis I., Gravigger P., Ideotheatron - Dimeli Publ., Athens, 1998

15. CLARKE A., *Mysteries of the World,* trans. Aidini A., Cactus Publ., Athens, 1981

16. DANEZIS M., THEODOSIOU S., *Cosmology of the Intellect, Introduction to Cosmology (includes appendix: Cybernetics and Contemporary Physics, Man as Receiver and Processor of Information (the illusion of the senses) by Georgiou G. and Drouga A.),* Diavlos Publ., Athens, 2003

17. *Daniel-Old Testament,* Biblical Society Publ., London, 1955

18. Däniken E. von, *The Second Coming has already begun,* Gr. tr. Arachovitis G., Notos Publ., Athens, 1996

19. DECHARME P., *Greek Mythology,* 1884, trans. Fragkias A., ed. Vrettakos N., Historika Vivlia Publ., Athens, n. d.

20. DEUTSCHE BIBELGESELLSCHAFT, *Novum Testamentum Graece (New Testament),* Nestle-Aland Publ., Stuttgart, 1979-2001

21. EVANGELOPOULOS D., *Chthonian Mysteries: The Big Enigma of the Hollow Earth,* Metaekdotiki S.A., Archetypon Publ., Athens, 2002

22. *Exodus-Old Testament,* Biblical Society Publ., London, 1955

23. *First Apocalypse of James (The),* Nag Hammadi Library, Codex V, En. tr. Schoedel W. R., The Gnostic Society Library,
http://www.gnosis.org/naghamm/1ja.html

24. *Genesis-Old Testament,* Biblical Society Publ., London, 1955

25. GAZIS A., *Dictionary of the Greek language,* published, supervised, edited, and paid for by Garpolas K., O. and Matakides Ch., S., Vienna, Austria, 1835

26. GIANNOPOULOS I., *Classified File: Hollow Earth,* Esoptron Publ., Athens, 2000

27. GIANNOULAKIS P., *Hollow Earth,* Metaekdotiki S.A., Archetypon Publ., Thessaloniki, 1999

28. GIANNOULAKIS P., KAVAKOPOULOS L., *The Truth about UFOs and Extraterrestrial Conspiracies,* Metaekdotiki S.A., Archetypon Publ., Athens, 2004

29. GOLEMAN D., *Emotional Intelligence: Why the 'EQ' is more significant than the 'IQ',* Gr. tr. Papastavrou A., Hellenica Grammata Publ., Athens, 1997

30. *Gospel of John (New Testament),* Biblical Society Publ., London, 1955

31. *Gospel of Luke (New Testament),* Biblical Society Publ., London, 1955

32. *Gospel of Matthew (New Testament),* Biblical Society Publ., London, 1955

33. GRAVIGGER P., *Chaldean Oracles,* Ideotheatron - Dimeli Publ., Athens, 1998

34. GRAVIGGER P., *Philosophical and Ceremonial/Ritual Hymns of the Ancient Greek Mystics,* from the Sphinx Library, Ideotheatron - Dimelē Publ., Athens, 2000

35. GREENE R., *Power: 48 Laws, a creation of Joost Elffers,* trans. Livadopoulou S., Esoptron Publ., Athens, 2000

36. GRIMAL P., *Dictionary of the Greek and Roman Mythology,* ed. Atsalos V., University Studio Press - Scientific Books and Periodical Publ., Thessaloniki, 1991

37. GUIRAND F., *World Mythology,* Eng. trans. from the French 'MYTHOLOGIE GÉNÉRALE' by Tetenes N., ed. Petridis M. G., Biblos Publ., 1953

38. HAWKING S., *The Universe in a Nutshell,* trans. Petraki M., Katoptro Publ., Athens, 2001

39. HERMES TRISMEGISTUS, *Hermetic Texts, Volume One,* trans. Rodakis P., Tzaferopoulos A., Paraskinio Publ., Athens, 1990

40. HERMES TRISMEGISTUS, *Hermetic Texts, Volume Two,* trans. Rodakis P., Tzaferopoulos A., Paraskinio Publ., Athens, 2002

41. HERMES TRISMEGISTUS: *The founder of Monotheism 9000 B.C.,* Ioannidis P. K., Dion Publ., Thessaloniki, 1997, 2001

42. HESIOD, *Theogony,* trans. Girgenis S., Zitros Publ., Thessaloniki, 2001

43. *Hidden Worlds, from the series Mysteries of the World, original series 'Enigma',* Domi S.A. Publ., Athens, n. d.

44. ICKE D., *Rebels of Consciousness,* trans. Perissaki P., of *'The Robots' Rebellion'* Esoptron Publ. Athens, 1998

45. ICKE D., *Revealing the Great Conspiracy (David Icke interviewed by Jon Rappoport),* trans. Tsoli N., Esoptron Publ. Athens, 2002

46. ICKE D., *Tales from the Time Loop,* trans. Aspiotou V., Esoptron Publ., Athens, 2005

47. ICKE D., *The Secret of All Times,* trans. Mastakouris Th., ; Esoptron Publ. Athens, 2002

48. KALLERGI D., *The Twelve Olympian Gods,* Ideotheatron Publ., Athens, 1998

49. KALOGERAKIS G., *Prometheus' Testament on the Creation and the Greeks,* Dion - Psaras Books Publ., Thessaloniki, 2001

50. KALOGERAKIS G., *The Return of the Gods: Universal Cause and Effect or Divine Providence?,* Dion - Psaras Books Publ., Thessaloniki, 2000

51. KLOURAS N., PERLEPES S. P., *General and Inorganic Chemistry, Volume One: Atomic Structure, Periodical System, Atomic Properties,* Greek Open University Publ., Patrai, 2000

52. KOULAKIS G., *The Great Etymological Dictionary,* Malliaris - Paedia Publ., Thessaloniki, 1993

53. KRAPPE A., *World Mythology,* Gr. tr. Vokos N., ed. Kourakis D., Spyropoulos Brothers - Koumoundoureas K. O. E. Publ., Athens, 1957

54. LELOUP J. Y., *The Gospel of Mary (Magdalene),* trans. Kouroussi A., Enalios Publ., Athens, 2005

55. LELOUP J. Y., *The Gospel of Philip (The Gnostic Gospel of Philip),* trans. Papathanasopoulou D., Enalios Publ., Athens, 2006

56. LELOUP J. Y., *The Gospel of Thomas (The Gnostic Gospel of Thomas)*, trans. Papathanasopoulou D., Enalios Publ., Athens, 2006

57. LIDDELL & SCOTT, *The Abridged Great Dictionary of the Greek Language*, Pelekanos Publ., Athens, 2007

58. LIVRAGA RIZZI J. A., *The elemental spirits of nature*, Gr. tr. Planas G. A., New Acropolis Publ., Athens, 1986

59. *Major Hellenic Lexicon (M. E. L)*, (electronic form) Tegopoulos - Fytrakis Publ.

60. MARCINIAK B., *'Gaia' Pleiadian Keys to the Living Library*, Gr. tr. Matzorou E., Kryon LTD Publ., Athens, 2004

61. MARGIORIS N., *De-symbolization of the Greek Mythology*, Omakoeio Athenon Publ., 1988

62. MARRS T., *L.U.C.I.D. Project*, Liakopoulos Publ., 2006

63. *Mysteries of Antiquity, from the series Mysteries of the World, original series 'Enigma'*, Domi S.A. Publ., Athens, n. d.

64. *Mysteries of the Earth, from the series Mysteries of the World, original series 'Enigma'*, Domi S.A. Publ., Athens, n. d.

65. *Mysteries of the East, from the series Mysteries of the World, original series 'Enigma'*, Domi S.A. Publ., Athens, n. d.

66. *Mysteries of the West, from the series Mysteries of the World, original series 'Enigma'*, Domi S.A. Publ., Athens, n. d.

67. NATIONAL GEOGRAPHIC SOCIETY, *'The Gospel of Judas' (Codex Tchacos)*, tr. Kasser R., Meyer M., Wurst G., in coll. w/ Gaudard F., Lambrakis Publ., Athens, 2006 [Eng. tr. *http://www.nationalgeographic.com/lostgospel/_pdf/GospelofJudas.pdf*]

68. *Near East Texts: The Epic of Gilgamesh - Enuma Elish (The Saga of Creation)*, trans. Skartsi X. S., Skartsis S. L., Kastaniotis Publ., Athens, 1989

69. *New School Encyclopedia: For You Children*, Avlos Publ., Athens, n. d.

70. *Orphic Hymns, Modern Gr.* trans. Magginas S., Ideotheatron Publ., Athens, 2000

71. PADMASAMBHAVA, *The Tibetan Bible of the Dead*, intro, trans, design Liakopoulos E., Esoptron Publ. Athens, 1992

72. PANTAZIDIS I., *Homeric Lexicon*, ed. Konstadinides M., Sideris I. N. Publ., Athens, 1930

73. PAPASTAVROU A., *Letters to Anonymous*, Papastavrou A. Publ., Athens, 1967

74. PAPASTAVROU A., *World within World, Psychic and Other Phenomena*, Tucson, Arizona, USA, 1959, Makris Publ., Athens, n. d.

75. PHILOSTRATUS, *Life of Apollonius of Tyana*, intro, trans, notes Tzaferopoulos A., Georgiades Publ., Greek Library, Athens, 1995

76. PLATO, *Critias*, trans. Koutroumpas G., Georgiades Publ., Athens, 2001

77. PLATO, *Phaedo*, trans. Athanasopoulos J. K., Georgiades Publ., Athens, 2003

78. PLATO, *The Republic*, Mod. Gr. tr. Griparis G., Ancient Greek Writers Library, Athens, n. d.

79. PLATO, *Timaeus*, Mod. Gr. tr. Koutroumpas G., Georgiades Publ., Athens, 2001

80. RICHEPIN J., *Greek Mythology*, trans. Tetenes N., ed. Marinatos S., Biblos Publ., 1953

81. SADOUL J., *The Treasure of the Alchemists*, trans. Petrakopoulou M., Neos Stathmos Publ., n. d.

82. SAKELLARIOS G., *Pythagoras, The Teacher of the Centuries*, Ideotheatron Publ., Athens, 1963

83. SAKELLARIOU CH., *Dictionary of Synonyms*, Sideris I. N. Publ., Athens, 2005

84. SALLUSTIUS, *Of Gods and the World*, Mod. Gr. tr. Gravigger P., Ideotheatron - Dimeli Editions, Athens, 1999

85. *Secret Messages, from the series Mysteries of the World, original series 'Enigma'*, Domi S.A. Publ., Athens, n. d.

86. *Secret Societies (Collective works)*, Metaekdotiki LTD, Archetypo Publ., Athens, 2002

87. *Secret Worlds (Collective works)*, Secret Library Series, Anichneftes Publ., Thessaloniki, 1998

88. SINGH S., *Big Bang*, trans. Spanou A., Travlos Publ., Athens, 2005

89. STAMATAKOS J., *Ancient Greek Dictionary*, Bibliopromitheftiki Publ., Athens, 2002

90. STAMKOS G., KAVAKOPOULOS L., *Conspiracy Theories*, Metaekdotiki S.A., Archetypon Publ., Athens, 2003

91. STEINER R., *Apocryphal Science, Hyper-sensed World View Synopsis*, trans. Panagos G., Tropos Zois Publ., Athens, 1995

92. STEINER R., *At the Gates of Anthroposophy*, trans. Alexiou Th., Anthroposophy Publ., Athens, 1994

93. STEINER R., *From the Akashic Chronicle - Cosmic Memory*, trans. Alexiou Th., Anthroposophy Publ., Athens, 1995

94. *The Bible of Creation 'Sefer Yetzirah'*, trans. Siafarikas Th., Iamblichus Publ., Athens, 1990

95. THEODOSIADIS N., *Leprechauns, series: Fantastic Worlds*, Metaekdotiki LTD, Archetypon Publ., Thessaloniki, 1998

96. TIME LIFE INTERNATIONAL, *The Human Body*, 'Lycios Apollo' Scientific Library - Chryssos Typos publ., 1970

97. TRIANTAFILLIDIS M., *Common Modern Greek Dictionary*, Modern Greek Studies Institute, Aristotelian University, Triantafillidis Foundation, Thessaloniki, 1998, 2005

98. TZIROPOULOU-EUSTATHIOU A., *Greek Word - How the Greek language inseminated the global Logos*, Georgiades Publ., Athens, 2003

99. VAGIONAKIS K., *Introduction to Natural Sciences, Volume Four: Oscillation and Harmonious Movement, Introduction to the Mechanics of Fluids*, Greek Open University Publ., Patrai, 2008

In Electronic Form:

100.   ARISTOPHANES, *Ornithes, (Birds)*
http://www.gutenberg.org/ebooks/27315

101.   *The (First) Apocalypse of James,* Nag Hammadi Library, Codex V, trans. Schoedel W. R., The Gnostic Society Library.
http://www.gnosis.org/naghamm/1ja.html

102.   *The Apocryphon of John*, Nag Hammadi Library, NH Codex III, 1(SHORT VERSION), NH Codex IV,1 (LONG VERSION), trans. Waldstein M., Wisse F., The Gnostic Society Library, *http://www.gnosis.org/naghamm/apocjn-short.html* [SHORT VERSION]
http://www.gnosis.org/naghamm/apocjn-long.html [LONG VERSION]

103.   *The Apocryphon of John* (The Secret Book of John), Nag Hammadi Library, Eng. trans. Davies S., The Gnostic Society Library,
http://www.gnosis.org/naghamm/apocjn-davies.html

104.   *The Apocryphon of John (The Secret Book of John)*, (COMBINATION OF 4 MANUSCRIPTS) Nag Hammadi Library, Eng. tr. Frederik Wisse, The Gnostic Society Library *http://www.gnosis.org/naghamm/apocjn.html*

105.   *DOMI Encyclopedia*, (electronic form)

106.   *Gospel of Philip (The)*, The Gnostic Society Library, The Nag Hammadi Library, Eng. tr. from Coptic: Wesley W. Isenberg
http://www.gnosis.org/naghamm/gop.html

107.   *Gospel of Philip (The)*, Metalogos, The Ecumenical Coptic Project, Eng. tr. from Coptic: Paterson Brown T. *http://www.metalog.org/files/philip.html*

108.   *Gospel of Philip (The)*, Eng. tr. Paterson Brown T.
http://www.metalog.org/files/philip.html

109.   *Gospel of Thomas (The)*, Early Christian Writings, Eng. tr. BEATE BLATZ
http://www.earlychristianwritings.com/thomas/gospelthomas70.html

110.   *Gospel of Thomas (The)*, Sacred Texts, Eng. tr. Thomas O. Lambdin
http://www.sacred-texts.com/chr/thomas.htm

111.   Gospel of Thomas *(The)*, The Ecumenical Coptic Project
http://www.metalog.org/files/thomas.html

112.   *Gospel of Thomas (The)*, The Gnostic Society Library, Eng. tr. Stephen Patterson and Marvin Meyer, *http://www.gnosis.org/naghamm/gosthom.html*

113.   *Gospel of Truth (The),* Nag Hammadi Library, tr. Paterson Brown T.
http://www.metalog.org/files/valent.html;

114.   *Infancy Gospel of Thomas (The), (Thomas' account of the infancy of the Lord)*, First Greek form, En. tr. Roberts A., Donaldson J.
http://www.earlychristianwritings.com/infancythomas.html; HOMEPAGE
http://www.earlychristianwritings.com/text/infancythomas-a-roberts.html; TEXT PAGE

Periodicals:

1. *AVATON,* Issue 64, September 2006, Archetypo Publ.
2. *HELLENIC NEXUS,* Issue 12, February - March 2006, Esoptron Publ.
3. *HELLENIC NEXUS,* Issue 2, July 2004, Esoptron Publ.
4. *IDEOTHEATRON,* Volume A, Issues 1-8 (1998-1999), Ideotheatron Publ.
5. *ILISSOS,* Issue 80, 1970
6. *ILISSOS,* Issue 95, 1972
7. *NATURE,* August 2001
8. *SCIENCE ILLUSTRATED,* Special Edition 'Evolution', January 2007
9. *STRANGE,* Issue 26, October 2000, Archetypo Publ.
10. *STRANGE,* Issue 45, June 2000, Archetypo Publ.
11. *STRANGE,* Issue 49, November 2002, Archetypo Publ.
12. *STRANGE,* Issue 57, summer 2003, Archetypo Publ.
13. *STRANGE,* Issue 75, March 2005, Agnosto Publ.
14. *STRANGE,* Issue 80, September 2008, Agnosto Publ.
15. *STRANGE,* Issue 112, August 2008, Agnosto Publ.
16. *STRANGE,* Special Collector's Edition 'Extraterrestrials and UFOs', Agnosto Publ.
17. *TRITO MATI [Third Eye],* Issue 85, March 2000, Esoptron Publ.
18. *TRITO MATI [Third Eye],* Issue 153, July 2007, Esoptron Publ.

DVD, Documentaries

1. *'A Papyrus (scroll) from the time of Jesus'*, (Documentary), Discovery Channel, 2004
2. *'The Maya Prophecy'*, (Documentary), History Channel, 2005
3. *'What The Bleep Do We Know'*, (Docudrama), Director: William Arntz, Betsy Chasse, Mark Vicente, Production: Lord Of The Wind, 2004, http://www.whatthebleep.com/

Web Pages

1. A NEW HUMAN SPECIES WHICH LIVED BEFORE 18,000 YEARS, CHALLENGES THE HISTORY OF EVOLUTION (GENEALOGY OF MAN) Guardian, October 28, 2004
    http://www.physics4u.gr/news/2004/scnews1653.html
2. ADDITIONAL DIMENSIONS OFFER NEW POSSIBILITIES TO SOLVE OLD MYSTERIES, Nima Arkani-Hamed Article, SLAC Research Library
    http://www.physics4u.gr/articles/fifthdim.html

3.   AIR FRANCE 447 ELECTRICAL PROBLEMS AND THE SOUTH ATLANTIC ANOMALY
     *http://www.examiner.com/x-11224-Baltimore-Weather-
     Examiner~y2009m6d4-Air-France-447-electrical-problems-and-the-South-
     Atlantic-Anomaly*

4.   ALIEN IMPLANTS: Article published by Kostas Kiapekos, Ch. editor of 'Super-
     natural' magazine, in 'Mystery' magazine, (25-09-07, 14:33)
     http://www.inout.gr/archive/index.php/t-15979.html

5.   APOPHIS
     http://el.wikipedia.org/wiki/99942_Άποφις

6.   ASTEROID ARRIVAL IN 2019
     http://www.supernatural.gr/news_asteroid_2019.htm

7.   ASTEROID THREATENS THE EARTH, PATHFINDER NEWS, March 3rd, 2007:
     Scotsman news
     http://www.pathfinder.gr/periscopio/asteroid-hit-earth.html

8.   ATHENIAN AND MACEDONIAN NEWS AGENCY
     http://www.ana-mpa.gr/anaweb/

9.   BACK TO THE FUTURE THROUGH…TIME-HOLES: 'TA NEA' Athens newspa-
     per, June 10th, 2000
     http://www.physics4u.gr/news/2000/scnews51.html

10. BILL HAMILTON'S INTERVIEW (EXCERPT)
     http://www.boomspeed.com/joseph2/J-Rod2.htm

11. CAN WE FIND A PLACE IN A PARALLEL UNIVERSE? Comment on max Teg-
     mark's article in Scientific American Magazine: June 2003
     http://www.physics4u.gr/articles/2003/paralleluni.html

12. CHUPACABRA, 1st Photo
     http://www.ghoststudy.com/new6/para_files/chupacabra02.jpg

13. CHUPACABRA, 2nd Photo
     http://www.hufos.net/images/chupacabra.jpg

14. CHUPACABRA, 3rd Photo
     http://www.acemprol.com/download/file.php?id=11128&mode=view

15. CLAY-MINERAL CRYSTALLIZATION CASE STUDY
     http://www.bltresearch.com/xrd.php

16. CONCERNS ABOUT THE CERN EXPERIMENT
     http://www.inout.gr/showthread.php?p=176548#post176548

17. COSMIC WEB
     http://www.physics4u.gr/news/2008/scnews3311.html

18. COSMOLOGICAL COMPOSITION, Remote Sensing Tutorial (RST) of NASA and
     Indiana Univ., Physics Dpt. Principal Author: Dr. Nicholas M. Short, Sr.
     http://rst.gsfc.nasa.gov/Sect20/Cosmological_composition.jpg

19. DARK ENERGY CAN TEAR US TO PIECES: space.com, December 30, 2008
     http://www.physics4u.gr/news/2009/scnews3593.html

20. DARK ENERGY, Article by Robert Reynolds Caldwell, 1st part, 4th part, Phys-
     ics World magazine, May 2004
     http://physicsweb.org/articles/world/17/5/7

21. DARK ENERGY, 10 YEARS AFTER, Eugenides Foundation-Planetarium, Article: Alexis Delivorias
    http://www.eugenfound.edu.gr/frontoffice/portal.asp?cpage=RESOURCE&cre src=570&cnode=28

22. DARK MATTER ACCUMULATES FIRST AND THEN THE GALAXY IS FORMED: NASA News, June 16, 2006
    http://www.physics4u.gr/news/2006/scnews2503.html

23. DID THE CREATION OF THE LIVING WORLD OCCUR BY CHANCE? A POINT OF VIEW OPPOSITE TO THE DARWINIAN THEORY
    http://www.physics4u.gr/articles/2003/creationvital.html

24. DOES OUR CONSCIOUSNESS FUNCTION IN A QUANTUM WAY?: LINK E. Manousakis 28 /10/ 07
    http://arxiv.org/PS_cache/arxiv/pdf/0709/0709.4516v1.pdf
    http://tech.pathfinder.gr/xpaths/x-science/564485.html

25. EARTH'S MAGNETIC FIELD WEAKENS BY 10% OVER THE PAST 150 YEARS
    http://www.redorbit.com/news/space/22057/earths_magnetic_field_weakens_b y_10_percent/

26. EARTH'S NATURAL 'SHIELD' IS DIMINISHING, September 25, 2008
    http://www.ert.gr
    http://www.apn.gr/news/world-news/

27. EL CHUPACABRA FROM DISCOVERY CHANNEL
    http://www.discoverychannel.co.uk/paranormal/cryptozoology/chupacabras/in dex.shtml

28. EL CHUPACABRA FROM NATIONAL GEOGRAPHIC
    http://www.tv.com/national-geographic-channel-is-it-real/chupacabra/episode/552653/summary.html

29. EMBIOGENESIS: Physics4u.Gr
    http://www.physics4u.gr/articles/2003/creationvital.html

30. ENVIRONMENTAL POLICIES AS A COVER-UP FOR THE GENOCIDE AND EN-SLAVEMENT OF HUMANITY, Vicky Chryssou, 20/05/2009
    http://periballondiki.blogspot.com/2009/05/blog-post_8215.html

31. EXTRATERRESTRIALS - MYTH OR REALITY
    http://www.physics4u.gr/news/2000/scnews18.html

32. FREE GREEK ENCYCLOPEDIA
    http://www.live-pedia.gr

33. GENEALOGY OF MAN, Part 1: physics4u.gr
    http://www.physics4u.gr/articles/2005/originofhuman1.html
    http://www.physics4u.gr/news/2004/scnews1653.html
    http://www.physics4u.gr/news/2005/scnews1895.html

34. GREEKS THE SONS OF THE GODS, Gerasimos Kalogerakis
    http://www.blackstage.gr/moon.htm
    http://ellania.pblogs.gr

35. GREENHOUSE EFFECT ON MARS TOO! OVERHEATING DOESN'T THREATEN EARTH ONLY: 'TA NEA' Athens Newspaper
    http://digital.tanea.gr/Default.aspx?d=20070817&nid=5608613

36. HITLER WAS AN ANTI-SMOKER TOO…
http://periballondiki.blogspot.com/2009/06/blog-post.html
http://www.bmj.com/archive/7070nd2.htm

37. J-ROD AND MICROBIOLOGIST DAN B. BURISCH, PH.D. © 2002 by Linda
Moulton Howe
http://www.boomspeed.com/joseph2/j-rod.htm
http://www.boomspeed.com/joseph2/j-rod2.htm

38. LIVING ON THE EDGE OF CHAOS
http://www.physics4u.gr/5lessons/lesson4.html

39. LOVE IS A CHEMICAL PHENOMENON, NEUROSCIENTISTS CONFIRM
http://www.in.gr/news/article.asp?lngEntityID=973620&lngDtrID=252:
in.gr/news
http://el.science.wikia.com/wiki/αγάπη

40. MAGNETIC GATES OPEN AND CLOSE CONTINUOUSLY LETTING PARTICLES
PASS THROUGH AND REACH EARTH FROM THE SUN (OR) STRANGE PORTAL
CONNECTS EARTH TO SUN; HIGH-ENERGY-PARTICLES CAN TRAVEL THE 93
MILLION MILES DURING BRIEF OPENING
http://www.arvanitidis.gr/?s=flux+transfer+event&submit=Searchhttp://www
.msnbc.msn.com/id/27525165/#.TysHVeTAG7s

41. MAGNETIC-SHIELD CRACKS FOUND; BIG SOLAR STORMS EXPECTED, Victoria
Jaggard in San Francisco, National Geographic News, December 17, 2008
http://news.nationalgeographic.com/news/2008/12/081217-solar-
breaches.html

42. MAITREYA = 666: The Number of the Beast Revealed
http://www.youtube.com/watch?v=BVkusRzq4Xo

43. MAITREYA'S FIRST INTERVIEW, Share International magazine January - February 2009 (Benjamin Creme) 11 January 2009
http://www.share-gr.org/new/mast0901.html
http://share-international.org/magazine/old_issues/2009/2009-01.htm

44. MAITREYA'S MAGAZINE, SHARE INTERNATIONAL, Issue December 2008,
Questions & Answers with Benjamin Creme
http://www.share-gr.org/new/QA0812.html

45. MAITREYA'S MAGAZINE, SHARE INTERNATIONAL, Issue July-August 2009,
Questions & Answers with Benjamin Creme
http://www.share-gr.org/new/QA0907-08.html

46. MAITREYA'S MAGAZINE, SHARE INTERNATIONAL, Issue June 2009, Questions
& Answers with Benjamin Creme
http://www.share-gr.org/new/QA0906.html

47. MAITREYA'S MAGAZINE, SHARE INTERNATIONAL, Issue March, Questions &
answers with Benjamin Creme
http://www.share-gr.org/new/QA0903.html

48. MAITREYA'S MAGAZINE, SHARE INTERNATIONAL, Issue May 2009, Questions
& answers with Benjamin Creme
http://www.share-gr.org/new/QA0905.html

49. MAITREYA'S MISSION (MY-'TRAY-AH) 'THE SON OF MAN' Questions & Answers with Benjamin Creme
    http://www.share-gr.org/02-02.htm
50. MAITREYA'S TEACHINGS ON RELIGION, DISCUSSION OF THE IMPACT OF RELIGION ON HUMAN SUFFERING, AND THE ROLE OF CLERGY.
    http://www.share-international.org/ARCHIVES/M_teachings/Mt_religion.htm
51. MASS EXTINCTIONS OF SPECIES ON EARTH DURING THE PALEOZOIC-MESOZOIC ERAS: Physics4u, January 2004
    http://www.physics4u.gr/articles/2004/massextinction.html
52. M-BRANES AND THE DREAMS FOR UNIFICATION: Physics4u
    http://www.physics4u.gr/articles/2007/M-branes.html
53. MEGIDDO TUNNEL
    http://www.geocities.com/sfetel/gr/plumb_waters_g.htm#menu
    http://web.archive.org/web/20050525010642/
    http://www.geocities.com/sfetel/gr/plumb_waters_g.htm
54. MYSTERIOUS GIANT HOLE DISCOVERED IN THE UNIVERSE: Associated Press: Washington 25/08/07, 00:42 Washington (AP)
    http://www.in.gr/news/default.asp
55. MYSTERIOUS PHENOMENON IN OUR GALACTIC NEIGHBORHOOD; DARK ENERGY IS AROUND US: MSNBC, March 16, 2005
    http://www.physics4u.gr/news/2005/scnews1853.html
56. NASA PLANS TO SEND ASTRONAUT ONTO ASTEROID: The Guardian 17/11/06
    http://www.physics4u.gr/news/2006/scnews2664.html
57. NEW MODEL ALLOWS TIME-TRAVEL: BBC & New Scientist, June 17, 2005
    http://www.physics4u.gr/news/2005/scnews2007.html
58. NO PARADOX FOR TIME TRAVELERS (Mark Buchanan; New Scientist, June 2005)
    http://www.newscientist.com/article/dn7535-no-paradox-for-time-travellers.html
59. OFFICIAL WEBSITE OF MAITREYA: 'Maitreya will shout fervently'
    http://www.share-gr.org
60. ORTHODOX GROUP OF DOGMA RESEARCH
    http://www.oodegr.com/oode/grafi/kd/exwxr.pig1.htm#span
61. OUR SOLAR SYSTEM'S BOUNDARIES
    http://www.physics4u.gr/blog/?p=768
62. PARALLEL UNIVERSES BY MAX TEGMARK, (Part 1) From Scientific American, June 2003
    http://www.physics4u.gr/articles/2003/paralleluni1.html
    http://www.scientificamerican.com/article.cfm?id=parallel-universes
63. PARALLEL UNIVERSES BY MAX TEGMARK, Metanexus Institute, Views: 27-02-2002
    http://www.metanexus.net/magazine/ArticleDetail/tabid/68/id/5685/Default.aspx
64. PARALLEL UNIVERSES MAKE QUANTUM SENSE
    http://www.newscientist.com/article/mg19526223.700-parallel-universes-make-quantum-sense.html
    http://www.physics4u.gr/articles/2007/parallel_universes_quantum_sense.html

65. PARALLEL WORLDS
   http://news.pathfinder.gr/periscopio/3476.html
66. PARTHENOGENESIS AND OTHER MIRACLES, posted by: KAROLOS2 -
   28/03/2009 (Eleftherotypia newspaper)
   http://wwkarolos.blogspot.com/2009/04/blog-post.html
67. PARTHENOGENESIS, KOMODO DRAGONS (December 22, 2006)
   http://news.pathfinder.gr/scitech/366824.html
68. PHYSICISTS DEVELOP EXPERIMENT TO TEST STRING THEORY: San Diego Univ.,
   California, January 23, 2007
   http://www.physics4u.gr/news/2007/scnews2727.html
69. PLANT ABNORMALITIES, BLT RESEARCH TEAM, INC. (William C. Levengood)
   http://www.bltresearch.com/plantab.php
70. PLASMA
   http://el.wikipedia.org/wiki/Πλάσμα_(Φυσική)
   http://en.wikipedia.org/wiki/Plasma_(physics)
71. QUANTUM FUNCTION OF THE BRAIN
   http://www.physics4u.gr/artcles/qbrain1.html
72. QUANTUM MEMORIES SHOULD MIMIC OURS: NATURE, 6/8/2001
   http://www.nature.com/news/1998/010809/full/news010809-4.html#1
   http://www.physics4u.gr/news/2001/scnews290.html
73. QUANTUM WORMHOLES COULD CARRY PEOPLE, 18:10 23 May 2002 by
   Charles Choi
   http://www.physics4u.gr/news/2002/scnews640.html
   http://www.newscientist.com/article/dn2312-quantum-wormholes-could-carry-people.html
74. QUINTESSENCE AS ANOTHER CAUSE OF COSMIC ACCELERATION PART 3, –
   WHY DOES IT HAPPEN NOW IN THE HISTORY OF THE UNIVERSE? Physics World
   , November 2006
   http://www.physics4u.gr/articles/2006/quintessence3.html
75. RETROSPECTIVE DISTORTION
   http://www.skepdic.com/retfalse.html
76. SCIENTIFICALLY 'APPROVED' EBOLA VIRUS: THE SOLUTION FOR THE SALVA-
   TION OF THE PLANET! Article by Christos Vagenas, published in Hellenic
   Nexus magazine.
   http://www.nexushellas.gr/index.php?option=com_content&task=view&id=121
77. SHARK PARTHENOGENESIS: Scientists confirmed the 2nd ever Shark Parthenogenesis: CNN (October 14th, 2008)
   http://news.pathfinder.gr/misc/510310.html
   *http://www.powermediaplus.com/news/archive.aspx?newsTypeID=1&newsID
   =2974*
78. SIX DIMENSIONS
   http://www.physics4u.gr/news/2000/scnews4.html
79. SOLAR WIND, HELIOPAUSE, HELIOSPHERE: astronomia.gr
   http://www.astronomia.gr/wiki/index.php?title

80. SOUTH ATLANTIC ANOMALY (S. A. A.)
    http://heasarc.gsfc.nasa.gov/docs/rosat/gallery/display/saa.html
    http://www.aviso.oceanobs.com/en/news/idm/2007/iom200710/index.html
    http://www.examiner.com/x-11224-Baltimore-Weather-
    Examiner~y2009m6d4-Air-France-447-electrical-problems-and-the-South-
    Atlantic-Anomaly
81. SPACE-TIME - BLACK HOLES - PARALLEL UNIVERSES
    http://www.physics4u.gr/5lessons/lesson5.html
82. STRING THEORY
    http://www.physics4u.gr/news/2000/scnews4.html
83. SUN'S POWER HITS NEW LOW, MAY ENDANGER EARTH? National Geographic News, September 24, 2008, Anne Minard
    http://news.nationalgeographic.com/news/2008/09/080924-solar-wind.html
84. SUN'S RAYS TO ROAST EARTH AS POLES FLIP, 'The Observer' Sunday November 10, 2002, GMT Article history
    http://www.guardian.co.uk/world/2002/nov/10/science.research
    http://www.physics4u.gr/news/2002/scnews732.html
85. THE ANCESTOR OF ALL HUMAN SPECIES LIVED 6-7 MILLION YEARS AGO: Reuters, April 6, 2005
    http://www.physics4u.gr/news/2005/scnews1895.html
86. THE BLACK HOLE UNIVERSE MIGHT EXPLAIN DARK ENERGY: New Scientist, November 2007
    http://www.newscientist.com/article/mg19626243.600-blackhole-universe-might-explain-dark-energy.html
87. THE DISCLOSURE PROJECT
    http://en.wikipedia.org/wiki/The_Disclosure_Project
88. THE EXPANDING UNIVERSE: FROM SLOWDOWN TO SPEED UP, physics4u.gr, from SciAm.com, February 2004
    http://www.physics4u.gr/articles/2004/fromslowingtospeeding.html
89. THE EXPANSION OF THE UNIVERSE - SNAP Space Observatory
    http://www.physics4u.gr/articles/expuniv1.html
90. THE GEOGRAPHIC REGION OF ARMAGEDDON, TEL MEGIDDO
    http://wikimediafoundation.org/
91. THE GNOSTIC SOCIETY LIBRARY The (First) Apocalypse of James Translated by William R. Schoedel
    http://www.gnosis.org/naghamm/1ja.html
92. THE GNOSTIC SOCIETY LIBRARY, The Apocryphon of John Collection [The Secret Revelation of John - The Secret Book of John]
    http://www.gnosis.org/naghamm/apocjn.html
    http://www.gnosis.org/naghamm/apocjn-davies.html
93. THE GOLDILOCKS ENIGMA: Why does the Universe have just the right conditions for life to appear on Earth? Sources: The Guardian, Physics4u, April 2007
    http://www.physics4u.gr/articles/2007/universe_and_man.html
94. THE KALUZA-KLEIN THEORY, Physics4u.Gr
    http://www.physics4u.gr/strings/string6.html

95. THE LOST MATTER OF THE UNIVERSE FOUND IN THE COSMIC WEB: Science Daily, May 20, 2008
   http://www.physics4u.gr/news/2008/scnews3327.html

96. THE MOST IMPORTANT FACTS IN PHYSICS IN 2002 AS RECORDED BY PHYSICS WEB
   http://www.physics4u.gr/articles/2002/bestof2002.html

97. THE MURDEROUS, THE MALE, THE FEMALE BRAIN': science news.gr
   http://www.typos.com.cy/nqcontent.cfm?a_id=30744

98. THE MYSTERY OF THE MOON
   http://www.diodos.gr/content/view/77/36/

99. THE OCEAN CURRENTS GENERATORS OF THE MAGNETIC FIELD OF EARTH MONDAY, June 15th, 2009: physics4u.gr
   http://www.physics4u.gr/blog/?p=672

100. THE PORTAL OF THE GREEK LANGUAGE
   http://www.greek-language.gr

101. THE PROBLEM OF DARK MATTER AND THE EXPANSION OF THE UNIVERSE
   http://www.physics4u.gr/news/2001/scnews169.html

102. THE SECOND LAW OF THERMODYNAMICS, VARIOUS CASES OF ENTROPY AND THE EVOLUTION OF LIFE
   http://www.physics4u.gr/articles/2002/secondlaw1.html

103. THE STORY OF THE DARK MATTER THEORY, Article: October 2005
   http://www.physics4u.gr/articles/2005/historydarkmatter.html

104. THE SUN'S SURFACE IS STRANGELY QUIET, April 29, 2009
   http://www.apn.gr/news/world-news/

105. THE TOP 15 NEWS STORIES ABOUT SPACE IN 2006 – COSMIC COLLISION REVEALS DARK MATTER, Physics4u.Gr, January 2007
   http://www.physics4u.gr/articles/2007/top_space_stories_2006.html

106. THE UNIVERSE EXISTED BEFORE THE BIG BANG, physics4u.gr: NEWGEN January, 2000
   http://www.physics4u.gr/news/2000/scnews87.html

107. THEORY INTERPRETS THE BEHAVIOR OF DARK MATTER ASSUMING THE EXISTENCE OF THREE ADDITIONAL DIMENSIONS: Science News.gr, 09/09/2005
   http://www.sciencenews.gr/index.php?option=com_cont

108. TIME IN PHYSICS - TIME-MACHINES
   http://x.e-e-e.gr/real_x_files/science/time_travels/index.html

109. TIMES ON LINE: NEWS AND VIEWS FROM THE TIMES AND SUNDAY TIMES
   http://www.timesonline.co.uk/tol/news/

110. WHAT IS HIDDEN BEHIND THE MOON, MYTHS AND PROOF
   http://www.blackstate.gr/moon.htm

111. WHAT IS TIME? 5TH LECTURE
   http://www.physics4u.gr/5lessons/lesson5.html

112. WHAT THE BLEEP DO WE KNOW, Official Website of movie
   http://www.whatthebleep.com/

113. WHY DOES THE UNIVERSE HAVE THE IDEAL CONDITIONS FOR THE APPEAR-
     ANCE OF LIFE ON EARTH? Physics4u: The Guardian, April 2007
     http://www.physics4u.gr/articles/2007/universe_and_man.html
114. WIKIPEDIA: THE FREE ENCYCLOPEDIA
     http://el.wikipedia.org/wiki/
115. WORMHOLES DO EXIST (DRAWING)
     http://www.physics4u.gr/news/2008/scnews3242.html
     http://stavrochoros.pblogs.gr/tags/fysiki-gr.html
116. WORMHOLES DO EXIST, CLAIMS RUSSIAN SCIENTIST: in.gr & BBC 12-04-
     2000
     http://www.physics4u.gr/news/2000/scnews52.html